Legal Aid in Criminal Proceedings

Legal Aid in Criminal Proceedings

James Parry, LL. B.
Associate Solicitor, E. Rex Makin & Co

Consultant editor
Paul Carr, MA
Barrister, Head of Court Services and Justices Clerk,
Essex (North)

Butterworths
London, Edinburgh, Dublin
1997

United Kingdom	Butterworths a Division of Reed Elsevier (UK) Ltd, Halsbury House, 35 Chancery Lane, LONDON WC2A 1EL and 4 Hill Street EDINBURGH EH2 3JZ
Australia	Butterworths, SYDNEY, MELBOURNE, BRISBANE, ADELAIDE, PERTH, CANBERRA and HOBART
Canada	Butterworths Canada Ltd, TORONTO and VANCOUVER
Ireland	Butterworths (Ireland) Ltd, DUBLIN
Malaysia	Malaysian Law Journal Sdn Bhd, Kuala Lumpur
New Zealand	Butterworths of New Zealand Ltd, WELLINGTON and AUCKLAND
Singapore	Reed Elsevier (Singapore) Pte Ltd, SINGAPORE
South Africa	Butterworths Publishers (Pty) Ltd, DURBAN
USA	Michie, Charlottesville, VIRGINIA

A CIP Catalogue record for this book is available from thje British Library.

ISBN 0 406 04605 0

Typeset by Ponting–Green Publishing Services, Chesham, Buckinghamshire
Printed by Redwood Books, Trowbridge, Wiltshire

Preface

This book is intended to provide assistance with the practical problems that arise under the criminal legal aid scheme in England and Wales. It has been written for use by court staff charged with the administration of the scheme and solicitors and their clerks who specialise in criminal legal aid work, and is intended to be an easily digested source of information for everyday use. Although the book deals primarily with the decision-making process in the magistrates' court, it also covers the procedures adopted by the Crown Court and the Court of Appeal. Emphasis is placed on magistrates' courts simply because the majority of legal aid applications are submitted to and determined by those courts. In order to assist the reader an attempt has been made to collect together all the relevant statutory and other reference material, including the relevant Lord Chancellor's Department Circulars, so as to provide a comprehensive range of materials. The relevant case law has been summarised in a digest of cases.

Informal research by the author during presentation of training seminars to magistrates' courts staff and solicitors suggests that many of the problems encountered by professional users of the scheme and those who administered it were created by a failure to understand the needs and concerns of each other.

Magistrates' courts staff tend to regard the problems that they encounter at a local level as being unique to their particular court, whereas, in fact, the problems are usually exactly the same as those in other courts and, in many cases, effective and satisfactory solutions to them have been discovered. The independent nature of magistrates' courts tends to work against an everyday informal exchange of information between different courts and, in relying on their own devices, a lot of time and energy are expended in re-inventing the wheel whenever a new problem is encountered.

A further cause of concern to magistrates' court staff was that they often report that they feel are being pressurised into making instant decisions by defence advocates in circumstances where there is insufficient information to do so. If that decision is to refuse an order, or an amendment to an order, the subsequent complaint often provides the extra details that would have resulted in a decision to grant the application. Mutual frustration arises on the part of both the court staff, who feel they could have provided a better service if they had been provided with all the relevant information in the first place, and on the part of the solicitor, who considers that the court is merely placing bureaucratic obstacles in his way so as to prevent him representing his client.

Solicitors are concerned that they should be able to predict which cases will attract legal aid and require a prompt and efficient consideration of each application so that they can embark on the task of representing their clients as soon as possible. They are constrained in assisting the court with the provision of documents by their clients who are frequently reluctant to contact their solicitor until the day of their first court appearance, when they never bring any documentation with them, but expect instant help and assistance.

Recent pressure from central government to ensure that magistrates' courts were properly administering the legal aid scheme and consequential amendments to further tighten the requirements for the production of documentary evidence has tended to increase the frustration between court staff and solicitors. On the one hand court staff have been told that if they do not improve their administration of the scheme it will be taken from them, yet on the other hand solicitors encounter frequent changes in the rules and requests for more and more documents.

This book sets out to explain what the requirements are and to identify common problems; and in doing so overcome the difficulties that arise between those who control the scheme and those who are paid by it. The book covers the mechanics of obtaining legal aid and amending such orders. A small section is included on obtaining payments from the fund, but taxation of bills is not covered in great detail as many works exist on this subject.

My thanks are due to those who have assisted me in the production of this book, including the team at Butterworths whose encouragement and advice is particularly valuable. Special thanks are due to Ian Coates and Nicola Dimcek at Liverpool magistrates' court. Ian Coates is a principal court clerk who co-wrote and presented the training course Legal Aid in Criminal Courts' with me, which provided the original ideas for this book. His assistance in designing the outline structure for the book was of great assistance. Nicola Dimcek provided support in the production of that course, including the production of the handout material, with numerous revisions, some of which has been incorporated into this book.

James N R Parry
November 1996

CONTENTS

Preface v
Table of statutes xi
Table of statutory instruments xiii
Table of cases xv

Chapter One Alternatives to Funding Criminal Litigation other than Criminal Legal Aid Orders 1
Advice, assistance and representation 1
Conclusion 7

Chapter Two Sources of State Funded Representation other than a Criminal Legal Aid Order 9
Introduction 9
Legal advice and assistance 9
Advice by way of representation (ABWOR) 10
The Court Duty Solicitor Scheme 20
The Police Station Duty Solicitor Scheme 26

Chapter Three Criminal Legal Aid Scheme – Methods of Application 27
The scope of the Criminal Legal Aid Scheme 27
Competent authorities to grant legal aid orders and method of application 28
Timing of applications 32
Content of applications 33

Chapter Four The Criminal Legal Aid Scheme Means Test 35
Introduction 35
The requirement to provide a statement of means 35
The requirement to provide documentary evidence 37
Powers to grant 'conditional orders' pending the receipt of documentation 38
The assessment of resources (over 16 year olds) 38
The assessment of resources (under 16 year olds) 39
Passporting applicants to free legal aid 40
Full means enquiries 40
Calculating the amount of income received each week 45

Chapter Five The Merits Test: Deeming Provisions 61
Overview 61
Appeals 61

Bail applications 62
Bail Act offences 62
Cross-examination of child witnesses 63
Committal for trial 63
Committal for sentence 63
Remands for pre-sentence reports 64
Sentencing hearings 64

Chapter Six The Merits Test: Discretionary Provisions 67
Overview 67
The application form 69
Satisfying the statutory criteria 69
Case studies 81

Chapter Seven Legal Aid Contribution Orders 93
The issue of contribution orders 93
The 'collecting court' 97
The duration of contribution orders and the date payments fall due 99
The court's powers to withhold orders until contributions from capital are paid 101
Changes in a legally assisted person's, or an appropriate contributor's, financial circumstances 101
The court's powers to seek further information during the life of the case 107

Chapter Eight Enforcing Criminal Legal Aid Contribution Orders 109
Enforcing payments of a legal aid contribution order 109
Powers to refund overpayments or remit further contributions and correct mistakes 125

Chapter Nine The Criminal Legal Aid Scheme – Renewals of Applications 129
Common reasons for the rejection of legal aid applications on merit 129
Renewals of applications in the magistrates' court 130
Reviews of applications by the Legal Aid Board Area Committee 132
Renewals of applications for proceedings in the Crown Court 138
Renewals of applications before the Court of Appeal 138
Other forms of renewal 138
Judicial review 140

Chapter Ten The Criminal Legal Aid Scheme – The Nature and Amendment of Criminal Legal Aid Orders 141
Nature of representation under criminal legal aid orders 141
Amendment of legal aid orders 146

Chapter Eleven Costs and the Criminal Legal Aid Scheme 159
The refund or remittal of a successfully legally aided defendant's contributions as an alternative to a defendant's costs order 159
The refund or remittal of an unsuccessful legally aided defendant's contributions where the contributions paid exceed the solicitor's bill 161
Work done prior to the grant of a legal aid order 162

The scope of the order – work done under the legal aid order 164
The power to make defendant's costs in relation to legally assisted persons 167
Time limits and relevant taxing authorities 170
Methods of claimng costs 171
Standard fees in magistrates' courts 171
Avenues of appeal against taxation 175

Chapter Twelve Criminal Legal Aid Scheme – Future developments 177
The problems 177
The solutions 178

APPENDICES

Appendix A Guidance and Circulars issued by the Lord Chancellor's Department 183
A1 Legal Aid in Criminal Proceedings 185
A2 Guidance on the Interests of Justice Test for the Grant of Criminal Legal Aid 199
A3 Administration of Legal Aid in Magistrates' Courts 211
A4 Guidance to Granting Authorities on the Legal Aid in Criminal Proceedings (General)(Amendment) Regulations 1995 223
A5 Guidance to Court Staff for Calculation of Legal Aid Contributions 1996/97 228
A6 Guidance on Changes to Criminal Legal Aid Means Testing to come into Effect on 1 June 1996 231

Appendix B Article 6 European Convention on Human Rights 237

Appendix C Legal Aid Board Duty Solicitor Arrangements 1994 239

Appendix D Legal Aid Act 1988 257

Appendix E Statutory Instruments 315
E1 Legal Aid in Criminal and Care Proceedings (General) Regulations 1989 315
E2 Legal Advice and Assistance Regulations 1989 355
E3 Legal Advice and Assistance (Scope) Regulations 1989 382
E4 Legal Aid in Criminal and Care Proceedings (Costs) Regulations 1989 387

Appendix F Eligibility and Payment Rates from April 1996 427

Appendix G Digest of Cases 433

Appendix H National Mode of Trial Guidelines 453

Index 459

Table of statutes

References in this Table to *Statutes* are to Halsbury's Statutes of England (Fourth Edition) showing the volume and page at which the annotated text of the Act may be found. Page references printed in **bold** type indicate where the Act is set out in part or in full.

PAGE

Attachment of Earnings Act 1971 (22 *Statutes* 466) 124
Bail Act 1976 (12 *Statutes* 662)
  s 6 62
Children Act 1989 (6 *Statutes* 387) 17
Children and Young Persons Act 1933 (6 *Statutes* 18)
  s 53 65
Criminal Evidence Act 1898 (17 *Statutes* 130)
  s 1(f) 80
Criminal Justice Act 1967 (12 *Statutes* 358)
  s 9 76
Criminal Justice Act 1982 (12 *Statutes* 802)
  s 3 .... 65, 66
  17 124
Criminal Justice Act 1987 (12 *Statutes* 1100)
  s 4 172
  20(b) 29
Criminal Justice Act 1988 (17 *Statutes* 242)
  s 32 80
  34A 63, 80
Criminal Justice Act 1991 (12 *Statutes* 1484)
  s 53 172
Criminal Justice (International Co-operation) Act 1990 (12 *Statutes* 1408)
  s 25 28
Domestic Proceedings and Magistrates' Courts Act 1978 (27 *Statutes* 816)
  s 2, 6, 7, 19 17
Legal Aid Act 1974 108
  s 28(5) 27
Legal Aid Act 1988 (24 *Statutes* 9) 23, 25, 30, 33, 78, 168, 169, **257–313**
  s 2(2) 1
  3(1) 169
  8(1) 9
  9(11) 29
  Pt V (ss 19—26) 35
  s 19(1) 27
  (5) 20, 28, 114, 120
  20(2) 29
  (4)(a) 29
  (b) 29, 32
  (bb) 29
  (5) 29
  (8) 28, 29
  21(1) 2, 9, 27
  (2) 9, 27, 35, 67

PAGE

Legal Aid Act 1988–*contd*
  s 21(3) 67
  (a) 63
  (b) 61
  (c) 14, 62
  (d) 64
  (5) 9, 27, 35, 62, 163
  (6) 163
  (7) 53, 68, 81, 117, 132
  22 .... 61, 67, 69, 129
  (2) 135
  (a) 63, 69, 72, 73
  (b) 74
  (c) 37, 75
  (d) 79
  (e) 80
  23(1) 96
  (7) 126, 161
  24(1) 52, 101
  25(3) 166
  39 40
  (1) 59, 91
  (b) 107
  (2), (3) 107
  Sch 3
  Pt I
  para 1 97
  2(4) 120
  5 98
  (1), (2) 117
  6 117
  (a), (b) 115
  7, 8 117
Legal Aid Act 1996 119
Magistrates' Courts Act 1980 (27 *Statutes* 143) 98
  s 6(1) 172
  (2) 30, 33, 76, 172
  12 76
  13 118
  64(1)(a), (b) 120
  75–78 124
  80 120
  82(4) 124
  83(1) 119
  84(1) 120
  88, 94 124
  95 .... 120, 160, 161

PAGE

Magistrates' Courts Act 1980 –*contd*
s 96 ... 121
102 ... 76
115 ... 27
125 ... 119
127 ... 107
135, 136 ... 124
Offences against the Person Act 1861 (12 *Statutes 87)*
s 47 ... 82
Pension Schemes Act 1993 ... 47
Pensions Act 1995 ... 47
Police and Criminal Evidence Act 1984 (12 *Statutes* 845)
Code C
para 3.6—3.11 ... 6
6, 6D ... 6

PAGE

Powers of Criminal Courts Act 1973 (12 *Statutes* 571)
s 1 ... 172
21(1) ... 64
Prosecution of Offences Act 1985 (12 *Statutes* 937)
s 16 ... 2
(1) ... 125
(6) ... 168
17(3) ... 3
19 ... 2
19A ... 3
Public Health Act 1936 (35 *Statutes* 117)
s 99 ... 27
Public Order Act 1986 (12 *Statutes* 1060)
s 4 ... 85
Social Security Contributions and Benefits Act 1992 (40 *Statutes* 492) ... 47

Table of statutory instruments

Page references printed in **bold** type indicate where the regulation is set out in part or in full.

PAGE

Costs in Criminal Cases (General) Regulations 1986, SI 1986/1335 .... **315–354**
reg 15, 16 .... 166, 169
Legal Advice and Assistance Regulations 1989, SI 1989/340 .... **355–381**
reg 6 26
7 20
14(2A) 11
Legal Advice and Assistance (Scope) Regulations 1989, SI 1989/550 .... **382–386**
reg 7(1)(a), (b) 10
(2) 62
(a)–(c) 13
(d) 13, 15
(3), (4) 13
Legal Aid (General) Regulations 1962, SI 1962/148
reg 6(5) 107
Legal Aid in Criminal and Care Proceedings (Costs) Regulations 1989, SI 1989/343 ... **387–426**
reg 5 173
(1) 170, 171
(1A) 170
(5) 164
6 173
7 172
8(1) 170
(2) 171
12 163
(1) 174
13 163
(1)–(3) 174
14(1), (2), (7) 174
15(1), (6)–(9), (12)–(14) 174
16(3)–(6) 174
17(2) 170
Sch 1
Pt III
para 1 173
3 171
4(2) 171
Legal Aid in Criminal and Care Proceedings (General) Regulations 1989, SI 1989/344 35
reg 3 105
(1) 39
(a)–(c) 170
4 170
5 105

PAGE

Legal Aid in Criminal and Care Proceedings (General) Regulations 1989–*contd*
reg 8(2) 30
10 .... 36, 105, 108, 115, 139, 152
11(1) 30
(a), (b) 28, 31
(2) 31
(a)–(c) 30
(3) 30, 31
12, 13 95
14(1), (2) 130, 132
(4) 131
(5) 132
(6) 131, 132
(7) 131
15(2)(a) 133, 150
(b), (c) 134
16(1) 134
(2)(a), (b) 134
(3), (4) 134
17(1), (2) 134
(3) 138
18(1) 31
(a) 30, 32
(b)–(d) 30
(2) 31
19 .... 93, 95
(2) 32, 138
20 .... 93, 95, 138
22(1)(b) 32
(5)(a), (b) 32
(6) 32
21(1)–(6) 138
22(3) 138
23 .... 54, 131, 139
(1) 36
(2) 28
(2A) 37
(3) 36, 39, 105
(4)(a)–(c) 36
24(1) 37, 103, 107, 120
(2) 103, 108
26(2A) 37, 108
(a) 38
(b) 38, 39
(3) 40
27 96
(1) 93
(2) 94

PAGE

Legal Aid in Criminal and Care Proceedings (General) Regulations 1989–*contd*
reg 29(1) 99, 100, 105
(2) 53, 100, 105
(3) 101
(4) 126
30(2) 101
31 .... 101, 114
32 108
(1)(a), (b) 106
33 108
(a), (b) 103, 106
34 127
35(1) 125, 159, 160
(a) 126
(2) 161
(3) 160
36(1)(a) 111
(b) 112
(2) 111, 112
(3) 113
(b) 114
(4) 115
37 109
(1)(a) 106, 117
(b), (c) 117
39 126
40(1) 93, 142, 146, 154
(a) 31
(2) 31, 32, 93
41 146
(1)(a) 153
(b) 105, 152, 153
(d) 103, 108
(2) 130
(3) 115
(4)(a), (b) 115
44(1), (2) 141
(3)(a) 141, 152
(4)–(6) 142
(7) 33, 163
45(1) 143, **144**
(2) 143
46 .... 143, 144
48(3) 142, 153
(4) 142
49 .... 143, 144, **145**
50 .... 146, 154
(1) 144, **145**
(2) 102, 154
51 146
(1) 150
(a), (b) 151
(2) 149, 150, 151
(3) 150
(4)(a), (b) 151
(5) 151
(6) 149
(a) 150
(b)(i), (ii) 150
54 .... 146, 157
(1)(e) 167
55 157

PAGE

Legal Aid in Criminal and Care Proceedings (General) Regulations 1989–*contd*
reg 55(a) 167
56 .... 102, 154
Sch 2
Form 1 .... 30, 31, 40, 41, 42, 54, 66, 69, 70, 71, 72, 73, 74, 76, 79, 80, 81, 83, 84, 85, 86, 87, **88–92**, 134
2 .... 30, 93, 95, 130, 131, 138, 139
3 .... 134, 135
4 138
5 .... 28, 40, 41, 44, 54, 66, 103, 104, 120
6 .... 93, 96, 101
7 101
9 .... 111, 112, 125
10 .... 112, 125
11 .... 31, 93, 131, 139
11A 93
14 .... 115, 125
Sch 3
para 1(1) 43
(a)–(c) 39
(2) 42
2 42
2A 1
(1), (3) 45
3 47
4(1) 44
6 46
7(a), (b) 46
8 46
(2)(a) 47
(b) 48
9 .... 46, 50
10–14 46
15(1), (2) 50
17, 18 .... 50, 51
19 .... 47, 50
20, 21 50
Sch 4 52
Legal Aid in Criminal and Care Proceedings (General) (Amendment) (No 2) Regulations 1993, SI 1993/1895 37
Legal Aid in Criminal and Care Proceedings (General) (Amendment) Regulations 1994, SI 1994/807 37
Legal Aid in Criminal and Care Proceedings (General) (Amendment) Regulations 1996, SI 1996/436
reg 4 1
Legal Aid in Criminal and Care Proceedings (General) (Amendment) (No 3) Regulations 1996, SI 1996/1258
reg 10(b) 38, 40
Magistrates' Courts (Attachment of Earnings) Rules 1971, SI 1971/809 124
Magistrates' Courts Rules 1981, SI 1981/552
r 99 111

Table of cases

PAGE

B

Baker v West Sussex Justices (1983) 148 JP 129, 128 Sol Jo 48 .... 143, 445
Benham v United Kingdom (1995) Independent, 3 February, ECtHR 120, 437
Bold, ex p. See R v Clerk to South Cheshire Justices, ex p Bold

C

Cullen v Trimble (1872) LR 7 QB 416, 37 JP 115, 41 LJMC 132, 20 WR 701, 26 LT 691 100

D

DPP v Peacock [1989] Crim LR 372 119

H

Hobby v Hobby [1954] 2 All ER 395, [1954] 1 WLR 1020, 118 JP 331, 98 Sol Jo 474 6

P

Practice Note [1989] 2 All ER 479, sub nom Practice Direction [1989] 1 WLR 618, 89 Cr App Rep 133 .... 153, 446
Practice Note [1990] 3 All ER 979, [1990] 1 WLR 1439, [1990] NLJR 1534 .... 70, 453
Practice Note (criminal law: costs) [1991] 2 All ER 924, sub nom Practice Direction [1991] 1 WLR 498, 93 Cr App Rep 89 .... 3, 126, 160

R

R v Birmingham Justices, ex p Wyatt [1975] 3 All ER 897, [1976] 1 WLR 260, 61 Cr App Rep 306, 140 JP 46, 119 Sol Jo 726, DC 64, 65
R v Bury Justices, ex p N [1987] QB 284, [1986] 3 All ER 789, [1986] 3 WLR 965, 84 Cr App Rep 186, 150 JP 575, [1987] Crim LR 52, 130 Sol Jo 879, [1986] LS Gaz R 3836, [1986] NLJ Rep 916 .... 134, 446
R v City of Cambridge Justices, ex p Leader (1979) 144 JP 148, 124 Sol Jo 187 .... 440, 446
R v Clerk to South Cheshire Justices, ex p Bold (1996) Times, 15 July 120, 437
R v Crawley Justices, ex p Ohakwe (1994) 158 JP 781 .... 28, 435
R v Crown Court at Cambridge, ex p Hagi (1979) 144 JP 145 444
R v Crown Court at Inner London, ex p Bentham [1989] 1 WLR 408, 153 JP 262, [1989] Crim LR 450, 21 HLR 171, 133 Sol Jo 785 .... 27, 434
R v Crown Court at Isleworth, ex p Willington [1993] 2 All ER 390, [1993] 1 WLR 713, [1992] 33 LS Gaz R 39, 136 Sol Jo LB 259 .... 152, 441
R v Crown Court at Liverpool, ex p Lord Chancellor (1993) 158 JP 821 .... 142, 448
R v Crown Court at Liverpool, ex p McCann [1995] RTR 23, [1995] Crim LR 425 ...... 20, 28, 133, 139, 140, 436
R v Davis (1986) 8 Cr App Rep (S) 64, CA 63, 437
R v Derby Justices, ex p Kooner [1971] 1 QB 147, [1970] 3 All ER 399, [1970] 3 WLR 598, 54 Cr App Rep 455, 134 JP 680, 114 Sol Jo 620, DC 152, 447
R v Edgehill [1963] 1 QB 593, [1963] 1 All ER 181, [1963] 2 WLR 170, 47 Cr App Rep 41, 106 Sol Jo 1054, CCA 206, 443
R v Egan (1996) Times, 14 October 437
R v Guildford Justices, ex p Scott [1975] Crim LR 286, 119 Sol Jo 237 .... 152, 153, 447
R v Highbury Corner Magistrates and Islington London Borough Council, ex p Watkins [1992] RA 300 437

PAGE

R v Highbury Corner Magistrates' Court, ex p D J Sonn & Co (a firm) [1995] 4 All ER 57, [1995] 1 WLR 1365, 159 JP 605 .... 33, 442
R v Highgate Justices, ex p Lewis (1977) 142 JP 78, [1977] Crim LR 611, 121 Sol Jo 712, CA 438
R v Highgate Justices, ex p Petrou [1954] 1 All ER 406, [1954] 1 WLR 485, 118 JP 151, 98 Sol Jo 180, DC 120
R v Hollywood (1990) 12 Cr App Rep (S) 325, 154 JP 705, [1990] Crim LR 817, CA 64
R v King's Lynn Justices, ex p Fysh [1964] Crim LR 143, 107 Sol Jo 932 206
R v Legal Aid Board, ex p RM Broudie & Co (1994) 138 Sol Jo LB 94 164
R v Legal Aid Board, ex p Hepstonstalls [1995] 33 LS Gaz R 23 .... 63, 436
R v Leigh Justices, ex p Kara (1980) 72 Cr App Rep 327, [1981] Crim LR 628 443
R v Liverpool City Justices, ex p McGhee (1993) 158 JP 275, [1993] Crim LR 609 .... 64, 69, 80, 81, 444
R v Liverpool City Justices, ex p RM Broudie & Co (1994) 159 JP 330, 138 Sol Jo LB 95 ... 442
R v Liverpool City Magistrates' Court, ex p Pender [1993] 2 All ER 929, [1993] 1 WLR 1148, [1993] 13 LS Gaz R 37, 137 Sol Jo LB 210 .... 115, 139, 140, 440
R v Liverpool City Magistrates' Court, ex p Pender (No 2) [1994] 2 All ER 897, [1994] 1 WLR 964, 158 JP 129, [1993] 37 LS Gaz R 51 .... 105, 108, 139, 440, 446
R v Liverpool City Magistrates' Court, ex p Shacklady [1993] 2 All ER 929, [1993] 1 WLR 1148, [1993] 13 LS Gaz R 37 .... 115, 139, 140, 440
R v Macclesfield Justices, ex p Greenhalgh (1979) 144 JP 142 440
R v Manchester Stipendiary Magistrate, ex p Hill [1983] 1 AC 328, [1982] 3 WLR 331, [1982] RTR 449, 126 Sol Jo 526, sub nom Hill v Anderton [1982] 2 All ER 963, 75 Cr App Rep 346, 146 JP 348, [1982] Crim LR 755, HL 28
R v Newham Justices, ex p Mumtaz (1990) 154 JP 597, [1990] Crim LR 589 .... 33, 38, 68, 108, 162, 438
R v Newton (1982) 77 Cr App Rep 13, 4 Cr App Rep (S) 388, [1983] Crim LR 198, CA 75
R v O'Brien [1985] 1 All ER 971, [1985] 1 WLR 464, 81 Cr App Rep 25, 149 JP 289, [1985] Crim LR 225, 129 Sol Jo 247, [1985] LS Gaz R 847, [1985] NLJ Rep 207 .... 143, 445
R v Redbridge Magistrates' Court, ex p Guppy (1995) 159 JP 622 .... 20, 28, 120, 133, 436
R v Serghiou [1966] 3 All ER 637n, [1966] 1 WLR 1611, 50 Cr App Rep 312, 110 Sol Jo 789, CA 64, 206, 443
R v Solihull Justices, ex p Johnson (1976) 140 JP Jo 189 .... 143, 163, 444
R v South Western Justices, ex p Doyle and Bennett (1 November 1995, unreported) ... 38, 107, 439
R v Stubbs [1982] 1 All ER 424, [1982] 1 WLR 509, 74 Cr App Rep 246, 146 JP 166, 126 Sol Jo 227, CA 449
R v Tullett [1976] 2 All ER 1032, [1976] 1 WLR 241, 62 Cr App Rep 225, 140 JP 502, [1976] Crim LR 193, 120 Sol Jo 95 439
R v Winter [1980] Crim LR 659, CA 449
Ridehalgh v Horsefield [1994] Ch 205, [1994] 3 All ER 848, [1994] 3 WLR 462, [1994] 2 FLR 194, [1994] Fam Law 560, [1994] BCC 390, CA 169
Roberts v Duce [1974] Crim LR 107, 122 NLJ 1012 107

S

Simms v Moore [1970] 2 QB 327, [1970] 3 All ER 1, [1970] 2 WLR 1099, 54 Cr App Rep 347, 134 JP 573, 114 Sol Jo 416 6

W

Welch v Redbridge Justices (1984) 148 JP 474 .... 33, 162, 446
Whittall v Kirby [1947] KB 194, [1946] 2 All ER 552, 45 LGR 8, 111 JP 1, [1947] LJR 234, 90 Sol Jo 571, 175 LT 449, 62 TLR 696, DC 75

Chapter One

Alternatives to Funding Criminal Litigation other than Criminal Legal Aid Orders

This chapter will examine the alternatives that exist to enable criminal litigation to be funded from sources other than criminal legal aid orders.

Although, as yet, there is no mandatory requirement to consider whether any alternative source of funding exists for defending a criminal charge, there is evidence that Parliament is beginning to move in that direction, as proper officers are now able to take into account the financial resources of persons who have been providing funds for a defence to a criminal charge prior to the application, or maintaining an applicant for a criminal legal aid order. These will be regarded as those of the applicant when determining the applicants financial eligibility for legal aid.[1]

A further reason for including this topic within a text on this subject is to provide some alternative avenues of funding should an application for criminal legal aid fail, or where criminal legal aid is not available – for example to fund prosecutions.

ADVICE, ASSISTANCE AND REPRESENTATION

The Legal Aid Act 1988 differentiates between advice, assistance and representation in determining the level of service that a solicitor or barrister might provide under different sections of the scheme[2]. It is therefore essential that the distinction between these terms is fully understood.

'Advice' means any written or oral comments on the application of English law as it applies to the particular circumstances of the person who seeks the advice.

'Assistance' means assistance in taking any of the steps that a person might take in relation to the particular circumstances of the application of English law that has arisen. This allows a solicitor either to take some action on behalf of the client, or to assist the client to take some action himself.

'Representation' is a more comprehensive service and includes assistance with all steps preliminary to any proceedings and advice on the merits of any appeal, together with preparation and advocacy during the proceedings.

In considering the alternatives that exist in the place of full legal aid it must be recognised that these sources may provide advice and/or assistance but may

1 Para 2A, Sch 3 of the Legal Aid in Criminal and Care Proceedings (General) Regulations 1989 as amended by Reg 4 of the Legal Aid in Criminal and Care Proceedings (General) (Amendment) Regulations 1996.

2 S 2(2) of the Legal Aid Act 1988 contains definitions of each term from which the following summary has been extracted.

stop short of full representation. Such alternative sources of help can be divided into five distinct groups:

1. client funded self help;
2. commercial or trade schemes;
3. state schemes other than a full legal aid order;
4. pro bono work undertaken by the legal profession; and
5. volunatary sector schemes.

For the purpose of identifying the sources of each type of assistance, the examples given below have been grouped according to the source of funding that maintains the scheme.

1. Client funded self help

Although the title of this work assumes that the defendant to a criminal charge will require assistance in the provision of legal services, it is appropriate to consider that a defendant has a right to represent himself or to select and pay for lawyers without the intervention of the state. This may be the only method of bringing a private prosecution in a magistrates' court, as criminal legal aid orders are not available for the purpose of mounting a prosecution at that stage[3].

Such costs can normally be recovered by way of a costs order, if either the representation leads to a successful outcome, or where the opposition does some act or makes some omission that wastes costs. Consequently, it is appropriate to consider briefly the scope of such orders at this stage.

Private payment of solicitors and counsel

Where the defendant has the means to do so, he is free to select the services of any solicitor and barrister who will act for him, and pay for their services from his own resources. The advantage to a defendant who chooses to do this is that he will not be restricted to the level of representation that is permitted under a legal aid order and he could, if he wished, instruct Queen's Counsel to defend a case of having no television licence in the magistrates' court.

Where the defence succeeds the defendant will be only able to recover those costs reasonably incurred under a defendant's costs order.

Costs incurred as a result of unnecessary or improper acts or omissions

An order can be made against parties to criminal proceedings where costs have been incurred as a result of the conduct of that party rather than by the conduct of their legal representative[4]. Where costs are incurred because of the acts of legal representatives, see 'Wasted costs orders' below.

Defendant's costs orders

Where a defendant in criminal proceedings successfully defends his case at trial, or where he is discharged at committal or where the case is otherwise discharged or not proceeded with, a defendant who has incurred expense may seek the refund of those costs actually and reasonably incurred[5]. Where the applicant was convicted of some offences but acquitted of others, he may be able to secure

3 S 21(1) of the Legal Aid Act 1988.
4 S 19 of the Prosecution of Offences Act 1985.
5 S 16 of the Prosecution of Offences Act 1985.

payment of some of his costs[6]. Costs will not be withheld unless there is some positive reason for doing so, for example where the defendant has escaped conviction on some technicality that has no merit or where he has misled the prosecution as to the strength of the case against him[7].

This method is only of limited assistance to those defendants who can afford to fund the proceedings themselves in the first instance. The risks are that in the event of a conviction no refund of the costs will be available and for this reason solicitors will always ensure that funds are available to cover their disbursements and profit costs prior to trial, save in an exceptional case, since disappointed defendants are not prone to pay their bills.

Where costs are granted, bills are submitted to either the magistrates' court or the Crown court for taxation and, once a sum has been calculated, costs are paid from central funds, which in the magistrates' court means the fines and fees account. Eventually an account adjustment is effected at central government level and such payments constitute a debit on the legal aid account.

Private prosecutor's costs from central funds

Where a prosecutor is an individual, rather than a public authority or an individual acting on behalf of such an authority, and the offence charged is an indictable offence, prosecution costs can be ordered to be paid from central funds[8]. If the proceedings are taken over by the Crown Prosecution Service the power ceases to be available, although costs incurred prior to the take over can be recovered.

This power may assist persons bringing private prosecutions, as the award of costs is not dependent on securing a conviction, but the amount that is payable may not be the full amount incurred if the court is of the opinion that it is inappropriate that the prosecutor should recover the full amount expended by him[9].

Wasted Costs Orders

Where a legal representative causes costs to be expended by an opponent due to some unnecessary act or omission on his behalf, costs may be awarded or disallowed against that representative or anyone employed by him[10]. Whilst such orders do not enable proceedings to be funded at the outset, they do protect a private paying client against the wasteful excesses of his opponent.

2. Commercial or trade schemes

Insurance policies

Where a defendant is charged with a motoring offence such as careless driving, where a conviction would expose the insurer to civil liability the insurer will often provide legal representation in the criminal proceedings to protect its interests. In such circumstances the insured defendant is unlikely to be allowed a choice of solicitor but will have agreed in his contract of insurance to accept

6 Para 2 (1) and (3) of *Practice Direction* [1991] 1 WLR 498.
7 Para 2(1) of *Practice Direction* [1991] (ibid).
8 S 17 of the Prosecution of Offences Act 1985.
9 S 17(3) of the Prosecution of Offences Act 1985.
10 S 19A of the Prosecution of Offences Act 1985.

the advice and representation of a solicitor nominated by the insurance company.

There also some specialist policies of legal insurance that will provide the services of a solicitor or barrister to persons charged with criminal offences. Increasingly these policies are being incorporated into household or motoring policies as add-on extras.

Law centres

Many large cities have law centres, funded by local authorities and legal aid receipts, that offer legal advice and representation in criminal proceedings in a locality. These are non-profit making institutions that may conduct representation themselves, but more usually instruct local solicitors on behalf of dependants if legal aid is available.

Medical Defence Union

The Medical Defence Union is an example of a professional trade union that will provide legal assistance to its members, in this case doctors, charged with criminal offences arising out of their professional duties.

Motoring organisations

Motoring organisations will provide advice and sometimes legal representation to their members when their members are charged with criminal offences related to the use of their motor vehicles. An increasing number of schemes exclude alcohol related offences from representation under them.

Trade unions

Trade unions will often offer legal advice and representation to their members if the proceedings arise from, or will affect, their employment. Members of such institutions are not normally free to instruct representatives of their choice but will be restricted to those engaged by the union on their behalf.

3. State schemes other than a full legal aid order

Advice and assistance schemes

Advice and assistance schemes provide advice and assistance from a solicitor in certain circumstances, but the extent of the advice and assistance given will fall short of that available under a full legal aid order. See Chapter 2 for a full discussion of this scheme.

Court Duty Solicitor scheme[11]

The Court Duty Solicitor scheme pays for the attendance of a local solicitor with a criminal practice to attend at the magistrates' court where he or she will be available for consultation by any unrepresented defendant until the court concludes, or until it is clear that the duty solicitor is no longer required[12]. The scope of the service requires the duty solicitor to:

11 The full arrangements and conditions of this scheme are contained within the Legal Aid Board Duty Solicitor Arrangements, which are reproduced at Appendix C.

12 Para 52 of the Legal Aid Board Duty Solicitor Arrangements 1994.

(i) provide advice to any defendant who is in custody[13];
(ii) make a bail application for a defendant who is in custody, unless the defendant has previously received assistance with such an application[14];
(iii) represent a defendant who is in custody and wishes to enter a guilty plea to an offence, unless the solicitor considers the case should be adjourned in the interests of justice or the defendant[15];
(iv) advise and represent a defendant who is before the court in respect of a breach of a court order or in relation to unpaid fines where there is a risk of imprisonment and such advice is considered necessary by the solicitor[16];
(v) advise and represent any defendant who is not in custody where the solicitor believes such advice and representation is necessary[17];
(vi) assist a defendant to apply for a criminal legal aid order. The duty solicitor is required to establish from the defendant which solicitor the defendant chooses to represent him and insert his or her name on the application, as the defendant's right to select an advocate of his own choosing is preserved under these arrangements[18].

The scheme expressly prohibits the provision of advice and assistance where:

(i) the advice and assistance is required in committal proceedings or during a not guilty trial[19];
(ii) where the offence is not punishable by imprisonment, unless there are circumstances which the solicitor considers exceptional[20];
(iii) advice and assistance is required at an adjourned hearing, unless the defendant has not received any advice from any solicitor in the same case, or where the defendant has been brought back before the court in breach of a court order or having failed to pay the fine and is at risk of imprisonment[1];
(iv) any member of the duty solicitor's firm is representing the Crown Prosecution Service in the same court room[2].

Local arrangements may also affect the running of the scheme in individual courts and the duty solicitor is often responsible for ensuring that the nominated solicitors of those held in custody on new matters or arrest warrants are contacted before court. Where the case is not concluded on the day, the duty solicitor may only continue to act for a defendant where the defendant has been informed of his right to select any solicitor of his or her own choosing and where there is no solicitor already acting for the defendant in the proceedings.

The Green Form scheme

In criminal matters the Green From scheme allows a solicitor to provide up to two hours' advice and assistance to clients who qualify on financial grounds. There is no merits test provided the proceedings are within the scheme. This scheme is fully discussed in Chapter 2.

13 Para 50(1)(a) of the Legal Aid Board Duty Solicitor Arrangements 1994.
14 Para 50(1)(b) of the Legal Aid Board Duty Solicitor Arrangements 1994.
15 Para 50(2)(a) of the Legal Aid Board Duty Solicitor Arrangements 1994.
16 Para 50(2)(b) of the Legal Aid Board Duty Solicitor Arrangements 1994.
17 Para 50(2)(c) of the Legal Aid Board Duty Solicitor Arrangements 1994.
18 Para 50(2)(d) of the Legal Aid Board Duty Solicitor Arrangements 1994.
19 Para 51(1) of the Legal Aid Board Duty Solicitor Arrangements 1994.
20 Para 51(1) of the Legal Aid Board Duty Solicitor Arrangements 1994.
1 Para 51(2) of theLegal Aid Board Duty Solicitor Arrangements 1994.
2 Para 51(3) of the Legal Aid Board Duty Solicitor Arrangements 1994

Police Station Duty Solicitor scheme

The Police Station Duty Solicitor scheme provides for free legal advice to be given to anyone held in police custody. The right to free legal advice whilst in custody is guaranteed[3], save in very exceptional circumstances. Advice is provided from local panels of solicitors who are completely independent of the police and experienced in private criminal defence practice. The solicitor's only role is to protect and advance the legal rights of his client[4] and such representation is in addition to the rights of a youth or a mentally disordered person to have an appropriate adult present[5]. Solicitors claim their remuneration from the Legal Aid Board.

4. Pro bono work undertaken by the legal profession

Court staff

Generally the role of a court's staff is to administer the affairs of the court and in some circumstances to provide legal advice to the court. However, whilst they are not necessarily under a duty to do so, court staff will often provide advice and assistance to defendants to criminal charges and private prosecutors and as such provide pro bono help.

Court staff are unable to provide advice as to plea, as this would interfere with their impartiality, but they are able, and do, provide advice on procedural matters and will explain the effect of the court's orders. They are also able to help with problems over listings and provide initial advice on obtaining representation. In many courts initial advice is provided by leaflets distributed with summonses or handed to persons charged with criminal offences by custody officers.

In court, a magistrates' court clerk has a duty to assist an unrepresented defendant[6], but this stops short of conducting the case on the defendant's behalf[7] and is usually confined to indicating when questions can be asked. The court clerk will not usually have any advance knowledge of the defence case and the assistance provided will be restricted by this factor.

Free interviews

Most solicitors offer an initial free interview at which basic information is given to persons facing criminal proceedings and eligibility for Green Form assistance or a full legal aid order is assessed. Further representation will be dependent on payment of a fee or the existence of some assistance to meet the costs of representation. Conditional fees, whereby payment is only made where the solicitor obtains a successful solution, are not available in criminal cases.

Pro bono work

In some circumstances, usually where established clients face proceedings for which criminal legal aid is not available, solicitors will provide free representation. Whilst this is usually a commercially-driven decision to ensure client

3 Para 6, Code C of the Police and Criminal Evidence Act 1984.
4 Para 6D, Code C of the Police and Criminal Evidence Act 1984.
5 Code C, paras 3.6–3.11 of the Police and Criminal Evidence Act 1984.
6 *Simms v Moore* [1970] 3 All ER 1.
7 *Hobby v Hobby* [1954] 2 All ER 395.

loyalty, pro bono work may also be undertaken in cases of special interest. One specific example of such free representation is those cases where appeals against the death penalty have been brought before the Privy Council. In such cases, representation is normally provided by counsel without charge.

5. Voluntary sector schemes

Citizens' Advice Bureaux

Citizens' Advice Bureaux are located in most towns and cities throughout England and Wales and are listed in most phone books in the 'useful numbers' section.

They provide advice and assistance on a wide range of personal and legal problems which may be resolved through the intervention of the centre's staff or by an onward referral to specialist help. Some branches have volunteer solicitors in attendance at certain times.

In defending criminal matters, help is usually available to decipher summonses and other court documentation, provide general advice on the likely penalty and plea, assist in the completion of guilty plea forms and statements of means. Assistance is also provided in contacting solicitors where appropriate.

Pressure groups

Organisations such as the Animal Liberation Movement, CND and less radical organisations such as Taxidrivers' Federations have been known to fund the defence of members and supporters who have been charged with offences that have arisen during protests and rallies to support their cause.

CONCLUSION

Although it is not necessary to consider the alternative sources of legal advice and assistance that may be available to a person applying for a criminal legal aid order, it is appropriate to be aware that in the event that legal aid is not granted, alternative resources might be available. Some advocates have been heard to say, in support of their client's application for legal aid: 'If you refuse to grant my client a legal aid order, you deny him access to justice'. In many cases that assertion may be misleading, as it is not always the case.

Chapter Two

Sources of State Funded Representation other than a Criminal Legal Aid Order

This chapter considers alternative sources of legal advice and representation provided by the state to persons who are suspected of having committed criminal offences, or against whom proceedings have been commenced. The chapter will consider:

1. Legal Advice and Assistance (the Green Form Scheme)
2. Assistance by Way of Representation (ABWOR)
3. The Court Duty Solicitor scheme
4. The Police Station Duty Solicitor scheme and free legal advice at police stations from a defendant's own solicitor.

The chapter will outline the eligibility criteria and methods of application. Tables setting out the financial eligibility rates and remuneration rates are set out in Appendix H.

INTRODUCTION

The power to make a full criminal legal aid order only applies where the applicant is charged in criminal proceedings[1] and can satisfy the eligibility tests as to merits and means[2]. In the absence of any other scheme a person detained at a police station in order that allegations against him can be investigated, or persons who are facing a police application for a warrant of further detention before charge, would be without any right to representation. Similarly, persons unable to satisfy the provisions within the regulations as to the production of documentary evidence to support their statement of means, might be denied representation at a time where some important decisions are to be made as to the future conduct of the case, especially in relation to bail. To overcome these difficulties a range of schemes exists to fill the gaps in representation that can occur under the criminal legal aid scheme. These will be examined in turn.

LEGAL ADVICE AND ASSISTANCE

This scheme is frequently referred to as the 'Green Form Scheme', owning to the colour of the standard application form. Subject to certain exclusions, such as wills and conveyancing matters, legal advice and assistance is available to persons who qualify on the grounds of means, in respect of any question of law[3].

1 S 21(1) of the Legal Aid Act 1988 makes legal aid available to the 'accused or convicted' person.
2 S 21(2) and (5) of the Legal Aid Act 1988.
3 S 8(1) of the Legal Aid Act 1988.

The Legal Aid Board will not remunerate a solicitor who provides advice and assistance in relation to a matter which is not a question of English law. For the purpose of criminal proceedings in England or Wales, that restriction is likely to be of little consequence.

The scheme is not tested on merits, but is subject to a means test. This test is administered by the solicitor, who calculates whether the applicant is eligible by completing the relevant sections on the application form and then applying the means test from data supplied to him on a 'key card'. Applicants qualify if their disposable income, that is their gross income less standard allowances[4], is less than £76 per week. A single applicant may have capital resources of up to £1,000 and there are additional allowances for dependants in respect of capital and income. Applicants are automatically passported through the means test if they receive disability working allowance, family credit, income based job seekers' allowance or income support.

The scheme provides assistance in the early stages of the case and will allow the solicitor to perform the equivalent of two hours' work. Frequently this will be utilised in taking initial instructions and completing an application for a criminal legal aid order, but this part of the scheme can also be used to write letters to obtain the documentary evidence that is required to accompany the application.

It was standard practice to have the Green Form endorsed to extend it to allow representation in court, in circumstances where the court approved a solicitor's proposal to provide representation by him so that the case could proceed that day (see paragraph 2.1 below), but as this extends the scope of the Green Form to an application for ABWOR, the Legal Aid Board require that the form ABWOR 1 be completed and endorsed by the court. It is to be noted that the financial limits differ in respect of the Green Form and ABWOR.

ADVICE BY WAY OF REPRESENTATION (ABWOR)

Advice by Way of Representation (ABWOR) is available in respect of the following criminal proceedings in magistrates' courts:

1. where a person has not been refused representation under any other scheme that provides advice and assistance in respect of the same proceedings, and where the court:
   (i) is satisfied that the case should proceed (although this does not necessarily mean that it will be concluded) that day; and
   (ii) is satisfied that the accused person would not otherwise be represented; and
   (iii) requests a solicitor who is in the precincts of the court to provide representation; or
   (iv) approves a proposal from a solicitor who is within the precincts of the court to provide representation[5].
2. in relation to applications for a warrant of further detention[6];
3. where a person has not been refused representation under any other scheme that provides advice and assistance in respect of the same proceedings to provide representation:

4 See Appendix H, para 1.1.
5 Reg 7(1)(a) of the Legal Advice and Assistance (Scope) Regulations 1989.
6 Reg 7(1)(b) of the Legal Advice and Assistance (Scope) Regulations 1989.

FIG 1: APPLICATION FOR ADVICE AND ASSISTANCE – THE GREEN FORM

Legal Aid

Green Form

GF 1 Key Card

LEGAL AID BOARD LEGAL AID ACT 1988

To be used by solicitors with NO franchise contract which covers the category of work into which this green form falls

Legal aid account no:

Ref:

(Copy from extension authority before sending claim)

- **If you have a franchise contract covering the category of work into which this claim falls, complete form GF7.**
- **If you give advice and assistance about making a will you must submit form GF4 with your claim.**
- **You should keep a copy of the entire green form.**

Client's details

Please use block capitals **Delete the one which does not apply* Male/Female*

Surname: ______ First names: ______

Address: ______

______ Postcode: ______

National Insurance No: ______ Date of birth: ______

Capital details

(give these details even if the client gets income support, family credit or disability working allowance)

How many dependants (partner, children or other relatives of his/her household) does the client have? ______

Give the total savings and other capital which the client has (and if relevant his or her partner)

Client: £ ______

Spouse (or person living as if a spouse of the client): £ ______

Total: £ ______

A

Income details

Does the client get Income Support, Family Credit or Disability Working Allowance?

☐ Yes: ignore the rest of this section ☐ No: give the total gross weekly income of

The client: £ ______

The client's spouse (or person living as if a spouse of the client): £ ______

Total: £ ______

B

Calculate the total allowable deductions: Income tax: £ ______

National Insurance contributions: £ ______

Spouse (or person living as if a spouse of the client): £ ______

Attendance allowance, disability living allowance, constant attendance allowance and any payment made out of the Social Fund: £ ______

Dependent children and other dependants:

Age	*Number*	
Under 11	______	£ ______
11 to 15	______	£ ______
16 to 17	______	£ ______
18 and over	______	£ ______

C D E F G

Less total deductions: £ ______

Total weekly disposable income: £ ______

Client's declaration

I confirm that:

- I am over the compulsory school-leaving age (or, if not, the solicitor is advising me under Regulation 14(2A) Legal Advice & Assistance Regulations 1989);
- I have/have not *(delete whichever one is not correct)* previously received help from a solicitor on this matter under the green form; and
- I understand that I might have to pay my solicitor's costs out of any property or money which is recovered or preserved for me.

As far as I am aware, the information on this page is correct. I understand that if I give false information I could be prosecuted.

Signed: ______ **Date:** ___/___/___

96/02/06

Attach a completed Form GF3 as proof of every financial extension

Category of problem

Please tick the relevant box

☐ Personal injury *(G)* ☐ Debt *(E)* ☐ Housing *(D)* ☐ Welfare benefits *(H)* ☐ Crime *(C)* ☐ Immigration *(J)* ☐ Employment *(F)*

☐ Consumer/general contract *(K)*

☐ Matrimonial/family: *please also tick one of the following boxes:*

(A) ☐ Petitioner in divorce or judicial separation

(M) ☐ Respondent in divorce or judicial separation

(N) ☐ Child support assessment

(B) ☐ Other family matters *(please specify in the summary)*

☐ Other *(L) specify in the summary*

Solicitor charge

Has any money or property been recovered for the client? ☐ No: go on to the next section ☐ Yes: please give details:

Summary of work

Has a legal aid certificate or order been granted or applied for? ☐ No ☐ Yes: give the reference:

Please give below a brief summary of the work done:

Breakdown of work done

Please give a breakdown of the work done. If an extension has been granted, record below only the carry forward total times spent, and any subsequent work undertaken. Complete in chronological order, continuing on a separate sheet if necessary

FEE EARNER'S INITIALS	DATE D M Y	TRAVEL Hrs Mins	ATTENDANCE Hrs Mins	PREPARATION Hrs Mins
Totals carried forward from any extension(s) granted:		:	:	:
		:	:	:
		:	:	:
		:	:	:
		:	:	:
		:	:	:
		:	:	:
		:	:	:
		:	:	:
		:	:	:
		:	:	:
Time old rate		:	:	:
Costs old rate		£	£	£
Time current rate		:	:	:
Costs current rate		£	£	£
Total costs		£	£	£

Letters and Telephone Calls *(not telephone advice calls)*

		Number	£
Letters written	old rate:		
	current rate:		
Telephone calls	old rate:		
	current rate:		
	Total		

Details of disbursements

	£	VAT
Counsel's fees:		
Mileage:		
Other disbursements:		
Totals		

	Claimed	Area office use only Assessed
Profit costs:	£	£
VAT on profit costs:	£	£
Total disbursements:	£	£
VAT on disbursements:	£	£
Total claim:	£	£

➤ I certify that all the information given in this claim is correct: I have not claimed and will not otherwise claim for the same items from the Legal Aid Fund and I have held a valid practising certificate throughout the conduct of this matter.

Solicitor's personal signature: ______________ Date: / / Sol ref: ______________

Name & address of firm/office: ______________

May 1995

(i) to make an application for bail[7];
(ii) where the defendant is in custody but wishes the case to be concluded that day, provided that the solicitor believes this is in the defendant's best interests and that the case should not be adjourned in the interests of justice[8];
(iii) where the defendant is brought before the court as a result of a failure to obey an order of the court and where such a failure may lead to an order of imprisonment being made[9];
(iv) in the case of a defendant who is not in custody, where the solicitor believes the person requires ABWOR[10].

4. where the defendant is brought before the court in respect of failure to pay a fine or other monetary order made on conviction, where that failure may lead to imprisonment[11].

If the proceedings relate to committal or are where the defendant has pleaded 'not guilty', ABWOR is not available, unless the solicitor considers that there are exceptional circumstances[12]. There is no guidance as to what might constitute 'exceptional circumstances' and it seems reasonable to suggest that in the majority of cases any such circumstances will almost certainly amount to grounds for obtaining a full legal aid order. If a solicitor determines exceptional circumstances exist and provides representation, he runs the risk that the Legal Aid Board will disagree with his interpretation and disallow his claim for payment.

A closer examination of the criteria that provide ABWOR in magistrates' courts suggests that in many cases alternative sources of advice and assistance will be available.

1. Unrepresented defendants requiring the assistance of a solicitor already at court

Where courts are faced with unrepresented defendants who have attended at the court it is usual for those persons to be referred to the duty solicitor, rather than any other solicitor who happens to be present, and in this regard the first element of the criteria for representation that has been identified seems to duplicate the duty solicitor scheme.

Circumstances where this particular part of the ABWOR scheme may be of assistance will be where there is no duty solicitor available, for whatever reason, or where a solicitor attends court to deal with a particular client and comes across another established client who has failed to give him instructions in a matter that is to proceed that day. This limb of the criteria may also be of assistance where the duty solicitor cannot deal with a case referred to him because of a conflict of interest or other professional problem, and the case can then be referred to another solicitor who happens to be present in court.

Where this limb of ABWOR is used the court is required to endorse the form ABWOR 1 to show that it has extended the scope of the scheme to cover representation to the court. It was standard practice for the Green Form to be

7 Reg 7(2)(a) of the Legal Advice and Assistance (Scope) Regulations 1989.
8 Reg 7(2)(b) of the Legal Advice and Assistance (Scope) Regulations 1989.
9 Reg 7(2)(c) of the Legal Advice and Assistance (Scope) Regulations 1989.
10 Reg 7(2)(d) of the Legal Advice and Assistance (Scope) Regulations 1989.
11 Reg 7(4) of the Legal Advice and Assistance (Scope) Regulations 1989.
12 Reg 7(3) of the Legal Advice and Assistance (Scope) Regulations 1989.

endorsed in such circumstances, but if this is done the Legal Aid Board will return the claim and require the correct form to be endorsed.

2. Warrants of further detention

A defendant facing an application for a warrant of further detention prior to charge is ineligible for a full legal aid order as 'criminal proceedings' have not been commenced. There is clear distinction between this application and an application for a remand to local custody or police station cells after charge, as in the latter case a full legal aid order may be obtained.

ABWOR allows for representation to be provided on a means tested basis and the defendant may select the solicitor of his choice rather than being reliant on the services of the duty solicitor.

3. Bail applications

A full legal aid order must be granted, if the applicant qualifies in relation to his means, for so much of the proceedings as relates to bail, where he has already been remanded in custody by the court, and where he wishes to apply for bail and be represented whilst doing so, in circumstances where he was not represented at the hearing at which he was remanded in custody[13].

The restricted nature of this provision means that a defendant who is to be remanded in custody in respect of a case that would not otherwise attract legal aid would not be eligible for representation, even though his liberty is at stake. This would affect, for example, a person held in custody where the grounds for refusing bail are that he has already breached his bail in the same proceedings but the charge is of such a minor nature, perhaps a drunk and disorderly charge, that a legal aid order would not be granted. If such a person were remanded in custody he would not be eligible for representation until the second hearing.

The availability of ABWOR provides a solution to that problem by allowing representation, subject only to assessment of means, without any restriction in respect of applications for bail. This will allow representation at the first hearing where bail is to be considered, provided no other application for representation has been made and refused.

4. Concluding a case that day where the defendant is in custody

Where the defendant has not sought representation through any other application that has been refused, and is held in custody and wishes his case to be disposed of that day, a solicitor may provide representation under ABWOR, provided that the solicitor does not form the opinion that the case should be adjourned in the client's interests or the interests of justice.

In the majority of such cases this will mean that disposal will be by way of a guilty plea. The question arises as to the circumstances in which a solicitor would seek to have the case adjourned in the interests of the client or the interests of justice. Examples may include those cases where a defendant discloses a valid defence but insists on the entry of a guilty plea to negate prosecution objections to bail. The duty of client confidentiality and the requirement to act on the client's instructions or to withdraw will avoid any overt assertions that the

13 S 21(3)(c) of the Legal Aid Act 1988.

interests of the client require an adjournment, as the solicitor is bound to withdraw and respect his client's privilege, and it is therefore unlikely that the second limb of the criteria will have much effect.

5. Failure to obey orders of the court

ABWOR is available to persons brought before the court in respect of a failure to obey the orders of the court, providing that no other application for representation has been made and refused and the applicant qualifies for ABWOR on means. The scope of this provision appears to extend to both monetary and non-monetary orders and consequently allows representation, for example, in the following cases.

Financial court orders:

- Community charge or council tax enforcement hearings at the committal stage
- Means enquiries in respect of maintenance or affiliation arrears
- Means enquiries in respect of arrears accrued under legal aid contribution orders at the committal stage
- Proceedings to estreat sums imposed in consequence of ordering a bind over
- Estreating sums from sureties in bail cases

Non-financial court orders

- Breach of bail

6. Persons who are not in custody, but who, in the opinion of the solicitor, require ABWOR

The vague terms in which this provision is drafted make it difficult to establish ground rules as to what circumstances might suggest themselves as meriting ABWOR. In cases of mental infirmity, for example, it may be preferable to seek a full legal aid order and thereafter obtain authority to commission psychiatric reports, if the condition and subject matter merit such a step. In very simple cases it may be that the intervention of a solicitor on the day of the court hearing may enable the matter to be concluded speedily and efficiently, but great care is needed to ensure that the defendant's interests are not prejudiced. In most cases such representation as is required in respect of this class of case will be provided by the duty solicitor, unless he or she is unavailable or one of the other constraints applies, and it would seem that this provision is only likely to be used where a solicitor unexpectedly encounters one of his established clients needing urgent but prompt assistance.

It is to be noted that the burden of deciding whether the defendant requires assistance rests with solicitor and not the court[14].

7. Failure to pay fines or other monetary orders imposed on conviction

This part of ABWOR allows representation in respect of monetary orders imposed on conviction. Although the phrase 'on conviction' implies that the

14 Reg 7(2)(d) of the Legal Advice and Assistance (Scope) Regulations 1989.

FIG 2: APPLICATION FORM FOR ABWOR – ABWOR 1

Application for Assistance by way of Representation

Key Card

ABWOR 1

Application number: ______________ LEGAL AID BOARD LEGAL AID ACT 1988

Applicant's details *Please use block capitals*

Surname *Mr/Mrs/Miss/Ms:* ______________

First names: ______________

Date of birth: ___/___/___ Occupation: ______________

Permanent address: ______________

Capital details *(give these details even if the client gets income support, family credit or disability working allowance)*

A

How many dependants (partner, children or other relatives in his/her household) does the client have? ______

Give the total savings and other capital which the client has (and if relevant his or her partner)

Client: £ ______

Partner (if living with the client as man and wife): £ ______

Total: £ ______

Income details

B

Does the client get Income Support, Family Credit or Disability Working Allowance?

☐ Yes: ignore the rest of this section ☐ No: Please give the total weekly income of

The client: £ ______

The client's partner (if living with the client as man and wife): £ ______

Total: £ ______

Calculate the total allowable deductions: Income tax: £ ______ C

National Insurance contributions: £ ______ D

Partner (if living with the client as man and wife): £ ______ E

Attendance allowance, disability living allowance, constant attendance allowance and any payment made out of the Social Fund: £ ______ F

Dependent children and other dependants:

Age	*Number*	
Under 11	______	£ ______
11 to 15	______	£ ______
16 to 17	______	£ ______
18 and over	______	£ ______

G

Less total deductions: £ ______

Total weekly disposable income: £ ______

Weekly contribution: £ ______

Solicitor's details *Please use block capitals*

Conducting solicitor: ______________ Legal Aid account number: ______________

Name and address of firm: ______________

Dx no: ______________ Fax no: ______________

Tel no: ______________ Ref no: ______________

I certify that the conducting solicitor holds a current practising certificate and will not act or delegate the conduct of this matter while not certificated. *(To be signed by or on behalf of the conducting solicitor)*

Signature: ______________ **Date:** ___/___/___

Please tick the type of proceedings this application relates to: ***(tick one box only)*** ☐ Matrimonial or family ☐ Other

PAGE 2

The proceedings

▸ Please complete this section even if you have granted ABWOR under devolved powers

My client requires assistance by way of representation for ☐ ***taking*** ☐ ***defending proceedings relating to***

☐ Financial provision under Section 2 DPMCA 1978 [1]

☐ Agreed payments under Section 6 DPMCA 1978 [2]

☐ Confirmation of voluntary payments where the parties live apart or there is an interim maintenance order under Sections 7 & 19 DPMCA 1978 [3]

☐ Variation/revival or revocation of financial provision [4]

☐ Proceedings under the Children Act 1989 *(please specify in your client's statement precisely the order(s) sought or opposed)*

☐ Variation of residence or contact [6]

☐ Protection or exclusion order *(including breach)* [7]

☐ Mental Health Review Tribunal [10]

☐ Disciplinary proceedings before a prison governor [11]

☐ Representation before a Discretionary Lifer Panel [18]

☐ Other [13] *(please state)*

(This includes grants by the court - no statement needed, but the client must sign the form)

____

____

____

Date of hearing (if known): ___ / ___ / ___

Please give any of the following information that is relevant:

Opponent's surname *Mr/Mrs/Miss/Ms:* ____________________

Opponent's first names: ____________________

Opponent's address: ____________________

Opponent's date of birth: __________ Occupation: __________

Date of marriage: ___ / ___ / ___ Date the parties last lived together: ___ / ___ / ___

Name of child: ________________ Age: ______

Name of child: ________________ Age: ______

Name of child: ________________ Age: ______

Name of child: ________________ Age: ______

Franchised firms only

Do you want to receive the preferential payment on account?

☐ Yes ☐ No If 'yes', are you registered for VAT? ☐ Yes ☐ No

Have you granted Approval by Way of Representation under devolved powers in this case?

☐ Yes: please give the information asked for below ☐ No: ignore the rest of this section

I granted approval for Assistance by Way of Representation to my client on: ___ / ___ / ___

I granted the approval in the following terms *(please write the description in full and give the wording code)*:

____

____

________________________ Wording code: ______

with, if relevant, the following limitation *(please write the limitation in full and give the wording code)*:

____

________________________ Wording code: ______

Please give the ABWOR case code: ________

Now please give brief reasons for approving ABWOR in the statement section on page 3 and ask your client to sign and date it

PAGE 3

Statement of case

Please set out below a statement in support of your application (unless ABWOR has been granted by the court). If relevant, include details of your opponent's financial resources (if known) and corroborative evidence in support. If the application relates to child maintenance make the basis of the court's jurisdiction clear. Except in the case of step-children, child maintenance will only be covered if this is expressly stated in the ABWOR approval. If the application relates to proceedings before a Mental Health Review Tribunal, attach any relevant report.

➤ As far as I am aware, the financial information on the front of this form is correct. I understand that if I give false information I could be prosecuted.

➤ I authorise the Legal Aid Board to request the Clerk to the Justices to enforce any order for costs made in my favour in the proceedings, for which approval may be given, or to write off such costs if he considers they are irrecoverable or only recoverable at unjustified expense.

Signed by the client: ______________________ **Date:** ___ / ___ / ___

PAGE 4

For official use only

Granted/refused ______________ Case Code: ______________

Description wording codes
and/or non-standard text: ______________

Condition and limitation
wording codes (if any): ______________

October 1993

order should be made at the time of conviction, in practice many fines, compensation and costs orders will not be made until some time later, when pre-sentence reports have been obtained. It would seem unnecessarily harsh to strictly interpret the regulations in a restrictive way that excludes representation if there was a delay between conviction and sentence. In any event other provisions, such as the definition of criminal proceedings within the Legal Aid Act[15], have been generously defined[16] in similar circumstances and the effect of those decisions is certainly persuasive in this respect.

The usefulness of this provision within ABWOR has probably been abated as full legal aid orders can now be obtained in respect of proceedings to enforce compensation orders in criminal proceedings[17] and it is widely accepted that this power extends to include orders for costs and fines made in the same circumstances.

THE COURT DUTY SOLICITOR SCHEME

The Court Duty Solicitor scheme provides for the attendance of a locally based solicitor at a magistrates' court in order that he might be on hand to provide advice and assistance free to persons who are in custody or otherwise appearing before the magistrates' court and require his assistance. The advice and assistance provided are forms of ABWOR[18] provided under arrangements made by the Legal Aid Board[19]. The scheme is administered by local committees[20] who select suitably qualified solicitors[1] to the panel and draw a rota of solicitors who will attend the magistrates' court to provide the advice and assistance.

Unlike other forms of ABWOR, the advice and representation can be provided without any reference to the person's finances[2] and no written application is required. The solicitor obtains his payment through the submission of a standard report.

Where a person is discovered in custody by a duty solicitor and they either choose to be represented by a solicitor of their own choosing, or are an established client of another firm of solicitors, the duty solicitor's role is to communicate with the other firm or solicitor and advise them of their client's imminent appearance before the court. If a person who has received advice or assistance from a duty solicitor decides that he wishes that solicitor to continue to represent him, the defendant must be informed of his freedom to select any solicitor of his choosing before he is invited to nominate that solicitor. The duty solicitor cannot be paid under a legal aid order for work done in respect of clients he is assisting as duty solicitor as the schemes are not intended to duplicate one another.

The range of assistance and representation that can be provided is otherwise identical to that available under ABWOR.

15 S 19(5) of the Legal Aid Act 1988.
16 See for example *R v Redbridge Magistrates' Court, ex p Guppy* (1995) 159 JP 622 and *R v Crown Court at Liverpool, ex p McCann* [1995] RTR 23.
17 *R v Redbridge Magistrates' Court,* ex p Guppy (1995) 159 JP 622.
18 Reg 7 of the Legal Advice and Assistance Regulations 1989.
19 Legal Aid Board Duty Solicitor Arrangements 1994.
20 Para 6 of the Legal Aid Board Duty Solicitor Arrangements 1994.
1 Paras 31 and 32 of the Legal Aid Board Duty Solicitor Arrangements 1994.
2 Para 7(3) of the Legal Aid Board Duty Solicitor Arrangements 1994.

FIG 3: REPORT BY COURT DUTY SOLICITOR

DSC

LEGAL AID BOARD
LEGAL AID ACT 1988

REPORT BY COURT DUTY SOLICITOR

Legal Aid

for official use only

Please complete sections 1, 2 & 3 of this report form.
You should retain the first copy; the remaining two copies should be sent within 3 months of attendance at court to the area office in whose area the court you attended as duty solicitor is situated.
If you provide "advice and representation" to more than 16 defendants, please complete section 3 only of another form with details of the additional defendants. Sections 1 & 2 of this form should be fully completed to cover all the defendants.

SECTION 1

1. Name of duty solicitor: ....
2. Firm name: ....
3. Address of firm: ....
   .... Office telephone no: (.............. STD) ....
4. Name of court attended: .... magistrates/juvenile/both (delete as appropriate)
5. Date of attendance: ....
6. Time spent in attendance at court:
   (a) morning session .... am to .... am/pm
   (b) afternoon session .... pm to .... pm
   (c) total time spent at court (excluding lunch recess and any time spent attending existing clients) for which remuneration is claimed .... hours .... minutes.
7. Travel:
   (a) if you are claiming for travel, delete one or other of the following:-
      (i) I was not required to be in attendance at the court but was called in by the court to provide "advice and representation", or
      (ii) I had left the court where I acted as duty solicitor but was recalled by the court to provide "advice and representation" to another defendant.
   (b) time spent in travelling from your office to the court, and return .... hours .... minutes
   (c) if travel by car, state mileage .... miles
8. I certify that:
   (i) the above information is correct
   (ii) I provided "advice and representation" to .... defendants and certify that the information set out in Section 3 is correct OR I attended court but no defendant required "advice or representation" *(delete as appropriate).*
   (iii) the time for which remuneration as duty solicitor is claimed was spent solely for the purpose of providing "advice and representation", and
   (iv) the time for which remuneration as duty solicitor is claimed is not and will not be the subject of any other claim for remuneration (ie for green form or criminal legal aid).
   Signature of duty solicitor ....
9. DECLARATION AS TO CERTIFICATION: I HEREBY DECLARE THAT I HAVE AT ALL TIMES DURING THE CONDUCT BY ME OF THE MATTER TO WHICH THE CLAIM RELATES HELD A VALID PRACTISING CERTIFICATE.

Signed by Conducting Solicitor

NOTICE OF ASSESSMENT **FOR OFFICIAL USE ONLY**

Your costs have been assessed as set out below. If the assessment is accepted please return this form duly signed where indicated. If the assessment is not accepted you may appeal in writing within 21 days to the Area Committee in support of your claim as originally submitted or on any item in it if you so wish. This form should be returned with your representations.

Attendance at Court £
Travelling time £
Travelling expenses £
VAT £

Assessment

.... Date
Authorised Signatory
Legal Aid Area No.

I accept this assessment

.... Date
Duty Solicitor

Oakley Press PLC Nov. 1989

COPY FOR ACCOUNTS DEPARTMENT

SECTION 2

CLAIM FOR COSTS

A	LEGAL AID ACCOUNT NO.	Attendance at Court £	p	Travelling time* £	p	Travelling expenses* £	p	V.A.T.† £	p

*can only be claimed if you are called in to the court
†only complete if your firm is registered for V.A.T.

SECTION 3

DETAILS OF DEFENDANTS PROVIDED WITH ADVICE AND REPRESENTATION

Defendants' names (initials & surname)

Do NOT include defendants for whom the only service provided was to contact their own solicitor

Please tick relevant columns

Defendants' names	defendant				charge				assistance provided by duty solicitor		result of hearing (where duty solicitor represents): plea				sentence (if applicable)			adjourn/remand: custody		adjourn/remand: on bail		
	adult	juvenile	in custody	on bail/summons	indictable/either way	summary (non-motoring)	motoring	fine default, etc.	advice *without* representation	representation	guilty	not guilty	mixed plea	no plea taken	custodial	suspended sentence	fine, other	no bail application	unsuccessful bail application	contested bail application	uncontested bail application	other result e.g. bind over
	1	2	1	2	1	2	3	4	1	2	1	2	3	4	1	2	3	4	5	6	7	8

FOR AREA OFFICE USE ONLY

Region No.

No. of Defendants

Date of Attendance

D D M M Y Y

Court Identifier

Provisional Assessment Indicator

FOR AREA OFFICE USE ONLY

Payment of duty solicitor's claim authorised

Signed: ______________________ Date: ______________________

AUTHORISED SIGNATORY LEGAL AREA NO.

FOR ACCOUNTS DEPARTMENT USE ONLY

B	CONTROL TOTAL £	p

FOR AREA OFFICE USE ONLY

Date of receipt of claim

FIG 4: ABWOR CLAIM FORM FOR ATTENDANCE AT A POLICE STATION

DSPS 1

LEGAL AID BOARD - LEGAL AID ACT 1988

ADVICE AT POLICE STATIONS REPORT

Legal Aid

Area Reference

Date of receipt of claim

Total claim £

This form should be completed whether you acted as own solicitor or 24-hour duty solicitor.

Please complete Sections 1,2,3,4 and 5

Section 6 should be completed where a client has been represented on an application for a warrant of further detention or extension of such a warrant

You should retain the copy of this form marked "*Solicitor's Copy*".

The remaining two copies should be sent to your Legal Aid Area Office.

Claims for standby and hotel expenses should be made on form DSPS 2.

SECTION 1

Office Use Only

Client's surname **Initials**

Client's address

I acted as	*Tick one box*
own solicitor	*1*
24-hour rota duty solicitor	*2*
24-hour panel duty solicitor	*3*
24-hour back-up duty solicitor	*4*
both own and duty solicitor	*5*

Police Station where client was located

Date of first attendance (day, month, year)

Was your client	*Tick one box*
an adult (civilian)	*6*
a juvenile (civilian)	*7*
a Services person being investigated by Services police: Army *8* Navy *9* RAF *10*	

State offence for which client is being investigated (If more than one, state the most serious)

Is this offence	*Tick one box*
an arrestable offence	*11*
a non-arrestable offence	*12*

Did you advise and assist the client when he/she was attending the police station	*Tick one box*
voluntarily	*13*
under arrest	*14*
both	*15*

Did you advise the client	*Tick one box*
in office hours	*16*
out of office hours	*17*
both	*18*

If you acted as duty solicitor, was advice given by a duty solicitor's representative? **YES** *19* **NO** *20*

Legal Aid Account No.

Solicitor's Reference

VAT Registration No. (if required)

LBF APRIL 95

SECTION 2 WORK DONE

Visits to Police Station	**1st visit**	**2nd visit**	**3rd visit**	**4th visit**
From				
To				
Use 24-hour clock for times				

Own solicitor	Time (in mins)	Cost Claimed £ p	Office Use £ p
Travelling			
Waiting			
Advice and assistance at station			
Sub Total			
Duty Solicitor			
Travelling			
Waiting and advising at station			
Sub Total			
Telephone calls			
Total time on advice and assistance calls			
No. of advice and assistance calls			
No. of routine calls			
Sub Total			
ABWOR			
Sub total profit costs			
VAT on profit costs			
Total profit costs inc. VAT			
Disbursements and travel			
Total disbursements *(enter details in Section 3 & 6 overleaf)*			
Mileage *(if appropriate)*			
VAT on travel and disbursements *(where appropriate)*			
Total disbursements and travel inc. VAT			

Has your client previously received advice and assistance in respect of this matter **YES** **NO** *(If 'yes' please see section 3)*

Date **Signed (for solicitor)**

DECLARATION AS TO CERTIFICATION: I hereby declare that I have at all times during the conduct by me of the matter to which the claim relates held a valid practising certificate.

.... Signed by Conducting Solicitor

Duty Solicitor Region **Scheme identifier**

Provisional Assessment Y N

Signed Authorised Signatory

Legal Aid Area No. **Date**

ACCOUNTS DEPARTMENT'S COPY

Duty and own solicitors use this form.

SECTION 3

Details of disbursements *Please include the amount of VAT (if any) on disbursements where indicated below*		
Disbursements £	:	:
VAT on disbursements £	:	:
(include these amounts in 'Disbursements' and 'VAT on travel and disbursement' boxes in section 2)		

If the client has previously received advice and assistance in respect of this matter, please state the date of the advice, the amount of the claim and the name and the address of the solicitor

Does the office have a crime franchise?

Tick one box	Yes		No	

If the office does not have a crime franchise and you have exceeded the costs limit, please explain why it was necessary in the interests of justice that advice and assistance was given as a matter of urgency.

For office use		
Authority to exceed costs limit		
Granted		
Refused		
Date		
Signed		

SECTION 4

Details and category of the person advising

Duty Solicitor	= 1	Accredited representative	= 5
Duty Solicitor Representative	= 2	Probationary representative	= 6
Own Solicitor	= 3	Immigration representative	= 7
Trainee Solicitor representative	= 4		

For initial telephone advice

Name					
Date		Category (1 - 7)		PIN no.	

For first attendance at police station

Name					
Date		Category (1 - 7)		PIN no.	

For any subsequent attendance at police station

Name					
Date		Category (1 - 7)		PIN no.	
Name					
Date		Category (1 - 7)		PIN no.	
Name					
Date		Category (1 - 7)		PIN no.	

Type of case: *Tick one box only*

Immigration		Indictable only		either way		summary	

SECTION 5

Solicitor's name

Firm's name, address and telephone number

Document exchange number

SECTION 6

To be completed only if you represented a client on an application for a warrant of further detention or an extension of such a warrant (ABWOR)

Total time spent *(Use 24-hour clock for times)*	
From	
To	

	Time (in mins)	Claim for costs: Claimed £ p	Claim for costs: Assessed £ p
Travelling		:	:
Personal attendance		:	:
Preparation		:	:
Waiting for advocacy			
Waiting		:	:
Advocacy		:	:
Letters and telephone calls			
No. of letters written		:	:
No. of telephone calls		:	:
Total for Section 6 so far		:	:
(enter this amount in 'ABWOR' box in Section 2)			
Travel expenses			
Mileage *(if appropriate)*		:	:
(include this amount in 'Travel expenses' box in Section 2).			

Details of disbursements *Please include the amount of VAT (if any) on disbursements where indicated below*		
Disbursements £	:	:
VAT on disbursements £	:	:
(include these amounts in 'Disbursements' and 'VAT on travel and disbursement' boxes in section 2)		

FIG 5: POLICE STATION DUTY SOLICITOR STANDBY CLAIM FORM

DSPS 2

Area Reference

LEGAL AID BOARD
LEGAL AID ACT 1988

Advice at Police Stations Standby Claim

Legal Aid

This form should only be completed where you are claiming a standby payment or hotel expenses. If you have given advice and assistance to any clients at a police station, you must submit all the relevant DSPS 1 forms with this form.

Section 1 must always be completed. Section 2 covers hotel expenses and Section 3 standby claims. Any standby claimed on this form should not be for a period of more than 24 hours.

You should retain the copy of this form marked "*Solicitor's Copy*", the remaining two copies should be sent to your area office.

Please submit DSC (Report by Court Duty Solicitor) form with this form if you were in attendance at court as court duty solicitor during the period for which you are claiming a standby payment.

SECTION 1

Solicitor's name

Firm's name, address and telephone number

Solicitor's Reference

Document Exchange No.

VAT Registration No. *(if required)*

Legal Aid Account No.

Does the office have a crime franchise?
Tick one box Yes No

Date

Signed (for solicitor)

DECLARATION AS TO CERTIFICATION

I hereby declare that I have at all times during the conduct by me of the matter to which the claim relates, held a valid practising certificate.

Signed by Conducting Solicitor.

SECTION 2 CLAIM FOR HOTEL EXPENSES

Hotel expenses *Please submit receipts*	£ :	£ :
VAT	£ :	£ :
Total	£ :	£ :

SECTION 3 CLAIM FOR STANDBY PAYMENT

Name of rota

Date on rota duty

Did you change your rota period on duty?
Tick one box Yes No

If yes, please give the name and address of solicitor with whom you changed

Time (use 24 hour clock) Start	Finish	No. of hours on duty

Total number of DSPS 1 forms submitted with this form

Were you also in attendance as court duty solicitor?
Tick one box Yes No

For office use

1	Check duty solicitor rota		
2	Number of hours on rota		
3	Maximum eligible standby payment	£	:
4	Less 50% or amount claimed if less (excluding VAT)	£	:
5	Total Standby payment	£	:
	VAT	£	:
	TOTAL	£	:

Duty Solicitor Region | Scheme Identifier

Total standby payment	£	:
VAT	£	:
TOTAL	£	:

Date of receipt of claim

Signed Authorised Signatory

Legal Aid Area No. Date

LBF AUGUST 94

ACCOUNTS DEPARTMENT'S COPY

THE POLICE STATION DUTY SOLICITOR SCHEME

The Police Station Duty Officer scheme provides for legal advice to be provided free of charge to any person detained in a police station. The scheme provides for a panel of duty solicitors to be appointed[3] by a local committee. In practice the same committee selects both court and police station duty solicitors.

The scheme is a form of ABWOR[4] and provides for funding for a defendant's own solicitor, rather than the duty panel solicitor, to attend at the police station. Where a firm maintains its own call-out rota for its solicitors, the Board will not make payment of the standby fee, which is payable to duty solicitors even if they are not called.

Duty solicitors who attend at the police station are required to attend a training course prior to their selection[5]. In addition, clerks who attend on behalf of duty solicitors are required to be accredited by passing examinations that deal with all aspects of police station work[6].

Payment is made on the basis of claim forms submitted by the duty solicitor directly to the Legal Aid Board.

3 Paras 33 to 37 of the Duty Solicitor Arrangements 1994.
4 Established under reg 6 of the Legal Advice and Assistance Regulations 1989.
5 Para 33(3) of the Duty Solicitor Arrangements 1994.
6 Sch 2 to the Duty Solicitor Arrangements 1994.

Chapter Three

Criminal Legal Aid Scheme – Methods Of Application

This chapter will cover:

1. The scope of the criminal legal aid scheme
2. Authorities competent to grant criminal legal aid orders
3. Method of application
4. The timing of applications
5. Content of applications

THE SCOPE OF THE CRIMINAL LEGAL AID SCHEME

The criminal legal aid scheme exists, in part, to honour the United Kingdom's obligations as a signatory to the European Convention on Human Rights[1]. Consequently, in assessing whether legal aid should be granted to any one individual, the competent authority will be required to determine whether it is in the interests of justice to grant an order. In order to do this two tests will be applied, the first being whether the applicant's finances are such that he or she requires assistance[2] and the second whether the merits of the application are such that a grant of representation is required[3].

Criminal legal aid is available to any person charged with a criminal offence, or who is the subject of criminal proceedings commenced by way of information, that is to be determined before a magistrates' court, the Crown Court, the Criminal Division of the Court of Appeal or the Courts Martial Appeal Court[4]. Criminal legal aid is not available to the prosecution except to enable an individual, who is not acting in an official capacity, to resist an appeal to the Crown Court in respect of an earlier conviction in the magistrates' court[5]. There are grounds for believing that the power to allow a private prosecutor to resist an appeal from the findings of a magistrates' court would extend to proceedings that are not truly criminal in nature, such as proceedings under section 99 of the Public Health Act 1936[6].

'Criminal Proceedings' is defined by the Act so as to include proceedings relating to applications for persons to be bound over to keep the Peace[7], or for

1 Art 6(3)(c) of the European Convention on Human Rights.
2 S 21(5) of the Legal Aid Act 1988.
3 S 21(2) of the Legal Aid Act 1988.
4 S 19(1) of the Legal Aid Act 1988.
5 S 21(1) of the Legal Aid Act 1988.
6 *R v Crown Court at Inner London, ex p Bentham* [1989] 1 WLR 408, although this point was decided on the basis of s 28(5) of the Legal Aid Act 1974, which whilst similar in nature is not identical to the existing provision.
7 Under s 115 Magistrates' Courts Act 1980.

the estreatment of any recognisance[8]. The definition also extends to proceedings dealing with an offender 'in respect of any sentence' and this has been held to include applications to vary any order made on conviction of an offender, including applications for the restoration of a driving licence[9] and proceedings to enforce payment of a compensation order[10]. Orders cannot be granted to resist applications for monies seized under section 25 of the Criminal Justice (International Co-operation) Act 1990, where monies are thought to be the proceeds of drugs trafficking[11].

COMPETENT AUTHORITIES TO GRANT LEGAL AID ORDERS AND METHOD OF APPLICATION

The basic provisions determining competence to grant criminal legal aid orders are contained within the Legal Aid Act 1988, which defines which courts may grant such orders. Those provisions are supplemented by the Legal Aid in Criminal and Care Proceedings (General) Regulations 1989, which extend the basic provisions so as to allow justices' clerks, their nominated subordinates and officers of the Crown Court to grant orders without reference to a court. The regulations also set out the methods by which applications which have been unsuccessful may be renewed and the authorities that may consider such applications[12]. This section will set out the basic provisions and will then move on to consider the extent of the jurisdiction to grant legal aid orders within each court. In doing so the procedures that must be adopted will discussed.

Figure 1 provides an overview of the courts competent to consider legal aid applications.

1. Magistrates' courts

Magistrates' courts become competent to grant legal aid orders as soon as a defendant is charged with an offence[13] and, in theory, the use of computerisation, which allows the police to enter cases directly onto magistrates' courts' systems, should enable magistrates' courts to be able to verify instantly whether proceedings have been commenced. Where the proceedings are by way of information, the proceedings commence as soon as a valid information is accepted[14], although in practice an application for legal aid is unlikely to be submitted until after a summons has been issued and served, because it is unlikely that the defendant in the proceedings will be aware of them.

Applications for criminal legal aid orders may be made to the justices' clerk in writing on Form 5[15], or may be made orally to the court[16]. In either case the application must be supported by a statement of means on Form 5[17], unless one

8 S 19(5) of the Legal Aid Act 1988.
9 *R v Crown Court at Liverpool 159 JP 622, ex p McCann* [1995] RTR 23.
10 *R v Redbridge Magistrates' Court, ex p Guppy*, (1995) 159 JP 622.
11 *R v Crawley Justices, ex p Ohakwe* (1994) 158 JP 781.
12 Renewal procedures are dealt with in Chapter 8.
13 S 20(8) of the Legal Act 1988.
14 *R v Manchester Stipendary Magistrate, ex p Hill* [1983] 1 AC 328.
15 Reg 11(1)(a) of the Legal Aid in Criminal and Care Proceedings (General) Regulations 1989.
16 Reg 11(1)(b) of the Legal Aid in Criminal and Care Proceedings (General) Regulations 1989.
17 Reg 23(2) of the Legal Aid in Criminal and Care Proceedings (General) Regulations 1989.

FIG 1: AUTHORITIES COMPETENT TO CONSIDER APPLICATIONS FOR CRIMINAL LEGAL AID ORDERS IN THE FIRST INSTANCE

COURTS COMPETENT TO CONSIDER CRIMINAL LEGAL AID APPLICATIONS

MAGISTRATES' COURTS.	CROWN COURT.	COURT OF APPEAL/ COURT MARTIAL APPEAL COURT.	HOUSE OF LORDS.
Magistrates' courts 1. After charge but before first appearance. s20(8). 2. During any criminal proceedings before it. s 20(2)	**Magistrates' courts** 1. When sitting as examining justices. s 20(5) 2. On committal for trial or sentence. s 20(4)(a) 3. On notice of transfer. s 20(4)(b) &(bb) **Crown Court** 1. During any criminal proceedings before it. s 20(2) **Court of Appeal and House of Lords** 1. When ordering a retrial.	**Crown Court** 1. On appeals under s9(11) Criminal Justice Act 1987 s 20(b) 2. To obtain leave to appeal s 20(b) Court ofAppeal/Court Martial Appeal Court. 1. During any criminal proceedings before it. s 20(2)	**Court of Appeal/Court Martial Appeal Court.** 1. On granting leave to appeal

Note All references within this diagram refer to the Legal Aid Act 1988.

of the rare exceptions applies that will avoid the necessity of lodging a such a statement[18]. In the majority of cases applications are submitted to the justices' clerk in order that they can be considered prior to the first date of hearing.

The term 'justices' clerk' includes any person duly authorised by him to discharge his duties under the Legal Aid Act 1988 and this allows applications to be determined by court clerks or administrative officers, thereby increasing the ability of the court to consider legal aid applications promptly.

Where the application is being made in respect of proceedings that are to take place before the Crown Court, the application for legal aid may be made orally to the magistrates' court at the conclusion of the proceedings before that court[19]. If the proceedings before the Crown Court are commenced by way of transfer, or by committal under section 6(2) of the Magistrates' Courts Act 1980, or as a result of notice of appeal being given in relation to a magistrates' courts decision, the application for legal aid may be made to the justices' clerk in such a form as he requires[20].

Where an application is submitted to the clerk to the justices or a magistrates' court the application may be granted or refused[1], but the court must keep records of the reasons for its decision and these must be disclosed to the applicant or to his or her solicitor with the notice of refusal[2]. Guidance issued to justices' clerks[3] suggests that the reasons should be noted on Form 1 which must then be copied and sent to the applicant if the application is refused. A legal aid order cannot be made until the court or the justices' clerk has considered a statement of means, unless the applicant is not required to furnish the court with one[4]. If the application is made orally to the court, the court may refer the application to the justices' clerk for consideration[5] and he may grant or refuse it.

The court effectively applies two tests when considering the application, the first being a means test to determine whether or not the applicant's resources are such that he requires legal aid, and the second, the interests of justice test. These tests are set out separately within this text at Chapters 4 and 6 below.

If the application is refused the court must issue the following documents to the applicant and his solicitor:

1. the notice of refusal – Form 2[6];
2. a copy of the court's record of the reasons for the decision[7] – which in most cases will mean a photocopy of the application form, endorsed to show the reasons for the refusal. Good practice would suggest that the reasons for the decision should be supplied in all cases, even where there is no right of renewal to the area committee;
3. the completed Form 1 – if there is a right of renewal to the area committee and this has not been supplied to satisfy 2 above[8].

18 See Chapter 4 for a full discussion of when a statement of means is required.
19 Reg 18(1)(a) of the Legal Aid in Criminal and Care Proceedings (General) Regulations 1989.
20 Reg 18(1)(b) to (d) of the Legal Aid in Criminal and Care Proceedings (General) Regulations 1989.
1 Reg 11(1) of the Legal Aid in Criminal and Care Proceedings (General) Regulations 1989.
2 Reg 8(2) of the Legal Aid in Criminal and Care Proceedings (General) Regulations 1989.
3 Para 8-20 of the 'Guidance to granting authorities on the Legal Aid In Criminal and Care Proceedings (General) (Amendment) Regulations 1995' – Lord Chancellor's Department 24.3.95 (reproduced in Appendix A).
4 Reg 11(3) of the Legal Aid in Criminal and Care Proceedings (General) Regulations 1989.
5 Reg 11(2) of the Legal Aid in Criminal and Care Proceedings (General) Regulations 1989.
6 Reg 12(2)(a) of the Legal Aid in Criminal and Care Proceedings (General) Regulations 1989.
7 Reg 12(2)(b) of the Legal Aid in Criminal and Care Proceedings (General) Regulations 1989.
8 Reg 12(2)(c) of the Legal Aid in Criminal and Care Proceedings (General) Regulations 1989.

FIG 2: OVERVIEW OF APPLICATION PROCESS IN MAGISTRATES' COURTS

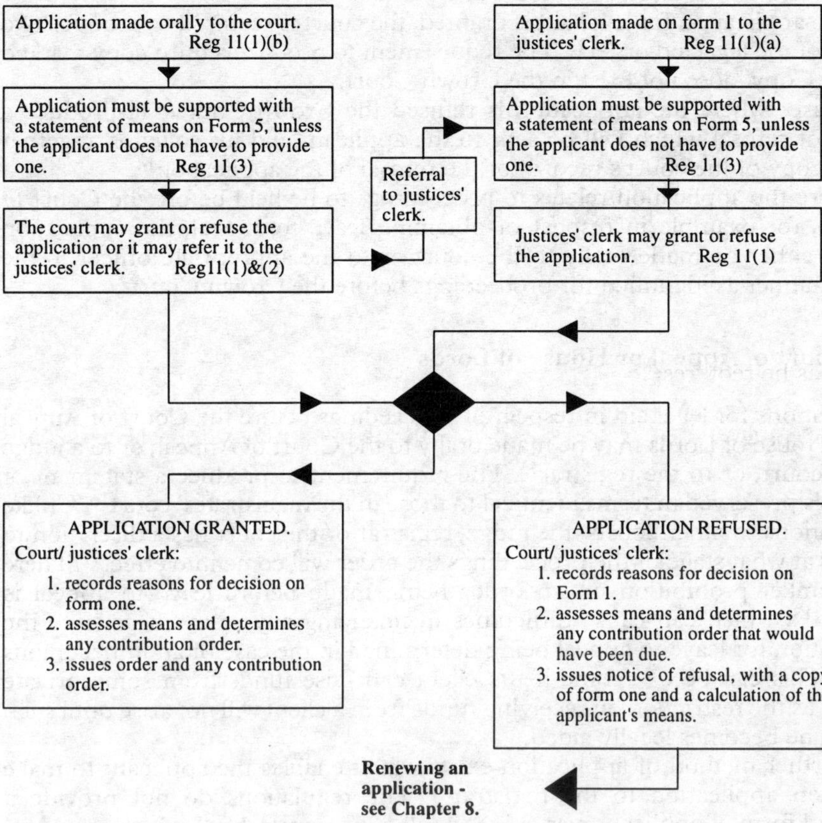

The procedure for renewing failed applications is discussed in Chapter 8 below.

Where the application has been granted the court or justices clerk must supply the following:

1. a legal aid order on Form 11 – one copy to the legally assisted person and two copies to the solicitor, one being marked 'Board Copy'[9]; and
2. where a contribution order has been made, a contribution order in Form 6 shall be sent to the legally assisted person , the person ordered to pay the contribution and the assigned solicitor.

2. Crown Court

Where proceedings are to take place before the Crown Court and a legal aid order has been made in the magistrates' court, an application can be made to the appropriate officer of the Crown Court on Form 1[10]. Identical rules apply in the Crown Court as to the production of a statement of means[11] and

9 Reg 40(1)(a) & 40(2) of the Legal Aid in Criminal and Care Proceedings (General) Regulations 1989.
10 Reg 18(1) of the Legal Aid in Criminal and Care Proceedings (General) Regulations 1989.
11 Reg 18(2) of the Legal Aid in Criminal and Care Proceedings (General) Regulations 1989.

supporting documents as in exist in the magistrates' court. Applications for legal aid can also be made orally to the Crown Court[12].

If the application for legal aid is granted, the court is required to produce two copies of the legal aid order[13]. The requirement to produce a third copy marked 'Board Copy' does not exist in the Crown Court.

In cases where the application is refused the Crown Court will produce a notice of refusal which will be sent to the applicant and his solicitor, together with a copy of the court's record for the refusal of the application[14].

Where the application relates to proceedings to be held before the Court of Appeal, for example in respect of obtaining leave to appeal, the application should either be made orally to the court or to the appropriate officer in the same manner as identified for proceedings before the Crown Court.

3. Court of Appeal or House of Lords

Applications for legal aid in respect of proceedings before the Court of Appeal or the House of Lords may be made orally to the Court of Appeal, or to a judge of the court, or to the registrar[15]. The requirement to produce a statement of means is preserved in terms identical to those in the magistrates' court[16]. Unlike applications to other courts, the judge, registrar or the court has a discretion to specify at what stage of the proceedings the order will come into effect[17]. There is a blanket prohibition on an order being made before leave to appeal is granted[18], which can cause difficulties in financing any research prior to the application for leave to appeal being determined in the case of an impecunious client. This can be overcome if the client can raise funds from some private source, as the restriction on receiving funds from a client will not arise until such time as he becomes legally aided.

A further method of application exists which enables the applicant to make a written application to the registrar[19]. The regulations do not provide a standard form of application as exists for all other courts, but leave the registrar free to direct the application to be made in a format of his choosing. Whatever form is selected the application will have to be supported by a statement of means in Form 5 with the production of the relevant documentation.

Where the Court of Appeal or the House of Lords orders a re-trial to be heard by a lower court, an application may be made to the Court of Appeal, a judge of that court, or the registrar in the same manner as that prescribed in respect of proceedings before it.[20]

TIMING OF APPLICATIONS

Generally solicitors will wish to submit applications for legal aid as soon as is practicable, in order to ensure that all their work is properly funded from the

12 Reg 18(1)(a) of the Legal Aid in Criminal and Care Proceedings (General) Regulations 1989.
13 Reg 40(2) of the Legal Aid in Criminal and Care Proceedings (General) Regulations 1989.
14 Reg 19(2) of the Legal Aid in Criminal and Care Proceedings (General) Regulations 1989.
15 Reg 22(1) of the Legal Aid in Criminal and Care Proceedings (General) Regulations 1989.
16 Reg 22(5)(b) of the Legal Aid in Criminal and Care Proceedings (General) Regulations 1989.
17 Reg 22(6) of the Legal Aid in Criminal and Care Proceedings (General) Regulations 1989.
18 Reg 22(5)(a) of the Legal Aid in Criminal and Care Proceedings (General) Regulations 1989.
19 Reg 22(1)(b) of the Legal Aid in Criminal and Care Proceedings (General) Regulations 1989.
20 S 20(4) of the Legal Aid Act 1988.

outset. If there is a delay in the submission of a legal aid order and urgent work has to be carried out prior to the commencement of the order, the solicitor can claim for that work if he can satisfy the taxing authority that the work was urgent, there was no undue delay in submitting the application and the work was undertaken by the solicitor assigned under the order[1]. This power to claim for work done retrospectively applies where the court does not consider the legal aid application until after the proceedings have been concluded, as it is now settled law that the court retains its jurisdiction to grant a legal aid order beyond the conclusion of the substantive proceedings.[2] This retained jurisdiction removes the need for courts to consider granting conditional orders or to back date orders, which are practices disapproved of by the High Court[3].

There may be circumstances where a solicitor will need to consider whether or not the contributions that would be payable during the early stages of a case will exceed the level of the solicitor's fees for that work. If this is the case, there may be merit in postponing an application for legal aid until later in the proceedings, but, if this course of action is undertaken where there are co-defendants, there is an inherent risk that when legal aid is granted the order will be assigned to a solicitor not of the applicant's choosing because he has already been retained under a legal aid order in respect of defendant with whom the applicant has no conflict.

Examples of circumstances where delay might prove beneficial include cases where the magistrates' courts proceedings will eventually lead to an uncontested committal for trial under section 6(2) of the Magistrates' Courts Act 1980 or where there is likely to be a lengthy delay before summary trial.

CONTENT OF APPLICATIONS

Research commissioned by the Legal Aid Board in 1992[4] revealed a disparate rate of percentage grant rates in magistrates' courts ranging from 35% at one magistrates' court to a rate of 100% at some others. The report also found that court clerks charged with determining such applications attached differing levels of importance to the various criteria expressed within the Legal Aid Act and that, generally, the content of applications with which they were presented was of a poor standard. The Report's findings appear to be confirmed by the comments of court staff during seminars run by the author.

An application seems more likely to succeed if it contains more than simple statements that assert that the criteria apply without any apparent reasoning. Less weight is attached to applications where standard phrases are used, particularly where, for example, the assertion is that the applicant is at risk of a custodial sentence when the offence is only punishable with a fine. If documentary evidence is available to support what is being said, this should always be included, as it is difficult to reject it and covering letters can be effective in imparting more complex information than can be included in the application form.

1 Reg 44(7) of the Legal Aid in Criminal and Care Proceedings (General) Regulations 1989.

2 *R v Highbury Corner Magistrates' Court, ex p Sonn Co* [1995] 4 All ER 57.

3 See in addition to *Ex p Sonn Co, Welch v Redbridge Justices* (1984) 148 JP 474 and *R v Newham Justices, ex p Mumtaz* (1990) 154 JP 597.

4 *In the Interests of Justice? The Determination of Criminal Legal Aid Applications by Magistrates' Courts in England and Wales* Young, Maloney and Saunders, (1992) Legal Aid Board.

The lesson for applicants and their solicitors is a simple one. It is that a properly prepared, comprehensive, application will succeed in circumstances where other applications might fail.

Chapter Four

The Criminal Legal Aid Scheme Means Test

INTRODUCTION

The availability of legal aid in criminal proceedings is regulated by Part V of the Legal Aid Act 1988. Legal aid shall be granted 'where it appears to the competent authority desirable to do so in the interests of justice'[1]. Subsequent provisions establish circumstances where the merits element of the test is automatically satisfied and, in other cases, the criteria on which the competent authority's discretion as to merits can be judged. In all cases, however, a criminal legal aid order cannot be granted unless the applicant can satisfy the means test:

> 'Representation shall not be granted to any person unless it appears to the proper officer that his financial resources are such as, under regulations, make him eligible for representation under this Part.[2]'

The regulatory framework is established within the Legal Aid in Criminal and Care Proceedings (General) Regulations 1989 (as amended). These provisions require that the means test must be administered when granting legal aid. It follows that no grant of legal aid can be made until this has been done and the practical effect of this provision is that the means test is determined before the merits test is considered.

The test must be viewed in context and it is worth remembering that 90%–95% of applicants receive free legal aid, 75% having been passported to free legal aid as a result of receipt of certain state benefits. Contribution receipts for the year 1993/94 amounted to approximately £4 million; however this amounted to only 0.89% of the total cost of criminal legal aid, which was in the region of £450 million[3]. There have been recent governmental concerns about the effectiveness of the means test and consequential amendments to the regulations, which now impose stringent rules requiring the production of documentary evidence to support the applicant's statement of means. These amendments have largely been prompted by the failure of the National Audit Office to certify the legal aid account for four successive years.

THE REQUIREMENT TO PROVIDE A STATEMENT OF MEANS

The general rule is that every applicant seeking a grant of criminal legal aid must provide a statement of his means on the standard Form 5 and provide the

1 S 21(2) of the Legal Aid Act 1988.
2 S 21(5) of the Legal Aid Act 1988.
3 Source - Hansard 6/3/95.

documentary evidence required by that form[4]. In the case of persons who have not attained the age of 16 years, the court or proper officer can require the applicant, ie the youth, or an appropriate contributor, or both, to provide such a statement[5]. In practice it is rare for a court to seek such a statement from both youth and appropriate contributor, most courts being content with an application from one of the parents, usually the mother. This practice would seem to have evolved because of the rarity of a youth having independent earnings, such as might be due to a child actor or model.

There are three exceptions to the general rule that enable accused persons seeking legal aid to avoid providing details of their means on Form 5.

1. Applicants passported to free legal aid[6]

This subject is fully dealt with below. However, applicants who are in receipt of income support, family credit or disability working allowance are exempt from providing a full statement of means and need only complete the abbreviated declaration at section 5 on Form 1, the merits application form. Evidence must still be provided that confirms receipt of the benefit specified by the applicant.

2. Applicants who have already submitted a statement of means in the same case where there has been no change in the applicant's circumstances[7]

This provision is more limited than the statement at section 5(b) on Form 1 suggests. That statement states 'I have already provided a statement of means to the _______ magistrates' court and there has been no change in my financial position. (A new statement is required if there has been any change).' Regulation 23(4)(b) of the 1989 General Regulations, as amended, inserts the caveat that the statement of means must be provided in the same case. Use of this provision is therefore restricted to applications to add offences to an existing order or to circumstances where a fresh application for legal aid is being made under Regulation 10, where an original order in the same proceedings was revoked or withdrawn, or where a legal aid order is being sought to cover proceedings before the Crown Court.

3. Where the applicant is unable to provide a statement of his means by virtue of some mental or physical disability[8]

This provision may be useful in those rare cases where the defendant has some mental condition that prevents him giving a true account of his means. The proper officer or the court will need sufficient evidence to certify his reasons for utilising this exception to the general rule. Such evidence may be readily obtained from the custody record, particularly if the police have made use of their surgeon or a psychiatrist or where the services of the court's psychiatric

4 Reg 23(1) of the Legal Aid in Criminal and Care Proceedings (General) Regulations 1989.
5 Reg 23(3) of the Legal Aid in Criminal and Care Proceedings (General) Regulations 1989.
6 Reg 23(4)(c) of the Legal Aid in Criminal and Care Proceedings (General) Regulations 1989.
7 Reg 23(4)(b) of the Legal Aid in Criminal and Care Proceedings (General) Regulations 1989.
8 Reg 23(4)(a) of the Legal Aid in Criminal and Care Proceedings (General) Regulations 1989.

nurse can be obtained. This evidence may also be useful in supporting an application for a grant on merits under the provisions of section 22(2)(c) of the 1988 Act.

Physical conditions that prevent the submission of a statement of means are harder to envisage. It is unlikely that if an applicant were in custody the court would accept that that applicant could not give an account of his financial circumstances. It may be that without access to his accounts he would wish to add a caveat within section 4 of Form 5 to the effect that the information had been provided to the best of his or her recollection without recourse to his accounts or financial records and, in addition, provide an explanation at section 6 informing the court that his incarceration prevented the submission of documents at that time. A similar approach may have to be adopted where the police have seized documentation.

THE REQUIREMENT TO PROVIDE DOCUMENTARY EVIDENCE

Until 1993 the requirement to produce documentary evidence, such as wage slips and evidence of the receipt of state benefits, was merely a matter of good practice that could be enforced by diligent courts through requests being made for the provision of further information under Regulation 24(1) of the 1989 General Regulations as it existed in its unamended state. A Lord Chancellor's Department Circular of 1 April 1992 [MCD(92)1] gave the impression at paragraph 10 that the requirement to provide 13 wage slips was mandatory and justices' clerks lacked any discretion to waive this requirement. The circular went on to state at paragraph 12 that it was also a mandatory requirement under the regulations to ensure that documentary evidence to verify receipt of benefits should also be provided. This inaccurate determination of the law was challenged and the offending statements were withdrawn in a parliamentary statement to the House of Commons, it being conceded that these requirements could only reflect good practice and that justices' clerks could not be compelled to request further information under the ambit of Regulation 24(1) of the 1989 general regulations.

Following that challenge, further amending regulations were laid before Parliament in the form of the Legal Aid in Criminal and Care Proceedings (General)(Amendment)(No 2) Regulations 1993 (SI 1993/1895) and the Legal Aid in Criminal and Care Proceedings (General)(Amendment) Regulations 1994 (SI 1994/807). The combined effect of these two new statutory instruments was to amend Form 5 and to make the provision of the documentary evidence described in the note fields of the form a mandatory requirement.

The current position is that documentary evidence must be provided to support every statement of means[9] except where there is a reasonable written reason why this cannot be done[10].

It seems to follow that if documentary evidence cannot be provided it is acceptable to provide a written explanation for non production and the court or proper officer must then consider the application on the basis of that information. If the court is dissatisfied with the failure to provide that informa-

9 Reg 23(2A) of the Legal Aid in Criminal and Care Proceedings (General) Regulations 1989.
10 Reg 26(2A) of the Legal Aid in Criminal and Care Proceedings (General) Regulations 1989.

tion, it must deal with the application in accordance with the powers available to it, namely:

(a) refuse representation if the court or proper officer considers, on the basis of the information available, that the applicant's financial resources are not such that he requires assistance; or

(b) deem his disposable income and capital as exceeding the limits below which no contribution is payable by virtue of Schedule 4 and fix the contribution by him at such an amount as the court or proper officer may determine or (in the case of an assisted person) redetermine[11].

These provisions would not allow the court to ignore the information provided as regard must be had to the information available (although this could include information as to lifestyle that had been disclosed by the prosecution)[12], but, for example, if the court or proper officer could justify the decision, the court may conclude that an applicant had underestimated his income.

Where applicants do not produce documentation to confirm the receipt of benefits that would passport them to free legal aid, the proper officer is to regard them as if they did not receive such a benefit[13]. In practical terms this will mean they have to compete the full statement of means rather that the shortened declaration on Form 1 and the proper officer will have to apply the means test. In almost every case the result will be a nil contribution as the level of benefit is likely to be less than is allowed under the free limit.

POWERS TO GRANT 'CONDITIONAL ORDERS' PENDING THE RECEIPT OF DOCUMENTATION

Legal aid can only be granted where the applicant's means, or those of an appropriate contributor, have been properly assessed, even if this means postponing a decision until further enquiries are completed[14]. In some courts the practice of making a conditional grant of legal aid has arisen, where a letter will accompany the legal aid order which suggests that if documenatry evidence is not provided within a specified period, the order will be revoked. This practice has been held to be unlawful[15], as the regulations only permit a court to dispense with documentary evidence where there is a reasonable cause that prevents the production of it. If this reason is accepted by the proper officer enquiries can only be resumed once the cause of the failure has ceased to exist.

THE ASSESSMENT OF RESOURCES (OVER 16 YEAR OLDS)

An applicant's means are assessed on the basis of his or her own income and that of his spouse. The term spouse is loosely defined for the purpose of these

11 Reg 26(2A)(a) and (b) of the Legal Aid in Criminal and Care Proceedings (General) Regulations 1989.
12 *R v Newham Justices, ex p Mumtaz* (1990) 154 JP 597.
13 Reg 10(b) of the Legal Aid in Criminal and Care Proceedings (General) (Amendment) (No 3) Regulations 1996.
14 *R v Newham Justices, ex p Mumtaz* (1990) 154 JP 597.
15 *R v South Western Justices, ex p Doyle and Bennett* (1 November 1995, unreported)

regulations and includes any man and woman who live together as man and wife[16]. There are circumstances where application may be made to disregard the income of a spouse, namely where:

1. the person concerned and his spouse are living separate and apart[17];
2. where the spouse has a contrary interest in the proceedings in respect of which an application for legal has been made[18];
3. in all the circumstances of the case, it would be inequitable to do so[19].

These circumstances are fully discussed below.

THE ASSESSMENT OF RESOURCES (UNDER 16 YEAR OLDS)

If the applicant is under the age of 16 years, the regulations require the assessment of his means and those of an appropriate contributor[20]. An appropriate contributor is defined as[1]:

(a) the applicant's father, or any person adjudged to be his father;
(b) his mother; or
(c) his guardian.

The regulations do not provide for any exceptions that allow the court or proper officer to disregard an appropriate contributor's means in the same ways as a spouse's means can be ignored, even where the youth is residing in local authority accommodation. It is also clear that a youth's social worker is not competent to sign the statement of means form, as there is no requirement upon a local authority to assume responsibility for a child's legal costs whilst in their care.

This can create problems for a youth applying for legal aid if parents refuse to co-operate in providing a statement of means. These problems can be overcome if the youth completes a full statement of means in his or her own right and declares the name and address of the appropriate contributor in box 4 which invites the declaration of 'further information'. A covering letter should outline the steps that have been taken to secure the provision of a statement of means from the youth's parents and invite the court to utilise its powers under Regulation 24 of the general regulations to compel the appropriate contributor to produce the required information. If this information is still not forthcoming the court or proper officer can determine that the appropriate contributor's means exceed the free limit and fix such a contribution as seems appropriate.[2] The court or proper officer would also have power to refuse the application, but, where the default is not of the applicant's making but is the fault of a third party, this course of action would seem unjust.

16 Para 1, Sch 3 of the Legal Aid in Criminal and Care Proceedings (General) Regulations 1989.
17 Para 1(1)(a), Sch 3 of the Legal Aid in Criminal and Care Proceedings (General) Regulations 1989.
18 Para 1(1)(b), Sch 3 of the Legal Aid in Criminal and Care Proceedings (General) Regulations 1989.
19 Para 1(1)(c), Sch 3 of the Legal Aid in Criminal and Care Proceedings (General) Regulations 1989.
20 Reg 23(3) of the Legal Aid in Criminal and Care Proceedings (General) Regulations 1989.
1 Reg 3(1) of the Legal Aid in Criminal and Care Proceedings (General) Regulations 1989.
2 Reg 26(2A)(b) of the Legal Aid in Criminal and Care Proceedings (General) Regulations 1989.

PASSPORTING APPLICANTS TO FREE LEGAL AID

Applicants for criminal legal aid who receive one of four specified state benefits, namely income support, family credit or disability working allowance, income based job seekers allowance or who has a spouse, or an appropriate contributor, who is in receipt of one of those benefits, is entitled to receive free legal aid and the court or proper officer need not carry out a means test[3]. In order to obtain the benefit of this provision the applicant should complete the abbreviated means section within Form 1 (see Figure 1) with details of the benefit received, his or her national insurance number and the name and address of the paying benefit office.

The application must also be accompanied by documentary evidence that confirms current eligibility to receive that specific benefit, otherwise the court must disregard the passporting element of the regulations and carry out a full means test[4]. Guidance has been issued to magistrates' courts that they should not accept documents such as UB40 cards that make no mention of the type of benefit received. Acceptable evidence would normally include a copy of the pages of a benefits book specifying the benefit paid, a letter from the paying authority, usually the Department of Social Security, or a statutory breakdown of the benefits payable. In some areas the DSS have been willing to supply return of fax confirmations to solicitors on a standard pro-forma. Confirmation by the applicant on oath that he is in receipt of one of these benefits is unlikely to be persuasive as it adds little to the declaration on the application form that renders the applicant liable to prosecution if he provides false, or withholds relevant, information[5].

If there is a reasonable excuse for the non-production of such documentation, such as its seizure by the police or because the applicant was arrested and has been held in police or court custody and has had no opportunity to collect his documentation, the reason should be recorded for the attention of the competent authority. The current law seems to be that the court may be persuaded by such a reason and declare itself satisfied as to the applicant's financial eligibility, but, at some later stage, the court may make a request for the provision of supporting documentation. For a detailed commentary on this aspect of the test see the section 'documentary evidence' below.

Figure 2 provides a summary for identifying cases that can be passported to free legal aid.

FULL MEANS ENQUIRIES

In any case where the applicant cannot be passported to free legal aid a full means enquiry will have to be conducted. This will necessitate the applicant completing Form 5, (shown at Figure 3) the statement of means in full. In practice this form is usually pre-printed and attached to the Form 1 supplied free of charge by magistrates' courts.

3 Reg 26(3) of the Legal Aid in Criminal and Care Proceedings (General) Regulations 1989.
4 Reg 10(b) of the Legal Aid in Criminal and Care Proceedings (General) (Amendment) (No 3) Regulations 1996.
5 S 39 of the Legal Aid Act 1988.

FIG 1: THE ABBREVIATED STATEMENT OF MEANS IN FORM 1

5. Your Financial Position: (*Tick the box which applies*)

a) ☐ I receive Income Support, Family Credit or Disability Working Allowance, and I authorise the court to make such enquiries of the Benefits Agency as it considers necessary. I consent to the disclosure of information to confirm that I am in receipt of benefit.
(*You may also tick this box if your spouse or partner receives one of these benefits and you are living together*)

Give:
i) the address of the Social Security Office dealing with the benefit

ii) National Insurance number of person receiving benefit

iii) Type of benefit

You should produce documentary evidence that you are receiving the benefit (e.g. order book). If you do not produce documentary evidence the court will assume that you are not recieving benefit and you will have to complete a Form 5 (statement of means).

b) ☐ I have already given a statement of my means to the court and there has been no change in my financial position. (*A new statement is required if there has been any change*)

c) ☐ I attach a statement of my means in these proceedings (*details of income and expenditure*)

d) ☐ I am under 16 and I attach a statement of my parents' means. If you are unable to give a statement of their means, give their name and address.

FIG 2: IDENTIFYING CASES FOR PASSPORTING TO FREE LEGAL AID

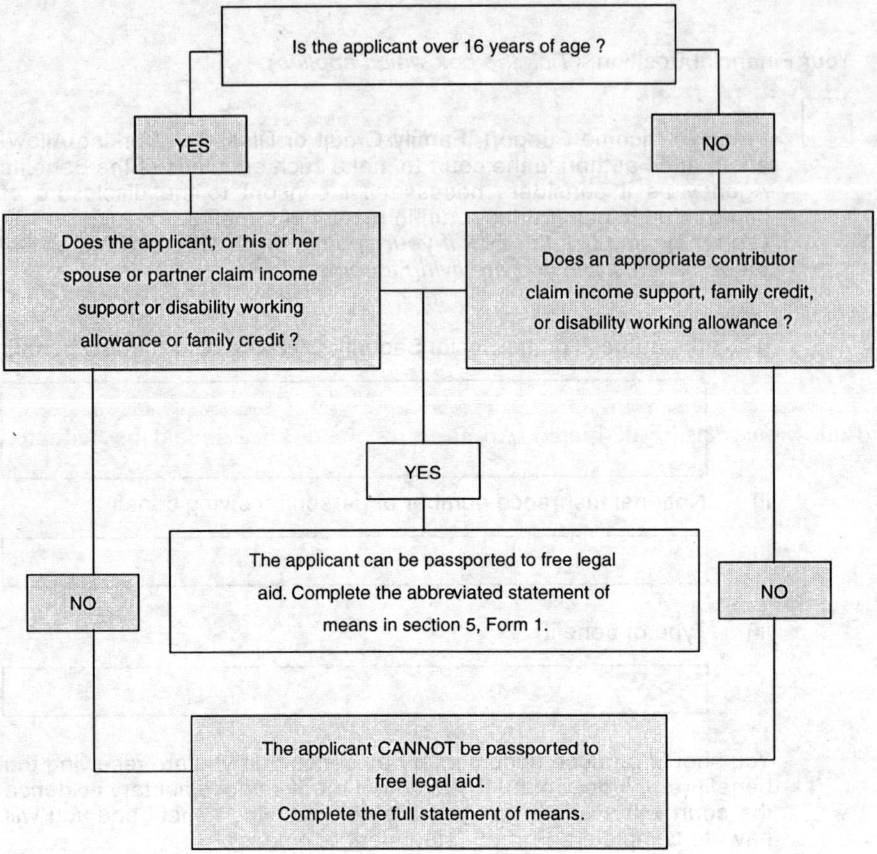

1. Spouses and co-habitees

The income and capital of spouses and co-habitees is to be regarded as the applicant's and must consequently be declared. A spouse means, for these purposes any man and woman living together in the same house.[6] Homosexual or lesbian couples are consequently excluded from this classification and are entitled to separate assessment, even though they may have a substantial joint income which would ordinarily prevent a party to a marriage receiving legal aid in similar circumstances.

Difficulties can arise if the spouse or co-habitee refuses to provide details of his or her earnings. In such circumstances a written explanation should be given on the statement of means to explain the deficiency and provide as many details as possible. The court or proper officer can then make an estimate of the earnings of the spouse[7]. Justices' clerks and their assistants may be able to turn to justices on their benches who have specific local knowledge of the industry to which the non co-operating spouse belongs to determine the average local rate of pay for a particular job.

6 Para 2, Sch 3 of the Legal Aid in Criminal and Care Proceedings (General) Regulations 1989.
7 Para 1(2), Sch 3 of the Legal Aid in Criminal and Care Proceedings (General) Regulations 1989.

For details of how to deal with the situation where a non earning spouse has to pay a contribution because of their partner's earnings and is unable to do so because of non co-operation see the section dealing within enforcement in Chapter 7.

Difficulties can arise in calculating the respective liability of spouses who are jointly or simultaneously charged with offences which attract legal aid, but where no contrary interest exists between them that would allow a separate assessment of resources (see below). A means test must be applied to both spouses individually, but if no account is taken of the contributions payable by each of them an overpayment would result. The correct approach would appear to be to deal with the applications in the chronological order in which they were received, or if received simultaneously, dealing with the one on top first. The first calculation should take account of the joint earnings and make allowance for dependants and other deductible expenses in full and the contribution should be determined. The second spouse's application should be determined in the same way with both incomes being considered and all allowable expenses and allowances being deducted. An additional allowance should be deducted from the disposable income, that being the amount paid each week as legal aid contribution by the first spouse.

A slightly different approach is required in relation to any capital contribution. If it is possible to attribute ownership of any specific asset to either spouse this should be done, otherwise the capital should be allocated to each spouse equally (ie by dividing the total capital sum in two). Thereafter each spouse should be allowed the free allowance of £3,000 from his or her share and any excess should be collected as the capital contribution.

The general rule that a spouse's or co-habitee's income must be included in the assessment of means can be overcome where one of the following exceptions applies[8].

The applicant and the spouse are living separate and apart

This may include circumstances where the spouses are judicially separated but are living in the matrimonial home pending its sale, but it is likely that the court would require some additional evidence of this status before accepting such an explanation, such evidence might be solicitors' letters that pre-date the legal aid application or court orders.

The spouse has a contrary interest in the proceedings in respect of which an application for legal aid has been made

This frequently occurs where one spouse has assaulted the other or where one spouse has stolen from the other, but where this has not precipitated a separation. It may also included circumstances where both spouses are jointly charged and where a conflict of interest exists between them so as to require separate representation.

Where, in all the circumstances it would be equitable to do so

This is clearly a discretionary power that will cater for unusual circumstances. It may include occasions such as where an applicant is mentally ill and has come

8 Para 1(1), Sch 3 of the Legal Aid in Criminal and Care Proceedings (General) Regulations 1989.

into contact with the criminal justice system, despite the best efforts of his or her spouse. It was once suggested to the author that this provision should extend to a spouse who had a substantial villa in Spain, which she enjoyed visiting, on the grounds that it would have to be sold to discharge the applicant's legal costs and that this would be inequitable as it would cause family friction. This reasoning was not sufficiently compelling to allow use of this provision and the decision was not challenged.

2 Income

The documentary evidence that will normally be required, in relation to income, is as follows:

Wage slips

Three monthly or thirteen weekly wage slips are described as being the 'best evidence' within the notes on Form 5. Fewer may suffice if accompanied by, for example, a reasonable explanation for the deficiency. Such explanations may include the fact that the applicant has only been in employment for ten weeks. One wage slip may suffice if cumulative totals for the financial year are included and a sufficient period has elapsed to give a meaningful average.

Accounts

Where the applicant or the appropriate contributor is self employed, frequent difficulties arise where the applicant has not been trading for sufficient time to have certified accounts. Alternatives that may be considered are loan applications that have been verified by a bank or financial institution, tax assessments, business plans or cash flow forecasts which are accompanied by a letter from a bank manager or accountant who confirms they are reasonable and accurate, assessments for government payments such as the enterprise allowance scheme. There are circumstances that might suggest some other form of corroboration is available and this should be discussed with the court concerned but any deficiency can be covered by a written explanation (see above).

State benefits

Evidence of non exempt state benefits should be included. Photocopies of allowance books of Benefit Agency assessments will normally suffice. It is worth noting that applicants frequently fail to declare child benefit even when they declare eligible children on the same form.

Any other income

Evidence in appropriate form will be required. This could be bank statements where money such as maintenance payments are credited directly to the bank or, in other cases, receipt books or a cash book.

It is important to note that all sources of income must be declared, irrespective of whether that income was earned or created in the United Kingdom or elsewhere[9]. Earned income and unearned income is to be included even if it

9 Para 4(1), Sch 3 of the Legal Aid in Criminal and Care Proceedings (General) Regulations 1989.

may be akin to an exempting state benefit, for example a student grant that is below income support levels.

3. Resources of third parties

The general rule that only the resources of the applicant, an appropriate contributor or the spouse of either are to be considered can be set aside where one of the following situations exists:

1. where the applicant or an appropriate contributor has directly or indirectly transferred resources to another person; or
2. where the applicant or an appropriate contributor has been maintained by some other person; or
3. where the resources of some other person have been made available to the applicant or an appropriate contributor for the purpose of these proceedings or to maintain his general living expenses[10].

References to 'other person' includes limited and private companies, partnerships, trustees or any body of persons[11]. If such circumstances exist the proper officer can treat the resources of the other person as being the resources of the applicant[12].

The effect of this provision is wide in its application as it would catch the wealthy parent of a person over 16 years of age who is still allowing his son or daughter to reside at home and is being provided with subsidised or free food and accommodation. Similarly a person charged with a motoring offence in which his insurers had an interest and had carried some preliminary investigations at their own expense would also be caught by this provision. In many ways the effect is to identify people who might have an alternative source of funding that would enable them to secure privately funded representation. They are therefore removed from eligibility under the scheme, without asking the question 'is there any other method of securing representation available to you?' The power to treat a third person's resources as those of the applicant remains discretionary.

CALCULATING THE AMOUNT OF INCOME RECEIVED EACH WEEK

When completing the statement of means form, income should be declared as the amount received each week. The Audit Commission found that some courts were converting monthly sums to weekly amounts by the simple expedient of dividing the sum by four. This practice should have now ceased and the conversion should be carried out in accordance with the following formula:

$$\frac{\textit{Monthly amount x 12}}{52} = \text{weekly amount}$$

Conversion of annual payments to weekly amounts can be achieved by dividing the annual sum by 52.

10 Para 2A(1), Sch 3 of the Legal Aid in Criminal and Care Proceedings (General) Regulations 1989.
11 Para 2A(3), Sch 3 of the Legal Aid in Criminal and Care Proceedings (General) Regulations 1989.
12 Para 2A(1), Sch 3 of the Legal Aid in Criminal and Care Proceedings (General) Regulations 1989.

All payments should be quoted a gross figures. Tax and national insurance can be claimed as allowances[13] later in the form. The form allocates a column for the spouse's income to be included separately from that of the applicant.

All sums received should be converted to weekly amounts and added together. The sum obtained is the gross weekly income figure from which deductions and allowances will be made.

The figure obtained will be based on an historical account of the applicant's fortunes and there are circumstances where reliance on such a figure would create an injustice – for example where as a result of the proceedings the applicant has been suspended on basic pay and has lost the right to any overtime or other allowance. Where such a discrepancy exists the court should be notified and documents that support this change in circumstances should also be provided. This information can be given on the statement of means form in section 4, 'Further Information', but it may also be expedient to draw the assessing officer's attention to the existence of this special factor in a covering letter.

1. Allowances and deductions from income[14]

Having obtained the gross weekly figure various allowances can be made and certain items can be disregarded. For ease of reference the deductions and allowances are dealt with by subject heading and are not therefore in the order that they appear in the regulations.

Non passporting state benefits[15]

There are a number of benefits that do not entitle an applicant to free legal aid but are none the less to be disregarded. Consequently if they form the applicant's only income the applicant will receive free legal aid. These benefits are:

1. disability living allowance
2. attendance allowance
3. constant attendance allowance
4. housing benefit
5. any payment made out of the social fund.

In practice this means that the total of these benefits is to be deducted from the gross figure obtained above.

Expenses of employment[16]

Under this heading any compulsory deduction such as tax and national insurance is to be deducted from the gross figure. The full list of qualifying deductions is:

13 Para 7(a) and (b), Sch 3 of the Legal Aid in Criminal and Care Proceedings (General) Regulations 1989.

14 Paras 6 to 14, Sch 3 of the Legal Aid in Criminal and Care Proceedings (General) Regulations 1989.

15 Para 6, Sch 3 of the Legal Aid in Criminal and Care Proceedings (General) Regulations 1989.

16 Para 7, Sch 3 of the Legal Aid in Criminal and Care Proceedings (General) Regulations 1989.

1. *Tax* – the total amount of any tax payable on that income
2. *National Insurance Contributions* – the total amount of any contributions payable under the Social Security Contributions and Benefits Act 1992
3. *Pension Contributions* – the amount of any contribution paid, whether under a legal obligation or not to an occupational or personal scheme within the meaning of the Pension Schemes Act 1993 and the Pensions Act 1995 – this therefore provides for any contributions paid to an employer's pension scheme or to a private scheme to be allowed in full, although it is likely that account would have to be taken of the capital value of any private scheme, but this sum could, in the discretion of the assessing officer be disregarded on the grounds that access to the capital sum is restricted until retirement age is reached.
4. *Child Care* – reasonable expenses in respect of the making of reasonable provision for the care of any dependent child living with the person concerned because of that person's absence from the home by reason of employment – this would seem to embrace any child minding or day-care nursery charges at the local market rate. In certain circumstances it might justify allowing the costs of a nanny's wages, if the employment of a nanny was 'reasonable'.

2. Housing costs

The nature of the allowances will differ according to an individual's circumstances depending on whether he is an owner occupier, tenant or lodger. The full list of allowances is as follows:

Rent

The full annual net rent can be deducted[17]. 'Net rent' means the full rent paid less any proceeds from sub-letting any part of the premises or any sums received in respect of housing benefit.

Mortgage payments

A full deduction is to be made on any payments of interest or capital in respect of the interest payments relating to the first £100,000 of any mortgage or heritable security charged on the house in which the householder resides or has an interest[18]. Where the applicant has more than one dwelling, allowance for mortage interest may only be applied to the first £100,000 of the total mortgage debts. It is not therefore possible to claim £100,000 worth of interest payments against each property.

It is to be noted that this section of the Schedule is dealing with deductions from income and therefore it is unlikely that this provision would allow a person facing a particularly heavy capital contribution to reduce his mortgage on his main dwelling in the knowledge that the consequential increase in equity on that dwelling would be disregarded, as this would constitute deprivation in the terms of paragraph 3 of Schedule 3 and could properly be set aside by the assessing officer (see Deprivation and Conversion below).

17 Para 8(2)(a), Sch 3 of the Legal Aid in Criminal and Care Proceedings (General) Regulations 1989.
18 Para 19, Sch 3 of the Legal Aid in Criminal and Care Proceedings (General) Regulations 1989.

Insurances and household maintenance[19]

A reasonable amount may be allowed for the costs of any repairs or maintenance and to meet any necessary insurance premium in respect of the applicant's dwelling.

Domestic rates, water rates and council tax[20]

A deduction in respect of any of the above expenses may be claimed in respect of the applicant. The provision appears to cater for current payments only and is silent on the question of any arrears.

Rent or board payments made by a non-householder[1]

Where the applicant is not a householder he is entitled to receive a deduction respect of his reasonable housing costs. Where the payment of board and lodgings includes the provisions of meals the Lord Chancellor's Department guidance to justices' clerks suggests that only half the total payment should be allowed. The logic behind this guidance appears to be that an applicant is supposed to feed and clothe himself out of the free limit of £47.00, which is equivalent to the corresponding income support rate. Were a person whose meals are provided as part of his rental payment to receive a full allowance in respect of his board he would be placed in a more preferential position to a person of identical means who was a householder. It is important to consider that the LCD's document is only guidance and is not part of the regulations and must only be followed if it is reasonable to do so. This allows the proper officer a measure of discretion to allow a greater or lesser amount of the board payment if local conditions so dictate.

3. Calculating the contribution from income

The Lord Chancellor's Department has provided magistrates' courts and Crown Court officers with guidance as to the mechanics of the calculation in a circular that accompanied the latest revision to the regulations. This guidance incorporates a pro-forma that guides assessing officers through the calculation. The relevant part of that form is reproduced below.

The rates quoted within this section were the rates in force at the time of going to print. they are subject to annual updating, usually in April or May of each year. Full tables of allowances and payments rates are produced in Appendix F.

> *Part Two: Assessment.*
>
> Income
>
> Enter here the total average weekly net income of the applicant, including that of his partner (where appropriate). Do *not* include attendance allowance, disability living allowance, housing benefit, constant attendance allowance paid as an increase to a disablement pension, and payments out of the social fund.
>
> **Total net weekly income £..........(A)**

19 Para 8(2)(b), Sch 3 of the Legal Aid in Criminal and Care Proceedings (General) Regulations 1989.

20 Para 8(2)(b), Sch 3 of the Legal Aid in Criminal and Care Proceedings (General) Regulations 1989.

1 Para 9, Sch 3 of the Legal Aid in Criminal and Care Proceedings (General) Regulations 1989.

Allowances from income.

Enter here the total net amount of weekly allowances against income under the following headings:

a. *Maintenance of Dependants*

(i) Partner living with the applicant :-

Rate £27.30 £..........

(ii) Dependant children living with the applicant

18 and over Rate £37.90. £..........

16 and 17 Rate £28.85. £..........

11 to 15 Rate £24.10. £..........

under 11 Rate £16.45. £..........

(iii) Any other dependants for whom the applicant must provide, at the rates set out at (b) above.

£..........

(iv) **Total dependants allowances £........(B)**

b. *Council Tax*

Enter the total weekly amount of Council Tax payable by the applicant and by his partner only (if appropriate). Deduct any amount paid by Council Tax Benefit.

£..........(C)

c. *Housing Expenses*

Enter the total amount spent on housing including rent or mortgage repayments, water and sewerage charges. Deduct any amount met by housing benefit. Where the applicant pays for board and lodging allow an amount for accommodation costs that is (that is excluding food costs included in the total payment) reasonable in all the circumstances.

£..........(D)

d. *Travelling Expenses*

Enter the total amount spent on travelling to and from the place of employment.

£.............(E)

e. *Any other expenses for which an allowance should be made*

£.............(F)

CALCULATION:

TOTAL DISPOSABLE INCOME = A – (B + C + D + E + F)
= J

If J is £49 or less the contribution is nil.

If is more than £49 the weekly contribution is £1 for every £3, or part of £3, by which the disposable income exceeds £48.

To calculate:

$$\text{Total Weekly Contribution} = \frac{\textit{Total Disposable Income (J)} - 48}{3}$$

4 Capital and savings

This section of the form requires the applicant and his or her spouse to declare any savings or capital that they might possess. Any item or resource of value is determined as capital[2] and must be declared. If the asset is not a financial asset, such as share certificates, that can be readily valued, open market value should be declared, or if this cannot be agreed, the amount which the proper officer considers reasonable[3].

From the court's point of view this area of a person's financial affairs causes the greatest difficulty and may have given rise to some of the more notorious grants of legal aid, where the legally assisted person was subsequently shown by the press to have substantial wealth and was sometimes worth millions of pounds. This difficulty arises because unless the name of the applicant is well known to the assessing court or proper officer, the only information that will be available is that which is declared or ventilated in open court. It follows that except in very rare circumstances the court will not discover any undeclared assets because it has no powers of investigation other than to ask the legally assisted person. The only practical solution available to the courts is to cause any discovered frauds to be properly investigated.

5. Allowances and deductions from capital

Certain items of capital are not to be included in the assessment, following the provisions of Schedule 3, paragraphs 17 to 21, but such assets must still be declared:

Residential property[4]

The first £100,000 of any equity in the legally assisted person's only or main dwelling is exempt from the means assessment. It follows that any equity in a second home will be taken into account in full.

The value of the main or only dwelling has to be declared on the form with effect from the 1 June 1996. In accordance with the usual guidance as to the need for documentary evidence to support the information on the statement of means, applicants will need to able to justify the value they place on their homes. Sources of such proof may be the contract documentation if the house was recently purchased, mortage valuation report togther with any published information, such as the Halifax report on house prices, since that report was made, or an estate agent's valuation.

This exception gives rise to the most frequent error occurring on statement of means forms submitted to magistrates' courts, as applicants frequently answer the question 'Do you own a house or property other than your main or only dwelling?' in the affirmative in circumstances where this is inappropriate. This may be due to poor reading of the question. The result is that certificates are withheld pending receipt of the capital contribution that follows such a statement being made.

2 Para 15(1), Sch 3 of the Legal Aid in Criminal and Care Proceedings (General) Regulations 1989.

3 Para 15(2), Sch 3 of the Legal Aid in Criminal and Care Proceedings (General) Regulations 1989.

4 Para 19, Sch 3 of the Legal Aid in Criminal and Care Proceedings (General) Regulations 1989.

Household furniture and personal effects[5]

Household furniture and personal effects of the only or main residence are to be disregarded, save in exceptional circumstances. It follows that the contents of a second home are to be taken into account.

In this context exceptional circumstances would probably allow the proper officer to take into account a legally assisted person's collection of original Picassos or a classic car collection, but this proposition has yet to be tested.

Articles of personal clothing[6]

Articles of personal clothing can be disregarded save in exceptional circumstances. This may catch a person with an extensive collection of haute couteur dresses.

Business assets

Save in exceptional circumstances, no sum shall be included in the amount of the capital of the person concerned in respect of any business assets owned by him.

Interpretation of this exemption must turn on what can properly be regarded as 'exceptional circumstances'. This term would seem to allow the proper officer or court to disregard the assets of a trader who is solely dependent on them to continue his trade – for example the assets of a plumber which consist of the tools of his trade, a van and a modest amount of stock – yet take account of the share holdings of the chairman of a multinational company where his assets are so substantial that funding his own defence would not cause him to cease trading. It is always important to remember that if a person who is refused legal aid on the grounds that the substantial nature of his business assets make him financially ineligible and that person is later discharged or acquitted in respect of the charges he faces, he will not suffer an injustice as he will normally be able to recover his reasonably incurred costs from central funds.

Tools and equipment of trade[7]

Tools and equipment of trade could probably be regarded as a business asset in most cases, but this exemption may give relief to an employed person who is required to own and maintain his own equipment, such as a professional musician who has to own an instrument on which he can perform.

The schedule also allows certain savings to be disregarded at paragraph 17, namely savings of mobility allowance, attendance allowance, income support, family credit, disability working allowance and payments made out of the social fund. These are unlikely to occur with any degree of regularity.

6. Capital sums subject to freezing orders

In certain cases the prosecuting authorities have the power to obtain a High Court Order freezing the assets of an accused person. These assets are still assessable in respect of an application for criminal legal aid orders and must be

5 Para 18, Sch 3 of the Legal Aid in Criminal and Care Proceedings (General) Regulations 1989.
6 Para 18, Sch 3 of the Legal Aid in Criminal and Care Proceedings (General) Regulations 1989.
7 Para 18, Sch 3 of the Legal Aid in Criminal and Care Proceedings (General) Regulations 1989.

declared. Difficulties are often perceived if the proper officer or court determines that the existence of these sums makes the applicant ineligible for legal aid under the means test. Defence practitioners should bear in mind that the usual order drafted by the Crown Prosecution Service, which has a central office to deal with such matters, includes a clause that allows the accused person access to the capital, with the prior consent of the CPS, for the purposes of funding his defence. From the practitioner's point of view this may be beneficial, given the higher rates of remuneration that are available where a case is non-legally aided.

7. Calculation of the capital contribution

The court or proper officer will add together all resources of value and financial assets to arrive at a gross capital figure. From this will be deducted all allowable items to arrive at a net figure.

A free capital limit of £3,000 currently exists[8] and therefore this sum will be deducted from the net capital value and any sums in excess of this amount will fall to be collected as a capital contribution. The court has power under section 24(1) of the Legal Aid Act 1988 to withhold the order until the capital contribution is paid, as this sum falls due on making the order.

8. The application of the means test

There is no fixed upper limit for legal aid in criminal cases and therefore the court or proper officer must determine whether or not the applicant's liability to contribute to the costs of his case exceeds the likely value of the case in terms of the eventual bill that would be submitted.

The court or proper officer is unlikely to be able to apply the test until the calculations described above have been carried out. There will then be available details of the amount of the contribution that falls to be paid from income throughout the life of the case and details of a capital sum that is due immediately the order is made.

The assessment is complicated owing to the indeterminate period of the contribution from income. Prior to the amendment of the 1989 general regulations the contribution order from income lasted for a fixed period of twenty six weeks; however, that limitation has been removed and the order now lasts for the life of the case. The consequences are that if the case is concluded within seven days of the order being made nothing is due from income, but if the case lasts 100 weeks, then 100 weekly payments are due. In assessing the value of the likely contribution from income it is suggested that the court or proper officer should take account of the average time a case of the type in issue takes to be concluded and multiply the weekly payment by the number of weeks within this period. These figures form part of the court's Management Information Statistics (MIS) and are readily ascertainable.

Having determined the value of the capital and income contributions the court or proper officer should then decide the likely fee that would be payable if the applicant was not legally aided. In the magistrates' court guidance as to the likely worth of a case will be available by examining the bills taxed by the court as a result of applications for orders for costs from central funds. In the

8 Sch 4 of the Legal Aid in Criminal and Care Proceedings (General) Proceedings 1989.

Crown Court the court will have experience of taxing bills submitted in respect of legal aid orders and can therefore rely on this experience in determining the case's worth. If the value of the contribution exceeds the worth of the case the applicant has failed the test and legal aid should be refused on means. If there is any doubt this must be resolved in the applicant's favour[9].

Operation of the means test may be complicated in circumstances where the value of applicant's capital resources are such that he would fail the test, but the resources are not readily convertible into a cash asset. In such cases the proper officer may exercise his discretion to allow an order to be granted, but to postpone collection of the capital lump sum for a reasonable period[10], which will allow the applicant to arrange for the sale or conversion of the asset. Such cases are likely to be rare and must be considered on their individual merit. Some assurance will be required to satisfy the proper officer that steps have been put in place to ensure the asset is to be applied to the applicants legal aid costs, so as to avoid the problems of enforcement at a later stage.

9 S 21(7) of the Legal Aid Act 1988.
10 Reg 29(2) of the Legal Aid in Criminal and Care Proceedings (General) Regulations 1989.

FIG 3: THE FULL STATEMENT OF MEANS FORM (FORM 5)

Statement of Means by Applicant or Appropriate Contributor for Legal Aid purposes

Form 5
Regulation 23
(also known as
Crown Court Form 5132)

To apply for criminal legal aid you must complete this form unless you can prove that you are in receipt of Income-based Jobseeker's Allowance, Income Support, Family Credit or Disability Working Allowance and have provided documentary evidence that you receive one of those benefits when you completed Form 1. *(See Section 5 of Form 1 headed* **Your Financial Position).** If you are not yet sixteen, then your mother or father may also be asked to complete one. If you have applied for legal aid for a child of yours who is aged sixteen or over **you** do not need to fill in this form. **Your child** should complete it, giving details of his or her **own income.**

To avoid delay in your application being considered please complete the form as fully and carefully as possible and provide the information and documentary evidence the form requires. If you cannot provide the documentary evidence you must explain why at Section 5.

1 Personal Details (please use BLOCK letters)

1. Surname ☐ Mr ☐ Mrs ☐ Miss ☐ Ms ☐
2. Forenames ☐
3. Date of birth ☐
4. Home address ☐
5. Marital status (please tick one box)
   Single ☐ Single and living together ☐ Widow(er) ☐
   Married ☐ Married but separated ☐ Divorced ☐
6. Are you claiming legal aid for a dependent child who is not yet sixteen? YES ☐
   If YES, give the following details about the child
   Surname ☐ NO ☐ (go to section 2)
   Forenames ☐
   Date of birth ☐
   Home address (if different from yours) ☐
   Your relationship to the child (eg. father) ☐

2 Financial details - Part A : Income

In this section you are asked to give details of the money you receive. If you are living with your spouse or partner then you must provide details of the income of your spouse or partner as well. The details will be used to work out whether you have to pay a contribution towards legal aid and if so how much.
The assessment is based on weekly income so your answers must show the amount you get *each week*.
If any of the sections do not apply, write NONE in the space.

		Amount received		
Work	Employer's name and address	**Your Income**	**Income of Spouse or Partner**	**Official use**
Enter gross earnings ***per week*** (before tax and insurance), including overtime, commission or bonuses. You must attach documentary evidence of the pay you have received over the past 13 weeks. Three monthly or 13 weekly wage slips would be the best evidence.		£	£	
If you are self-employed write SELF EMPLOYED. Show your gross earnings and attach the most recent accounts, showing gross income.		£	£	
Part time work Enter gross earnings ***per week*** (before tax and insurance) from any part time job not included above and attach documentary evidence.		£	£	
State Benefits Enter ***weekly amounts*** eg. from unemployment benefit, child benefit, etc. Say which benefit(s) you get in the space provided. You should produce evidence of the benefit payment (eg. order book).	Types of benefit	£ £ £	£ £ £	
Money from property Enter ***weekly amounts*** (before any deductions) of money from sub-letting a house or rooms and attach documentary evidence.		£	£	
Any other income Please give details and ***weekly amounts*** and attach documentary evidence.		£	£	

Important: If the information you have given above is going to change soon, please give details of the changes in Section 5 of this form.

2 Financial details - Part B : Capital and Savings

**Please give details of all your capital and savings.
If you are living with your spouse or partner you must also give details of their capital and savings.**

Property

*Note in the questions which follow the value of the equity means the sum which you would receive from the sale of the property after paying the mortgage or other loan on it.

1. **Main Dwelling** *(tick appropriate box)*
Do you or your spouse/partner own the house or property which you treat as your main dwelling?

	You	Spouse or Partner
	Yes ☐ No ☐	Yes ☐ No ☐

If so, please provide the following information

i) What is the value of the equity* in your main dwelling? ☐

ii) What is your main dwelling worth now, that is, what is its market value? ☐

iii) What is the mortgage on your main dwelling? ☐

2. **Other Houses or Property** *(tick appropriate box)*
Do you or your spouse/partner own a house or property other than the house or property which you treat as your main dwelling?

	You	Spouse or Partner
	Yes ☐ No ☐	Yes ☐ No ☐

If so, please provide the following information

i) What is the value of the equity* in the house(s)/other property? ☐

ii) What are the house(s)/other property worth now, that is, what are their market values? ☐

iii) What are the mortgages on the houses(s)/other property ☐

		You	Spouse or Partner	Official Use
Savings Give details of white your savings are, and the amounts. Include money in any bank, building society, National Savings Certificates, cash, stock and shares or any other investments. You should produce pass books etc.		£	£	
Articles of Value Give details of any articles of value that you own, (eg. jewellery, furs, paintings) with their approximate value. You may be asked to produce valuation certificates.		£	£	

3 Allowances and Deductions

1. Enter Tax and National Insurance Contributions deducted from your earnings ***per week.***

	You		Spouse or Partner
Tax		Tax	
N.I.		N.I.	

2. Enter the NUMBER of dependants **who are living with you.** If you are claiming legal aid for a child, please include that child. ***N.B. Dependants are the people you and your spouse or partner look after financially.***

Spouse or Partner	Children 18 and over	Children 16 and 17	Children 11 to 15	Children under 11

Others (please say who)

3. If you pay maintenance to any dependant who does **NOT** live with you, please give details of the amounts you, or your spouse or partner, pay.

Age(s) of dependant(s)	Your relationship to the dependant	Amount per week

You should supply copies of agreements or court orders.

4. Give the amounts of Council Tax which you and your spouse or partner pay.

(a) The amount of Council Tax paid. You must provide evidence of this (eg. the demand from the local authority).

£ ☐ a week ☐ a month ☐ a year

(b) Is Council Tax benefit received? YES ☐ NO ☐

(please say how much)

£ ☐ a week ☐ a month ☐ a year

---

5. Give the following details of housing expenses of you and your spouse/partner. If you own more than one house only give details for the house in which you live. If you are paying the expenses of a dependant who is not living with you, enter the details in the spaces on the right. You should produce rent books, evidence of mortgage instalments, and evidence of water and sewerage charges. It is in your interests to provide evidence of any other expenses claimed and you may be required to provide this.

		Amount for dependant(s)
Rent	£ / week	£ / week
Mortgage payment	£ / week	£ / week
Ground rent	£ / week	£ / week
Service charge	£ / week	£ / week
Water and sewerage charges	£ / week	£ / week
Board and lodging	£ / week	£ / week
Bed and Breakfast	£ / week	£ / week

3 Allowances and Deductions (continued)

	You	Your spouse or partner
6. How much does it cost you and your spouse or partner ***each week*** to travel to and from work?	£	£
7. Give details of any other expenses which you think the court should know about. You may include any payments on court orders, and contributions to approved pension schemes, **but not**: money for food, clothing or heating. You should produce documentary evidence of the payments.	£	£

4 Further Information

1. Have you directly or indirectly transferred any resources (such as sums of money, stocks or shares, the equity value in your home or any other valuable items) to another person since you became aware that these proceedings would be brought? If so, please give details.

2. Has another person been paying your legal fees and expenses in respect of these or other proceedings before you applied for legal aid? If so, please give details.

3. Are the resources of another person available to you eg. is another person providing you with free accommodation or paying your bills? If so, please give details.

4. Please give any other financial information that you think that the court should have when deciding upon your application for legal aid. You should also include any future changes in circumstances that might alter your position.

5 If you have not produced documentary evidence of all income/benefits that you receive and each allowance you have claimed, you must explain why you cannot do so.

6 Declaration

If you knowingly make a statement which is false, or knowingly withhold information, you may be prosecuted. If convicted, you may be sent to prison for up to three months, or be fined, or both *(section 39(1) Legal Aid Act 1988).*
After your application has been considered by the court, you may be asked to give further information or to clarify information or to provide further proof of the information that you have given.
If your financial position changes in any way after you have submitted this form, you must tell the court. This is a requirement of the Legal Aid Regulations.

I declare that to the best of my knowledge and belief, I have given a complete and correct statement of my income, savings and capital (and that of my spouse or partner)* (and that of my child).**
I authorise the court to make such enquiries of the Benefits Agency as it considers necessary and I consent to the disclosure of information to confirm that I am in receipt of benefit.

Signed Date

* Delete if you are single or if you are not living with your spouse or partner
** Delete if legal aid is not sought for your child

Chapter Five

The Merits Test: Deeming Provisions

This chapter will deal with those circumstances where the applicant is passported through the merits test by the operation of the Legal Aid Act 1988 or other legislation. The effect of case law has also generated some circumstances where applicants are effectively passported through the merits element of the test and this chapter will also deal with those circumstances. Whether legal aid is ultimately granted will also depend on whether the means test is satisfied, and this is discussed in Chapter 4.

OVERVIEW

There are two prime sources capable of giving rise to mandatory grants of criminal legal aid. The most authoritative of these is the Legal Aid Act 1988[1], which establishes four distinct circumstances where a legal aid certificate must granted, subject only to the means of the applicant being such that legal aid should be granted. In practical terms this provision operates to passport applicants through the merits test in the same way that receipt of income support satisfies the means test. Secondary sources are to be found within other statutes and case law. Applicants who are reliant on these secondary sources may find that the application has to be fully argued before the competent authorities to ensure a grant is achieved.

In order to provide an easily accessible discussion of all the various authorities that enable applicants to be passported through the merits test we have approached the different circumstances in turn.

APPEALS

There is no mandatory right to legal aid for every appeal. In the case of an appeal from the magistrates' court to the Crown Court it seems that the grant is discretionary and must be viewed alongside section 22 of the Act, as would an application at first instance. A similar situation seems to exist for appeals from the Crown Court to the Court of Appeal.

The only exception to this general rule is that legal aid must be granted where the prosecutor appeals, or applies for leave to appeal, to the House of Lords[2]. It follows that if the defence should appeal to the House of Lords they will have to satisfy the usual criteria. The restricted power to grant under this provision

1 S 21(3) of the Legal Aid Act 1988.
2 S 21(3)(b) of the Legal Aid Act 1988.

is further curtailed by the need to satisfy the means test within section 21(5) of the Act and its subordinate regulations.

BAIL APPLICATIONS

1. First hearing

There is no statutory provision that enables a criminal legal aid order to be granted irrespective of means for any bail application, even if that certificate is limited to bail applications and despite some magistrates' courts assuming such a power. This can produce difficulties where documentary evidence cannot be brought to court in time for the first bail hearing. The solution seems to lie in making an application to extend the green form for the first application[3].

2. Second hearing

Where a person who has been brought before a magistrates' court in pursuance of a remand in custody when he may again be remanded or committed in custody, and, is not but wishes to be legally represented before the court (not having been represented when he was so remanded), he must be granted a legal aid order for so much of the proceedings as relates to bail, provided that he satisfies the means test[4].

The drafting of this provision makes it virtually useless in practical terms, as it is rare that a defendant who is likely to be remanded in custody is not represented by the duty solicitor, or a solicitor of his own choosing, at the first hearing and where he was so represented the provision ceases to apply. It cannot be argued that a decision by the police to refuse bail to a defendant amounts to the first decision to remand the accused in custody, as the ordinary meaning of the term 'remand'[5] relates to a judicial decision taken by a court.

Further difficulties arise because, although a certificate issued under this provision can be limited to such part of the proceedings as relates to bail, the grant is still means tested and the usual problems that occur in relation to the production of documents will arise. If it is accepted that persons who are remanded in custody are usually facing more serious offences, or have previous convictions that would aggravate a more minor offence, the strategy of seeking limited certificate is further devalued, as there will probably be grounds for seeking a full unrestricted certificate.

This provision is unusual as it provides the only example within the Act of a power being given to competent authorities to issue a restricted certificate. All other grants have effect for the whole of the proceedings including preliminary applications and advice as to an appeal.

BAIL ACT OFFENCES

There is no statutory authority that compels a grant of criminal legal aid for offences charged under section 6 of the Bail Act 1976, but it has been decided

3 See Reg 7(2) of the Legal Advice and Assistance (Scope) Regulations 1989.
4 S 21(3)(c)of the Legal Aid Act 1988.
5 Remand – to adjourn a hearing to a future date, and to order that the defendant, unless he is admitted to bail, be kept in custody (Osbourne's Concise Law Dictionary, 7th edn 284).

that such proceedings constitute a separate case[6], for the purpose of fixed fees, and consequently separate certificates should be obtained.

There are grounds to believe that representation must be granted for such offences as the Court of Appeal has held that counsel should be invited to make what ever representations are appropriate in such cases, and where the defendant is not represented he should be afforded the opportunity of being represented. Where the established procedure has not been followed the Court of Appeal has overturned convictions[7]. Magistrates' courts appear reluctant to accept that they must grant legal aid orders in such circumstances.

CROSS-EXAMINATION OF CHILD WITNESSES

Defendants in cases of a violent or sexual nature are prohibited from directly cross-examining child witnesses[8]. The consequence of this provision seems to be to compel a grant of legal aid provided that the accused's means satisfy the appropriate test, as a refusal would prevent an accused from advancing his defence. The appropriate authority's attention could properly be drawn to such circumstances by using box i, in section 7 of Form 1.

COMMITTAL FOR TRIAL

1. Offence of murder

Legal aid must be granted where a person is committed on a charge of murder[9]. As with all such grants it is subject to the means test. In practical terms it is unlikely that it will be necessary to rely on this provision, as most proper officers are easily persuaded, at an early stage of the proceedings, that the mandatory life sentence that will be imposed on conviction for an offence of murder amounts to a sentence that would deprive an accused of his liberty.

2. Other cases

The fact that an accused person has exercised his right to elect trial by jury in an otherwise straightforward case of a relatively minor nature does not compel the court to grant a legal aid order and the merits test must be properly applied.

COMMITTAL FOR SENTENCE

Where a magistrates' court commits a defendant for sentence it must have reached the decision that its powers of punishment are insufficient to enable it to properly deal with the defendant. Almost inevitably this will mean that it has in mind a custodial sentence which will, in its self, satisfy the merits test[10]. It

6 *R v Legal Aid Board, ex p Hepstonstalls* [1995] 33 LS Gaz R 23.
7 *R v Davis* (1986) 8 Cr App Rep (S) 64.
8 S 34A of the Criminal Justice Act 1988.
9 S 21(3)(a) of the Legal Aid Act 1988.
10 S 22(2)(a) of the Legal Aid Act 1988.

has been held, prior to the enactment of the present Act, that legal aid should be granted in such circumstances[11].

It seems that in any case where a magistrates' court declines jurisdiction at mode of trial, the court has in mind that a heavier sentence than it can pass is likely to be appropriate on conviction. It therefore follows that a criminal legal aid certificate should be issued in such circumstances, as the magistrates' court is certifying that were the prosecution case to be substantiated at its highest, the magistrates' court's powers of six months' imprisonment and a £5,000 fine are likely to be insufficient. As a custodial penalty seems likely the applicant qualifies for a grant of legal aid.

REMANDS FOR PRE-SENTENCE REPORTS

Many magistrates' courts will automatically grant a criminal legal aid certificate to any defendant who is remanded, either on bail or in custody, for the preparation of a pre-sentence report, however there is no statutory obligation for this to be done and if the bench have indicated that they will impose a community penalty this practice becomes increasingly difficult to justify[12].

Legal aid must be granted where an accused person has been remanded in custody for the preparation of reports as to sentence[13]. By using the phrase 'for sentence or otherwise to be dealt with' it is clear that Parliament had in mind that this provision should safeguard those persons likely to be made the subject of hospital orders as well as those who were to receive a more conventional sentence.

SENTENCING HEARINGS

There is no specific requirement that compels the grant of legal aid to every defendant awaiting sentence. The Legal Aid Act makes no specific provisions at this stage of criminal proceedings and therefore the authorities that compel the offer of legal aid are derived from other enactments.

First sentence of imprisonment

Where a person is to receive their first sentence of imprisonment the defendant must be represented, or have refused to apply for representation, or have been refused legal aid because it did not appear that his means were such as required a grant of legal aid[14]. If a sentence of imprisonment is imposed in contravention of this rule it will be invalid[15]. This rule does not apply where a suspended sentence of imprisonment is the only suitable sentence[16].

11 *R v Serghiou* [1966] 3 All ER 637n.
12 Following *R v Liverpool City Justices, ex p McGhee* [1993] Crim LR 609.
13 S 21(3)(d) of the Legal Aid Act 1988.
14 S 21(1) of the Powers of Criminal Courts Act 1973.
15 *R v Birmingham Justices, ex p Wyatt* [1976] 1 WLR 260.
16 *R v Hollywood* (1990) 12 Cr App Rep (S) 325.

Sentence of detention in a young offender institution

A court shall not pass a sentence of detention in a young offender institution where the accused person is not represented, unless he has declined to apply for a grant of legal aid, or his application has been refused on the grounds that his means were such that he does not require representation[17].

It is likely that the effect of a court ignoring this provision would be to render the sentence invalid[18] although no direct authority appears to have tested this point.

Courts may encounter difficulties where the means of appropriate contributors and not the accused person have to be taken into account. It seems that the Criminal Justice Act 1982 requires that the accused's means should be examined, and therefore by implication not the means of his parent or guardian. It may be that courts will be persuaded that legal aid should be granted to the accused and the relevant contribution should be recovered from the appropriate contributor, even where the contribution payable is such that legal aid would normally be refused on the grounds of sufficiency of means. The difficulties of obtaining the co-operation of appropriate contributors in cases involving youths has been dealt with in Chapter 4.

Sentence of custody for life where offender is under 21

Where a court is dealing with an offender aged under 21 years, who has been convicted of an offence of murder or another offence where a sentence of life imprisonment is fixed by law in the case of an adult, it must impose a sentence of custody for life. In such circumstances a legal aid order must be granted unless the offender declines to apply for legal aid, or the application was refused on the basis of his means[19].

Sentences of detention – section 53 of the Children and Young Persons Act 1933

This provision caters for those limited cases where a child or young person may be tried on indictment. In the case of a child the only qualifying offences are cases of homicide, in the case of a young person aged between 10 and 17 inclusive the offence must be one for which an adult could receive at least 14 years' imprisonment. There is a further exception for persons aged over 16 years charged with an offence of indecent assault, for which an adult could receive a term of 10 years' imprisonment, which is an offence whereby persons over 16 years may be tried on indictment.

When sentencing a child or young person tried on indictment Crown Court must grant a legal aid, or have found that the accused has refused to apply for legal aid or that legal aid has been refused upon assessment of the youth's means before it can impose any sentence of detention[20].

17 S 3 of the Criminal Justice Act 1982.
18 Following *R v Birmingham Justices, ex p Wyatt* [1976] 1 WLR 260.
19 S 3 of the Criminal Justice Act 1982.
20 S 3 of the Criminal Justice Act 1982.

Secure training orders

Courts must ensure that a young person who is to made the subject of a secure training order is not so sentenced unless he has applied for legal aid and been refused on the grounds that his means are not such so that he requires representation, or that he has failed to apply for legal aid[1].

Method of application

Given the restrictive nature of this last group of offences it is unlikely that practitioners will be required to rely on these provisions to any great extent as, in the majority of cases, there will be sufficient information to secure a grant of criminal legal aid before the power to insist upon a mandatory grant becomes available.

Applicants, or their solicitors, in making their application will need to comply with the usual requirements of submitting Forms 1 and 5, if the application is being submitted to a proper officer in the magistrates' court.

When completing Form 1 the most appropriate box to use to draw the proper officer's attention to there being reasons which passport the applicant through the merit test will be the final box on the form, 'other reasons'.

j) Any other reasons (Give full particulars)	☐		

It may also be appropriate to draw the proper officer's attention to the passported nature of the application by the use of a covering letter providing full details of the criteria relied upon.

1 S 3 of the Criminal Justice Act 1982.

Chapter Six

The Merits Test: Discretionary Provisions

This chapter will deal with the excercise of the court's discretion in the application of the merits test when determining applications for criminal legal aid. Extensive guidance on this subject was disseminated to justices clerks in a joint circular issued by the Justices' Clerks Society, The Lord Chancellor's Department and the Legal Aid Board[1]. We have reproduced that circular in Appendix A2 and, in order to avoid repetition of the information within that document, this chapter has been structured to follow the format of Form 1 and to give guidance on how that form can be properly be completed. Each question on the form has been cross referenced to the criteria within section 22 of the Legal Aid Act 1988 and, where appropriate, sources of supporting information are discussed.

The application of the merits test is also discussed by the structured decision-making template provided by sections 5 to 12 of the decision tree issued by the Lord Chancellor's Department in May 1996[2]. For ease of reference this has been reproduced in Appendix A1.

Although both documents purport to provide guidance to magistrates' courts, their content provides a basic good practice guide that has much to commend it to all competent authorities seized of legal aid applications. From the practitioner's viewpoint they provide an insider's view of the processes and decision-making stratagem that will be employed by proper officers.

OVERVIEW

All grants of legal aid are discretionary and can only be made where the applicant is able to satisfy the competent authority that it is in the interests of justice to make such an order[3]. There are some circumstances where the applicant is automatically deemed to have satisfied this test[4] and these have been fully explored in Chapter 5.

In the absence of any factor that deems the applicant to have satisfied the merits test, the application will be considered, on an individual basis, against the statutory criteria contained within section 22 of the Legal Aid Act 1988. The list within the statute is not an inclusive or exhaustive list, and it is possible for an applicant to qualify for a grant of legal aid on some extraneous ground, or

1 *Guidance on the Interests of Justice Test for the Grant of Legal Aid* – The Lord Chancellor's Department, Justices' Clerks Society and The Legal Aid Board – May 1994.

2 *Guidance on the procedures for considering applications to magistrates' courts for an initial grant of legal aid* – The Lord Chancellor's Department, Justices' Clerks Society and The Legal Aid Board – May 1996.

3 S 21(2) of the Legal Aid Act 1988.

4 See for example s 21(3) of the Legal Aid Act 1988.

because a combination of factors, that cannot satisfy a proper officer on their own, are of such weight, when considered together, that legal aid should be granted in the interests of justice.

In such cases it will be necessary for the applicant to provide sufficient information to a competent authority to allow it to conclude that the test has been satisfied. This places an unequivocal burden on the applicant to produce an adequate amount of information to allow a proper, informed decision to be reached and where the information is thought to be inadequate or incomplete a proper officer appears to be entitled to postpone the decision pending the receipt of further information from the applicant[5]. This view is supported by Lord Widgery[6], who held that there must be adequate knowledge of the circumstances of a case before a decision to grant legal aid was made. He stated that it was to be hoped that all parties would co-operate in providing information to magistrates' courts. Although this decision was handed down prior to the enactment of the Legal Aid Act 1988, which gave statutory weight to Lord Widgery's criteria, there can be little doubt that the principle remains good law, as otherwise the inevitable consequence would be that a competent authority confronted by an inadequate application would simply refuse to make an order.

The contrary argument, that section 21(7) of the 1988 Act (which provides that where any doubt whether representation shall be granted to any person shall be resolved in that person's favour) applies to inadequate applications is clearly un-sustainable. If it were a valid argument at its highest it would allow an applicant to present a blank application and demand that as it raises the question of whether legal aid shall be granted it must be resolved in his favour. Such a situation would be nonsensical. Having said that, where there is a persistent failure to consider fully completed applications, or pedantic requests for more and more information, this might amount to a refusal to adjudicate and will be reviewable by the High Court.

In determining applications, the competent authority may take into account:

1. the information given within the application form;
2. any supporting documentation, including copies of antecedent histories, covering letters or experts; reports[7];
3. any oral representations, which should be recorded by the justices' clerk on the application form so as to maintain a proper record of the reasons for the decision[8]; and
4. any other valid information, which may include taking account of the prosecution summary of the case during bail applications[9].

5 Para 5 *Guidance on the procedures for considering applications to magistrates' courts for an initial grant of legal aid* – The Lord Chancellor's Department, Justices' Clerks Society and The Legal Aid Board – May 1996.

6 *R v Highgate Justices, ex p Lewis* [1977] Crim LR 611.

7 Para 6(c) *Guidance on the procedures for considering applications to magistrates' courts for an initial grant of legal aid* – The Lord Chancellor's Department, Justices' Clerks Society and The Legal Aid Board – May 1996.

8 Para 6(c) *Guidance on the procedures for considering applications to magistrates' courts for an initial grant of legal aid* – The Lord Chancellor's Department, Justices' Clerks Society and The Legal Aid Board – May 1996.

9 *R v Newham Justices, ex p Mumtaz* (1990) 154 JP 597 where information was provided by the prosecution of the nature of the applicant's financial resources and provoked an enquiry by the justices' clerk.

A further important consideration is that the criteria within section 22 of the 1988 Act are not exclusive and there may be other reasons for making a legal aid order than those disclosed within the statute[10]. Similarly, the criteria are not mutually exclusive and, if none of the criteria is in itself satisfied to an extent that is sufficient to merit a grant of legal aid, the test can be satisfied if, taking all of the information into consideration, it would be in the interests of justice to make an order[11].

THE APPLICATION FORM

The application form, Form 1, is structured to guide applicants through the criteria set out in section 22 of the 1988 Act. There are a series of preliminary questions in sections 1 to 7 of the form that are designed to identify the applicant, the proceedings to which the application relates and to establish whether, should the merits test be satisfied, he is passported to free legal aid. Then, at section 7, a series of ten questions are asked which progressively analyse the statutory criteria. The space afforded to these questions is not extensive and in borderline cases, where greater explanation may be needed to explain why the criteria apply to the applicant, it is perfectly acceptable to refer the proper officer to a covering letter. Such letters should be structured to cover each of the criteria in turn, so as to enable proper officers and magistrates to follow the structured decision-making process with which they are familiar.

Solicitors or others assisting applicants to complete legal aid forms should ensure the information provided is complete. Many examples exist of letters being sent to justices' clerks which criticise decisions to refuse legal aid orders on the grounds that ample information existed that would have ensured a grant. Unfortunately, all too often an examination of the application form reveals the information that is disclosed in the letter of complaint was never endorsed upon the application form. Applicants and their representatives should be aware that much of the information they possess in the opening stages of proceedings simply has not been disclosed to the court, particularly as the court does not automatically receive advance information or copies of defendant's records. Additionally, on a human level, whilst it is unlikely that proper officers would indulge in a war of attrition, undeserved criticism of a court's legal aid section is not going to ensure the greatest co-operation from its staff. Care should also be taken to ensure that any remarks recorded on application forms are clearly legible, as it is common complaint that a substantial proportion of applications have to be returned because they are illegible.

SATISFYING THE STATUTORY CRITERIA

1 Section 22(2)(a) – the risk of a custodial sentence

This element of the statutory criteria is addressed at question a) in section 7 of form 1 which states that:

10 *R v Liverpool City Justices, ex p McGhee* [1993] Crim LR 609.
11 *R v Liverpool City Justices, ex p McGhee* (ibid).

a) It is likely that I will lose my liberty *(You should consider seeing a solicitor before answering this question)* ☐	Details	

In determining whether an applicant will receive a sentence that will deprive an accused person of his liberty, the competent authority is being asked to consider whether or not the applicant is at risk of a custodial sentence. Although the imposition of a community penalty, such as a community service order, imposes a restriction on the liberty of an offender this has been held not to amount to deprivation of liberty and insufficient to satisfy the criteria on its own, although the imposition of a community penalty is one of the factors that might be taken into account[12].

In order to decide whether this criterion will apply, those advising applicants should consider the following points.

Does the offence carry a custodial penalty?

If there is no power to imprison this element of the criterion cannot apply, but none the less applications are made, through solicitor's offices, that state this ground applies for offences such as no television licence or drunk and disorderly. When this occurs the impression given is either that the applicant's solicitor does not know what he is talking about, or the application has been grossly overstated. In either case the effect is to devalue any further submissions on the form.

What is the usual tariff sentence for this offence?

This information may come from a number of sources, including the Magistrates' Association Guidelines, Court of Appeal decisions and knowledge of local sentencing practices. In addition, where the National Mode of Trial Guidelines[13] indicate that the circumstances of an offence indicate that it should be tried before a jury in the Crown Court this will support an application on the ground of a likely custodial sentence, given that the magistrates' powers of sentence are being declared to be insufficient. The National Mode of Trial Guidelines are reproduced at Appendix H.

The Magistrates' Association Guidelines indicate that the following offences have custody as the entry point when considering sentence[14]:

- Aggravated vehicle taking
- Assault on a police officer
- Burglary of a dwelling house
- Driving whilst disqualified
- The supply of class A and B drugs
- Violent disorder
- Wounding

12 *R v Liverpool City Justices, ex p McGhee* (ibid).
13 *Practice Note* [1990] 1WLR 1439.
14 Magistrates' Association, 28 Fitzroy Square, London, W1P 6DD.

Local sentencing practices

Local sentencing practices are less easily identified without the benefit of local knowledge, but where a particular court treats particular offences with the imposition of a custodial penalty to deal with some local problem, account should be taken of this. Proper officers will be able to establish their justices' sentencing practices by an examination of the court's statistics which are required to kept for monitoring by the Lord Chancellor's Department.

What aggravating features are presented by the applicant's personal circumstances or antecedents?

Aggravating features might include those circumstances where an applicant has indicated to his solicitor that he will not co-operate with community penalties, where there is a lengthy record of past offending, a history of a lack of co-operation with non-custodial disposals or the offence was committed whilst on bail. The presence of any one of these elements is capable of raising the sentence above the 'usual' tariff and should be set out so the proper officer can properly consider them.

A prompt to identify those cases where the sentence might be affected by the existence of a pre-existing non-custodial sentence is given by the second question:

b) I am subject to a:			
suspended or partly suspended prison sentence	☐		
conditional discharge	☐		
probation order	☐		
supervision order	☐		
deferment of sentence	☐		
community service order	☐		
care order	☐		
combination order	☐		
Give details as far as you are able, including the nature of the offence and when the order was made.			

The fullest possible details of all outstanding orders should be given and, where it is appropriate to do so, the circumstances of the original offence for which the order was imposed should be given. If the offence for which the order was made and the offence for which the application is being made are similar in nature, the fact that the order is in force will be an aggravating feature.

Having gathered this information together, the first two questions can be completed. This should be done in such a way as to state what the likely sentence is going to be and why. If there is insufficient space for this on the form, a covering letter should be used. If a copy of the applicant's antecedents is to hand a copy of the record should be included with the application, as this will avoid the possibility of a request being made for it later by the proper officer.

If legal aid was refused at the outset of the proceedings and it subsequently becomes apparent that the justices have a custodial sentence in mind or are considering committing the applicant to the Crown Court for sentence, the application for legal aid should be renewed. In many courts, applications will be granted on this ground whenever the justices order pre-sentence reports, as custody has become a realistic option at that point.

2. Section 22(2)(a) – a sentence that would lead to the loss of the applicant's livelihood

c) It is likely that I will lose my livelihood. ☐		

This element of the criterion may supplement the preceding section, as in many cases a loss of livelihood will be the inevitable consequence of a sentence. It will also apply in cases where the punishment of the court is of a more minor nature but the mere fact of a conviction will lead to the applicant being dismissed from his employment.

There is a basic requirement that the applicant must have a livelihood to lose for this criterion to apply. In circumstances where the applicant is unemployed he will not lose his livelihood on conviction, even if the result of the conviction will be that he will be ineligible for employment in his chosen field. In such circumstances an argument that his reputation will be seriously damaged, because he will be deemed ineligible for employment in the profession or trade for which he is qualified, is likely to be more appropriate.

Where the applicant is still employed but has been suspended from that post, on full pay or otherwise, pending the outcome of these proceedings, this provision will almost certainly apply.

It may also apply in relatively minor motoring cases if the applicant is liable to a 'totting up' disqualification and the intervention of a solicitor may lead to this being avoided either by an argument that mitigating circumstances exist, or, less commonly, an application to show special reasons apply why the applicant should not have his licence endorsed.

Where this criterion is to be used it is important to be able to justify why a grant of legal aid will avoid the mischief that will lead to the loss of livelihood. It may be self evident in cases where the offence is being denied, but where there is to be a guilty plea some explanation may be required, as in the absence of any reason to suppose representation will assist the applicant to retain his livelihood, the competent authority may conclude a grant of representation is not in the interests of justice on this ground.

Examples of where this criterion would apply are:

- a person in a position of trust charged with a minor offence of dishonesty (eg a postman, cashier or police officer charged with an offence of theft);
- a person with responsibility for children or other vulnerable persons charged with an offence of a sexual or immoral nature even where this may not be immediately evident (eg a bus driver charged with importuning who has responsibility for driving a school bus);
- a taxi driver charged with having a motor vehicle in an un-roadworthy condition.

In all the above examples some measure of explanation will be required to ensure that the proper officer or the court is fully cognisant of all the relevant factors when making his decision.

If documentary evidence exists to support what is being relied on, such as an employer's letter setting out the reasons for suspending the applicant, this should be exhibited with the application.

3. Section 22(a) – The applicant will suffer serious damage to his reputation

d) It is likely that I will suffer serious damage to my reputation.	☐		

It can be argued that any conviction will damage someone's reputation. For a person of good character this will represent the loss of his good name, where for a person with a criminal record a further conviction will compound his bad name. However, the Legal Aid Act is not concerned with mere damage, but with *serious* damage. In assessing what amounts to serious damage the court or proper officer will have to have regard to all the circumstances, including the nature of the offence, the applicant's record if any, the likely plea or the effect of the mitigation to be advanced, the applicant's personal circumstances and the likely penalty. In deciding on whether a person will suffer serious damage to his reputation one of the first factors that will need to be considered is the nature of the offence. Many offences will attract a greater degree of social disgrace than some other offences that attract similar penalties. In addition, the nature of such an offence may be more serious depending on the occupation or religious belief of the applicant. By way of example consider two applications reliant on this criterion:

1. The applicant is an unmarried middle aged man charged with an offence of kerb crawling. He intends to plead guilty but is concerned that if his case is reported in the local press he will be subjected to some ridicule amongst the locals at his local pub. He remembers only too well that last time this happened he was accused of being an 'amateur' and was criticised for his lack of stamina by the barman, who secured two identical convictions in one evening.
2. The applicant is a local Muslim elder, who resides in an area where street prostitution has been a particular problem. He was instrumental in leading a local group of residents in lawful protests to have the police take direct action to control and deal with the problem and he runs a local community centre, which aims to keep the Muslim youth off the streets at night. He is now charged with kerb crawling and intends to plead not guilty. He is concerned that should he be convicted he will be disgraced by the community. He believes they will express their dissatisfaction by removing their sons and daughters from his youth club.

The examples are perhaps extreme but they illustrate several points. Clearly the serious damage to a person's reputation must be the type of damage that would be thought of as serious by any right thinking members of the community. A little light-hearted teasing by a more experienced offender is unlikely to satisfy the test. The author was once privileged to have considered an application submitted by a young man charged with taking and driving away a Reliant Robin three-wheeled motor car. He argued that he should receive legal aid because his friends were in the habit of taking more powerful hot hatchbacks and his street credibility would be damaged. The application did not succeed.

The second point illustrated by the examples is that some reputations are more fragile than others. Priests of all sects and denominations, those with the care or moral guidance of children, and persons in public life seem to be particularly vulnerable to social disgrace when charged with criminal proceedings. It is a morally difficult question as to whether such groups of people should have easier access to legal aid than others who pursue a different lifestyle, but this is a question that has been determined by Parliament and in implementing the rules a competent authority is effectively looking for a reason to grant an order. It seems to follow that in such circumstances the proper officer is directed by Parliament to consider whether serious damage will be done to an individual's reputation and as this is a subjective test individual characteristics that affect the strength of an applicant's reputation must be considered.

This criterion may also be applicable to a person who is training, such as a scholar or student, or someone otherwise preparing for a particular career or vocation, but who has not yet entered employment which would enable him to claim a loss of livelihood, who would lose the opportunity to follow his chosen career if he were convicted or sentenced in a particular way. A conviction for a minor offence of dishonesty would be potentially prohibitive to a person reading law who intended to seek admission as a solicitor or barrister, for example. Similarly, and perhaps more frequently encountered, are applicants for legal aid who are seeking to enter the armed forces, but who will be rendered ineligible if they receive certain sentences.

The criterion is also likely to be affected by the seriousness and nature of the offence. It is submitted that offences of serious child abuse will almost inevitably attract intense social disgrace, which may sometimes be evidenced by hate mail or threats of violence prior to conviction, and would almost certainly justify a grant of legal aid under this heading even to a person with a substantial criminal record, even if other criteria cannot be satisfied. On the other hand minor offences of drunkenness are unlikely to seriously affect a person's reputation even if they are of good character.

4. Section 22(2)(b) – The determination of the case may involve the consideration of a substantial question of law

A substantial question of law is involved ☐ *(You will need the help of a solicitor to answer this question).* *(Please give authorities to be quoted with law report references).*		

To qualify for a grant of legal aid under this heading the applicant must identify a 'substantial' question of law, which could either go to the facts of the matter or could be procedural in nature. The application form suggests that the help of a solicitor is needed to answer the question and requires the identification of relevant law reports and references. This creates a considerable problem for the solicitor who is unlikely to wish to undertake detailed research until such preparation is properly funded under a legal aid order. Additionally some questions of law may arise from new legislation which has not been challenged in any reported decision. In such circumstances it is submitted that a statement which identifies the legal argument to be advanced and the nature of the challenge may suffice, but, as always, the fullest possible details should be given.

Where there is to be a guilty plea it is unlikely that the criteria will be met unless there is a substantial challenge to the basis of sentencing, either through pursuing a special reasons[15] argument so as to enable the court to avoid endorsing a driving licence or imposing a disqualification argument or through a Newton[16] hearing, to determine the factual basis of the sentence.

It is difficult to accurately define what will and will not amount to a 'substantial question of law' but it would seem that it must beyond the type of question that the applicant could be expected to resolve on his own. It may apply where the proceedings are of such complexity that merely understanding the legal issues involved is extremely complex, such as in serious fraud cases.

It is not possible for the court to grant a limited order in criminal proceedings that would enable advice to be sought from counsel as to the merit of the legal argument to be advanced, as is the case with civil orders. Where it is proposed to take counsel's opinion, an outline argument will have to be presented to the proper officer together with a statement of the intended steps that are to be taken. If this involves obtaining an expert's report, the applicant might also qualify for legal aid on the basis of tracing expert witnesses and, if the matter proceeds to trial, expert cross-examination of the expert (see below). Once a legal aid order has been obtained, if the proceedings relate to a case before the magistrates' court the certificate will require amendment before counsel's opinion can be sought (see Chapter 9). The only other method by which initial research into a substantial question of law can be undertaken prior to the grant of a legal aid order is through the use of the two hours work permitted under the Green Form Scheme, although a considerable proportion of this will almost certainly have been utilised in obtaining initial instructions. If the restrictions imposed on the research of the question of law are such that it prevents all the authorities being cited in the application, this should be drawn to the attention of the proper officer.

5. Section 22(2)(c) – The accused may be unable to understand the proceedings or to state his own case because of his inadequate knowledge of English, mental illness or other mental or physical disability

Inadequate knowledge of English

This section contemplates persons who cannot understand English to enable them to follow the proceedings and would almost certainly embrace any foreign national or citizen of England and Wales who does not have English as a first language, and where the trial is not to be conducted in his own language. The only circumstances where trials are likely to be conducted in a language other than English is in Wales, where a right to trial in Welsh exists.

The right to legal aid in such circumstances is in addition to the rights to an interpreter, and the fact that an interpreter is required is a reasonable guide that this criterion applies.

The provision requires an understanding of English to an extent that enables the applicant to be able to follow the proceedings and to state his own case. The question arises as to whether this requires the applicant to be able to read and

15 *Whittall v Kirby* [1947] KB 194.
16 *R v Newton* (1982) 77 Cr App Rep 13.

I shall be unable to understand the court proceedings or state my own case because: i) My understanding of English is inadequate ☐ ii) I suffer from a disability ☐ *(Give full details)*		

write. Although criminal proceedings are conducted orally in open court, there is an increasing tendency for much of the evidence to be served in writing for agreement[17]and in some cases the whole proceedings are based on written material if a guilty plea is to be entered in the defendant's absence[18]. In committal cases the evidence will be served in writing[19] in the hope that a short form committal can be undertaken[20]. In all these cases a defendant who cannot read or write will suffer substantial prejudice as he will not be able to follow the proceedings himself. In the absence of any assistance it would seem he must be eligible for legal aid in such matters, even though they may be minor in nature.

In minor cases where no written English will be involved, such as a disorderly person who is to be bound over, or a person charged with being drunk and disorderly, all the relevant evidence is likely to be presented orally and consequently an inability to read and write will be of no consequence. The nature and seriousness of the offence must therefore be a consideration of the proper officer.

A further problem frequently presents itself with applicants for legal aid who are youths with a poor grasp of English, even if English is their first and only language. The argument that can be presented is that their comprehension and their powers of expression are inadequate to allow them to understand what is being said against them and to reply adequately to those allegations themselves. In evaluating such claims proper officers must have regard to the individual applicant. Indications that the criterion are met might include those circumstance where the youth is attending a special school or has been evaluated by the local authority as having special educational needs, even if these do not amount to a mental illness or disability. The solicitor may be able to assist by obtaining details of any special school arrangements and providing an assessment of the ease with which instructions could be taken.

Regional dialects are in themselves unlikely to provide adequate grounds for finding an inadequate knowledge of English exists, unless there is some additional factor that would prevent understanding or create a inability to state the applicant's case.

Mental illnesses or disability

Unreported research within the Liverpool Magistrates' Court, prior to the appointment of a Community Psychiatric Nurse to screen defendants held in the court's Bridewell, demonstrated that police officers, court staff and solicitors frequently failed to detect the signs of mental illness or impairment. One of the reasons for such failure is the formal nature of the proceedings, which may

17 Under s 9 of the Criminal Justice Act 1967.
18 S 12 of the Magistrates' Courts Act 1980.
19 S 102 of the Magistrates' Courts Act 1980.
20 S 6(2) of the Magistrates' Courts Act 1980.

enable an impaired or mentally ill person to disguise the signs of their illness. It is only in extreme cases where the symptoms of such problems manifest themselves in such an overt way that enables all who come into contact with the impaired person to readily identify mental illness. Despite schemes that are intended to divert mentally ill people from the criminal justice system the practice of care in the community has meant that courts are frequently dealing with defendants who are suffering from some mental impairment that would fall short of grounds for declaring them unfit to plead but would none the less affect their understanding of what is taking place around them.

In some cases solicitors will have had prior dealings with potential applicants for legal aid on these grounds and will therefore be alerted to the difficulties. In other cases the information that a person is suffering from such illness or disability may come from the following sources:

1. The police custody record – which may reveal residence at an address or hostel that is associated with the treatment of mental illnesses or disabilities, the possession of prescribed drugs used in the treatment of mental illnesses[1], or an examination by a police surgeon to determine whether the person was fit to be detained or interviewed.
2. Court escort officers – for example Group 4 officers, where they have cause to be concerned as to the mental or physical well-being of their charges.
3. Bail information officers – who may discover such information when making enquiries into detained person's suitability for bail.
4. Community Psychiatric Nurses (CPNs) – where available, who will screen persons detained for court and will have access to medical records to establish any existing treatment programmes. Often CPNs will accept referrals from solicitors who are concerned as to the mental state of their clients who are on bail. Their observations may assist in obtaining legal aid and also in providing information that can be used to support an application to obtain a full psychiatric report, for which an authority is needed from the Legal Aid Board[2].
5. Court staff – where the person has appeared unrepresented and it has become apparent that he requires the assistance of a solicitor.
6. Friends or relatives of the person concerned – who may attend court and volunteer information.
7. Where a disability has been registered, such as blindness or deafness, the registration documents.
8. Notifications of assessment as provided by the Department of Social Security during the assessment of eligibility for certain benefits.
9. The person concerned – who may recognise his own difficulties and tell his solicitor about them.

A solicitor may suspect a mental problem exists but this is denied by the person concerned, even though such a denial may be one of the symptoms of the illness. In the absence of being able to seek further information, it may be difficult for these concerns to be expressed on the application form, which the applicant should read and sign. It is suggested that in these circumstances such concerns

1 A useful list of such drugs is given in the pocket guide that accompanies the police station accredited representatives pack, published by the Law Society, and further information may be obtained from dictionaries dealing with prescribed drugs.
2 See Chapter 9.

can properly be expressed in a covering letter from the solicitor to the proper officer dealing with the matter.

The question arises as to what degree of impairment is required to trigger a grant of legal aid. The 1988 Act is phrased in such a way as to avoid the need to establish that a recognised mental illness exists, as a mental or physical disability will suffice. The level of the impairment will have to be sufficient to prevent that applicant following the proceedings or stating his own case, but beyond that there will be a need to examine the circumstances of each applicant individually.

Self-induced intoxication, or the long term effects of substance abuse, create a further problem. Many drug addicts feel the need to support themselves through court hearings by taking whatever substance they abuse immediately before the hearing, so that when they appear before the court they are experiencing the effects of the drug that was consumed. In some cases courts respond to intoxicated defendants by having them taken into custody until they sober up and can be dealt with, but in some cases the effects of withdrawal can disorientate the subject even more, which tempts the court into dealing with them there and then. In such circumstances, unless the court can be sure that holding someone in custody will result in them being rendered fit to take part in the proceedings, representation under a legal aid order may be appropriate.

Courts are urged to obtain supporting information[3] to confirm the existence of such impairment, particularly where it is suggested that the impairment or illness will be compounded during the proceedings. As General Practitioners frequently charge for producing even basic certificates of their patients' illnesses, solicitors may be unwilling to incur such expense prior to the grant of legal aid and the court has no power to grant a limited certificate to enable such information to be obtained. It is suggested that solicitors should look to obtain such confirmation from one of the sources identified above, or else make an application for legal aid orally to the court where the applicant's characteristics can be directly observed.

Physical illnesses or disabilities

The fact that an applicant for a criminal legal aid order has a broken leg is irrelevant, as it will not prevent him following the proceedings or stating his own case, although it might motivate the court staff to ensure that the case is heard in an easily accessible court room and allow the justices to grant the applicant permission to remain seated throughout the proceedings. On the other hand disabilities such as deafness, blindness or the infliction of a severe stammer brought on or compounded by stress may affect the ability of the subject to state his own case.

Unless the disability is manifestly obvious to persons who come into contact with the sufferer the court will probably require some confirmation from an independent source such as general practitioner or social worker or other health care worker.

3 Para 10(b)(ii) of the *Guidance on the Interests of Justice Test for the Grant of Criminal Legal Aid* – Lord Chancellor's Department, Justices' Clerks Society and the Legal Aid Board, May 1994 (reproduced at Appendix A2).

6. Section 22(2)(d) – The nature of the defence is such as to involve the tracing and interviewing of witnesses or expert cross-examination of a witness for the prosecution

There are two distinct elements to this criterion: the first deals with the tracing and interviewing of witnesses for the defence and the second deals with the need for expert cross-examination of witnesses for the prosecution.

Tracing and interviewing of witnesses

There are many cases, particularly those involving allegations of drunkenness, where defendants claim to have a large number of witnesses who can give material evidence as to what took place during an incident, but in many cases there is very little prospect of tracing those witnesses, or, even if they were found, it is unlikely that they would be able to provide any material evidence.

g) Witnesses have to be traced and/or interviewed on my behalf. *(State circumstances)* ☐		

In order to satisfy the criteria to obtain legal aid under this heading the court needs to be satisfied that witnesses exist and that representation is needed to trace them. It follows that in a straightforward case where the names and addresses of the witnesses are known to the applicant, such representation is unnecessary. In a more complicated case, there may be witnesses who can only be traced with difficulty and where representation is appropriate.

By way of example consider a case where the applicant is charged with assault occasioning actual bodily harm. He denies the offence and says that at the time he was on a train, but he did not retain the ticket. During the journey he had a conversation with a local person, but he did not obtain their address. The magistrates have declined jurisdiction on the case and reporting restrictions now apply to the committal proceedings. In order to trace this witness it is proposed to apply to the court for the reporting restrictions to be lifted and to advertise in local papers and at the station to trace the person who was speaking with the applicant. In such circumstances it would be appropriate to obtain a legal aid order as there are identified steps that can be taken to trace the witness and it is unlikely that an unrepresented person could deal with the applications to lift reporting restrictions or the placing of effective advertisements so that he is not prejudiced by them and to ensure they are effective.

The above application has to be contrasted with an application that was received by a court to trace two males called Patrick and Michael whom the applicant encountered whilst drinking in a Liverpool pub and who would confirm that the applicant was not present at a burglary. The only identifiable attributes of these males was that they spoke with Irish accents. This application was refused on the basis that it failed to disclose any realistic prospect of tracing either male. It was suggested that the applicant might be more successful in his quest if he returned to the pubs at which he had met them.

It would be a legitimate consideration to take into account whether or not the applicant is at liberty to conduct any enquiries on his own account to trace the witnesses. Where the applicant is in custody, or has bail conditions that keep him out of an area at which he might expect to locate his witnesses, it is clear that he will need assistance which can be properly arranged under a legal aid order.

If a criminal legal aid order is granted, the authority of the Legal Aid Board's Area Office should be sought before instructing private enquiry agents or advertising expenses (see Chapter 9).

Expert cross-examination

h) The case involves expert cross-examination of a prosecution witness *(Give brief details)* ☐		

In order for this element of the criterion to apply there must be the prospect of a trial or committal hearing or other proceedings, such as a Newton hearing, taking place, at which evidence will be challenged. If there is to be no such trial, there will be no evidence that will be in issue and no cause for expert cross-examination.

Where the applicant seeks legal aid to allow expert cross-examination of the prosecution witnesses he will be required to justify why this is necessary. There must be some factor that requires a standard of advocacy over and above that which an unrepresented defendant could be expected to display, as otherwise this criterion would act as a gateway to provide every one who is pleading not guilty to a criminal charge, no matter how minor, to obtain representation.

The need for expert cross-examination is not exclusively confined to those occasions when expert witnesses are to give evidence[4], although where an expert is to give evidence of a specialist nature representation will usually be desirable. It may also apply where some complicated issue needs careful exploration, perhaps, for example, where character is in issue but where the applicant's 'shield'[5], that prevents his previous convictions being disclosed to the court, needs to be maintained.

7. Section 22(2)(e) – it is in the interests of someone other than the accused that the accused be represented

i) It is someone else's interest that I am represented ☐		

This criterion allows the court to consider the interests of someone other than the applicant. It has a particular application where the offence involves a child witness or complainant and is of a violent or sexual nature so that direct cross-examination of the witness is prohibited[6].

4 *R v Liverpool City Justices, ex p McGhee* [1993] Crim LR 609.
5 S 1(f) of the Criminal Evidence Act 1898.
6 S 32 and 34A of the Criminal Justice Act 1988, and see Chapter 5.

Where there is no statutory prohibition that prevents the applicant directly cross-examining his alleged victim this criterion may still be applied, particularly if the victim is vulnerable through age or infirmity, or where the nature of the offence will involve particularly personal or embarrassing issues being put to the complainant. Most sexual offences against the person would qualify under this heading, even if no other criteria are applicable.

It may be that where the applicant is known to be particularly disruptive or abusive the interests of the court are served by him being represented, if for no other reason than it helps to preserve the dignity of the court. In such limited circumstances it may be appropriate to grant an order under this heading. There appears to be no limitation to confine the power to consider the range of persons who might benefit from this provision to participants in the proceedings.

Difficulties arise where it is thought desirable to grant representation under this section to attempt to prevent a defendant from embarking on an unnecessary or improper course of conduct within the proceedings, such as unnecessary cross-examination of witnesses, as the advocate assigned under the order will be compelled to comply with his instructions, in so far as it proper to do so. If the instructions are contrary to the advocate's code of conduct the only avenue available to the advocate is to withdraw. In any event, defendants cannot be compelled to accept representation.

8. Any other reason

Courts and proper officers must not confine their deliberations to the statutory criteria alone as they are not exhaustive[7]. Consequently, if the applicant raises any other points within his application that ought to be taken into account, the proper officer has power so to do.

j) Any other reasons *(Give full particulars)* ☐		

It also follows that if none of the criteria that have been discussed above are sufficient in themselves to allow an order to be granted, the court or proper officer may consider the application as a whole and if the cumulative weight of the matters raised are sufficient an order may be granted. If after all the relevant information has been gathered a doubt remains as to whether an order should be granted, then the applicant must be given the benefit of that doubt[8] and an order will be made.

CASE STUDIES

The following case studies have been designed to demonstrate how legal aid applications are affected by the manner in which the application form is completed. Each case study presents a summary of the allegation, a poorly

7 *R v Liverpool City Justices, ex p McGhee* [1993] Crim LR 609.
8 S 21(7) of the Legal Aid Act 1988.

completed application form, which has been completed using details that have appeared on actual legal aid application forms submitted to magistrates' courts and a further, more detailed, application.

The information within each application is not intended for use on live applications because the use of standard words and phrases is generally inappropriate in circumstances where each application should properly reflect the individual applicant and offence.

Case one

The applicant is a 44-year old male who is charged with assault occasioning actual bodily harm contrary to section 47 of the Offences Against the Person Act 1861. The complainant is a 10-year old boy who was a passenger on a school bus driven by the applicant. It is alleged that the applicant struck the boy about the ear for no apparent reason, causing mild swelling and discomfort. The incident was witnessed by several other school children.

The applicant's instructions are that he was driving the bus on a busy high street at about ten minutes to nine when the boy ran forward to the front of the bus and began to interfere with the mechanism that operated the door. The applicant was concerned that if the door opened the boy could fall from the bus and injure himself and, by running around at the front of the bus, he was endangering the other passengers and road users by blocking the driver's line of sight and distracting him from keeping a proper lookout. In order to retrain the boy the applicant reached out to grab him but inadvertently caught his ear.

As a result of this complaint the applicant has been suspended from work and has been told he will be dismissed if the complaint is proved. The applicant understands that the boy has a very poor discipline record at school and was recently expelled from another school for causing damage and stealing from the school's kitchen.

The case has attracted a great deal of local interest and press comment.

The court's decision in respect of this application was that it should be refused on the basis of the following:

1. Although the offence carries the possibility of a custodial sentence, local sentencing practices suggest that a custodial sentence is only likely where there has been a breach of trust, very serious injury or some other aggravating feature. None of these has been disclosed within this application.
2. Although the applicant is suspended from his employment it is not suggested he will be dismissed and therefore he does not seem to be at risk of losing his livelihood.
3. Whilst all convictions damage a person's reputation the application discloses no evidence of serious damage or any adverse effects that will be suffered by the applicant if he is convicted.
4. It is noted that the applicant is pleading not guilty but there is nothing within the application that suggests any complex question of law exists or any dispute other than matters of fact are in issue. No difficulty in tracing witnesses has been disclosed.
5. The applicant's means have been assessed separately and the manner in which the prosecution is represented is a matter for them and is not a matter the court needs to consider in dealing with this application.

7. Reasons for wanting Legal Aid

- To avoid the possibility of your application being delayed or legal aid being refused because the court does not have enough information about the case you must complete the rest of this form.
- When deciding whether to grant you legal aid, the court will need to know the reasons why it is in the interests of justice for you to be represented.
- If you need help completing this form, and especially if you have previous convictions, you should see a solicitor. He may be able to advise you free of charge or at a reduced fee.

Note: If you plead **NOT GUILTY** neither the information in this form nor that in your statement of means will be made available to the members of the court trying your case unless you are convicted or you consent. If you are acquitted, only the financial information you have given in your statement of means will be given to the court.

Tick any boxes which apply and give brief details or reasons in the spaces provided.

		Details	Reasons for grant or refusal *(for court use only).*
a) It is likely that I will lose my liberty *(You should consider seeing a solicitor before answering this question)*	[x]	*The offence carries a custodial sentence*	
b) I am subject to a:			
suspended or partly suspended prison sentence	[ ]	*I am of good character.*	
conditional discharge	[ ]		
probation order	[ ]		
supervision order	[ ]		
deferment of sentence	[ ]		
community service order	[ ]		
care order	[ ]		
combination order	[ ]		
Give details as far as you are able, including the nature of the offence and when the order was made.			
c) It is likely that I will lose my livelihood.	[x]	*I have been suspended from my employment until this case is dealt with.*	
d) It is likely that I will suffer serious damage to my reputation.	[x]	*A conviction will damage my good name.*	
e) A substantial question of law is involved *(You will need the help of a solicitor to answer this question).* *(Please give authorities to be quoted with law report references).*	[x]	*I am pleading not guilty.*	
f) I shall be unable to understand the court proceedings or state my own case because:			
i) My understanding of English is inadequate	[ ]		
ii) I suffer from a disability. *(Give full details)*	[ ]		
g) Witnesses have to be traced and/or interviewed on my behalf. *(State circumstances)*	[x]	*I am pleading not guilty and there will be a trial.* *There were other pasengers on the bus.*	
h) The case involves expert cross-examination of a prosecution witness *(Give brief details)*	[x]	*See above.*	
i) It is someone else's interest that I am represented	[ ]		
j) Any other reasons *(Give full particulars)*	[x]	*I cannot afford a solicitor but I am pleading not guilty and I want a solicitor.* *The prosecution will have one.*	

7. Reasons for wanting Legal Aid

- To avoid the possibility of your application being delayed or legal aid being refused because the court does not have enough information about the case you must complete the rest of this form.
- When deciding whether to grant you legal aid, the court will need to know the reasons why it is in the interests of justice for you to be represented.
- If you need help completing this form, and especially if you have previous convictions, you should see a solicitor. He may be able to advise you free of charge or at a reduced fee.

Note: If you plead **NOT GUILTY** neither the information in this form nor that in your statement of means will be made available to the members of the court trying your case unless you are convicted or you consent. If you are acquitted, only the financial information you have given in your statement of means will be given to the court.

Tick any boxes which apply and give brief details or reasons in the spaces provided.

		Details	Reasons for grant or refusal *(for court use only).*
a) It is likely that I will lose my liberty *(You should consider seeing a solicitor before answering this question)*	[x]	*The is an allegation of an assault by a 44 year old bus driver on a child of 10 who was a passenger on the school bus driven by the applicant. Although a custodial sentence is unusual for this type of offence the breach of trust and difference in age mkaes such likely if the is a conviction.*	
b) I am subject to a:		*I am of good character, but I have been suspended from my employment pending the outcome of these proceedings.*	
suspended or partly suspended prison sentence	[ ]		
conditional discharge	[ ]		
probation order	[ ]		
supervision order	[ ]		
deferment of sentence	[ ]		
community service order	[ ]		
care order	[ ]		
combination order	[ ]		
Give details as far as you are able, including the nature of the offence and when the order was made.			
c) It is likely that I will lose my livelihood.	[x]	*I have been told that if I am convicted of this offence I will be dismissed by ny employers. I have attached a copy of their letter to me that confirms this.*	
d) It is likely that I will suffer serious damage to my reputation.	[x]	*If I am convicted of an offence such as this not only will I lose my good name but I will be unable to gain employment driving public service vehicles ortaxis. My reputation will be seriously damaged in this respect.*	
e) A substantial question of law is involved *(You will need the help of a solicitor to answer this question).* *(Please give authorities to be quoted with law report references).*	[x]	*Given the child's age and the fact that I believe he has been expelled from school because of his dishonesty and for damaging property difficult evidential questions as regards character and the admissability of a childs record of behaviour at shcool will be raised during the trial. I do not have sufficient knowledge to deal with these matters myself.*	
f) I shall be unable to understand the court proceedings or state my own case because:			
i) My understanding of English is inadequate	[ ]		
ii) I suffer from a disability.	[ ]		
(Give full details)			
g) Witnesses have to be traced and/or interviewed on my behalf. *(State circumstances)*	[x]	*I need to obtaib access to the complainant's school record or trace officers of the education department to determine whether the complainant was expelled from school for dishonetsty and causing damage, and to obtain admissible statements from such persons. I have been told that it is unlikely that disclosure of school records will be allowed in the absence of a witness summons or a solicitor's letter.*	
h) The case involves expert cross-examination of a prosecution witness *(Give brief details)*	[x]	*The complainant is 10 years old. He will need careful cross examination to avoid any possibility of him becoming distressed. I think that the prosecution may have evidence from some of the other children on the bus and they will need careful cross examination for similar reasons.*	
i) It is someone else's interest that I am represented	[ ]	*I am alleged to have been violent to a child of 10 years of age. Although I dispute the allegation it would not be appropriate for me to directly cross-examine a child in these circumstances as it might distress the child to have to face his assailant. Such questioning is best carried out by an independent advocate.*	
j) Any other reasons *(Give full particulars)*	[x]	*The case has become a matter of local interest and comment in the press. For justice to be seen to be done it would be preferable if I was represented by a solicitor.*	

Following receipt of the notice of refusal the applicant transfers his instructions to another firm of solicitors who renew the application by submitting a fresh Form 1, together with other appropriate documents to the proper officer.

This application was granted by the court on the grounds that the offence was aggravated by the difference in the ages of the complainant and the applicant and, given the nature of the circumstances in which the applicant was employed at the time of the assault, may aggravate a fairly minor assault to such an extent that there is a likelihood of a custodial sentence being imposed. Additionally, because of the age of the child and the nature of the allegation would not be appropriate for the child to be directly cross-examined by the applicant. It was not necessary to consider the other elements of the application as it was clear that legal aid should be granted in this case.

Case two

The applicant is a male youth aged 18 who contacts you after he has been charged with an offence of stealing a pair of jeans from a well known high street store. It is his intention to plead guilty.

The applicant has two previous offences recorded against him, one for an offence under section 4 of the Public Order Act 1986, for which he was conditionally discharged for six months. This offence was recorded against him two years ago. The other offence is three years old and relates to a charge of shoplifting, where a packet of batteries were stolen, for which he was fined. The applicant lives with his parents and is unemployed. Local sentencing practices suggest the offence would be dealt with by way of a fine.

On taking the applicant's instructions you notice that the applicant has a severe stutter which makes it difficult to understand him and this seems to get worse whenever he becomes concerned about what he is telling you.

For the reasons disclosed on the form the court refused to grant the application.

7. Reasons for wanting Legal Aid

- To avoid the possibility of your application being delayed or legal aid being refused because the court does not have enough information about the case you must complete the rest of this form.
- When deciding whether to grant you legal aid, the court will need to know the reasons why it is in the interests of justice for you to be represented.
- If you need help completing this form, and especially if you have previous convictions, you should see a solicitor. He may be able to advise you free of charge or at a reduced fee.

Note: If you plead **NOT GUILTY** neither the information in this form nor that in your statement of means will be made available to the members of the court trying your case unless you are convicted or you consent. If you are acquitted, only the financial information you have given in your statement of means will be given to the court.

Tick any boxes which apply and give brief details or reasons in the spaces provided.

		Details	Reasons for grant or refusal *(for court use only).*
a) It is likely that I will lose my liberty *(You should consider seeing a solicitor before answering this question)*	x	*This offence is one which carries a custodial penalty and I have previous offences which make matters worse.*	*Now spent – not relevant.*
b) I am subject to a: suspended or partly suspended prison sentence	☐		
conditional discharge	☐	*Imposed two years ago.*	*Not agreed – fine most likely penalty*
probation order	☐		
supervision order	☐		
deferment of sentence	☐		
community service order	☐		
care order	☐		
combination order *Give details as far as you are able, including the nature of the offence and when the order was made.*	☐		
c) It is likely that I will lose my livelihood.	x		
d) It is likely that I will suffer serious damage to my reputation.	x	*A conviction will make my record worse.*	*This will not cause serious damage as the applicant is not a good character.*
e) A substantial question of law is involved *(You will need the help of a solicitor to answer this question). (Please give authorities to be quoted with law report references).*	x		
f) I shall be unable to understand the court proceedings or state my own case because: i) My understanding of English is inadequate	☐		
ii) I suffer from a disability. *(Give full details)*	☐	*I am a youth and I cannot be expectred to understand what is going on.*	*Applicant is 18 years old and can be expected to understand procedure on a plea of guilty.*
g) Witnesses have to be traced and/or interviewed on my behalf. *(State circumstances)*	x		
h) The case involves expert cross-examination of a prosecution witness *(Give brief details)*	x		
i) It is someone else's interest that I am represented	☐		
j) Any other reasons *(Give full particulars)*	x	*I need a lawyer because the police have got one.*	*Not relevant.*

7. Reasons for wanting Legal Aid

- To avoid the possibility of your application being delayed or legal aid being refused because the court does not have enough information about the case you must complete the rest of this form.
- When deciding whether to grant you legal aid, the court will need to know the reasons why it is in the interests of justice for you to be represented.
- If you need help completing this form, and especially if you have previous convictions, you should see a solicitor. He may be able to advise you free of charge or at a reduced fee.

Note: If you plead **NOT GUILTY** neither the information in this form nor that in your statement of means will be made available to the members of the court trying your case unless you are convicted or you consent. If you are acquitted, only the financial information you have given in your statement of means will be given to the court.

Tick any boxes which apply and give brief details or reasons in the spaces provided.

		Details	Reasons for grant or refusal *(for court use only).*
a) It is likely that I will lose my liberty *(You should consider seeing a solicitor before answering this question)*	☐		
b) I am subject to a: suspended or partly suspended prison sentence conditional discharge probation order supervision order deferment of sentence community service order care order combination order *Give details as far as you are able, including the nature of the offence and when the order was made.*	 ☐ ☐ ☐ ☐ ☐ ☐ ☐ ☐		
c) It is likely that I will lose my livelihood.	☐		
d) It is likely that I will suffer serious damage to my reputation.	☐		
e) A substantial question of law is involved *(You will need the help of a solicitor to answer this question).* *(Please give authorities to be quoted with law report references).*	☐		
f) I shall be unable to understand the court proceedings or state my own case because: i) My understanding of English is inadequate ii) I suffer from a disability. *(Give full details)*	 ☐ ☒	I suffer from a severe stutter that gets worse whenever I am subjected to things that cause me stress. It will prevent me telling the court all that they need to know and is very embarrassing.	Agreed – although this is a minor offence it is imperative that the applicant's mitigation can be placed before the court. His disability suggests he cannot do this unaided and no one other than a solicitor has a right of audience before this court.
g) Witnesses have to be traced and/or interviewed on my behalf. *(State circumstances)*	☐	Solicitors note: We can confirm that taking instructions from the applicant was extremely difficult as his stutter became severely debilitating even in the calm surroundings of our office. We do not believe he would be able to present his own mitigation without the assistance of an advocate. As this disability is self-evident we do not propose to seek confirmaiton from his doctor as this would be a waste of public funds.	
h) The case involves expert cross-examination of a prosecution witness *(Give brief details)*	☐		
i) It is someone else's interest that I am represented	☒	The court will have difficulty understanding the applicant because of his disability.	
j) Any other reasons *(Give full particulars)*	☐		

FIG 1: THE APPLICATION FORM FOR A CRIMINAL LEGAL AID ORDER (FORM 1)

Liverpool City Magistrates' Court
Application for Legal Aid in Criminal Proceedings
Magistrates or Crown Court

Form 1
Regulations 11 & 18

I apply for Legal Aid -

For the purpose of proceedings before the | Liverpool | Magistrates' / Youth Court*

1. Personal Details: *(Please use BLOCK letters and BLACK ink)*

a) Surname

e) Date of birth

b) Forenames

c) Permanent address

d) Present address
(If different from above)

2. Case Details:

a) Describe briefly what it is you are accused of doing, eg. "stealing £50 from my employer", "kicking a door causing £50 damage".

b) Date of offence

c) The following other person(s) is / are charged in this case.

d) Give reasons why you and the other persons charged in this case, if any, should not be represented by the same solicitor.

3. Court Proceedings: *(Complete section a or b whichever applies)*

a) I am due to appear before | the Liverpool Magistrates' / Youth Court* | on 19 at am/pm

or

b) I appeared before | the Liverpool Magistrates' / Youth Court* | on 19 at am/pm

and *(tick whichever applies)*

☐ my case has been transferred to the Crown Court for trial
☐ I was convicted and committed for sentence to the Crown Court
☐ I was convicted and / or sentenced and I wish to appeal against the | conviction and/or sentence*

* Cross out whichever does not apply

1

4. Outstanding Matters:

a) If there are any other outstanding criminal charges or cases against you, give details including the court where you are due to appear (only those cases that are not yet concluded)

5. Your Financial Position: *(Tick the box which applies)*

a) ☐ I receive Income-based Jobseeker's Allowance, Income Support, Family Credit or Disability Working Allowance and I attach documentary evidence that I am receiving such a benefit *(e.g. order book)*
(You may also tick this box if your spouse or partner receives any of these benefits and you are living together)

i) the address of the Social Security office or Jobcentre dealing with the benefit

ii) National Insurance number of person receiving benefit

iii) Type of benefit

If you do not produce documentary evidence that you are receiving benefit, the court will assume that you are not receiving benefit and you will also have to complete a Form 5 (statement of means). If you cannot produce evidence you should give your reasons below.

b) ☐ I have already given a statement of my means to the ______ Court and there has been no change in my financial position. *(A new statement is required if there has been any change)*

c) ☐ I attach a statement of my means in these proceedings *(details of your income and expenditure)*

d) ☐ I am under 16 and I attach a statement of my parents means. If you are unable to provide a statement of their means, give their name and address

6. Legal Representation:

Note

a) If you do not give the name and address of a solicitor the court will select a solicitor for you.

b) You must tell the solicitor that you have named him/her, unless he/she has helped you complete this form.

c) If you have been charged along with another person or persons, the court may assign a solicitor other than the solicitor of your choice

a) The solicitor I wish to act for me is

b) Give the firm's name and address (if known)

2

7. Reasons for wanting Legal Aid:

- To avoid the possibility of your application being delayed or legal aid being refused because the court does not have enough information about the case, you must complete the rest of this form.
- When deciding whether to grant legal aid, the court will need to know the reasons why it is in the interests of justice for you to be represented.
- If you need help in completing this form, and especially if you have previous convictions, you should see a solicitor. He/she may be able to advise you free of charge or at a reduced rate.

Note: If you plead **NOT GUILTY** neither the information in this form nor that in your statement of means will be made available to the members of the court trying your case unless you are convicted or you consent. If you are acquitted, only the financial information you have given in your statement of means will be given to the court.

Tick any boxes which apply and give brief details or reasons in the space provided

	Details	Reasons for grant or refusal *(for court use only)*
a) It is likely that I will lose my liberty *(You should consider seeing a solicitor before answering this question)* ☐		
b) I am subject to a : suspended or partly suspended prison sentence ☐ conditional discharge ☐ probation order ☐ supervision order ☐ deferment of sentence ☐ community service order ☐ care order ☐ combination order ☐ *Give details as far as you are able, including the nature of the offence and when the order was made*		
c) It is likely that I will lose my livelihood ☐		
d) It is likely that I will suffer serious damage to my reputation ☐		
e) A substantial question of law is involved ☐ *(You will need the help of a solicitor to answer this question)*		

(Please give authorities to be quoted with law reports references)

3

		Details	Reasons for grant or refusal *(for court use only)*
f) I shall be unable to understand the court proceedings or state my own case because: i) My understanding of English is inadequate ii) I suffer from a disability *(Give full details)*	☐ ☐		
g) Witnesses have to be traced and/or interviewed on my behalf *(State circumstances)*	☐		
h) The case involves expert cross examination of a prosecution witness *(Give brief details)*	☐		
i) It is in someone else's interests that I am represented	☐		
j) Any other reasons: *(give full particulars)*	☐		

8. Declaration:

If you knowingly make a statement which is false, or knowingly withhold information, you may be prosecuted. If convicted, you may be sent to prison for up to three months or be fined or both *(section 39 (1) Legal Aid Act 1988).* After your application has been considered by the court, you may be asked to give further information or to clarify information or to provide further proof of the information you have given.
If you stop receiving Income-based Jobseeker's Allowance, Income Support, Family Credit, Disability Working Allowance or if your financial position changes in any way after you have submitted this form, you must tell the court. This is a requirement of the Legal Aid regulations. I understand that, if I do not produce all the information which the court needs, it may make such enquiries of the Benefits Agency as it considers necessary and I authorise it so to do. I consent to the disclosure of information to confirm that I am in receipt of benefit.

I understand that the court may order me to make a contribution to the costs of Legal Aid, or to pay the whole costs if it considers that I can afford to do so and, if I am under 16, may make a similar order with respect to my parents.

Signed **Dated:**

4

For Court use only

Any additional factors considered when determining the application, including any information given orally.

Decision on the interests of justice test

I have considered all available details of all the charges and it is / is not * in the interests of justice that representation be granted because:

Signed ______ Proper Officer

Date ______

* Cross out whichever does not apply

Chapter Seven

Legal Aid Contribution Orders

This chapter deals with:

1. The issue of contribution orders.
2. The 'collecting court'.
3. The duration of contribution orders and the dates payments fall due.
4. The power of the court to withhold legal aid until capital contributions are paid.
5. Changes in a legally aided person's, or an appropriate contributor's, financial circumstances.
6. The court's powers to seek further information during the life of the case.

THE ISSUE OF CONTRIBUTION ORDERS

Where the court has calculated that an applicant for a criminal legal aid order, or an appropriate contributor who is associated with the application, is liable to make a contribution from income or capital if a legal aid order is made, the court or proper officer will then decide whether or not the merits of the application are such that is in the interests of justice to grant the application. It is only when the decision to grant a criminal legal aid order has been made that the contribution order comes into effect.

If the competent authority determines not to make an order the notice of refusal should be endorsed to show the contribution that would have fallen due, had an order been made.[1] The statutorily prescribed form of refusal is Form 2[2] and it contains the necessary declaration as to the contribution that would have fallen due at paragraph two (see Figure 2).

If it has been decided to grant an order and a contribution falls due, the court, or proper officer, must issue a legal aid order on Form 11, if the grant was in a magistrates' court[3], or Form 11A if the issuing court is the Crown Court[4] and, in either case a contribution order[5] on Form 6 which also shows the calculations that were used. In practice this tends to take the form of three separate documents, namely:

1 Reg 20 of the Legal Aid in Criminal and Care Proceedings (General) Regulations 1989.
2 Reg 19 and Form 2, Sch 2 of the Legal Aid in Criminal and Care Proceedings (General) Regulations 1989.
3 Reg 40(1) and Form 11, Sch 2 of the Legal Aid in Criminal and Care Proceedings (General) Regulations 1989.
4 Reg 40(2) and Form 11A, Sch 2 of the Legal Aid in Criminal and Care Proceedings (General) Regulations 1989.
5 Reg 27(1) and Form 6, Sch 2 of the Legal Aid in Criminal and Care Proceedings (General) Regulations 1989.

FIG 1: AN OVERVIEW OF THE PROCESS OF ISSUING CONTRIBUTION ORDERS

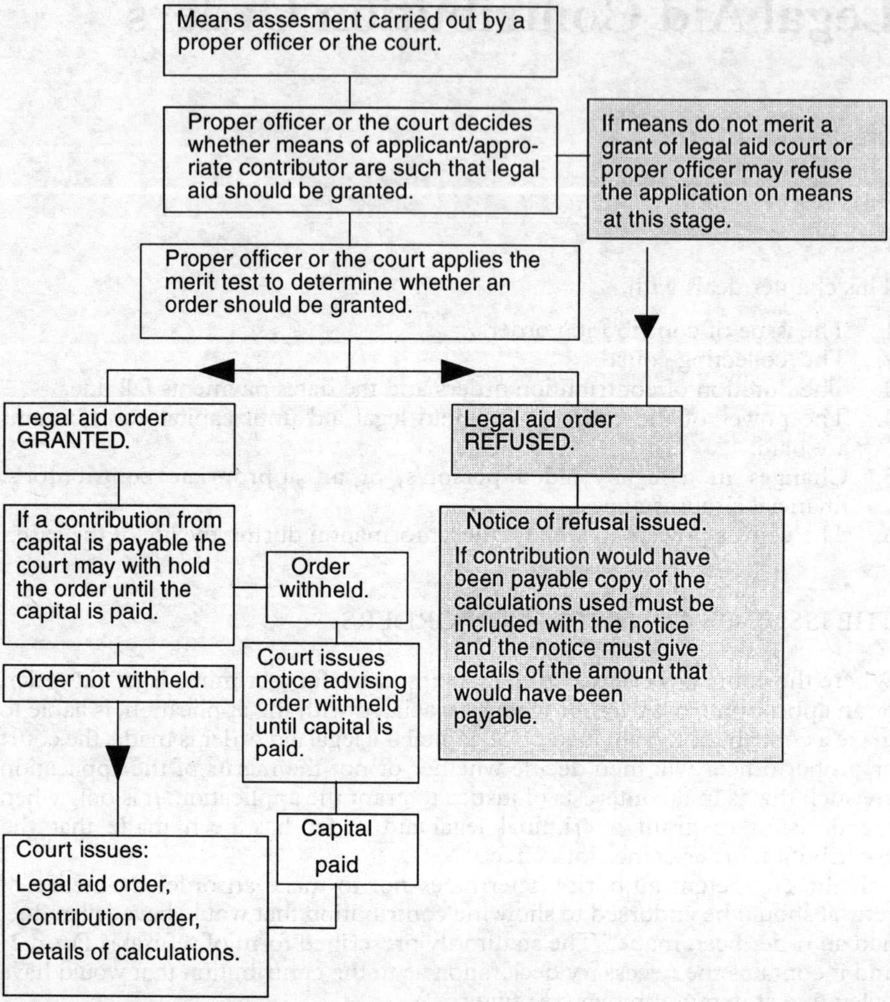

(i) the legal aid order;
(ii) the contribution order; and
(iii) a form showing the calculations used.

The contribution order is reproduced at Figure 4 and the form showing the calculations used is shown at Figure 5.

Three copies of the contribution order will be required and must be distributed as follows:

(1) to the legally assisted person;
(2) to the legally assisted person's solicitor (or counsel if the legal aid order provides for the services of counsel only); and
(3) to the collecting court (see below)[6].

6 Reg 27(2) of the Legal Aid in Criminal and Care Proceedings (General) Regulations 1989.

FIG 2: FORM 2 – CERTIFICATE OF REFUSAL TO GRANT A CRIMINAL LEGAL AID ORDER

NOTIFICATION OF REFUSAL TO GRANT LEGAL AID AND DETERMINATION OF CONTRIBUTION.

Regs.12,13,19 and 20.

To:

Your application for legal aid has been refused by the court/a judge of the court/a justice of the peace/ a proper officer on the following grounds:

(a) it does not appear desirable to make an order in the interests of justice. A statement of reasons for this decision is enclosed, and/or

(b) it does not appear that your means are such that you require assistance in meeting the costs you may incur.

If legal aid had been granted you would have been required to pay a contribution of £ per week from income and £ from capital [payable on] towards the costs of your case/legal aid would have been conditional on immediate payment of £ . .

You are entitled:

(i) to apply for legal aid to an area committee (in some cases where your application has been refused under paragraph (a) above). If you wish to do this you should complete form 3. You must apply within 14 days of this notification.

(ii) to renew your application to the court [to the Crown Court] at any time If you wish to do so you should complete the bottom part of this form and return the whole form to the court at the address stated.

(iii) in any event to apply for legal aid to the court of trial on the day of the trial.

Signed:
Justices' Clerk/An Officer of the Crown Court.

Date:

I wish to renew my application for legal aid to the court.

I have/have not made application to an area committee.

Signed:
Date:

NOTE: (i) You should enclose any additional or new information you think is relevant to your application.

(ii) If there has been any change in your financial circumstances you must complete and enclose a new statement of means form.

(iii) If you have made an application to an area committee you should enclose a copy of the notification of the decision.

FIG 3: FORM 6 – LEGAL AID CONTRIBUTION ORDER

LEGAL AID CONTRIBUTION ORDER Form 6; Reg 27.

TO:

In accordance with the provisions of section 23(1) Legal Aid Act 1988 the Court (area committee) orders you to contribute towards the costs of representation to be provided to you under a legal aid order:-

The contribution required is:-

a contribution from disposable capital is one lump sum of £......... This must be paid on or before........ 199......

contributions from disposable income payable at the rate of £.........per week/per month for so long as the legal aid order is in force. The first instalment must be paid on or before.............199......

This money should be paid to the Clerk to the Justices, ... Magistrates' Court.

Signed:
Date:

NOTES:

The figures overleaf show how the contribution was calculated. If you are not satisfied with the calculations used you may apply to this court for your means to be redetermined. If your means change you must inform the court which is hearing your case IMMEDIATELY so that the contribution can be reassessed and changed if necessary. If you do not want legal aid on these terms, you MUST inform the court IMMEDIATELY by tearing off and returning the slip below. If your legal aid is revoked you may still have to pay some money towards any costs already incurred.

If you would prefer to pay monthly, you should inform the Clerk to the Justices who will decide whether you should pay weekly or monthly.

Tear off along here.

I, of (address) have been granted legal aid by the Court at

I hereby apply for my legal aid order to be withdrawn. I understand I may be required to pay any costs that have already been incurred.

RETURN THIS FORM IMMEDIATELY TO: [Name and Address of the Court]

Signed . . . .
Dated. . . . .

FIG 4: SPECIFIED FORM SHOWING CALCULATIONS USED TO DETERMINE CONTRIBUTION

LEGAL AID CONTRIBUTION ORDER – CALCULATIONS USED.

Part One- Figures used.

(1) Average weekly net INCOME			£	A)
(2) Allowances against income	-dependants		£	
	-housing		£	
	-travel		£	
	-others		£	
	Total Allowances		£	(B)
(3) Total CAPITAL			£	

Part Two- Calculation of contribution from income.

(1) Disposable income is (A) – (B) = £
Contribution is Disposable income – 47, divided by 3 = £

NOTE: Contributions are rounded to the nearest whole pound. The minimum contribution is £1.

Part Three-Summary.

Your contribution from INCOME is £......................per week/month.

Your contribution from CAPITAL is £......................

Please turn to the contribution order for details of how and when to pay.

As a matter of good practice some magistrates' courts will include a leaflet advising legally assisted persons of their rights and obligations under a legal aid contribution order and this leaflet may also provide further information about the payment options that are available in that particular magistrates' court. Such a document will usually highlight the need to tell the court about any changes in income and expenditure that will affect the contribution order. Payment options might include the facility to pay by direct debit or standing order, 'Transcash' through Post Offices in addition to the options of attending at the court's cash office or sending cheques and postal orders through the post. It is also possible that the explanation within such a notice will explain how to pay in circumstances where the collection of funds has been contracted out to another agency by the collecting court.

THE 'COLLECTING COURT'

This term is used to denote the court that will be responsible for collecting the contributions that fall due under the order. The collecting court can be determined by reference to Schedule 3, Part 1, Paragraph 1 of the Legal Aid Act 1988 which directs that the collecting court shall be named within the contribution order and shall be:

(a) the magistrates' court that made the legal aid contribution order; or
(b) where the contribution order was made in respect of proceedings that had been transferred, or committed for trial, or sentence, from a magistrates' court, or was made in respect of an appeal against the decision of a magistrates' court, the collecting court will be the magistrates' court in which the proceedings originated; or
(c) in any other case, a magistrates' court nominated by the court making the order.

In a case that falls within group (c) above the order will usually be made by a Crown Court and the most appropriate magistrates' court to nominate is the one in whose petty sessional division the legally assisted person resides, as this avoids the need for a transfer order to be made at a later stage.

1. Transfer of the collecting court

Paragraph 5 of Schedule 3 allows a 'Transfer Order' to be made where it appears to the collecting court that the person subject to the contribution order is residing in a different petty sessions area. The consequences of making such an order are twofold, namely:

(a) payments under the order are enforceable in the petty sessions area specified in the transfer order; and
(b) as from the date of the transfer order, a magistrates' court for the petty sessions area specified in the order shall be substituted for the court which made the transfer order as the collecting court in relation to the contribution order.

This means that the court nominated in the transfer order will be required to collect any outstanding or remaining payments and enforce payment in default. Some magistrates' courts have declined to accept transferred contribution orders from neighbouring or more remote areas until the substantive proceedings, for which the legal aid order has been made, have been concluded. There may be some justification for thinking that transfer orders can only be made during the enforcement stage, when it is known exactly how much money has to be collected. However, closer examination of the statute does not appear to restrict the court's powers to transfer a contribution order at any time and there is nothing within the Act that suggests a court's consent is required before it can be nominated in a transfer order. As magistrates' courts face great pressure to ensure they perform as well as possible in the opening and closing of collection accounts, prudent magistrates' clerks will undoubtedly wish to transfer all contribution order accounts in cases where the contributor lives in another petty sessions division.

There is no specified form for a transfer order and this is not an order that can be made by a Justices' Clerk or a nominated proper officer. The correct procedure appears to be for the order to be made by a properly constituted magistrates' court[7] and, thereafter, for a certified memorandum of order to be drawn up from the court's register which can be dispatched to the new collecting court together with any relevant account history and a record of the enforcement action taken to date. On receipt, the newly nominated collecting court will be required to open an account and take any necessary enforcement action. The

7 See s 121 of the Magistrates' Courts Act 1980 in relation to constitution of magistrates' courts.

newly appointed court may also have to adjust the account to take account of the final taxation of the solicitor's bill[8].

THE DURATION OF CONTRIBUTION ORDERS AND THE DATE PAYMENTS FALL DUE

1. Contributions from income

Contributions from income are calculated to establish a weekly sum that must be paid into the collecting court. Such weekly payments must be made for the duration of the case[9] and consequently the final amount payable cannot be specified in the order. The first payment falls due seven days after the contribution order is made and payments fall due every seven days thereafter[10].

Figure 5 provides a diagrammatic reconstruction of an account history showing due dates for payment. It is to be noted that should a case be completed

FIG 5: ACCOUNT EXAMPLE – CONTRIBUTIONS FROM INCOME

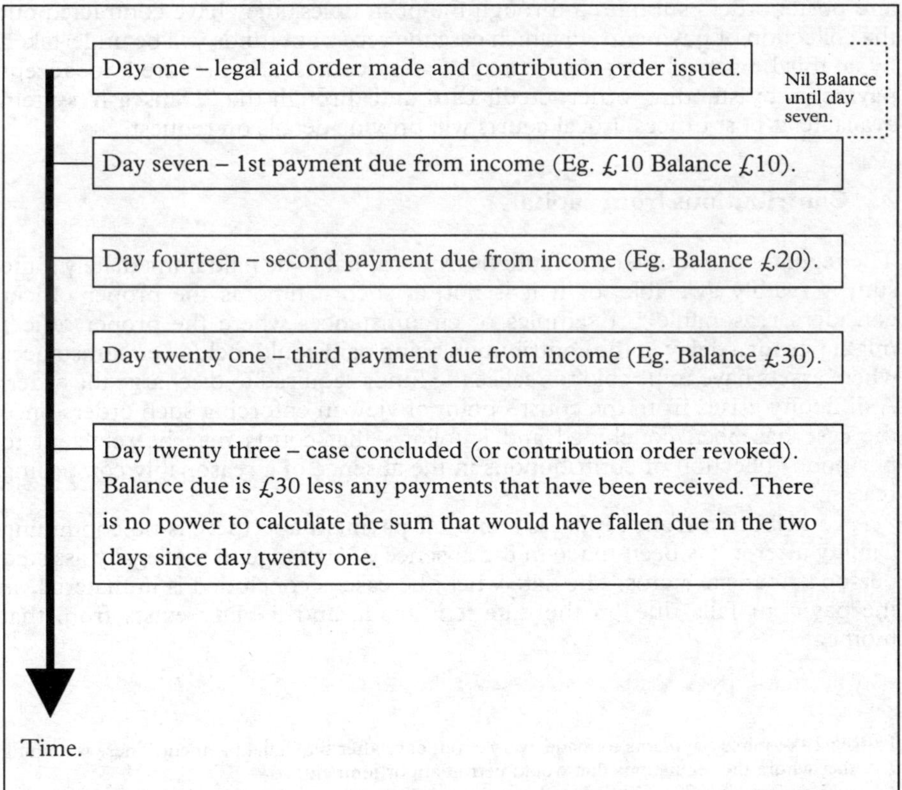

8 See ss 7 and 8 below for a commentary on enforcement action and account adjustments.
9 Reg 29(1) of the Legal Aid in Criminal and Care Proceedings (General) Regulations 1989.
10 Reg 29(1) of the Legal Aid in Criminal and Care Proceedings (General) Regulations 1989.

within seven days of the making of a contribution order no payments from income fall due. It also follows that where a case is concluded on a date that is not a payment date the account balance remains that which existed on the last payment date. The regulations do not permit a collecting court to apportion the weekly sum due so as to reflect the notional sum that would have fallen due since the last payment date[11].

A collecting court has no power to withhold legal aid orders until a contribution from income is paid[12]. If the only contribution is from income the legal aid order must be released to the legally aided person and his solicitor. The court's powers to deal with non-payment are dealt with separately in section 7 below.

If payments of a contribution order from income on a weekly basis causes the legally aided person or the appropriate contributor some difficulty, the proper officer of the collecting court does have a discretion to allow it to be paid on a fortnightly or monthly basis[13]. The proper officer should be approached in advance of making monthly payments as, if the court has an efficient enforcement programme, the order could be revoked within the period between payments.

Methods of payment into collecting courts differ from area to area. All magistrates' courts accept payments of cash, at their own cash office counter, and postal orders submitted through the post, unless they have contracted out the collection of payments, in which case the receipt of funds will be undertaken by a third party. Increasingly magistrates' courts are prepared to accept payments by standing order, credit card and through the 'Transcash' system available at post offices. Local courts will provide details on request.

2. Contributions from capital

The regulations require contributions from capital to be paid immediately if the sum is readily available, or if it is not, at such a time as the proper officer considers reasonable[14]. Examples of circumstances where the proper officer might permit a delay in the contribution being paid could include circumstances where assets have to be sold to realise the funds required to discharge the order. A difficulty arises from the court's point of view in enforcing such orders once the case has been concluded and it follows that courts may be reluctant to postpone collection of contributions in the absence of a reasonably compelling reason.

A contribution from capital is a one-off payment and there is no continuing liability after it has been made in the absence of a change in the legally assisted person's financial status. The date when the case is concluded is immaterial, as the payment falls due on the date it is made and liability exists from that moment.

11 Reg 29 requires payments to made every seven days after the initial payment. There is nothing other within the regulations that would permit apportionment.

12 *Cullen v Trimble* (1872) 37 JP 115 determined that magistrates' courts could only do that which they were empowered to do by statute. Consequently, in the absence of any specific authority enabling the court to withhold the order any attempt to do so would be unlawful and the court could be compelled to issue the order by an order for judicial review.

13 Reg 29(1) of the Legal Aid in Criminal and Care Proceedings (General) Regulations 1989.

14 Reg 29(2) of the Legal Aid in Criminal and Care Proceedings (General) Regulations 1989.

THE COURT'S POWERS TO WITHHOLD ORDERS UNTIL CONTRIBUTIONS FROM CAPITAL ARE PAID

Where a capital contribution is to be paid, is readily available and is ordered to be paid forthwith, the legal aid order must be withheld and will not take effect until the contribution is paid in full[15].

FIG 6: FORM 7 – NOTICE OF WITHHOLDING OF A LEGAL AID ORDER

NOTICE OF WITHHOLDING OF A LEGAL AID ORDER

Form 6; Reg 29.

TO:

The ____________________ Court has made an order granting you legal aid in respect of the proceedings before it / the ____________________ Court. It has also made an order, a copy of which is attached, requiring you to make a contribution out of capital towards the cost of your case.

In accordance with regulation 29(3) of the Legal Aid in Criminal and Care Proceedings (General) Regulations 1989 the court requires you to make an immediate payment of that capital contribution to the Clerk to the Justices.

NOTE: ***You will NOT receive the legal aid order until you have made this payment and your solicitor and counsel will not be covered by the order until it has been received.***

A copy of this notice has been sent to your solicitor/counsel.

The procedure is that the court will notify both the legally assisted person, any appropriate contributor and the assigned solicitor using Form 7 (see Figure 5). The payment will normally be made to the court which makes the order[16] rather than any collecting court and on receipt of the payment the order can be released. Courts may consider it to be appropriate to ensure that funds have cleared to their account before releasing the order.

CHANGES IN A LEGALLY ASSISTED PERSON'S, OR AN APPROPRIATE CONTRIBUTOR'S, FINANCIAL CIRCUMSTANCES

1. The duty to report changes

A legally assisted person or an appropriate contributor must report any change in their financial circumstances which occurs after the submission of his statement of means and which might affect the terms of any existing contribution order or, if no contribution order has been made, might make him liable to contribute towards the costs of the legal aid order[17]. If such a person intentionally refuses to provide the court with details of a relevant change in his financial circumstances and his legal representative becomes aware of this, the legal

15 S 24(1) of the Legal Aid Act 1988.
16 Reg 30(2) of the Legal Aid in Criminal and Care Proceedings (General) Regulations 1989.
17 Reg 31 of the Legal Aid in Criminal and Care Proceedings (General) Regulations 1989.

FIG 7: DEALING WITH CHANGES IN FINANCIAL CIRCUMSTANCES

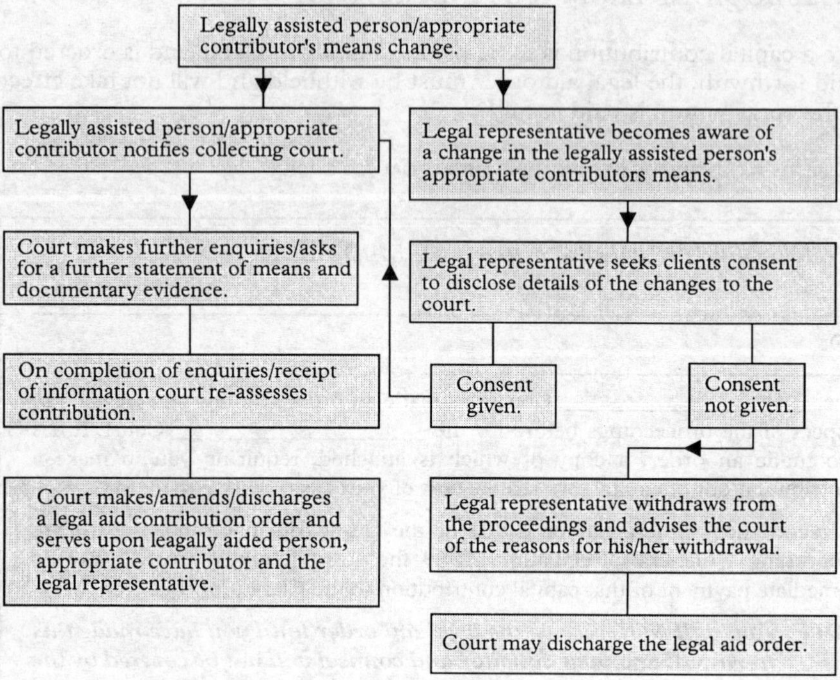

representative will have a duty to report the change to the court, notwithstanding any professional privilege that might normally apply[18]. The Law Society has issued guidance to solicitors that states:

> 'Where the client is legally aided in a criminal matter the duty to disclose all relevant information remains with the client. However if the solicitor becomes aware of information which indicates that the client's circumstances have changed, or that the client did not disclose relevant information at the outset, the solicitor must advise the client that unless the client informs or permits the solicitor to inform the clerk to the justices or the appropriate officer of the Crown Court, the solicitor will have to cease acting'[19].

Should the legal representative withdraw, the court will be bound to re-assign the legal aid order to another solicitor unless it forms the view that some conduct of the legally aided person makes this inappropriate and requires the court to exercise its discretion to withdraw the order[20]. On a strict construction of the statute it follows that mere withdrawal will be insufficient to protect the legal aid fund and will not discharge the legal representative's duty to disclose an abuse of legal aid, although the view of the profession differs slightly[1]. A solicitor

18 Reg 56 of the Legal Aid in Criminal and Care Proceedings (General) Regulations 1989.
19 Para 5.04 of the *Guide to the Professional Conduct of Solicitors 1993*, The Law Society.
20 Reg 50(2) of the Legal Aid in Criminal and Care Proceedings (General) Regulations 1989.
1 Para 5.04 *Professional Conduct of Solicitors*, suggests that the client's consent to disclose the withheld information should be sought and if that is withheld the solicitor should withdraw. Problems may follow, in which case solicitors should seek the advice of the Law Society on an individual basis to ensure they are protected both from allegations they have allowed the fund to be abused and from their client's accusations of breach of privilege.

or barrister would appear to be permitted under the regulations to advise the court of the reasons for his or her withdrawal, thereby empowering the court to make its own enquiries or withdraw the legal aid order.

2. Form of notification of a change in financial circumstances

The regulations do not impose any standard form for notifying a change in the financial circumstances of a legally assisted person or an appropriate contributor; however, the court will require sufficient information to carry out a further means assessment and in many cases this will mean that a new statement of means will be required together with relevant documentary evidence. If the court is dissatisfied with the information that has been provided, or it has reason to believe that the applicant's means have changed, the court has power to require the legally assisted person or the appropriate contributor to complete a new statement of means on Form 5 with all the accompanying documentation and any further information that the proper officer might require.[2] If the legally assisted person or the appropriate contributor fails to comply with an instruction to provide this information, the court would seem to be unable to revoke the order, as the power to do so only applies if a request for documentary evidence was made by the court in circumstances where a reasonable explanation had originally been provided to justify the non-production of documents[3]. The court's remedy would appear to be to re-assess the order on the basis of the information that is available[4] and if there is a consequential increase in the amount to be paid under the contribution order which aggrieves the contributor, a further re-assessment can be undertaken when the required information is provided by him to the court.

In advising a legally assisted person of the extent of the information that is likely to be required reference to the check list at table one may be of assistance, although this will not bind the proper officer in any way and he may require further details.

Where a doubt arises as to the information that may be required, the court's proper officer should be consulted.

3. Determining when a re-assessment is required

The regulations specify various circumstances where the court will be bound to carry out a re-assessment of the legally assisted person's or the appropriate contributor's means with a view to varying the contribution order. For ease of reference these have been listed in Table 2.

In the final case listed, that of a youth attaining 16 years of age, the regulations do not provide a specific remedy. The regulations referred to appear to be applicable in the circumstances. If the court will not reassess the contribution order it would be open to the legally assisted person to seek the discharge of the

2 Reg 24(1) of the Legal Aid in Criminal and Care Proceedings (General) Regulations 1989.
3 Reg 24(2) and 41(1)(d) of the Legal Aid in Criminal and Care Proceedings (General) Regulations 1989.
4 Reg 33(a) of the Legal Aid in Criminal and Care Proceedings (General) Regulations 1989.

TABLE 1: DOCUMENTARY EVIDENCE WHICH MAY BE REQUIRED TO NOTIFY A CHANGE IN FINANCIAL CIRCUMSTANCES

Change in financial circumstances.	*Notification and documents required.*
Loss of employment and claim for unemployment benefit.	Letter of dismissal from employer and copy of application form for DSS benefits (preferably stating the type of benefit applied for). Details of any final lump sum or redundancy pay should be disclosed.
Start of employment and cessation of receipt of a qualifying benefit.	Letter setting out terms of employment and stating wage to be paid. Full statement of means on Form 5 including documentary evidence of all outgoings.
Wage/salary increase or decrease.	Letter from employer setting out new rates of pay. Confirmation from legally assisted person that all other details given on the statement of means remain the same.
Commencement of receipt of a qualifying benefit (income support, family credit or disability working allowance).	Copy of the DSS letter advising that the benefit will be paid.
Youth attaining 16 years of age.	Letter from appropriate contributor seeking discharge of any existing contribution order. Full statement of means from youth with full documentary evidence.
Increase in capital[5].	Bank, building society or other independent statements setting out total capital held and a letter from the contributor detailing the increase.
Increase/decrease in allowable expenditure.	Documentary evidence setting out the increase or decrease in expenditure (eg letter from a building society advising the contributor of the change in mortgage payment due to an interest rate change) and, if necessary, a written explanation justifying the change.

5 The regulations do not permit a re-assessment of the contribution order where the legally assisted person's capital assets have fallen in value (see Reg 33(b) of the Legal Aid in Criminal and Care Proceedings (General) Regulations 1989) and consequently no notification of capital expenditure after the initial assessment has been made would be required.

TABLE 2: FINANCIAL LIMITS OF CHANGE TO COMPEL RE-ASSESSMENT

CHANGE IN CIRCUMSTANCES	MINIMUM/MAXIMUM CHANGE TO REQUIRE RE-ASSESSMENT
1. **Increase in disposable income.**	Re-assessment required if increase is more than **£750.00 per annum.**
2. **Reduction in disposable income.**	Re-assessment required if reduction is more than **£300.00 per annum.**
3. **Increase in disposable capital.**	Re-assessment required if increase is more than **£750.00 during a year.**

legal aid order[6] which will have the effect of terminating the contribution order as such a contribution order (from income) only remains in force for the period of time during which the legal aid order is in force[7]. As regards the payment of any capital sum, this would remain due, if it had not already been paid, as such a sum falls to be paid when the contribution order is made[8]. Once the legal aid order has been discharged, the former legally assisted person, namely the youth, may make a fresh application for legal aid orally to the court at any hearing[9] and *his* means must be assessed rather than those of any appropriate contributor as he is now an adult and the powers to treat him as an under 16-year old do not apply[10].

If the youth attains the age of 16 after the application is submitted to the court but before a legal aid order is granted the position is much clearer as the regulations provide that the youth shall be treated as if he was under 16[11]. It therefore follows that it will be preferable to delay the submission of the application until after the youth's 16th birthday if there is a likelihood of a contribution order being made as this will avoid the need for the action already described to vary the order. Given that courts tend to process properly completed applications within 24 to 36 hours, the consequential delay is likely to be minimal.

Where a change in a contributor's financial position has been brought about by a change in the applicable allowances (eg where a further child has been born during the currency of the order) or an increase in an allowable expense, such as a mortgage the court will look to see how this has affected the disposable income before deciding whether to redetermine the amount of the contribution order. In practical terms this means the proper officer will have recalculate the disposable income in the first instance to discover the effect the change has had.

6 Reg 41(1)(b) of the Legal Aid in Criminal and Care Proceedings (General) Regulations 1989.
7 Reg 29(1) of the Legal Aid in Criminal and Care Proceedings (General) Regulations 1989.
8 Reg 29(2) of the Legal Aid in Criminal and Care Proceedings (General) Regulations 1989.
9 Reg 10 of the Legal Aid in Criminal and Care Proceedings (General) Regulations 1989 and *R v Liverpool City Magistrates' Court, ex p Pender (No 2)* [1994] 2 All ER 897.
10 Regs 3 and 23(3) of the Legal Aid in Criminal and Care Proceedings (General) Regulations 1989.
11 Reg 5 of the Legal Aid in Criminal and Care Proceedings (General) Regulations 1989.

TABLE 3: DETERMINING WHETHER RECALCULATION REQUIRED

FINANCIAL CHANGE	RECALC?	EFFECT	REG.[12]
No contribution order in force:			
Further information becomes available after the initial calculation.	YES	Recalculation may lead to a contribution order being made. Order will take effect from the date it is made.	32(1)(a)
The circumstances upon which the initial calculation was performed alter.	YES	Recalculation may lead to a contribution order being made. Order will take effect from the date it is made.	32(1)(b)
Contribution order in force:			
Contributor begins receipt of an exempting benefit.	YES	Contribution period is terminated. Any arrears may be enforced but no further payments will fall due.	37(1)(a)
Contributor's disposable income increases by more than £750.00 per year.[13]	YES	Contribution will be increased unless there has been a corresponding increase in allowable expenses.	33(a)
Contributor's disposable income is reduced by more than £300.00 per year.[14]	YES	Contribution will be reduced unless there has been a corresponding reduction in allowable expenses.	33(a)
Contributor's disposable capital increases by more than £750.00.	YES	Capital contribution will be increased – the balance not yet collected will fall due immediately.	33(b)
Youth attains 16 years of age.	YES	Youth is entitled to separate assessment of his means and appropriate contributor may seek discharge of the order against him and the youth becomes liable to contribute if his means do not entitle him to free legal aid.	32(1)(b) for youth and 33(a) for contributor.

12 All references are to the Legal Aid in Criminal and Care Proceedings (General) Regulations 1989 (as amended).

13 This would include circumstances where an allowance or allowable expenditure has changed thereby affecting the amount of disposable income.

14 This would include circumstances where an allowance or allowable expenditure has changed thereby affecting the amount of disposable income.

4. Failure to disclose a change in circumstances

An offence is committed where any person intentionally fails to comply with the regulations as to the information required to be furnished by him[15], which carries a maximum penalty on summary conviction of three months' imprisonment or a level four (£2,500) fine. This offence can be committed by a legally assisted person who fails to notify any change in his circumstances that would affect his legal aid contribution order or might lead to such an order being made[16]. It is important to note that the normal time limit that requires information to be laid in respect of a summary offence within six months of the date upon which the offence was committed[17] does not apply[18], but proceedings must be brought within two years of the date of the offence[19].

THE COURT'S POWERS TO SEEK FURTHER INFORMATION DURING THE LIFE OF THE CASE

The court has a limited power of investigation, which in practice is limited to requesting further information or supporting documentary evidence. It had been thought that the court could make a legal aid order on the basis of information supplied in a statement of means which was not supported by the provision of documentary evidence and, thereafter, impose a condition that the documents be produced within a given period, usually 14 to 21 days, from the date of order. In order to enforce that condition the court would threaten to withdraw the order in the event of non-compliance. This procedure has been found to be unlawful as the court's powers to deal with an application in the absence of documentary evidence are limited to circumstances where there is a reasonable, written, reason that persuades the proper officer that it is impractical for documentation to be produced. Once such a reason has been found the court cannot make any further enquiry until there are grounds for believing that the cause of the prohibition on the production of documents no longer applies[20]. In circumstances where such an order was made the court will have to be reasonably certain that there is a prospect that a further request can be made before exercising its powers to compel the production of further information.

The basic powers to make further enquiries arise within the regulations. These allow the court or proper officer to require, at any time after the submission of a statement of means, further evidence of any information given in a statement of means, or any change in his financial circumstances together with such additional information as the court or proper officer may direct[1]. This power is broad in its extent, but the difficulty for the court or proper officer is

15 S 39(1)(b) of the Legal Aid Act 1988.
16 See, for example, *Roberts v Duce* [1974] Crim LR 107 where a student failed to notify an increase in his further education grant. He was convicted of an offence of failing to comply with Reg 6(5) of the Legal Aid (General) Regulations 1962, predecessor of the current regulations. He appealed on the grounds that his grant was not income. That appeal was dismissed.
17 S 127 of the Magistrates' Courts Act 1980.
18 S 39(2) of the Legal Aid Act 1988.
19 S 39(3) Legal Aid Act 1988.
20 *R v South Western Justices, ex p Doyle and Bennett* (1 November 1995, Unreported).
1 Reg 24(1) of the Legal Aid in Criminal and Care Proceedings (General) Regulations 1989.

FIG 8: PROCESS FOR THE REQUEST OF FURTHER INFORMATION

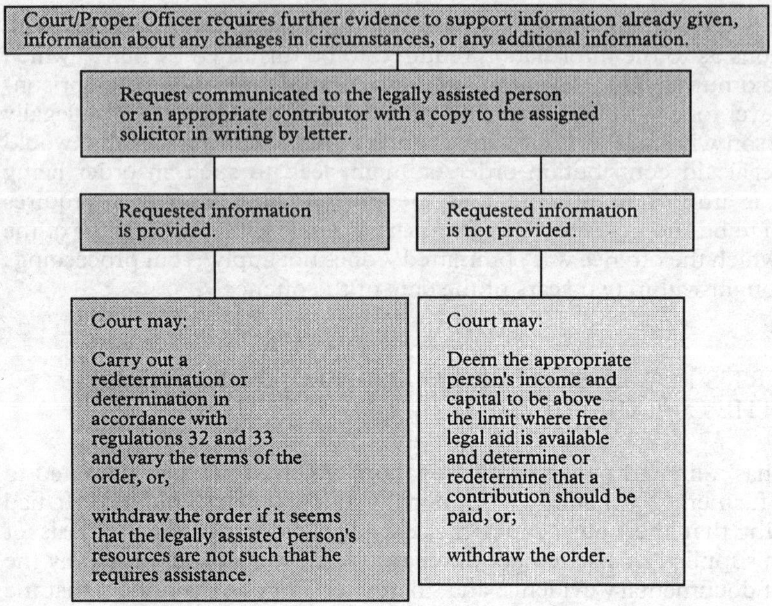

knowing where to look. In reaching this decision the appropriate authority can have regard to any evidence adduced by or on behalf of the prosecution[2].

Figure 8 above sets out the procedure that will be adopted by the court when it seeks further information from appropriate contributors or legally assisted persons. If such a person fails to comply with the request of the proper officer there is power to revoke the order[3]. If this were to happen the former legally assisted person would be able to make an application for a further legal aid order[4], but the requirement to produce the required documentation or further information could also be renewed and the court could refuse representation[5] or delay a decision until the information was provided[6].

Proposals exist for the establishment of a special unit within the Legal Aid Board that will be able to accept referrals from court staff in particularly complex cases so that special investigations as to a person's means might be undertaken, It remains to be seen whether, if these proposals come into force, any extra powers to seek better particulars will be introduced.

2 See, for example, *R v Newham Justices, ex p Mumtaz* (1990) 154 JP 597 – in this case the clerk to the justices became concerned that evidence adduced during a bail application that gave details of the accused's lavish life style did not accord with the information given on the statement of means. The clerk to the justices sought further information and delayed calculating the accused's means until it was received. This was held to be a right and proper exercise of the clerk's powers but it must be noted that this case considered the regulations made under the Legal Aid Act 1974, although the current regulations are almost identical in their provisions as regards further information.

3 Regs 24(2) and 41(1)(d) of the Legal Aid in Criminal and Care Proceedings (General) Regulations 1989.

4 Reg 10 of the Legal Aid in Criminal and Care Proceedings (General) Regulations 1989 and *R v Liverpool City Magistrates' Court, ex p Pender (No 2)* [1994] 2 All ER 897.

5 Reg 26(2A) of the Legal Aid in Criminal and Care Proceedings (General) Regulations 1989.

6 *R v Newham Justices, ex p Mumtaz* (1990) 154 JP 597.

Chapter Eight

Enforcing Criminal Legal Aid Contribution Orders

This chapter will deal with:

1. Enforcing payment of contribution orders.
2. Powers to refund overpayments or remit further contributions and correct mistakes.

ENFORCING PAYMENT OF A LEGAL AID CONTRIBUTION ORDER

The collecting court is charged with the duty to enforce the collection of contributions that are not paid by an appropriate contributor or legally assisted person. If the court has made use of the power to withhold a legal aid order until the capital contribution is paid[1] there will be no need to enforce the capital element of the contribution order as there will be no valid legal aid order, and therefore no cost to public funds, until the capital element has been received by the court. The majority of enforcement action will be required to enforce payments from income.

For ease of explanation and to reflect the practicalities of the action required the process can be broken down into two separate stages:

1. **Enforcement whilst the legal aid order is in force or during the contribution period.** (*Stage one enforcement*)
   In most cases the contribution period will cover the whole of the period whilst the legal aid order is in force. The only exceptions are likely to be where the contribution period came to an end prior to the conclusion of the proceedings. This might be brought about where a legally assisted person begins to receive income support, family credit or disability working allowance, but there are arrears of contributions that arose before he became eligible to receive that benefit.
2. **Enforcement action after the contribution period has ended.** (*Stage two enforcement*)
   This will take place when ever the contribution period comes to an end[2].

Figure 1 provides an overview of the enforcement process.

1 Page 101 above.
2 See Reg 37 of the Legal Aid In Criminal and Care Proceedings (General) Regulations1989.

FIG 1: AN OVERVIEW OF THE ENFORCEMENT OF LEGAL AID CONTRIBUTION ORDERS

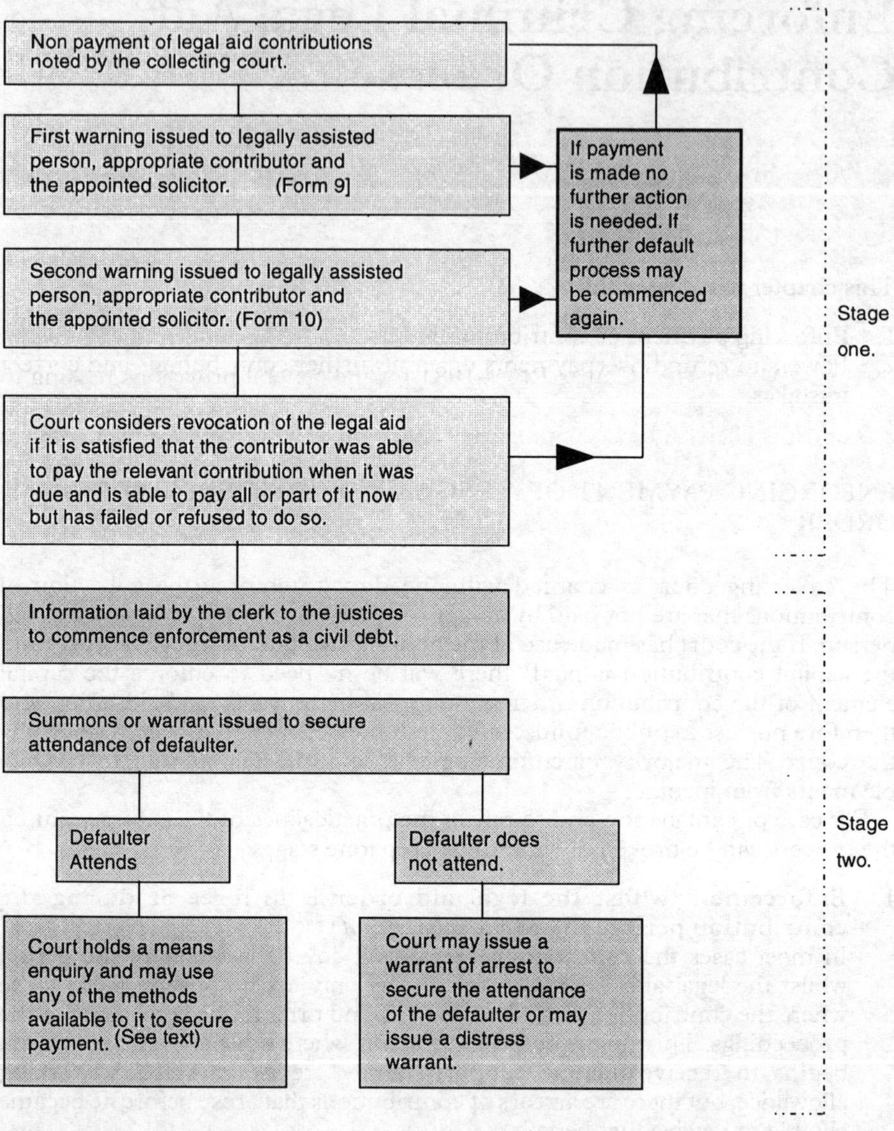

1. Stage one enforcement

The collecting court is charged with monitoring the receipt of payments of legal aid contributions. In the event that arrears accumulate whilst the legal aid order remains in force the court will wish to use this stage one procedure to encourage payment, or to minimise the loss to public funds that would be created if the legal aid order were to remain in force without collection of the contributions being made.

Many collecting courts will be assisted in the management of legal aid accounts by the accounting packages that have been designed for magistrates' courts computer systems. Almost all of these will produce reports that will highlight legal aid accounts that have fallen into arrears and many will produce the appropriate documentation. In courts without the benefit of computerisation the enforcement process is easily managed if a systematic approach is adopted by the court. Generally the number of legal aid contribution accounts is very low, often about 5% of the total figure of live legal aid orders, and consequently the task of the enforcement officer is less daunting than it might seem.

In practical terms no action can be taken until the income portion of the contribution order has been live for 14 to 21 days. This is because the first payment will not have fallen due until the seventh day after the order was made and some account should be taken of the time taken to effect payment by post. After 14 days or so the court can detect arrears and can undertake the first stage of enforcement. This requires the dispatch of a standard warning on Form 9. This form is reproduced at Figure 2 below. The rules of service are unclear as the regulations do not specify any specific methods; however, reference to rule 99 of the Magistrates' Courts Rules 1981 for the general provisions relating to service of documents in magistrates' courts would suggest that service by first class post is likely to be acceptable. The form must be sent to the legally aided person and the solicitor or barrister assigned under the order[3]. The regulations do not cater for an appropriate contributor defaulting in payments of the contribution order. Good practice would suggest that a copy of the notice should be sent to an appropriate contributor in addition to the legally assisted person and the solicitor or barrister assigned under the order.

FIG 2: FIRST WARNING FOR NON-PAYMENT OF LEGAL AID CONTRIBUTIONS

Notification of Arrears of Payment of Contribution Order — Form 9, Reg 36(1)(a)

To:

You have fallen into arrears in the payment of instalments in respect of your legal aid contribution order. You have missed instalments of £ and are now £ in arrears.

You must pay this sum to the Clerk to the Justices at Magistrates' Court, WITHIN SEVEN DAYS OF RECEIPT OF THIS NOTICE. If you fail to do so this court will consider revoking legal aid.

A copy of this form has been sent to your solicitor/counsel.

Signed

Dated

Once Form 9 has been sent to the defaulter a reasonable period must be allowed for the default to be remedied. The form specifies that a response must be made within seven days of receipt of the form. When the delays occasioned by the use of the postal system are taken into account, the court would seem precluded from taking any further action for a period of at least 14 days.

Once a sufficient period of time has elapsed and if the default has not been remedied further action may be taken by sending the defaulter a warning that

3 Reg 36(2) of the Legal Aid in Criminal and Care Proceedings (General) Regulations 1989.

the court is considering revoking his legal aid order. Again the statutory form, Form 10 which is reproduced at Figure 3, must be used by the court[4]. The distribution of the document is identical to that already required in dealing with Form 9. This warning not only warns of the consequences of further default but also provides an opportunity for the defaulter to provide the court with an explanation as to why the arrears have accrued. In many cases the explanation tendered to the court will disclose grounds for making further enquiries into the contributor's means or to vary or discharge the contribution order. In such circumstances regard must be had to the principles discussed above so that a proper determination can be made as to whether it is necessary to recalculate the contribution order.

FIG 3: WARNING OF REVOCATION

Warning of revocation of Legal Aid Order for Non-payment of Contribution — Form 10, Reg 36(1)(b)

To:

You were recently sent a warning of arrears in respect of your legal aid contribution order. The arrears now stand at £ . The court is now considering revoking your legal aid. You are entitled to explain to the court why you have fallen into arrears, and to invite the court not to revoke you legal aid.

If you wish to do this YOU MUST RETURN THIS FORM TO THIS COURT WITHIN SEVEN DAYS otherwise your legal aid might be revoked.

A copy of this form has been sent to your solicitor/counsel.

Signed:
Dated:

I have fallen into arrears because:

Signed:
Dated:

If as a result of the use of either of these warnings payments are brought up to date, the enforcement process can be abandoned and recommenced if there is any further default. There is no specific provision within the regulations that would require the steps already taken to be repeated if the default was remedied and then reoccurs, but it would seem unjust not to do so if there was a substantial period of time between the original and subsequent defaults.

Once Form 10 has been sent to the defaulter a further period of time must be allowed for any response to be received, a 14 to 21 day period should be allowed for the reasons already discussed above.

If, after the two warnings the defaulter has not remedied the defect the case can be referred to a court so that consideration can be given to revoking the order. Although the power to revoke cannot be exercised by a proper officer there is no requirement to give notice of the hearing and arrange for the legally

4 Reg 36(2) of the Legal Aid in Criminal and Care Proceedings (General) Regulations 1989.

aided person to appear before the court. In circumstances where the substantive matters for which legal aid was granted are to come before a court at a convenient time, it may be appropriate for the justices to be asked to consider the question of revocation in the presence of the legally assisted person and his advocate as a supplementary issue.

The procedure at such hearings is not established, but the justices will need to be informed of the account history and to have sight of any representations made by the legally assisted person before they exercise their discretion to revoke the legal aid order[5]. The test that must be applied by the justices is two fold and a check list is set out in Figure 4 below.

FIG 4: THE TEST TO DETERMINE WHETHER TO REVOKE A LEGAL AID ORDER FOR NON-PAYMENT OF CONTRIBUTIONS

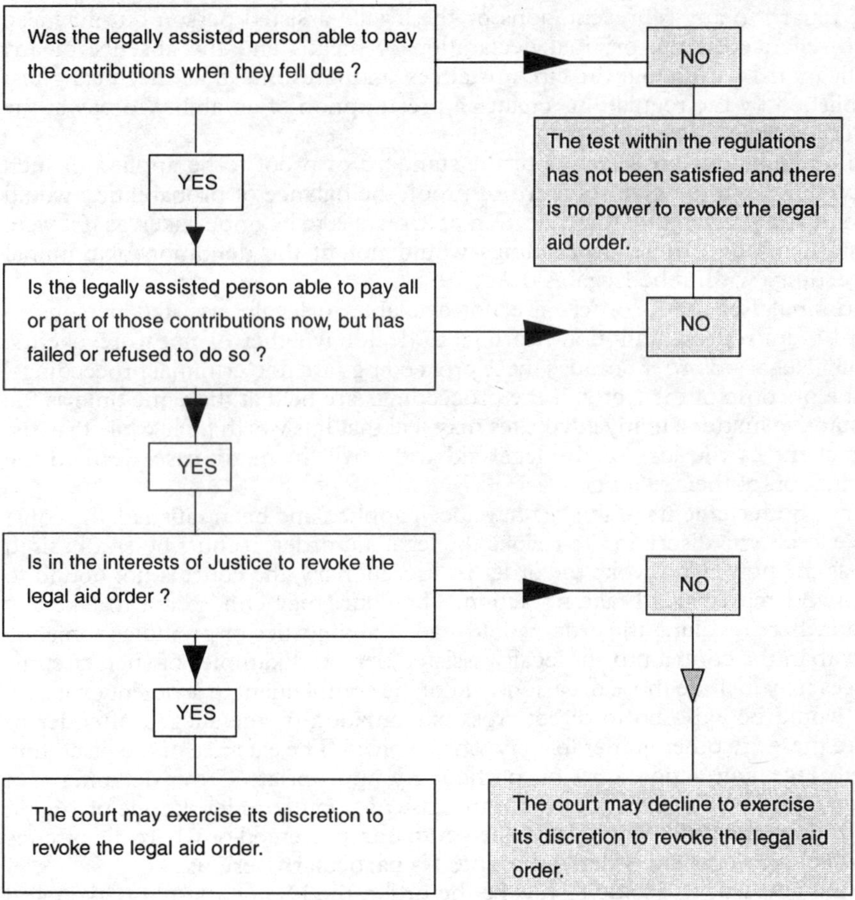

The first element of the test is to determine whether the legally assisted person was able to pay the legal aid contribution when it was due. To some extent this will be a matter of historical record. Provided the original determination of the amount of the contribution was correctly performed, there is a statutory

5 Reg 36(3) of the Legal Aid in Criminal and Care Proceedings (General) Regulations 1989.

presumption that the contributor could afford to pay since that is the rationale of the means test. The legally assisted person is under a duty to notify the court or proper officer of any change in his financial circumstances that would affect his ability to contribute towards the order[6] and if he has not done so, the court would be acting reasonably were it to infer that in the absence of such notification the legally assisted person remained able to pay the contributions as they fell due.

The second element of the test requires the court to examine whether or not the legally assisted person is able to pay all or part of the contribution but has failed or refused to do so[7]. Refusal rarely occurs but would require the court to be satisfied of some deliberate intent on the part of the contributor not to pay. Establishing failure will be much easier for the court, as an examination of the court's accounts will determine whether or not there has been any payment towards the legal aid contributions. In determining ability to pay, the court must have regard to any representations by the legally assisted person but may also place reliance on the original declaration of means and the absence of any notification of a change in circumstances and presume that the means test established by the regulations creates a presumption of an ability to pay at the prescribed rate.

The regulations are silent as to the standard of proof to be applied in such proceedings but the civil standard of proof, the balance of probabilities, would seem to apply given that the collection of arrears is to be undertaken as if it were a civil debt[8] and these proceedings would not fit the definition of criminal proceedings within the Legal Aid Act 1988[9].

Criminal Legal Aid orders are not available to legally assisted persons to afford them representation at hearings to decide whether or not to revoke the criminal legal aid order because these proceedings are not 'criminal proceedings' for the purpose of the Act[10]. If the proceedings are held at the same time as the substantive matters, many advocates may feel that it is worth their while to assist their client as the loss of the legal aid order will in many cases lead to the termination of their retainer.

Once both elements of the test have been applied and been satisfied, the court may exercise its discretion to revoke the legal aid order. It must be emphasised that as the power to revoke the order is discretionary, the court is not bound to do so and may instead take no action. The court may choose not to take any action where revoking the order would lead to an injustice or prejudice someone other than the contributor or legally assisted person. Examples of such circumstances may include those occasions where the complainant in a violent or sexual case would be exposed to direct cross-examination by the alleged offender or where there are other vulnerable persons involved. The exercise of the discretion not to take any action may be particularly appropriate if the defaulter is a reluctant appropriate contributor in the case of a youth under the age of 16 and to withdraw the order would leave the youth unrepresented or where the offence for which the legal aid order was granted is particularly serious.

If the court does decide to revoke the order, the legally assisted person and

6 Reg 31 of the Legal Aid in Criminal and Care Proceedings (General) Regulations 1989.
7 Reg 36(3)(b) of the Legal Aid in Criminal and Care Proceedings (General) Regulations 1989.
8 See this chapter below.
9 S 19(5) of the Legal Aid Act 1988.
10 S 19(5) of the Legal Aid Act 1988.

his solicitor or barrister must be notified of the decision on Form 14[11] and copies of that form shall be sent to:

(1) the legally assisted person; or
(2) the solicitor assigned (unless the order nominates only a barrister in which case the notice shall be sent to the barrister)[12].

The consequences of revoking the order are that the legal aid ceases to have any effect from the date of revocation but the former assigned solicitor or barrister is entitled to claim against the legal aid fund for the work undertaken to that date[13]. A solicitor assigned under an order is required to send all the papers relating to the substantive case to the legally assisted person on revocation[14], or if only a barrister is assigned under the order the papers must be sent to the instructing solicitor[15], although in practice there may a sufficient lien on the papers to enable the bill to be submitted and taxed. The advocates assigned under the order must submit their claim for payment to the taxing authority within the time limit which will begin to run at the date of revocation[16].

A further legal aid order can be issued for the same case but the clerk to the justices or nominated proper officer is not competent to grant such an order[17]. A further order can only be obtained by making an oral application to a properly constituted magistrates' court[18] which is asked to deal with the substantive matter or an incidental application relating to the case. The requirement that the application must be made 'to the court of trial or in other proceedings' has been held to allow an application to be made at any hearing before the justices[19].

2. Stage two enforcement

This stage of the enforcement process begins when either the substantive proceedings are concluded, or when the legal aid order is revoked or withdrawn and the substantive proceedings are still continuing[20]. This allows a court to commence this stage of enforcement immediately after it has revoked a legal aid order owing to the appropriate contributor's failure to maintain contributions from income. There is no requirement that compels the court to await final taxation of the contributor's bill before undertaking this stage of enforcement. If there is an eventual overpayment this will be refunded to the legally assisted person in due course after taxation and making payments on the due date will not create any injustice.

A further limitation exists if the defaulter is a member of the armed forces and the court has been notified that the Paymaster General will collect the contributions due by direct deductions from the serviceman's pay. In such circumstances the court is prohibited from taking any action to recover arrears

11 Form 14, Sch 2 of the Legal Aid in Criminal and Care Proceedings General) Regulations 1989 and Figure 5 this chapter.
12 Reg 41(3) of the Legal Aid in Criminal and Care Proceedings General) Regulations 1989.
13 Reg 36(4) of the Legal Aid in Criminal and Care Proceedings General) Regulations 1989.
14 Reg 41(4)(b) of the Legal Aid in Criminal and Care Proceedings General) Regulations 1989.
15 Reg 41(4)(a) of the Legal Aid in Criminal and Care Proceedings General) Regulations 1989.
16 See Chapter 8 for a full discussion of claiming costs against legal aid orders.
17 *R v Liverpool City Magistrates' Court, ex p Shacklady and Pender* [1993] 2 All ER 929.
18 Reg 10 of the Legal Aid in Criminal and Care Proceedings (General) Regulations 1989.
19 *R v Liverpool City Magistrates' Court, ex p Pender* [1993] 2 All ER 929.
20 Para 6(a) and (b), Sch 3 of the Legal Aid Act 1988.

FIG 5: OVERVIEW OF THE STAGE TWO ENFORCEMENT PROCESS

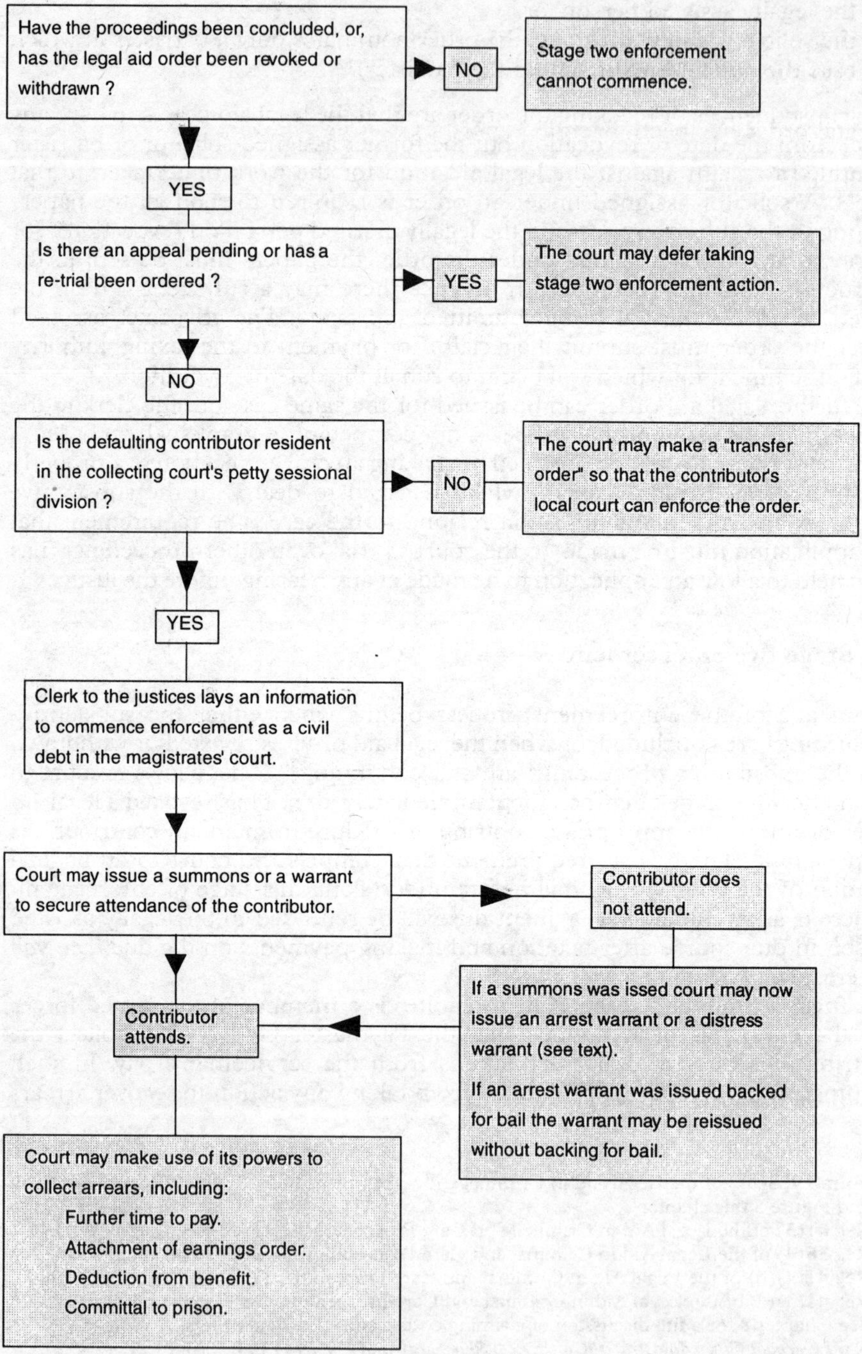

until such time as the court is notified that the person concerned has left the services[1].

The court may postpone stage two enforcement action if an appeal is pending, or where a re-trial has been ordered[2], however this power is discretionary and circumstances may exist where the court would not be willing to agree to such a deferment. Courts will wish to take into account whether the appellant is funding these further proceedings under a legal aid order. If the original order has been extended and the means of the legally assisted person or his appropriate contributor have not changed, he would still be liable to maintain his contributions from income, as the contribution period will not have ended,[3] and stage two enforcement action could not be commenced[4]. The only exceptions to this general rule are where the appellant has received an immediate custodial sentence[5] or where the court has remitted any sums that would fall due after the conclusion of the original proceedings[6]. The regulations do not assist in dealing with the circumstances of an appellant who received an immediate custodial sentence but who is subsequently released on bail pending appeal. If the general rule is followed any such doubts must be resolved in favour of the legally assisted person[7] and courts could not be criticised for finding that the contribution period had ended on the date that the sentence was imposed as this would seem to be strict interpretation of the regulations.

If the defaulting contributor lives outside the petty sessional division of the magistrates' court that made the order a 'transfer order'[8] may be made[9]. Such an order has the effect of transferring all the duties of the collecting court to the magistrates' court in whose area the defaulter resides[10]. The Act does not require the solicitor's bill to be taxed by the appropriate authority prior to transfer, neither does it require any consent on the part of the receiving magistrates' court. There is no defined form of order and it would therefore seem that a memorandum of the court's order will suffice together with the usual documentation that would accompany a transfer of fine order. Use of this procedure will be of assistance to magistrates' courts in maintaining their collection rates, which is important given that such rates form part of the statistical base which determines the amount of their budget.

On receipt of a transferred legal aid order, the new collecting court may embark on stage two enforcement action as if it had always had conduct of the order. To assist in following this text, reference may be made to the structured enforcement process set out in Figure 6.

The Justices' Clerks Accounting Manual[11] suggests that clerks to the justices should make use of the procedure established by the Legal Aid Act 1988 for collecting arrears of contributions[12] and that recalcitrant payers should be made

1 Para 7, Sch 3 of the Legal Aid Act 1988.
2 Para 8, Sch 3 of the Legal Aid Act 1988.
3 Reg 37(1)(a) of the Legal Aid in Criminal and Care Proceedings (General) Regulations 1989.
4 Para 6, Sch 3 of the Legal Aid Act 1988.
5 Reg 37(1)(c) of the Legal Aid in Criminal and Care Proceedings (General) Regulations 1989.
6 Reg 37(1)(b) of the Legal Aid in Criminal and Care Proceedings (General) Regulations 1989.
7 S 21(7) of the Legal Aid Act 1988.
8 See Chapter 7.
9 Para 5(1), Sch 3 of the Legal Aid Act 1988.
10 Para 5(2), Sch 3 of the Legal Aid Act 1988.
11 This document is issued to justices' clerks by the Lord Chancellor's Department and sets out the standard accounting procedures that are to be adopted by magistrates' courts.
12 Para 4.9.5, p 130 of the Justices' Clerks Accounting Manual.

aware of the court's powers[13]. Some courts will give consideration to the issue of a warning letter prior to commencement of the statutory enforcement process as this can be a cost-effective method of recovering a proportion of the arrears in many cases. The model for such a letter will be a standard civil or contractual debt recovery letter. A typical example of such a letter, in this case used by Liverpool Magistrates' Court, is reproduced at Figure 7. If such a letter is used the commencement of the enforcement action will have to be delayed to allow a response.

FIG 6: ARREARS RECOVERY LETTER BEFORE STAGE TWO ENFORCEMENT ACTION

A Magistrates Court
The Town Centre
Newtown

A. Defaulter
1 High Street
Newtown

Dear Sir

LEGAL AID CONTRIBUTION ORDER ARREARS
AMOUNT OUTSTANDING £100.00

You were recently ordered to pay a contribution towards the costs of your legal representation. As the [proceedings have now been concluded] [the order has been revoked] I am now required to collect the outstanding arrears which are now due.

I require payment of the sum set out above in full within seven days. You must pay this sum now even if your solicitor has told you that his bill will be less than the amount you have already paid. If I am advised by the Legal Aid Board that your solicitor has been paid less than the court has received from you I will refund any overpayment.

If you do not bring your account up to date within the next seven days I will commence legal action to recover the sum due. A cost of £30.00 may be added to your account to recover the costs of taking this action. The court may issue a distress warrant that will allow your goods to seized and sold and the proceeds used to clear this debt.
Yours faithfully

Clerk to the Justices.

If despite the enforcement letter the account is not settled, stage two proceedings may now be commenced by the clerk to the justices laying an information for recovery of the arrears[14]. For the purposes of this process the clerk to the justices is the complainant and it therefore seems necessary for him to lay the complaint before a Justice of the Peace, as it would appear improper for him to use his own powers to commence an action in which he has an interest. The form of such a complaint is the standard form of complaint for a civil debt (see Figure 8).

13 Para 4.9.5, p 130 of the Justices' Clerks Accounting Manual.
14 The procedure is the same as for the recovery of sums due under affiliation orders and is regulated by s 13 of the Magistrates' Courts Act 1980.

Once a complaint has been issued the court may either issue a summons or issue a warrant to secure the attendance of the defaulter[15]. In the majority of cases most courts will find it preferable to issue a summons as this enables a more flexible, efficient and cost-effective approach to be taken to the enforcement process.

The issue of a summons provides the court with a further opportunity to warn defaulters of the consequences of further failure or refusal to pay contributions as an explanatory leaflet can be enclosed with the summons. The text of one such leaflet is shown together with the summons in Figure 9. The costs of the production of such a leaflet are easily recovered if it has any success in recovering the outstanding arrears. The author's experience is that approximately 45% of defaulters that have reached this stage of the enforcement process will respond to such a document, either by contacting the court to reach an agreed scheme of repayments or by settling the debt in full.

The court can compel the defaulter to complete a statement of means, which need not be in the form required by the Legal Aid Act 1996, for the purpose of

FIG 8: COMPLAINT FOR RECOVERY OF ARREARS

______________________ Magistrates' Court
Code ______

Date: __________ 199_.
Account number: __________.
Debtor: __________________.
Address: __________________
____
____

The complaint of: __________________, Clerk to the Justices, __________ Magistrates' Court, ______________________ in the county of __________.

Who upon oath states that on ______ day of ________ 199__, the above named debtor was ordered by the [______________ Magistrates' Court] [the Crown Court at ______________] to pay a legal aid contribution order in the following terms:-

£____.__ per week from income and
£____.__ as a lump sum, being a contribution from capital

and the debtor is now in default of payment.

Amount paid: £____.__
Total Amount due: £____.__
Amount of default: £____.__

Taken and sworn before me

Justice of the Peace

15 S 83(1) of the Magistrates' Courts Act 1980. It is important to note that the restrictions on the issue of warrants under s 125 of the Magistrates' Courts Act do not apply do means enquiries *DPP v Peacock* [1989] Crim LR 372.

the means enquiry hearing[16]. It is also possible for the court to require the defaulter to complete a further Form 5[17], although the usual sanction of revoking the legal aid order would be invalid at this stage of the proceedings.

Courts will have to fix the date of an enforcement hearing prior to the issue of the summons in order that details of the date can be included on that document. There is nothing that requires legal aid contribution orders to be recovered at a special hearing and the hearing can therefore take place during a normal list in the adult or youth court, dependent on the age of the defaulter, or, if the court's list is sufficiently large to accommodate a separate fines default court, the matters can be listed with means enquiry cases.

Legal representation cannot be obtained under the Criminal Legal Aid Scheme to provide representation at means enquiry hearings in relation to legal aid contribution orders as a legal aid order is not made upon, or in connection with, a conviction. Consequently, proceedings to recover arrears of contributions do not fall within the definition of 'criminal proceedings' within section 19(5) of the Legal Aid Act 1988 whereas a compensation order made in criminal proceedings has been held to do so[18]. It is likely that this position will remain unchanged until new legislation is introduced that reflects the decision of the European Commission in relation to the imprisonment of Community Charge defaulters[19] as the High Court has refused to declare that criminal legal aid is available in such proceedings[20], but should the statutory framework be amended to allow representation for means enquiries into civil debts in magistrates' courts it is likely that it would embrace legal aid contribution orders. Other forms of assistance may be available – see Chapter 1.

The costs of the clerk to the justices in bringing default proceedings can be recovered from the defaulter[1], but, in the unlikely event that a complaint for the recovery of arrears was dismissed or not proceeded with, the defaulter's costs can be recovered from the clerk to the justices[2]. In either case the costs awarded must not exceed those actually incurred[3].

The procedure at the hearing is identical to any other means enquiry hearing and as court clerks and practitioners will be aware of the process no detailed commentary is required in a work of this type.

Mention should be made however, of the powers within the Magistrates' Courts Act 1980 that are specifically preserved in relation to legal aid contribution order enforcement hearings.[4] These powers allow the court to:

1. apply the monies found on a defaulter at a means enquiry against the debt which is being enquired into[5]; and
2. remit all or part of the outstanding arrears.[6]

16 S 84(1) of the Magistrates' Courts Act 1980.
17 Reg 24(1) of the Legal Aid in Criminal and Care Proceedings (General) Regulations 1989.
18 *R v Redbridge Magistrates' Court, ex p Guppy* (1995) 159 JP 622.
19 *Benham v United Kingdom*, (1995) Independent, 3 February, ECt HR.
20 *Ex p Bold* [1996] 27 LS Gaz R 28 which the suggestion that where justices were considering imprisoning a community charge defaulter for prison for non-payment of the debt were entertaining a criminal sanction was rejected.
1 S 64(1)(a) of the Magistrates' Courts Act 1988.
2 S 64(1)(b) of the Magistrates' Courts Act 1988.
3 *R v Highgate Justices, ex p Petrou* [1954] 1 All ER 406.
4 Para 2(4), Sch 3 of the Legal Aid Act 1988.
5 S 80 of the Magistrates' Courts Act 1980.
6 S 95 of the Magistrates' Courts Act 1980.

FIG 9: SUMMONS FOR ARREARS AND ADVISORY LEAFLET

In the [Insert name of court] Magistrates' Court.
Code:[Insert court code]

Date: 199 .
Account number:[Insert court's account reference number]

To: [Insert name of defaulter]

MATTER OF COMPLAINT: That on [insert date contribution order was made] you were order to pay a legal aid contribution order by the [insert name of court] court requiring payments of:

£ [amount] from your income, and,
£ [amount] from your capital,
and £ [amount of arrears] is now outstanding and you are therefore in default of payment.

COMPLAINANT: [Name of Clerk to the Justices]
[Name and address of collecting court]

AMOUNT ORDERED TO BE PAID	£
AMOUNT PAID	£
TOTAL DEFAULT	£

You are hereby summoned to appear on the [date] at [time] at the [name of court] magistrates' court, [address of court] to consider the complaint and for an enquiry to be made as to your means you have had since the order was made and to show cause why you should not be committed to prison in accordance with section 96, Magistrates' Court Act 1980 in default of payment.

Justice of the Peace

LEGAL AID CONTRIBUTIONS ENFORCEMENT HEARING.

You have been summoned to appear before the court as you have not paid all or part of the legal aid contribution order you were required to pay as a condition of your legal aid order.

This leaflet explains what will happen at the court hearing and what orders that the court can make.

AT THE HEARING

The court will want to know why you have not paid the payments that have fallen due and it will need to know if your financial circumstances changed since you got the order.

You can help the court and yourself if you fill in the enquiry form attached to this leaflet, as it will make sure you remember to tell us everything that is important. If your financial circumstances changed, for example if you lost your job or went on to short time working, the court will need to know the date this happened and

the effect it had on your pay. If you have a letter from your employer or wage slips that show the change you must bring these with you when you come to court.

The court cannot take any notice of your solicitor's final bill, even if it is less than you have paid, until the Legal Aid Board or the Crown Court tell us how much they paid on your behalf. If you have overpaid by the time this happens we will return the overpayment to you.

ORDERS THAT CAN BE MADE BY THE COURT

When you appear before the court, the court can make one of the following orders:

1. A FURTHER PAYMENT ORDER – this will allow you to continue to pay the order at a weekly rate that will be fixed by the court after it has heard about your financial circumstances.

2. AN ATTACHMENT OF EARNINGS ORDER – the court will tell your employer that you owe the court money and that the court has ordered him/her to take money from your wages and send it to the court until the debt is cleared. The court will fix two amounts, the first is called a *protected earnings rate* , this ensures that you receive the amount the court thinks you need to live on each week from your employer. The second rate is the *normal deduction rate*, the amount that will normally be taken from your wages. If taking the full amount would mean that you receive less than the protected rate your employer will reduce the amount to ensure you receive the protected earnings fixed by the magistrates. Your employer may make a charge for deducting these payments and you will have to pay that charge.

3. A DISTRESS WARRANT – this means the court will employ bailiffs to seize your goods and sell them so the money raised can be used to clear your debt. The bailiff will charge a fee for doing this and you will have to pay that and the amount of the unpaid contributions.

4. AN ORDER COMMITTING YOU TO PRISON – if the magistrates believe that none of the other methods will work and they find that you have wilfully refused to pay this order or that you have culpably neglected to pay it the magistrates can send you to prison. They can do this at the hearing or they can suspend the order so that you can pay the arrears off at a weekly rate, but if you miss a payment they will issue the warrant enabling you to be taken to prison. The length of the sentence depends on the amount you owe.

IF YOU FAIL TO ATTEND AT THE HEARING

The magistrates may issue a warrant for your arrest. This will mean that you will be arrested and you may be kept in police custody until the court can deal with you. Alternatively the court may decide to deal with your case and issue a distress warrant.

YOU CAN GET FURTHER HELP FROM:

1. the solicitor who acted for you or from any other solicitor who is prepared to help you;
2. the Citizens' Advice Bureau [insert address and telephone numbers]; and
3. you can contact the court's collecting office at [insert address and telephone number].

Means Enquiry Form

NAME .... **DATE OF BIRTH**.....................

ADDRESS..

....

ACCOUNT NUMBER...

Personal Details

I am single / married / cohabiting / separated / divorced.*
Who lives in your household ?: Number of adults:
Number of children:
Does anyone in your household have a disability or any special needs ? YES/NO

If YES please give details..

....

.....................**Do you have to pay for this ?** YES/NO

I am employed / self employed / unemployed.*

Take home pay from your employment or the amount of benefit you receive. £......................

If you receive a DSS benefit please tell us the type of benefit you get and which office pays it to you. ....

....

Take home pay / benefit of your partner. £......................
Amount of any other payments you get. £......................
What are they for ?....................................

TOTAL INCOME: £

EXPENSES:

Rent/ Mortgage	£......................
Council tax	£......................
Gas/Electricity/other fuel	£......................
Hire Purchase/Catalogue	£......................
County Court Orders	£......................
Other Court Orders (eg fines)	£......................

TOTAL PAYMENTS: £

HOW DO YOU INTEND TO PAY THIS DEBT?.....................................

NOTE: YOU SHOULD BRING YOUR WAGE SLIPS AND COPIES OF THE BILLS OR COURT ORDERS YOU HAVE TOLD US ABOUT TO COURT WHEN YOU COME.

If the court imposes a term of imprisonment in default of payment the debt is not automatically discharged as it would be if it were a fine, but the court is prohibited from imposing another term of imprisonment for the same debt[7]. In practical terms once the period of imprisonment is served the court is unlikely to be able recover the debt by using its own powers of enforcement and it may decide that it is more cost-effective to write off the debt (see below).

As the amounts are to be collected as if they were arrears under a maintenance order the following powers are also available to the court under the terms of the Magistrates' Courts Act:

1. Power to dispense with immediate payment – (section 75 of the Magistrates' Courts Act);
2. Attachment of earnings orders (Attachment of Earnings Act 1971 and Magistrates' Courts (Attachment of Earnings) Rules 1971);
3. Money Payment Supervision Order – (section 88 of the Magistrates' Courts Act 1980);
4. Attendance Centre Order (if defaulter is under 21) – (section 17 of the Criminal Justice Act 1982);
5. Issue of a distress warrant – (sections 76 to 78 of the Magistrates' Courts Act 1980);
6. Short period of detention – (section 135 of the Magistrates' Courts Act 1980) (for detention in the court house) (section 136 of the Magistrates' Courts Act 1980)(for overnight detention in a police station); and,
7. Imprisonment in default – (section 82(4) of the Magistrates' Courts Act 1980).

3. Enforcement timetable

In order to establish an efficient system of recovery of outstanding amounts court staff may find it appropriate to draw up a standard timetable that will set guidelines to identify when appropriate enforcement action should be taken. This will ensure a routine is adopted that identifies cases where action is needed. The compilation of a list of standard instructions that reflect the statutory requirements is recommended to justices' clerks by the Lord Chancellor's Department[8]. Whatever action is taken should be documented[9] and a write off system should be established to dispose of irrecoverable amounts.[10]

Figure 10 sets out a draft timetable by which enforcement action could be regulated. The time scales indicated within that timetable can be regard as the minimum times in which enforcement action can reasonably be undertaken. If the periods between enforcement actions is further reduced difficulties arise ensuring that documents have been served on a defaulter and that he has been given sufficient opportunity to respond.

7 S 94 of the Magistrates' Courts Act 1980.
8 Paras 4.11.1 and 4.9.6 of the Justices' Clerks Accounting Manual.
9 Para 4.9.4 of the Justices' Clerks Accounting Manual.
10 Para 4.10.1 of the Justices' Clerks Accounting Manual – amounts written off must be recorded and the Lord Chancellor's Department notified in accordance with the proceed established with section E1 of the Accounting Manual of which paras 4.8 to 4.8.2 relate solely to write-offs on legal aid accounts.

POWERS TO REFUND OVERPAYMENTS OR REMIT FURTHER CONTRIBUTIONS AND CORRECT MISTAKES

1. Remission of contributions

At the conclusion of the substantive criminal proceedings the court has the power to remit any legal aid contributions that have, or should have, been paid by the appropriate contributor under the terms of the legal aid contribution order if the legally assisted person was acquitted[11]. The terminology of this provision differs slightly from that which regulates the payments of a defendant's costs order. The power to make a defendant's costs order arises 'where an information is not proceeded with, or examining justices decide not to commit for trial, or the accused is acquitted after summary trial'[12]. This difference in terminology

FIG 10: ENFORCEMENT TIMETABLE

STAGE ONE

Day 0	Contribution Order made. Contribution period starts. Information leaflet issues to contributor setting out his rights and obligations under the order.
Day 7	First payment from income due under order. Payments now fall due on every seventh day.
Day 21	Routine monitoring of account to establish whether payments made and order up to date. If the account is in arrears Form 9 (1st statutory warning) is issued.
Day 35	Routine monitoring of account to establish that account has been brought up to date and remains in credit. If the account is not up to date Form 10 (second statutory warning) is issued.
Day 49	If no reasonable response received in relation to Form 10 case referred to court for the consideration of an order revoking the grant of legal aid to be taken. Any written representations received from the defaulter are placed before the court. If order revoked Form 14 (notice of revocation) issued.

STAGE ONE ENDS.

STAGE TWO

Day 49	Consideration given to making a transfer order if the defaulter lives outside the court's petty sessions division, otherwise warning letter issued.
Day 70	Complaint laid before a justice of the peace by the clerk to the justices. Summons and advisory leaflet issued to defaulter.
Day 105	Enforcement hearing.

11 Reg 35(1) of the Legal Aid in Criminal and Care Proceedings (General) Regulations 1989.
12 S 16(1) of the Prosecution of Offences Act 1985.

may be more than a question of mere semantics as on strict construction of the regulations a legally aided person will not be able to recover his contributions where the proceedings to which he is subject are discontinued, discharged or withdrawn as he has not been acquitted in the true sense of the word.

Despite the apparent distinction between the power to award costs and to refund legal aid contributions most magistrates' courts appear to use the guidance within the *Practice Direction (Crime: Costs)*[13] to determine whether contributors should have their contributions returned. This directs that where an information is not proceeded with or the accused is acquitted the court should normally make a defendant's costs order [refund legal aid contributions] unless there are positive reasons for not doing so. Two specific examples are then cited as being positive reasons for not doing so, namely:

1. that the accused brought suspicion on himself by his own conduct and thus misled the prosecution into thinking that the case against him was stronger than it was; and
2. the he was acquitted on a technicality which has no merit, but there was ample evidence to support a conviction.

It seems that by placing reliance on this guidance the courts have avoided creating a distinction between the position of a legally aided defendant and a privately funded defendant where the legally aided person is in a less beneficial position than the person who has sufficient means to fund his own cause.

The court also has power to remit any contribution that falls due after the conclusion of the proceedings[14]; however, this power is only likely to be of use where the proper officer has postponed the payment of a capital sum to a fixed date after the conclusion of the proceedings, as in the majority of cases the contribution period will end with the close of the proceedings[15].

2. Repayment of contributions

Where the total collected under a legal aid contribution order exceeds the amount paid on taxation to the legally assisted person's legal representatives the taxing authority, either the Legal Aid Board in relation to representation in the magistrates' court, or the Crown Court's taxing officer, in relation to Crown Court work, will inform the collecting court of the amount paid to the solicitor. The collecting court will then refund any overpayment directly to the appropriate contributor[16].

It is important to note that the collecting court can only make a refund of the overpayment when it receives notification from the taxing authority. Consequently, when a legally assisted person complains about monies still being held when he understands that his solicitor's bill was less than that collected under the contribution order, the court should direct him to take the matter up with his solicitor or the taxing authority as the collecting court has no jurisdiction to interfere with the taxation process.

13 [1991] 1WLR 498.
14 Reg 35(1)(a) of the Legal Aid in Criminal and Care Proceedings (General) Regulations 1989.
15 Reg 29(4) of the Legal Aid in Criminal and Care Proceedings (General) Regulations 1989.
16 S 23(7) of the Legal Aid Act 1988 and Reg 39 of the Legal Aid in Criminal and Care Proceedings (General) Regulations 1989.

3. The correction of mistakes

Where there has been an error in the calculation of a contribution order the court may rectify this, if it appears just and equitable to do so, and vary or revoke the contribution order[17]. Clearly, in exercising its discretion, the court or proper officer must be able to state why it was just and equitable to vary or to decline to vary the order. A balanced decision will require the proper officer or the court to consider the effect on the legally assisted person, the appropriate contributor and the loss of revenue to the state.

17 Reg 34 of the Legal Aid in Criminal and Care Proceedings (General) Regulations 1989.

Chapter Nine

The Criminal Legal Aid Scheme – Renewals Of Applications

This chapter will deal with renewing legal aid applications that failed on the grounds that it did not appear to the competent authority that the merits of the application justified a grant of legal aid. Such applications may be renewed to either the court or the Legal Aid Board Area Committee. For ease of reference the chapter has been structured to deal with each individual avenue of appeal separately, as shown below:

1. Renewals of applications in the magistrates' court.
2. Reviews of applications by the Legal Aid Board Area Committee.
3. Renewal of applications for proceedings in the Crown Court.
4. Renewals of applications before the Court of Appeal.
5. Other forms of renewal.
6. Judicial review.

As it will only be necessary to renew an application that has been unsuccessful at first instance the chapter will commence with a brief analysis of the most common reasons for a written application being rejected by the proper officer.

COMMON REASONS FOR THE REJECTION OF LEGAL AID APPLICATIONS ON MERIT

In 1992 a report[1] was published that documented the manner in which legal aid applications were resolved by magistrates' courts. It disclosed grant rates that differed from 100% in some courts to 35% in one magistrates' court[2]. The report attributed the reason for the variations in approach on a number of factors including the importance individual court clerks attached to the criteria within section 22 of the Legal Aid Act 1988 and the poor quality of legal aid applications submitted on a defendant's behalf[3].

The report also discovered that applicants rarely complete applications themselves and that this is invariably done either by the solicitor acting in the case or, usually, by a solicitor's clerk. An examination of two firms side by side revealed that the firm that used non-qualified staff submitted poorer applications than the firm that used solicitors to prepare the applications[4].

Whilst the need to delegate considerable amounts of legal aid work to non-qualified staff in a busy criminal legal aid practice is accepted by most

1 'In the Interests of Justice? the Determination of Criminal Legal Aid Applications by Magistrates' Courts in England and Wales' – Report to the Legal Aid Board, Young , Young Maloney and Saunders (1992).
2 Appendix 4, 'In the Interests of Justice . . .', ibid.
3 Chapter 21, sections 21.3 and 21.20, ibid.
4 Chapter 21, section 21.21, ibid.

practitioners, the lesson for solicitors is clear and is that non-qualified staff will benefit from adequate training to ensure they are able to extract the necessary information from a client's instructions so as to be able to prepare a well-reasoned application that is difficult to refuse.

The difficulty in individual perceptions of the relevance of the criteria to individual court clerks has largely been addressed by the requirement that reasons for the grant or refusal of any legal aid application are to be recorded by proper officers. Such reasons are scrutinised by auditors when they make their inspection of a magistrates' court's legal aid operation.

RENEWALS OF APPLICATIONS IN THE MAGISTRATES' COURT

It is always open to an applicant who has been refused a grant of criminal legal aid for proceedings in the magistrates' court on the merits of the application to renew the application to either the magistrates' court or an authorised proper officer acting on behalf of the justices' clerk[5]. Unlike the procedure which enables the Legal Aid Board Area Committee to review refusals in the case of indictable or either-way offences, this procedure is available in relation to applications for legal aid in respect of all classifications of offences.

The procedural requirements are straightforward but differ slightly depending on whether the applicant decides to make an oral application before the court or to make an application to the proper officer.

1. Oral applications to a magistrates' court

The application can be made at any time after the initial refusal but the applicant must produce the form of refusal, Form 2, to the court at the time the application is made[6]. The rationale behind this requirement is to prevent applicants who are able to renew applications to the court or seek a review of the application before an area committee from taking both forms of appeal simultaneously and thereby obtaining two legal aid orders for the same proceedings. Should applicants succeed in doing that, the second legal aid order would be invalid in any event[7], but two claims for costs could be submitted inadvertently, with the risk that this would not be detected, creating a loss to public funds if an overpayment was made. Until the introduction of the unique numbering system that now applies to all criminal legal aid orders, there was little prospect of duplicate claims being detected by the manual payment system operated by the Legal Aid Board.

Having lodged the notification of refusal, the application is made orally to the court. The magistrates will be required to give their reasons for refusing to grant a legal aid order and issue a further notice of refusal[8]. Where it is possible to renew an application to the Legal Aid Board Area Committee this can be undertaken after a renewal to the magistrates' court.

5 Reg 14(1) of the Legal Aid in Criminal and Care Proceedings (General) Regulations 1989.
6 Reg 14(2) of the Legal Aid in Criminal and Care Proceedings (General) Regulations 1989.
7 Reg 41(2) of the Legal Aid in Criminal and Care Proceedings (General) Regulations 1989.
8 Reg 14(2) of the Legal Aid in Criminal and Care Proceedings (General) Regulations 1989.

FIG 1: RENEWALS TO MAGISTRATES' COURTS – OVERVIEW

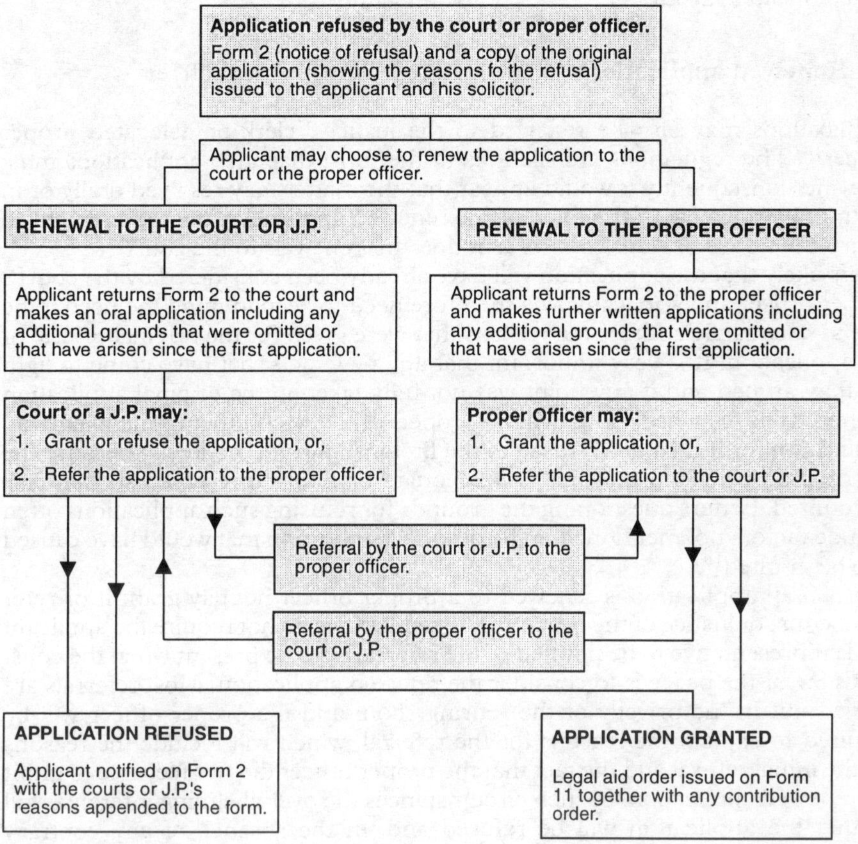

In determining the application the magistrates' courts options are either to grant or refuse the application or to refer to a proper officer[9]; however, this can only be done after the court has considered a statement of means[10], which in practice will have already been done by a proper officer who determined the original application[11].

If the court elects to refer the application to a proper officer the only options available to him are to grant the application or to refer it back to the court or a justice of the peace[12]. If the proper officer returns the application to the court or to a single justice of the peace he may also find himself in the position of having to advise in relation to any question of law or mixed fact and law that arises from the application but he would otherwise be precluded from assisting the justice determine the application. In practice the mere return of the application to the court may carry implicit advice that the application should be refused, even though it could be argued that the inability of the court to decide whether the application should be granted or refused of its own motion may

9 Reg 14(4) of the Legal Aid in Criminal and Care Proceedings (General) Regulations 1989.
10 Reg 14(7) of the Legal Aid in Criminal and Care Proceedings (General) Regulations 1989.
11 As Reg 23 of the Legal Aid in Criminal and Care Proceedings (General) Regulations 1989 compels him to do this.
12 Reg 14(6) of the Legal Aid in Criminal and Care Proceedings (General) Regulations 1989.

suggest there is a reasonable doubt so that the application should be resolved in the applicant's favour[13].

2. Renewed applications to the justices' clerk/proper officer

Applications may also be renewed to the justices' clerk or delegated proper officer[14]. The regulations are silent as to the form that such applications must take and consequently it would appear that the matter may resolved orally or in writing. Irrespective of the form of the renewed application the requirement to return the notice of refusal exists as it does for renewals to the court[15].

It is likely that the application will have already been considered by the court's proper officer and applicants will therefore need to keep in mind the need to be able to adequately address the reasons that were given for the original refusal of the application. It is very important that any new facts that have come to light are fully argued and if any point was not fully taken in the original application it should be clarified now. Many proper officers comment that when an application for legal aid is refused in the first instance it is generally because the information provided to them is inadequate or poorly presented so that it is discounted. Letters questioning the grounds for refusing such applications often include factors not mentioned in the original application that would have caused it to be granted[16].

When an application is renewed to a proper officer he may grant it or refer it to a court or justice of the peace[17]. The regulations do not require the applicant or his representative to be notified of the referral or to be present when the court or justice of the peace is to consider the referred application. Most referrals are carried out in the privacy of the retiring room and the proper officer will be required to explain the reasons for the referral, which will include the reasons for the initial refusal and the fact that the proper officer did not feel able to grant the renewed application. In such circumstances the overwhelming inference will be that the application will be refused and, in the absence of any contrary representations, this is likely.

When an application is referred to a court or to a justice of the peace the application must be granted or refused[18]. There is no power to refer the application back to the proper officer and any attempt to do so could amount to a refusal to adjudicate which would allow the applicant to seek an order of mandamus.

REVIEWS OF APPLICATIONS BY THE LEGAL AID BOARD AREA COMMITTEE

In certain circumstances applications that have been refused at first instance in the magistrates' court can be renewed to the Legal Aid Board Area Committee. Although the regulations distinguish between a renewal in the magistrates' court

13 S 21(7) of the Legal Aid Act 1988.
14 Reg 14(1) of the Legal Aid in Criminal and Care Proceedings (General) Regulations 1989.
15 Reg 14(2) of the Legal Aid in Criminal and Care Proceedings (General) Regulations 1989.
16 The authors research during presentations of the course 'Legal Aid in Criminal Courts' (Coates and Parry) to magistrates' courts staff.
17 Reg 14(6) of the Legal Aid in Criminal and Care Proceedings (General) Regulations 1989.
18 Reg 14(5) of the Legal Aid in Criminal and Care Proceedings (General) Regulations 1989.

FIG 2: CHECK LIST: CAN THE APPLICATION BE RENEWED TO THE AREA COMMITTEE?

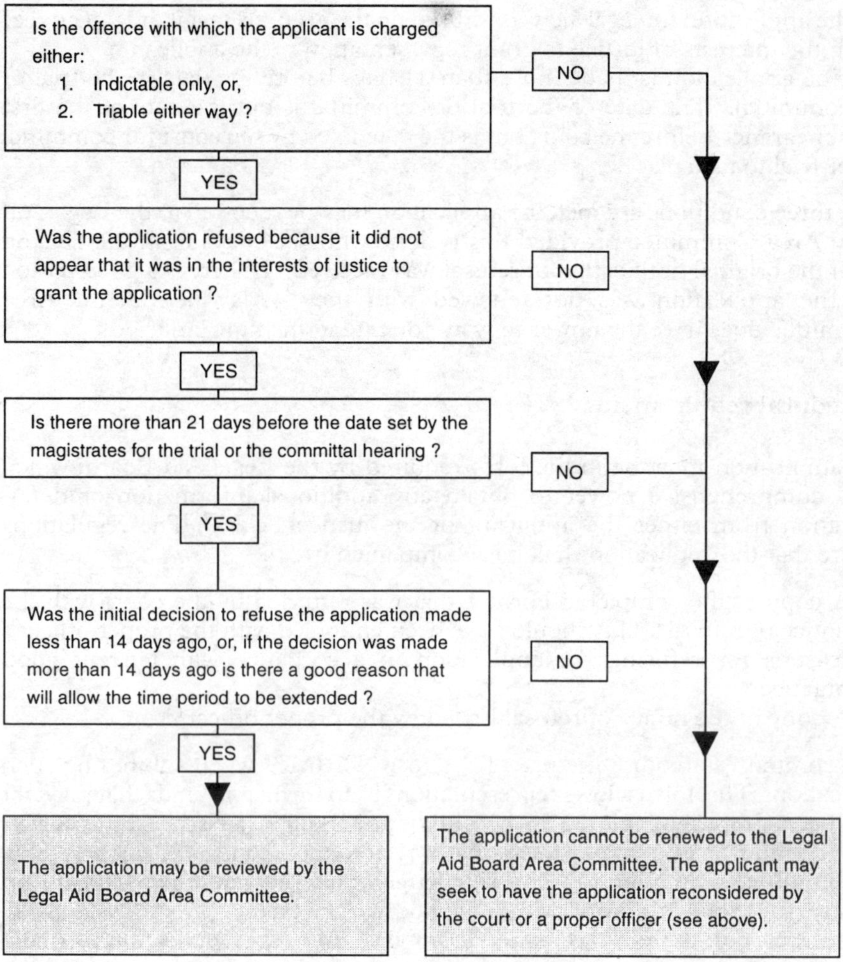

and a review by the committee there is little in practice to divide the two methods as both are forms of appeal against the initial decision.

Applications may be reviewed by the Area Committee if:

1. The applicant is charged with an offence which is indictable, or triable either way, or he has been brought before a magistrates' court to be dealt in respect of a sentence imposed for such an offence or in relation to an order made in connection with such an offence[19]. This provision would allow applications to be renewed to the area committee if the application was to cover proceedings such as the removal of a disqualification imposed as part of a sentence[20] or during proceedings to enforce unpaid fines[1] and in any other

19 Reg 15(2)(a) of the Legal Aid in Criminal and Care Proceedings (General) Regulations 1989.

20 As it has been held that such proceedings come within the scope of the criminal legal aid scheme – see *R v Crown Court at Liverpool, ex p McCann* [1995] RTR 23.

1 As criminal legal aid is available for such proceedings – see *R v Redbridge Magistrates' Court, ex p Guppy* (1995) 159 JP 622.

enforcement proceedings, even if those proceedings can only be determined in the magistrates' court.

2. the application for legal aid was refused on the grounds that it did not appear in the interests of justice to grant representation to the applicant.[2]
3. The application is made more than 21 days before the date of the trial or committal.[3] The date of the trial or committal is not the date of the first appearance before the court but is the date fixed by the court for committal or trial to take place.[4]

If the three conditions are met, the application may be renewed to the Legal Aid Board Area Committee provided this is done within 14 days from the date on which the original notification of refusal was received[5]. If there is a good reason why the application was not renewed with the 14 day period, the Area Committee does have the power to waive or extend the time limit[6].

Procedural requirements

The application must be in the form required by the Legal Aid Board, which has a comprehensive power to obtain any additional information or documentation from either the applicant or the justices' clerk[7]. The regulations require that the application shall be accompanied by:

1. A copy of the completed Form 1 that was returned by the court with the notice of refusal[8]. This should have been endorsed with the proper officer's reasons for refusing the application in accordance with current good practice[9].
2. A copy of the notice of refusal issued by the proper officer[10].

Area committees require the use of the form CRIM 9 when submitting such applications. This form allows representations as to further grounds that may not have been properly explored to be outlined, although the size of the spaces allowed within the form may mean that it is preferable to use the form to draw the committee's attention to a covering letter which sets out the grounds relied on more fully than is allowed within the body of the form.

The area committee may either grant or refuse the application[11]. If the decision of the committee is to grant the application it is bound to make a contribution order in the terms calculated by the justices' clerk[12]. In those circumstances where the justices' clerk would have withheld the order until a capital contribution was paid, the Area Committee will send the order to the

2 Reg 15(2)(b) of the Legal Aid in Criminal and Care Proceedings (General) Regulations 1989.
3 Reg 15(2)(c) of the Legal Aid in Criminal and Care Proceedings (General) Regulations 1989.
4 *R v Bury Justices, ex p N (a minor)* [1986] 3 All ER 789, which was considered on an examination of previous but similarly worded regulations.
5 Reg 16(1) of the Legal Aid in Criminal and Care Proceedings (General) Regulations 1989.
6 Reg 16(3) of the Legal Aid in Criminal and Care Proceedings (General) Regulations 1989.
7 Reg 16(4) of the Legal Aid in Criminal and Care Proceedings (General) Regulations 1989.
8 Reg 16(2)(a) of the Legal Aid in Criminal and Care Proceedings (General) Regulations 1989.
9 Para 13 to 20 of the 'Guidance to Granting Authorities on Legal Aid in Criminal and Care Proceedings (General) (Amendment) Regulations 1995' Lord Chancellor's Department 24.3.1995.
10 Reg 16(2)(b) of the Legal Aid in Criminal and Care Proceedings (General) Regulations 1989.
11 Reg 17(1) of the Legal Aid in Criminal and Care Proceedings (General) Regulations 1989.
12 Reg 17(2) of the Legal Aid in Criminal and Care Proceedings (General) Regulations 1989.

FIG 3: APPLICATION FORM FOR A REVIEW BY THE AREA COMMITTEE (FORM 3)

Legal Aid

Application in criminal proceedings

➤ **Please read the notes overleaf before completing this form in block capitals.**

➤ **Do NOT use this form for an application for authority for prior expenditure. Complete form CRIM10 instead.**

CRIM 9

LEGAL AID BOARD LEGAL AID ACT 1988

Legal Aid Order number (please copy this from the refusal or order) LA

Has this application been granted over the telephone? ☐ YES ☐ NO

Defendant's details

Surname: *Mr/Mrs/Miss/Ms* ____ First Names: ____

Address: ____

____

____ Occupation: ____

Solicitor's details

Name of Solicitor: ____ Initials: ____ Title: ____

Name & Address of firm: ____

____

____

Legal Aid account no: ____ Reference: ____ DX No: ____

Tel No: ____ Fax No: ____

Application type

Please refer to the notes overleaf, then tick the appropriate application type

Review of refusal of legal aid	01	Instruct Q.C. without junior	04	Withdrawal of Legal Aid Order	06
Assignment of counsel	03	Change solicitor	05		

Court / charge details

Court Name:

Nature of Charges (including statute and section):

Likely Plea: Date of next hearing:

Purpose of next hearing:

Give the full reasons for the application. In review cases please give full reasons why it is in the interests of justice for legal aid to be granted (refer to the criteria set out in Section 22 (2) Legal Aid Act 1988 [formerly known as the "Widgery criteria"]). If a solicitor has been assigned to act for co-defendants, please give details of any conflict of interest to justify separate representation.

Give a brief summary of the prosecution case. You may attach the advance disclosure or extracts.

Give a summary of the defence or mitigation. Attach your client's statement and details of any previous convictions, if available in either case.

Solicitor's signature: ____ **Date:** ____ / ____ / ____

FIG 3 Cont'd

Important notes

1. Review applications sent without a copy of the original legal aid application (which is available from the court which dealt with the application) may be refused. In such cases a further application for review to the Area Committee (as opposed to a renewed application to the court) is not possible. **Review applications sent without a copy of the notification of refusal will be rejected.**
2. Applications to assign counsel or change solicitor must first be made to the clerk at the court. When applying to the area office in such cases you must send a copy of the application made to the court and a copy of the court's notice of refusal. **Where these applications are sent without a copy of the notification of refusal they will be rejected.**
3. Check that the application has been sent to the appropriate area office and, except on review applications, that a legal aid order is held which covers the proceedings. The Board will deal with applications on the basis of the information sent by the solicitor and an Area Committee only has jurisdiction where it is the correct Area Committee and there is the appropriate legal aid cover.
4. Send applications to the Area Office in whose area the court is situated. A covering letter is not needed but you can continue on a separate sheet of paper if necessary.

For area office use only

COURT CODE: DATE:

DECISION:

RF2	Request further information	
G10	Granted - Delegated	
G12	Granted - Committee	
R21	Refused - Committee	

CL4	Out of Time	
W10	Withdrawn	
CL5	No Jurisdiction	

DOCUMENT CODES AND STANDARD WORDINGS CODES REQUIRED:

SUMMARY FOR COMMITTEE:

September 1993

FIG 4: NOTIFICATION OF A DECISION OF THE AREA COMMITTEE ON A REVIEW OF REFUSAL TO GRANT LEGAL AID

Legal Aid
England and Wales

LEGAL AID BOARD
Liverpool Area Office

Direct Dial Lines: Legal 0151-243 3901 Emergency Applications 0151-243 3902
Civil Finance 0151-243 3903 ABWOR Applications 0151-243 3904
Green Form Extensions 0151-243 3904 Criminal Applications/Authorities 0151-243 3905
Franchising 0151-243 3907

Dear

Legal Aid Order number:

Your application for legal aid has been considered by the Area Committee who have decided to refuse it for the reasons set out below.

There is no right of appeal against that decision although you may renew your application to the Court at any time and may in any event apply for legal aid to the court on the day of the trial.

You may wish to discuss this decision with your solicitor.

Yours faithfully,

AREA MANAGER

REASONS FOR REFUSAL

In your case the Area Committee considered that it does not appear desirable to make a legal aid order in the interests of justice on any of the following grounds:-

1 You are likely to lose your liberty.
2 You are likely to lose your livelihood.
3 You are likely to suffer serious damage to your reputation.
4 A substantial question of law is involved.
5 You are unable to understand the proceedings or state your own case because:-
   (a) Your knowledge of English is inadequate.
   (b) You suffer from a disability.
6 Your case involves tracing and/or interviewing witnesses or expert cross-examination of a prosecution witness.
7 It is in someone else's interests that you are represented.

The committee reached this decision because:

CRIM/1 (5/95)

Cavern Walks, 8 Mathew Street, Liverpool, Merseyside L2 6RE DX 14208
Switchboard 0151 236 8371

justices' clerk in order that it might be withheld and so that it cannot be released until the capital sum is paid to the justices' clerk.[13]

Irrespective of whether the Area Committee determines to grant or refuse the application, it must give notice to the applicant, his solicitor and the justices' clerk on Form 4 of the outcome of the application.

RENEWALS OF APPLICATIONS FOR PROCEEDINGS IN THE CROWN COURT

Applications for grants of criminal legal aid in respect of proceedings before the Crown Court will have been initially considered by an appropriate officer of the Crown Court who will have determined the outcome of the application and whether any contribution would have been due[14]. Where it has been determined that the application is to be refused the appropriate officer will notify the applicant and his solicitor on Form 2[15].

Where application has been refused the applicant may renew it either to the appropriate officer of the Crown Court or orally to the court itself[16]. No form of application is specified by the regulations, save for the requirement that the notice of refusal must be returned with the application[17].

If the application has been renewed to the appropriate officer he may either grant the application or refer it to a judge of the court[18], whereas the court has the discretion to grant or refuse the application outright or refer it to an appropriate officer[19]. On referral an appropriate officer may either grant or refuse the application or refer it to a judge[20] who must either grant or refuse the application[1]. In essence the procedure is little different from that which exists in the case of a renewal in the magistrates' court.

RENEWALS OF APPLICATIONS BEFORE THE COURT OF APPEAL

If an application for a criminal legal aid order in respect of proceedings before the Court of Appeal has been refused by the registrar the applicant may renew the application orally to the Court of Appeal[2].

OTHER FORMS OF RENEWAL

Applications for criminal legal aid orders may be made at any time, orally to the court or to a judge of the court or the registrar of the Court of Appeal under

13 Reg 17(3) of the Legal Aid in Criminal and Care Proceedings (General) Regulations 1989.
14 Reg 19(b) and 20 of the Legal Aid in Criminal and Care Proceedings (General) Regulations 1989.
15 Reg 19(2) of the Legal Aid in Criminal and Care Proceedings (General) Regulations 1989 and see Chapter 7, Fig 2 for the form of the notice.
16 Reg 21(1) of the Legal Aid in Criminal and Care Proceedings (General) Regulations 1989.
17 Reg 21(2) of the Legal Aid in Criminal and Care Proceedings (General) Regulations 1989.
18 Reg 21(3) of the Legal Aid in Criminal and Care Proceedings (General) Regulations 1989.
19 Reg 21(4) of the Legal Aid in Criminal and Care Proceedings (General) Regulations 1989.
20 Reg 21(6) of the Legal Aid in Criminal and Care Proceedings (General) Regulations 1989.
1 Reg 21(5) of the Legal Aid in Criminal and Care Proceedings (General) Regulations 1989.
2 Reg 22(3) of the Legal Aid in Criminal and Care Proceedings (General) Regulations 1989.

FIG 5: RENEWAL PROCEDURE IN THE CROWN COURT – OVERVIEW

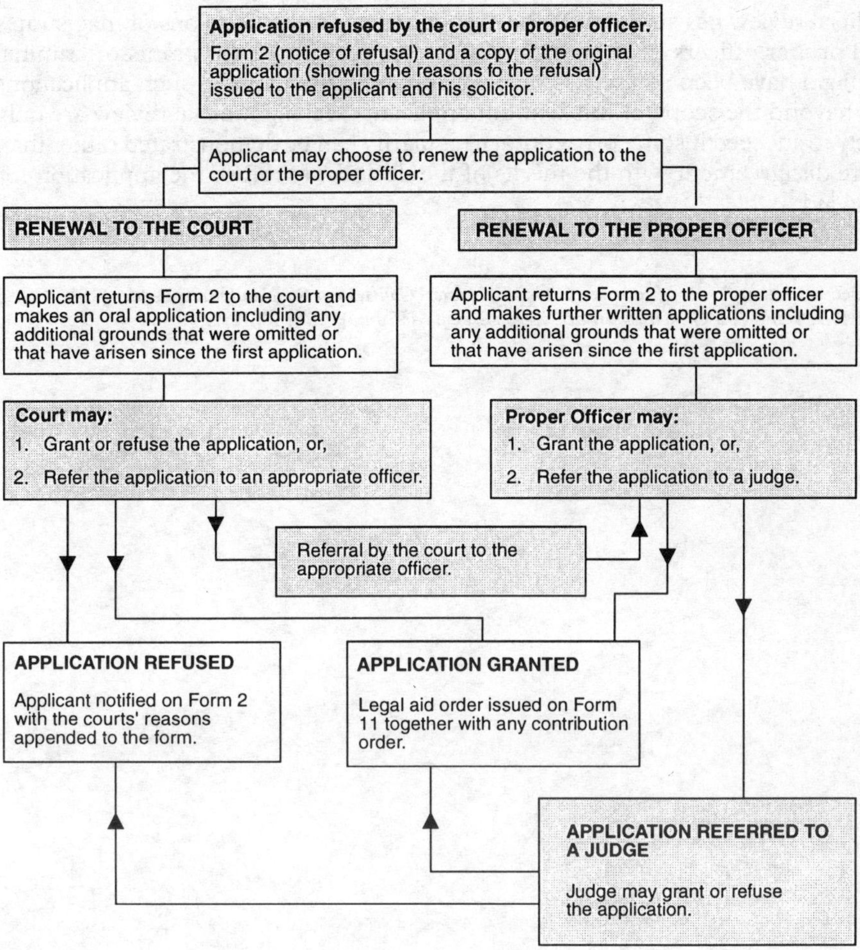

the scope of Regulation 10 of the Legal Aid in Criminal and Care Proceedings (General) Regulations 1989. This power is not restricted to the court of the trial but can be exercised at any hearing at which the substantive proceedings come before the court[3] and applies even where there has been a previous legal aid order which has been withdrawn or revoked[4].

The court will be required to determine the applicant's means[5] but there are no other rules as to the form of such applications, save that they cannot be determined by a justices' clerk or proper officer[6].

3 *R v Liverpool Magistrates' Court, ex p Pender (No 2)* [1994] 2 All ER 897.
4 *R v Liverpool City Magistrates' Court, ex p Shacklady and Pender* [1993] 2 All ER 929.
5 As Reg 10 preserves the effect of Reg 23 of the Legal Aid in Criminal and Care Proceedings (General) Regulations 1989.
6 *R v Liverpool City Magistrates' Court, ex p Shacklady and Pender* [1993] 2 All ER 929. and *R v Crown Court at Liverpool, ex p McCann* [1995] RTR 23.

JUDICIAL REVIEW

Judicial review has successfully been sought against the decisions of magistrates and proper officers in circumstances where applications for grants of criminal legal aid have been refused[7]. The procedural requirements of such applications are beyond the scope of this text but applicants seeking judicial review are only likely to succeed if some procedural irregularity can be demonstrated rather than mere disagreement with the merits of the decision to refuse the application for legal aid.

7 See for example *R v Liverpool City Magistrates' Court, ex p Shacklady and Pender* [1993] 2 All ER 929 and *R v Crown Court at Liverpool, ex p McCann* [1995] RTR 23.

Chapter Ten

The Criminal Legal Aid Scheme – The Nature and Amendment of Criminal Legal Aid Orders

This chapter will:

1. define the nature of representation provided by a legal aid order;
2. identify the extent to which legal aid orders can be amended to alter the nature of representation or to allow unusual expenditure to be incurred;
3. identify the competent authorities that may grant such amendments; and
4. discuss how unsuccessful applications to amend orders may be renewed.

NATURE OF REPRESENTATION UNDER CRIMINAL LEGAL AID ORDERS

In order to be able to determine when it is necessary to amend a legal aid order it is necessary to understand the nature of representation that is permissible under the basic order. There are three areas of concern:

1. the level of representation permitted under the order; by which we mean whether the order will allow representation by a solicitor only, a solicitor and counsel, or counsel alone;
2. the assignment of the solicitor and counsel; with reference to the ability of the applicant to select advocates of his or her own choosing; and
3. the ability of the legal representatives to incur costs under the order; thereby ensuring that they receive proper payment for the work they do.

1. Level of representation

The basic level of representation allowed under a criminal legal aid order provides for the services of a solicitor and counsel[1] with the following exceptions:

Magistrates' courts

1. Representation shall only be by a solicitor unless the case is indictable (which includes an offence which is triable either way) and is unusually grave or difficult[2];
2. Even if an offence in the magistrates' court qualifies for representation by counsel because of its nature and gravity, representation by counsel is not allowed for so much of the proceedings as relates to bail[3].

1 Reg 44(1) of the Legal Aid in Criminal and Care Proceedings (General) Regulations 1989.
2 Reg 44(3)(a) of the Legal Aid in Criminal and Care Proceedings (General) Regulations 1989.
3 Reg 44(2) of the Legal Aid in Criminal and Care Proceedings (General) Regulations 1989.

Crown courts

1. In the Crown Court a legal aid order may provide for representation by counsel only in appeal or trial proceedings, if it appears to the court that it is matter of urgency that legal aid be granted and there is no time to instruct a solicitor[4].
2. A legal aid order may allow representation by a solicitor only if the proceedings are such that the solicitor has a right of audience[5].
3. The legal aid order may specify that representation shall be by counsel alone[6].

This basic level of representation can be amended so that the order includes representation by more than one counsel, or by Queens counsel in the following prescribed circumstances[7]:

1. during a trial in the Crown Court, or on appeal from that court on a charge of murder, or;
2. during a trial in the Crown Court, or on appeal from that court in connection with a charge that appears to be a matter of exceptional difficulty, gravity or complexity so that representation by two counsel is desirable in the interests of justice.

Legal aid orders that provide for the services of two counsel can only be made by magistrates' courts on a charge of murder and such orders must only provide for the services of a Queen's Counsel and junior counsel[8]. In the Crown Court a circuit judge or a High Court Judge may make a two counsel order that provides for representation by:

1. a Queen's Counsel and junior counsel;
2. a Queen's Counsel with noting junior counsel;
3. two junior counsel; or
4. a junior counsel with noting junior counsel[9].

In all cases the representation permitted by the order will be at the basic level until an application to amend the order is considered and granted, as such decisions cannot be taken retrospectively. The consequences of not amending the order is that payment will only be made for the level of representation allowed on the face of the order[10].

Where orders are granted to cover proceedings in the magistrates' court and those proceedings then become the subject of committal proceedings the legal aid order can be amended so that it allows representation both before the justices and at the Crown Court[11]. Such orders are termed 'through orders'. Good practice suggests through orders should be granted at the earliest opportunity and many courts automatically grant such orders in respect of offences that are triable either way.

4 Reg 44(5) of the Legal Aid in Criminal and Care Proceedings (General) Regulations 1989.
5 Reg 44(6) of the Legal Aid in Criminal and Care Proceedings (General) Regulations 1989.
6 Reg 44(4) of the Legal Aid in Criminal and Care Proceedings (General) Regulations 1989.
7 As set out within Reg 48 of the Legal Aid in Criminal and Care Proceedings (General) Regulations 1989.
8 Reg 48(4) of the Legal Aid in Criminal and Care Proceedings (General) Regulations 1989.
9 Reg 48(3) of the Legal Aid in Criminal and Care Proceedings (General) Regulations 1989.
10 *R v Crown Court at Liverpool, ex p Lord Chancellor* (1993) 158 JP 821.
11 Reg 40(1) of the Legal Aid in Criminal and Care Proceedings (General) Regulations 1989.

2. Assignment of solicitors and counsel

Within those general rules a person applying for a legal aid order is generally free to select the solicitor and counsel of his or her choice[12]. Under these arrangements it is permissible for one solicitor or counsel to be nominated by, and to act for more than one legally assisted person under legal aid orders[13]. In the case of co-defendants this freedom of choice is restricted as the court or proper officer granting legal aid must assign all subsequent legal aid orders to the solicitor who was the first to be appointed under a legal aid order, unless the solicitor assigned under the legal aid order certifies that there is a conflict that would prevent him acting for more than one defendant[14]. This rule requires the appointed solicitor, not the disappointed solicitor, to certify that the conflict exists. It is not sufficient to rely on a pre-existing solicitor–client relationship to overcome this rule and it therefore follows that an early application is essential if established clients are not to be represented by other firms. If a conflict does arise the court is not free to select any other solicitor but must assign a solicitor who was nominated by a least one of the remaining co-accused[15].

In circumstances where there is more than one defendant represented by one solicitor under the terms of legal aid orders and counsel is to be assigned the solicitor may instruct different counsel for each defendant[16].

FIG 1: ASSIGNING LEGAL AID ORDERS – APPLYING THE RULE IN *REGINA V SOLIHULL JUSTICES*

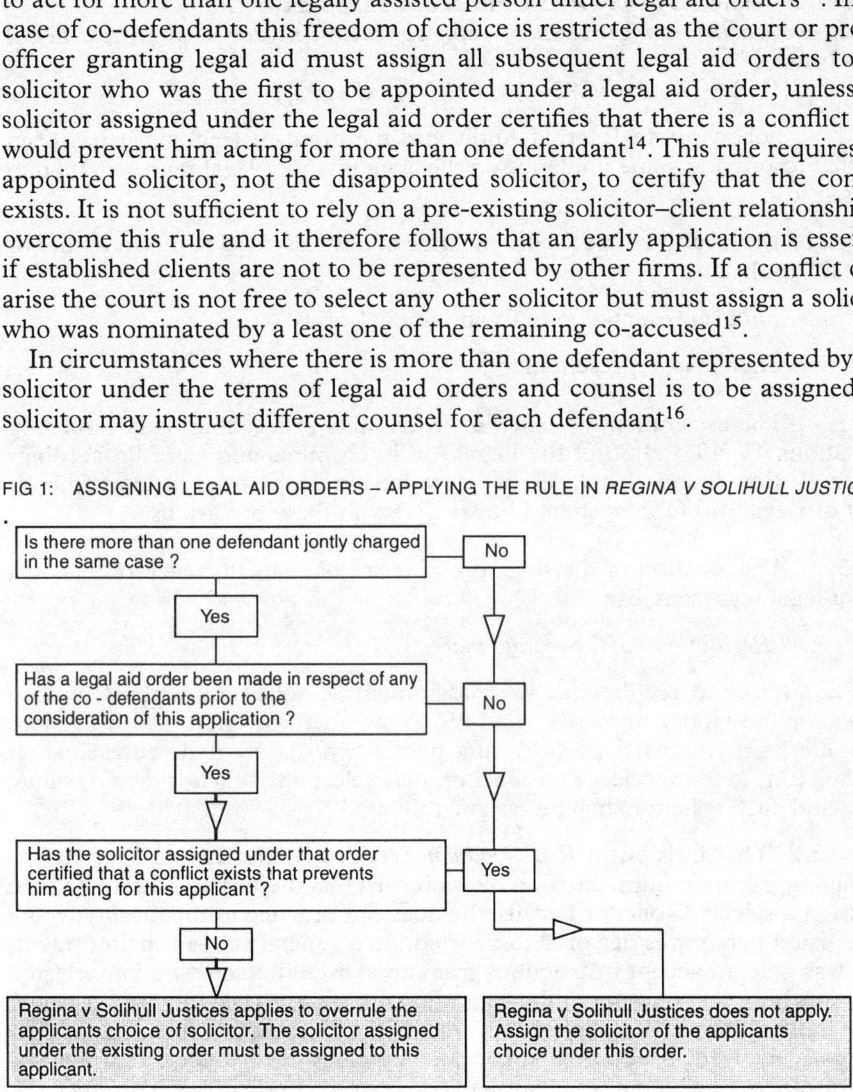

12 Reg 45(1) and (2) of the Legal Aid in Criminal and Care Proceedings (General) Regulations 1989 for proceedings other than those in the Court of appeal and House of Lords and Regulation 46 of the Legal Aid in Criminal and Care Proceedings (General) Regulations 1989.
13 Reg 49 of the Legal Aid in Criminal and Care Proceedings (General) Regulations 1989.
14 *R v Solihull Justices, ex p Johnson* (1976) 140 JP Jo 189.
15 *Baker v West Sussex Justices* (1983) 148 JP 129.
16 *R v O'Brien* [1985] 1 All ER 971.

Where a legally assisted person wishes to change the solicitor or barrister assigned under the legal aid order, or the solicitor or barrister wishes to withdraw from his obligations under the order, an application must be made to amend the order[17].

Guidance Issued by the Lord Chancellor's Department:
Guidance on the assignment of representation under a Criminal Legal Aid Order
(Issued as LCD Circular JC93(1) on 29 March 1993).

1. Following an Internal Audit into the grant of legal aid it has been decided to provide some guidance on the assignment of legal representation in relation to:-

i. the location of a solicitor in terms of costs of travel to the court and/or legal aid applicant;

ii. joint representation in multi-handled cases;

iii. change of representation.

2. The assignment of solicitors in criminal proceedings is governed by regulations 45, 49 and 50 of the Legal Aid in Criminal and Care Proceedings (General) Regulations 1989. All those involved in the granting, and/or amendment of Legal Aid Orders should be familiar with these provisions.

3. The location of the solicitors in terms of costs of travel to the court and/or legal representative.

3.1 *Regulation 45(1) provides that*:-

'... subject to regulations 46 (Assignment of solicitor for the Court of Appeal or the House of Lords), and 49 (Assignment of one solicitor to more than one legally assisted person), any person who is granted representation entitling him to the services of a solicitor, may select any solicitor who is willing to act and such solicitor shall be assigned to him.'

3.2 The decision in *R v Goodwin*, certified by the Taxing Master (see the Taxing Compendium, decision S7) confirms that there is no power to refuse to assign a selected solicitor because he does not practice in the locality where the assisted person resides or is to be tried. As a general rule a solicitor ought, if he was able, to accept instructions from an assisted person who has selected him, but there was nothing in the legislation which compelled him to. It would be a proper reason to decline a retainer due to the fact that under the regulations the costs involved in accepting may not be wholly recovered. There may be circumstances in which it was reasonable to instruct a solicitor at a distance but this will not always be the case.

3.3 In *R v Goodwin* the Taxing Master held that the determining officer had correctly made his assessment on the basis of what should reasonably have been allowed a local solicitor. The representation that the defendant had a free choice of solicitor was incorrect. An assisted person was entitled to a

17 Reg 50(1) of the Legal Aid in Criminal and Care Proceedings (General) Regulations 1989.

reasonable choice of solicitors. The relevant regulations conferred on a person to whom legal aid was granted – the right to select any solicitor *who was willing to act*.

3.4 When considering assignment under a criminal Legal Aid Order the 'proper officer' should, where considered appropriate, bring to the attention of a solicitor whose practice is some distance from the legally assisted person and/or court the decision in *R v Goodwin*. However, if the solicitor is still prepared to act for the legally assisted person, he should be so assigned under the Legal Aid Order.

4. Joint representation in multi-handed cases.

4.1 *Regulation 49 provides that*:-

'. . . a solicitor may be assigned to two or more legally assisted persons whose cases are to be heard together, unless the interests of justice require that such persons be separately represented'.

4.2 In multi-handed cases consideration should be given to the possibility of assigning a solicitor to more than one defendant. Unless the 'proper officer' is already satisfied that joint comments from the solicitor concerned before taking any decision.

4.3 It would not be proper to assign joint representation in cases where there is a conflict of interests between the defendants. It may also *not* be desirable to assign joint representation where the defendant concerned are existing clients of different solicitors, or where there would be more than three defendants assigned to a particular solicitor. This is by no means an exhaustive list, and there may be other good reasons why joint representation would not be appropriate.

5. Change of representation.

5.1 *Regulation 50(1) provides that*:-

'. . . a court having power to make a Legal Aid Order may, on application, amend any such order by substituting for any legal representative or representatives previously assigned under the order any legal representative or representatives whom the court could have assigned if it had been making the Legal Aid Order'.

5.2 Before a case comes to trial there may be an application under Regulation 50(1) to amend the Legal Aid Order by substituting a different solicitor. Such an application must clearly state the reasons why it is felt necessary to amend the order, together with any comments from the existing solicitor. The existing solicitors should also inform the court of the extent of the preparation already undertaken. If the granting of an application to amend the order is likely to lead to a delay in bringing the case on for trial the Resident Judge should be consulted.

Legal services and agencies division (PL1)

cc Circuit administrators
Court administrators
Circuit taxing directors
Training centre

3. Authority to incur costs under the order

As a general rule the solicitor or barrister with conduct of the case for which legal aid is granted has a discretion to incur such costs as are just and reasonable, with the inevitable consequence that if the costs cannot be justified on taxation they will be disallowed by the appropriate authority. If it appears that it will be necessary to incur any unusual or excessive expenditure in relation to proceedings in the magistrates' or Crown Courts, the representative assigned under the order may seek prior authority from the Legal Aid Board's Area Committee

FIG 2: AMENDMENT TO LEGAL AID ORDERS – OVERVIEW

NOTE: All references to regulations refer to the Legal Aid in Criminal and Care Proceedings (General) Regulations 1989.

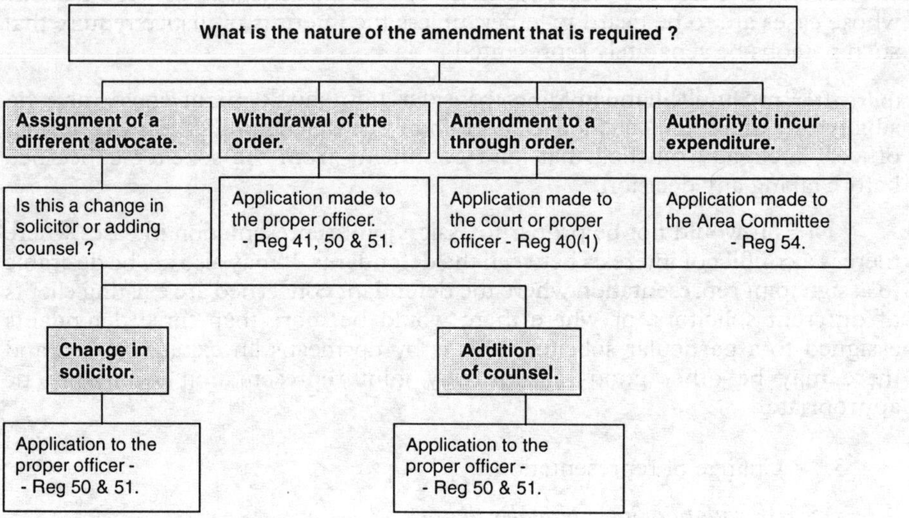

Figure 2 provides a diagrammatic overview of the process of amending criminal legal aid orders. In order to provide readers with a detailed commentary on the method of application and guidance as to the criteria to be employed each type of amendment will be examined in turn, together with the avenues of appeal that exist if the initial application is rejected.

AMENDMENT OF LEGAL AID ORDERS

1. Assignment of a different solicitor under the order

Circumstances occasionally arise where defendants to criminal charges become dissatisfied with the advice they receive from their solicitors, or where the advice tendered is unpalatable, or where conflicts of interest arise, either between the defendant and the solicitor's other clients or between the defendant and the solicitor's professional duty. Where such defendants are legally aided they are not free simply to transfer the legal aid order to a new solicitor, as they must first satisfy a competent authority that it is in the interests of justice to do so.

In assessing whether it is in the interests of justice to reassign the order to another solicitor the proper officer, or a court if the application is being renewed, will need to consider the requirements of all the stakeholders involved and the reason for the request. They will therefore consider:

1. the reason why the request is being made;
2. the interests of the legally assisted person;
3. the interests of other parties to the proceedings, particularly if granting the request is likely to cause further delay or expense;
4. the interests of the solicitor assigned under the order;
5. the interests of the proposed solicitor;
6. the interests of the State, which will have to fund any additional expense incurred by the amendment.

In order to ensure that all those views that can properly be considered are considered some courts have devised a non-statutory application process with the co-operation of local Law Societies that uses a common application form, which is completed by the legally assisted person, with his grounds for making the application, and is sent to the putative solicitor for his agreement to act and thereafter to the solicitor holding the order, so that he might consent to the application or make such observations as are appropriate. A sample of such a form is shown at Figure 3.

Despite the use of application forms there is no requirement for an application to be in any specific form, although there are rules as to whom the application must be directed.

Examples of cogent reasons for allowing the reassignment of the nominated solicitor under the order might include the following, although this list is not intended to be exhaustive.

Professional difficulties

Professional difficulties includes a range of problems including those circumstances where a legally aided person has disclosed that he has committed an offence but none the less persists in pursuing a defence that is deliberately misleading. In such circumstances the solicitor under the order cannot continue to act for the legally assisted person if he will be required to deliberately mislead the court and would wish to withdraw, but he or she would still be precluded from explaining the reasons for that withdrawal.

Conflict of interest

Conflict of interest is clearly anticipated by the *Solihull Justices* case[18] and arises where more than one defendant is being represented by a solicitor under a legal aid order and their instructions differ so that material issues of fact are indisposed between them. The most typical example is where each of the co-accused blames the other for the commission of the offence.

Breakdown of the solicitor–client relationship

Where it is impossible for a working relationship to develop or continue between the solicitor and his client. One example of such circumstances was where a solicitor's client stole the solicitor's portable compact disc player from the solicitor's office during an attendance for instructions on a criminal case; others

18 Footnote 14, ibid.

FIG 3: APPLICATION FORM FOR THE RE-ASSIGNMENT OF A LEGAL AID ORDER

REQUEST FOR TRANSFER OF LEGAL AID

Part 1 (to be completed by the defendant)

To: The Clerk to the Justices
Liverpool Magistrates' Court
107 Dale Street
LIVERPOOL
L2 2JQ

I ....hereby authorise

(name of applying solicitor) ....
to take over my outstanding case/cases before your court from
(name of appointed solicitor) ....

The matter/matters outstanding are: (give full details of the offences)

....
....

I further request that any legal aid order(s) relating to these matters be transferred to

....

The reasons why I want to change solicitors are:

....
....
....
....
....

Signed .... Date ....

Part 2 (to be completed by the applying solicitor)

To: (enter details of appointed solicitor)

Your client has approached this firm and requested that the outstanding matters against him/her at Liverpool Magistrates' Court, as detailed in Part 1, be transferred to us. I would be obliged if you would signify your consent or dissent to this request to transfer Legal Aid by completing the relevant section of Part 3 and returning this form to us within 5 working days.

Signed .... Date ....

Part 3 (to be completed by the appointed solicitor)

To: **(give name and address of applying solicitor)**

** **We agree to our client's request that the outstanding matters against him/her at Liverpool Magistrates' Court, as shown in Part 1, be transferred to your firm. The relevant case numbers as shown on our copy of the legal aid orders are:**

....

....

** **We cannot agree to our clients request that the outstanding matters against him/her at Liverpool Magistrates Court, as shown in Part 1, be transferred to your firm. The reasons for this objection are:**

....

....

....

....

....

****(delete as appropriate)**

Signed .... **Date** ....

Part 4 (to be completed by the Clerk to the Justices)

To: **(enter details of applying solcicitor)**

** **This request for transfer of legal aid has been refused. Your attention is drawn to Regulation 51(2) & 51(6) of the 1989 Regulations which indicate your possible rights concerning this refusal.**

** **I do not agree that it is in the interest of justice for these matters to be transferred despite an agreement by the two solicitors and this request has been refused. Your attention is drawn to Regulation 51(2) & 51(6) of the 1989 Regulations which indicate your possible rightos concerning this refusal.**

Copies of the original legal aid application and the statement of means are attached for your information.

** **(delete as appropriate)**

Signed

Malcolm Marsh
Clerk to the Justices **Date** ....

include theft of solicitor's motor cars or assault upon the legally assisted person's advocate.

Geographical constraints

Where proceedings are committed or transferred to courts in locations that can more easily and cost effectively be dealt with by a local solicitor.

Client followings

Where in ongoing or complex proceedings the solicitor with conduct of the matter transfers to a different practice it might be appropriate to allow his legally aided clients to follow the solicitor, but proper officers would need to be aware of the effect of restraint of trade clauses that might embroil them in civil disputes.

Examples of applications that are unlikely to succeed would include those cases where the reassignment of legal aid was designed to delay the proceedings or to intimidate or inconvenience prosecution witnesses. Other examples might include circumstances where there is sustainable evidence of touting or other non-professional practices.

Method of application and renewal

Applications to amend legal aid orders by assigning a different advocate must be accompanied by a statement of the grounds on which the applicant relies and should be directed to the courts proper officer, who may grant or refuse the application[19]. If the application is refused the application may always be renewed to the court[20], but it can only be renewed to the Legal Aid Board's Area Committee as an alternative if:

1. an application to extend the order in the same way has not previously been refused by the Area Committee[1]; and
2. the application was made no more than 14 days after the date of committal for trail or sentence where the substantive proceedings are in the Crown Court[2]; or
3. the application is made not less than 14 days before the date fixed for committal or trial in respect of proceedings being held in the magistrates' court[3].

It is to be noted that the procedures allowing applications to amend legal aid orders to be renewed differ from renewals of applications for the grant of a criminal legal aid order. In the case of a renewal to amend an order it is not necessary for the application to relate to an indictable or either-way offence, but in the case of a renewed application for a grant of legal aid in the first instance the substantive proceedings must be either way or indictable[4].

Where an application is renewed to a court, the court may grant or refuse the application or may refer it to a proper officer[5]. A proper officer in either the Crown Court or a magistrates' court may grant an application which is referred

19 Reg 51(1) of the Legal Aid in Criminal and Care Proceedings (General) Regulations 1989.
20 Reg 51(2) of the Legal Aid in Criminal and Care Proceedings (General) Regulations 1989.
1 Reg 51(6)(a) of the Legal Aid in Criminal and Care Proceedings (General) Regulations 1989.
2 Reg 51(6)(b)(i) of the Legal Aid in Criminal and Care Proceedings (General) Regulations 1989.
3 Reg 51(6)(b)(ii) of the Legal Aid in Criminal and Care Proceedings (General) Regulations 1989.
4 Reg 15(2)(a) of the Legal Aid in Criminal and Care Proceedings (General) Regulations 1989.
5 Reg 51(3) of the Legal Aid in Criminal and Care Proceedings (General) Regulations 1989.

FIG 4: APPLICATION AND RENEWAL PROCEDURE

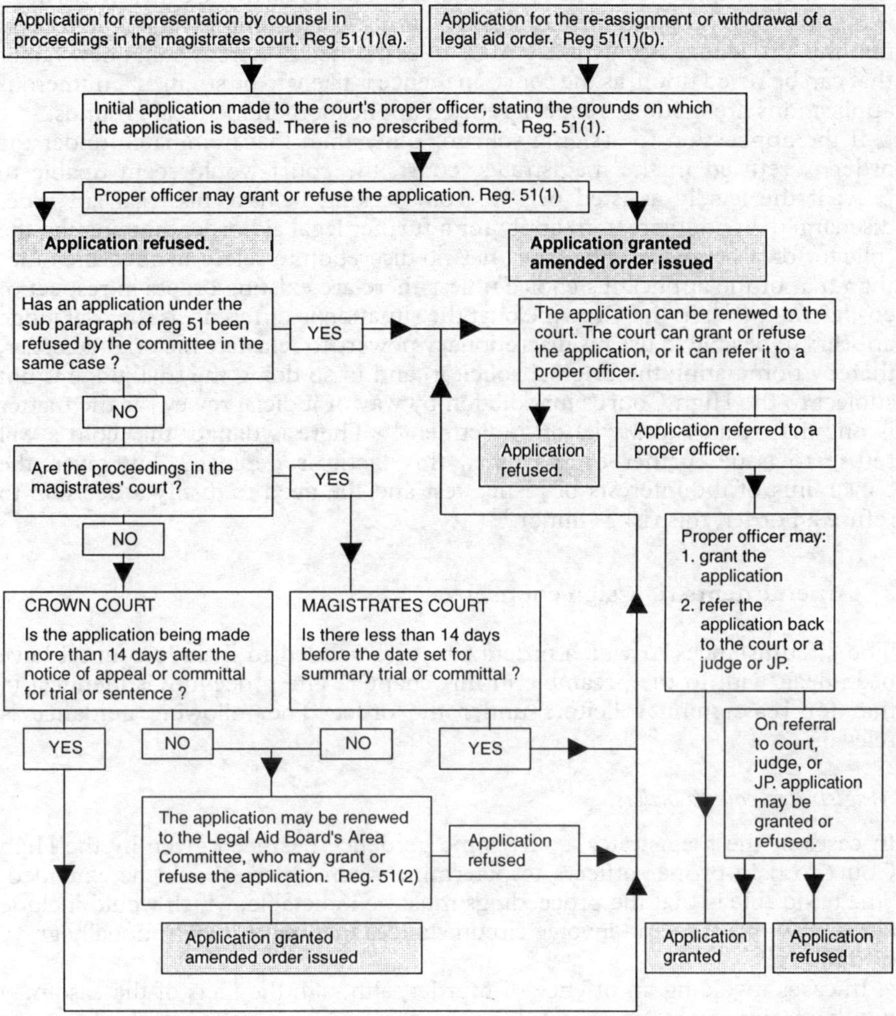

to him by a court, but he may not refuse the application[6]. If a proper officer, who is a justices' clerk, or a person delegated by a justices' clerk, is not prepared to grant an application that is referred to him, he may refer it back to the court or to a justice of the peace[7], and the court or justice of the peace may grant or refuse the application[8]. Where a proper officer is an officer of the Crown Court or the Registrar of the Court of Appeal he may grant the application[9] or refer it to a judge of the court, who may grant or refuse the application[10].

If the application is refused by the Legal Aid Board's Area Committee there would seem to be no prohibition to further applications being made, for the

6 Reg 51(4)(a) of the Legal Aid in Criminal and Care Proceedings (General) Regulations 1989.
7 Reg 51(4)(b) of the Legal Aid in Criminal and Care Proceedings (General) Regulations 1989.
8 Reg 51(5) of the Legal Aid in Criminal and Care Proceedings (General) Regulations 1989.
9 Reg 51(4)(a) of the Legal Aid in Criminal and Care Proceedings (General) Regulations 1989.
10 Reg 51(5) of the Legal Aid in Criminal and Care Proceedings (General) Regulations 1989.

same amendment, on the same grounds, provided that the application is made to the court. Similarly, further applications can be made to the court where there is no right of renewal to the Legal Aid Board's Area Committee. It would seem that this procedure is only likely to be of assistance if there is some new factor that can be relied upon, as the court's patience is likely to be strained if numerous applications are made to renew a refused application on identical grounds.

If the application to assign a solicitor other than that nominated under the order is refused in the magistrates' court, the court would seem unable to prevent the legally assisted person from seeking to have his legal aid order discharged[11] and, thereafter, apply for a further legal aid order, nominating the solicitor of his choice[12]. The court has no discretion to select an advocate other than that of the applicant's choice unless there are existing orders in respect of co-defendants[13]. In the Crown Court the situation is different, as the trial judge appears to be able to use his discretionary powers to reinstate the original order, thereby nominating the original solicitor, and in so doing the trial judge is not subject to the High Court's jurisdiction by way of judicial review, as the matter is one that relates to a trial on indictment[14]. There is danger that courts will refuse to issue further orders when this tactic is deployed, but given the constraints of the interests of justice test and the need to justify a decision to refuse an order, this risk is minor.[15]

2 Amendments to assign counsel

The circumstances in which orders can be amended to include counsel have been dealt with to the preamble in this chapter. The procedure is identical to that for reassigning solicitors under the order. The following guidance is relevant.

Magistrates' court's orders

In cases in the magistrates' court some guidance has been given by the High Court to help proper officers to determine when orders should be extended. The basic rule is that the proceedings must be indictable, which would include either-way offences and involve circumstances that make it exceptionally grave or difficult[16].

In cases involving an offence of murder, although the facts of the case may not themselves create any great difficulty, the offence is undoubtedly grave and representation should normally be extended to counsel[17]. In cases that do not involve murder, the fact that there may be numerous offences disclosed is not a reason to extend the certificate for counsel[18]. In many cases it will be apparent that no useful purpose will be served in objecting to evidence at the committal stage; however, if there are reasons for supposing that counsel might discover a

11 Reg 41(1)(b) of the Legal Aid in Criminal and Care Proceedings (General) Regulations 1989
12 As permitted by Reg 10 of the Legal Aid in Criminal and Care Proceedings (General) Regulations 1989.
13 See *R v Solihull Justices, ex p Johnson* (ibid).
14 *R v Crown Court at Isleworth, ex p Willington* [1993] 1 WLR 713.
15 For a full discussion of this point see 'Enforcement Of Contribution Orders During Currency Of Criminal Legal Aid Orders' (1993) 157 JPN 739 at p 741.
16 Reg 44(3)(a) of the Legal Aid in Criminal and Care Proceedings (General) Regulations 1989.
17 *R v Derby Justices, ex p Kooner* [1971] 1 QB 147
18 *R v Guildford Justices, ex p Scott* [1975] Crim LR 286.

sensible basis for a submission of no case to answer or a sound forensic technical reason why certain statements should not be admitted so that witnesses might be called, and perhaps give evidence, the justices might be persuaded to grant an extension to counsel at the committal stage[19].

Crown Court orders

The amendment of order in the Crown Court is governed by the Practice Direction issued in 1989:

Practice Note[20]

1. Regulation 48(3) of the 1989 General Regulations enables a High Court or circuit judge to make a legal aid order which provides for the services of two counsel.
2. If such an application is made to the Crown Court it shall be placed before the resident or designated judge of the Court except where the substantive case is to be heard by a named High Court Judge in which case the application shall be placed before him.
3. The above does not apply if the application is made during a pre-trial review or during the trial. In those cases the judge seized of the matter shall determine the application.
4. In case of doubt the judge concerned or the presiding judge of the circuit should make such direction as he considers appropriate.

No further guidance exists as to the circumstances in which such applications will be granted, save in serious fraud cases where it is the accepted practice for Queen's Counsel and two junior counsel to be instructed on the basis of the compexity of the case. The reason for this lack of guidance appears to be that the High Court routinely declines jurisdiction to entertain judicial reviews in such matters on the basis that such decisions are matters of discretion relating to a trial and cannot be challenged in that way.

3. Withdrawal of a legal aid order

This procedure applies to those circumstances where an application to withdraw a legal aid order has been refused. In practice this situation very rarely arises, as there is usually very little opposition by proper officers to the withdrawal of legal aid orders, but it is dealt with in this text for the sake of completeness.

An application to withdraw a legal aid order may arise in the following circumstances:

1. Where a legally assisted person does not wish to accept the order on the terms on which it is offered[1], usually as a result of the contribution order element of the order being too high.
2. At the request of the legally assisted person[2]. This may arise to avoid the consequences of a refusal to reassign the order[3], or because of a change in

19 *R v Guildford Justices, ex p Scott* [1975] Crim LR 286.
20 [1989] 2 All ER 479.
1 Reg 41(1)(a) of the Legal Aid in Criminal and Care Proceedings (General) Regulations 1989.
2 Reg 41(1)(b) of the Legal Aid in Criminal and Care Proceedings (General) Regulations 1989.
3 See 'Other forms of renewal' below.

the legally assisted person's financial circumstances that would result in the imposition of a large contribution order.

3. Where all the legal representatives assigned under the order withdraw and submit that the conduct of the legally assisted person is not such that would enable the court to reassign the order[4]. This is only likely to be relevant in cases where the legally assisted person fails to notify the court of a relevant change in his financial circumstances and refuses consent to enable his solicitor to do so. In such circumstances the solicitor would be bound to withdraw[5] and, thereafter, to advise the court of the reasons for this withdrawal so as to discharge his duty under the regulations[6].

The procedure for making, and renewing, such applications is identical to that for the amendment of an order by reassigning it to another solicitor and reference should be made to the previous section.

4. Amendment to a through order

Where legal aid orders are granted in respect of indictable or either-way offences during the magistrates' court proceedings, that order may specify that it is only valid in the magistrates' court, or it may allow representation in both the magistrates' court and the Crown Court. An order that permits representation in both courts is termed a 'through order'.

In the case of purely indictable offences many magistrates' courts will issue a through order as a matter of course, but for either-way cases there seems to be a tendency to wait until either committal takes place, or at least, mode of trial is determined. There may be good cause for this hesitation as a 'through order' can only be made by examining justices[7]. If a through order is not made at the outset of the proceedings the order can be amended to a through order by the courts at any hearing[8]. The procedure on application and renewal is the same as for amending the solicitor assigned under the order[9].

5. Applications to incur expenditure

An application can only be made for an authority to incur expenditure if the expense is related to one of the following items:

1. obtaining a written report from an expert (but note that the authority obtained from the committee does not cover the expense of the expert's attendance at court to give evidence, should this be necessary);
2. employing someone other than an expert to provide a written report or opinion;
3. bespeaking transcripts of shorthand notes or tape recordings (including police interviews);
4. instructing Queen's Counsel without junior counsel where an order allows representation by solicitor and one counsel;

4 Reg 50(2) of the Legal Aid in Criminal and Care Proceedings (General) Regulations 1989.
5 Para 5.04, Professional Code of Conduct of Solicitors.
6 Reg 56 of the Legal Aid in Criminal and Care Proceedings (General) Regulations 1989.
7 Reg 40(1) of the Legal Aid in Criminal and Care Proceedings (General) Regulations 1989.
8 Reg 40(1) and 50 of the Legal Aid in Criminal and Care Proceedings (General) Regulations 1989.
9 See section 1 above.

FIG 5: APPLICATION FORM FOR PRIOR AUTHORITY TO INCUR EXPENDITURE IN CRIMINAL PROCEEDINGS. CRIM 10

Application for prior authority for expenditure in criminal proceedings

Legal Aid

➤ **Please read the notes overleaf before completing this form in block capitals.**

CRIM 10

LEGAL AID BOARD LEGAL AID ACT 1988

App Type 02

Legal Aid Order number (please copy this from the order) LA

Has this application been granted over the telephone? ☐ YES ☐ NO

Defendant's details

Surname: *Mr/Mrs/Miss/Ms* ______ First Names: ______

Address: ______

Date of birth: / / Occupation: ______

Solicitor's details

Name of Solicitor: ______ Initials: ______ Title: ______

Name & Address of firm: ______

Legal Aid account no: ______ Reference: ______ DX No: ______

Tel No: ______ Fax No: ______

Court/charge details

Court Name:

Nature of charges (including statute and section):

Likely plea: Date of next hearing:

Purpose of next hearing:

Give the full reasons for the application and state clearly the purpose of the authority sought; in the case of a medical report indicate whether as to fitness to plead and/or plea and/or disposal:

Give a brief summary of the prosecution case. You may attach the advance disclosure or extracts:

Give a summary of the defence or mitigation. Attach your client's statement and details of any previous convictions, if available in either case:

Type of Expenditure e.g. medical report

Details of Charging Rates per hour
(Do not include VAT) Please read the notes overleaf

Preparation

Travel (do not include travelling expenses)

Total authority you are seeking

Name and address of expert or other person you want to instruct:

Type of expertise and qualifications:

Only applicable to medical reports: Consultant: ☐ NO ☐ YES

Are there any other defendants who would benefit from the expenditure and with whom there is no conflict of interest?

☐ NO ☐ YES: What consideration has been given to a joint instruction?

Have alternative quotes been obtained?

☐ NO ☐ YES: What were the amounts quoted?

Solicitor's signature: ______ **Date:** / /

Specific Information required

1. Court attendance fees of expert witnesses cannot be authorised - these are payable from Central Funds in the absence of a court direction to the contrary. Solicitors should consider what fee is likely to be allowed (if necessary, by asking the court) so that instructions are not given to an expert whose full court attendance fee is unlikely to be allowed by the court. The costs of medical reports ordered by the court to assist in sentencing are also payable from Central Funds and will not be authorised.
2. In Intoximeter or excess alcohol cases, include the reading or blood level, the nature or amount of alcohol consumed before and after driving with the times of consumption and the times of the test. In "hip flask" cases, also give details of any corroborative evidence.
3. The absence of alternative quotes will not, in itself, lead to a refusal to incur expenditure.
4. Check that the application has been sent to the appropriate area office and that a legal aid order is held which covers the proceedings. The Board will deal with applications on the basis of the information sent by the solicitor and an Area Committee only has jurisdiction where it is the correct Area Committee and there is the appropriate legal aid cover.
5. Send applications to the Area Office in whose area the court is situated. A covering letter is not needed but you can continue on a separate sheet of paper if necessary.

For area office use only

COURT CODE: DATE:

DECISION:

RF2	Request further information	
G10	Granted - Delegated	
G12	Granted - Committee	
R21	Refused - Committee	

CL4	Out of Time	
W10	Withdrawn	
CL5	No Jurisdiction	

DOCUMENT CODES AND STANDARD WORDINGS CODES REQUIRED:

SUMMARY FOR COMMITTEE:

L.B.F. September 1993

5. performing an act which is unusual in nature or involves unusually large expenditure (for example excessive travel).[10]

Although it is not a mandatory requirement that prior authority be obtained most prudent solicitors will do so, as if an unusual expenditure was incurred, there is a risk that it will be disallowed on taxation in the absence of a specific authority that it shall be paid.

An application can be made by telephone in very urgent cases, but it is more usual for written applications to be submitted to the Board's Area Office. Where the application is granted over the telephone the Area Office will usually require the submission of a written application to support what was said during the telephone conversation.

The Legal Aid Board requires the form CRIM 10 to be used. This form is quite simple to complete but does require the solicitor to have obtained the name, address and qualifications of the person who is going to be instructed and details of their fee. If the Board considers that the fee to be claimed is excessive, it may only grant authorisation to a lower level than that which was requested.

The application will initially be considered by an authorised officer who may grant the application, but in cases of doubt the application will be referred to the full committee who will determine the outcome. In some cases, usually where there is a large expense or a particularly complicated issue, the committee can invite the applicant's solicitor to attend to justify the application.

If an application is made to incur such expenditure and is refused by the area committee a solicitor is allowed to take funds from his client to finance that expense, even though the general rule is that he cannot receive any funds from a legally assisted person[11]. It is important to stress that the power to receive funds, or costs from sources other than the Legal Aid Fund, only arises in respect of a legally aided client after he ceases to be legally aided, or to fund enquiries or reports if there has been an application to incur that expenditure and it has been refused.

10 Reg 54 of the Legal Aid in Criminal and Care Proceedings (General) Regulations 1989.
11 Reg 55 of the Legal Aid in Criminal and Care Proceedings (General) Regulations 1989.

Chapter Eleven

Costs and the Criminal Legal Aid Scheme

This chapter will deal with the following:

1. the refund or remittal of a successful legally aided defendant's contributions as an alternative to a defendant's costs order;
2. the refund or remittal of an unsuccessful legally aided defendant's contributions where the contributions paid exceed the solicitor's bill;
3. work done prior to the grant of a legal aid order;
4. the scope of the order–work done under the legal aid order;
5. the power to a make defendant's costs order in relation to legally assisted persons;
6. time limits and relevant taxing authorities;
7. methods of claiming costs;
8. standard fees in magistrates' courts; and
9. avenues of appeal against taxation.

The chapter does not examine the taxation process in depth as this is a process undertaken by Central Taxing Units at the Crown Court or the Legal Aid Board's Area office and is a complex process beyond the scope of this work. In practice the taxation of legal aid bills follows the same principals as taxation of any other bills and these are comprehensively covered by other works.

THE REFUND OR REMITTAL OF A SUCCESSFUL LEGALLY AIDED DEFENDANT'S CONTRIBUTIONS AS AN ALTERNATIVE TO A DEFENDANT'S COSTS ORDER

Where a person has been required to contribute to the costs of his defence through a legal aid contribution order he has effectively contributed costs on account. This places that person in a similar position to a person who is funding his own defence and has placed funds on account of costs with his solicitor. In the latter case, where those defendant's reasonable costs were paid from central funds by way of a defendant's costs order, the funds are usually paid to the solicitor, but actually belong to the defendant. The solicitor will then pay them over to the defendant, who is left in the position he would have been if the charges had not been made against him.

In the case of legally assisted person paying a contribution the remedy that places the defendant, in respect of the costs of his defence, in the same financial position that existed prior to him being granted legal aid, is achieved through a refund of those contributions that have been paid and the remittal of any unpaid contributions that have fallen due[1]. The power to remit or repay contributions

1 Reg 35(1) of the Legal Aid in Criminal and Care Proceedings (General) Regulations 1989.

FIG 1: OBTAINING THE REFUND OR REMITTAL OF LEGAL AID CONTRIBUTIONS WHERE THE DEFENCE HAS SUCCEEDED

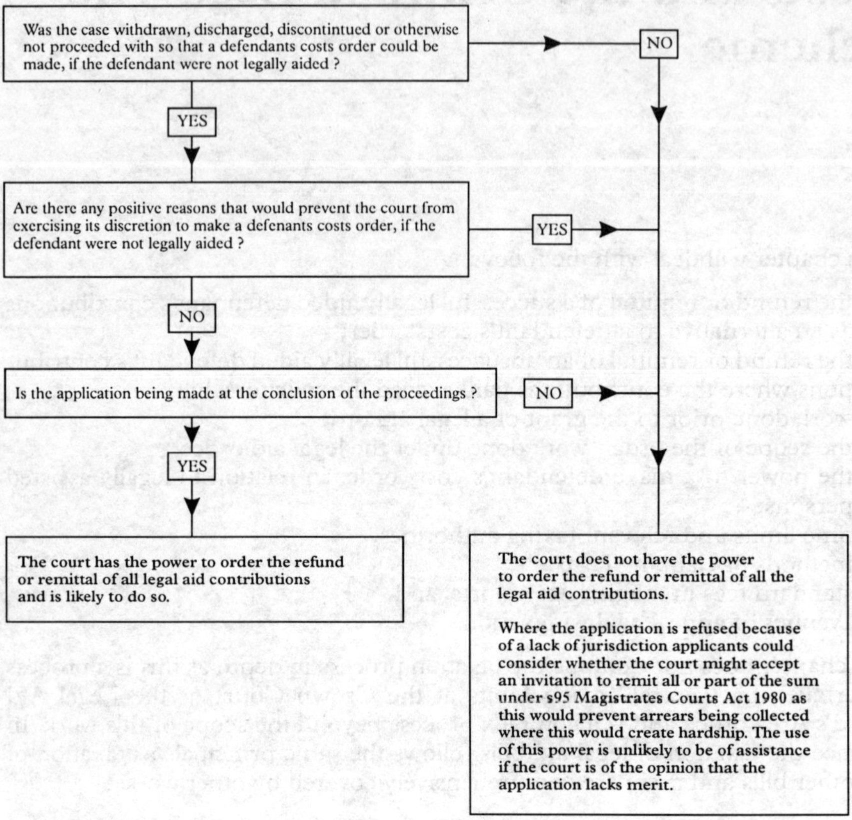

is to be exercised 'where the court thinks fit', but in practice this means that a court will refund the contributions where it would have made a defendant's costs order.

The general rule is set out in the *Practice Direction (Crime: Costs)*[2] that a defendant's costs order, and therefore an order to refund contributions, should be made in any case where the case is dismissed, withdrawn, discharged or otherwise not proceeded with, unless there are positive reasons for not doing so. The Practice Direction then indicates examples of where the exception might apply, such as cases where there was sufficient evidence to support a conviction, but the defendant escaped conviction by use of a technicality which has no merit, or where the defendant caused suspicion to fall upon himself and in doing so misled the prosecution as to the strength of the case against him.

The power to order the refund of contributions is only excercisable at the conclusion of the proceedings[3], or by a court hearing an appeal which is either successful or unsuccessful[4]. This can cause difficulties where cases are dis-

2 [1991] 1 WLR 498.
3 Reg 35(1) of the Legal Aid in Criminal and Care Proceedings (General) Regulations 1989.
4 Reg 35(3) of the Legal Aid in Criminal and Care Proceedings (General) Regulations 1989.

continued and no application is made at the conclusion of the proceedings. In discontinued cases it is not necessary to have the case re-listed so that an application for costs can be made, as the application for a defendant's costs order can be made direct to the court clerk within three months of the date of discontinuance. This power does not extend to legal aid contributions on a strict interpretation of the regulations, although many courts informally allow such applications to be heard afterwards by a clerk or a full court. If courts refuse to entertain such applications it will be necessary to have the proceedings reinstated for the specific purpose of making the application for a refund.

If a legal aid order has been revoked prior to the case being dismissed, discharged or disposed of in some other way that would enable a contribution order to be made, the power to refund contributions is preserved[5]. In those cases where enforcement action has been taken to recover unpaid arrears prior to the conclusion of the case and additional court costs or bailiff's fees have been added to the account, the amount due to be refunded will be the amount due under the basic contribution order. If the court feels it is equitable to remit the costs of enforcing the payments that were not made when they were due, the court will have to use its powers of remittal under the Magistrates' Courts Act 1980[6] where different criteria apply. In such circumstances the court will be bound to take into account the reason for the non-payment at the due date and the level of culpability on the part of the legally assisted person or the defaulting appropriate contributor.

THE REFUND OR REMITTAL OF AN UNSUCCESSFUL LEGALLY AIDED DEFENDANT'S CONTRIBUTIONS WHERE THE CONTRIBUTIONS PAID EXCEED THE SOLICITOR'S BILL

In circumstances where a defence has not succeeded, or where it was successful but the court declined to exercise its discretion and order the refund or remittal of the contributions, there will be occasions when the amount paid by the legally assisted person, or the appropriate contributor, exceeds the amount paid on taxation to the solicitor. In such cases any excess will be paid back to the legally aided person or the appropriate contributor without the need for any formal application[7].

There will inevitably be some delay from the date that the proceedings are concluded and the refund being made because the collecting court must wait until the taxation process has been completed and it has been notified of the result by the taxing authority before it can adjust the account. It follows that there is an onus on the solicitor to submit his bill without undue delay in such cases to ensure his client's funds are returned as soon as possible. Courts are not able to accept a copy of the bill as submitted for taxation by the solicitor as authority for adjusting the account as the amount claimed may be varied on taxation and may not include counsel's fees which are submitted direct to the taxing authority in some cases.

5 Reg 35(2) of the Legal Aid in Criminal and Care Proceedings (General) Regulations 1989.
6 S 95 of the Magistrates' Courts Act 1980.
7 S 23(7) of the Legal Aid Act 1988.

FIG 2: REFUNDING OVERPAYMENTS OF CONTRIBUTIONS AFTER TAXATION

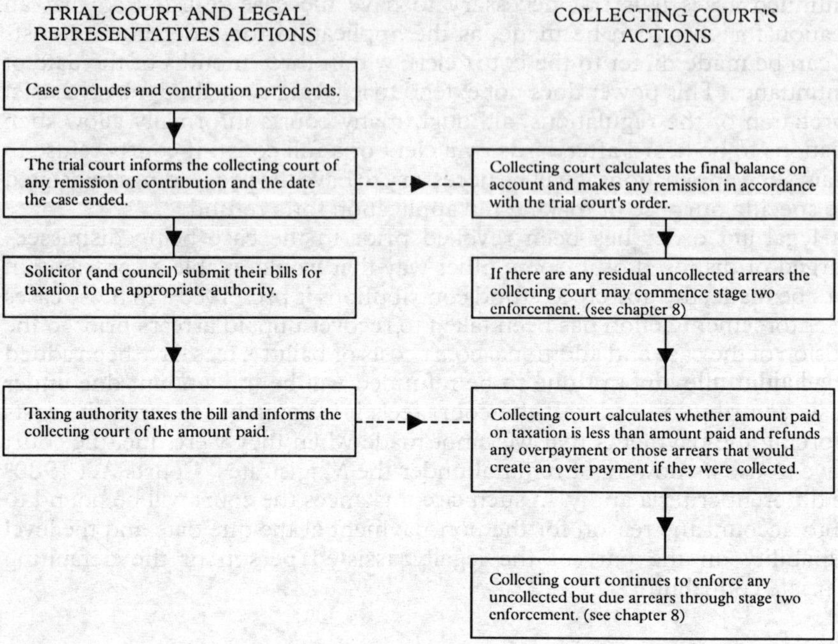

WORK DONE PRIOR TO THE GRANT OF A LEGAL AID ORDER

Instructions to justices' clerks emphasise that legal aid orders can only be dated on the date that they are made[8]. This advice has been confirmed by the High Court[9] which was asked to consider a case where an application was made to the justices who declined to deal with it and determined that it should be referred to the clerk to the justices. The application still had not been considered some seven days later, when a further application was made that argued, not only that the application should be granted, but that it should be dated as of the date of submission. The High Court disagreed with this submission and held that such an order can only be granted on the date upon which it is made.

This position has been preserved in circumstances where further enquiries have been made into an applicant's means, because of contradictory information given by the prosecution which has cast doubt on the validity of the information within the applicant's statement of means[10]. Here it was held that the clerk to the justices was entitled to wait until he had received an answer to his questions before he considered whether or not to grant the application, because the Act required that a court shall not make a legal aid order unless it appears that [the applicant's] disposable income and disposable capital are such that he requires assistance. In such a case no order could be made until the applicant had discharged that burden and therefore the argument that the order should be dated on the date upon which the original application had been submitted was

8 Para 6.1 of the Justices' Clerks Accounting Manual.
9 *Welch v Redbridge Justices* (1984) 148 JP 474.
10 *R v Newham Justices, ex p Mumtaz* (1990) 154 JP 597.

not relevant, as at that time there were no grounds on which to make an order. Although both these decisions were made under old legislation, the present Act preserves the same provisions in almost identical form[11].

The importance to solicitors of providing sufficient information to the court to enable it to provide a prompt decision, without requests for further information, is highlighted by these decisions, as is the importance solicitors attach to the court providing an efficient turn round of legal aid applications.

An efficient solicitor can mitigate the effect of these decisions providing that he has taken steps to ensure that he has properly argued his client's application so that it will be granted and if he has made use of ABWOR or the green form scheme in cases where his client is eligible for such advice as pre-legal aid certificate costs may be sourced from those schemes.

If a solicitor's client is not eligible for advice and assistance under either ABWOR or the green form scheme urgent work undertaken prior to the grant of a legal aid can be deemed to be work done under the order if[12]:

(i) the interests of justice required that representation or advice be provided as a matter of urgency – which would seem to include representation at any early court hearings, particularly if the court directs that progress be made that day, or action taken by the solicitor to secure or preserve evidence, such as video tapes, for example, that might otherwise be destroyed;

(ii) that there was no undue delay in making an application for legal aid – this provision is a little less clear than might have been intended. There may be a delay in a defendant instructing a solicitor and once instructed the solicitor acts with all due dispatch to secure a legal aid order. The question arises as to whether delay on the part of the defendant in instructing his solicitor amounts to a delay that negates the power to deem work done after the instructions as work done under the order. This point does not appear to have been tested and the question is one that must be resolved by taxing officers on a case by case basis;

(iii) the representation or advice was provided by the solicitor who was subsequently assigned under the order – this element of the criteria can cause problems where the applicant for a legal aid order has co-accused who may have been granted representation already, or whose applications have preceded that of the person who requires urgent representation. The risk to the solicitor is that if the order is assigned to some other solicitor who represents a co-defendant with whom there is no conflict[13], the solicitor undertaking the urgent work will not be paid.

The Costs Appeals Committee[14] has considered the effect of this provision and has emphasised that each case must be reviewed on its own merits; however, it has indicated that the criteria are likely to be met where there is a hearing within ten days of the original instructions being given and an application for legal aid was made no more than seven days after the initial instructions were received[15].

11 See now ss21(5) and 21(6) of the Legal Aid Act 1988.

12 Reg 44(7) of the Legal Aid in Criminal and Care Proceedings (General) Regulations 1989.

13 As is permitted by *R v Solihull Justices, ex p Johnson* (1976) 140 JP Jo 189.

14 This committee is established by the Legal Aid Board to review decisions relating to the taxation of claims for costs made under the Act where the board is the taxing authority and the solicitor is dissatisfied with a decision of an Area Committee. Before such reviews can take place the area committee must have certified a point of general principle applies – see Regs 12 and 13 of the Legal Aid in Criminal and Care Proceedings (Costs) Regulations 1989.

15 Paras 17–24, Part I, Legal Aid Handbook 1995, Legal Aid Board.

The guidance offered by the Costs Appeals Committee is not exhaustive and there may be circumstances in individual cases where the periods suggested are exceeded yet a claim for urgent work would still be appropriate.

In all cases the solicitor making the claim must provide sufficient information to justify his claim and specify what special circumstances arose[16] if he is to succeed in claiming such payments. If he is relying on the fact that a hearing was to take place within ten days of the initial instructions, for example, he would need to supply the dates on which instructions were received, the date upon which the legal aid application was submitted and the date on which the hearing took place.

If there was a delay in considering a legal aid application on the part of the court which forms the basis of the application for payment for urgent work, the solicitor might consider seeking a written confirmation of the delay from the court and an explanation as to why the delay arose. This written explanation can then be submitted with the claim to justify the delay in the making of the order.

The question arises as to whether a solicitor can be party to making a claim for a defendant's costs order to cover such work that was undertaken prior to the grant of a legal aid order. This situation is considered in the next section.

THE SCOPE OF THE ORDER – WORK DONE UNDER THE LEGAL AID ORDER

In general the legal aid order covers all the work necessary to conduct the defence from the date the order is made until the conclusion of the proceedings. The order will allow work to be done before the defendant appears in court and also allows advice to be given on the merits of an appeal after the case has been concluded.

The order provides for certain minimum standards of representation and if these are thought to be insufficient applications must be made to amend the order[17]. Similarly, where it is proposed to undertake certain types of work an application should be made for approval by the Legal Aid Board's Area Committee to ensure that no point will be taken on taxation as to the necessity of taking those steps.

Guidance is available in certain area as to exactly what may be claimed under the legal aid order in the form of 'points of general importance' which have been decided by the Legal Aid Board's Costs Appeals Committee. These are dealt with below:

Photocopying[18]

Photocopying is to be treated as part of the normal overheads of a solicitor's practice and will not generally be remunerated separately. In exceptional circumstances, however, the actual costs of the copying, if it was done by contractors outside the office, or the actual commercial costs will be allowed on taxation. 'Exceptional circumstances' means 'unusual or out of the ordinary'[19].

16 Reg 5(5) of the Legal Aid in Criminal and Care Proceedings (Costs) Regulations 1989.
17 See Chapter 9.
18 CRIMLA 1.
19 *R v Legal Aid Board, ex p RM Broudie* (1994) 138 Sol Jo LB 94.

Letters to clients confirming dates of hearings and the final outcome of the case[20]

Claims for writing to clients to inform them of the next hearing date and the final outcome of the case are matters for the discretion of the solicitor with conduct of the case, but will be allowed on taxation.

Medical/psychiatric reports for use as mitigation[1]

The general rule is that medical or psychiatric reports will only be allowable if prior authority to incur the expenditure was obtained. In most cases this will not pose any problem to solicitors as the content of a psychiatric report may well have been considered to establish whether the defendant was fit to plead or if he had a psychiatric defence due to lack of mental capacity.

Foreign language ability of the solicitor applied during the conduct of the cased[2]

Where the solicitor makes use of his own capabilities to speak a foreign language and thereby avoid the need to engage an interpreter, enhanced rates may be claimed and allowed on taxation.

Work done after/before the reassignment of the order

Once a solicitor is no longer assigned under an order he may not claim for any work done in respect of that case[3]. Equally the new solicitor assigned under the order may not claim for the work he has done before its transfer[4], as a legal aid order was already in force.

Attendance at formal remand hearings[5]

Unless a solicitor has a representation to make on the client's behalf, or the hearing provides a convenient and cost-efficient opportunity to take further instructions from a client who is remanded in custody, attendance at formal remand hearings should not normally be necessary. Consequently claims for unnecessary attendances will not be allowed on taxation.

Attendance on clients remanded at a distance from a court at which the solicitor usually practices[6]

Where a client is remanded in custody by a court at which the solicitor usually practices the costs of attending on the client will normally be allowed, even if the client is held at a considerable distance from the solicitor's office, unless the nature of the case makes it practical for instructions to be taken at court, or the client is to be released on bail or moved to a local place of remand. All the circumstances of the case will fall to be considered when determining such claims, including the nature and seriousness of the case.

20 CRIMLA 2.
1 CRIMLA 3.
2 CRIMLA 4.
3 CRIMLA 6.
4 CRIMLA 29.
5 CRIMILA 7.
6 CRIMLA 9.

Attendance on clients remanded in custody from a court at which the solicitor does not usually practice[7]

The solicitor may be permitted to claim for attending on clients remanded in custody if all the circumstances of the case merit this and it is not practical to take instructions in court. Similar considerations apply as to the previous situation.

Separate representation by counsel[8]

Where two or more defendants are represented by the same firm of solicitors and the circumstances of the case justify it, separate advocates may represent each of the defendants in court. In-house solicitors, solicitor agents or assigned counsel may be used. The fact that this provision exists to enable separate representation in court does not affect the rules that regulate when a solicitor should withdraw from a case because of a conflict of interests between two or more clients. Neither will the use of separate representation automatically justify the payment of an enhanced rate[9].

Compliance with a court order or an undertaking given to the court[10]

Any costs or disbursements incurred in complying with an order of the magistrates' court or an undertaking given to such a court will be assessed in accordance with the normal rules. As a consequence of this decision a solicitor could not overcome a refusal by the Legal Aid Board's Area Committee to allow him to incur specific expenditure on the grounds that he had given an undertaking to the court or the step had been ordered by the court. The risk that costs incurred in this way will not be met on taxation remains a valid one.

Use of enquiry agents[11]

All the circumstances of the reasons for use of an enquiry agent will be considered when determining whether his fee will be allowed on taxation. Where the taxing authority determines that no profit costs should be allowed in respect of the instruction of the enquiry agent, they may still allow an amount in respect of the actual fee incurred.

Witness expenses[12]

Witness expenses are not payable out of the legal aid fund unless a court has directed that they may not be claimed from central funds[13]. Provisions exist which allow witnesses to recover their costs and amounts for loss of earnings from central funds irrespective of whether the defendant is successful in his defence or not, or whether they appeared to give evidence on behalf of the prosecution or the defence[14].

In summary, if a solicitor is to ensure he is remunerated for all the work he does in relation to the defence of his client, he must be certain that work is

7 CRIMLA 21.
8 CRIMLA 11.
9 CRIMLA 17.
10 CRIMLA 27.
11 CRIMLA 25.
12 CRIMLA 15.
13 S 25(3) of the Legal Aid Act 1988.
14 Regs 15 and 16 of the Costs in Criminal Cases (General) Regulations 1986.

allowable per se, or alternatively seek the authority of the Legal Aid Board to ensure it will be allowed on taxation. Where an unusual or particularly expensive step is contemplated such authority may be sought as a matter of right, even if it does not relate to the obtaining of a report or transcript[15]. Such authority might be to confirm that travel to a distant court will be allowed or in exceptional cases to enable a solicitor to travel abroad to conduct relevant enquiries in a foreign country, if that is merited by the facts of the case.

THE POWER TO MAKE DEFENDANT'S COSTS IN RELATION TO LEGALLY ASSISTED PERSONS

The general rule is that where a legal aid order has been made, the legal representative(s) that provides representation under the order may not receive or be a party to the making of any payment from any other source other than those made from the legal aid fund by the Legal Aid Board or from the Lord Chancellors[16]. The latter case will embrace those circumstances where payment is made by the central taxing units attached to the Crown Court who tax those bills that relate to criminal cases concluded in the Crown Court. This general rule therefore requires that payments may only be received by the solicitor if they are payments under the order and he may only be a party to the making of payments to a third party if they are payments funded from the order.

The only exceptions to this rule, within the legal aid regulations, are where expenses or fees are incurred in the following circumstances:

(i) preparing, obtaining or considering a report, opinion or further evidence from an expert witness or some other sources; or
(ii) producing transcripts of tape recorded interviews or shorthand notes made in any proceedings, including interviews at police stations,

provided that an application has been made to the Legal Aid Board's Area Committee to incur such and expenditure and that application has been refused.

If either of the above criteria is satisfied, payments may be accepted by the solicitor to cover the expenditure that was not authorised by the Area Committee and would not therefore be payable on taxation under the legal aid order. This provision cannot be used to cover work done before the issue of a certificate where an existing order was revoked or the claim is in relation to work done prior to the transfer of an existing order[17].

The general rule prevents solicitors using the legal aid scheme as a form of a contingency insurance scheme, so that they hold a legal aid order, but if the client is successful in his defence and is eligible to claim his expenses under a defendant's costs order no claim is made under the legal aid as a claim under the defendant's costs order will ensure the solicitor is remunerated at a higher rate.

The question arises as to whether a person is legally aided, and therefore subject to the application of the general rule in circumstances where the expenses he incurs are not payable under the scope of a legal aid order. For the sake of clarity several distinct circumstances will be considered.

15 Reg 54(1)(e) of the Legal Aid in Criminal and Care Preceedings (General) Regulations 1989.
16 Reg 55(a) of the Legal Aid in Criminal and Care Proceedings (General) Regulations 1989.
17 CRIMLA 8 and CRIMLA 29.

1. Pre-legal aid order costs – no change in the legally assisted person's circumstances[18]

As has been seen above, the date on which the legal aid order is granted and becomes effective is the date upon which the decision to grant is made and no earlier. In the absence of the rule that enables urgent work undertaken before the order was made to be remunerated as if it were work done under the order, it would be a straightforward approach to say that the person was legally aided only from the date of the order and in that case any costs incurred prior to that date were not costs of a legally aided person and so not subject to the rule that prevents payment of them being made from a source other than legal aid.

The existence of the rule complicates the position that prevents the application of such a straightforward solution. Additional complications are imposed by the fact that many persons who subsequently receive a legal aid order will have received assistance from the green form scheme or ABWOR prior to the grant of the order. The question arises as to whether assistance provided under these schemes qualifies as 'legal aid' for the purposes of the rule that would exclude payments from other sources.

In such cases some solicitors argue that pre-certificate costs are claimable from central funds if they decline to submit a claim under the green form. Their argument appears to be that it is part of the adversarial process to maximise their claim for costs. This approach appears to be flawed as it creates a situation of contingency funding not authorised by the current Law Society rules. A 'Rule 15 letter' is the standard device employed by solicitors that meets the requirement that a solicitor advises his client, in writing, of the exact terms under which he is retained and the fees that will be charged[19]. If payment is to made on a privately funded basis, such a letter will confirm to a court or a taxing master whether or not the defendant is contractually responsible for the fees claimed in any claim for pre-legal aid order costs from central funds. If there is no contractual liability for such costs there is an argument that the expenses have not been properly incurred and if they have been so incurred they fall outside the criteria that would enable them to be met from central funds[20].

Such claims may also be ethically doubtful if the solicitor had failed or omitted to advise his client of the availability of legal, as a solicitor is required to consider and advise his client where legal aid is, or is likely to be, available to him[1]. In this context it is clear from the terminology of the rule, that the term 'legal aid' extends to all forms of advice and assistance under the Legal Aid Act 1988. If the solicitor has failed to do this, or has provided the advice and then failed to act promptly upon his client's instructions so that legal advice and assistance ceased to be available, it could be argued that the State has no obligation to underwrite expenses not recoverable under a legal aid order through the solicitor's failure to act properly. It would clearly be inappropriate to reward such incompetence at a higher rate as would be the case if the payment were made under a defendant's costs order.

Where courts or taxing officials form the opinion that the claim for costs is merely in order to maximise the solicitor's costs there are two distinct ways in

18 See also *Applications for Pre-Legal Aid Certificate Costs – A Lawful Order?*, James N R Parry (1995) 104 JP&LGL 104.
19 Rule 15 of the Solicitors' Practice Rules 1990.
20 S 16(6) of the Prosecution of Offences Act 1985.
1 Para 5.01 of the The Guide to the Professional Conduct of Solicitors, 6th edn.

which they might approach the problem. The first would be for the court to refuse to exercise its discretion to make an order for defendant's costs to be paid from central funds. The second method is for the appropriate taxing authority to require the solicitor to produce proof that a contractual obligation existed that would compel the legally assisted person to pay such costs that have been incurred, but are not recoverable under the legal aid order, and that full and proper consideration was given to the client's eligibility for legal advice, assistance and representation under the Legal Aid Act 1988. If the solicitor cannot produce such proof, it seems open to the taxing authority to conclude that the costs were not properly incurred and therefore that they should be disallowed on taxation.

2. Pre-legal aid order costs – where the circumstances of the applicant have changed so as to make him eligible for legal aid

There may occasionally be circumstances where a defendant to criminal charges who has initially financed his defence from his own funds suffers some financial catastrophe, such as bankruptcy, that makes him eligible for legal aid at some point during the proceedings. If his defence were successful, it would be inequitable if he could not recover his own expenses from central funds. In this instance proof will probably exist that the client had agreed, to pay his solicitor's costs and supporting information would generally be available to explain the change in the defendant's circumstances. In such circumstances the objections raised in the previous section would not apply. Consequently, it seems perfectly proper for an order from central funds to be made in such circumstances.

3. Witness expenses

Witness expenses are not allowable under a legal aid order and therefore may be properly claimed from central funds under provisions other than the Legal Aid Acted[2].

4. Wasted Costs – orders against legal representatives

The fact that the party to an action is legally aided does not affect the liability of a legal representative for wasted costs as the grant of a legal aid order only affects the rights of third parties in specified circumstances[3]. In deciding whether to make such orders the court must bear in mind the particular vulnerability of legal representatives acting for assisted persons[4].

5. Expenses not covered by the legal aid order

A successful defendant to criminal proceedings may incur some expenses that are not recoverable under a legal aid order. For example, if the proceedings are to be dealt with at a court some distance from the defendant's home he may incur expenses in relation to travel and accommodation that are reasonable in

2 Regs 15 and 16 of the Costs in Criminal Cases (General) Regulations 1986.
3 S 3(1) of the Legal Aid Act 1988.
4 *Ridehalgh v Horsefield* [1994] 3 All ER 848.

their nature having regard to all the circumstances of the case. Whilst there is no provision that enables a defendant to recover lost earnings or contributions he has made in respect of a legal aid order (although these may well be refunded to him – see above) from central funds, some commentators believe that these costs can be recovered under a defendant's costs order[5].

TIME LIMITS AND RELEVANT TAXING AUTHORITIES

Solicitors and counsel are required to submit their claims for costs to the appropriate authority within three months from the conclusion of the criminal proceedings[6]. An exception exists in the case of solicitors undertaking work in the magistrates' court where the legally aided defendant is wanted on warrant. In such cases claims for costs must be submitted no earlier than six weeks after the date on which the warrant was issued and no later than 19 weeks after that date[7].

In any of the above cases the appropriate authority has discretion to accept a claim out of time and extend the time limit in exceptional circumstances, but it may also consider whether or not the reason for the delay is such that it justifies reducing the amount paid on taxations[8].

The appropriate authority is determined by the court in which the proceedings were conducted. They are listed in Figure 3.

FIG 3: DETERMINING THE APPROPRIATE AUTHORITY

NOTE: All references are to the Legal Aid in Criminal and Care Proceedings (General) Regulations 1989

Court	Appropriate Authority	Regulation
Court of Appeal	Registrars of the Court of Appeal	3(1)(a)
Crown Court (Criminal Proceedings)	Officer appointed by the Lord Chancellor – in practice either an officer of the Crown Court or a member of a Central Taxing Unit	3(1)(b)
Crown Court (Appeals from the magistrates' court)	Legal Aid Board	4
Magistrates' courts	Legal Aid Board	3(1)(c)

5 See for example *Greenslade on Costs*, page 10.7.
6 Reg 5(1) of the Legal Aid in Criminal and Care Proceedings (Costs) Regulations 1989 in the case of solicitors and reg 8(1) of the Legal Aid in Criminal and Care Proceedings (Costs) Regulations 1989 in the case of the counsel.
7 Reg 5(1A) of the Legal Aid in Criminal and Care Proceedings (Costs) Regulations 1989.
8 Reg 17(2) of the Legal Aid in Criminal and Care Proceedings (Costs) Regulations 1989.

METHODS OF CLAIMING COSTS

The claim for costs are required to be submitted to the appropriate authority in 'such a form and manner as [the appropriate authority] may direct'[9]. In practice this means the use of one of a number of standard forms, which are available free of charge from local Legal Aid Board Area Offices. These forms are listed at Figure 4.

FIG 4: FORMS FOR CLAIMING COSTS UNDER CRIMINAL LEGAL AID ORDERS

CLAIMAINT	FORM
Assigned counsel	CRIM 11
Unassigned counsel	CRIM 12
Solicitor claiming lower standard fee	CRIM 13
Solicitor claiming higher standard fee or a non-standard fee	CRIM 14 CRIM 15
Application for payment on account (franchise holders only)	CRIM 19

The appropriate authority may also require sight of the case papers and may make such other enquiries as it feels are appropriate in determining the bill.

STANDARD FEES IN MAGISTRATES' COURTS

Standard fees have been introduced in relation to a wide variety of magistrates' court proceedings. The fee payable is largely determined by the category of the work undertaken, although if counsel is assigned or costs are allowed at an enhanced rate the standard fee regime no longer applies[10].

The standard fee is designed to remunerate the solicitor or counsel in respect of his 'core costs', which is any of the following work undertaken in relation to the cased[11].

1. any preparation including listening to or viewing any tape recorded transcripts of police interviews;
2. routine letters and telephone calls;
3. advocacy including bail applications in either a magistrates' court or the Crown Court;
4. work done by a fee earner acting as an agent for the solicitor assigned under the order;
5. unassigned counsel's preparation travelling and waiting time, preparation and advocacy.

9 Regs 5(1) and 8(2) of the Legal Aid in Criminal and Care Proceedings (Costs) Regulations 1989.
10 Para 3, Sch 1, Part III of the Legal Aid in Criminal and Care Proceedings (Costs) Regulations 1989.
11 Para 4(2), Sch 1, Part III of the Legal Aid in Criminal and Care Proceedings (Costs) Regulations 1989.

The categories of standard fee are set out in Figure 5 and determine the level of payment.

FIG 5: CATEGORIES OF STANDARD FEE

	CATEGORY ONE	CATEGORY TWO	CATEGORY THREE
1.	Guilty pleas	Contested trials	Committal proceedings under s 6(2) Magistrates' Courts Act including cases that are withdrawn or discontinued.
2.	Uncontested proceedings arising out a breach of a magistrates' court order but including breaches of a Crown Court probation order, community service order, or suspended sentence.	Proceedings fully prepared for trial in a magistrates' court but disposed of by way of a guilty plea on the date of trial before the opening of the prosecution case.	Committal proceedings discontinued or withdrawn before the court has fixed a date for s 6(1) committal.
3.	Proceedings (other than committal proceedings) which discontinued or withdrawn.	Proceedings fully prepared for trial disposed of by way of the prosecution offering no evidence or a bind over on the date of trial before the prosecution case is opened.	Proceedings transferred under s 4 Criminal Justice Act 1987, or s 53 Criminal Justice Act 1991.
4.	Proceedings (other than committal proceedings) which relate to summary or either way offences which result in a bind over.	Contested proceedings relating to breach of a magistrates' court order (including those Crown Court orders specified in category 1.3)	
5.	Proceedings arising out of a deferment of sentence (including any subsequent sentencing hearing) under s 1 Powers of Criminal Courts Act 1973.	Proceedings where mixed pleas are entered.	

There are two standard fee rates: a lower standard fee and a higher standard fee. The rate which is paid is determined by an assessment of the 'core costs', which have already been identified.

The lower standard fee will be paid where the core costs do not exceed the lower limit[12]. If the costs are within the band between the lower limit and the higher limit the higher standard fee will be paid, but where the higher limit is exceeded a determination will be carried out and the amount actually incurred will be paid[13].

12 See Appendix H, para 4.2, post, for the lower and higher limit rates and the standard fee levels.
13 Reg 7 of the Legal Aid in Criminal and Care Proceedings (Costs) Regulations 1989.

FIG 6: DETERMINING THE STANDARD FEE PAYABLE

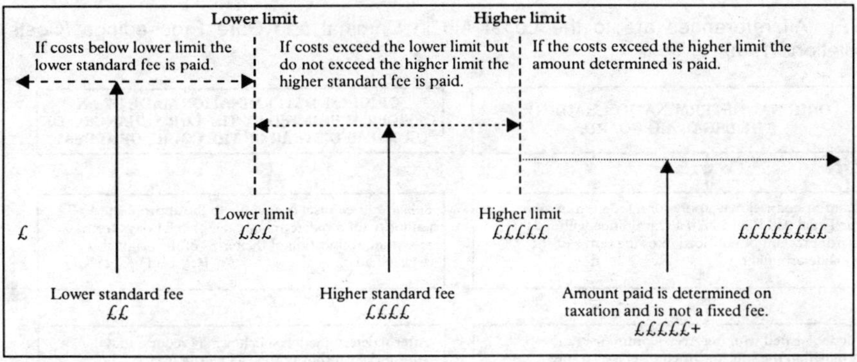

In addition to the standard fee, payments will be made in respect of travelling and waiting of both fee earners and unassigned counsel and any disbursements incurred in relation to the conduct of the case[14].

Where a solicitor represents more than one defendant, or a defendant has more than one charge, a single standard fee will be paid that will embrace the work done in respect of all matters that amount to 'one case'[15]. The phrase 'a case' means in this context, *'proceedings relating to one or more charges . . . which are preferred or laid at the same time or which are founded on the same facts or which form part of a series of offences'*[16]. It has been established by the Legal Aid Board's Costs Appeals Committee that the fact that the all the offences are offences of dishonesty and were disposed of on the same day does not, in its self, indicate that there is only one case[17]. In applying the test the Legal Aid Board recommend applying three separate elements of the definitions[18]:

(i) Were the charges preferred or laid at the same time? – in other words do the charges appear on the same charge sheet or in the same information, even though they may be dissimilar? If the charges were preferred or laid at the same time only one fixed fee will be payable.
(ii) Do the charges have a common factual origin? – this would apply to charges laid as alternatives, for example simple possession of drugs and possession of drugs with intent to supply. In such cases one, fixed fee would be paid in respect of both charges.
(iii) Do the charges form part of a series of offences? – here the test is satisfied if some similar features exist which suggest the charges arise from a series of similar conduct that would allow them to be dealt with together, even though they may have been laid in different magistrates' courts.

In applying this test it is immaterial how many legal aid orders exist, that all the hearings were in the same or different courts, or that the matters were heard

14 Reg 6 of the Legal Aid in Criminal and Care Proceedings (Costs) Regulations 1989.
15 Reg 5 of the Legal Aid in Criminal and Care Proceedings (Costs) Regulations 1989.
16 Para 1, Sch 1, Part III of the Legal Aid in Criminal and Care Proceedings (Costs) Regulations 1989.
17 CRIMLA 40.
18 Legal Aid Handbook 1995, The Legal Aid Board, p 156.

FIG 7: CHALLENGING A DETERMINATION OF COSTS UNDER A CRIMINAL LEGAL AID ORDER

NOTE: All references are to the Legal Aid in Criminal and Care Proceedings (Costs) Regulations 1989.

ORIGINAL DETERMINATION MADE BY THE LEGAL AID BOARD.

↓

Solicitor or counsel may apply for a redetermination by the Legal Aid Board's Area Committee within 21 days from receipt of notification of the terms of the original determination. Reg. 12(1).

↓

If still dissatisfied with the Area Committee's determination the solicitor or counsel may apply to the Area Committee to certify a point of general importance. Reg. 13(1).

↓

If a point of general importance is certified by the Area Committee the colicitor or counsel may appeal to the Legal Aid Board within 21 days from the date upon which he received notification that a point of general importance had been certified. Reg. 13(2).

↓

The Legal Aid Board may:
(i) reverse
(ii) affirm, or
(iii) amend

the decision of the Area Committee. Reg 13(3).

ORIGINAL DETERMINATION MADE BY AN OFFICER APPOINTED BY THE LORD CHANCELLOR OR THE REGISTRAR OF THE COURT OF APPEAL.

↓

Solicitor or counsel may apply to the appropriate authority for a redetermination within 21 days from receipt of notification of the terms of the original determination. Reg 14(1) & (2).

↓

After redetermination solicitor may request that the appropriate authority state its reason for the determination and the authority must comply with such a request, if it was made within 21 days of notification of the decision. Reg 14(7).

↓

If still dissatisfied the solicitor or counsel may appeal against the determination to a taxing master within 21 days from the date which the reasons were received. Reg 15(1).

↓

The Lord Chancellor may make representations to the Taxing Master, if it is in the public interest to do so, but a right of reply is given to the appellant. Reg 15(6)–(9).

↓

The Taxing Master may alter or confirm the decision and shall notify the appellant, the appropriate authority and the Lord Chancellor of his decision. Reg 15(12) & (13).

↓

Costs incured in bringing an appeal before a Master may be allowed unless the decision challenged was confirmed or reduced. Reg 15(14).

↓

If still dissatisfied the solicitor or counsel may apply to the Taxing Master to certify a point of general impotance, within 21 days of receipt of notificiation of the Taxing Masters decision. Reg 16(1) & (2).

↓

Where the Taxing Master certifies a point of general importance the solicitor or counsel may appeal to the High Court within 21 days from the date upon which notification of the Taxing Master's decision to certify the point of general importance was received. The Lord Chancellor will be the respondant to the poceedings. Reg 16(3)–(6).

on the same day. In applying the test each set of charges must be examined on an individual basis to see if that particular set of matters constitutes a series.

These tests will be applied by the Legal Aid Board as they are the appropriate authority to determine costs in the magistrates' court.

AVENUES OF APPEAL AGAINST TAXATION

Where a legal representative is dissatisfied with the determination of his fee by the appropriate authority he may challenge the decision and seek a re-determination. The procedure that must be adopted differs depending on who the appropriate authority is. These routes of appeal have been summarised in Figure 7.

Where an appeal is lodged the general rule is that the authority charged with determining the appeal may demand to see such documentation to support the claim as it feels appropriated. Where applications are made to the Legal Aid Board's Area Committee the Committee will usually allow the solicitor or counsel to appear before it to make any oral representations that are considered necessary; however, this right is not contained within the regulations and the Committee will usually give its decision at a later date, after private consideration of the solicitor's representations.

Chapter Twelve

Criminal Legal Aid Scheme – Future Developments

This chapter assesses the future of the criminal legal aid scheme in the light of the Government's White Paper, '*Striking the Balance*'[1].

THE PROBLEMS

In common with the legal aid scheme generally, criminal legal aid has enjoyed a bad press. Cases where legal aid has been granted to individuals who are apparently wealthy, such as the Maxwell brothers, Azil Nadir and Darius Guppy have provoked media outrage which has been coupled with further publicity surrounding the conviction of a minority of solicitors who have chosen to abuse the criminal legal aid scheme.

This public disquiet has come at a time when the government has been facing its own internal difficulties in relation to legal aid generally. The Committee of Public Accounts 34th Report[2] drew attention to legal aid fraud, which it attributed to two material problems; solicitors grossly overstating their claims and claimants understating their means[3]. This report prompted the appearance of Sir Thomas Legg KCB, QC, the Permanent Secretary and Clerk of the Crown in Chancery, Lord Chancellor's Department and Mr Steve Orchard before the Parliamentary Public accounts Committee on 6 March 1995 in order to allow them, in part, to explain why the legal aid account was not certified by the Comptroller and Auditor General for four years running[4]. Sir Thomas Legg attributed the qualification of the accounts as a result of the failure of justices' clerks properly to apply the means test by securing the necessary provision of documentary evidence[5].

The application of the interest of justice test was also called into question by the Committee[6], who sought to discover why legal aid appeared to be granted on the differing perceptions of justices' clerks as they assess the seriousness of cases. This was a question that Sir Thomas was unable to answer, save to point to the joint guidance issued by the Legal Aid Board, the Justices' Clerks Society and the Lord Chancellor's Department[7].

That meeting prompted a direct approach to both the Chairman of the Justices' Clerks Society and the Chairman of the Law Society by letter of 28

1 *Striking the Balance*, Cmd 3305, HMSO, June 1996.
2 House of Commons Paper HC282, HMSO.
3 Para 28.
4 Para 156 of the Minutes of Evidence taken before the Committee of Public Accounts, 6 March 1995.
5 Ibid, paras 159–168.
6 Ibid, paras 20–25.
7 '*Guidance on the Interests of Justice Test for the Grant of Criminal Legal Aid*', May 1994 (see Appendix A2).

April 1995 in which Sir Thomas sought to remind the profession of the requirements of the Legal Aid Act and its subordinate legislation, and seek co-operation to ensure its proper application. In addition, audits have been carried out in magistrates' courts of their legal aid operations to establish whether there has been any improvement in the standards of compliance. Despite these initiatives it is widely predicted that the 1995/6 accounts will again be qualified, the first time that a government department has suffered this misfortune for five consecutive years.

In addition to these problems, the government has been concerned at the rising costs of the legal aid scheme. Figure 1 shows the increase in expenditure of the criminal legal aid scheme, but corresponding increases have also taken place in relation to the civil scheme, where expenditure increased from under £100 million in 1984/85 to over £600 million in 1995/96. This increase in expenditure has proved difficult to finance at a time of public spending restraint.

FIG 1: INCREASE IN COSTS – CRIMINAL LEGAL AID FROM 1984/5 to 1994/5

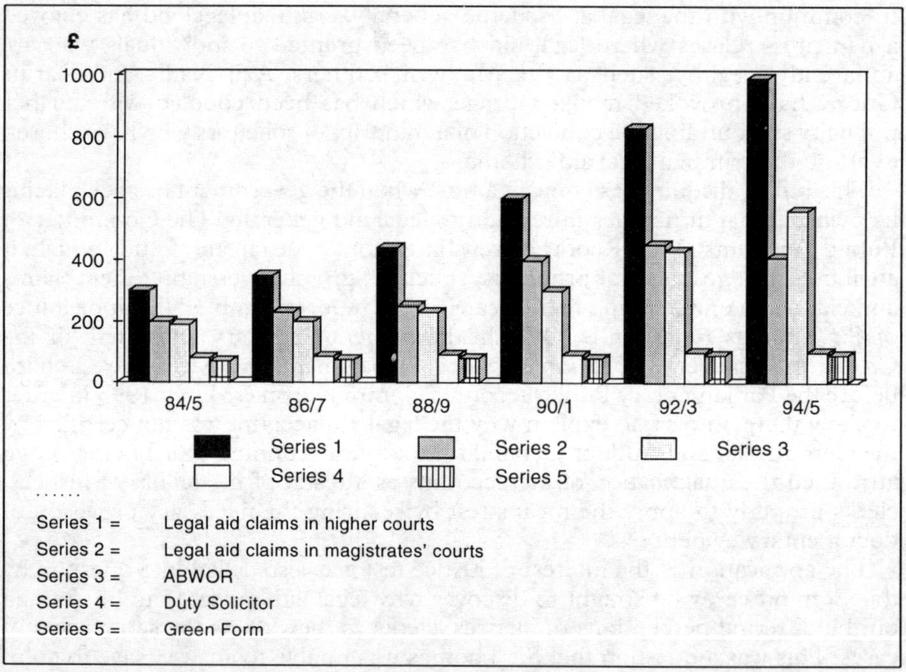

In order to overcome these problems and identify solutions, the government has undertaken a discussion process through publication of two Green Papers[8], which have prompted much discussion within the profession and the media.

THE SOLUTIONS

While the United Kingdom remains a signatory to the European Convention on Human Rights[9] an obligation exists to supply legal representation to persons

8 '*Legal Aid for the Apparently Wealthy*' and '*Legal Aid – Targeting Need*'.
9 See Appendix B.

charged with criminal offences where the interests of justice require that they are represented but where they cannot afford to provide such representation themselves. This requirement limits the power of central government to abolish the scheme in its entirety and leaves it with the burden of producing a cost-efficient and effective system that provides representation to those who need it. The Government's proposals to do this are contained within the White Paper '*Striking the Balance*'.

The key points within the White Paper in relation to criminal legal aid are:

(i) Contracting for routine criminal cases.
(ii) Restricting freedom of choice to any firm who is contracted to provide representation in criminal cases.
(iii) Establishing contracts for Crown Court cases on a cost per case basis.
(iv) Providing one-off contracts for very expensive cases.
(v) The current interests of justice test will be retained.
(vi) The Legal aid Board will assume responsibility for administering the test and determining applications.
(vii) Advice and assistance at police stations will continue to be free.
(viii) Fixed contributions will be paid for persons not on a passporting benefit during the early stages of a case, whilst those on passporting benefits will receive representation free.
(ix) More substantial help will be based on an in depth assessment of means.

Whilst the White Paper is short on the detail of how such measures are to be implemented it is clear that many of the proposals will require primary legislation. It is also a matter of fact that amendments to the legal aid scheme must provide legal assistance to those who are charged with a criminal offence but cannot afford to provide legal representation themselves. In this regard the Government's decision not to amend the interests of justice criteria is a very welcome step to ensuring the future of a legal aid scheme of some kind.

Any statement of policy by a Government facing an imminent election is one that may not be implemented. In this instance, however, the Opposition have broadly welcomed the measures proposed in the document and Paul Boateng, the opposition spokesman on legal affairs, is quoted as saying that these proposals do not hit lawyers hard enough[10].

The move towards the award of block contracts to franchised firms will force those who have been reluctant to consider franchising to do so quickly, because if they do not there will little chance of retaining any of the existing legal aid market. Newly formed firms will also face the difficulty of having to be established before they can obtain contracts. Given that over 95% of defendants to criminal charges receive legal aid there will be little prospect of such firms establishing a profitable criminal practice without the certainty of a block contract.

There must also be some doubt as to the advisability of removing the interests of justice test away from magistrates' courts to the Legal Aid Board. The Legal Aid Board is a bureaucracy that has been criticised for its delays in considering civil legal aid applications. In criminal cases where legal aid is needed, it is required quickly in order to minimise the period spent in custody before trial and to ensure that relevant evidence is preserved where necessary. If there are delays in the process of such applications, the inevitable consequence is that a

10 '*Striking the Wrong Note*', Roger Smith, Law Society Gazette 93/26 (10.7.96).

benefit that is designed to protect the individual from the overbearing power of the state will achieve the opposite and create injustice.

Magistrates' courts have a proportion of their funds determined on the basis of the length of time that cases take from inception to conclusion, and recognise that one of the features that delay cases is delay in legal aid being granted, whereas it is hard to see what incentive exists to encourage the Legal Aid Board to efficiently process such applications. One proposal being considered is that the franchisee should be permitted to grant legal aid. If such a proposal is adopted, great pressure would be placed upon the monitors of the scheme to ensure the quality of such decisions was not motivated by financial gain on the part of the service provider.

The Board is also unlikely to be able to respond adequately to local sentencing patterns as it will not have the benefit of direct liaison with the court. This may lead to legal aid being granted in cases where magistrates would not impose a severe sentence and refused in other cases that will be regarded by a bench in one locality as being much more serious than in another. If the Board adopts the views of the harshest bench in order to remove doubts as to when legal aid should be granted, the likely consequence will be an increase in the number of legal aid orders granted.

Despite the problems that may arise in implementing the proposed changes there is one further argument that mitigates against them which arises from the Government's own figures. Since 1992 the cost of criminal legal aid has levelled

FIG 2: COMPARISON BETWEEN THE COSTS OF CIVIL LEGAL AID AND CRIMINAL LEGAL AID FROM 1992/3 TO 1995/6[11]

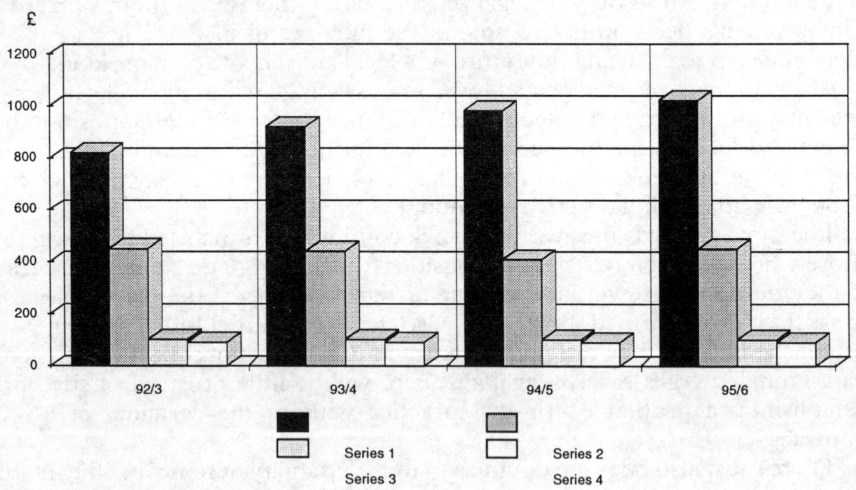

Series 1 = Cost of civil legal aid
Series 2 = Cost of criminal legal aid
Series 3 = Cost of duty solicitor scheme
Series 4 = Cost of green form scheme

11 Source: Chart C(ii) '*Striking the Balance*' (ibid).

out, whereas the costs in civil cases has continued to grow. If this trend is maintained, the existing fixed fee structure may in its self be sufficient to attain the Government's aims.

Some doubt must remain as to whether these proposals will improve the legal aid scheme by preventing abuse of it by claimants or those who rely on it for payment or whether they will merely impose a new administrative regime on the existing scheme.

Appendix A

Guidance and Circulars issued by the Lord Chancellor's Department

Appendix A1

Legal Aid in Criminal Proceedings

Legal Aid in Criminal Proceedings

Guidance on the procedures for considering applications to magistrates' courts for an initial grant of legal aid

MAY 1996

This "decision tree" is issued by the Lord Chancellor's Department, the Legal Aid Board and the Justices' Clerks' Society. It is designed to provide at-a-glance reference both to the statutory provisions governing the grant of criminal legal aid and to good practice guidance. It is not a statement of the law, but is intended for use in conjunction with the relevant statutory material and guidance.

Reference to the following guidance is made in this document:

- **Interests of justice test for the grant of criminal legal aid**
  (issued jointly by the Lord Chancellor's Department, the Justices' Clerks' Society and the Legal Aid Board, 3 May 1994) ***APPENDIX A***
- **Recording of reasons**
  (issued by the Lord Chancellor's Department, 24 March 1995) ***APPENDIX B***
- **Administration of legal aid in magistrates' courts**
  (issued by the Lord Chancellor's Department, 1 April 1992, as amended 26 June 1992) ***APPENDIX C***
- **Changes to the Legal Aid in Criminal and Care Proceedings (General) Regulations 1989**
  (issued by the Lord Chancellor's Department, 16 August 1993) ***APPENDIX D***
- **Calculation of legal aid contributions 1996/97**
  (issued by the Lord Chancellor's Department, 11 March 1996) ***APPENDIX E***
- **Changes to criminal legal aid means testing to come into effect on 1 June 1996**
  (issued by the Lord Chancellor's Department, May 1996) ***APPENDIX F***
- **The Justices' Clerks' Accounting Manual (JCAM)**
  (issued by the Lord Chancellor's Department)
- **The Magistrates' Association Sentencing Guidelines (MASG)**
  (issued by the Magistrates' Association)
- **The Legal Aid Good Practice Guide**
  (issued by the Justices' Clerks' Society) **(JCSGPG)**

Abbreviations of statutory material:

LAA 1988	Legal Aid Act 1988
1989 Regs	Legal Aid In Criminal and Care Proceedings (General) Regulations 1989 (as amended)
PCCA 1973	Powers of Criminal Courts Act 1973
CJA 1982	Criminal Justice Act 1988
CYPA 1933	Children and Young Persons Act 1933

Other abbreviations:

A	Applicant
Appn	Application

Written and Oral Applications

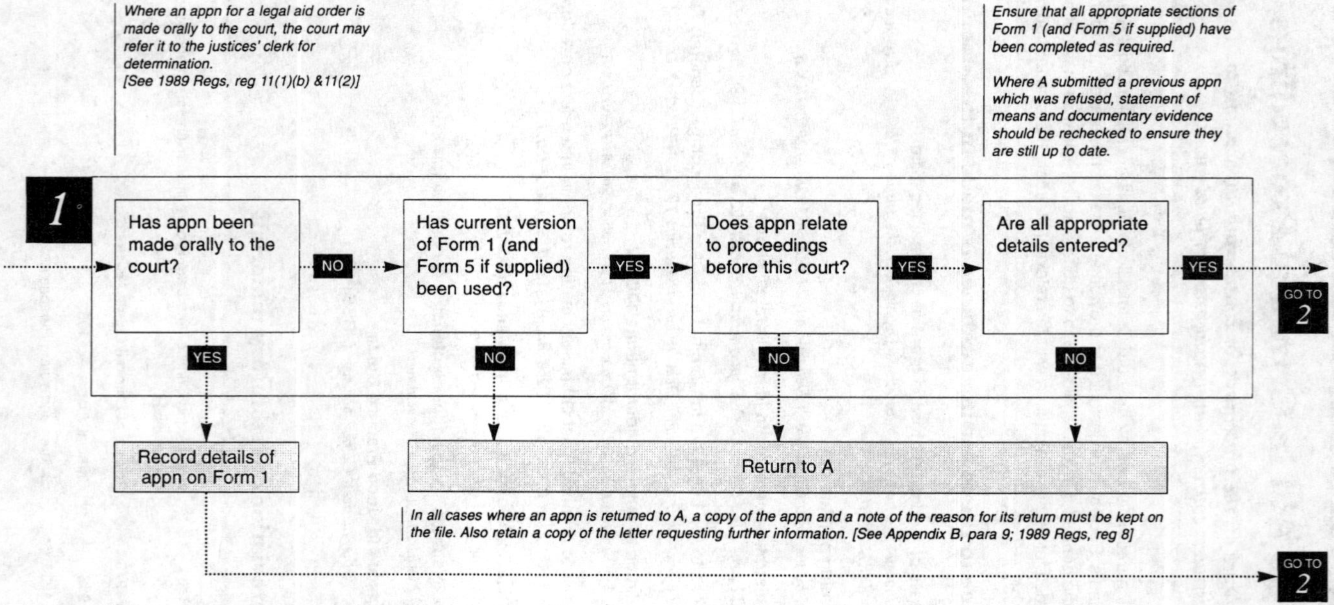

Assessment of Means PASSPORTING BENEFITS

LAA 1988 Section 21(5)

Passporting Benefits:
Currently income support, family credit and disability working allowance. (From 7/10/96 also income based job seeker's allowance.) If an applicant can prove receipt of any of these benefits, a statement of means is not required, and no contribution is payable.
[See 1989 Regs, regs 23(4)(c) and 26(3)]

Proof of receipt of benefit could be an order book specifying the benefit or, in the case of family credit and disability working allowance, the letter notifying the award of the benefit. In the absence of any other evidence, ask A to obtain a stamped confirmation from his/her local Benefits Agency Office (or from 7/10/96 a jobcentre in the case of income based job seekers allowance). [See 1989 Regs, reg 23(4)(c) and Appendix D, para 3 (i)(a)]. Form 1, section 5 requires A to attach documentary evidence of passporting benefits and provides for A to authorise the court to make enquiries of the local Benefits Agency Office to confirm receipt of benefit. If documentary evidence is not provided A must complete Form 5. [See Appendix F]

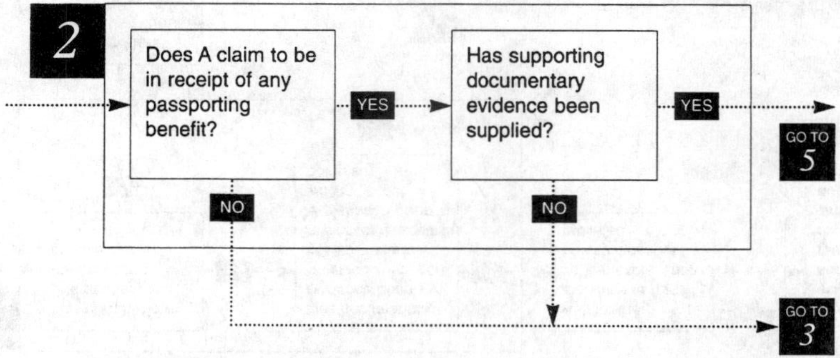

(**Remember:** check all statements of means and evidence supplied, including evidence of passporting benefits, for inconsistencies with case papers. See also 1989 Regs, reg 31 re change of circumstances)

Assessment of Means (cont'd) STATEMENT OF MEANS

LAA 1988 Section 21(5)

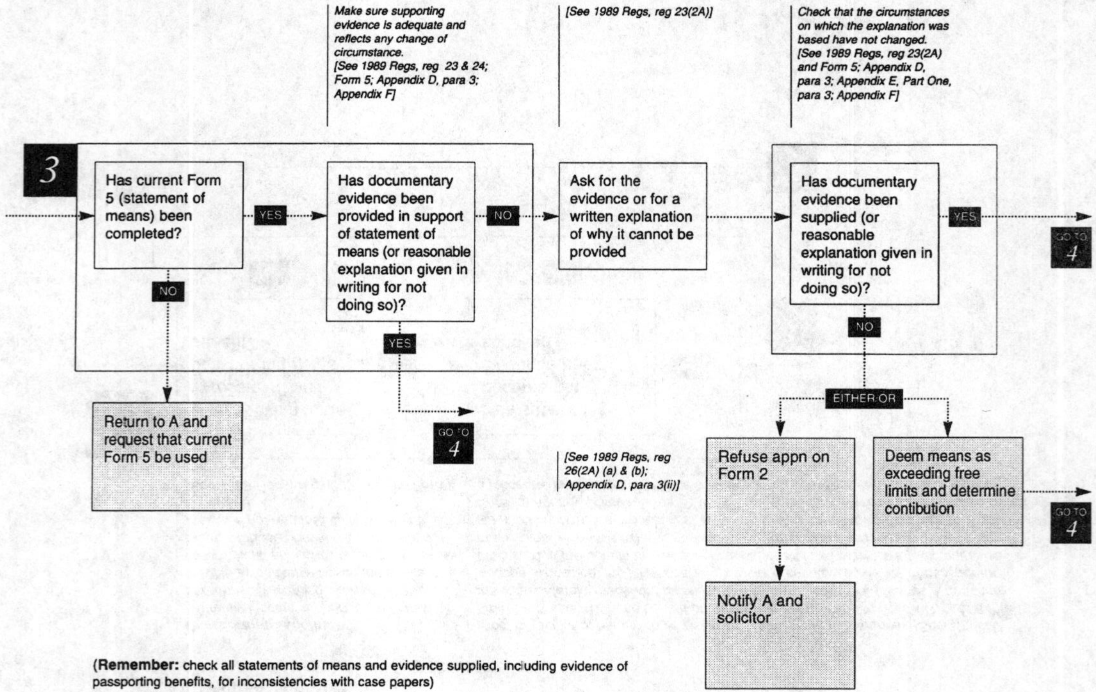

(**Remember:** check all statements of means and evidence supplied, including evidence of passporting benefits, for inconsistencies with case papers)

Assessment of Means (cont'd) CALCULATION OF CONTRIBUTIONS

LAA 1988 Section 21(5) & 23

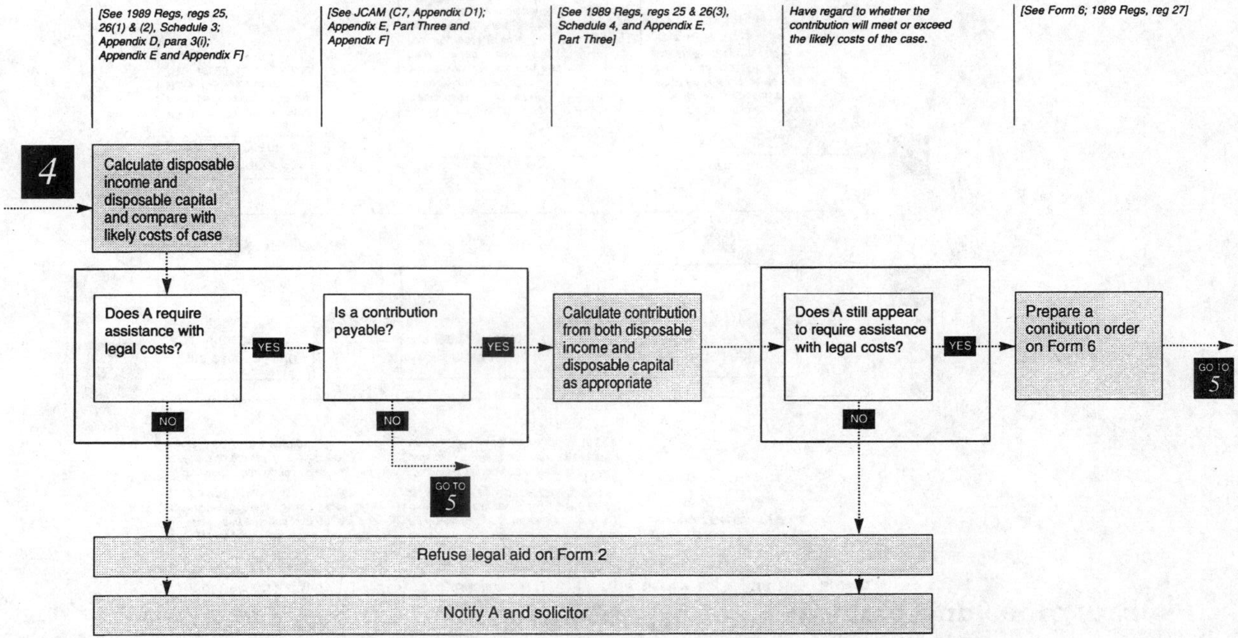

(**Remember:** check all statements of means and evidence supplied, including evidence of passporting benefits, for inconsistencies with case papers)

Statutory Requirement for Legal Aid to be Granted Subject to Means

LAA 1988, Section 21(3) & (11); PCCA 1973, Section 21(1); CYPA 1933, Section 53(2); CJA 1982, Section 3

***Categories** [See Appendix A, para 3]:*
a) A has been charged with murder and committed for trial in Crown Court: LAA 1988 s.21(3)(a);
b) prosecutor has appealed, or applied for leave to appeal, to the House of Lords: LAA 1988 s.21(3)(b);
c) court is about to impose a prison term on A who has not previously served a term of imprisonment: PCCA 1973 s.21(1) as amended by Sch. 16 CJA 1982;
d) court is about to impose a term of detention or make an order for detention under CYPA 1933, s.53(2): CJA 1982 s.3;
e) court is about to pass a sentence of custody for life: CJA 1982 s.3.

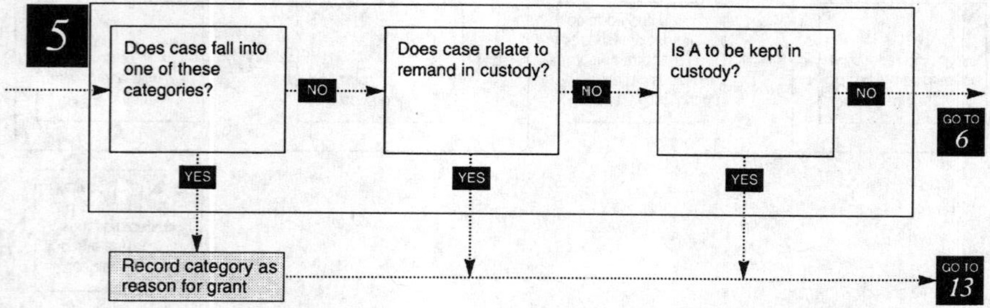

Reasons for grant or refusal must be recorded in full on Form 1 in every case. [See 1989 Regs, reg 8 and Appendix B]

Has A been brought to court in pursuance of a remand in custody/local authority accommodation and may again be remanded or committed in custody, and wishes to be legally represented (having not been legally represented when he was so remanded)? LAA 1988 s.21(3)(c) & 21(11)

Is A to be kept in custody/local authority accommodation for enquiries or a pre-sentence report to be made? LAA 1988 s.21(3) & (11)

Deprivation of Liberty

LAA 1988 Section 22(2)(a); Appendix A, Para 8(a)

Have regard to:
- *the seriousness and circumstances of offence;*
- *aggravating circumstances tending to increase seriousness and the likely sentence;*
- *previous convictions;*
- *mitigating circumstances tending to reduce seriousness and the likely sentence;*
- *any known offence mitigation [See MASG];*
- *any local sentencing guidelines;*
- *the decision in R -v- Liverpool City Magistrates ex parte McGhee*
- *likelihood of either immediate or suspended sentence, detention under CYPA 1933 s.32(2), hospital or guardianship order.*

[See Appendix A, para 8(a)(viii)]

There are statutory restrictions on a court passing certain sentences on a person who is not legally represented. [See Appendix A, para 3(d)]

Legal aid should normally be granted, subject to means, if court is:
a) committing A to Crown Court for sentence; or
b) considering a recommendation for deportation; or
c) considering making a hospital order.
[See Appendix A, para 8(a)(ix)]

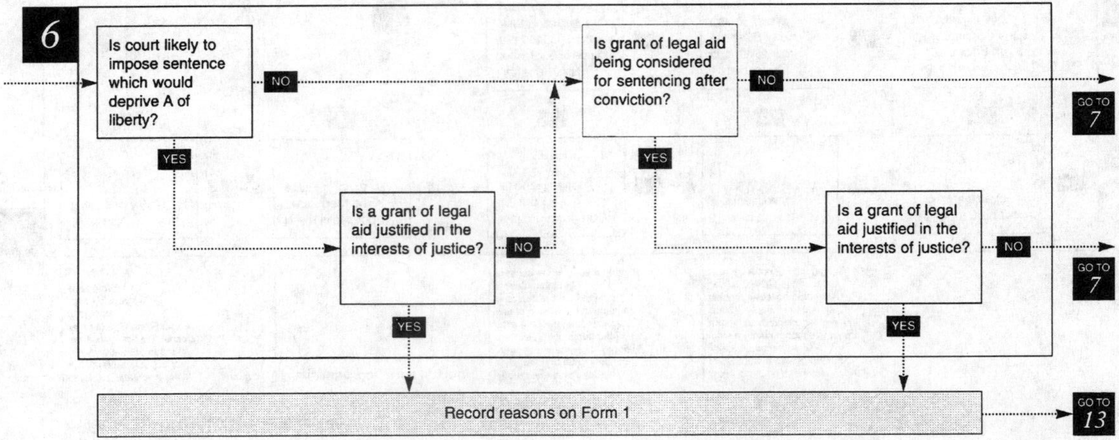

Loss of Livelihood

LAA 1988, Section 22(2)(a); Appendix A, para 8(b)

Consider whether, if the charge is proved, the fact of the conviction or the likely sentence will cause a real risk of A losing his/her livelihood. [See Appendix A, para 8(b)(i)-(iv)]

Disqualification from driving:

There can seldom be justification to grant legal aid to resist a mandatory driving disqualification alone arising from a drink/driving charge unless a cogent argument is put forward that special reasons apply. [See Appendix A, para 8(b)(iv)]

Grant could be justified in exceptional circumstances, eg if A could show that the disqualification could result in a real risk of losing job. It is good practice for courts to request evidence from A that he/she may be dismissed. [See Appendix A, para 8(b)(iv)]

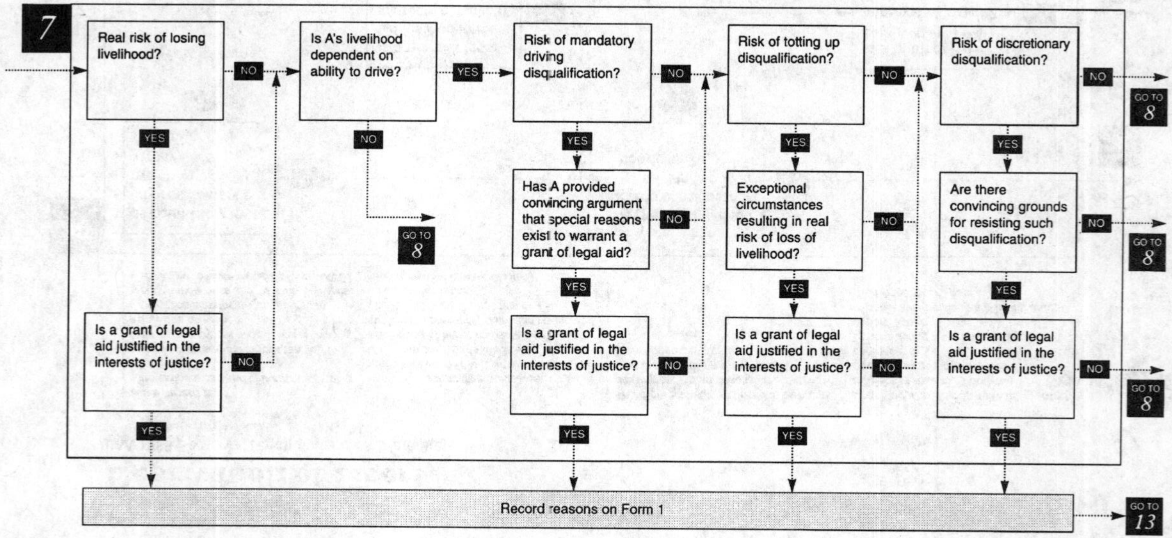

Serious Damage to Reputation

LAA 1988, Section 22(2)(a); Appendix A, para 8(c)

*Consider whether, if the charge is proved, it is likely there would be **serious** damage to A's reputation, because either:*
- *the nature of the offence, or*
- *A's circumstances (other than social class) would lead to disgrace or damage to A's standing, out of proportion to the penalty.*

The damage to reputation will generally only be serious if the offence is serious.

*A previous conviction for a **like** or **more serious** offence will usually mean A has already lost his/her reputation and this criterion will not apply.*
*A previous conviction for **an offence of a different kind** may mean that A's reputation has not already been lost in the way that he/she now risks losing it. Criterion could still apply. [See Appendix A, para 8(c)]*

Factors such as religious background may mean A stands to lose reputation in a way that another person would not.
If A is undertaking professional or vocational training he/she may be at risk of suffering damage to reputation so serious that he/she may lose future livelihood.
[See Appendix A, para 8 (c)(iv) & (v)]

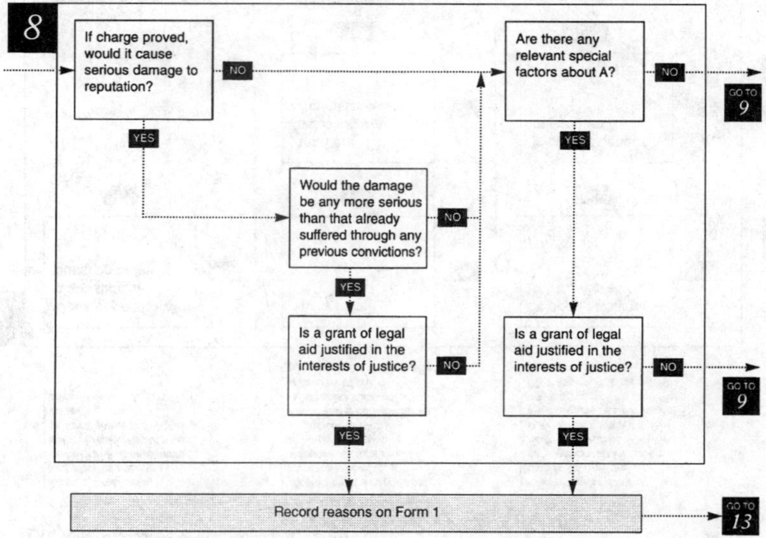

Substantial Question of Law

LAA 1988, Section 22(2)(b); Appendix A, para 9

Does appn show a ***substantial*** *question of law which A cannot handle without representation and which is relevant to A's case?*
[See Appendix A, para 9(i)]

Examples of exceptional circumstances:
• special reasons in drink/driving cases, (e.g. laced drinks)
• sentencing considerations which raise substantial questions of law.
[See Appendix A, para 9(i)]

Preliminary advice can usually be provided satisfactorily under Green Form or by advice from the duty solicitor, except where the charges are serious or complex.
[See Appendix A, para 9(iii)]

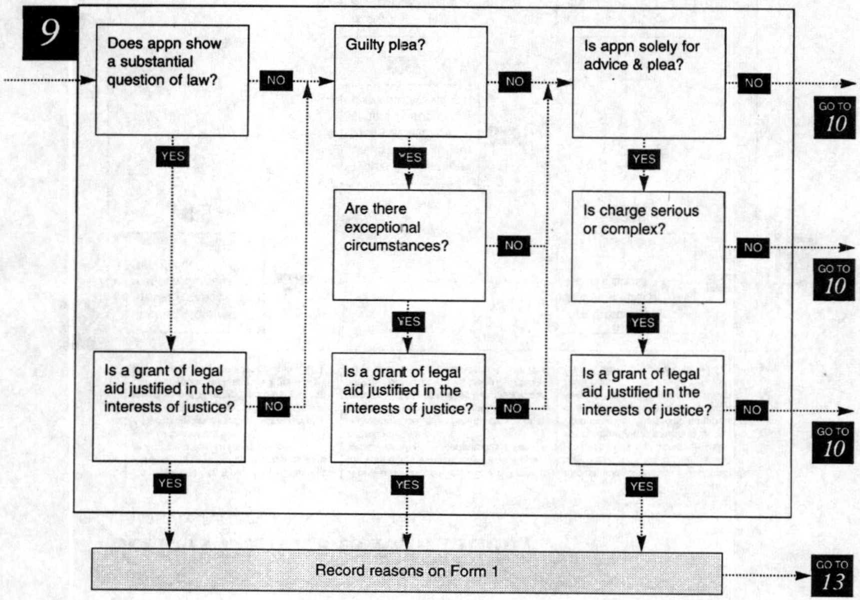

Unable to understand the Proceedings or to State Own Case

LAA 1988, Section 22(2)(c); Appendix A. paras 10(a) & (b)

Have regard to whether A will be able to understand the proceedings or state his/her own case. Consider the complexity of the case. The availability of an interpreter is not normally a sufficient ground for refusal. [See Appendix A, para 10(a)]

Remember, inability to read and write is unlikely in itself to justify grant.

[See Appendix A, para 10(b)]

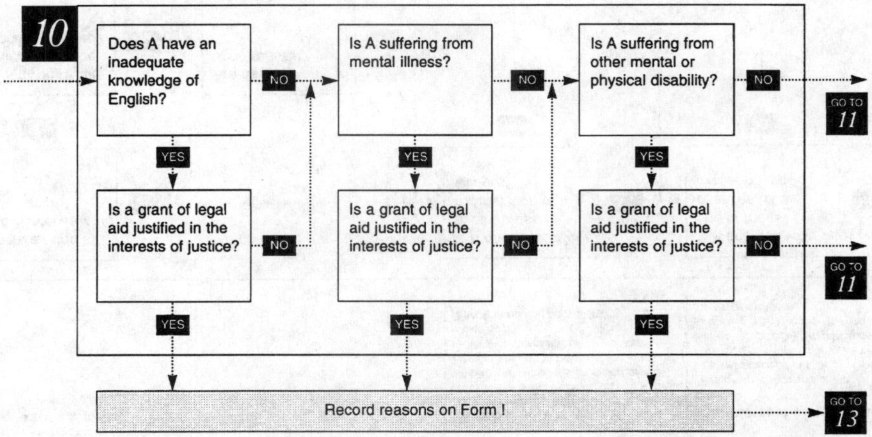

Tracing and Interviewing Witnesses; Expert Cross-Examination of a Witness

LAA 1988, Section 22(2)(d) & (e); Appendix A, paras 11(a) & (b)

[See Appendix A, para 11(a)]

Legal aid should normally be granted (subject to means) when there is a need for professional cross-examination of a witness whether the witness is an expert or not. Have regard to the nature of the evidence rather than the status of the person providing it.
[See Appendix A, para 11(b)(ii)]

The interests of someone other than the accused:

Offences

- *A is charged with one of the offences specified in s.32(2) of the CJA 1988, in which case s.34A of that Act will prohibit him/her cross-examining a child victim or witness to the alleged offence;*
- *A is charged with a sexual offence and it is desirable the complainant is not cross-examined by A;*
- *A is charged with an offence against a very old or very young person.*

[See Appendix A, para 12]

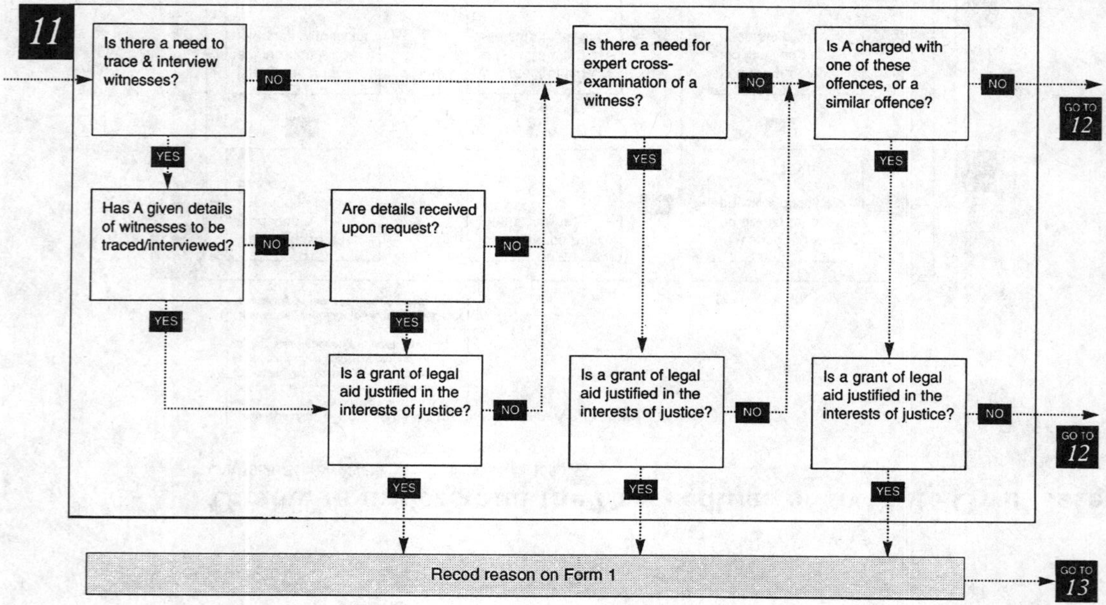

Other factors

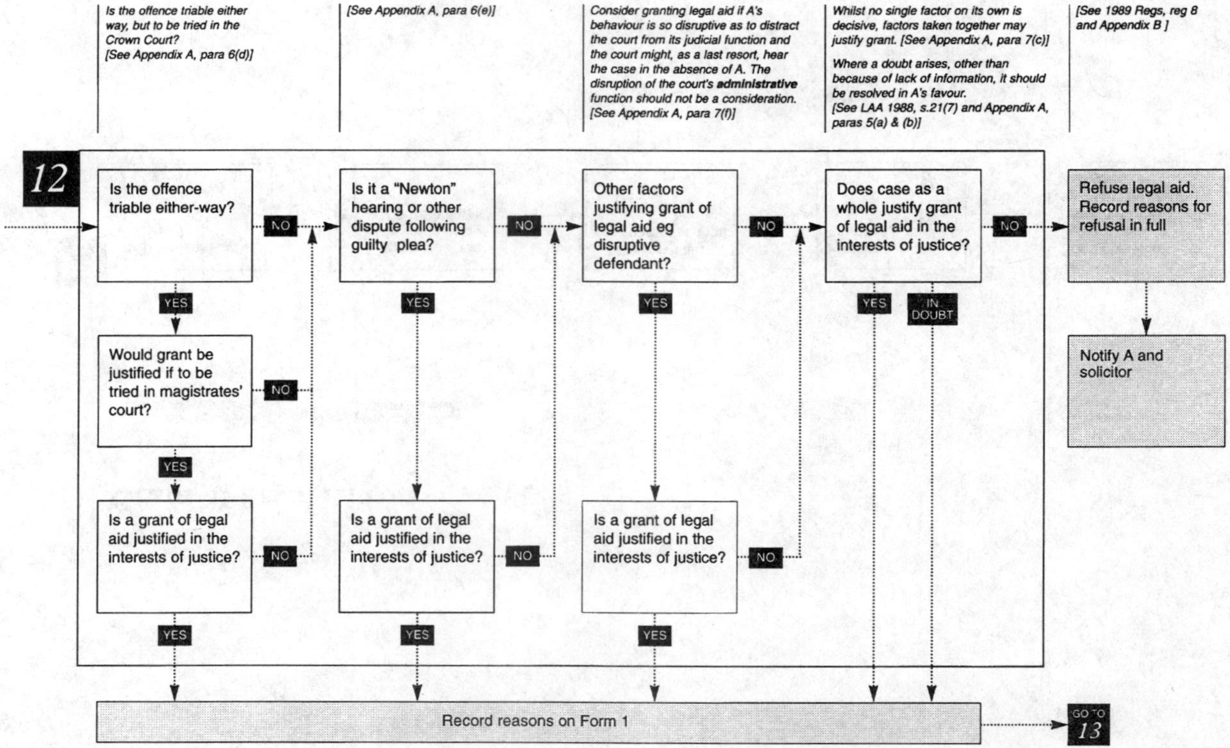

Grant of Legal Aid

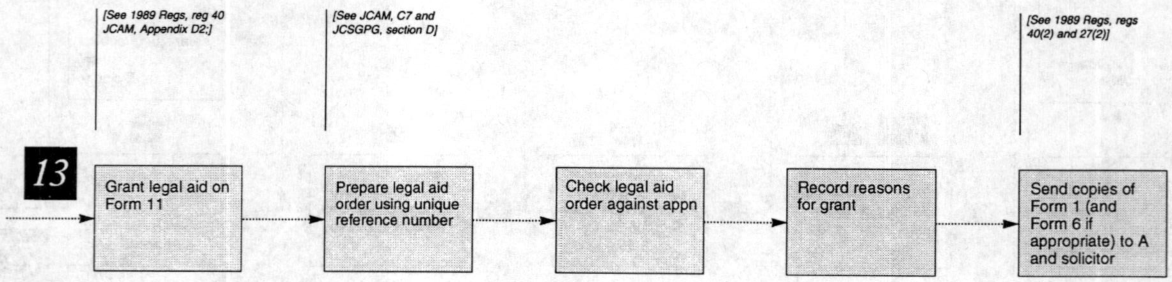

Appendix A2

Guidance on the Interests of Justice Test for the Grant of Criminal Legal Aid

LORD CHANCELLOR'S DEPARTMENT
TREVELYAN HOUSE
GREAT PETER STREET
LONDON SW1P 2BY

Telephone 071 210 8585

3 May 1994

Your reference
Our reference

Dear Sir/Madam,

This guidance is being issued to all magistrates' courts, Crown Court centres and Area Committees of the Legal Aid Board. It will also appear in future issues of the Legal Aid Handbook. It is issued jointly by the Lord Chancellor's Department, the Justices' Clerks' Society and the Legal Aid Board, and is intended for use by those considering applications for criminal legal aid.

The purpose of the guidance is to ensure that criminal legal aid is granted and refused only in accordance with the Legal Aid Act 1988, and that this can be demonstrated clearly through the proper recording of reasons for decisions. It also aims to promote greater consistency between different granting authorities in applying the statutory provisions. It is issued for guidance only; it does not affect the right and responsibility of granting authorities to exercise their discretion in every case in deciding whether it is in the interests of justice to grant legal aid.

It is intended that the guidance should be updated regularly. Any suggestions for revisions, comments on its practical use or questions should be directed to:

Melanie Field
Legal Aid Policy and Administration
Lord Chancellor's Department
Trevelyan House
30 Great Peter Street
London SW1P 2BY

(Telephone 071 210 8545)

Yours faithfully,

S F SMITH
Legal Aid Policy and Administration Division

LEGAL AID GUIDANCE

CONTENTS

Page

Introduction 1

CRITICISMS OF THE PRESENT SYSTEM 1
THE LAW 2
EXERCISE OF DISCRETION 3
INSUFFICIENT INFORMATION 4

LEGAL AID APPLICATIONS – GENERAL CONSIDERATIONS 4

THE INTERESTS OF JUSTICE CRITERIA – DETAILED CONSIDERATIONS 5

SECTION 22(2)(a) 6

Likelihood of deprivation of liberty 6
Loss of livelihood 8
Serious damage to reputation 8

SECTION 22(2)(b) 9

Consideration of a substantial question of law 9

SECTION 22(2)(c) 10

Inadequate knowledge of English 10
Mental or Physical disability 10

SECTION 22(2)(d) 11

Trace and interview witnesses 11
Expert cross examination of a prosecution witness 11

SECTION 22(2)(e) 12

In the interests of someone else that the accused be represented 12

LEGAL AID GUIDANCE

1. *Introduction*

This guidance is issued jointly by the Lord Chancellor's Department, Legal Aid Board and Justices' Clerks' Society, and is recommended for use by justices' clerks and their staff, Area Committees of the Legal Aid Board, the Crown Court and practising lawyers when considering and completing applications for legal aid in criminal proceedings.
It supersedes previous guidance, 'Legal Aid in Criminal Proceedings' and 'Guide-lines for the Consideration of Legal Aid Applications', issued by the Justices' Clerks' Society in 1990 and 1991 respectively. This new guidance is issued following a recent research report, commissioned by the Legal Aid Board, into why grant rates for criminal legal aid vary from court to court[1], the implementation of the Criminal Justice Acts 1991 and 1993 and case-law thereunder, and the Magistrates' Association's Sentencing Guidelines 1993.

2. *Criticisms of the Present System*

Uncertainty over whether legal aid in criminal cases was being granted in the magistrates' courts in accordance with the requirements of the Legal Aid Act 1988 and regulations thereunder resulted in the Comptroller and Auditor-General being unable to approve the Lord Chancellor's Department's Legal Aid Account in 1990/91, 1991/92 and 1992/93. That uncertainty has increased following the findings of the research report referred to at paragraph 1 above.

The report was commissioned by the Legal Aid Board. Its findings were:

- differences between courts in granting legal aid are attributable to the approaches of individual clerks;
- grants are more likely to be made according to court clerks' perception of the seriousness of the case, rather than according to the statutory criteria;
- applications for legal aid are often of poor quality, and the information provided to courts is frequently inadequate.

Consequently, the Lord Chancellor has directed that guidance be issued to remind justices' clerks of the requirements of the Legal Aid Act 1988 and to promote greater consistency of approach to the consideration of criminal legal aid applications generally.

3. *The Law*

(a) Justices' clerks and other granting authorities are reminded that there is no authority to grant legal aid other than in accordance with the Legal Aid Act 1988. They are further reminded that the discretion granted to them under that Act should be exercised reasonably; that is, in a way which takes into

1 R. Young, T. Moloney and A. Sanders, 'In the Interests of Justice? The Determination of Criminal Legal Aid Applications by Magistrates' Courts in England and Wales'. Legal Aid Board; September 1992.

account the relevant factors and does not take into account any that are irrelevant. Relevant factors here include, but are not limited to, the 'interests of justice criteria' discussed from paragraph 7 onwards. The Lord Chancellor will shortly lay before Parliament regulations directing granting authorities to record the specific reasons why they consider that particular applications do or do not meet the criteria under which they have been made. This will apply to applications determined by magistrates, by justices' clerks or by Area Committees of the Legal Aid Board.

(b) Section 21(5) of the Legal Aid Act 1988 provides that legal aid shall not be granted unless the applicant's financial resources are such as to require assistance in meeting the costs of legal representation. Section 21(2) provides that, subject to means, representation may be granted where it is desirable in the interests of justice. Regulation 11(3) of the Legal Aid in Criminal and Care Proceedings (General) Regulations 1989 requires that a legal aid order shall not be made until the court or the justices' clerk has considered the applicant's statement of means, unless the applicant is incapable of furnishing such a statement on account of his physical or mental condition. Guidance on the financial test is contained in the Justices' Clerks Accounting Manual, and in the Circular issued every March to those courts with responsibility for the grant of legal aid. Copies of that Circular are available from the Lord Chancellor's Department on request.

(c) The factors set out in section 22(2) have no application in those instances where statute provides that legal aid *shall* be granted to a person whose means are such that he cannot meet the likely cost of representation. These provisions are:

(3) 'Subject to subsection (5) below, representation must be granted –

(a) where a person is committed for trial on a charge of murder, for his trial;

(b) where the prosecutor appeals or applies for leave to appeal to the House of Lords, for the proceedings on the appeal;

(c) where a person charged with an offence before a magistrates' court –

(i) is brought before the court in pursuance of a remand in custody when he may be again remanded or committed in custody, and

(ii) is not, but wishes to be, legally represented before the court (not having been legally represented when he was so remanded),

for so much of the proceedings as relates to the grant of bail, and

(d) where a person:

(i) is to be sentenced or otherwise dealt with for an offence by a magistrates' court or the Crown Court, and

(ii) is to be kept in custody to enable enquiries or a report to be made to assist the court,

for the proceedings on sentencing or otherwise dealing with him.'

(d) Moreover, there are statutory restrictions on a court passing certain sentences on a person who is not legally represented, unless either he applies for legal aid and the application is refused on the ground that it does not appear his means are such that he requires assistance; or he refuses or fails to apply for legal aid. Accordingly, an applicant whose means are insufficient to meet the cost of legal representation *shall* be granted legal aid before the court passes or makes any of the following sentences or orders:

(i) A sentence of imprisonment on a person who has not been previously sentenced to imprisonment by a court in any part of the UK (Powers of Criminal Courts Act 1973, s.21(1));

(ii) A sentence of detention in a young offender institution under the Criminal Justice Act 1982, s.lA (Criminal Justice Act 1982, s.3);

(iii) A sentence of custody for life under the Criminal Justice Act 1982, s.8(2) (Criminal Justice Act 1982, s.3);

(iv) An order for detention under the Children and Young Persons Act 1933, s.53(2) (Criminal Justice Act 1982, s.3).

4. *Exercise of Discretion*

(a) This guidance is intended to assist those determining applications for the grant of criminal legal aid in the interpretation of the limits of their discretion. It is issued for guidance only. It does not affect the right and responsibility of granting authorities to exercise their discretion in every case in deciding whether the interests of justice test (including the criteria in section 22 of the Legal Aid Act 1988) has been met.

(b) Section 21(7) of the Legal Aid Act 1988 provides that 'where a doubt arises whether representation under this Part should be granted to any person, the doubt shall be resolved in that person's favour'.

5. *Insufficient Information*

(a) If it is not possible to make a proper determination because insufficient information has been provided on the application form, or some detail needs clarification, it is suggested that this does not constitute a 'doubt' for the purposes of section 21(7). In such circumstances, further detail should be requested from the applicant or the applicant's solicitor. Section 21(7) should only come into play if, once all the appropriate information has been provided, a genuine doubt remains as to whether a grant of legal aid should be made.

(b) The granting authority is entitled to sufficient information to enable it to reach a properly informed decision on the grant of legal aid, and is entitled to ask for, and receive, such information. If an application does not contain sufficient information, further details should be sought. When seeking further information, the granting authority may declare to the applicant that the application will not be considered for grant until such time as the information is received and that it would be prudent for him to await a final decision before incurring any further costs.

6. *Legal Aid Applications – General Considerations*

(a) Every application for legal aid must be considered on its merits and must be determined in accordance with the provisions of Part V of the Legal Aid Act 1988.

(b) The specific criterion or other interests of justice consideration which is relied upon must be identified clearly in the application form.

(c) The decision must always be based on the information contained in the form of application for legal aid, together with any other oral or written information provided by or on behalf of the applicant, particulars of the offence(s) alleged as set out in the information(s) before the court, and any other relevant particulars which may be properly taken into account as a result of statements made in open court during the course of the proceedings against the applicant. If the decision to grant or refuse legal aid is influenced by information provided orally, then *the relevant information provided should be clearly recorded on the application.*

(d) In respect of offences triable either-way, the approach to the grant of legal aid should be the same whether the offence is to be tried in the Crown Court or the magistrates' court; accordingly, for example, an accused charged with an offence triable either-way, who does not merit legal aid for summary trial, should not automatically be granted legal aid simply because he elects to be tried at the Crown Court.

(e) It is suggested that the need for a Newton hearing (ie. a dispute on the facts following a plea of guilty) may justify a grant of legal aid if, for example, witnesses need to be traced by a legal representative or expert cross-examination is necessary. This may also apply for other disputes of fact and/or law arising after a guilty plea.

7. *The Interests of Justice Criteria – Detailed Considerations*

(a) The factors set out in Section 22 of the Legal Aid Act 1988 apply to proceedings by way of a trial by or before a magistrates' court or the Crown Court or on an appeal to the Crown Court against conviction.

(b) Section 22(2) specifies five factors which must be taken into account when a competent authority is determining whether it is in the interests of justice that representation be granted.

(c) In some cases the interaction of two or more of the factors may dictate that legal aid should be granted when neither by itself would have sufficed. For example, whereas a minor question of law could normally be dealt with under the Green Form Scheme, or a person's knowledge of English may be adequate rather than good, those two factors in combination could merit a grant of legal aid. Where such interaction is used this should clearly be noted on the application form.

(d) The five factors (considered below) are not exhaustive:
Section 22(2) states that 'The factors to be taken into account . . .

shall include the following . . .'. In *R v Liverpool City Justices, ex p McGhee* it was stated that '. . . these magistrates were plainly wrong in regarding the factors statutorily identified [in section 22(2)(a)–(e)] as being exhaustive and there may be, according to the circumstances of a particular case, other than the identified factors which have to be taken into consideration in deciding whether or not the justice of the case requires that legal aid should be granted.'

(e) While some applications may rely on all or several of the factors, an application which relies on only one must be given equal consideration. It also follows from *McGhee* that reliance on none of the statutory factors is not necessarily fatal. When a nonstatutory factor is held to have founded or supported the grant of legal aid this should be clearly specified on the application form.

(f) For example, where the behaviour of a defendant is so disruptive as to distract the court from the exercise of its judicial function, that alone could justify a grant of legal aid if the presence of a lawyer would mitigate the distraction – if only, as a last resort, enabling the court to continue the hearing in the absence of the defendant but in the presence of his legal representative. It is further suggested that behaviour which affects the court's administrative performance is outside the scope of section 22 and cannot, therefore, be the basis for a grant of legal aid.

8. *SECTION 22(2)(a)* – THE OFFENCE IS SUCH THAT IF PROVED IT IS LIKELY THAT THE COURT WOULD IMPOSE A SENTENCE WHICH WOULD DEPRIVE THE ACCUSED OF HIS LIBERTY OR LEAD TO LOSS OF HIS LIVELIHOOD OR SERIOUS DAMAGE TO HIS REPUTATION

(a) *likelihood of deprivation of liberty*

(i) The person considering the application must be provided with sufficient information to enable him to be satisfied that, in the event of a conviction, the accused's liberty would be at risk. Accordingly, information about the seriousness and circumstances of the offence alleged should be taken into account, including details of any aggravating circumstances which, in the event of the accused being convicted, might expose him to a more severe sentence than would normally be the case. Details relating to previous convictions should also be supplied for the purposes of determining seriousness. Regard should also be had to the gravity of the offence. Where any aggravating factors influence the decision on the grant of legal aid, these should be clearly recorded.

(ii) It is recommended that reference in appropriate cases be made to 'The Magistrates' Association Sentencing Guidelines' issued on 20 September 1993, which provide examples of seriousness indicators' (aggravating factors and mitigating factors) for various types of offence.

(iii) The onus is on the applicant to state why such a sentence is likely.

(iv) Legal aid should normally be granted where there is a real and practical (as opposed to theoretical) risk of imprisonment or other form of deprivation of liberty. For example, an offender of previous good character, charged with possessing a small quantity of cannabis, would have difficulty in establishing that he was likely to lose his liberty because, although the offence is punishable with three months' imprisonment on summary conviction, it would be most unusual for any court to pass a custodial sentence for such an offence.

(v) For the purpose of determining whether the accused is likely to lose his liberty etc. regard should be had to the sentencing approaches of courts generally and, in particular, to the sentencing approach of the court before which the accused is appearing.

(vi) The likelihood of conviction should not be taken into account; the grant of legal aid should not be based on the merits of the defence; conviction should always be assumed.

(vii) 'Deprivation of liberty' includes any sentence of imprisonment, whether immediate or suspended; detention in a young offender institution; custody for life; detention under section 53(2) of the Children and Young Persons Act 1933; hospital and guardianship orders.

(viii) As noted above, section 22(2)(a) refers specifically to the likelihood of deprivation of liberty and it has been a matter of some debate whether community sentences are capable of falling within that category. This debate has now been settled by the judgement in *R v Liverpool City Justices, ex p McGhee*. In giving judgement, Rose LJ said that '. . . I am not persuaded . . . that the risk of a community service order amount[s] to a risk of deprivation of liberty within the meaning of that section' [section 22(2)(a)]. In concurring, Waller J said '. . . I am also clear that the words in section 22(2)(a) "The offence is such that if proved it is likely that the court would impose a sentence which would deprive the accused of his liberty", do not include a community service order'. The judgement went on to state that the possibility of a community service order being made might be a factor to be considered when considering whether or not to grant legal aid, and Rose LJ made plain that this should not be taken to imply that legal aid should be granted if community service was likely. It was, however, a factor other than the listed factors which could be taken into account in particular cases.

(ix) Legal aid should normally be granted:

(a) upon a committal to the Crown Court for sentence (*R v Serghiou* [1966] 3 All ER 637n);

(b) where the court is considering making a recommendation for deportation (*R v Edgehill* [1963] 1 All ER 181);

(c) where the court is considering making a hospital order (*R v King's Lynn Justices, ex p Fysh* [1964] Crim LR 143).

(x) A grant of legal aid for mitigation only might be appropriate, for example, when the court's assessment of the gravity of the case is substantially altered by factors which come to light after conviction. Courts should also bear in mind the statutory restrictions on imposing certain sentences as referred to at paragraph 3(d) of these notes.

(b) *loss of livelihood*

(i) It follows from the provisions of the Act that the granting authority should consider how likely it is that loss of livelihood will result from a sentence imposed by the court on conviction. It is suggested that legal aid should only be granted where there is a real risk of loss of livelihood.

(ii) The applicant must explain why he believes that it is likely that he will lose his livelihood. In some cases this will be obvious, eg. a bank clerk accused of an offence of dishonesty; in others it may be obscure, eg. a teacher convicted of indecency with a child is likely to lose his livelihood, but a coach driver convicted of a similar offence might not appear so vulnerable until he explains to the court that he drives school buses. The likely loss of livelihood should be a direct consequence of the conviction or the sentence.

(iii) It is suggested that loss of livelihood would normally refer to current livelihood. Therefore, someone who is not currently employed would be less likely to meet this criterion, although other criteria under section 22 may be met, such as 'serious damage to reputation' (eg. see paragraph 8(c)(v) below).

(iv) Assertions that disqualification from driving will result in a loss of livelihood should be examined critically. There can seldom be justification to grant legal aid to resist a mandatory driving disqualification alone arising from a drink/driving charge unless a cogent argument as to special reasons can be put forward. Though a grant could be justified in exceptional circumstances (eg. if the applicant could show that the disqualification would result in a real risk of dismissal), legal aid would not usually be justified where the accused sought to avoid a 'totting-up' disqualification, having acquired twelve or more penalty points.

(c) *serious damage to reputation*

(i) In many cases, conviction will damage the accused's reputation. However, section 22 refers to *serious* damage. It is considered that this would relate to those cases in which the offence, or the offender's circumstances, are such that the disgrace of conviction, or consequent damage to the applicant's standing, would greatly exceed the direct effect of the penalty which might be imposed. 'Reputation' for these purposes is a question of good character, including honesty and trustworthiness. Social class and position should not be taken into account. The loss of reputation consequent on a conviction for dishonesty is absolute and not relevant to the amount.

(ii) As a general rule, offences of varying degrees of seriousness attract different levels of damage to reputation. The Act refers to *serious* damage as justifying the grant of legal aid.

(iii) An effective plea in mitigation for any charge may lessen the severity of the sentence and thereby lessen the seriousness of the damage to reputation. An applicant who either has a previous conviction for a *like* offence or a conviction for a more serious offence can be assumed to have lost reputation and the criterion will not apply. However, the fact that a person has previous convictions should not preclude consideration of legal aid under this head. For example, it may be that someone with a previous conviction for a minor assault might still suffer serious damage to reputation if convicted of an offence of dishonesty or a sexual offence.

(iv) In deciding upon the seriousness of the damage to reputation, it is suggested that special factors about the accused, for example religious background, might aggravate the damage to reputation caused by a conviction which may not have the same effect on another person. This could also apply, for example, to someone engaged in voluntary work such as drug use prevention, where a conviction for possession of a drug could particularly undermine their integrity.

(v) Consideration should be given to whether an accused who is undertaking vocational or professional training might suffer damage to reputation so serious that there is a risk that future livelihood might be lost.

9. *SECTION 22(2)(b)* – THE DETERMINATION OF THE CASE MAY INVOLVE CONSIDERATION OF A SUBSTANTIAL QUESTION OF LAW

(i) Legal aid should only be granted under this criterion if a question of law is raised which the applicant cannot be expected to deal with unaided and is a substantial question and is relevant to the applicant's case. It should be noted that this criterion may also apply when legal aid is being considered for an appeal against conviction.

If the applicant intends to plead guilty, the likelihood of substantial questions of law arising must generally be remote, though there may be exceptions, such as some 'special reasons' (such as laced drinks) in drink/driving cases. There may also be some instances in which sentencing considerations could give rise to a substantial question of law.

(ii) The defence solicitor should specify the point of law on the application form. Quite often issues coming before the courts involve mixed questions of fact and law but again, in such circumstances, to justify grant of legal aid the question of law must be a *substantial* one.

(iii) Except in circumstances where the applicant faces serious or complex charges, legal aid should not generally be granted solely for the purpose of obtaining advice as to the appropriate plea, since this can rarely be described as a substantial question of law. Preliminary advice as to plea can usually be provided satisfactorily by advice from the duty solicitor or from any solicitor under the green form scheme.

10. *SECTION 22(2)(c)* – THE ACCUSED MAY BE UNABLE TO UNDERSTAND THE PROCEEDINGS OR TO STATE HIS OWN CASE BECAUSE OF HIS INADEQUATE KNOWLEDGE OF ENGLISH, MENTAL ILLNESS OR OTHER MENTAL OR PHYSICAL DISABILITY

(a) *inadequate knowledge of English*

(i) Legal aid should not be granted unless the applicant's knowledge is sufficiently poor to prevent him from following the proceedings or conducting his case. It is suggested that the fact that the services of an interpreter are available is not a sufficient ground for refusing legal aid under this criterion.

(ii) The accused's difficulties of comprehension may differ with the complexity of the case; he may be able to manage in a very straightforward case but may be unable to do so in a more complex one. Courts should, therefore, consider carefully whether the stated impediment to understanding is likely to be operative in the particular case.

(iii) Generally, it is the ability to understand spoken English which is important. It should be borne in mind that, while the language of the courts is often technical, it is the responsibility of those working in the courts to use plain English. A lack of fluent literacy will not, in most cases, impair the accused's ability to prepare and present his case. Relevant factors could include the degree of literacy, the complexity of the case and the extent of reading required.

(b) *mental or physical disability*

(i) Legal aid should be granted if the applicant is unable to follow the proceedings or properly conduct his case by reason of substantial physical disability, for example deafness or blindness, or by reason of mental disorder, mental impairment or subnormality.

(ii) Courts may think it appropriate to request a medical report or certificate, especially in cases where it is claimed that the applicant is suffering from a form of mental illness that is likely to worsen significantly due to a court hearing and, as a consequence, is unlikely to be able to represent himself properly.

11. *SECTION 22(2)(d)* – THE NATURE OF THE DEFENCE IS SUCH AS TO INVOLVE THE TRACING AND INTERVIEWING OF WITNESSES OR EXPERT CROSS-EXAMINATION OF A WITNESS FOR THE PROSECUTION

(a) *trace and interview witnesses*

(i) Details of the witnesses, and why there is a necessity for representation to trace and/or interview them, should be included in the application. If details of witnesses are not included, consideration of the legal aid application should be deferred until the applicant has provided the court with sufficient information to make a determination.

(b) *expert cross-examination of a Prosecution witness*

(i) In cases where the applicant requires legal aid for the benefit of expert cross-examination of prosecution witnesses, he should be expected to explain why this is necessary.

(ii) It should be noted that section 22(2)(d) refers to expert cross-examination of a witness and *not* only to cross-examination of an expert witness. Giving judgement in *R v Liverpool City Justices, ex p McGhee*, Rose LJ said 'These justices . . . were clearly under the misapprehension . . . that because expert witnesses were not to be called, the factor identified in part of section 22(2)(d) was not satisfied. That, in itself, as it seems to me, is sufficient to flaw the approach of these justices'.

Thus, legal aid should be granted under this heading when there is a need for professional cross-examination of a witness. This may very likely be the case when the evidence is provided by an expert, since an accused person would rarely be capable, for example, of cross-examining a medical or handwriting expert. It may also apply in other cases, such as those where shades of emphasis in the evidence can make an action appear more sinister than it was in fact. But in considering applications under this heading, the emphasis should be clearly on the nature of the evidence, rather than on the status of the person providing the evidence.

12. *SECTION 22(2)(e)* – IT IS IN THE INTERESTS OF SOMEONE OTHER THAN THE ACCUSED THAT THE ACCUSED BE REPRESENTED

(i) It should be borne in mind when considering legal aid under this heading that section 34A of the Criminal Justice Act 1988 provides that a defendant charged with certain offences specified in section 32(2) of that Act shall not cross-examine in person any child witness who is an alleged victim or alleged witness to the commission of the offence.

(ii) It is suggested that legal aid should also be considered when, for example, the accused is charged with a sexual offence where it is desirable that the complainant should be spared the great strain of being cross-examined by a person whom they believe has committed a sexual offence against them.

(iii) This principle may also apply where the alleged victim or witness of, for example, an offence against the person or a burglary is very young or elderly, when cross-examination by the accused might put them under undue strain.

Appendix A3

Administration of Legal Aid in Magistrates' Courts

Note: Paragraph 10 of the attached circular was withdrawn by the Lord Chancellor's Department on the 26th June 1992 and should be disregarded.

LORD CHANCELLOR'S DEPARTMENT
TREVELYAN HOUSE
GREAT PETER STREET
LONDON SW1P 2BY
Telephone 071–210 8500

Your reference
Our reference MAG/92 7/15/1
The Clerk to the Justices

1 April 1992

Dear Sir or Madam,

LORD CHANCELLOR'S DEPARTMENT CIRCULAR NO. MCD(92)1

ADMINISTRATION OF LEGAL AID IN MAGISTRATES' COURTS

A. INTRODUCTION
B. BACKGROUND
C. APPLICATION FORMS AND THEIR CONSIDERATION
D. CASE REFERENCE NUMBERS
E. CONTRIBUTIONS – FINANCIAL ALLOWANCES
F. SIGNATURE AND RECORDING ENQUIRIES MADE
G. CHECKING AND AUTHORISATION OF LEGAL AID ORDERS AND CONTRIBUTION ORDERS
H. DATE ON LEGAL AID ORDER
I. RAISING OF IMPOSITIONS
J. REVIEW OF FINANCIAL ELIGIBILITY WHEN CASE IS CONCLUDED
K. NON-COMPLIANCE WITH TERMS OF CONTRIBUTION ORDER
L. WRITE-OFF OF LEGAL AID CONTRIBUTION ORDERS
M. LOCAL POLICY AND PROCEDURES
N. REVIEW OF POLICY AND PROCEDURES
O. CONCLUSION

A. INTRODUCTION

This circular sets out what needs to be done to ensure the efficient, effective and economic administration of legal aid in the magistrates' courts. The 1990/91 Criminal Legal Aid Account was qualified by the Comptroller and Auditor General as there was 'significant and material uncertainty as to the propriety and regularity of substantial sums of criminal legal aid expenditures'. In their work on behalf of the Home Office, the Lord Chancellor's Department's Internal Audit Division had expressed similar concerns in their audit. The circular states these concerns and provides advice and guidance on the correct administrative procedures. It has been prepared following consultation between the Home Office, the Lord Chancellor's Department, the Legal Aid Board and the Justices' Clerks' Society.

B. BACKGROUND

2. In his report on the qualification of 1990/91 Appropriation Account covering expenditure on legal aid the Comptroller and Auditor General set out the following key points which had arisen from the National Audit Office examination of that expenditure:

- insufficient information on the grounds for applications and whether these fulfilled the statutory conditions designed to establish the need for legal aid; for example, the 'real danger of a custodial sentence' was frequently quoted as grounds for an award with little or no supporting evidence that this was in practice a significant risk for the crime concerned or for the court involved;
- doubts on whether all applications were considered by a properly authorised officer;
- lack of evidence as to the extent and depth of checks on applicants' income, with many grants being determined in the absence of sufficient information and contributions frequently assessed without the applicant's financial circumstances being corroborated;
- variations and shortcomings in the supporting documentation and in the care with which applications were prepared and submitted;
- inconsistencies and delays in the monitoring and enforcement of contributions orders and sums outstanding and in write-off procedures;
- a general lack of guidance and instruction to encourage improved procedures and consistency of treatment within and between courts.

3. These conclusions were supported by the findings of the 1990/91 examination of justices' clerks accounts by the Lord Chancellor's Department's Internal Audit Division.

4. Expenditure on criminal legal aid included in the 1990 91 Account totalled £333 million. This comprised £175 million paid in respect of proceedings in magistrates' courts and £158 million in higher criminal courts. Statistics show that some 99 per cent of all awards of criminal legal aid, which provide the underlying authority for payments to solicitors and counsel, are granted by the magistrates' courts. In 1990 there were 548,000 applications for criminal legal aid in magistrates' and juvenile courts of which 503,000 (92 per cent) were granted. There were also 136,064 applications filed in magistrates' courts for

legal aid in respect of representation in the Crown Court, of which 135,214 (99 per cent) were granted.

5. The Accounting Officers for the Home Office and the Lord Chancellor's Department appeared before the House of Commons Public Accounts Committee on 20 January 1992 to answer questions following the qualification of the account. At that appearance the Accounting Officers undertook to remind justices' clerks of the importance of applying the statutory regulations relating to the grant of legal aid and ensuring the effective and efficient management of the legal aid system. This circular provides that reminder together with advice and guidance which it is hoped will be helpful.

6. From 1 April 1992, of course, the responsibility for justices' clerks' accounts moved from the HOme Office to the Lord Chancellor's Department. This will, for the first time, bring together in one department the responsibility both for statute and regulation governing the administration of legal aid and the audit of its efficient operation in magistrates' courts. It would have been likely that in the event of that change, even without the benefit of audit findings, closer scrutiny and attention would have been applied in this area There is already in progress a review by the Lord Chancellor's Department of the financial conditions for legal aid and the Legal Aid Board is conducting research into the application of the interests of justice criteria for the grant of legal aid. The conclusions of both the review and the research will be carefully considered with a view to introducing any changes necessary to improve the criminal legal aid system. In the meantime justices' clerks should ensure that the guidance in this circular is followed.

C. APPLICATION FORMS AND THEIR CONSIDERATION

7. The audit examination found many variations of the legal aid application form (Form 1) in use, some omitting altogether space for information necessary on which to decide whether the interests of justice criteria listed in section 22 of the Legal Aid Act 1988 were met. It also found there were a large number of cases where there was either insufficient or no evidence of income on the statement of means form and legal aid had been granted (Form 5). If these two forms are not completed in full or there is insufficient information to enable proper consideration to be given to the application, then the application should be returned with a request that the missing information be provided, in the absence of which the application should be refused.

8. The examination of the interests of justice criteria must be both thorough and critical. The authorised officer must be satisfied that the reasons advanced by the applicant stand up to examination e.g. that there really does exist a real danger of the court awarding a custodial sentence. Justice clerks should ensure that authorised officers are familiar with both the criteria and the guidance on the consideration of legal aid applications produced be the Justices' Clerks' Society.

9. Justices' clerks are reminded that a legal aid order must not be made until the court or the justices' clerk has considered the applicant's statement of means, unless the applicant is incapable of furnishing such a statement on account of

his physical or mental condition. Legal aid should not be granted unless the applicant's financial resources are such that he requires assistance in meeting the costs of legal representation. Accordingly, where the statement of means indicates that a financial contribution would be due, justices' clerks should ensure that regard is given to the likely cost of representation and to whether the applicant would be able to afford it without recourse to legal aid.

10. Justices' clerks are reminded that the statement of means form requires legal aid applicants in employment to submit, as evidence of income, three monthly or 13 weekly pay slips. If the evidence is not provided, there is insufficient information to enable a proper consideration to be given to an application for legal aid, and the application should be returned with a request that the evidence be provided. In its absence the application must be refused. There is no discretion to waive this requirement.

11. Similarly, applicants who claim to be in receipt of any social security benefit, but particularly Income Support, Family Credit or (from 6 April 1992) Disability Working Allowance which entitle the applicant to free legal aid, should be asked to produce evidence of receipt of the benefit. This could be the notification of the award or an order book for example. Form S requires, at section 2, every applicant in receipt of Income Support, Family Credit or Disability Working Allowance to provide the address of the relevant Benefits Agency office and a reference number. Justices' clerks are required to ensure that this information is provided. Arrangements for justices' clerks to make checks with local Benefit Agency offices are being sought. A further circular will be issued on this in due course.

12. Regulation 4 of the Legal Aid in Criminal and Care Proceedings (General) Regulations 1989 is amended as from 1 April 1992, to make clear that only the prescribed application form (Form I) and the prescribed statement of means form (Form 5) should be used. Both forms should be properly and fully completed before a legal aid application is considered.

13. It is important that those authorised by justices' clerks to decide on the grant of legal aid know precisely the limits of the authority delegated to them. Authorised officers should normally be qualified court clerks or senior administrative staff who have been given special training to undertake the task. Justices' clerks should ensure the quality of decision making by sampling cases on a regular basis.

D. CASE REFERENCE NUMBERS

14. You will be aware that the Justices' Clerks' Society and the Legal Aid Board have now agreed a common reference numbering system for legal aid applications and solicitors' bills. Justices' clerks were asked to adopt this system with effect from 1 January 1992. The Legal Aid Board is to introduce a new form by July 1992 which solicitors must use when submitting bills for work in the magistrates courts. The new form will require the legal aid order number to be entered on it. Justices' clerks are asked to ensure that all staff who are involved in legal aid work are aware of the new numbering systems and of the need to quote the legal aid order reference number, as well

as the name of the solicitor involved, in any correspondence with the legal aid area office.

15. At present, where a legal aid order is made in respect of an offence or offences, and the same defendant is charged with a subsequent offence or offences which will be dealt with at the same time, magistrates' courts either endorse the new offence(s) on the existing order or make a new order or orders. If another order is made it is possible for solicitors wrongly to claim twice for the same work. When the new numbering system is introduced, justices' clerks are asked to make sure that they either endorse all offences that are to be dealt with at the same time on the original legal aid order, or if not, they use the same reference number for any legal aid order or orders made in these circumstances. This will prevent double claiming.

E. CONTRIBUTIONS – FINANCIAL ALLOWANCES

16. Guidance for the use of justices' clerks and others on how legal aid contributions should be calculated is updated annually to reflect changes in dependants' allowances eligibility limits and contributions. The latest guidance is contained in Lord Chancellor's Department Circular JC(92) 1. However, the audit review highlighted that there is no clear guidance on what expenditure may be allowable in the calculations. A note which it is hoped will assist in this respect is at Annex A. This should be read in conjunction with the latest Lord Chancellor's Department circular.

17. Allowances against income and capital 'disregards' will be considered as part of the review of financial conditions (para 6). Depending on the outcome of the review, it may be possible to issue more specific instructions. In the meantime, officers conducting means assessments who exercise their discretion in respect of income or capital should obtain evidence of the amount which is claimed and also attach to the papers a note explaining the reasons for allowing (or refusing to allow) the additional amounts.

F. SIGNATURE AND RECORDING ENQUIRIES MADE

18. As it stands, Form 1 requires the signature of the justices' clerk and a statement of reasons for refusal of an application only where the refusal is on interests of justice grounds and the applicant may apply to an area committee. Accordingly there is no evidence of authorisation where an application is granted nor are reasons given when an application is refused on financial grounds. It is proposed to revise the form. In the meantime justices' clerks should ensure that the reason for refusal and a signature are given even where reference to the justices' clerk is not necessary and that where a grant is made the words 'reason for refusal' and the note below are struck through and the word 'granted' and a signature provided in the space below. Where the reason for grant is not immediately apparent from the information provided on the form, a brief explanation should be given.

19. Where prior to the grant of legal aid enquiries are made in respect of information on either Form 1 or 5 notes should be placed on the file as a

permanent record of the scrutiny given, any separate supporting evidence provided and the action taken.

G. CHECKING AND AUTHORISATION OF LEGAL AID ORDERS AND CONTRIBUTION ORDERS

20. The internal audit examination of accounts showed that in almost half of the courts visited Legal Aid Orders and legal aid contribution orders were sent to the applicant and the assisted person's solicitor without any check either as to their accuracy or their authorisation.

21. Justices' clerks are reminded of the need to ensure that all orders produced as a result of judicial decision should be checked for accuracy and properly authorised before despatch.

H. DATE ON LEGAL AID ORDER

22. The audit review discovered a divergence of practice between courts regarding the date of legal aid orders. Some courts show the date on the legal aid order (Form 11) as the date on which the application was received and others the date on which the order was made.

23. In urgent cases regulation 44 (7) of the Legal Aid in Criminal and Care Proceedings (General) Regulations 1989 allows discretion to pay for work carried out prior to the date of a legal aid order. Justices' clerks are reminded that orders should not be backdated and that the date shown must be the actual date the order is approved and signed regardless of any delays incurred after receipt or the reasons for them.

I. RAISING OF IMPOSITIONS

24. In all courts visited the internal auditors found that a copy of the contribution order was used to create an imposition i.e. an accounting record. However, in almost 60% of the instances examined there was no independent verification that the imposition raised agreed with the legal aid contribution order. In a number of instances it was also noted that there was no check to ensure that an account had been raised in respect of each legal aid contribution order issued.

25. Justices' clerks are reminded of the need to establish and maintain procedures to verify that all and only authorised and accurate impositions are created and brought to account.

J. REVIEW OF FINANCIAL ELIGIBILITY WHEN CASE IS CONCLUDED

26. The audit examination found inadequate formal arrangements for the review of the financial circumstances of those in receipt of legal aid despite the fact that additional or changed information is frequently available to the court

during the disposal of the case which may indicate that a legal aid contribution might be payable or could be varied.

27. Justices' clerks should always ensure that the financial situation of a legally aided defendant is reviewed when the case is heard. Where not already undertaken, a system should be introduced to ensure that the Bench is asked to review cases to identify whether the financial circumstances of a legally aided defendant have changed. Some courts have adopted a system of flagging case papers where legal aid has been awarded and attaching up-to-date information on any contributions paid, before each hearing.

K. NON-COMPLIANCE WITH TERMS OF CONTRIBUTION ORDER

28. Where a legally aided person fails to pay a legal aid contribution due, section 24 of the Legal Aid Act 1988 allows the court to revoke the grant of legal aid, provided it is clear that the person was able to pay but has failed or refused to do so. The audit review concluded that existence of section 24 was often overlooked.

29. In order to improve the incidence of compliance with the terms of legal aid contribution orders, justices' clerks are reminded that this power is available to the court and that the possibility of losing legal aid should be made dear to recalcitrant payers. In providing this power in primary legislation Parliament intended courts to revoke legal aid for non-payment of financial contributions in appropriate cases, notwithstanding that the interests of justice test continues to stand.

30. The Act requires that both tests, interests of justice and ability to make a contribution, should be separately considered and decided. It is important that case files are documented to indicate that, where appropriate, consideration has been given to revocation of an order and the reason for any decision reached.

31. As part of the review of financial conditions (para 6) careful consideration will be given to the efficiency and effectiveness of enforcement of legal aid contribution orders. Instructions will be issued following, and subject to, the outcome of the review. In the meantime, justices' clerks should continue to enforce legal aid orders in accordance with the provisions of section 24 of the Legal Aid Act 1988 and schedule 3 to the Act. In particular, justices' clerks are reminded that amounts due under contribution orders are enforceable in the same way as affiliation orders under section 93 of the Magistrates' Courts Act 1980. This provides for enforcement orders to be made on complaint. A contribution order may not be enforced until the proceedings are concluded or until the grant is revoked or withdrawn. Subject to this, justices' clerks should ensure that there is a system of regular examination of contribution orders and that action is taken to enforce payment.

L. WRITE-OFF OF LEGAL AID CONTRIBUTION ORDERS

32. The internal audit review found that very few courts systematically monitored legal aid contribution orders for the purpose of writing-off

irrecoverable amounts. Where systems had been established they tended to be inconsistent and unreliable in their application with the result that most courts retained outstanding and irrecoverable legal aid contributions in their accounts dating back many years.

33. Justices' clerks are reminded of the need to establish and maintain a system for identifying irrecoverable accounts so that they can request authority to write them off. Write-off schedules should be regularly submitted to the Lord Chancellor's Department in accordance with established requirements (Home Office circulars Nos 22/1983 & 18/1986). Justices' clerks are reminded that schedules of write-off in respect of legal aid contributions should be kept separate from those relating to the write-off of fines.

M. LOCAL POLICY AND PROCEDURES

34. The audit review found that in some instances no local instructions had been produced on the policy and procedures for the administration of legal aid. Locally produced administrative instructions, which should clearly define the limits of responsibility for those involved in the process, are important (para 1.4 of the memorandum accompanying Home Office circular No 88/1981) and it is recommended that justices' clerks should put them in place where they do not already exist. However, such guidance must not override the statutory conditions for granting criminal legal aid by suggesting, for example, that for certain types of case legal aid will always be either granted or refused.

N. REVIEW OF POLICY AND PROCEDURES

35. Justices' clerks are reminded of their responsibilities as set out in the Standards of Accounting Controls in Magistrates' Courts (Home Office circular No 88/1981). It is important that policies and procedures are set out in writing and made known to all staff. These policies and procedures should be kept under review both as to their continuing appropriateness and to ensure that there is compliance with them.

O. CONCLUSION

36. This circular draws attention to the importance of adhering to both the regulations covering the grant of legal aid and the minimum accounting and procedural control standards laid down in Home Office circulars. A list of the main points which it contains is at Annex B. It has also drawn attention to the financial conditions review and research into legal aid currently in hand, the conclusions of which will be reported in due course. Auditors from both the National Audit Office and the Lord Chancellor's Department's Internal Audit Division on their visits to courts will continue to scrutinise the administration of legal aid to establish adherence to the regulations and to identify areas of good practice.

37. It is intended, during the course of the year, to issue to the service a consolidated accounts circular in the form of an accounts manual in loose leaf

format which will include legal aid matters. The project has already started and it is planned to launch the manual with a series of seminars which will be announced in due course.

38. Any enquiries about his circular should be addressed to:
Robin Woodland (Legal Aid Policy)
Lord Chancellor's Department
Legal Aid Division
Trevelyan House
30 Great Peter Street
LONDON
SW1P 2BY
Telephone: 071210 8800
Ray Pawson (Accounts)
Magistrates' Courts Division
Address as above
Tel: 071 210 8500 (Switchboard)

Yours faithfully,

E A Grant

Copies: The Clerk to the Magistrates' Courts Committee
The Director of Public Prosecutions
Chief Crown Prosecutor
The Circuit Administrator
The Court Administrator
The Crown Court Chief Clerks

Annex A

LEGAL AID CONTRIBUTIONS – ALLOWANCES AGAINST INCOME AND CAPITAL

INCOME

The allowances which may be made against income as set out in schedule 3 to the Legal Aid in Criminal and Care Proceedings (General) Regulations 1989. The main allowances to be made are:

i) income tax and national insurance;
ii) maintenance of dependants;
iii) housing expenses – including rent, mortgage payments, water and sewage charges, community charge, an allowance for repairs and insurance and board and lodging if this is appropriate;
iv) the cost of travel to work;
v) child minding expenses in connection with employment;
vi) sums payable under court orders (other than payments in respect of the proceedings in which the application for legal aid is being made);
vii) pension scheme contributions.

Premiums on mortgage linked endowment policies should be allowed. Where the cost of meals is included in any payment for lodgings, only half of that payment should be allowed.

Paragraph 13 of schedule 3 allows the proper officer to make any other allowances which he or she considers to be reasonable in the circumstances of the case. Generally the repayment of loans, hire purchase and other forms of credit such as credit cards should not be allowed because the lower limit is intended to cover these. However officers conducting assessments may wish to consider allowing debt repayments (e.g. arrears of rent, mortgage, loans or H.P.) which are actually and regularly paid from income. It may also be thought reasonable to allow loans for house improvement and loans taken out to clear debts. Other expenditure which the assessing officer may consider allowing includes trade union and professional association subscriptions.

Paragraph 8 of schedule 3 makes dear that deductions for housing expenses are allowed for the applicant's main or only dwelling. However there may be very exceptional cases in which the assessing officer might feel it appropriate to make an allowance for a second home – where the applicant works at a considerable distance from his family or where the main home is being built or is undergoing considerable renovation for example.

It should be kept in mind that the income limit for free legal aid for criminal cases is somewhat higher than the limit for civil cases. Accordingly, many discretionary items of expenditure might reasonably be regarded as being covered. Officers conducting means assessments must be certain that discretionary allowances are fully justified in all the circumstances of the case and keep a note of their reasons with the papers.

CAPITAL

Paragraph 18 of the schedule provides that household furniture and effects, articles of personal clothing and tools and equipment of trade should not be included as capital except save in exceptional circumstances. *Paragraph 16* provides that savings of mobility allowance and for a period not exceeding 12 months, any arrears of attendance or mobility allowance and income support or family credit and in addition any payments made out of the social fund shall be disregarded. In addition, *paragraph 20* gives the assessing officer discretion to disregard other amounts of capital. Assessing officers should remember that the lower capital limit provides substantial cover for contingencies and capital which has been saved as a float for a particular purpose should not be disregarded. However, the assessing officer may wish to consider disregarding capital where the applicant relies to a large extent on income from his capital. There may also be exceptional circumstances where for example, the applicant is moving home, is holding the proceeds from the sale of his old home but has not yet exchanged contracts on his new property.

ANNEX B

LORD CHANCELLOR'S DEPARTMENT CIRCULAR No.CD(92)1

ADMINISTRATION OF LEGAL AID IN MAGISTRATES' COURTS – AUDIT 1990/91

SUMMARY OF MAIN POINTS

- The examination of the interest of justice criteria must be thorough and critical (Paragraph 8)
- Authorised officers should be familiar with the criteria and the guidance on legal aid application produced by the Justices' Clerks' Society (paragraph 8)
- A legal aid order should not be made until the applicant's means have been considered (paragraph 9)
- Where a financial contribution is due, regard must be had to the likely cost of representation (paragraph 9)
- Evidence of income must be provided (paragraph 10)
- Applicants must provide the address of the relevant Social Security office and a reference number if they are in receipt of Income Support, Family Credit or Disability Working Allowance (paragraph 11)
- Legal aid forms should be properly completed before an application is considered (paragraph 12)
- Checks should be made by justices' clerks to ensure the quality of decision making (paragraph 13)
- The common reference numbering system should be used (paragraph 14)
- Guidance is provided on the application of financial allowances in calculating legal aid contributions (paragraph 16)
- Form 1 should always have the signature of the officer granting or refusing the application and reasons should be shown where appropriate (paragraph 18)
- Files should contain information on enquiries made to determine whether an application should be approved (paragraph 19)
- Orders should be thoroughly checked and properly authorised (paragraph 21)
- The date shown on the legal aid order must be the actual date it is approved and signed (paragraph 23)
- Justices' clerks must establish and maintain procedures to verify that all and only authorised and accurate impositions are created and brought to account (paragraph 25)
- The financial situation of a legally aided defendant should be reviewed when the case is heard (paragraph 26)
- Action should be taken to ensure compliance with legal aid contribution orders (paragraph 29 et seq.)
- Systems should be established and maintained to identify irrecoverable legal aid contributions so that write off action can be pursued (paragraph 33)
- Local administrative information should be in place (paragraph 34)
- Standards of accounting must be maintained (paragraph 35)

Appendix A4

Guidance to Granting Authorities on the Legal Aid in Criminal and Care Proceedings (General) (Amendment) Regulations 1995 (SI 1995/542)

General

1. These regulations amend the Legal Aid in Criminal and Care Proceedings (General) Regulations 1989 by:

a) requiring magistrates' courts to provide copies of the application forms for criminal legal aid free of charge; and
b) requiring the proper officer to keep records of all applications for criminal legal aid, showing the reasons for deciding whether individual applications should be granted or refused; and
c) amending criminal legal aid Forms 1, 2, 3, 4 and S.

2. These changes come into force on 1 May 1995. The Justices' Clerks' Society and the Legal Aid Board were amongst those consulted on these regulations in draft.

Supply of free forms by magistrates' courts

3. Criminal legal aid application forms (Forms 1 and 5) are prescribed by Regulation. Traditionally, they have been supplied free of charge by magistrates' courts. However, recently some courts have started charging solicitors for supplying these forms, or told them to arrange their own supply. The Lord Chancellor does not consider this to be acceptable practice and these regulations provide for the free supply of application forms by magistrates' courts. These forms should therefore be made available free of charge to applicants and their solicitors from 1 May 1995.

Recording reasons

4. Uncertainty over whether legal aid in criminal cases was being granted in accordance with the Legal Aid Act 1988 (the Act) and regulations thereunder resulted in the National Audit Office (NAO) being unable to approve the Lord Chancellor's Department's Legal Aid Account in 1990/91 and each year since. This meant, in effect, that Parliament could gain no assurance that the money it had voted for criminal legal aid was being spent only in accordance with the law. The main focus of this criticism has been with regard to financial eligibility for legal aid, and this has been addressed separately.

5. However, the NAO also commented that there was insufficient information on the grounds for applications under the interests of justice test, and

whether these fulfilled the statutory conditions designed to establish need for legal aid. It referred to the example of the 'deprivation of liberty' criterion (section 22(2)(a) of the Act) and stated that this '. . . was frequently quoted as grounds for an award with little or no supporting evidence that this was in practice a significant risk for the crime concerned or for the court involved.'

6. As part of the attempt to overcome the criticisms made by the NAO, in May 1994 the Lord Chancellor's Department, the Justices' Clerks' Society and the Legal Aid Board issued joint guidance on the interests of Justice test for the grant of criminal legal aid. That guidance was the subject of consultation in draft, with copies going for comment to 16 interested bodies. Paragraph 3(a) of the guidance noted that the Lord Chancellor would shortly be laying before Parliament regulations directing granting authorities to record the specific reasons why they consider that particular applications do or do not meet the criteria under which they have been made. That is the aim of these regulations.

7. The new regulations are not designed to change the scope of criminal legal aid, or the nature of the interests of justice test, or the specific criteria listed in section 22(2) of the Act. They are not intended to influence the decisions reached by granting authorities one way or the other, but simply to ensure that a sufficient record exists of the reasons for the decision. Once the reasons underlying the grant or refusal of criminal legal aid are clearly recorded, the uncertainties uncovered by the NAO should be removed.

Keeping a record

8. It is the responsibility of the proper officer of each court to ensure that a record is kept of all legal aid applications made. The record can be, and usually will be, Form 1 and, where appropriate, Form 5. Legal aid files should be retained in accordance with the relevant Records Schedule.

9. A record must be kept even where the application is not pursued when further enquiries are made. Thus, if an application is returned to the applicant because of insufficient information having been provided, a copy of the application and a note of the reason for its return must be kept on the file. If a letter is sent requesting further information, a copy of the letter should be kept with the original application.

10. The record must show whether the application was granted, refused on the interests of justice ground, or refused on financial grounds. Where the decision to grant or refuse legal aid is made on the interests of justice ground, as opposed to financial grounds alone, the record must include a statement of reasons for the decision (see paragraphs 18 to 20 below).

11. Where an application is reviewed by the Area Committee of the Legal Aid Board, a copy of Form 4 (or equivalent) setting out the Committee's decision will be forwarded to the court to which the original application was made. Both this and the court's original decision must be retained on the file.

12. In any case where the application is refused on the interests of justice ground, a copy of the record must be sent to the applicant and his or her

solicitor. In most cases, this will simply involve sending a photocopy of pages 3, 4 and 5 of the completed Form 1. In cases where the applicant is entitled to apply for review to the Area Committee of the Legal Aid Board, a copy of the completed Form 1 must be sent in any event (regulation 12(2)).

Reasons for grant or refusal

13. The applicant will have ticked one or more boxes in section 7 of Form 1 ('Reasons for wanting legal aid'), and completed details in the boxes provided. The proper officer will then consider the reasons and details given to determine whether or not a grant of legal aid is justified, in accordance with the interests of justice test. The proper officer should note in the space provided by each factor whether or not the reasons given justify a grant of legal aid. For example, by '7(a) It is likely that I will lose my liberty', the proper officer might note '*This court unlikely to impose a custodial sentence for possession of a small quantity of cannabis*' or '*Custodial sentence likely in this court for breach of probation order.*'

14. If the information justifying the decision is already on the form, clear cross-referencing is acceptable to avoid the need to duplicate information. For example, if the applicant has ticked box 7(a) ('It is likely that I will lose my liberty'); has written '*Nature of offence*' in the details box, and has described the offence clearly in section 2 of the form, the proper officer can, provided that local sentencing policy is not a factor, simply write '*No*' or '*Not for this offence*' or '*Agreed*' in the reasons box. The less detail there is elsewhere on the form, the more detail will be needed in the reasons box. Other grounds may be less susceptible to this approach. For example, if an applicant offering no defence to a charge of driving with excess alcohol has ticked box 7(c) ('It is likely that I will lose my livelihood') and written '*Effect of disqualification*' in the details box, the entry in the reasons box might be '*No – disqualification mandatory penalty for this offence*'.

15. If the proper officer considers that a single factor justifies the grant of legal aid, there is no need to go on to consider the other factors relied upon by the applicant. If, however, none of the factors relied upon by the applicant is considered to justify a grant, the proper officer should go on to consider any other interests of justice factors he or she considers to be relevant to the application. These factors may include factors not listed on Form 1 or in section 22(2) of the Act. Any such factors considered should be noted in the appropriate box on Form 1. It should be remembered that in cases to which section 22 of the Act applies, the proper officer must consider those of the interests of justice criteria set out in section 22(2) which he or she considers to be relevant to the application.

16. Where all the relevant factors have been considered, and none on its own justifies a grant, the proper officer must then consider the application as a whole to determine whether two or more factors taken together Justify a grant, and this must be reflected in the record (see paragraph 19 below).

17. Where the applicant has failed the financial test prior to consideration of the interests of justice test, it is not necessary to go on to consider the interests of justice. Therefore, no statement of reasons is required.

Statement of reasons

18. In the majority of cases, it is not necessary to write a lengthy statement of reasons for grant or refusal in the box at the end of the form. Usually, a note along the lines of '. . . *see (a) above*' will suffice.

19. However, it may sometimes be necessary for a more detailed statement of reasons to be given. In cases where information given orally is the basis for the decision, a full statement of the reasons for the decision will always be necessary. Likewise, where a number of factors taken together are the reason for grant, a statement such as ' . . . *while the question of law involved is not a substantial one, and the defendant's knowledge of English is adequate although not fluent, I consider that the combination of these two factors justifies a grant of legal aid*' would be required. Again, where the justification for grant is the resolution of a doubt under section 21(7) of the Act, a full statement of reasons should be given.

20. When considering how much detail to include in the statement of reasons, it is important to remember that the information should be sufficient to enable anyone inspecting the records to be able to see clearly that legal aid has been granted or refused in accordance with the Act and regulations; it must be clear from the record why the grant of legal aid was or was not thought to be in the interests of justice.

Forms

Form 1

21. A number of changes have been made to this form:

a) the wording has been revised so that it more accurately reflects the criteria set out in section 22(2) of the Legal Aid Act 1988;

b) a section has been added for completion by applicants in receipt of means-tested benefits, to remove the requirement for a separate statement of means (Form 5) to be completed in these cases and thus reduce the amount of paperwork for courts;

c) a new section has been added for the proper officer to complete with a statement of the reasons for his or her decision on the interests of Justice test. The new section includes a statement that all available details of all the charges have been considered, and this section must be signed by the proper officer. The new Form 1 is designed to provide the statement of reasons required by the regulations with the minimum of additional work for the court.

Form 2

22. This form has been amended to reflect the change to regulation 12(2) which provides that a copy of the record (which will contain the statement of reasons for refusal) should be sent to the applicant in every case where the application was refused on the interests of justice.

Form 3

23. A change has been made to the notes at the end of the form, so that the applicant must provide the court with a copy of any additional information made available to the Area Committee. This is to ensure that the court is able to keep a full record of the application on the file. A copy of Form 4 (or equivalent), setting out the Committee's decision, will also be sent to the court to be retained on the file.

Form 4

24. This form is used by the Area Committee of the Legal Aid Board. The wording has been revised so that it more accurately reflects the criteria set out in section 22(2) of the Legal Aid Act 1988.

Form 5

25. This form has been amended as a result of the inclusion in Form 1 of a section for completion by applicants in receipt of means-tested benefits. Thus, Form 5 will no longer be required in these cases.

Decision tree

26. A 'decision tree', designed to be used as a reference sheet when considering applications for criminal legal aid, will be issued to granting authorities after further consultation. The decision tree will set out the various stages involved in this process, and will refer the user to more detailed guidance where appropriate.

Justices' Clerks Accounting Manual

27. Amendments to the Justices' Clerks Accounting Manual reflecting the changes introduced by these regulations will be made in due course.

Appendix A5

Guidance to Court Staff for Calculation of Legal Aid Contributions 1996/97

PART ONE: NOTES FOR GUIDANCE

1. This guidance covers only financial assessments and calculation of contributions. It does not cover the 'interests of justice' test.

2. Spouse or Partner

In this guidance, reference to *partner* applies to a husband and wife or a man and woman living together in the same household as if they were husband and wife.

3. Supporting evidence of means

The applicant is required to submit documentary evidence in support of the information in his statement of means. Appropriate evidence necessary is suggested in Form 5. Where this evidence is not provided, and the applicant does not supply a written explanation of why it was not practicable to do so, the proper officer should require the evidence to bc produced, or require a reasonable explanation in writing.

4. Grant without evidence of means

When an applicant provides a reasonable explanation of why it is not practicable to provide evidence at the time of the application, the court may grant legal aid and may require that evidence is produced at a later date, if it will then be practicable for the applicant to provide it. In these circumstances, the court must ensure that the necessary evidence is produced. If it is not produced, the court may withdraw the order.

5. Refusal of legal aid

Legal aid may be refused if it appears that the applicant does not require assistance, or if the documentary evidence is deficient and no reasonable explanation is given, and the proper officer is not satisfied on the information before him that the applicant's resources are such that he requires assistance. Alternatively, the proper officer may deem the applicant's disposable income and capital to exceed the level below which no contribution is payable, and fix a contribution at such level as he thinks fit.

6. Income Support, Family Credit, and Disability Working Allowance

If the applicant or his partner is in receipt of income support, family credit or disability working allowance, the contribution from income or capital will be NIL and there is no need to carry out an assessment.

PART TWO: ASSESSMENT

I. Income

Enter here the total average weekly net income of the applicant, including that of his partner (where appropriate). Do not include attendance allowance, disability living allowance, housing benefit, constant attendance allowance paid as an increase to a disablement pension, and payments made out of the social fund.

Total net income £............ (A)

Allowance from income

Enter here the total amount of weekly allowances against income under the following headings:

a. *Maintenance of Dependants*

i Partner living with the applicant:–

Rate £27.30 £............

ii. Dependant children living with the applicant:–

18 and over	Rate £37.90	£............
16 and 17	Rate £28.85	£............
11 to 15	Rate £24.10	£............
Under 11	Rate £16.45	£............

iii. Any other dependants for whom the applicant must provide, at the rates set out at (ii) above.

£............

iv. Total dependants' allowances £............ (B)

b. *Council Tax*

Enter the total weekly amount Council Tax payable by the applicant and by his partner only (if appropriate). Deduct any amount met by Council Tax Benefit.

£............ (C)

c. *Housing Expenses*

Enter the total amount spent on housing including rent or mortgage repayments, water and sewerage charges. Deduct any amount met by housing benefit. Where the applicant pays for board and lodging allow an amount for accommodation costs (that is, excluding food costs included in the total payment) as is reasonable in all the circumstances.

£............ (D)

d. *Travelling Expenses*

Enter the total amount spent on travelling to and from the place of employment.

£............ (E)

e. *Any other expenses for which allowance should be made*

£............ (F)

Total allowance from income (B+C+D+E+F)

£............ (G)

II Capital

Enter here the total capital of the applicant, including that of his partner (where appropriate). Do *not* include those capital resources to be disregarded under Schedule 3 (eg value of main residence, furniture, personal clothing and tools of trade).

Total Capital £............ (H)

PART THREE: CALCULATION OF CONTRIBUTION

1. INCOME

Total disposable income (A) – (G) =

£............ (J)

f. If (J) is £49 or less, the contribution is NIL.

g. If (J) is more than £49, the weekly contribution is £1 for every £3, or part of £3, by which disposable income exceeds £48.

$$\text{Total Weekly contribution (K)} = \frac{\text{Total Disposable Income (J)} - 48}{3}$$

Weekly contributions are payable for the duration of the legal aid order.

2. CAPITAL

h. If (H) is £3,000 or less, the contribution is NIL.

i. If (H) exceeds £3,000, the contribution is the full amount of the excess.

Capital Contribution = All disposable income in excess of £3,000.

ANNEX A

TABLE OF EXAMPLES OF WEEKLY CONTRIBUTIONS

Weekly Disposable Income		Weekly Contribution
£49 and below		NIL
More than £49 but not exceeding	£51	£1
£51	£54	£2
£54	£57	£3
£57	£60	£4
£60	£63	£5
£63	£66	£6
£66	£69	£7
£69	£72	£8

Weekly contributions are payable for the duration of the legal aid order.

Appendix A6

Guidance on Changes to Criminal Legal Aid Means Testing to come into Effect on 1 June 1996

1. I refer to the guidance issued on 11 March 1996 which, amongst other things, outlined the proposals intended to tighten up means assessments for the apparently wealthy and indicated that there would be some consequential changes to Form 5. It also indicated that there would be some further amendments to both Forms 1 and 5 and some additional regulation changes. The guidance set out below now outlines these changes, most of which come into force on June 1. Copies of the regulations accompany this guidance.

PART 1: THE LEGAL AID IN CRIMINAL AND CARE PROCEEDINGS (GENERAL) (AMENDMENT) REGULATIONS 1996

2. The Lord Chancellor has made regulations altering legal aid eligibility following his consultation last year about legal aid for the apparently wealthy. The changes in respect of criminal legal aid are contained in the Legal Aid in Criminal and Care Proceedings (General) (Amendment) Regulations 1996.

The treatment of the assisted person's dwelling house

3. The most important change concerns the treatment of an assisted person's dwelling house, which previously has been wholly exempt for eligibility purposes. Now for advice and assistance, civil and criminal legal aid the following rules will apply as from 1 June 1996:

- For the purposes of computing disposable capital the net value of the property will be taken into account in so far as it exceeds £100,000.
- For the purposes of computing disposable capital the extent to which any mortgage debt or charge over the property can reduce the value of the interest in the property is limited to £100,000.
- For the purposes of computing disposable income the deduction against income allowed for mortgage payments is limited to that payable on the first £100,000 of any mortgage (for example, if mortgage debt is £200,000, only half the amount actually paid will be taken into account).
- There are also provisions for second and subsequent dwellings which provide that the total amount of mortgage debt to be allowed for all properties cannot exceed £100,000.

4. The effect of these changes is that for capital, one will need to take into account the value of an assisted person's home, reduce this by the amount of mortgage or by £100,000, which is ever is the less, to produce a net equity figure. If this exceeds £100,000, the excess over £100,000 is taken into account as the capital of the assisted person.

Several examples are set below for information:

Example 1: Where the market value of a property is £200,000 and the mortgage liability is £75,000.

5. Then £75,000 is below the £100,000 maximum limit so simply deduct the £75,000 from £200,000 (which gives £125,000 as the equity value.) There is however a limit of £100,000 on the amount of equity value in a house which is ignored in the legal aid means assessment. Therefore deduct this £100,000 from the equity value (£125,000) to give the amount of equity which would be treated as disposable capital in the capital means assessment. In this example the amount of equity treated as capital would be £25,000.

6. To calculate the mortgage repayment allowable against income in this example. As there is a limit of £100,000 and the mortgage in this instance is only £75,000 then all of the mortgage repayment is allowable against income.

Example 2: Where the market value of a property is £275,000 and the mortgage liability is £160,000.

7. Then £160,000 is above the £100,000 maximum limit so one should deduct £100,000 from £275,000 (which leaves an equity value of £175,000). There is however a limit of £100,000 on the amount of equity value in a house which is ignored in the legal aid means assessment. There deduct this £100,000 from the above figure (£175,000) to give the amount of equity which would be treated as capital in the capital means assessment. In this example the amount of equity treated as capital would be £75,000.

8. To calculate the mortgage repayment allowable against income in this example. As there is a limit of £100,000 and the mortgage is £160,000 then divide £100,000 by £160,000 and multiply the result by the weekly mortgage repayment figure. This will give you the amount allowable against income.

Example 3: Where the applicant has two properties one with a market value of £200,000 and a mortgage liability of £75,000 the second with a market value of £100,000 and a mortgage liability of £50,000.

9. Take the main property (assumed here to be the larger). The £75,000 mortgage liability is below the £100,000 maximum so the equity value in this residence is market value less mortgage liability i.e. £200,000 – £75,000 = £125,000. There is however a limit of £100,000 on the amount of equity

value in a house which is ignored in the legal aid means assessment. Therefore deduct this from the equity value i.e. £125,000 – £100,000 = £25,000. This gives the amount of equity which is to be treated as disposable capital in the means assessment i.e. £25,000.

10. For the second property the equity value is calculated by deducting the mortgage liability (but only up to a maximum of £100,000 for all properties owned) from the market value i.e. £100,000 – £25,000 (i.e. mortgage is £50,000 but £75,000 of the allowance has already been utilised in the above calculation) = £75,000. The limit of £100,000 on the amount of equity value in a house which is ignored in the legal aid means assessment only applies to the main residence and cannot be carried over to other properties. The total equity that is treated as disposable capital in this example is therefore £25,000 + £75,000 = £100,000.

11. To calculate mortgage repayment allowable. All repayments on the first residence will be allowed as the mortgage liability is £75,000 i.e. less than £100,000. No allowance will be made in respect of mortgage payments on a second property (paragraph 8 of schedule 3, Legal Aid in Criminal and Care Proceedings (General) Regulations 1989).

Example 4: Where an applicant has two properties, one with a market value of £140,000 and a mortgage of £150,000 (i.e. negative equity) and a second property with a value of £100,000 and a mortgage of £50,000.

12. Take the main property first. The limit on mortgage to be allowed is £100,000 so the value of the property is £140,000 less £100,000, namely £40,000. One then applies the £100,000 exemption which means that no capital is taken into account for this property.

13. Turning to the second property, no mortgage can be allowed against this property because the full allowance of £100,000 has already been taken up in the first property. Therefore, the full value of £100,000 is taken into account for this property and since it is not the main property there is no exemption. As a result the total disposable capital arising from the two properties comes to £100,000.

The treatment of the assets of friends and relatives

14. Also on 1 June 1996, for civil and criminal legal aid, an additional discretionary power is being introduced which allows the proper officer to take into account the assets of persons other than the applicant for legal aid. This regulation is designed to catch those who have access to substantial income or capital assets which are in the name of other people or companies. The regulation may be applied where the assisted person has transferred resources to another person; another person has been maintaining the assisted person in the proceedings, e.g. paying their legal expenses, or where any of the resources of the other person have been made available to the assisted person, e.g. paying general living expenses. It will not usually be necessary to investigate all the finances of the friends or relatives of the applicant. In general only those resources being made available to the

applicant should be considered and, if appropriate, included in the legal aid means assessment. There is a wide power to allow the proper officer to assess or estimate the value of those resources to the best of his judgement if detailed valuations are not available.

15. The question of how recent would a transfer of assets to another person have to be, to be caught by the new regulations is not easily answered. The proper officer will have to consider each case individually and use their discretion when carrying out a legal aid means assessment. The regulations are designed to catch people who have deliberately transferred assets in order to obtain legal aid. The date an offence (or the initial offence) is alleged to have been committed is likely to be a reasonable starting date, to consider if any assets have been transferred, for most cases. However, the proper officer will need to use their discretion to identify any earlier relevant transfer of assets depending on the circumstances of the case.

Additional guidance

Capital contributions

16. Schedule 4, of the Legal Aid in Criminal and Care Proceedings (General) Regulations 1989), states that contributions from disposable capital shall be equal to such an amount as disposable capital exceeds £3,000. Regulation 29 (2) requires immediate payment if the sum is readily available. If, as seems likely in cases where assessed disposable capital is in the form of equity in a house, the proper officer may order payment within a reasonable time. In accordance with Regulation 29 (3) in such circumstances the legal aid order is not withheld pending payment.

Capital disregard

17. Proper officers should also be aware of Paragraph 20 of Schedule 3 to the Regulations. This provision allows the disregard of sums which might constitute disposable capital taking into account their nature, or the circumstances of the case.

PART 2: THE LEGAL AID IN CRIMINAL AND CARE PROCEEDINGS (GENERAL) (AMENDMENT) (NO. 3) REGULATIONS 1996

Forms 1 and 5

(a) apparently wealthy

18. The statement of means – Form 5 – has been changed to take account of the Legal Aid in Criminal and Care Proceedings (General) (Amendment) Regulations 1996 referred to in Part 1. Part B of section 2 asks questions aimed at obtaining information relevant to the equity and mortgage liabilities in the applicant's dwelling and other properties. Section 4 has been amended to ask questions about transfer of resources by the applicant and whether the resources of another are available to the applicant either generally or in relation to court proceedings (Regs 14 and 15).

(b) passported applicants

19. Regulation 23(4)(c) provides that where 'it appears' that an applicant, appropriate contributor or their spouse is in receipt of a passporting benefit, they are not required to complete Form 5. That means that there must be a basis on which this can so appear to a court or proper officer. In Form 1 emphasis has been put on the applicant etc. providing documentary evidence in support of receipt of a passporting benefit and also on the need to ensure that the applicant completes a Form 5 if documentary evidence of receipt of a passporting benefit is not available at the time legal aid is granted (Reg 10).

20. In Form 5 the opening paragraph has been amended to make it clear that those applicants who can successfully prove receipt of a passporting benefit need not complete Form 5. The present wording fails to do this and is therefore misleading (Reg 12).

Further information from passported applicants

21. Current regulations do not allow the court or proper officer to ask for further information from assisted parties who have not completed a statement of means because they were in receipt of a passporting benefit. In particular this means that courts or proper officers cannot seek further information from those passported applicants who appear to have had a change in circumstances which might have caused a change in their legal aid status. Regulations 24(1) and 31 have therefore been amended to allow the court or proper officer to ask applicants who have not submitted a statement of means for further information (Regs 3 and 5).

22. Regulation 41(1)(d) has been amended to make revocation easier by freeing that regulation from the constraints of regulation 24(2). This amendment therefore broadens the existing regulation to include those applicants who have been passported to legal aid (Reg 6).

Regulation 41A

23. Regulation 41A 'Withdrawal for abuse of legal aid or for failure to provide information' is a new regulation. It is designed to import a provision similar to one which exists in the civil regulations. Regulation 41A will allow a legal aid order to be withdrawn if information provided is found to be false or misleading or the assisted person has failed to provide information when requested to do so (Reg 7). An order withdrawing legal aid under this regulation should be made on Form 14, which has been amended to provide for this (Reg 15).

Duty to report abuse

24. The present regulation 56 allows the assisted party's legal representative to inform the proper officer of any facts which have led the legal representative to know that the assisted party is abusing the legal aid scheme. The amendment widens the regulation by giving the legal representative an

additional duty of informing the proper officer of any circumstances within the assisted party's conduct which may have led the legal representative to believe that an abuse is taking place (Reg 8)

Income-based jobseekers allowance

25. The income based jobseekers allowance will become a new passporting benefit from 7 October. The regulations and forms have been amended now to prepare for this (Regs 2, 4, 9, 11 and 12).

ENQUIRIES

26. Enquiries about the contents of this circular should be referred to Stan Coats (0171 210 8784) or Chris Morter (0171 210 8787).

LEGAL AID DIVISION
LORD CHANCELLOR'S DEPARTMENT
10 MAY 1996

Appendix B

Article 6 European Convention on Human Rights

Article 6

1. In the determination of his civil rights and obligations or of any criminal charge against him, everyone is entitled to a fair and public hearing within a reasonable time by an independent and impartial tribunal established by law. Judgement shall be pronounced publicly by press and the public may be excluded from all or part of the trial in the interests of morals, public order or national security in a democratic society, where the interests of juveniles or the protection of the private life of the parties so require, or the extent strictly necessary in the opinion of the court in special circumstances where publicity would prejudice the interests of justice.
2. Everyone charged with a criminal offence shall be presumed innocent until proved guilty according to law.
3. Everyone charged with a criminal offence has the following minimum rights:
   (a) to be informed promptly, in a language which he understands and in detail, of the nature and cause of the accusation against him;
   (b) to have adequate time and the facilities for the preparation of his defence;
   (c) to defend himself in person or through legal assistance of his own choosing or, if he has not sufficient means to pay for the legal assistance, to be given it free when the interests of justice so require;
   (d) to examine or have examined witnesses against him and to obtain the attendance and examination of witnesses on his behalf under the same conditions as witnesses against him;
   (e) to have the free assistance of an interpreter if he cannot understand or speak the language used in court.

Appendix C

Legal Aid Board Duty Solicitor Arrangements 1994

ARRANGEMENT OF PARAGRAPHS

PART I - GENERAL

1. Transitional arrangements
2. Interpretation
3. Regions

PART II - THE DUTY SOLICITOR COMMITTEE

4. Appointment of Duty Solicitor Committee
5. Powers and duties

PART III - REGIONAL DUTY SOLICITOR COMMITTEES

6. Appointment of regional committee Members and size of Membership
7. Categories of membership
8. Appointment of regional committee lay members
9. Majority of members
10. Adjudication on appeals and exclusions
11. Period of service
12. Vacancies
13. Powers and duties - magistrates' courts
14. Powers and duties - police stations
15. Powers and duties - general
16. Applications for review and appeal by the Duty Solicitor Committee

PART IV - LOCAL DUTY SOLICITOR COMMITTEES

17. Size of membership
18. Categories of membership
19. Solicitor and lay members
20. Majority of members and conduct of meetings
21. Adjudication on selection or exclusion
22. Period of service
23. Vacancies
24. Duties
25. Detailed arrangements - magistrates' courts
26. Detailed arrangements - police stations
27. Detailed arrangements - general
28. Appeals to regional committee
29. Appeals to the Duty Solicitor Committee
30. Payment of administrators

PART V - SELECTION OF DUTY SOLICITORS

31. Application
32. Selection criteria - magistrates' courts
33. Selection criteria - police stations
34. Interview
35. Approval of applications
36. Rejection of applications
37. Appeals to regional committee
38. Reselection
39. Reselection criteria - magistrates' courts and police stations
40. Reselection criteria - continuing training
41. Representations about performance
42. Changes in circumstances - duty to report
43. Changes in rota

PART VI- DUTY SOLICITORS' REPRESENTATIVES

44. Application
45. Selection criteria
46. Interview
47. Appeal to regional committee
48. Reselection criteria

PART VII - SCOPE OF SERVICE - MAGISTRATES' COURTS

49. Defendant's right to instruct another solicitor
50. Services to be provided
51. Prohibition of certain services
52. Duty to remain at court

PART VIII - SCOPE OF SERVICE - POLICE STATIONS

53. Initial advice
54. Obligation to attend the suspect at the police station
55. Discretion to attend the suspect at the police station
56. Services personnel
57. Advice by duty solicitor's representative
58. Continued instructions

PART IX - COMMITTEES - GENERAL PROVISIONS

59. Election of chairman and vice-chairman
60. Quorum
61. Minutes
62. Regional committee sub-committee and procedure
63. Resignation
64. Disqualification
65. Committee members' expenses and fees
66. Consultation with local Law Societies

The following arrangements have been approved by the Board and come into effect on 1 October 1994.

PART I - GENERAL

Transitional Arrangements

1. A committee member appointed or reappointed under the Duty Solicitor Arrangements 1992 or any previous Arrangements or Scheme shall be deemed to have been appointed or reappointed under these Arrangements for the remainder of the period for which he or she was so appointed or reappointed and any decision validly made under the Duty Solicitor Arrangements 1992 or any previous Arrangements or Scheme shall be deemed to continue to have been validly made.

Interpretation

2. In these Arrangements, unless the context otherwise requires:

"the 1988 Act" means the Legal Aid Act 1988;

"advice" means "advice and assistance" under Part III of the 1988 Act;

"appropriate area committee" means the area committee in the area of which are situated the magistrates' courts at which advice and representation is provided or police stations at which advice is provided;

"appropriate regional committee" means the regional duty solicitor committee in the region of which are situated the magistrates' courts at which advice and representation is provided and police stations at which advice is provided;

"appropriate local committee" means the local duty solicitor committee appointed by the appropriate regional committee for the purpose of making arrangements whereby advice and representation is provided by duty solicitors at one or more specified magistrates' courts and advice is provided by duty solicitors to persons at police stations;

"appropriate local law society" means the society or societies in the district or districts of which are situated the magistrates' courts at which it is proposed to provide advice and representation or police stations at which it is proposed to provide advice;

"area committee" means the area committee appointed by the Board in respect of each legal aid area;

"Board" means the Legal Aid Board appointed under the 1988 Act;

"clerk of the court" means a justices' clerk or a member of the staff of a justices' clerk acting as a clerk in a magistrates' court;

"duty solicitor" means a solicitor who in accordance with arrangements made by the appropriate local committee is in attendance at a magistrates' court for the purpose of providing advice and representation or giving advice at a police station or both and, in each case, has been selected in accordance with these Arrangements;

"Duty Solicitor Committee" means the committee appointed by the Legal Aid Board;

"duty solicitor's representative" means any person selected in accordance with paragraph 45;

"lay member" means a person neither practising as a barrister or solicitor nor coming within any of the categories specified in paragraphs 7(2), (3), (5), (7), (9) and (10) or 18(3), (4), (6) and (7).

"local committee" means the committee appointed by the appropriate regional committee for the purpose of making arrangements whereby advice and representation is provided by duty solicitors at one or more magistrates' courts and advice is provided at police stations;

"local law society" means a society or group of societies which is for the time being recognised as a local law society by the Law Society and, in London, includes the London Criminal Courts Solicitors' Association;

"panel" and "panel cases" means an arrangement whereby the telephone service telephones the duty solicitors in the order in which they appear on the panel until finding one willing to give advice and assistance at a police station. The telephone service will then start with the next duty solicitor on the panel in respect of the next suspect requiring advice and assistance at a police station. The panel arrangement will also apply where the telephone service is unable to refer to a solicitor on a rota;

"police station" means a police station, or any other place where a constable is present or, except where expressly excluded by these Arrangements, any place where Services personnel are assisting with an investigation under paragraph 56;

"region" means one of the regions referred to in paragraph 3;

"regional committee" means the committee appointed by the Duty Solicitor Committee for each region for the purpose of making arrangements whereby duty solicitors shall be in attendance at magistrates' courts and police stations within that region;

"regulations" mean the Legal Advice and Assistance Regulations 1989, the Legal Advice and Assistance (Scope) Regulations 1989; the Legal Advice and Assistance (Duty Solicitor) (Remuneration) Regulations 1989 and the Legal Advice and Assistance at Police Stations (Remuneration) Regulations 1989 and all subsequent amendments to such regulations;

"representation" means "assistance by way of representation" under Part III of the 1988 Act;

"rota" means a rota of duty solicitors to give advice and representation at magistrates' courts and advice at police stations;

"Services Discipline Acts" mean the Army Act 1955, the Air Force Act 1955 and the Navy Discipline Act 1957;

"Services police" means members of the Royal Naval Special Investigations Branch, members of the Corps of Royal Military Police or Women's Royal Army Corps Provost, Royal Air Force Provost Officers or members of the Royal Air Force Police;

"Services person" means a person assisting with an investigation by the Services police;

"suspect" means a person who for the purposes of assisting with an investigation attends voluntarily at a police station or who accompanies a constable to a police station without having been arrested or who has been arrested and is being held in custody in a police station or other premises or a Services person assisting with an investigation by Services police under paragraph 56.

"telephone service" means the telephone service established by the Duty Solicitor Committee to receive initial requests for advice from suspects at police stations;

Regions

3. For the purposes of these Arrangements, England and Wales shall be divided into the regions which are set out in Schedule I.

PART II - THE DUTY SOLICITOR COMMITTEE

Appointment of Duty Solicitor Committee

4. The Duty Solicitor Committee is appointed by the Board and shall perform its duties and exercise its powers in accordance with any guidance and directions issued by the Board.

Powers and duties

5. (1) The Duty Solicitor Committee shall:

(a) review decisions of a regional committee under paragraph 16 and appeals from a local committee under paragraph 29. The Duty Solicitor Committee shall give the appellant reasons for its decision in connection with a review or an appeal;

(b) give such directions and guidance to regional committees as it considers necessary;

(c) maintain records and call for such reports from the regional and local committees as are necessary for the Committee to fulfil its responsibilities properly; and

(d) make reports and recommendations to the Board in respect of the provisions and operations of these Arrangements.

(2) The Duty Solicitor Committee may:

(a) modify any provision in these Arrangements in connection with the provision of advice and representation at particular courts or advice at particular police stations;

(b) remove from office for due cause any member of a regional committee or local committee.

(3) (a) Whether or not arrangements have been approved under paragraph 14 (2) or any such arrangements are still operating, the Duty Solicitor Committee may, if it thinks fit, recommend to the Board that it enter into a contract or contracts for the provision of advice under Part II of the 1988 Act at specified police stations, and the procedure for so doing.

(b) If the Board approves such recommendation the Duty Solicitor Committee shall, at the appropriate time,

(i) where arrangements have been approved under paragraph 14(2), give notice to the appropriate regional committee that from a specified date the approval under paragraph 14(2) for arrangements at specified police stations shall be of no effect; and

(ii) in all cases direct the appropriate regional committee not to approve arrangements for specified police stations without the prior approval of the Duty Solicitor Committee.

(4) (a) Whether or not arrangements have been approved under paragraph 13(1) or any such arrangements are still operating the Duty Solicitor Committee may, if it thinks fit, recommend to the Board that it enter into a contract or contracts for the provision of advice and representation under Part II of the 1988 Act at specified magistrates' courts and the procedure for so doing.

(b) If the Board approves such recommendation, the Duty Solicitor Committee shall, at the appropriate time,

(i) where arrangements have been approved under paragraph 13(1) give notice to the appropriate regional committee that from a specified date the approval under paragraph 13(1) for arrangements at specified magistrates' courts shall be of no effect; and

(ii) in all cases direct the appropriate regional committee not to approve arrangements for specified magistrates' courts without the prior approval of the Duty Solicitor Committee.

PART III - REGIONAL DUTY SOLICITOR COMMITTEES

Appointment of Regional Committee Members and size of Membership

6. The members of a regional committee shall be such as the regional committee shall from time to time appoint but shall not be fewer than 10 nor more than 35.

Categories of membership

7. The members of each regional committee shall be the following:

(1) at least one member of each local committee in the region following the appointment of a committee or committees under paragraphs 13(1)(c) and 14(1), one or more of such member or members to be a duty solicitor with considerable current experience of advocacy in criminal cases in magistrates' courts to be nominated by the appropriate local committee;

(2) one or more Justices of the Peace, nominated by the Magistrates' Association;

(3) one or more Justices' Clerks, nominated by the Justices' Clerks' Society;

(4) two lay members. Members of court staff are ineligible for appointment under this sub-paragraph;

(5) one or more representatives of the police force or forces in the region nominated by the chief officer(s) of police;

and may include:

(6) one member of the appropriate area committee, such member to be a solicitor advocate experienced in criminal law and nominated by the appropriate area committee;

(7) one or more representatives of the probation service or services in the

region nominated by that service or those services;

(8) one or more lay members. Members of court staff are eligible for appointment under this sub-paragraph;

(9) one or more representatives of the Crown Prosecution Service nominated by that Service;

(10) a stipendiary magistrate.

Appointment of regional committee lay members

8. Applicants for membership of the regional committee within the categories set out in paragraphs 7(4) and 7(8) shall, prior to appointment, be interviewed by the chairman or vice-chairman and a majority of members of the regional committee appointed under paragraphs 7(4) and 7(8) in order to ascertain the extent of the applicants' understanding of the role of regional committee lay members and the applicants' suitability for membership of the regional committee.

Majority of members

9. The majority of members of a regional committee shall be solicitors appointed under paragraphs 7 (1), (6), and (9).

Adjudication on appeals and exclusions

10. (1) A decision by a regional committee upon an appeal under paragraphs 15(7) or 47(1) or a decision to exclude or suspend under paragraphs 15(5) or 15(14) can only be made by the solicitor members appointed under paragraphs 7(1) and 7(6) and the lay members save that the other members of the regional committee may participate in the deliberations of the regional committee prior to the decision being made.

(2) A member of the local committee which has made the decision from which the appeal is being made shall not participate in the hearing and determination of such appeal.

Period of service

11. Every member of a regional committee shall be appointed for a period not exceeding three years and may be reappointed by the regional committee, subject to such consultation or nomination as is required by paragraph 7, for successive periods not exceeding three years until he or she has attained 70 years of age. A member shall be re-appointed only if he or she has attended at least half of all the meetings which were held during his or her membership unless the regional committee considers that there are special circumstances to permit re-appointment despite a lower level of attendance.

Vacancies

12. Any vacancy on a regional committee caused by the retirement or otherwise of members shall be filled by the regional committee in accordance with the provisions of this Part of these Arrangements.

Powers and duties - magistrates' courts

13. In accordance with the provisions of Regulations 6 and 7 of the Legal Advice and Assistance Regulations 1989 and subject to any directions and guidance given to it by the Duty Solicitor Committee and in consultation with the appropriate local law society every regional committee shall:-

(1) in consultation with the appropriate magistrates' courts:

(a) decide in which magistrates' courts in the region it would be appropriate, in accordance with guidance laid down by the Duty Solicitor Committee, for duty solicitors to be in attendance whether or not any defendant wishes to consult a duty solicitor;

(b) in relation to those magistrates' courts in the region which do not come within the provisions of paragraph 13 (1)(a), make such arrangements as it thinks fit for the provision of advice and representation in accordance with guidance laid down by the Duty Solicitor Committee;

(c) the regional committee shall establish and appoint the members of a local committee for the magistrates' courts coming within paragraph 13(1)(a) and (b) and shall supervise such committees; and

(d) consider and, if satisfied, approve arrangements prepared by the appropriate local committee in accordance with guidance laid down by the Duty Solicitor Committee for the provision of advice and representation by duty solicitors at magistrates' courts.

(2) consider and, if satisfied, approve applications under paragraph 25(4);

(3) if it thinks fit, withdraw its approval of existing arrangements for the provision of advice and representation at magistrates' courts and substitute other arrangements where in its view the substituted arrangements will provide an adequate service to the public taking into account the cost of providing such a service.

Powers and duties - police stations

14. In accordance with the provisions of Regulations 6 and 7 of the Legal Advice and Assistance Regulations 1989 and subject to any directions and guidance given to it by the Duty Solicitor Committee and in consultation with the appropriate local law society every regional duty solicitor committee:

(1) shall consider what arrangements are required for the provision of advice by duty solicitors at police stations in the region, establish and appoint the members of local committees for the purpose of making such arrangements and shall supervise such committees. Such local committees may be either the committees appointed under paragraph 13(1)(c), or committees appointed solely for the purposes of this sub-paragraph;

(2) shall consider and, if satisfied, approve arrangements prepared by the appropriate local committees in accordance with guidance laid down by the Duty Solicitor Committee for the provision of advice by duty solicitors at police stations;

(3) may approve the use of duty solicitors' representatives in connection with the provision of advice at police stations covered by a particular local committee and may limit their use to particular periods of time;

(4) may approve:

(a) a variation in the requirements in paragraph 33(2) that an applicant shall live or work within 45 minutes travel time of the relevant police station;

(b) a modification under paragraph 26(6);

(5) shall if it thinks fit, withdraw its approval of existing arrangements for the provision of advice at police stations and substitute other arrangements,

where in its view the substituted arrangements will provide an adequate service to the public taking into account the cost of providing such a service.

Powers and duties - general

15. In accordance with the provisions of Regulations 6 and 7 of the Legal Advice and Assistance Regulations 1989 and subject to any directions and guidance given it by the Duty Solicitor Committee in consultation, if appropriate, with the appropriate local law society every regional committee shall administer these Arrangements within its region and in particular, and without prejudice to the generality of the foregoing:-

(1) may if it thinks fit, consent to a proposal by a local committee submitted in accordance with paragraph 25(10), or direct a local committee, to exclude solicitors from providing advice and representation at magistrates' courts unless such solicitors are willing to provide advice at police stations as duty solicitors subject to the right of appeal against any such direction set out in paragraph 29;

(2) shall monitor the arrangements by local committees for advice and representation at magistrates' courts and advice at police stations;

(3) shall:

(a) require a local committee to take any steps specified by the regional committee to facilitate the provision of advice and representation by duty solicitors and ensure that arrangements exist for dealing with emergencies;

(b) amalgamate two or more local committees if in the view of the regional committee an improved service would be provided to the public by so doing;

(4) shall if not satisfied with the arrangements made by the appropriate local committee for the provision of advice and representation at any magistrates' court or advice at any police station, give notice to the appropriate local committee requiring it to provide adequate arrangements within the period specified in the notice which shall not be less than three calendar months. If at the end of that period the appropriate regional committee is still not satisfied with the arrangements it may, with the consent of the Duty Solicitor Committee, disband the appropriate local committee forthwith and appoint a new committee in its place;

(5) (a) may if it thinks fit, suspend for a period of up to 12 months or exclude a duty solicitor from providing either advice and representation at magistrates' courts or advice at police stations or both in the event of failure to satisfy any of the criteria set out in Part V, failure to carry out his or her duties or for some other good cause provided that the solicitor has been notified of any complaint against him or her and that he or she may make written representations or give notice of his or her intention to make oral representations within 21 days of the committee having notified him or her of the complaint;

(b) failure to accept a reasonable number of calls while on panel duty may be treated as sufficient reason to justify exclusion or suspension;

(c) if the committee decides to exclude or suspend the duty solicitor it shall provide him or her with a written statement of the reasons for its decision;

(d) when a solicitor is under investigation or has been charged with a criminal offence or is the subject of an investigation by the Solicitors Complaints Bureau, the chairman with the concurrence of two other members of the committee may suspend the solicitor for a period of up to six weeks without his or her having been notified of the complaint against him or her or having the opportunity to be heard. The period of suspension may be extended for good reason on one other occasion for a further period of six weeks by the chairman with the concurrence of two members of the committee;

(e) the effect of a decision to suspend or exclude shall be immediate, subject to the regional committee having a discretion to postpone the effect providing that the solicitor affected undertakes to submit a notice of an appeal under paragraph 16(2) within the period stipulated in that paragraph;

(6) may if it thinks fit, recommend to the Duty Solicitor Committee that any provision in these Arrangements be modified in connection with the provision of advice and representation at any specified magistrates' court or advice at specified police stations;

(7) shall determine appeals under paragraphs 28, 37, and 47, and in connection with such appeals:

(a) each appeal shall be by way of a rehearing;

(b) the appellant shall submit written representations when giving notice of appeal and shall send a copy of such representations to the appropriate local committee;

(c) the appropriate local committee may submit written representations about the appeal to the appropriate regional committee and if it does so shall send a copy of such representations to the appellant;

(d) The Board's staff may obtain and provide information relating to the appeal and they shall ensure that both the appellant and the local committee receive copies;

(e) the appellant shall have the right to make oral representations to the appropriate regional committee in support of the appeal. If the oral representations or any written representations subsequently submitted cover matters not covered in the written representations referred to in paragraph 15(7)(b) the regional committee has a discretion not to consider such additional matters unless the appellant has given 14 days notice to the Board's staff and the local committee;

(f) the appellant shall be given written reasons for the appeal decision;

(g) where the regional committee is of the opinion that the local committee has not complied with the procedure laid down in paragraphs 35, 36, 38, 45(2) and 48 or with any directions and guidance given by the Duty Solicitor Committee under paragraph 5 (1)(b) it may refer the matter back to the appropriate local committee for reconsideration;

(h) the regional committee may exclude the appellant from any other scheme or schemes in the relevant region on the basis of the regional committee's appeal findings provided that the appellant has received 21 days notice that the regional committee may consider exclusion from such other schemes;

(8) shall investigate complaints about the provisions of advice and representation at magistrates' courts and

advice at police stations by duty solicitors;

(9) may report to the Duty Solicitor Committee any circumstances where duty solicitors have inadequate access to defendants in custody or suspects at police stations or inadequate facilities to enable them to carry our their functions;

(10) may if it thinks fit, approve local instructions to duty solicitors made by a local committee under paragraph 27 (7)(a);

(11) shall supply to the Duty Solicitor Committee such reports, statistics, estimates and other information as the Duty Solicitor Committee may from time to time require;

(12) shall keep the police, courts and other relevant organisations in the region informed about the existence and responsibilities of the regional committee;

(13) may revoke any consent, direction or approval it has given under paragraphs 13(1)(d), 14(2), 14(3), 14(4), 14(5), 15(1), 15(10), 25(4) and 25(6);

(14) (a) may if it thinks fit, suspend for a period of up to 12 months or exclude a duty solicitor's representative from providing advice if satisfied that he or she has failed to satisfy any of the criteria set out in paragraph 45(1), or that there is some other good cause provided that the duty solicitor employing the representative has been notified of the complaint against the representative and that the appropriate duty solicitor may make written representations or give notice of his or her intention to make oral representations within 21 days of the committee having notified him or her of the complaint;

(b) if the committee decides to exclude or suspend the representative, it shall provide the appropriate duty solicitor with a written statement of the reasons for its decision;

(c) where a duty solicitor's representative is under investigation or has been charged with a criminal offence, the chairman with the concurrence of two other members of the committee may suspend a duty solicitor's representative for a period of up to six weeks without his or her having been notified of the complaint against him or her or having the opportunity to be heard. The period of suspension may be extended for good reason on one occasion for a further period of six weeks by the chairman with the concurrence of two members of the committee;

(d) the effect of a decision to suspend or exclude shall be immediate subject to the committee having discretion to postpone the effect providing that the appropriate duty solicitor undertakes to submit a notice of an appeal under paragraph 16(2) within the period stipulated in that paragraph;

(15) may for good reason remove an administrator appointed by a local committee under paragraph 27(5) and request the local committee to appoint another administrator;

(16) may in exceptional circumstances waive the relevant paragraph where a local committee makes a recommendation under paragraph 32(1)(f)(vi) subject to the applicant appearing before the regional committee.

Applications for review and appeal by the Duty Solicitor Committee

16. (1) Where a duty solicitor or representative is dissatisfied with the determination of an appeal under paragraph 15(7) he or she may submit a written request for a review to the Duty Solicitor Committee;

(2) Where a duty solicitor or duty solicitor's representative is excluded or suspended under paragraphs 15(5), 15(7)(h) or 15(14) he or she may appeal to the Duty Solicitor Committee;

(3) The request for a review or notice of an appeal must be given within 28 days of having been notified of the decision of the appropriate regional committee subject to the Duty Solicitor Committee having discretion to accept a request outside the period of 28 days for good reason;

(4) A request for a review shall include a statement of reasons for which it is claimed that the regional committee's decision was unreasonable;

(5) The conduct of an appeal to the Duty Solicitor Committee shall be conducted so far as may be appropriate in the same way as an appeal to a regional committee under paragraph 15(7).

PART IV - LOCAL DUTY SOLICITOR COMMITTEES

Size of membership

17. The members of a local committee shall be such as the appropriate regional committee shall from time to time appoint and shall not be fewer than four or more than 15.

Categories of membership

18. The members of each local committee shall be the following:

(1) at least three solicitors with considerable current experience of advocacy in criminal cases in magistrates' courts of whom the majority shall be duty solicitors but excluding solicitors employed on a full time basis by the Crown Prosecution Service;

(2) one lay member. Members of court staff are ineligible for appointment under this sub-paragraph;

and may also include:

(3) one or more Justices of the Peace or stipendiary magistrate;

(4) one or more Justices' Clerks;

(5) a solicitor with considerable current experience of advocacy in criminal cases in magistrates' courts employed on a full-time basis by the Crown Prosecution Service;

(6) one or more representatives of the Probation Service or Services nominated by that Service or those Services;

(7) one or more representatives of the police force or forces nominated by the chief officer(s) of police; and

(8) not more than two additional lay members. Members of court staff are eligible for appointment under this paragraph.

Solicitor and lay members

19. (1) Solicitor members appointed under paragraph 18(1) shall be appointed after consultation with the appropriate local law society;

(2) Applicants for membership of the local committee within the categories set out in paragraphs 18(2) and 18(8) shall, prior to appointment, be interviewed by the chairman or vice-chairman and a majority of members of

the local committee in order to ascertain the extent of the applicants' understanding of the role of the local committee lay member, and the applicants' suitability for membership of the local committee. An existing member of the local committee appointed under paragraphs 18(2), or (8) if there is one, shall be present at the interview failing which a member of the appropriate regional committee, appointed under paragraph 7(4) or (8), should be given notice of the interview and a reasonable opportunity to attend.

Majority of members and conduct of meetings

20. (1) The majority of members of a local committee shall be solicitors appointed under paragraph 18(1).

(2) A member of the relevant regional committee and/or a member of the Board's staff shall be entitled to attend local committee meetings and shall be given adequate notice of a meeting where notice is given of an intention to attend.

Adjudication on selection or exclusion

21. A decision by a local committee upon selection and reselection under paragraphs 35, 38, 45 or 48 or the exclusion or suspension under paragraphs 27(3) or 27(10) can only be made by the solicitor members appointed under paragraphs 18(1) or (5) and the lay members save that the other members of the local committee may participate in the deliberations of the local committee prior to the decision being made.

Period of service

22. Every member of a local committee shall be appointed for a period not exceeding three years and may be reappointed by the appropriate regional committee, subject to such consultation as is required under paragraph 23(2), for successive periods not exceeding three years until he or she has attained 70 years of age.

Vacancies

23. (1) Any vacancy on a local committee caused by retirement or otherwise may be filled by the appropriate regional committee;

(2) in the case of a solicitor appointed under paragraph 18(1) after consultation with the appropriate local law society.

Duties

24. (1) Each local committee shall help the Board to provide a quality service to the public;

(2) The appropriate local committee shall, subject to any directions given to it by the appropriate regional committee, make arrangements for advice and representation to be provided by duty solicitors at the court or courts and advice at police stations in connection with which the committee is appointed under paragraphs 13(1)(c) or 14(1) respectively;

(3) Arrangements made under paragraph 24(2) are subject to approval by the appropriate regional committee and shall come into effect only when they have been approved under paragraph 13 or 14 as appropriate;

(4) Each local committee shall meet a minimum of once a year or:

(a) to consider an application from a solicitor who wishes to become a duty solicitor or an application in respect of a duty solicitor's representative or to undertake the reselection of a duty solicitor or duty solicitor's representative, or

(b) at the request of the chairman of the relevant regional committee, or

(c) if a member of the local committee submits a request in writing to the chairman of the local committee, or

(d) to consider an audit report about the performance of duty solicitors under the arrangements provided by the local committee.

Detailed arrangements - magistrates' courts

25. In connection with providing advice and representation under Part VII the appropriate local committee:

(1) shall ensure that arrangements exist to inform all defendants, who are eligible for advice or representation in accordance with the provisions of paragraph 50, of the availability of the duty solicitor;

(2) shall ensure that arrangements exist for a duty solicitor to be present at court, or available to the court, as the regional committee may specify so as to provide advice and representation as specified in paragraph 50 to defendants who are eligible to receive such advice and representation;

(3) shall ensure that arrangements exist for defendants who wish to receive advice and representation by a duty solicitor as specified in paragraph 50 to receive such advice and representation;

(4) shall apply to the appropriate regional committee for approval where it is proposed that more than one duty solicitor is regularly to be on duty at the same court at the same time;

(5) shall ensure where practicable that arrangements are made to provide advice and representation where sittings in addition to ordinary sittings of courts are involved;

(6) may, with the consent of the appropriate regional committee, specify the maximum number of courts before which a solicitor may appear as duty solicitor;

(7) may require all duty solicitors appointed by the local committee whilst acting as duty solicitor, not to undertake any cases in connection with which he or she has previously received instructions;

(8) may make appropriate arrangements for duty solicitors to be assisted by representatives of voluntary organisations to make initial contact with defendants and provide advice to defendants and their families;

(9) shall use its best endeavours to ensure compliance with Part VII;

(10) may, with the consent of the appropriate regional committee, exclude solicitors from providing advice and representation at magistrates' courts unless such solicitors are willing to provide advice at police stations as duty solicitors.

Detailed arrangements - police stations

26. In connection with the provision of advice at police stations the appropriate local committee either by itself or in conjunction with other local committees:

(1) shall ensure that arrangements exist for suspects to receive advice at police stations in accordance with paragraphs 53 - 56;

(2) shall, with the approval of the appropriate regional committee under paragraph 14(2), ensure that arrangements exist for duty solicitors to be available at all times of the day and night to give advice at police stations by means of a rota or a panel arrangement or by a combination of both;

(3) may require a duty solicitor to be available to go to a police station with the least possible delay;

(4) may, with the consent of the appropriate regional committee, permit the provision by duty solicitors' representatives of advice at police stations;

(5) may, where the appropriate regional committee consents to the use of duty solicitors' representatives, decide to select only solicitors as duty solicitors' representatives;

(6) may, with the consent of the regional committee, modify the requirement of home or office in paragraph 33(2) to office only.

Detailed arrangements - general

27. In connection with the provision of advice and representation at magistrates' courts and advice at police stations the appropriate local committee:

(1) shall satisfy itself that duty solicitors are not improperly or unnecessarily prevented from providing advice and representation to defendants and advice to suspects and, if the committee is not so satisfied, it shall report the matter to the appropriate regional committee;

(2) shall be responsible for the selection of duty solicitors in accordance with the procedure specified in Part V;

(3) (a) may suspend for a period of up to 12 months or exclude a duty solicitor from providing advice and representation at magistrates' courts or advice at police stations or both if satisfied that he or she has failed to carry out his or her duties or to meet any of the criteria set out in Part V, or is in breach of any local instructions to duty solicitors made under paragraph 27(7)(a), or that there is some other good cause provided that the solicitor has been notified of the complaint against him or her and that he or she may make written representations or give notice of his or her intention to make oral representations within 21 days of the committee having notified him or her of the complaint;

(b) failure to accept a reasonable number of calls while on panel duty may be treated as sufficient reason to justify exclusion or suspension;

(c) if the committee decides to exclude or suspend the duty solicitor it shall provide him or her with a written statement of the reasons for its decision;

(d) when a solicitor is under investigation for or has been charged with a criminal offence or is the subject of an investigation by the Solicitors Complaints Bureau, the chairman with the concurrence of two other members of the local committee may suspend a duty solicitor for a period of up to six weeks without him or her having been notified of the complaint against him or her or having the opportunity to be heard. The period of suspension may be extended for good reason on one occasion for a further period of six weeks by the chairman with the concurrence of two members of the local committee;

(e) the effect of a determination to suspend or exclude shall be immediate, subject to the local committee having discretion to postpone the effect, providing that the duty solicitor affected undertakes to submit notice of an appeal within the period stipulated in paragraph 28. An exclusion should be notified by the local committee to the relevant regional committee;

(4) shall, where a rota is required, by itself or in conjunction with other local committees, arrange rotas of individual duty solicitors for periods not exceeding six months which may include more than one duty solicitor from the same firm, and send copies of the rota as appropriate to the court, the telephone service, each solicitor on the rota, the appropriate office of the Board and such other organisations as the committee may determine no less than four weeks before the expiration of the previous rota;

(5) may appoint one or more administrators to prepare and issue the rota or rotas of duty solicitors, to receive applications from solicitors who wish to become duty solicitors, to convene meetings of the committee and generally to deal with the day to day matters including liaison with the courts and police, where it wishes these functions to be undertaken by an administrator rather than by the relevant legal aid office;

(6) may apply to the appropriate regional committee to exercise its power of recommendation under paragraph 15(6) where the committee considers that modification of these Arrangements is required;

(7) with the approval of the appropriate regional committee:

(a) shall prepare local instructions to duty solicitors relating to the procedure to be adopted by duty solicitors to comply with Parts VII and VIII and

(b) may issue notes for guidance and publicity;

(8) shall, if so required, submit an annual report to the appropriate regional committee about the operation of the arrangements in the courts or police stations for which it is responsible;

(9) shall supply to the appropriate regional committee or the appropriate office of the Board such reports, statistics, estimates, local instructions to duty solicitors and other information as that committee may from time to time require;

(10) (a) may suspend for a period of up to 12 months or exclude a duty solicitor's representative from providing advice if satisfied that he or she has failed to satisfy any of the criteria set out in paragraph 45(1) or that there is some other good cause provided that the appropriate duty solicitor has been notified of the complaint against him or her and that the appropriate duty solicitor may make written representations or give notice of his or her intention to make oral representations within 21 days of the committee having notified him or her of the complaint;

(b) if the committee decides to exclude or suspend the representative it shall provide the appropriate duty solicitor with a written statement of the reasons for its decision;

(c) where a duty solicitor's representative is under investigation for or has been charged with a criminal offence, the chairman with the concurrence of two other members of the local committee may suspend a duty solicitor's representative for a period of up to six weeks without him or her having been notified of the complaint against him or her or having the opportunity to be heard. The period of suspension may be extended for good reason on one occasion for a further period of six weeks by the chairman with the concurrence of two members of the local committee;

(d) the effect of a determination to suspend or exclude shall be immediate, subject to the local committee having a discretion to postpone the effect providing that the appropriate duty solicitor undertakes to submit notice of an appeal within the period stipulated by paragraph 28;

(11) Where a duty solicitor or a duty solicitor's representative has been excluded an application under paragraphs 31 and 44 may not be made to a local committee to which the exclusion relates for a period of 12 months from the date of the decision to exclude or any appeal or review relating thereto. If after 12 months an application is made to a local committee to which the exclusion relates and that local committee refuses to remove the exclusion the local committee shall not entertain a further application if made within 12 months of the refusal to remove the exclusion;

(12) shall comply with any revocation by the appropriate regional committee under paragraph 15(13) subject to an appeal to the Duty Solicitor Committee under paragraph 29.

Appeals to Regional Committee

28. (1) Where a duty solicitor has been excluded or suspended from providing advice and representation at magistrates' courts or advice at police stations or both under paragraph 27(3) or not reselected under paragraph 38 he or she may appeal to the appropriate regional committee within 28 days of the decision being notified to him or her subject to that committee having discretion to accept an appeal outside the period of 28 days for good reason;

(2) Where a duty solicitor's representative has been excluded or suspended from providing advice under paragraph 27(10) or not reselected under paragraph 48, the appropriate duty solicitor may appeal in writing to the appropriate regional committee within 28 days of the decision being notified to him or her subject to that committee having discretion to accept an appeal outside the period of 28 days for good reason;

(3) Where a local committee refuses to remove an exclusion under paragraph 27(11) the duty solicitor or the appropriate duty solicitor for a duty solicitor's representative may appeal to the regional committee.

Appeals to Duty Solicitor Committee

29. Where a local committee objects to being required by the appropriate regional committee to exclude solicitors from providing advice and representation at magistrates' courts or advice at police stations under paragraph 15(1), or to a revocation by the appropriate regional committee under paragraph 15(13), the local committee may appeal in writing to the Duty Solicitor Committee within 28 days of the decision being notified to it, subject to the Duty Solicitor Committee having the power to accept an appeal outside the period of 28 days for good reason.

Payment of administrators

30. The administrators appointed under paragraph 27(5) above may be paid for any reasonable expenses actually incurred by them.

PART V - SELECTION OF DUTY SOLICITORS

Application

31. The appropriate local committee shall require solicitors who wish to become duty solicitors to complete a current application form in a form approved by the Duty Solicitor Committee obtained from and returned to the relevant office of the Board.

Selection criteria - magistrates' courts

32. (1) The criteria for the selection of a duty solicitor to provide advice and representation at a magistrates' court shall be as follows:-

(a) the applicant's office shall, in connection with a magistrates' court at which a duty solicitor is required to be in attendance under paragraph 13(1)(a), be within the area of that court or, if it is outside the area of the court, be reasonably accessible to the court for the convenience of any defendant who wishes to instruct the duty solicitor to continue to act for him or her;

(b) the applicant shall, in connection with a magistrates' court at which a duty solicitor is required to be in attendance under paragraph 13(1)(a), normally be in attendance at the office referred to in paragraph 32(1)(a) and that office shall be open during the majority of normal business hours;

(c) the applicant's office shall, in connection with a magistrates' court or courts not falling within paragraph 13(1)(a), be reasonably accessible to the court or courts taking into account relevant local considerations;

(d) the applicant shall hold a current practising certificate which may (in the discretion of the local committee) be conditional;

(e) the applicant shall be willing to act personally as duty solicitor and to undertake the majority of rota duties allocated to him or her;

(f) (i) the applicant, who must not be a special constable, shall regularly practise in criminal defence work;

(ii) the applicant shall have comprehensive experience of criminal defence work including advocacy in magistrates' courts throughout the previous twelve months, except in the circumstances in sub-paragraph (iii) below;

(iii) if the applicant has been in recent full-time employment as a prosecuting solicitor or in another similar position for a period of eighteen months he or she must have had comprehensive experience of criminal defence work throughout the previous six months;

(iv) the experience of criminal defence work referred to in sub-paragraphs (ii) and (iii) above need not have been gained in the magistrates' court or courts in connection with which the local committee is appointed;

(v) any interval of up to 12 months, during or at the end of the periods of experience required by sub-paragraphs (ii) and (iii) above, when the applicant was absent from work because of sickness, injury, pregnancy or confinement or for other good reason may be disregarded;

(vi) if the applicant does not comply with paragraphs 32(1)(f)(i)-(v) but the local committee considers that the applicant would make a competent duty solicitor the local committee may recommend to the regional committee in exceptional circumstances that the latter exercises its power under paragraph 15(16) to waive the relevant paragraph;

(g) subject to the approval or direction of the appropriate regional committee under paragraph 15(1), the applicant shall provide or be willing to provide advice at police stations as a duty solicitor and, where that sub-paragraph is in effect, the local committee shall exclude a duty solicitor from providing advice and representation at magistrates' courts if he or she is not willing to provide advice at police stations;

(h) the applicant shall be prepared, if selected as a duty solicitor, to carry out his or her duties so as not to discriminate on grounds of race, gender, sexual orientation, religion or disability;

(i) any other criteria as approved by the appropriate regional committee and the Duty Solicitor Committee.

(2) In assessing an application the local committee shall be satisfied that the solicitor is competent to provide advice and representation having regard to the nature, frequency and quality of the solicitor's advocacy including:

(a) an ability to provide advice and representation to a number of defendants in a limited time without the opportunity to prepare the cases before arriving at court;

(b) an adequate knowledge of the procedure in magistrates' courts; and

(c) an adequate knowledge of the law relating to the more common offences coming before the court.

(3) The applicant shall have attended an advocacy training course appropriate to advice and representation at magistrates' courts by a duty solicitor, unless he or she has substantial experience of defence advocacy.

(4) Where the applicant:

(a) has been charged with or convicted of a criminal offence since admission, or

(b) has been the subject of any adverse findings by the Adjudication Committee of the Solicitors Complaints Bureau or by the Solicitors Disciplinary Tribunal, or there are any hearings pending in either forum, or

(c) for other good reason

the committee considering the application has a discretion to reject the application, if it considers that to do so would be in the interests of suspects or defendants provided that it provides the applicant with written reasons for its decision;

(5) The applicant shall possess or have access to books and periodicals prescribed by the Duty Solicitor Committee.

Selection criteria - police stations

33. The criteria for the selection of a duty solicitor to provide advice at a police station shall be as follows:

(1) the criteria set out in paragraphs 32(1) (d) to (i) and 32(2), (3), (4) and (5);

(2) the applicant's home or office shall be within 45 minutes travel time of the relevant police station, and the applicant shall be prepared to make arrangements to be reasonably accessible to the relevant police station when on rota duty, except where adherence to these requirements would make it impracticable for a police station to be covered; in which case the relevant regional committee may agree for the requirement of 45 minutes travel time to be varied under paragraph 14(4). The applicant may, in the discretion of the committee, be required to satisfy the committee that he or she will be in a position to accept panel cases referred by the telephone service;

(3) the applicant shall have attended a course on advice at the police station unless he or she has substantial experience of that area of work;

(4) adequate experience of providing advice to persons arrested and held in custody at police stations;

(5) the applicant shall agree not to provide any money or other gifts to a suspect except items of refreshment and smoking materials for immediate consumption by the suspect.

Interview

34. (1) The appropriate local committee shall interview all applicants. Interviews may be conducted by a sub-committee of the local committee. Where the applicant has been approved by another local committee the appropriate local committee is under no duty to interview him or her but may in its discretion do so. An applicant cannot be rejected by the appropriate local committee without an interview;

(2) Any local committee or sub-committee when interviewing must include a lay member appointed under paragraph 18(2) or (8) provided that any member appointed under paragraph 18(8) is, in this case, not a member of court staff. If no such member can attend, one who is entitled to attend must agree to the interview being conducted in his or her absence;

(3) A member of the relevant regional committee from another part of the region may be included on any local committee or sub-committee when interviewing and selecting applicants;

(4) The composition of the local committee or sub-committee when interviewing applicants is otherwise subject to paragraph 21.

Approval of applications

35. If the applicant meets the criteria set out in paragraph 32 or 33 (whichever is appropriate) the appropriate local committee shall, within 60 days of the submission of the application, approve the application and give notice of such approval to the applicant.

Rejection of applications

36. If the committee decides not to allow the application it shall provide the applicant with a statement of the reasons for its decision, showing which of the criteria in paragraph 32 or 33 he or she does not meet and an explanation of why they have not been met.

Appeals to regional committee

37. (1) Where an application has been rejected under paragraph 36 the applicant may appeal to the appropriate regional committee within 28 days of the decision being notified to him or her subject to the appropriate regional committee having discretion to accept an appeal outside the period of 28 days for good reason;

(2) Where an appeal is referred back to the appropriate local committee under paragraph 15(7)(g), the local committee must approve or reject the application within 60 days;

(3) If the appropriate local committee has not approved an application within a period of 60 days from the date of its submission or from when it was referred back to it under paragraph 15(7)(g) the application shall be deemed to have been rejected and the applicant may within 28 days of the expiration of such period appeal to the appropriate regional committee subject to that committee having discretion to accept an appeal outside the period of 28 days for good reason.

Reselection

38. (1) A duty solicitor shall be subject to reselection by the appropriate local committee at least every five years;

(2) The duty solicitor shall, when subject to reselection, complete a current form approved by the Duty Solicitor Committee and obtained from the Board and shall return it to the Board within the time scale specified thereon failing which the duty solicitor will be deemed not to be seeking reselection;

(3) If the committee is satisfied that the duty solicitor meets the criteria set out in paragraph 39(1) and/or (2) (whichever is appropriate) and, if appropriate, paragraph 40, it shall reselect him or her and give him or her notice of such reselection. If it is not satisfied that he or she meets such criteria, the committee shall give him or her a statement of any representations received under paragraph 41 and shall invite him or her to an interview. Acceptance of the invitation to an interview must be submitted within 21 days of the committee having invited the duty solicitor to the interview. If having interviewed the duty solicitor the committee decides not to reselect the duty solicitor it shall provide him or her with a statement of the reasons for its decision;

(4) Reselection shall take place, in respect of all duty solicitors admitted during a particular year, to take effect on 31 December of the fifth following year.

Reselection criteria - magistrates' courts and police stations

39. (1) The criteria for the reselection of duty solicitors providing advice and representation at magistrates' courts shall be:

(a) continued ability to satisfy the criteria in paragraph 32;

(b) regularity of personal attendance at court as duty solicitor; and

(c) compliance with these Arrangements and instructions to duty solicitors made under paragraph 27(7)(a);

(2) The criteria for the reselection of duty solicitors providing advice at police stations shall be:

(a) continued ability to satisfy the criteria in paragraph 33 (1),(2),(4) and (5);

(b) the availability of the duty solicitor to receive telephone calls concerning requests for advice from suspects at police stations, and willingness to accept calls when a panel duty solicitor;

(c) the attendance of the duty solicitor at police stations in the circumstances set out in paragraph 54;

(d) the appropriate use of duty solicitors' representatives at police stations.

Reselection criteria - continuing training

40. Any duty solicitor wishing to be reselected whether providing advice and representation at a magistrates' court or advice at a police station or both must have undertaken a minimum of six hours tuition during the previous five years on a course or courses relevant to advice and representation at magistrates' courts or advice at police stations or both.

Representations about performance

41. The appropriate local committee shall, when considering reselection, take into account any representations received as to the performance of the duty solicitor or duty solicitor's representative, provided that where any such representations are received the duty solicitor, or appropriate duty solicitor where a representative is involved, shall be provided with a written statement of them and shall have an opportunity in any representations he or she may make under paragraphs 38 or 48 to respond.

Changes in circumstances - duty to report

42. A duty solicitor, or, in the case of a duty solicitor's representative, the appropriate duty solicitor, shall immediately notify the appropriate local committee in any of the following circumstances:-

(a) if his or her practising address changes or if his or her home address changes if the home address was relevant for selection under paragraph 33(2);

(b) if he or she or a representative is unable to comply with the criteria set out in paragraphs 32, 33, 39, or 40 where duty solicitors are concerned, or 45 in the case of representatives;

(c) on resignation giving one month's notice;

(d) if he or she or a representative of him or her is incapable of carrying out his or her duties for more than 28 days;

(e) if he or she or a representative of him or her is charged with or convicted of a criminal offence;

(f) if (where appropriate) a hearing by the Adjudication Committee of the Solicitors Complaints Bureau or by the Solicitors Disciplinary Tribunal is pending in respect of him or her; or

(g) where the Adjudication Committee of the Solicitors Complaints Bureau or the Solicitors Disciplinary Tribunal has made an adverse finding in respect of him or her or a representative of him or her.

Changes in rota

43. A duty solicitor may arrange for another duty solicitor to take his or her place on a rota provided that the telephone service, in connection with the provision of advice at police stations, the court and, if the local committee so requests, the local committee and its administrator in connection with the provision of advice and representation, are notified of any such arrangement.

PART VI - DUTY SOLICITORS' REPRESENTATIVES

Application

44. When the appropriate regional committee gives its consent to the use of duty solicitors' representatives under paragraph 14(3), only a current application form in a form approved by the Duty Solicitor Committee and obtained from the Board and submitted by the appropriate duty solicitor to the Board shall be considered by the appropriate local committee.

Selection criteria

45. (1) When an application is received in respect of a duty solicitor's representative, the local committee must be satisfied that the person referred to in the application:

(a) is in the full or part-time employment of, or a partner in the same firm as, the duty solicitor or duty solicitors whose name or names appear on the application form referred to in paragraph 44 (and if more than one duty solicitor, all such duty solicitors must be in the same firm), and is not in the employment of any other solicitor; and

(b) has had experience of providing advice at a police station, having gained such experience as the result of having worked in a solicitor's office; and

(c) (i) if a solicitor, has had at least four months experience of criminal cases as a solicitor or trainee solicitor; or

(ii) if a solicitor's clerk, has had at least three years experience of criminal defence work; or

(iii) if a trainee solicitor, has had at least six months experience of which four months are of criminal cases;

(d) is competent to act as a duty solicitor's representative;

(e) has received appropriate training;

(f) has access to books and periodicals prescribed by the Duty Solicitor Committee;

(g) if a solicitor, holds a current practising certificate which may (in the discretion of the local committee) be conditional;

(h) where the proposed representative:

(i) has been charged with or convicted of a criminal offence (in the case of a solicitor, since admission), or

(ii) if a solicitor, has been the subject of any adverse findings by the Adjudication Committee of the Solicitors Complaints Bureau or by the Solicitors Disciplinary Tribunal, or there are any hearings pending in either forum; or

(iii) for other good reason

the committee considering the application has a discretion to reject the application where if it considers that to do so would be in the interests of suspects provided that it provides the applicant with written reasons for its decision;

(i) is not a special constable; and

(j) has agreed not to provide any money or other gifts to a suspect except items of refreshment and smoking materials for immediate consumption by the suspect;

(2) If the committee decides not to allow the application it shall provide the applicant with a statement of the reasons for its decision showing which of the criteria in paragraph 45(1) he or she does not meet and an explanation of why they have not been met.

Interview

46. (1) The appropriate local committee, or a sub-committee of it, shall require the proposed representative to attend an interview; however, where that person has been approved by any other local committee the appropriate local committee is under no duty to interview him or her but may in its discretion do so. An application cannot be rejected by the appropriate local committee without an interview.

(2) Any local committee or sub-committee when interviewing must include a lay member appointed under paragraph 18(2) or (8) provided that any member appointed under paragraph 18(8) is not a member of court staff. If no such member can attend, one who is entitled to attend must agree to the interview being conducted in his or her absence.

Appeal to regional committee

47. (1) Where an application has been refused under paragraph 45(2), an appeal may be made by the appropriate duty solicitor to the appropriate regional committee within 28 days of the decision being notified to him or her subject to that committee having a discretion to accept an appeal outside the period of 28 days for good reason;

(2) If the appropriate local committee has not approved the application within a period of 60 days from the date of its submission, the application shall be deemed to have been rejected and the applicant may, within 28 days of the expiration of such period, appeal to the appropriate regional committee subject to that committee having a discretion to accept an appeal outside the period of 28 days for good reason;

(3) Where a duty solicitor's representative has not been reselected under paragraph 48 the appropriate duty solicitor may appeal to the appropriate regional committee within 28 days of the decision being notified to the duty solicitor subject to that committee having a discretion to accept an appeal outside the period of 28 days for good reason;

(4) Where an appeal is referred back to the appropriate local committee under paragraph 15(7)(g), the local committee must approve or reject the application within 60 days.

Reselection criteria

48. (1) A duty solicitor's representative shall be subject to reselection by the appropriate local committee at least every five years;

(2) The appropriate duty solicitor shall, where a representative is subject to reselection, complete a current application form approved by the Duty Solicitor Committee and obtained from the Board and shall return it to the Board within the time scale specified thereon failing which it will be deemed that the appropriate duty solicitor is not seeking reselection of the representative;

(3) If the committee is satisfied that the duty solicitor's representative meets the criteria set out in paragraph 45(1) and that the representative has undertaken a minimum of six hours tuition during the previous five years on a course relevant to advice at police stations it shall reselect him or her and give notice of such reselection to the duty solicitor;

(4) If it is not satisfied that he or she meets such criteria, the committee shall give the appropriate duty solicitor a statement of any representations received under paragraph 41 and shall invite the appropriate duty solicitor and the representative to an interview. Acceptance of the invitation to an interview must be submitted within 21 days of the committee having invited the representative to the interview;

(5) If the committee decides not to reselect the representative it shall provide the appropriate duty solicitor with a statement of the reasons for its decision;

(6) Reselection shall take place, in respect of all representatives admitted during a particular year, to take effect on 31 December of the fifth following year.

PART VII - SCOPE OF SERVICE - MAGISTRATES' COURTS

Defendant's right to instruct another solicitor

49. (1) A duty solicitor at a magistrates' court shall inform every defendant to whom he or she offers advice or representation that the defendant is entitled to instruct any solicitor. The duty solicitor shall then ask the defendant if he or she has a solicitor whom he or she wishes to represent him or her and if the defendant has such a solicitor the duty solicitor shall not act for the defendant save in the circumstances mentioned in sub-paragraph (2) below;

(2) If the defendant wishes to be represented by a named solicitor or firm but that solicitor or a member of the firm is not available, then provided the defendant so wishes, the duty solicitor may give advice and representation to him or her on that occasion but shall not thereafter act for the defendant in that matter unless the defendant specifically asks him or her to do so in writing.

Services to be provided

50. (1) A duty solicitor at a magistrates' court shall provide the following services to any defendant who wishes to receive advice and representation from the duty solicitor:-

(a) advice to a defendant who is in custody;

(b) the making of a bail application unless the defendant has received such assistance on a previous occasion.

(2) The duty solicitor shall subject to paragraph 51 (1) also provide:-

(a) representation of a defendant who is in custody on a plea of guilty where the defendant wishes the case to be concluded at that appearance in court, unless the duty solicitor considers that the case should be adjourned in the interests of justice or of the defendant;

(b) where necessary, advice and representation to a defendant who is before the court as a result of failure to pay a fine or other sum ordered on conviction or to obey an order of the court, and such failure may lead to the defendant being at risk of imprisonment;

(c) advice and, where appropriate, representation of any other defendant who is not in custody where, in the opinion of the duty solicitor, such defendant requires advice or representation;

(d) help to a defendant to make an application for a legal aid order in respect of any subsequent appearance of the defendant before the court. Where such an application is made the duty solicitor shall enquire whether the defendant wishes to instruct another solicitor to act for him or her. If the defendant does so wish, the duty solicitor shall insert the name of that solicitor in the application form.

Prohibition of certain services

51. (1) A duty solicitor shall not under paragraph 50 provide representation in committal proceedings or on a not guilty plea, nor save in circumstances which the duty solicitor considers exceptional, advice or representation to a defendant in connection with a non-imprisonable offence;

(2) On any adjourned hearing, a duty solicitor shall not, as duty solicitor, represent a defendant to whom he or she or any other duty solicitor has provided advice or representation in the same case except in connection with defendants coming within paragraph 50(2)(b);

(3) A duty solicitor shall not advise or represent any defendant at a sitting when that duty solicitor or any member of his or her firm is representing the Crown Prosecution Service in the same courtroom.

Duty to remain at court

52. A duty solicitor shall remain at the court until it has become clear to him or her after consulting the clerk of the court where practicable that advice and representation is not required by any defendant under paragraph 50.

PART VIII - SCOPE OF SERVICE - POLICE STATIONS

Initial advice

53. (1) A duty solicitor on a rota shall accept a case referred to him or her by the telephone service unless he or she is already engaged in connection with another suspect at a police station or at a hearing of an application for a warrant of further detention or an extension of such a warrant;

(2) The duty solicitor on rota or a duty solicitor on a panel who accepts a case from the telephone service shall provide initial advice by speaking directly to the suspect on the telephone, unless the duty solicitor is at or adjacent to the police station and can immediately advise the suspect in person. If the suspect is incapable by reason of drunkeness or violent behaviour of speaking to the duty solicitor, initial advice may be postponed. The duty solicitor shall make arrangements to provide initial advice as soon as the suspect is capable of speaking to him or her. Where the case is one to which paragraph 54(1) applies, the duty solicitor shall tell the suspect that the duty solicitor will attend the police station to provide advice and to attend the police interview and any identity parade, group identification or confrontation unless the duty solicitor is of the opinion that there are exceptional circumstances for not doing so, in which case the duty solicitor shall explain the circumstances to the suspect;

(3) The duty solicitor may only arrange for a duty solicitor's representative to give advice under paragraph 57 after the duty solicitor has provided advice under paragraph 53(2);

(4) Requests by suspects for the duty solicitor must be referred to the duty solicitor by the telephone service except where the duty solicitor is already at the same police station at which the suspect requests the services of the duty solicitor. In the latter event the duty solicitor must notify the telephone service where he or she has accepted the request from the suspect.

Obligation to attend the suspect at the police station

54. (1) After providing initial advice, the duty solicitor shall attend the suspect at the police station in person or by his or her duly authorised representative if paragraph 57 applies, in the following circumstances:

(a) where the suspect has been arrested in connection with an arrestable offence as defined under

Section 24 Police and Criminal Evidence Act 1984, and the police intend to interview the suspect; or

(b) where the police intend to resolve an issue of identification by holding an identity parade, group identification or confrontation; or

(c) where the suspect complains of serious maltreatment by the police;

(2) If exceptional circumstances exist which justify non-attendance at the police station, the duty solicitor shall explain his or her decision not to attend on the costs claim form;

(3) If a police interview and any identification parade, group identification or confrontation is postponed to a time when the duty solicitor is no longer on duty or, if on a panel, where it is no longer convenient to act as duty solicitor, he or she must make arrangements to ensure that the suspect continues to receive advice in connection with paragraph 53(2) either by the rota duty solicitor continuing to act as duty solicitor or by ensuring that the suspect continues to receive advice from another duty solicitor.

Discretion to attend the suspect at the police station

55. In circumstances other than those set out in paragraph 54 the duty solicitor shall exercise his or her discretion whether it is in the interests of the suspect that he or she, or his or her representative, attends the police station. In assessing whether attendance is necessary the duty solicitor shall have regard to:

(1) whether he or she is satisfied that he or she can provide advice and assistance on the telephone with sufficient confidentiality to deal adequately with the matter, and

(2) where the suspect is a juvenile or a person at risk there shall be a presumption that the duty solicitor will exercise his or her discretion in favour of attendance.

Services personnel

56. Where the suspect is a Services person at a Services establishment or elsewhere assisting with an investigation by the Services police and suspected of offences contrary to the Services Discipline Acts where:

(a) the investigation involves any offences which cannot be dealt with summarily, or

(b) the offence appears to the interviewing Services police to be serious,

the duty solicitor shall attend personally upon the suspect where he or she considers that such attendance is necessary for the protection of the suspect's interests.

Advice by duty solicitor's representative

57. The duty solicitor may, where it is appropriate to do so, arrange for a duty solicitor's representative employed by his or her firm to give advice to the suspect at a police station provided that the police are prepared to allow any clerk acting as a representative the same rights of access as the solicitor and provided that the representative can attend at the police station within 45 minutes. The suspect must be informed before advice is given in such circumstances of the status of the representative giving such advice. A duty solicitor's representative may not give advice to a Services person unless that representative is a solicitor.

Continued instructions

58. The duty solicitor may, when he or she has given advice to the suspect at the police station, indicate to the suspect that he or she may be instructed by the suspect to continue to act for him or her, except in cases under paragraph 56 which are dealt with under summary Service procedures, subject to:

(1) advising the suspect that the suspect is entitled to instruct any solicitor; the duty solicitor should then ask the suspect if he or she has a solicitor whom he or she wishes to instruct and if the suspect has such a solicitor the duty solicitor shall not act for the suspect;

(2) if the suspect initially indicated that he or she wished to receive advice from a named solicitor or firm but that solicitor or a member of the firm was not available, the duty solicitor shall not continue to act for the suspect in that matter unless the suspect specifically asks him or her to do so in writing and such written instructions are filed within seven days with the local committee or the administrator of it;

(3) if the duty solicitor does not continue to act for the suspect he or she must make available to any solicitor subsequently instructed by the suspect any relevant information about the suspect's case.

PART IX - COMMITTEES - GENERAL PROVISIONS

Election of chairman and vice-chairman

59. A committee shall, at the first meeting after its appointment and thereafter annually, elect a chairman and, in the case of a regional committee, a vice-chairman to hold office for such period not exceeding one year as the Committee may determine. A chairman or vice-chairman shall be eligible for re-election at the expiration of such period provided that no chairman or vice-chairman shall hold office for more than three years.

Quorum

60. A quorum shall consist of not less than one-third of the members of the committee or sub-committee or, where a committee is considering a matter where not all members are entitled to make decisions, one-third of such members who are entitled to make decisions in either case with a minimum of two members.

Minutes

61. A committee or a sub-committee shall keep minutes of its proceedings with the names of the members present at each meeting, and such minutes shall be signed by the chairman of the appropriate meeting.

Regional committee sub-committee and procedure

62. (1) Each regional committee may appoint a sub-committee of at least five members, two of whom must be lay persons (provided that there is a majority of solicitor and lay members) to which it may delegate all decisions, providing that the regional committee shall meet at least twice a year;

(2) Each regional committee may also appoint sub-committees of at least three members of whom one must be a lay person (provided that there is a majority of solicitor and lay members) to whom it may delegate the determination of appeals under paragraph 15(7) and suspensions and exclusions under paragraphs 15(5)and 15(14);

(3) The ruling of the chairman of a committee or sub-committee on any matter of procedure arising at that meeting of such committee or sub-committee shall be final and conclusive.

Resignation

63. A member of a committee may resign by giving notice in writing to the appropriate area office whereupon his or her office shall become vacant.

Disqualification and notification

64. (1) The office of a member of a regional or local committee shall be vacated by disqualification if:

(a) receiving order in bankruptcy is made against him or her;

(b) he or she becomes a patient within the meaning of the Mental Health Act 1959;

(c) he or she abstains without leave of the committee from attending meetings for one year,

(d) he or she ceases to be a nominee of the body or organisation he or she was nominated to represent, or

(e) there is good reason to disqualify him or her.

(2) A resolution of the appropriate regional committee declaring a member of a regional or local committee disqualified shall be conclusive as to the fact and ground of disqualification stated in the resolution.

Committee members' expenses and fees

65. (1) When attending meetings and conferences convened by the Board, members of the Duty Solicitor Committee and regional committees including sub-committees of regional committees shall be entitled to receive the following:

(a) travel expenses;

(b) subsistence allowances on such scale as the Board shall from time to time direct;

(c) other proper expenses;

(d) if they suffer loss, such fees as the Lord Chancellor may with the concurrence of the Treasury from time to time direct;

(e) if they are lay members who attend to hear appeals under paragraph 15(7) or to consider suspensions or exclusions under paragraphs 15(5) and (14), the fee referred to in paragraph (d) but subject to the meeting of the regional committee:

(i) being specifically convened to hear such appeals, suspensions and exclusions, or

(ii) a sub-committee being held outside normal office hours;

(2) When making monitoring visits to magistrates' courts and police stations, members of regional and local committees shall be entitled to receive the following:

(a) travel expenses;

(b) subsistence allowances on such scale as the Board shall from time to time direct, and

(c) other proper expenses.

(3) When attending local committee meetings in accordance with paragraph 20(2) of these Arrangements, regional committee members shall be entitled to receive the following:

(a) travel expenses;

(b) subsistence allowances on such scale as the Board shall from time to time direct, and

(c) other proper expenses;

(4) When attending local committee meetings, members appointed under paragraphs 18 (2) and (8) shall be entitled to receive child care expenses and, from a date to be decided by the Board, travel expenses;

(5) Regional committee members from other parts of the region attending interviews under paragraphs 34(3) or 46, and interviewees under paragraph 8, shall be entitled to receive travel expenses;

(6) When attending for interview in accordance with paragraph 8 or paragraph 19(2) of these Arrangements, applicants shall be entitled to receive the following:

(a) travel expenses;

(b) subsistence allowances on such scale as the Board shall from time to time direct, and

(c) other proper expenses.

Consultation with local Law Societies

66. Where consultation is required with a local law society under paragraphs 13, 14, 15, 19(1) and 23 the appropriate local law society shall have a period of 21 days in which to notify an intention to respond and 42 days in which to respond.

SCHEDULE 1

Region	Legal Aid Area Covered
1.	**No. 1 (London)** The London Boroughs of: Bexley Bromley Croydon Ealing Greenwich Hounslow Kingston Lambeth Lewisham Merton Richmond Southwark Sutton Wandsworth
2.	**No. 2 (South Eastern)** East Sussex Kent Surrey West Sussex
3A.	**No. 3 (Southern)** Berkshire Buckinghamshire Oxfordshire
3B.	**No. 3 (Southern)** Dorset Hampshire Isle of Wight
4A.	**No. 4 (South Western)** Cornwall Devon The following districts of Somerset: Sedgemoor Yeovil Taunton Deane
4B.	**No. 4 (South Western)** Avon Gloucestershire Wiltshire

The following districts of Somerset:
Glastonbury
Shepton Mallet
Wells
Frome

5. **No. 5 (South Wales)**
Dyfed
South Glamorgan
Mid Glamorgan
West Glamorgan
Gwent
The following districts of Powys:
Brecknock
Radnor

6A. **No. 6 (West Midland)**
Hereford & Worcester
Warwickshire
The following West Midlands Metropolitan Boroughs:
Solihull
Coventry

6B. **No. 6 (West Midland)**
The following districts of Staffordshire:
Cannock Chase
Lichfield
South Staffordshire
Tamworth
The following West Midlands Metropolitan Boroughs:
Birmingham
Sandwell
Dudley
Walsall
Wolverhampton

7A. **No. 7 (North Western)**
Greater Manchester

7B. **No. 7 (North Western)**
The following districts of Cumbria:
Barrow-in-Furness
South Lakeland
The following districts of Lancashire:
Blackburn
Burnley
Chorley
Hyndburn
Lancaster
Pendle
Ribble Valley
Rossendale

8A. **No. 8 (Northern)**
The following districts of Cumbria:
Northumberland
Tyne and Wear
Allerdale
Carlisle
Copeland
Eden

8B. **No. 8 (Northern)**
Cleveland
Durham
The following districts of North Yorkshire:
Hambledon
Richmondshire
Ryedale
Scarborough

9A. **No. 9 (North Eastern)**
West Yorkshire

The following districts of North Yorkshire:
Craven
Harrogate
Selby
York

9B. **No. 9 (North Eastern)**
The following districts of Humberside:
Beverley
Boothferry
Holderness
Kingston-upon-Hull
North Wolds
South Yorkshire

10A. **No. 10 (East Midland)**
Derbyshire
Lincolnshire
Nottinghamshire
The following districts of Humberside:
Cleethorpes
Glanford
Grimsby
Scunthorpe

10B. **No. 10 (East Midland)**
Leicestershire
Northamptonshire

11A. **No. 11 (Eastern)**
Cambridgeshire
Norfolk
Suffolk
Bedfordshire

11B. **No. 11 (Eastern)**
Hertfordshire
Essex

12A. **No. 12 (Chester and North Wales)**
Clwyd
Gwynedd
The following district of Powys:
Montgomery

12B. **No. 12 (Chester and North Wales)**
Cheshire
Shropshire
The following districts of Staffordshire:
East Staffordshire
Newcastle-under-Lyme
Stafford
Staffordshire Moors
Stoke-on-Trent

13. **No. 1 (London)**
The City of London
The London Boroughs of:
Camden
Hackney
Havering
Islington
Newham
Redbridge
Tower Hamlets
Waltham Forest

14. **No. 1 (London)**
The London Boroughs of:
Barnet
Brent
Enfield
Hammersmith
Haringey
Harrow
Hillingdon
Kensington & Chelsea
Westminster

15. **No. 15 (Merseyside)**
Merseyside
The following districts of Lancashire:
Blackpool
Fylde
Preston
South Ribble
Wyre
West Lancashire

LEGAL AID BOARD DUTY SOLICITOR (AMENDMENT) ARRANGEMENTS 1995

The following arrangements to amend the Legal Aid Board's Duty Solicitor Arrangements 1994 have been approved by the Legal Aid Board and will come into effect on 27th June 1995 and supersede the Duty Solicitor (Amendment) Arrangements 1994 which cease to have effect:

1. In paragraph 45(1)(i) delete the word "and";

2. After paragraph 45(1)(j) add:

   "(k)has registered under the Legal Aid Board's Legal Advice and Assistance at Police Stations Register Arrangements 1994 as specified in Schedule 1 subject:

   (i) thereafter to that person remaining on the register, and

   (ii) to the requirement to register not applying to an applicant who is a solicitor or, until 1 February 1997, a trainee solicitor."

3. After paragraph 65 (6) add:

   "(7)When attending centralised selection meetings in regions 1, 13 and 14, members appointed under paragraphs 18(1) and (5) shall be entitled to receive travel expenses."

SCHEDULE 1

Category of duty solicitor representative	**Requirement for Registration**
i) duty solicitor representative selected before 1 July 1993.	Register as a probationary or accredited representative from 1 February 1997.
ii) duty solicitor representative selected between 1 July 1993 and 31 January 1995.	Register as a probationary or accredited representative from 1 February 1996.
iii) A duty solicitor representative applicant considered for selection between 1 February 1995 and 31 January 1996.	Register as a probationary or accredited representative from 1 February 1995.
iv) A duty solicitor representative applicant considered for selection after 1 February 1996.	Register as an accredited representative from 1 February 1996.
v) A person who is no longer a duty solicitor representative but who is within a period of five years of selection or reselection.	Register as a probationary or accredited representative from 1 February 1996.
vi) A person who is no longer a duty solicitor representative and who was last selected or reselected more than five years ago.	Register as a probationary or accredited representative from 1 February 1995.

DUTY SOLICITOR (AMENDMENT No.2) ARRANGEMENTS 1995

The following arrangements to amend the Legal Aid Board's Duty Solicitor Arrangements 1994 have been approved by the Legal Aid Board and will come into effect on 1st October 1995:

1. The following paragraph should be added after paragraph 53(2):

   53(3) In addition to the requirements set out in paragraph 53(2), the duty solicitor shall, where a suspect is to be charged with an arrestable offence, advise on the implications of the caution which will be given when the suspect is charged and must also consider whether or not he or she should attend the police station at that time bearing in mind whether it is possible to give confidential telephone advice and the possible consequences of not making a statement when being charged.

2. Paragraphs 53(3) and 53(4) should be renumbered 53(4) and 53(5) respectively.

Appendix D

Legal Aid Act 1988

1988 CHAPTER 34

An Act to make new provision for the administration of, and to revise the law relating to, legal aid, advice and assistance

[29th July 1988]

BE IT ENACTED by the Queen's most Excellent Majesty, by and with the advice and consent of the Lords Spiritual and Temporal, and Commons, in this present Parliament assembled, and by the authority of the same, as follows:–

PART I PRELIMINARY

1 Purpose of this Act

The purpose of this Act is to establish a framework for the provision under Parts II, III, IV, V and VI of advice, assistance and representation which is publicly funded with a view to helping persons who might otherwise be unable to obtain advice, assistance or representation on account of their means.

Annotations
Commencement order: SI 1989 No 288.
This section does not extend to Scotland.

2 Interpretation

(1) This section has effect for the interpretation of this Act.

(2) 'Advice' means oral or written advice on the application of English law to any particular circumstances that have arisen in relation to the person seeking the advice and as to the steps which that person might appropriately take having regard to the application of English law to those circumstances.

(3) 'Assistance' means assistance in taking any of the steps which a person might take, including steps with respect to proceedings, having regard to the application of English law to any particular circumstances that have arisen in relation to him, whether by taking such steps on his behalf (including assistance by way of representation) or by assisting him in taking them on his own behalf.

[(3A) 'Mediation' means mediation to which Part IIIA of this Act applies; and includes steps taken by a mediator in any case–

(a) in determining whether to embark on mediation;
(b) in preparing for mediation; and
(c) in making any assessment under that Part.]

(4) 'Representation' means representation for the purposes of proceedings and it includes–

(a) all such assistance as is usually given by a [legal representative] in the steps preliminary or incidental to any proceedings;
(b) all such assistance as is usually so given in civil proceedings in arriving at or giving effect to a compromise to avoid or bring to an end any proceedings; and
(c) in the case of criminal proceedings, advice and assistance as to any appeal;

and related expressions have corresponding meanings.

(5) Regulations may specify what is, or is not, to be included in advice or assistance of any description, or representation for the purposes of proceedings of any description, to which any Part or provision of a Part of this Act applies and the regulations may provide for the inclusion, in prescribed circumstances, of advice or assistance given otherwise than under this Act.

(6) Advice, assistance and representation under this Act, except when made available under Part II, [shall only be by legal representatives], but in the case of Part II, may be by other persons.

[(7) Subject to section 59 of the Courts and Legal Services Act 1990, regulations–

(a) may prescribe the circumstances in which representation shall be only by one legal representative and may require him to be from a prescribed category;
(b) may regulate representation by more than one legal representative from any one or more prescribed categories.

(7A) If it is satisfied that the circumstances of a particular case in the Supreme Court or the House of Lords warrant a direction under this subsection, the Board or, in the case of criminal proceedings the competent authority, may direct that representation in that case shall be by one legal representative.

(7B) In subsection (7A), 'competent authority' shall be construed in accordance with section 20.]

(8) The Lord Chancellor may, if it appears to him to be necessary to do so for the purpose of fulfilling any obligation imposed on the United Kingdom or Her Majesty's Government in the United Kingdom by any international agreement, by order direct that such advice or assistance relating to the application of other laws than English law as is specified in the order shall be advice or assistance for any of the purposes of this Act.

(9) For the purposes of the application of subsection (8) above in the case of an obligation to provide for the transmission to other countries of applications for legal aid under their laws, the reference to advice or assistance relating to the application of other laws includes a reference to advice or assistance for the purposes of making and transmitting such an application.

(10) In this Act 'person' does not include a body of persons corporate or unincorporate which is not concerned in a representative, fiduciary or official capacity so as to authorise advice, assistance or representation to be granted to such a body.

(11) In this Act 'legally assisted person' means any person who receives, under this Act, advice, assistance or representation and, in relation to proceedings, any reference to an assisted party or an unassisted party is to be construed accordingly.

Annotations
Commencement order: SI 1989 No 288.
Sub-s (3A): prospectively added by the Family Law Act 1996, s 26(2), as from a day to be appointed.
Sub-ss (4), (6): words in square brackets substituted by the Courts and Legal Services Act 1990, s 125(3), Sch 18, paras 61(1), 63(3).
Sub-ss (7)–(7B): substituted, for sub-s (7) as originally enacted, by the Courts and Legal Services Act 1990, s 125(3), Sch 18, para 61(2).
This section does not extend to Scotland.

PART II LEGAL AID BOARD AND LEGAL AID

3 The Legal Aid Board

(1) There shall be established a body to be known as the Legal Aid Board (in this Act referred to as 'the Board').

(2) Subject to subsections (3) and (4) below, the Board shall have the general function of securing that advice, assistance and representation are available in accordance with this Act and of administering this Act.

(3) Subsection (2) above does not confer on the Board any functions with respect to the grant of representation under Part VI for the purposes of proceedings for contempt.

(4) Subsection (2) above does not confer on the Board any of the following functions unless the Lord Chancellor so directs by order and then only to the extent specified in the order.

The functions referred to are –

(a) determination of the costs of representation under Part IV;
(b) functions as respects representation under Part V other than determination of the costs of representation for the purposes of proceedings in magistrates' courts;
(c) < . . . >
(d) determination of the financial resources of persons for the purposes of this Act.

(5) Subject to subsection (6) below, the Board shall consist of no fewer than 11 and no more than 17 members appointed by the Lord Chancellor; and the Lord Chancellor shall appoint one of the members to be chairman.

(6) The Lord Chancellor may, by order, substitute, for the number for the time being specified in subsection (5) above as the maximum or minimum membership of the Board, such other number as he thinks appropriate.

(7) The Board shall include at least two solicitors appointed after consultation with the Law Society.

(8) The Lord Chancellor shall consult the General Council of the Bar with a view to the inclusion on the Board of at least two barristers.

(9) In appointing persons to be members of the Board the Lord Chancellor shall have regard to the desirability of securing that the Board includes persons having expertise in or knowledge of–

(a) the provision of legal services;
(b) the work of the courts and social conditions; and
(c) management.

(10) Schedule 1 to this Act shall have effect with respect to the Board.

Annotations
Commencement orders: SI 1988 No 1361, SI 1989 No 288.
Sub-s (4): para (c) repealed by the Children Act 1989, s 108(7), Sch 15.
This section does not extend to Scotland.

4 Powers of the Board

(1) Subject to the provisions of this Act, the Board may do anything–

(a) which it considers necessary or desirable to provide or secure the provision of advice, assistance and representation under this Act; or
(b) which is calculated to facilitate or is incidental or conducive to the discharge of its functions;

and advice, assistance and representation may be provided in different ways in different areas in England and Wales and in different ways in different fields of law.

(2) Without prejudice to the generality of subsection (1) above, the Board shall have power–

(a) to enter into any contract including, subject to subsection (7) below, any contract to acquire or dispose of land;
(b) to make grants (with or without conditions, including conditions as to repayment);
(c) to make loans;
(d) to invest money;
(e) to promote or assist in the promotion of publicity relating to the functions of the Board;
(f) to undertake any inquiry or investigation which the Board considers necessary or expedient in relation to the discharge of its functions; and
(g) to give the Lord Chancellor such advice as it may consider appropriate in relation to the provision of advice, assistance and representation under this Act.

(3) Subsection (1) above does not confer on the Board power to borrow money or to acquire and hold shares in bodies corporate or take part in forming bodies corporate.

(4) The powers to provide advice, assistance or representation under this Part and to secure its provision under this Part by means of contracts with, or grants or loans to, other persons or bodies–

(a) shall not be exercisable unless the Lord Chancellor so directs and then only to the extent specified in the direction; and
(b) if exercisable, shall be exercised in accordance with any directions given by him.

(5) The power to secure the provision of representation under Part IV by means of contracts with other persons shall only be exercisable in the classes of case prescribed in regulations.

(6) Advice, assistance and representation provided by the Board under this Part may be granted with or without limitations and may be amended, withdrawn or revoked.

(7) The power under subsection (2) above to enter into contracts to acquire or dispose of land shall not be exercised without the approval in writing of the Lord Chancellor.

(8) The Board may, from time to time, prepare and submit to the Lord Chancellor proposals for the assumption by it of any functions in relation to the provision of advice, assistance or representation under this Act.

Annotations
Commencement order: SI 1989 No 288.
This section does not extend to Scotland.

5 Duties of the Board

(1) The Board shall, from time to time, publish information as to the discharge of its functions in relation to advice, assistance and representation including the forms and procedures and other matters connected therewith.

(2) The Board shall, from time to time, furnish to the Lord Chancellor such information as he may require relating to its property and to the discharge or proposed discharge of its functions.

(3) It shall be the duty of the Board to provide to the Lord Chancellor, as soon as possible after 31st March in each year, a report on the discharge of its functions during the preceding twelve months.

(4) The Board shall deal in any report under subsection (3) above with such matters as the Lord Chancellor may from time to time direct.

(5) The Board shall have regard, in discharging its functions, to such guidance as may from to time be given by the Lord Chancellor.

(6) Guidance under subsection (5) above shall not relate to the consideration or disposal, in particular cases, of–

(a) applications for advice, assistance or representation;
(b) (b)supplementary or incidental applications or requests to the Board in connection with any case were advice, assistance or representation has been made available.

(7) For the purposes of subsection (2) above the Board shall permit any person authorised by the Lord Chancellor for the purpose to inspect and make copies of any accounts or documents of the Board and shall furnish such explanations of them as that person or the Lord Chancellor may require.

Annotations
Commencement order: SI 1989 No 288.
This section does not extend to Scotland.

6 Board to have separate legal aid fund

(1) The Board shall establish and maintain a separate legal aid fund.

(2) Subject to regulations, there shall be paid out of the fund–

(a) such sums as are, by virtue of any provision of or made under this Act, due from the Board in respect of remuneration and expenses properly incurred in connection with the provision, under this Act, of advice, assistance or representation;
(b) costs awarded to any unassisted party under section 13 or 18;
(c) any part of a contribution repayable by the Board under section 16(4) or 23(7); and
(d) such other payments for the purposes of this Act as the Lord Chancellor may, with the concurrence of the Treasury, determine.

(3) Subject to regulations, there shall be paid into the fund–

(a) any contribution payable to the Board by any person in respect of advice, assistance or representation under this Act;
(b) any sum awarded under an order of a court or agreement as to costs in any proceedings in favour of any legally assisted party which is payable to the Board;
(c) any sum which is to be paid out of property recovered or preserved for any legally assisted party to any proceedings;
(d) any sum in respect of the costs of an unassisted party awarded under section 13 or 18 which is repaid to the Board under that section;
(e) the sums to be paid by the Lord Chancellor in pursuance of section 42(1)(a); and
(f) such other receipts of the Board as the Lord Chancellor may, with the concurrence of the Treasury, determine.

Annotations
Commencement order: SI 1989 No 288.
This section does not extend to Scotland.

7 Accounts and audit

(1) The Board shall keep separate accounts with respect to–

(a) its legal aid fund; and
(b) the receipts and expenditure of the Board which do not relate to that fund;

and shall prepare in respect of each financial year a statement of accounts.

(2) The accounts shall be kept and the statement of accounts shall be prepared in such form as the Lord Chancellor may, with the approval of the Treasury, direct.

(3) The accounts shall be audited by persons to be appointed in respect of each financial year by the Lord Chancellor in accordance with a scheme of audit approved by him, and the auditors shall be furnished by the Board with copies of the statement and shall prepare a report to the Lord Chancellor on the accounts and statement.

[(4) No person shall be appointed auditor under subsection (3) above unless he is–

(a) eligible for appointment as a company auditor under section 25 of the Companies Act 1989; or
(b) a member of the Chartered Institute of Public Finance and Accountancy.]

(5) Upon completion of the audit of the accounts, the auditors shall send to the Lord Chancellor a copy of the statement of accounts and of their report, and the Lord Chancellor shall send a copy of the statement and of the report to the Comptroller and Auditor General.

(6) The Lord Chancellor and the Comptroller and Auditor General may inspect the accounts and any records relating to them.

(7) The Lord Chancellor shall lay before each House of Parliament a copy of every statement of accounts and report of the auditors sent to him under subsection (5) above.

(8) In this section 'financial year' means the period beginning with the day on which the Board is established and ending with 31st March next following and each subsequent period of 12 months ending with 31st March in each year.

Annotations
Commencement order: SI 1989 No 288.
Sub-s (4): substituted by SI 1991 No 1997, reg 2, Schedule, para 69.
This section does not extend to Scotland.

PART III ADVICE AND ASSISTANCE

8 Scope of this Part

(1) Subject to the provisions of this section, this Part applies to any advice or assistance and advice and assistance under this Part shall be available to any person subject to and in accordance with the provisions of this section and sections 9, 10 and 11.

(2) This Part only applies to assistance by way of representation if, and to the extent that, regulations so provide; and regulations may make such provision in relation to representation for the purposes of any proceedings before a court or tribunal or at a statutory inquiry.

(3) Advice or assistance of all descriptions or advice or assistance of any prescribed description is excluded from this Part, or is so excluded as regards any area, if regulations so provide; and if regulations provide for all descriptions to be excluded as regards all areas then, so long as the regulations so provide, this Part (other than this subsection) shall not have effect.

(4) Advice or assistance of any prescribed description is restricted to its provision to prescribed descriptions of persons if regulations so provide.

(5) This Part does not apply to advice or assistance given to a person in connection with proceedings before a court or tribunal or at a statutory inquiry at a time when he is being represented in those proceedings under any other Part of this Act.

Annotations
Commencement order: SI 1989 No 288.
This section does not extend to Scotland.

9 Availability of, and payment for, advice and assistance

(1) Advice and assistance to which this Part applies shall be available to any person whose financial resources are such as, under regulations, make him eligible for advice or assistance under this Part.

(2) If regulations so provide, advice or assistance to which this Part applies shall be available, in prescribed circumstances and subject to any prescribed conditions, to persons without reference to their financial resources.

(3) Subject to any prescribed exceptions, assistance by way of representation under this Part shall not be given without the approval of the Board.

(4) Approval under subsection (3) above may be given with or without limitations and may be amended, withdrawn or revoked.

(5) Except as provided by subsection (6) or (7) below, the legally assisted person shall not be required to pay to his [legal representative] any charge or fee.

(6) Except as provided by subsection (7) below, a legally assisted person shall, if his financial resources are such as, under regulations, make him liable to make a contribution, be liable to pay to his [legal representative], in respect of the advice or assistance, charges or fees of such amount as is determined or fixed by or under the regulations.

(7) A legally assisted person to whom advice or assistance is made available by virtue of regulations under subsection (2) above shall, in circumstances prescribed by the regulations and, if the regulations apply only to persons of a prescribed description, he is a person of that description, be liable to pay to his [legal representative], in respect of the advice or assistance, a fee of such amount as is fixed by or under the regulations (in lieu of a contribution under subsection (6) above).

Annotations
Commencement order: SI 1989 No 288.
Sub-ss (5)–(7): words in square brackets substituted by the Courts and Legal Services Act 1990, s 125(3), Sch 18, para 63(4).
This section does not extend to Scotland.

10 Financial limit on prospective cost of advice or assistance

(1) Where at any time (whether before or after the advice or assistance has begun to be given) it appears to a [legal representative] that the cost of giving advice or assistance to a person under this Part is likely to exceed the prescribed limit–

(a) the [legal representative] shall determine to what extent that advice or assistance can be given without exceeding that limit; and
(b) shall not give it (nor, as the case may be), instruct [an additional legal representative] to give it) so as to exceed that limit except with the approval of the Board.

(2) Approval under subsection (1)(b) above may be given with or without limitations and may be amended, withdrawn or revoked.

(3) For the purposes of this section the cost of giving advice or assistance shall be taken to consist of such of the following as are applicable in the circumstances, namely–

(a) any disbursements, that is to say, expenses (including fees payable to [an additional legal representative]) which may be incurred by the [legal representative] in, or in connection with, the giving of the advice or assistance; and
(b) any charges or fees (other than charges for disbursements) which would be properly chargeable by the [legal representative] in respect of the advice or assistance.

Annotations
Commencement order: SI 1989 No 288.
Sub-ss (1), (3): words in square brackets substituted by the Courts and Legal Services Act 1990, s 125(3), Sch 18, paras 61(3), 63(3), (4).
This section does not extend to Scotland.

11 Payment for advice or assistance otherwise than through legally assisted person's contribution

(1) This section applies to any charges or fees which, apart from section 9, would be properly chargeable in respect of advice or assistance given under this Part, in so far as those charges or fees are not payable by the legally assisted person in accordance with that section.

(2) Except in so far as regulations otherwise provide, charge or fees to which this section applies shall constitute a first charge for the benefit of the [legal representative]–

(a) on any costs which are payable to the legally assisted person by any other person in respect of the matter in connection with which the advice or assistance is given, and
(b) on any property which is recovered or preserved for the legally assisted person in connection with that matter.

(3) In so far as the charge created by subsection (2) above in respect of any charges or fees to which this section applies is insufficient to meet them, the deficiency shall, subject to subsection (5) below, be payable to the [legal representative] by the Board.

(4) For the purposes of subsection (2) above, it is immaterial, in the case of costs, whether the costs are payable by virtue of a judgment, order of a court or otherwise and, in the case of property, what its nature is and where it is situated and the property within the charge includes the legally assisted person's rights under any compromise or settlement arrived at to avoid proceedings or bring them to an end.

(5) For the purpose of determining what charges or fees would be properly chargeable, and whether there is a deficiency to be paid by the Board, charges or fees in respect of advice or assistance under this Part shall, in prescribed circumstances, be determined in such manner as may be prescribed.

Annotations
Commencement order: SI 1989 No 288.
Sub-ss (2), (3): words in square brackets substituted by the Courts and Legal Services Act 1990, s 125(3), Sch 18, para 63(4).
This section does not extend to Scotland.

12 Limit on costs against person receiving assistance by way of representation

(1) Where a person receives any assistance by way of representation in any proceedings before a court or tribunal or at a statutory inquiry, then, except in so far as regulations otherwise provide, his liability by virtue of an order for costs made against him with respect to the proceedings shall not exceed the amount (if any) which is a reasonable one for him to pay having regard to all the circumstances, including the financial resources of all the parties and their conduct in connection with the dispute.

(2) Regulations shall make provision as to the court, tribunal or person by whom that amount is to be determined and the extent to which any determination of that amount is to be final.

(3) None of the following, namely, a legally assisted person's dwelling house, clothes, household furniture and the tools and implements of his trade shall–

(a) be taken into account in assessing his financial resources for the purposes of this section, or
(b) be subject to execution or any corresponding process in any part of the United Kingdom to enforce the order,

except so far as regulations may prescribe.

Annotations
Commencement order: SI 1989 No 288.
Extent: sub-ss (1), (2) do not extend to Scotland.

13 Costs of successful unassisted parties

(1) This section applies to proceedings in which a person who receives assistance by way of representation is a party and which are finally decided in favour of an unassisted party.

(2) In any proceedings to which this section applies the court by which the proceedings are so decided may, subject to subsections (3) and (4) below, make an order for the payment by the Board to the unassisted party of the whole or any part of the costs incurred by him in the proceedings.

(3) Before making an order under this section, the court shall consider what order for costs should be made against the assisted party and for determining his liability in respect of such costs.

(4) An order under this section in respect of any costs may only be made if–

(a) an order for costs would be made in the proceedings apart from this Act;
(b) as respects the costs incurred in a court of first instance, those proceedings were instituted by the assisted party and the court is satisfied that the unassisted party will suffer severe financial hardship unless the order is made; and
(c) in any case, the court is satisfied that it is just and equitable in all the circumstances of the case that provision for the costs should be made out of public funds.

(5) Without prejudice to any other provision restricting appeals from any court, no appeal shall lie against an order under this section, or against a refusal to make such an order, except on a point of law.

(6) In this section 'costs' means costs as between party and party, and includes the costs of applying for an order under this section; and where a party begins to receive the assistance after the proceedings have been instituted, or ceases to receive the assistance before they are finally decided or otherwise receives the assistance in connection with part only of the proceedings, the reference in subsection (2) above to the costs incurred by the unassisted party in the proceedings shall be construed as a reference to so much of those costs as is attributable to that part.

(7) For the purposes of this section proceedings shall be treated as finally decided in favour of the unassisted party–

(a) if no appeal lies against the decision in his favour;
(b) if an appeal lies against the decision with leave, and the time limited for applications for leave expires without leave being granted; or
(c) if leave to appeal against the decision is granted or is not required, and no appeal is brought within the time limited for appeal;

and where an appeal against the decision is brought out of time the court by which the appeal (or any further appeal in those proceedings) is determined may make an order for the repayment by the unassisted party to the Board of the whole or any part of any sum previously paid to him under this section in respect of those proceedings.

(8) Where a court decides any proceedings in favour of the unassisted party and an appeal lies (with or without leave) against that decision, the court may, if it thinks fit, make or refuse to make an order under this section forthwith, but if an order is made forthwith it shall not take effect–

(a) where leave to appeal is required, unless the time limited for applications for leave to appeal expires without leave being granted;
(b) where leave to appeal is granted or is not required, unless the time limited for appeal expires without an appeal being brought.

(9) For the purposes of this section 'court' includes a tribunal.

Annotations
Commencement order: SI 1989 No 288.
This section does not extend to Scotland.

PART IIIA [MEDIATION]

[13A] [Scope of this Part]

[(1) This Part applies to mediation in disputes relating to family matters.

(2) 'Family matters' means matters which are governed by English law and in relation to which any question has arisen, or may arise–

(a) under any provision of–

(i) the 1973 Act;
(ii) the Domestic Proceedings and Magistrates' Courts Act 1978;
(iii) Parts I to V of the Children Act 1989;
(iv) Parts II and IV of the Family Law Act 1996; or
(v) any other enactment prescribed;

(b) under any prescribed jurisdiction of a prescribed court or tribunal; or
(c) under any prescribed rule of law.

(3) Regulations may restrict this Part to mediation in disputes of any prescribed description.

(4) The power to–

(a) make regulations under subsection (2), or
(b) revoke any regulations made under subsection (3),

is exercisable only with the consent of the Treasury.]

Annotations
This section is prospectively added by the Legal Aid Act 1988, s 26(1), as from a day to be appointed.
This section does not extend to Scotland.

[13B] [Provision and availability of mediation]

[(1) The Board may secure the provision of mediation under this Part.

(2) If mediation is provided under this Part, it is to be available to any person whose financial resources are such as, under regulations, make him eligible for mediation.

(3) A person is not to be granted mediation in relation to any dispute unless mediation appears to the mediator suitable to the dispute and the parties and all the circumstances.

(4) A grant of mediation under this Part may be amended, withdrawn or revoked.

(5) The power conferred by subsection (1) shall be exercised in accordance with any directions given by the Lord Chancellor.

(6) Any contract entered into by the Board for the provision of mediation under this Part must require the mediator to comply with a code of practice.

(7) The code must require the mediator to have arrangements designed to ensure–

(a) that parties participate in mediation only if willing and not influenced by fear of violence or other harm;
(b) that cases where either party may be influenced by fear of violence or other harm are identified as soon as possible;
(c) that the possibility of reconciliation is kept under review throughout mediation; and
(d) that each party is informed about the availability of independent legal advice.

(8) Where there are one or more children of the family, the code must also require the mediator to have arrangements designed to ensure that the parties are encouraged to consider–

(a) the welfare, wishes and feelings of each child; and
(b) whether and to what extent each child should be given the opportunity to express his or her wishes and feelings in the mediation.

(9) A contract entered into by the Board for the provision of mediation under this Part must also include such other provision as the Lord Chancellor may direct the Board to include.

(10) Directions under this section may apply generally to contracts, or to contracts of any description, entered into by the Board, but shall not be made with respect to any particular contract.]

Annotations

This section is prospectively added by the Family Law Act 1996, s 27, as from a day to be appointed.

This section does not extend to Scotland.

[13C] [Payment for mediation under this Part]

[(1) Except as provided by this section, the legally assisted person is not to be required to pay for mediation provided under this Part.

(2) Subsection (3) applies if the financial resources of a legally assisted person are such as, under regulations, make him liable to make a contribution.

(3) The legally assisted person is to pay to the Board in respect of the costs of providing the mediation, a contribution of such amount as is determined or fixed by or under the regulations.

(4) If the total contribution made by a person in respect of any mediation exceeds the Board's liability on his account, the excess shall be repaid to him.

(5) Regulations may provide that, where–

(a) mediation under this Part is made available to a legally assisted person, and
(b) (b)property is recovered or preserved for the legally assisted person as a result of the mediation,

a sum equal to the Board's liability on the legally assisted person's account is, except so far as the regulations otherwise provide, to be a first charge on the property in favour of the Board.

(6) Regulations under subsection (5) may, in particular, make provision–

(a) as to circumstances in which property is to be taken to have been, or not to have been, recovered or preserved; and
(b) as to circumstances in which the recovery or preservation of property is to be taken to be, or not to be, the result of any mediation.

(7) For the purposes of subsection (5), the nature of the property and where it is situated is immaterial.

(8) The power to make regulations under section 34(2)(f) and (8) is exercisable in relation to any charge created under subsection (5) as it is exercisable in relation to the charge created by section 16.

(9) For the purposes of subsections (4) and (5), the Board's liability on any person's account in relation to any mediation is the aggregate amount of–

(a) the sums paid or payable by the Board on his account for the mediation, determined in accordance with subsection (10);
(b) any sums paid or payable in respect of its net liability on his account, determined in accordance with subsection (11) and the regulations –

(i) in respect of any proceedings, and
(ii) for any advice or assistance under Part III in connection with the proceedings or any matter to which the proceedings relate,

so far as the proceedings relate to any matter to which the mediation relates; and
(c) any sums paid or payable in respect of its net liability on his account, determined in accordance with the regulations, for any other advice or assistance under Part III in connection with the mediation or any matter to which the mediation relates.

(10) For the purposes of subsection (9)(a), the sums paid or payable by the Board on any person's account for any mediation are–

(a) sums determined under the contract between the Board and the mediator as payable by the Board on that person's account for the mediation; or
(b) if the contract does not differentiate between such sums and sums payable on any other person's account or for any other mediation, such part of the remuneration payable under the contract as may be specified in writing by the Board.

(11) For the purposes of subsection (9)(b), the Board's net liability on any person's account in relation to any proceedings is its net liability on his account under section 16(9)(a) and (b) in relation to the proceedings.]

Annotations
This section is prospectively added by the Family Law Act 1988, s 28(1), as from a day to be appointed.
This section does not extend to Scotland.

PART IV CIVIL LEGAL AID

14 Scope of this Part

Part IV Civil Legal Aid

(1) This Part applies to such proceedings before courts or tribunals or at statutory inquiries in England and Wales as–

(a) are proceedings of a description for the time being specified in Part I of Schedule 2 to this Act, except proceedings for the time being specified in Part II of that Schedule, and
(b) are not proceedings for which representation may be granted under Part V,

and representation under this Part shall be available to any person subject to and in accordance with sections 15 and 16.

(2) Subject to subsection (3) below, Schedule 2 may be varied by regulations so as to extend or restrict the categories of proceedings for the purposes of which representation is available under this Part, by reference to the court, tribunal or statutory inquiry, to the issues involved, to the capacity in which the person seeking representation is concerned or otherwise.

(3) Regulations under subsection (2) above may not have the effect of adding any proceedings before any court or tribunal or at any statutory inquiry before or at which persons have no right, and are not normally allowed, to be represented by [a legal representative].

(4) Regulations under subsection (2) above which extend the categories of proceedings for the purposes of which representation is available under this Part shall not be made without the consent of the Treasury.

Annotations
Commencement order: SI 1989 No 288.
Sub-s (3): words in square brackets substituted by the Courts and Legal Services Act 1990, s 125(3), Sch 18, para 63(1).
This section does not extend to Scotland.

15 Availability of, and payment for, representation under this Part

(1) Subject to subsections (2) [to [(3D)]] below, representation under this Part for the purposes of proceedings to which this Part applies shall be available to any person whose financial resources are such as, under regulations, make him eligible for representation under this Part.

(2) A person shall not be granted representation for the purposes of any proceedings unless he satisfies the Board that he has reasonable grounds for taking, defending or being a party to the proceedings.

(3) A person may be refused representation for the purposes of any proceedings if, in the particular circumstances of the case it appears to the Board–

(a) unreasonable that he should be granted representation under this Part, or
(b) more appropriate that he should be given assistance by way of representation under Part III;

and regulations may prescribe the criteria for determining any questions arising under paragraph (b) above.

[(3A) Representation under this Part shall not be available –

(a) to any local authority; or
(b) to any other body which falls within a prescribed description, [or
(c) to a guardian *ad litem*,]

for the purposes of any proceedings under the Children Act 1989.

(3B) Regardless of subsection (2) or (3), representation under this Part must be granted where a child who is brought before a court under section 25 of the 1989 Act (use of accommodation for restricting liberty) is not, but wishes to be, legally represented before the court.]

[(3C) Subject to subsection (3A) but regardless of subsections (2) or (3), representation under this Part must be granted to the child in respect of whom the application is made, to any parent of such a child and to any person with parental responsibility for him within the meaning of the 1989 Act to cover proceedings relating to an application for the following orders under that Act–

(a) an order under section 31 (a care or supervision order);
(b) an order under section 43 (a child assessment order);
(c) an order under section 44 (an emergency protection order); or
(d) an order under section 45 (extension or discharge of an emergency protection order).

(3D) Subject to subsections (2) and (3), representation must be granted to cover proceedings relating to an appeal against an order made under section 31 of the 1989 Act to a person who has been granted representation by virtue of subsection (3C).

(3E) Subject to subsections (1) and (3A) but regardless of subsections (2) or (3), representation under this Part must be granted where a person applies to be or has been joined as a party to any of the proceedings mentioned in subsection (3C).]

[(3F) A person shall not be granted representation for the purposes of proceedings relating to family matters, unless he has attended a meeting with a mediator–

(a) to determine –
    (i) whether mediation appears suitable to the dispute and the parties and all the circumstances, and
    (ii) in particular, whether mediation could take place without either party being influenced by fear of violence or other harm; and
(b) if mediation does appear suitable, to help the person applying for representation to decide whether instead to apply for mediation.

(3G) Subsection (3F) does not apply–

(a) in relation to proceedings under–

(i) Part IV of the Family Law Act 1996;
(ii) section 37 of the Matrimonial Causes Act 1973;
(iii) Part IV or V of the Children Act 1989;

(b) in relation to proceedings of any other description that may be prescribed; or
(c) in such circumstances as may be prescribed.

(3H) So far as proceedings relate to family matters, the Board, in determining under subsection (3)(a) whether, in relation to the proceedings, it is reasonable that a person should be granted representation under this Part–

(a) must have regard to whether and to what extent recourse to mediation would be a suitable alternative to taking the proceedings; and
(b) must for that purpose have regard to the outcome of the meeting held under subsection (3F) and to any assessment made for the purposes of section 13B(3).]

[(3I) A person may be refused representation for the purposes of any proceedings if–

(a) the proceedings are marital proceedings within the meaning of Part II of the Family Law Act 1996; and
(b) he is being provided with marriage counselling under section 23 of that Act in relation to the marriage.]

(4) Representation under this Part may be granted by the Board with or without limitations and may be amended, withdrawn or revoked.

[(4A) A person may not be refused representation for the purposes of any proceedings on the ground (however expressed) that it would be more appropriate for him and a legal representative of his to enter into a conditional fee agreement (as defined by section 58 of the Courts and Legal Services Act 1990).]

(5) Where the case is one in which the Board has power to secure the provision of representation under this Part by means of contracts with other persons, the grant of representation under this Part may be limited under subsection (4) above as regards the persons who may represent the legally assisted person to representation only in pursuance of a contract made with the Board.

(6) Except in so far as he is required under section 16 to make a contribution, a legally assisted person shall not be required to make any payment in respect of representation under this Part and it shall be for the Board to pay his [legal representative].

(7) The Board's obligation under subsection (6) above is–

(a) in the case of representation provided in pursuance of a contract between the Board and the legally assisted person's [legal representative], to make such payments as are due under the contract; and
(b) in the case of representation provided otherwise than in pursuance of such a contract, to make such payments as are authorised by regulations.

(8) Nothing in subsection (6) above affects the duty of the [legal representative] to pay in the first instance expenses incurred in connection with

the proceedings that would ordinarily be paid in the first instance by a person's [legal representative].

Annotations
Commencement order: SI 1989 No 288.
Sub-s (1): first words in square brackets substituted by the Children Act 1989, s 99(2), figure in square brackets therein substituted by SI 1991 No 1924, art 2(a).
Sub-s (3A): added by the Children Act 1989, s 99(2); words in square brackets added by SI 1991 No 2036, reg 3.
Sub-s (3B): added by the Children Act 1989, s 99(2).
Sub-ss (3C), (3D), (3E): added by SI 1991 No 1924, art 2(b).
Sub-ss (3F)–(3I): prospectively added by the Family Law Act 1996, ss 23(9), 29, as from a day to be appointed.
Sub-s (4A): added by the Courts and Legal Services Act 1990, s 125(2), Sch 17, para 19.
Sub-ss (6)–(8): words in square brackets substituted by the Courts and Legal Services Act 1990, s 125(3), Sch 18, paras 61(4), 63(4).
This section does not extend to Scotland.

16 Reimbursement of Board by contributions and out of costs or property recovered

(1) A legally assisted person shall, if his financial resources are such as, under regulations, make him liable to make such a contribution, pay to the Board a contribution in respect of the costs of his being represented under this Part.

(2) The contribution to be required of him by the Board shall be determined by the Board in accordance with the regulations and may take the form of periodical payments or one or more capital sums or both.

(3) The contribution required of a person may, in the case of periodical payments, be made payable by reference to the period during which he is represented under this Part or any shorter period and, in the case of a capital sum, be made payable by instalments.

(4) If the total contribution made by a person in respect of any proceedings exceeds the net liability of the Board on his account, the excess shall be repaid to him.

(5) Any sums recovered by virtue of an order or agreement for costs made in favour of a legally assisted person with respect to the proceedings shall be paid to the Board.

(6) Except so far as regulations otherwise provide–

(a) any sums remaining unpaid on account of a person's contribution in respect of the sums payable by the Board in respect of any proceedings, and
(b) a sum equal to any deficiency by reason of his total contribution being less than the net liability of the Board on his account,

shall be a first charge for the benefit of the Board on any property which is recovered or preserved for him in the proceedings.

(7) For the purposes of subsection (6) above it is immaterial what the nature of the property is and where it is situated and the property within the charge includes the rights of a person under any compromise or settlement arrived at to avoid the proceedings or bring them to an end and any sums

received by virtue of an order for costs made in his favour in the proceedings (not being sums payable to the Board under subsection (5) above).

(8) The charge created by subsection (6) above on any damages or costs shall not prevent a court allowing them to be set off against other damages or costs in any case where a [legal representative's] lien for costs would not prevent it.

(9) In this section references to the net liability of the Board on a legally assisted person's account in relation to any proceedings are references to the aggregate amount of–

(a) the sums paid or payable by the Board on his account in respect of those proceedings to any [legal representative], and
(b) any sums so paid or payable for any advice or assistance under Part III in connection with those proceedings or any matter to which those proceedings relate, [and
(c) if and to the extent that regulations so provide, any sums paid or payable in respect of the Board's liability on the legally assisted person's account in relation to any mediation in connection with any matter to which those proceedings relate,]

being sums not recouped by the Board by sums which are recoverable by virtue of an order or agreement for costs made in his favour with respect to those proceedings or by virtue of any right of his to be indemnified against expenses incurred by him in connection with those proceedings.

(10) Where a legally assisted person has been represented in any proceedings in pursuance of a contract made with the Board on terms which do not differentiate between the remuneration for his and other cases, the reference in subsection (9)(a) above to the sums paid or payable by the Board on his account in respect of the proceedings shall be construed as a reference to such part of the remuneration payable under the contract as may be specified in writing by the Board.

[(11) For the purposes of subsection (9)(c) above, the Board's liability on any person's account in relation to any mediation is its liability on his account under section 13C(9)(a) and (c) above in relation to the mediation.]

Annotations
Commencement order: SI 1989 No 288.
Sub-s (8): words in square brackets substituted by the Courts and Legal Services Act 1990, s 125(3), Sch 18, para 63(2), (3).
Sub-s (9): in para (a) words in square brackets substituted by the Courts and Legal Services Act 1990, s 125(3), Sch 18, para 63(2), (3); para (c) and word 'and' immediately preceding it prospectively added by the Family Law Act 1996, s 28(2), as from a day to be appointed.
Sub-s (11): prospectively added by the Family Law Act 1996, s 28(3), as from a day to be appointed.
This section does not extend to Scotland.

17 Limit on costs against assisted party

(1) The liability of a legally assisted party under an order for costs made against him with respect to any proceedings shall not exceed the amount (if any) which is a reasonable one for him to pay having regard to all the circumstances, including the financial resources of all the parties and their conduct in connection with the dispute.

(2) Regulations shall make provision as to the court, tribunal or person by whom that amount is to be determined and the extent to which any determination of that amount is to be final.

(3) None of the following, namely, a legally assisted person's dwelling house, clothes, household furniture and the tools and implements of his trade shall–

(a) be taken into account in assessing his financial resources for the purposes of this section, or
(b) be subject to execution or any corresponding process in any part of the United Kingdom to enforce the order,

except so far as regulations may prescribe.

Annotations
Commencement order: SI 1989 No 288.
Extent: sub-ss (1), (2) do not extend to Scotland.

18 Costs of successful unassisted parties

(1) This section applies to proceedings to which a legally assisted person is a party and which are finally decided in favour of an unassisted party.

(2) In any proceedings to which this section applies the court by which the proceedings were so decided may, subject to subsections (3) and (4) below, make an order for the payment by the Board to the unassisted party of the whole or any part of the costs incurred by him in the proceedings.

(3) Before making an order under this section, the court shall consider what order for costs should be made against the assisted party and for determining his liability in respect of such costs.

(4) An order under this section in respect of any costs may only be made if–

(a) an order for costs would be made in the proceedings apart from this Act;
(b) as respects the costs incurred in a court of first instance, those proceedings were instituted by the assisted party and the court is satisfied that the unassisted party will suffer severe financial hardship unless the order is made; and
(c) in any case, the court is satisfied that it is just and equitable in all the circumstances of the case that provision for the costs should be made out of public funds.

(5) Without prejudice to any other provision restricting appeals from any court, no appeal shall lie against an order under this section, or against a refusal to make such an order, except on a a point of law.

(6) In this section 'costs' means costs as between party and party, and includes the costs of applying for an order under this section; and where a party begins to receive representation after the proceedings have been instituted, or ceases to receive representation before they are finally decided or otherwise receives representation in connection with part only of the proceedings, the reference in subsection (2) above to the costs incurred by the unassisted party

in the proceedings shall be construed as a reference to so much of those costs as is attributable to that part.

(7) For the purposes of this section proceedings shall be treated as finally decided in favour of the unassisted party–

(a) if no appeal lies against the decision in his favour;
(b) if an appeal lies against the decision with leave, and the time limited for applications for leave expires without leave being granted; or
(c) if leave to appeal against the decision is granted or is not required, and no appeal is brought within the time limited for appeal;

and where an appeal against the decision is brought out of time the court by which the appeal (or any further appeal in those proceedings) is determined may make an order for the repayment by the unassisted party to the Board of the whole or any part of any sum previously paid to him under this section in respect of those proceedings.

(8) Where a court decides any proceedings in favour of the unassisted party and an appeal lies (with or without leave) against that decision, the court may, if it thinks fit, make or refuse to make an order under this section forthwith, but if an order is made forthwith it shall not take effect–

(a) where leave to appeal is required, unless the time limited for applications for leave to appeal expires without leave being granted;
(b) where leave to appeal is granted or is not required, unless the time limited for appeal expires without an appeal being brought.

(9) For the purposes of this section 'court' includes a tribunal.

Annotations
Commencement order: SI 1989 No 288.
This section does not extend to Scotland.

PART V CRIMINAL LEGAL AID

19 Scope of this Part

(1) This Part applies to criminal proceedings before any of the following–

(a) a magistrates' court;
(b) the Crown Court;
(c) the criminal division of the Court of Appeal or the Courts-Martial Appeal Court; and
(d) the House of Lords in the exercise of its jurisdiction in relation to appeals from either of those courts;

and representation under this Part shall be available to any person subject to and in accordance with sections 21, 22, 23, 24 and 25.

(2) Representation under this Part for the purposes of the proceedings before any court extends to any proceedings preliminary or incidental to the proceedings, including bail proceedings, whether before that or another court.

(3) Representation under this Part for the purposes of the proceedings before a magistrates' court extends to any proceedings before a [youth court] or other magistrates' court to which the case is remitted.

(4) In subsection (2) above in its application to bail proceedings, 'court' has the same meaning as in the Bail Act 1976, but that subsection does not extend representation to bail proceedings before a judge of the High Court exercising the jurisdiction of that Court.

(5) In this Part–

'competent authority' is to be construed in accordance with section 20;

'Court of Appeal' means the criminal division of that Court;

'criminal proceedings' includes proceedings for dealing with an offender for an offence or in respect of a sentence or as a fugitive offender and also includes proceedings instituted under section 115 of the Magistrates' Courts Act 1980 (binding over) in respect of an actual or apprehended breach of the peace or other misbehaviour and proceedings for dealing with a person for a failure to comply with a condition of a recognizance to keep the peace or be of good behaviour [and also includes proceedings under section 15 of the Children and Young Persons Act 1969 (variation and discharge of supervision orders) and section 16(8) of that Act (appeals in such proceedings)];

'proceedings for dealing with an offender as a fugitive offender' means proceedings before a metropolitan stipendiary magistrate under section 9 of the Extradition Act 1870, section 7 of the Fugitive Offenders Act 1967 or section 6 of the Criminal Justice Act 1988; and

'remitted', in relation to a [youth court], means remitted under section 56(1) of the Children and Young Persons Act 1933;
and any reference, in relation to representation for the purposes of any proceedings, to the proceedings before a court includes a reference to any proceedings to which representation under this Part extends by virtue of subsection (2) or (3) above.

Annotations
Commencement order: SI 1989 No 288.
Sub-s (3): words in square brackets substituted by the Criminal Justice Act 1991, s 100, Sch 11, para 40.
Sub-s (5): in definition 'criminal proceedings' words in square brackets added by the Children Act 1989, s 99(3); in definition 'remitted' words in square brackets substituted by the Criminal Justice Act 1991, s 100, Sch 11, para 40.
This section does not extend to Scotland.

20 Competent authorities to grant representation under this Part

(1) Subject to any provision made by virtue of subsection (10) below, the following courts are competent to grant representation under this Part for the purposes of the following proceedings, on an application made for the purpose.

(2) The court before which any proceedings take place, or are to take place, is always competent as respects those proceedings, except that this does not apply to the House of Lords; and, in the case of the Court of Appeal and the Courts-Martial Appeal Court, the reference to proceedings which are to take place includes proceedings which may take place if notice of appeal is given or an application for leave to appeal is made.

(3) The Court of Appeal or, as the case may be, the Courts-Martial Appeal Court is also competent as respects proceedings on appeal from decisions of theirs to the House of Lords.

(4) The magistrates' court–

(a) which commits a person for trial or sentence or to be dealt with in respect of a sentence,
[(aa) which proceeds with a view to transferring proceedings to the Crown Court for trial,]

(b) which has been given a notice of transfer under section 4 of the Criminal Justice Act 1987 (transfer of serious fraud cases) [or section 53 of the Criminal Justice Act 1991 (transfer of certain cases involving children)], < . . . >
[(bb) which has been given a notice of transfer under Part I of the Schedule to the War Crimes Act 1991, or]

(c) from which a person appeals against his conviction or sentence,

is also competent as respects the proceedings before the Crown Court.

(5) The magistrates' court inquiring into an offence as examining justices is also competent, before it decides whether or not to commit the person for trial, as respects any proceedings before the Crown Court on his trial.

(6) The Crown Court is also competent as respects applications for leave to appeal and proceedings on any appeal to the Court of Appeal under section 9(11) of the Criminal Justice Act 1987 (appeals against orders or rulings at preparatory hearings).

(7) On ordering a retrial under section 7 of the Criminal Appeal Act 1968 (new trials ordered by Court of Appeal or House of Lords on fresh evidence) the court ordering the retrial is also competent as respects the proceedings before the Crown Court.

(8) Any magistrate' court to which, in accordance with regulations, a person applies for representation when he has been arrested for an offence but has nopt appeared or been brought before a court is competent as respects the proceedings in relation to the offence in any magistrates' court.

(9) In the event of the Lord Chancellor making an order under section 3(4) as respects the function of granting representation under this Part for the purposes of proceedings before any court, the Board shall be competent as respects those proceedings, on an application made for the purpose.

(10) An order under section 3(4) may make provision restricting or excluding the competence of any court mentioned in any of subsections (2) to (8) above and may contain such transitional provisions as appear to the Lord Chancellor necessary or expedient.

Annotations

Commencement order: SI 1989 No 288.

Sub-s (4): in sub-para (a) words underlined prospectively repealed, and sub-para (aa) prospectively added, by the Criminal Justice and Public Order Act 1994, ss 44, 168(3), Sch 4, Part II, para 67, Sch 11, as from a day to be appointed; in sub-para (b) words in square brackets added by the Criminal Justice Act 1991, s 53(5). Sch 6, para 9, word omitted repealed by the War Crimes Act 1991, s 3(2), and the Criminal Justice Act 1991, s 101(2), Sch 13; sub-para (bb) added by the War Crimes Act 1991, s 3(2), prospectively repealed by the Criminal Justice and Public Order Act 1994, s 168(3), Sch 11, as from a day to be appointed.

Sub-s (5): prospectively repealed by the Criminal Justice and Public Order Act 1994, s 168(3), Sch 11, as from a day to be appointed.
This section does not extend to Scotland.

21 Availability of representation under this Part

(1) Representation under this Part for the purposes of any criminal proceedings shall be available in accordance with his section to the accused or convicted person but shall not be available to the prosecution except in the case of an appeal to the Crown Court against conviction or sentence, for the purpose of enabling an individual who is not acting in an official capacity to resist the appeal.

(2) Subject to subsection (5) below, representation may be granted where it appears to the competent authority to be desirable to do so in the interests of justice; and section 22 applies for the interpretation of this subsection in relation to the proceedings to which that section applies.

(3) Subject to subsection (5) below, representation must be granted–

(a) where a person is committed for trial on a charge of murder, for his [proceedings against a person who is charged with murder are transferred to the Crown Court for trial, for that person's] trial;
(b) where the prosecutor appeals or applies for leave to appeal to the House of Lords, for the proceedings on the appeal;
(c) where a person charged with an offence before a magistrates' court
   (i) is brought before the court in pursuance of a remand in custody when he may be again remanded or committed in custody, and
   (ii) is not, but wishes to be, legally represented before the court (not having been legally represented when he was so remanded),

   for so much of the proceedings as relates to the grant of bail; and
(d) where a person–
   (i) is to be sentenced or otherwise dealt with for an offence by a magistrates' court or the Crown Court, and
   (ii) is to be kept in custody to enable enquiries or a report to be made to assist the court,

   for the proceedings on sentencing or otherwise dealing with him.

(4) Subject to any provision made under section 3(4) by virtue of section 20(10), in a case falling within subsection (3)(a) above, it shall be for the magistrates' court which commits [transfers the proceedings against] the person for trial, and not for the Crown Court, to make the grant of representation for his trial.

(5) Representation shall not be granted to any person unless it appears to the competent authority that his financial resources are such as, under regulations, make him eligible for representation under this Part.

(6) Before making a determination for the purposes of subsection (5) above in the case of any person, the competent authority shall, except in prescribed cases, require a statement of his financial resources in the prescribed form to be furnished to the authority.

(7) Where a doubt arises whether representation under this Part should be granted to any person, the doubt shall be resolved in that person's favour.

(8) Where an application for representation for the purposes of an appeal to the Court of Appeal or the Courts-Martial; Appeal Court is made to a competent authority before the giving of notice of appeal or the making of an application for leave to appeal, the authority may, in the first instance, exercise its power to grant representation by making a grant consisting of advice on the question whether there appear to be reasonable grounds of appeal and assistance in the preparation of an application for leave to appeal or in the giving of a notice of appeal.

(9) Representation granted by a competent authority may be amended or withdrawn, whether by that or another authority competent to grant representation under this Part.

(10) Regulations may provide for an appeal to lie to a specified court or body against any refusal by a magistrates' court to grant representation under thai Part and for that other court or body to make any grant of representation that could have been made by the magistrates' court.

[(10a) Where section 44A of the Criminal Appeal Act 1968 (death of convicted person) applies, the reference in subsection (1) above to the convicted person shall be construed as a reference to the person approved under that section.]

(11) Subsection (3) above shall have effect in its application to a person who has not attained the age of eighteen as if the references in paragraphs (c) and (d) to remand in custody and to being remanded or kept in custody included references to being committed under section 23 of the Children and Young Persons Act 1969 to the care of a local authority or a remand centre.

Annotations

Commencement order: SI 1989 No 288.

Sub-ss (3), (4): words underlined prospectively repealed and subsequent words in square brackets prospectively substituted by the Criminal Justice and Public Order Act 1994, s 44, Sch 4, Part II, para 68, as from a day to be appointed.

Sub-s (10A): added by the Criminal Appeal Act 1995, s 29, Sch 4, para 17.

This section does not extend to Scotland.

22 Criteria for grant of representation for trial proceedings

(1) This section applies to proceedings by way of a trial or before a magistrates' court or the Crown Court or on an appeal to the Crown Court against a person's conviction.

(2) The factors to be taken into account by a competent authority in determining whether it is in the interests of justice that representation be granted for the purposes of proceedings to which this section applies to an accused shall include the following–

(a) the offence is such that if proved it is likely that the court would impose a sentence which would deprive the accused of his liberty or lead to loss of his livelihood or serious damage to his reputation;
(b) the determination of the case may involve consideration of a substantial question of law;
(c) the accused may be unable to understand the proceeding or to state

his own case because of his inadequate knowledge of English, mental illness or other mental or physical disability;

(d) the nature of the defence is such as to involve the tracing and interviewing of witnesses or expert cross-examination of a witness for the prosecution;

(e) it is in the interests of someone other than the accused that the accused be represented.

(3) The Lord Chancellor may, by order, vary the factors listed in subsection (2) above by amending factors in the list or by adding new factors to the list.

Annotations
Commencement order: SI 1989 No 288.
This section does not extend to Scotland.

23 Reimbursement of public funds by contributions

(1) Where representation under this Part is granted to any person whose financial resources are such as, under regulations, make him liable to make a contribution, the competent authority shall order him to pay a contribution in respect of the costs of his being represented under this Part.

(2) Where the legally assisted person has not attained the age of sixteen, the competent authority may, instead of or in addition to ordering him to make a contribution, order any person–

(a) who is an appropriate contributor in relation to him, and

(b) whose financial resources are such as, under regulations, make him liable to make a contribution,

to pay a contribution in respect of the costs of the representation granted to the legally assisted person.

(3) Regulations may authorise the making of a contribution order under subsection (1) or (2) above after the grant of representation in prescribed circumstances.

(4) The amount of the contribution to be required under subsection (1) or (2) above by the competent authority shall be such as is determined in accordance with the regulations.

(5) A legally assisted person or appropriate contributor may be required to make his contribution in one sum or by instalments as may be prescribed.

(6) Regulations may provide that no contribution order shall be made in connection with a grant of representation under this Part for the purposes of proceedings in the Crown Court, the Court of Appeal or the House of Lords in a case where a contribution order was made in connection with a grant of such representation to the person in question in respect of proceedings in a lower court.

(7) Subject to subsection (8) below, if the total contribution made in respect of the costs of representing any person under this Part exceeds those costs, the excess shall be repaid–

(a) where the contribution was made by one person only, to him; and
(b) where the contribution was made by two or more persons, to them in proportion to the amounts contributed by them.

(8) Where a contribution has been made in respect of the costs of representing any person under this Part in any proceedings and an order for costs is made in favour of that person in respect of those proceedings, then, where sums due under the order for costs are paid to the Board or the Lord Chancellor under section 20(2) of the Prosecution of Offences Act 1985 (recovery regulations)–

(a) if the costs of the representation do not exceed the sums so paid, subsection (7) above shall not apply and the contribution shall be repaid;
(b) if the costs of the representation do exceed the sums so paid, subsection (7) above shall apply as if the costs of the representation were equal to the excess.

(9) References in subsection (8) above to the costs of representation include any charge or fee treated as part of those costs by section 26(2).

(10) In this Part–

'appropriate contributor', means a person of a description prescribed under section 34(2)(c); and
'contribution order' means an order under subsection (1) or (2) above.

Annotations
Commencement order: SI 1989 No 288.
This section does not extend to Scotland.

24 Contribution orders: supplementary

(1) Where a competent authority grants representation under this Part and in connection with the grant makes a contribution order under which any sum is required to be paid on the making of the order, it may direct that the grant of representation shall not take effect until that sum is paid.

(2) Where a legally assisted person fails to pay any relevant contribution when it is due, the court in which the proceedings for the purposes of which he has been granted representation are being heard may, subject to subsection (3) below, revoke the grant.

(3) A court shall not exercise the power conferred by subsection (2) above unless, after affording the legally assisted person an opportunity of making representations in such manner as may be prescribed, it is satisfied–

(a) that he was able to pay the relevant contribution when it was due; and
(b) that he is able to pay the whole or part of it but has failed or refused to do so.

(4) In subsection (2) above 'relevant contribution', in relation to a legally assisted person, means any sum–

(a) which he is required to pay by a contribution order made in connection with the grant to him of representation under this Part, and

(b) which falls due after the making of the order and before the conclusion of the proceedings for the purposes of which he has been granted such representation.

(5) Regulations with respect to contribution orders may–

(a) provide for their variation or revocation in prescribed circumstances;
(b) provide for their making in default of the prescribed evidence of a person's financial resources;
(c) regulate their making after the grant of representation;
(d) authorise the remission or authorise or require the repayment in prescribed circumstances of sums due or paid under such orders; and
(e) prescribe the court or body by which any function under the regulations is to be exercisable.

(6) Schedule 3 to this Act shall have effect with respect to the enforcement of contribution orders.

Annotations
Commencement order: SI 1989 No 288.
This section does not extend to Scotland.

25 Payment of costs of representation under this Part

(1) Where representation under this Part has been granted to any person the costs of representing him shall be paid–

(a) by the Lord Chancellor, or
(b) by the Board,

as the Lord Chancellor may direct.

(2) Subject to regulations, the costs of representing any person under this Part shall include sums on account of the fees payable to his [legal representative] and disbursements reasonably incurred by his [legal representative] for or in connection with his representation.

(3) The costs required by this section to be paid in respect of representing him shall not include any sum in respect of allowances to witnesses attending to give evidence in the proceedings for the purposes of which he is represented in any case where such allowances are payable under any other enactment.

Annotations
Commencement order: SI 1989 No 288.
Sub-s (2): words in square brackets substituted by the Courts and Legal Services Act 1990, s 125(3), Sch 18, para 63(3), (4).
This section does not extend to Scotland.

26 Payment for advice or assistance where representation under this Part is subsequently granted

(1) This section has effect where–

(a) advice or assistance under Part III is given to a person in respect of any matter which is or becomes the subject of criminal proceedings against him; and

(b) he is subsequently granted representation under this Part for the purposes of those proceedings.

(2) If the [legal representative] acting for the person under the grant of representation is the [one] who gave him the advice or assistance, any charge or fee in respect of the advice or assistance which, apart from this section, would fall to be secured, recovered or paid as provided by section 11 shall instead be paid under section 25 as if it were part of the costs of the representation.

(3) If a contribution order is made in connection with the grant of representation under this Part to him–

(a) any sum which he is required by virtue of section 9(6) or (7) to pay in respect of the advice or assistance (whether or not already paid) shall be credited against the contribution to be made by him under the contribution order; and
(b) section 25 shall have effect in a case to which subsection (2) above applies as if the charges and fees properly chargeable in respect of the advice or assistance were part of the costs of the representation under this Part and as if any such sum as is mentioned in paragraph (a) above which he has paid were part of the contribution made under the contribution order.

Annotations
Commencement order: SI 1989 No 288.
Sub-s (2): words in square brackets substituted by the Courts and Legal Services Act 1990, s 125(3), Sch 18, paras 61(5), 63(4).
This section does not extend to Scotland.

PART VI LEGAL AID IN SPECIAL CASES

Contempt proceedings

29 Representation in contempt proceedings

(1) This section applies to any proceedings where a person is liable to be committed or fined–

(a) by a magistrates' court under section 12 of the Contempt of Court Act 1981;
(b) by a county court under section 14, 92 or 118 of the County Courts Act 1984;
(c) by any superior court for contempt in the face of that or any other court;

and in this Act 'proceedings for contempt' means so much of any proceedings as relates to dealing with a person as mentioned in paragraph (a), (b) or (c) above.

(2) In any proceedings for contempt against a person the court may order that he be granted representation under this section for the purposes of the proceedings if it appears to the court to be desirable to do so in the interests of justice.

(3) In this section, 'superior court' means the Court of Appeal, the High Court, the Crown Court, the Courts-Martial Appeal Court, the Restrictive Practices Court, the Employment Appeal Tribunal and any other court exercising in relation to its proceedings powers equivalent to those of the High Court, and includes the House of Lords in the exercise of its jurisdiction in relation to appeals from courts in England and Wales.

Annotations
Commencement order: SI 1991 No 790.
This section does not extend to Scotland.

SUPPLEMENTARY

30 Supplementary

(1), (2)< . . . >

(3) In Part V, section 25 shall apply for the purposes of representation in proceedings for contempt as it applies for the purposes of representation under that Part in criminal proceedings.

Annotations
Commencement orders: SI 1989 No 288, SI 1991 No 790.
Sub-ss (1), (2): repealed by the Children Act 1989, ss 99(4), 108(7), Sch 15.
This section does not extend to Scotland.

PART VII GENERAL AND SUPPLEMENTARY

31 Act not generally to affect position of legal representatives or other parties

(1) Except as expressly provided by this Act or regulations under it–

(a) the fact that the services of [a legal representative] are given under this Act shall not affect the relationship between or rights of [the legal representative] and client or any privilege arising out of such relationship; and

(b) the rights conferred by this Act on a person receiving advice, assistance or representation under it shall not affect the rights or liabilities of other parties to the proceedings or the principles on which the discretion of any court or tribunal is normally exercised.

(2) Without prejudice to the generality of subsection (1)(b) above, for the purpose of determining the costs of a legally assisted person in pursuance of an order for costs or an agreement for costs in his favour (other than an order under Part II of the Prosecution of Offences Act 1985) the services of his [legal representative] shall be treated as having been provided otherwise than under this Act and his [legal representative shall be treated as having paid the fees of any additional legal representative instructed by him].

(3) A person who provides advice, assistance or representation under this Act shall not take any payment in respect of the advice, assistance or representation except such payment as is made by the Board or authorised by, or by regulations under, this Act.

(4) The revocation under this Act of a grant (or, in the case of Part III, of approval for a grant) of advice, assistance or representation to a legally assisted person shall not affect the right of any legal representative of his, arising otherwise than under a contract, to remuneration for work done before the date of the revocation.

Annotations

Commencement order: SI 1989 No 288.

Sub-ss (1), (2): words in square brackets substituted by the Courts and Legal Services Act 1990, s 125(3), Sch 18, paras 62(1), 63(1), (3).

This section does not extend to Scotland.

32 Selection and assignment of legal representatives

(1) Subject to the provisions of this section, a person entitled to receive advice or assistance or representation may [select the legal representative to advise, assist or act for him from among the legal representatives willing] to provide advice, assistance or representation under this Act.

(2) Where the Board limits a grant of representation under Part IV to representation in pursuance of a contract made by the Board, it may, as it thinks fit, assign to the legally assisted person [one or more legal representatives or direct that he may only select a legal representative from among those with whom such a contract subsists.]

(3) A person's right to select his [legal representative] is subject, in the case of representation under Part V, to regulations under subsection (8) below.

(4) Subsection (1) above does not confer any right of selection in relation to proceedings under section 29 for the purposes of proceedings for contempt.

(5) Where a court grants representation to a person for the purposes of proceedings for contempt, it may assign to him for the purposes of the proceedings any [legal representative] who is within the precincts of the court at the time.

(6) The selection by or assignment to a person of [legal representative] shall not prejudice the law and practice relating to the conduct of proceedings by a [legal representative] or the circumstances in which a [legal representative] may refuse or give up a case or entrust it to another.

(7) Regulations may provide that the right conferred by subsection (1) above shall be exercisable only in relation to [legal representatives] who are for the time being members of a prescribed panel.

(8) Regulations may provide as respects representation under Part V that subsection (1) above shall not apply in cases of any prescribed description and that in any such case a prescribed authority shall assign [one or more legal representatives] in accordance with regulations under section 2(7) to the person entitled to receive such representation.

[(9) None of the following persons may be selected or assigned under this section–

(a) a solicitor who is for the time being excluded from legal aid work under section 47(2) of the Solicitors Act 1974 (powers of Solicitors Disciplinary Tribunal);

(b) a barrister excluded from such work under section 42 of the Administration of Justice Act 1985 (exclusion of barristers from legal aid work);

(c) any other legal representative excluded from such work for disciplinary reasons by an authorised body.]

(10) Notwithstanding subsection (1) above, a [legal representative] who has been selected to act for a person under that subsection may himself select to act for that person, as the [legal representative's] agent, any other [legal representative] who is not for the time being excluded from selection.

Annotations

Commencement order: SI 1989 No 288.

Sub-ss (1)–(3), (5)–(8), (10): words in square brackets substituted by the Courts and Legal Services Act 1990, s 125(3), Sch 18, paras 62(2), 63.

Sub-s (9): substituted by the Courts and Legal Services Act 1990, s 125(3), Sch 18, para 62(2).

This section does not extend to Scotland.

33 Legal aid complaints against barristers and their exclusion from legal aid work

< . . . >

Annotations

Commencement order: SI 1989 No 288.

This section substitutes the Administration of Justice Act 1985, ss 41, 42.

This section does not extend to Scotland.

34 Regulations

(1) The Lord Chancellor may make such regulations as appear to him necessary or desirable for giving effect to this Act or for preventing abuses of it.

(2) Without prejudice to the generality of subsection (1) above, any such regulations may–

(a) make provision as to the matters which are or are not to be treated as distinct matters for the purposes of advice or assistance under Part III, as to the proceedings which are or are not to be treated as distinct proceedings for the purposes of representation under Part IV, and as to the apportionment of sums recoverable or recovered by virtue of any order for costs made generally with respect to matters or proceedings treated as distinct;

(b) regulate the procedure of any court or tribunal in relation to advice, assistance or representation under this Act or orders for costs made thereunder and authorise the delegation (subject to appeal) or the exercise of their functions by members, officers or other courts or the judges or members of other courts;

(c) regulate the availability of advice, assistance or representation (other than for the purposes of proceedings for contempt) and the making of contributions towards its provision by reference to the financial resources or, in prescribed cases, the aggregate financial resources, of persons and provide for the courts, persons or bodies who are to determine the financial resources of persons and the persons who are to be required or permitted to furnish information for those purposes;

(d) provide for the cases in which a person may be refused advice, assistance or representation or have the grant of it withdrawn or revoked by reason of his conduct when seeking or receiving advice, assistance or representation (whether in the same or a different matter);

(e) make provision for the remuneration and payment of the expenses of [legal representatives] and for the courts, persons or bodies by whom, and the manner in which, any determinations which may be required for those purposes are to be made, reviewed or appealed;

(f) make provision for the recovery of sums due to the Board and for making effective the charge created by this Act on property recovered or preserved for a legally assisted person and regulating the release or postponement of the enforcement of any charge (however created) in favour of the Board.

(3) Regulations may also modify this Act for the purposes of its application to prescribed descriptions of persons or in prescribed circumstances.

(4) Without prejudice to subsection (3) above, regulations may also modify this Act for the purposes of its application–

(a) in cases where its modification appears to the Lord Chancellor necessary for the purpose of fulfilling any obligation imposed on the United Kingdom or Her Majesty's Government in the United Kingdom by any international agreement; or

(b) in relation to proceedings for securing the recognition or enforcement in England and Wales of judgments given outside the United Kingdom for whose recognition or enforcement in the United Kingdom provision is made by any international agreement.

(5) Regulations made for the purposes mentioned in subsection (2)(b) above may include provisions–

(a) as to the determination of costs incurred in connection with proceedings not actually begun; and

(b) as to the cases in which and extent to which a person receiving advice, assistance or representation may be required to give security for costs, and the manner in which it may be so given.

(6) Regulations made for the purposes mentioned in subsection (2)(c) above may provide that the income or capital of a person in receipt of prescribed [benefits under Part VII of the Social Security Contributions and Benefits Act 1992 (income-related benefits)] is to be taken as not exceeding a prescribed amount.

(7) Regulations made for the purposes mentioned in subsection (2)(e) above may include provisions–

(a) imposing conditions for the allowance of remuneration and expenses;

(b) attaching financial penalties in the event of appeals or reviews of determinations being unsuccessful;

(c) authorising the making of interim payments of remuneration or in respect of expenses.

(8) Regulations made for the purposes mentioned in subsection (2)(f) above may include provisions–

(a) for the enforcement for the benefit of the Board of an order or agreement for costs made in favour of a legally assisted person;
(b) for making a [legal representative's] right to payment by the Board wholly or partly dependent on his performance of the duties imposed on him by regulations made for the purposes of that paragraph; and
(c) requiring interest to be charged at a prescribed rate in circumstances where enforcement of a charge in favour of the Board is postponed.

(9) The Lord Chancellor, in making regulations for the purposes mentioned in subsection (2)(e) above as respects any description of legal aid work, shall have regard, among the matters which are relevant, to–

(a) the time and skill which it requires;
(b) the general level of fee income arising from it;
(c) the general level of expenses of [legal representatives] which is attributable to it;
(d) the number and general level of competence of [legal representatives] undertaking it;
(e) the effect of the regulations on the handling of the work; and
(f) the cost to public funds of any provision made by the regulations.

(10) Before making regulations for the purposes mentioned in subsection (2)(e) above, the Lord Chancellor shall consult the General Council of the Bar and the Law Society.

(11) Regulations under this Act may make different provision for different descriptions of advice, assistance or representation, for different cases or classes of case, for different areas or for other different circumstances and for different descriptions of persons.

(12) Before making regulations as to the procedure of any court or tribunal, the Lord Chancellor shall so far as practicable consult any rule committee or similar body by whom or on whose advice rules of procedure for the court or tribunal may be made apart from this provision or whose consent or concurrence is required to any such rules so made.

(13) No regulations shall be made under this section which include provision for the purposes mentioned in subsection (2)(c) or (e) above except with the consent of the Treasury.

(14) <. . .>

Annotations

Commencement order: SI 1989 No 288.

Sub-ss (2), (8), (9): words in square brackets substituted by the Courts and Legal Services Act 1990, s 125(3), Sch 18, para 63(2), (5).

Sub-s (6): words in square brackets substituted by the Social Security (Consequential Provisions) Act 1992, s 4, Sch 2, para 97.

Sub-s (14): repealed by the Social Security (Consequential Provisions) Act 1992, s 3, Sch 1.

This section does not extend to Scotland.

35 Advisory Committee

(1) The existing advisory committee shall continue in being to advise the Lord Chancellor on such questions relating to the provision of advice, assistance

or representation under this Act as he may from time to time refer to them and to make recommendations or furnish comments to him on such matters as they consider appropriate.

(2) Appointments to the committee by the Lord Chancellor, whether by way of replacing existing members or making additional appointments, shall be made so as to secure that the committee is constituted of persons having knowledge of the work of the courts and social conditions.

(3) The Lord Chancellor may pay to the members of the advisory committee such travelling and other allowances as he may, with the consent of the Treasury, determine; and any expenses of the Lord Chancellor under this subsection shall be defrayed out of money provided by Parliament.

(4) It shall be the duty of the advisory committee to provide to the Lord Chancellor, as soon as possible after 31st March in each year, a report containing any advice, recommendations or comments of theirs on questions or matters arising during the preceding twelve months.

(5) The Lord Chancellor shall lay before each House of Parliament a copy of the annual report of the committee made to him under subsection (4) above.

(6) The Lord Chancellor may, by order dissolve the advisory committee on such day as is specified in the order and on that day this section shall cease to have effect except as regards the defrayal out of money provided by Parliament of the allowances falling to be paid thereafter under subsection (3) above.

(7) In this section 'the existing advisory committee' means the advisory committee in existence under section 21 of the Legal Aid Act 1974 at the passing of this Act.

Annotations
This section was repealed by SI 1995 No 162, except as specified in sub-s (6) above.
This section does not extend to Scotland.

36 Orders and regulations: general

(1) Any power under this Act to make an order or regulations shall be exercisable by statutory instrument.

(2) As respects orders under this Act other than orders under section 47–

(a) except in the case of an order under section 3(4) and 35(6), any instrument containing the order shall be subject to annulment in pursuance of a resolution of either House of Parliament;
(b) in the case of an order under section 3(4) or 35(6), no such order shall be made unless a draft of it has been laid before and approved by resolution of each House of Parliament.

(3) As respects regulations under this Act–

(a) except in the case of regulations under section 8, 14(2) and 32(7), any instrument containing the regulations shall be subject to annulment in pursuance of a resolution of either House of Parliament;
(b) in the case of regulations under section 8, 14(2) or 32(7), no such

regulations shall be made unless a draft of them has been laid before and approved by resolution of each House of Parliament.

Annotations
Commencement order: SI 1989 No 288.
This section does not extend to Scotland.

37 Laying of Board's annual reports before Parliament

The Lord Chancellor shall lay before each House of Parliament a copy of the annual report of the Board made to him under section 5(3).

Annotations
Commencement order: SI 1989 No 288.
This section does not extend to Scotland.

38 Restriction of disclosure of information

(1) Subject to the following provisions of this section, no information furnished for the purposes of this Act to the Board or any court or other person or body of persons upon whom functions are imposed or conferred by regulations and so furnished in connection with the case of a person seeking or receiving advice, assistance or representation shall be disclosed otherwise than–

(a) for the purpose of enabling or assisting the Lord Chancellor to perform his functions under or in relation to this Act,
(b) for the purpose of enabling the Board to discharge its functions under this Act,
(c) for the purpose of facilitating the proper performance by any court, tribunal or other person or body of persons of functions under this Act,
(d) with a view to the institution of, or otherwise for the purposes of, any criminal proceedings for an offence under this Act,
(e) in connection with any other proceedings under this Act, or
(f) for the purpose of facilitating the proper performance by any tribunal of disciplinary functions as regards [legal representatives].

(2) This section does not apply to information in the form of a summary or collection of information so framed as not to enable information relating to any particular person to be ascertained from it.

(3) Subsection (1) above shall not prevent the disclosure of information for any purpose with the consent of the person in connection with whose case it was furnished and, where he did not furnish it himself, with that of the person or body of persons who did.

(4) A person who, in contravention of this section, discloses any information furnished to the Board or any court or other person or body of persons for the purposes of this Act shall be liable on summary conviction to a fine not exceeding level 4 on the standard scale.

(5) Proceedings for an offence under this section shall not be brought without the written consent of the Attorney General.

(6) For the avoidance of doubt it is hereby declared that information furnished to [a legal representative] as such by or on behalf of a person seeking

or receiving advice, assistance or representation under this Act is not information furnished to the Board or a person upon whom functions are imposed or conferred as mentioned in subsection (1) above.

Annotations
Commencement order: SI 1989 No 288.
Sub-ss (1), (6): words in square brackets substituted by the Courts and Legal Services Act 1990, s 125(3), Sch 18, para 63(1), (5).
This section does not extend to Scotland.

39 Proceedings for misrepresentation etc

(1) If any person seeking or receiving advice, assistance or representation under this Act–

(a) intentionally fails to comply with regulations as to the information to be furnished by him, or
(b) in furnishing any information required by regulations knowingly makes any false statement or false representation,

he shall be liable on summary conviction to a fine not exceeding level 4 on the standard scale or to imprisonment for a term not exceeding three months or to both.

(2) Notwithstanding anything in the Magistrates' Courts Act 1980, proceedings in respect of an offence under subsection (1) above may be brought at any time within the period of six months beginning with the date on which evidence sufficient in the opinion of the prosecutor to justify a prosecution comes to his knowledge.

(3) Nothing in subsection (2) above shall authorise the commencement of proceedings for an offence at a time more than two years after the date on which the offence was committed.

(4) A county court shall have jurisdiction to hear and determine any action brought by the Board to recover the loss sustained by it on account of its legal aid fund by reason of–

(a) the failure of a person seeking or receiving advice, assistance or representation to comply with regulations as to the information to be furnished by him, or
(b) a false statement or false representation made by such a person in furnishing information for the purposes of this Act,
< . . . >

Annotations
Commencement order: SI 1989 No 288.
Sub-s (4): words omitted repealed by SI 1991 No 724, art 2(1)(m), (8), Schedule, Part I.
This section does not extend to Scotland.

40 Adaptation of rights of indemnity in cases of advice, assistance or representation in civil proceedings

(1) This section shall have effect for the purpose of adapting in relation to Parts III and IV any right (however and whenever created or arising) which a person may have to be indemnified against expenses incurred by him.

(2) In determining for the purposes of any such right the reasonableness of any expenses, the possibility of avoiding them or part of them by taking advantage of Part III or Part IV shall be disregarded.

(3) Where a person having any such right to be indemnified against expenses incurred in connection with any proceedings receives in connection with those proceedings advice, assistance or representation then (without prejudice to the effect of the indemnity in relation to his contribution, if any, under section 9 or 16) the right shall enure also for the benefit of the Board as if any expenses incurred by the Board on his account in connection with the advice, assistance or representation had been incurred by him.

(4) Where a person's right to be indemnified enures for the benefit of the board under subsection (3) above in a case where he has been represented in pursuance of a contract made with the Board on terms which do not differentiate between the remuneration for his and other cases, the reference in that subsection to any expenses incurred by the Board on his account shall be construed as a reference to such part of the remuneration payable under the contract as may be specified in writing by the Board.

(5) Where–

(a) a person's right to be indemnified against expenses incurred in connection with any proceedings arises by virtue of an agreement and is subject to any express condition conferring on those liable under it any right with respect to the bringing or conduct of the proceedings, and
(b) those liable have been given a reasonable opportunity of exercising the right so conferred and have not availed themselves of the opportunity,

the right to be indemnified shall be treated for the purpose of subsection (3) above as not being subject to that condition.

(6) Nothing in subsections (3) and (5) above shall be taken as depriving any person or body of persons of the protection of any enactment or, except as provided in subsection (5), as conferring any larger right to recover money in respect of any expenses than the person receiving advice, assistance or representation would have had if the expenses had been incurred by him.

Annotations
Commencement order: SI 1989 No 288.
This section does not extend to Scotland.

41 Application to Crown

This Act binds the Crown.

Annotations
Commencement order: SI 1989 No 288.
This section does not extend to Scotland.

42 Finance

(1) The Lord Chancellor shall pay to the Board out of money provided by Parliament–

(a) such sums as are required (after allowing for payments by the Board into its legal aid fund under paragraphs (a), (b), (c), (d) and (f) of section 6(3)) to meet the payments which, under subsection (2) of that section, are to be paid by the Board out of that fund; and

(b) such sums as he may, with the approval of the Treasury, determine are required for the other expenditure of the Board.

(2) The Lord Chancellor may, with the approval of the Treasury –

(a) determine the manner in which and times at which the sums referred to in subsection (1)(a) above shall be paid to the Board; and

(b) impose conditions on the payment of the sums referred to in subsection (1)(b) above.

Annotations
Commencement order: SI 1989 No 288.
This section does not extend to Scotland.

43 Definitions

In this Act–

'advice', 'assistance' and 'representation' have the meanings assigned to them by section 2(2), (3) and (4) respectively subject, however, to the other provisions of that section;

['authorised body' has the meaning assigned by section 119(1) of the Courts and Legal Services Act 1990;]

'the Board' has the meaning assigned to it by section 3(1);

'determination', in relation to the costs of advice or assistance or representation for the purposes of proceedings, includes taxation and assessment;

'financial resources', in relation to any person, includes any valuable facility which is available to him;

['legal representative' means an authorised advocate or authorised litigator, as defined by section 119(1) of the Courts and Legal Services Act 1990;]

['mediator' means a person with whom the Board contracts for the provision of mediation by any person.]

'order for costs' includes any judgment, order, decree, award or direction for the payment of the costs of one party to any proceedings by another party, whether given or made in those proceedings or not;

'prescribed' means prescribed by regulations made by the Lord Chancellor under this Act;

'proceedings for contempt' has the meaning assigned to it by section 29(1);

'regulations' means regulations made by the Lord Chancellor under this Act;

'sentence', in relation to a person, includes any order made on his conviction of an offence;

'solicitor' means solicitor of the Supreme Court;

'statutory inquiry' has the meaning assigned to it by [section 16(1) of the Tribunals and Inquiries Act 1992]; and

'tribunal' includes an arbitrator or umpire, however appointed, and whether the arbitration takes place under a reference by consent or otherwise.

Annotations
Commencement order: SI 1989 No 288.
Definitions 'authorised body' and 'legal representative' added by the Courts and Legal Services

Act 1990, s 125(3), Sch 18, para 60; definition 'mediator' prospectively added by the Family Law Act 1996, s 26(3), as from a day to be appointed; in definition 'statutory inquiry' words in square brackets substituted by the Tribunals and Inquiries Act 1992, s 18(1), Sch 3, para 21.

This section does not extend to Scotland.

PART VIII MISCELLANEOUS

Scottish provisions

44 Scottish provisions

The Legal Aid (Scotland) Act 1986 shall have effect subject to the amendments specified in Schedule 4 to this Act.

Annotations
Commencement order: SI 1988 No 1388.
This section applies to Scotland only.

Supplementary

45 Amendments, repeals and transitional provisions

(1) The enactments specified in Schedule 5 to this Act shall have effect subject to the amendments there specified.

(2) Subject to subsection (4) below, the enactments specified in Schedule 6 to this Act are repealed to the extent specified in the third column of that Schedule.

(3) Where any enactment amended or repealed by subsection (1) or (2) above extends to the United Kingdom or any part of it, the amendment or repeal has a corresponding extent.

(4) Schedule 7 to this Act shall have effect for the purpose of making the transitional and saving provisions set out there.

Annotations
Commencement order: SI 1989 No 288.

46 Amendments of Legal Aid Act 1974 pending repeal

The Legal Aid Act 1974 shall have effect subject to the amendments specified in Schedule 8 to this Act.

Annotations
This section does not extend to Scotland.

47 Short title, commencement and extent

(1) This Act may be cited as the Legal Aid Act 1988.

(2) Subject to subsections (3) and (4) below, this Act shall come into force on such day as the Lord Chancellor appoints by order and different days may be appointed for different provisions.

(3) Section 44 and Schedule 4 shall come into force on such day as the Secretary of State appoints by order and different days may be appointed for different provisions.

(4) Sections 35 (together with the repeal of section 21 of the Legal Aid Act 1974) and 46 shall come into force on the date on which this Act is passed.

(5) An order under subsection (2) or (3) above may contain such transitional and saving provisions as appear to the Lord Chancellor or, as the case may be, the Secretary of State necessary or expedient.

(6) This Act, with the exception of sections 12(3) and 17(3), section 44 and Schedule 4 and the amendments or repeals of the enactments referred to in section 45(3), above, extends to England and Wales only and section 44 and Schedule 4 extend to Scotland only.

SCHEDULE 1

The Legal Aid Board

Section 3

Incorporation and Status

1 The Board shall be a body corporate.

2 The Board shall not be regarded as the servant or agent of the Crown or as enjoying any status, immunity or privilege of the Crown; and the Board's property shall not be regarded as property of, or held on behalf of, the Crown.

Tenure of Members

3 Subject to paragraphs 4 and 5 any member of the Board shall hold and vacate office in accordance with the terms of his appointment, but a person shall not be appointed a member of the Board for a period of more than 5 years.

4 (1) The chairman or a member may resign office by giving notice in writing to the Lord Chancellor, and if the chairman ceases to be a member he shall cease to be the chairman.

(2) A person who ceases to be the chairman or a member shall be eligible for reappointment.

5 The Lord Chancellor may terminate the appointment of a member of the Board if satisfied that–

(a) he has become bankrupt or made an arrangement with his creditors;
(b) he is unable to carry out his duties as a Board member by reason of physical or mental illness;

(c) he has been absent from meetings of the Board for a period longer than six consecutive months without the permission of the Board; or
(d) he is otherwise unable or unfit to discharge the functions of a member of the Board.

Member's interests

6 (1) Before appointing a person to be a member of the Board, the Lord Chancellor shall satisfy himself that that person will have no such financial or other interest as is likely to affect prejudicially the exercise or performance by him of his functions as a member of the Board.

(2) The Lord Chancellor shall from to time satisfy himself with respect to every member of the Board that he has no such interest as is referred to in sub-paragraph (1) above.

(3) Any person whom the Lord Chancellor proposes to appoint as, and who has consented to be, a member of the Board, and any member of the Board, shall, whenever requested by the Lord Chancellor to do so, supply him with such information as the Lord Chancellor considers necessary for the performance by the Lord Chancellor of his duties under this paragraph.

7 (1) A member of the Board who is in any way directly or indirectly interested in a contract made or proposed to be made by the Board shall disclose the nature of his interest at a meeting of the Board; and the disclosure shall be recorded in the minutes of the Board, and the member shall not take any part in any deliberation or decision of the Board with respect to that contract.

(2) For the purposes of sub-paragraph (1) above, a general notice given at a meeting of the Board by a member of the Board to the effect that he is a member of a specified company or firm and is to be regarded as interested in any contract which may, after the date of the notice, be made with the company or firm shall be regarded as a sufficient disclosure of his interest in relation to any contract so made.

(3) A member of the Board need not attend in person at a meeting of the Board in order to make any disclosure which he is required to make under this paragraph if he takes reasonable steps to secure that the disclosure is made by a notice which is brought up and read out at the meeting.

Remuneration of members

8 (1) The Board may–

(a) pay to its members such remuneration; and
(b) make provision for the payment of such pensions, allowances or gratuities to or in respect of its members,

as the Lord Chancellor may, with the approval of the Treasury, determine.

(2) Where a person ceases to be a member of the Board otherwise than on the expiry of his term of office, and it appears to the Lord Chancellor that there are special circumstances which make it right for that person to receive

compensation, the Lord Chancellor may, with the consent of the Treasury, direct the Board to make that person a payment of such amount as the Lord Chancellor may, with the consent of the Treasury, determine.

Staff

9 (1) The Board shall appoint a person to be the chief executive of the Board who shall be responsible to the Board for the exercise of its functions.

(2) The Board may appoint such other employees as it thinks fit.

(3) The Board may only appoint a person to be its chief executive or the holder of any other employment of a specified description after consultation with, and subject to the approval of, the Lord Chancellor.

(4) The reference in sub-paragraph (3) above to employment of a specified description is a reference to any employment for the time being specified by the Lord Chancellor in a direction given for the purposes of that sub-paragraph.

(5) An appointment under this paragraph may be made on such terms and conditions as the Board, with the approval of the Lord Chancellor and consent of the Treasury, may determine.

10 (1) The Board shall make, in respect of such of its employees as, with the approval of the Lord Chancellor and the consent of the Treasury, it may determine such arrangements for providing pensions, allowances or gratuities, including pensions, allowances or gratuities by way of compensation for loss of employment, as it may determine.

(2) Arrangements under sub-paragraph (1) above may include the establishment and administration, by the Board or otherwise, of one or more pension schemes.

(3) If an employee of the Board–

(a) becomes a member of the Board; and
(b) was by reference to his employment by the Board a participant in a pension scheme established and administered by it for the benefit of its employees,

the Board may determine that his service as a member shall be treated for the purposes of the scheme as service as an employee of the Board whether or not any benefits are to be payable to or in respect of him by virtue of paragraph 8.

(4) Where the Board exercises the power conferred by sub-paragraph (3) above, any discretion as to the benefits payable to or in respect of the member concerned which the scheme confers on the Board shall be exercised only with the approval of the Lord Chancellor and consent of the Treasury.

Proceedings

11 (1) Subject to anything in regulations, the Board may regulate its own proceedings.

(2) The Board may make such arrangements as it considers appropriate for the discharge of its functions, including the delegation of specified functions and shall make such arrangements for the delegation of functions to committees and persons as may be prescribed.

(3) Subject to anything in regulations, committees may be appointed and may be dissolved by the Board, and may include, or consist entirely of, persons who are not members of the Board.

(4) A committee shall act in accordance with such directions as the Board may from time to time give, and the Board may provide for anything done by a committee to have effect as if it had been done by the Board.

(5) The validity of any proceedings of the Board or of any committee appointed by the Board shall not be affected by any vacancy among its members or by any defect in the appointment of any member.

Instruments

12 (1) The fixing of the seal of the Board shall be authenticated by the chairman or another member of the Board and by some other person authorised either generally or specially by the Board to act for that purpose.

(2) A document purporting to be duly executed under the seal of the Board, or to be signed on the Board's behalf, shall be received in evidence and, unless the contrary is proved, be deemed to be so executed or signed.

Allowances

13 The Board may pay to the members of any committee such fees and allowances as the Lord Chancellor may, with the consent of the Treasury, determine.

Annotations
Commencement order: SI 1988 No 1361.
This Schedule does not extend to Scotland.

SCHEDULE 2 CIVIL PROCEEDINGS: SCOPE OF PART IV REPRESENTATION

Section 14

PART I DESCRIPTION OF PROCEEDINGS

1 Proceedings in, or before any person to whom a case is referred in whole or in part by, any of the following courts, namely–

(a) the House of Lords in the exercise of its jurisdiction in relation to appeals from courts in England and Wales;

(b) the Court of Appeal;
(c) the High Court;
(d) any county court.

2 The following proceedings in a magistrates' court, namely–

(a) < . . . >
(b) proceedings under section 43 of the National Assistance Act 1948, section 22 of the Maintenance Orders Act 1950, section 4 of the Maintenance Orders Act 1958, or section 18 of the Supplementary Benefits Act 1976;
(c) proceedings in relation to an application for leave of the court to remove a child from a person's custody under section 27 or 28 of the Adoption Act 1976 or proceedings in which the making of an order under Part II or section 29 or 55 of the Adoption Act 1976 is opposed by any party to the proceedings;
(d) proceedings under Part I of the Maintenance Orders (Reciprocal Enforcement) Act 1972 relating to a maintenance order made by a court of a country outside the United Kingdom;
(e) < . . . >
(f) proceedings for or in relation to an order under Part I of the Domestic Proceedings and Magistrates' Courts Act 1978;
[(g) proceedings under the Children Act 1989;]
[(h) appeals under section 20, where they are to be made to a magistrates' court, and proceedings under section 27 of the Child Support Act 1991;]
[(i) proceedings under section 30 of the Human Fertilisation and Embryology Act 1990.]

3 Proceedings in the Employment Appeal Tribunal.

4 Proceedings in the Lands Tribunal.

5 Proceedings before a Commons Commissioner appointed under section 17(1) of the Commons Registration Act 1965.

6 Proceedings in the Restrictive Practices Court under Part III of the Fair Trading Act 1973, and any proceedings in that court in consequence of an order made, or undertaking given to the court, under that Part of that Act.

Annotations

Commencement order: SI 1989 No 288.

Para 2: sub-paras (a) and (e) repealed, and sub-para (g) added, by the Children Act 1989, s 108(4), (7), Sch 12, para 45, Sch 15; sub-para (h) added by SI 1993 No 1354, reg 2; sub-para (i) added by SI 1994 No 2768, reg 2.

This Schedule does not extend to Scotland.

PART II EXCEPTED PROCEEDINGS

1 Proceedings wholly or partly in respect of defamation, but so that the making of a counterclaim for defamation in proceedings for which representation may be granted shall not of itself affect any right of the defendant to the counterclaim to representation for the purposes of the proceedings and so that representation may be granted to enable him to defend the counterclaim.

2 Relator actions.

3 Proceedings for the recovery of a penalty where the proceedings may be taken by any person and the whole or part of the penalty is payable to the person taking the proceedings.

4 Election petitions under the Representation of the People Act 1983.

5 In a county court, proceedings for or consequent on the issue of a judgment summons and, in the case of a defendant, proceedings where the only question to be brought before the court is as to the time and mode of payment by him of a debt (including liquidated damages) and costs.

[**5A** Proceedings for a decree of divorce or judicial separation unless the cause is defended, or the petition is directed to be heard in open court, or it is not practicable by reason of physical or mental incapacity for the applicant to proceed without representation; except that representation shall be available for the purpose of making or opposing an application–

(a) for an injunction;
(b) for ancillary relief, excluding representation for the purpose only of inserting a prayer for ancillary relief in the petition;
(c) for an order relating to the custody of (or access to) a child, or the education or care or supervision of a child, excluding representation for the purpose only of making such an application where there is no reason to believe that the application will be opposed;
(d) for an order declaring that the court is satisfied as to arrangements for the welfare of the children of the family, excluding representation for the purpose only of making such an application where there is no reason to believe that the application will be opposed; or
(e) for the purpose of making or opposing any other application, or satisfying the court on any other matter which raises a substantial question for determination by the court.]

[**5B** Proceedings to the extent that they consist in, or arise out of, an application to the court under section 235A of the Trade Union and Labour Relations (Consolidation) Act 1992.]

6 Proceedings incidental to any proceedings excepted by this Part of this Schedule.

Annotations
Commencement order: SI 1989 No 288.
Para 5A: added by SI 1989 No 549, reg 2.
Para 5B: added by the Trade Union Reform and Employment Rights Act 1993, s 49(2), Sch 8, para 39.
This Schedule does not extend to Scotland.

SCHEDULE 3 CRIMINAL PROCEEDINGS: ENFORCEMENT OF CONTRIBUTION ORDERS

Sections 24, 30

PART I ORDERS MADE BY A COURT

Collecting court

1 In this Part 'collecting court', in relation to a contribution order, means a magistrates' court specified in the order; and the court so specified shall be–

(a) in a case where the court making the order is itself a magistrates' court, that court;
(b) in a case where the order is made on an appeal from a magistrates' court, or in respect of a person who was committed (whether for trial or otherwise by a magistrates' court) [against whom proceedings were transferred for trial or who was committed for sentence] to the Crown Court, the court from which the appeal is brought or, as the case may be, which committed him [transferred the proceedings against him or committed him for sentence]; and
(c) in any other case, a magistrates' court nominated by the court making the order.

Enforcement proceedings

2 (1) Any sum required to be paid by a contribution order shall be recoverable as if it had been adjudged to be paid by an order of the collecting court, subject to and in accordance with the provisions of this paragraph.

(2) Sections 17 (not more than one committal for same arrears) and 18 (power to review committal) of the Maintenance Orders Act 1988 shall apply as if a contribution order were a maintenance order.

(3) The collecting court may exercise, in relation to a contribution order, the power conferred by section 75 of the Magistrates' Courts Act 1980 (power to dispense with immediate payment); and for the purposes of that section any provisions made by the authority which made the order as to time for payment, or payment by instalments, shall be treated as made by the collecting court.

(4) The following provisions of the Magistrates' Courts Act 1980 shall apply as if a contribution order were enforceable as an affiliation order–

section 80 (application of money found on defaulter to satisfy sum adjudged);
section 93 (complaint for arrears);
section 94 (effect of committal on arrears); and
section 95 (power to remit arrears).

(5) Any costs awarded under section 64 of the Magistrates' Courts Act

1980 on the hearing of a complaint for the enforcement of a contribution order shall be enforceable as a sum required to be paid by that order.

3 (1) Without prejudice to paragraph 2, any sum required to be paid by a contribution order shall be enforceable by the High Court or a county court as if the sum were due to the clerk of the collecting court in pursuance of a judgment or order of the High Court or county court, as the case may be.

(2) The clerk of the collecting court shall not take proceedings by virtue of this paragraph unless authorised to do so by the court.

(3) This paragraph shall not authorise–

(a) the enforcement of a sum required to be paid by a contribution order by issue of a writ of fieri facias or other process against goods or by imprisonment or attachment of earnings; < . . . >

(b) < . . . >

4 (1) Any expenses incurred by the clerk of a magistrates' court in recovering any sum required to be paid by a contribution order shall be treated for the purposes of Part VI of the Justices of the Peace Act 1979 as expenses of the magistrates' courts committee.

(2) Any sum paid to a clerk of a magistrates' court in or towards satisfaction of a liability imposed by a contribution order shall be paid by him to the Lord Chancellor and section 61(4) of the Justices of the Peace Act 1979 (regulations as to accounts of justices' clerks) shall apply in relation to sums payable to the Lord Chancellor under this sub-paragraph as it applies in relation to sums payable to the Secretary of State under that section.

Transfer of enforcement proceedings to different court

5 (1) Where in relation to any contribution order it appears to the collecting court that the person subject to it is residing in a petty sessions area other than that for which the court acts, the court may make an order under this paragraph ('a transfer order') with respect to the contribution order specifying the other petty sessions area.

(2) Where a court makes a transfer order in relation to any contribution order–

(a) payment under the contribution order shall be enforceable in the petty sessions area specified in the transfer order; and

(b) as from the date of the transfer order, a magistrates' court for that petty sessions area shall be substituted for the court which made the transfer order as the collecting court in relation to the contribution order.

Limitations on enforcement by proceedings

6 Any sum due under a contribution order shall not be recoverable, and payment of any such sum shall not be enforced, under paragraph 2 or 3 until–

(a) the conclusion of the proceedings for the purposes of which the relevant grant of representation was made; or
(b) if earlier, the revocation or withdrawal of the relevant grant of representation.

7 Where a contribution order has been made in respect of a member of Her Majesty's armed forces and the Secretary of State notifies the collecting court that any sum payable under the order will be recovered by deductions from the person's pay, the collecting court shall not enforce payment of any sum unless and until the Secretary of State subsequently notifies it that the person is no longer a member of those forces and that sum has not been fully recovered.

Power to defer enforcement proceedings

8 The collecting court may defer recovering any sum due under a contribution order if–

(a) an appeal is pending in respect of the proceedings for the purposes of which the relevant grant of representation was made; or
(b) the person granted representation has been ordered to be retried.

Interpretation

9 In this Part–

(a) 'relevant grant of representation', in relation to a contribution order, means the grant of representation in connection with which the order was made; and
(b) references to the proceedings for the purposes of which a grant of representation has been made include, where the proceedings are proceedings before a magistrates' court which result–
   (i) in the legally assisted person being committed to the Crown Court for trial or sentence, or
   [(i)in the proceedings against the legally assisted person being transferred to the Crown Court for trial or in the legally assisted person being committed to the Crown Court for sentence, or]
   (ii) in his case being remitted to a [youth court] in pursuance of section 56(1) of the Children and Young Persons Act 1933,

the proceedings before the Crown Court or that [youth court].

Annotations

Commencement order: SI 1989 No 288.

Para 1: words underlined prospectively repealed and subsequent words in square brackets prospectively substituted by the Criminal Justice and Public Order Act 1994, s 44, Sch 4, Part II, para 69(2), as from a day to be appointed.

Para 3: in sub-para (3) words omitted repealed by SI 1991 No 724, art 2(1)(m), (8), Schedule, Part I.

Para 9: words underlined prospectively repealed and subsequent words in square brackets prospectively substituted by the Criminal Justice and Public Order Act 1994, s 44, Sch 4, Part II, para 69(3), as from a day to be appointed; second and final words in square brackets substituted by the Criminal Justice Act 1991, s 100, Sch 11, para 40.

This Schedule does not extend to Scotland.

PART II ORDERS MADE BY THE BOARD: LIMITATIONS ON ENFORCEMENT BY PROCEEDINGS

10 (1) Any sum due under a contribution order shall not be recoverable, and payment of any such sum shall not be enforced until–

(a) the conclusion of the proceedings for the purposes of which the relevant grant of representation was made; or
(b) if earlier, the revocation or withdrawal of the relevant grant of representation.

(2) In this paragraph–

(a) 'relevant grant of representation', in relation to a contribution order, means the grant of representation in connection with which the order was made; and
(b) the reference to the proceedings for the purposes of which the relevant grant of representation was made includes, where the proceedings are proceedings before a magistrates' court which result–

(i) in the legally assisted person being committed to the Crown Court for trial or sentence, or
[(i) in the proceedings against the legally assisted person being transferred to the Crown Court for trial or in the legally assisted person being committed to the Crown Court for sentence, or]
(ii) in his case being remitted to a [youth court] in pursuance of section 56(1) of the Children and Young Persons Act 1933,

the proceedings before the Crown Court or that [youth court].

11 Where a contribution order has been made in respect of a member of Her Majesty's armed forces and the Secretary of State notifies the Board that any sum payable under the order will be recovered by deductions from the person's pay, the Board shall not enforce payment of any sum unless and until the Secretary of State subsequently notifies it that the person is no longer a member of those forces and that sum has not been fully recovered.

Annotations
Commencement order: SI 1989 No 288.
Para 10: in sub-para (2) words underlined prospectively repealed and subsequent words in square brackets prospectively substituted by the Criminal Justice and Public Order Act 1994, s 44, Sch 4, Part II, para 69(4), as from a day to be appointed; second and final words in square brackets substituted by the Criminal Justice Act 1991, s 100, Sch 11, para 40.
This Schedule does not extend to Scotland.

SCHEDULE 4 AMENDMENTS OF LEGAL AID (SCOTLAND) ACT 1986 (C 47)

Section 44

PART I DIRECT PAYMENT OF FEES AND OUTLAYS BY LEGALLY ASSISTED PERSON

< . . . >

Annotations

Commencement order: SI 1988 No 1388.

This Part amends the Legal Aid (Scotland) Act 1986, ss 4, 16, 17, 32, 33, 36; repealed in part and prospectively repealed in part as from a day to be appointed, by the Law Reform (Miscellaneous Provisions) (Scotland) Act 1990, s 74, Sch 9.

This Schedule applies to Scotland only.

PART II LIABILITY OF LEGALLY ASSISTED PERSON FOR EXPENSES TO BE ASSESSED IN ALL CASES

< . . . >

Annotations

Commencement order: SI 1988 No 1388.

This Part amends the Legal Aid (Scotland) Act 1986, ss 18, 19, 20.

This Schedule applies to Scotland only.

PART III BOARD'S PROPERTY TO BE RATEABLE

< . . . >

Annotations

Commencement order: SI 1988 No 1388.

This Part amends the Legal Aid (Scotland) Act 1986, Sch 1.

This Schedule applies to Scotland only.

SCHEDULE 5 MINOR AND CONSEQUENTIAL AMENDMENTS

Section 45

< . . . >

Annotations

Commencement order: SI 1989 No 288.

This Schedule contains amendments only.

SCHEDULE 6 Repeals

Section 45

Chapter	Short title	Extent of repeal
1967 c 80	The Criminal Justice Act 1967	Section 90
1974 c 4	The Legal Aid Act 1974	The whole Act
1974 c 47	The Solicitors Act 1974	Section 75(d) In Schedule 3, paragraph 10
1975 c 72	The Children Act 1975	Section 65 In Schedule 3, paragraph 82
1976 c 36	The Adoption Act 1976	In Schedule 3, paragraph 18
1976 c 63	The Bail Act 1976	Section 11
1976 c 71	The Supplementary Benefits Act 1976	In Schedule 7, paragraphs 33 and 35
1977 c 38	The Administration of Justice Act 1977	In Schedule 1, Part I
1977 c 45.	The Criminal Law Act 1977	In Schedule 12, the entry relating to the Legal Aid Act 1974
1978 c 22	The Domestic Proceedings and Magistrates' Courts Act 1978	In Schedule 2, paragraphs 45 and 52
1979 c 26	The Legal Aid Act 1979	The whole Act
1979 c 55	The Justices of the Peace Act 1979	In Schedule 2, paragraph 27
1980 c 5	The Child Care Act 1980	In Schedule 5, paragraph 36
1980 c. 30	The Social Security Act 1980	In Schedule 4, paragraph 9
1980 c 43	The Magistrates' Courts Act 1980	In Schedule 7, paragraphs 126 to 129
1981 c 49	The Contempt of Court Act 1981	Section 13 In Schedule 2, Part I
1982 c 27	The Civil Jurisdiction and Judgments Act 1982	Section 40(1)
1982 c 44	The Legal Aid Act 1982	The whole Act
1982 c 48	The Criminal Justice Act 1982	Section 25(2) Section 29(3) Section 60(4)
1983 c 41	The Health and Social Services and Social Security Adjudications Act 1983	In Schedule 1, paragraph 3
1984 c 42	The Matrimonial and Family Proceedings Act 1984	In Schedule 1, paragraph 18
1984 c 60	The Police and Criminal Evidence Act 1984	Section 59
1985 c 23	The Prosecution of Offences Act 1985	Section 16(8) In section 19(2)(b), the words '(including any legal aid order)' In section 21(1), the definition of 'legal aid order'
1985 c 61	The Administration of Justice Act 1985	Sections 45 and 46 In Schedule 7, paragraphs 1 to 3
1986 c 28	The Children and Young Persons (Amendment) Act 1986	Section 3(3)

Chapter	Short title	Extent of repeal
1986 c 47	The Legal Aid (Scotland) Act 1986	In section 4(2)(c), the words 'for the purposes of this Act' In section 16, subsection (1) and, in subsection (2), the words 'in this section and' In section 17, subsections (3) to (8) Section 18(1) In section 32(a), the words ', out of the Fund' In Schedule 1, paragraph 2(4)
1986 c 50	The Social Security Act 1986	In Schedule 10, paragraphs 46, 47 and 56
1986 c 55	The Family Law Act 1986	Section 64
1987 c 38	The Criminal Justice Act 1987	In Schedule 2, paragraphs 7 and 8.

Annotations
Commencement order: SI 1989 No 288.

SCHEDULE 7 TRANSITION

Section 45

Preliminary

1 In this Schedule–

'the 1974 Act' means the Legal Aid Act 1974; and
'the appointed day' means the day appointed by the Lord Chancellor under section 47(2) of this Act for the coming into force of section 3(2) thereof.

The Legal Aid Fund

2 (1) On the appointed day the legal aid fund ('the Old Fund') maintained by the Law Society under section 17 of the 1974 Act shall be wound up.

(2) If, as at the appointed day, after taking account of all receipts and expenses of the Law Society attributable to their functions under the 1974 Act and the Legal Aid Act 1982 ('the 1982 Act'), there is in relation to the Old Fund any surplus or deficit–

(a) such surplus shall be paid by the Law Society to the Lord Chancellor; and
(b) such deficit shall be made up by payment to the Law Society by the Lord Chancellor of the amount of the deficit.

(3) Notwithstanding their repeal by this Act–

(a) sections 15(9) and 18 of the 1974 Act shall continue to have effect for the purposes of requiring the Law Society to account for the Old Fund and to report on the discharge of its functions under that Act up to the appointed day; and

(b) section 17(5) of that Act shall continue to have effect for the purposes of any determination as to the expenses or receipts of the Law Society;

and, if the appointed day falls on a day which is not the last day of the financial year (for the purposes of the said section 18), references in those sections to the financial year shall be construed as references to the period commencing on the day immediately following the end of the last complete financial year and ending with the appointed day.

(4) The Lord Chancellor shall pay to the Law Society such expenses incurred after the appointed day in connection with their functions under sections 15(9) and 18 of the 1974 Act as appear to him to be reasonable.

(5) Any payments received by the Lord Chancellor under sub-paragraph (2)(a) above shall be paid by him into the legal aid fund established by the Board under section 6.

(6) Any amount required to be paid by the Lord Chancellor under sub-paragraph (2)(b) or (4) above shall be defrayed out of money provided by Parliament.

Rights, obligations and property

3 (1) Subject to paragraph 2, on the appointed day all rights, obligations and property of the Law Society which are referable to its functions under the 1974 Act and the 1982 Act shall become rights, obligations and property of the Board.

(2) Any payments which are required to be made into or out of the Old Fund in connection with legal aid or advice or assistance under the 1974 Act shall, on and after the appointed day, be paid to or by the Board.

Transfer of functions

4 (1) Any grant of legal aid under Part I of the 1974 Act which is in force immediately before the appointed day shall, on and after the appointed day, have effect as a grant by the Board of representation under Part IV of this Act.

(2) Any approval given in connection with the grant of legal aid or advice or assistance under Part I of the 1974 Act which is in force immediately before the appointed day shall, on and after the appointed day, have effect as an approval by the Board in connection with the corresponding advice, assistance or representation under Part III or IV of this Act.

(3) Anything which, immediately before the appointed day, is in the process of being done by or in relation to the Law Society in connection with any function which it has relating to legal aid or advice or assistance under Part I of the 1974 Act, may be continued, on and after the appointed day, by or in relation to the Board.

Legal aid contribution orders

5 Notwithstanding their repeal by this Act, the provisions of the 1974 Act and the 1982 Act with respect to legal aid contribution orders shall continue to have effect in relation to any such order made in connection with a legal aid order made by virtue of section 28(11A) of the 1974 Act (legal aid for proceedings for contempt).

The Board: transfers of employment

6 (1) The Board shall make, not later than such date as the Lord Chancellor may determine, an offer of employment by the Board to such of the persons employed immediately before that date by the Law Society for the purpose of their functions under the 1974 Act as fall within such descriptions as the Lord Chancellor designates for the purposes of this paragraph or are persons whom the Board wishes to employ.

(2) The terms of the offer shall be such that they are, taken as a whole, not less favourable to the person to whom the offer is made than the terms on which he is employed on the date on which the offer is made.

(3) An offer made in pursuance of this paragraph shall not be revocable during the period of 3 months commencing with the date on which it is made.

7 (1) Where a person becomes an employee of the Board on acceptance of an offer made under paragraph 6, then, for the purposes of [the Employment Rights Act 1996], his period of employment with the Law Society shall count as a period of employment by the Board, and the change of employment shall not break the continuity of the period of employment.

(2) Where an offer is made under paragraph 6 to any person, none of the agreed redudancy procedures applicable to employees of the Law Society shall apply to him.

(3) Where a person employed by the Law Society ceases to be so employed–

(a) on becoming a member of the staff of the Board on accepting an offer under paragraph 6, or

(b) having unreasonably refused such an offer,

< . . . > he shall not be treated for the purposes of any scheme in force under section 19 of the 1974 Act as having been retired on redundancy.

(4) Where a person to whom an offer under paragraph 6 has been made continues in employment in the Law Society after having not unreasonably refused that offer he shall be treated for all purposes as if no offer under paragraph 6 had been made to him.

8 (1) Any dispute as to whether an offer purporting to be made under paragraph 6 complies with that paragraph shall be referred to and be determined by an industrial tribunal.

(2) An industrial tribunal shall not consider a complaint referred to it under sub-paragraph (1) above unless the complaint is presented to the tribunal before the end of the period of 3 months beginning with the date of the offer of

employment or within such further period as the tribunal considers reasonable in a case where it is satisfied that it was not reasonably practicable for the complaint to be presented before the end of the period of 3 months.

(3) An appeal shall lie to the Employment Appeal Tribunal on a question of law arising from the decision of, or in proceedings before, an industrial tribunal under this paragraph.

(4) Except as mentioned in sub-paragraph (3) above, no appeal shall lie from the decision of an industrial tribunal under this paragraph.

9 (1) In the event of the Board assuming under section 3(4) any of the functions specified in that subsection the Lord Chancellor shall by regulations make such provision corresponding to paragraphs 6, 7 and 8 in respect of employees to whom this paragraph applies as appears to him to be appropriate.

(2) This paragraph applies to persons employed–

(a) in the civil service of the State, or
(b) by a magistrates' courts committee,

and so employed wholly or mainly in connection with the functions referred to in sub-paragraph (1) above.

Pensions

10 Any arrangements made by the Law Society under section 19 of the 1974 Act in respect of any pension shall be treated on and after the appointed day (so far as may be necessary to preserve their effect) as having been made under paragraph 10(2) of Schedule 1 to this Act, and any pension scheme administered by the Law Society immediately before the appointed day shall be deemed to be a pension scheme established and administered by the Board under that paragraph and shall continue to be administered accordingly.

Representation in affiliation proceedings: transitory provision

11 Until the repeal of the Affiliation Proceedings Act 1957 by the Family Law Reform Act 1987 takes effect, Schedule 2 to this Act shall be taken to include proceedings in the Crown Court or a magistrates' court for or in relation to an affiliation order within the meaning of the Affiliation Proceedings Act 1957.

Annotations

Commencement orders: SI 1988 No 1361, SI 1989 No 288.

Para 7: in sub-para (1) words in square brackets substituted by the Employment Rights Act 1996, s 240, Sch 1, para 36; in sub-para (3) words omitted repealed by the Employment Rights Act 1996, s 242, Sch 3, Part I.

This Schedule does not extend to Scotland.

SCHEDULE 8 TRANSITORY AMENDMENTS OF LEGAL AID ACT 1974

Section 46

< . . . >

Annotations
This Schedule amends the Legal Aid Act 1974.
This Schedule does not extend to Scotland.

Appendix E1

Legal Aid in Criminal and Care Proceedings (General) Regulations 1989

1989 No. 344
Made – – – 3rd March 1989

PART I GENERAL

1 Citation, commencement and application

(1) These Regulations may be cited as the Legal Aid in Criminal and Care Proceedings (General) Regulations 1989 and shall come into force on 1st April 1989.

(2) < . . . >

Annotations
Para (2): revoked by SI 1991 No 1925, reg 2.

2 Revocations

The Regulations specified in Schedule 1 are hereby revoked.

3 Interpretation

(1) In these Regulations, unless the context otherwise requires,–

'the Act' means the Legal Aid Act 1988;

'applicant' means, in relation to an application for legal aid made on behalf of a person who has not attained the age of 17 by his parent or guardian, that person and, in the case of any other application for legal aid, the person making the application;

'appropriate authority' means an officer or body authorised to determine costs under the Legal Aid in Criminal and Care Proceedings (Costs) Regulations 1989;

'appropriate contributor', in relation to a person who has not attained the age of 16, means–

(a) his father (or any person who has been adjudged to be his father) or his mother; or
(b) his guardian;

'appropriate officer' means, in the case of the Crown Court, the Chief Clerk or an officer designated by him to act on his behalf;

'appropriate area committee' means the area committee in whose area is situated the court to which an application for or concerning a legal aid order has been made;

'area committee' and 'Area Director' have the meanings assigned to them by regulation 4 of the Civil Legal Aid (General) Regulations 1989

'Area Director' includes any person duly authorised to act on his behalf;

['attendance allowance' means an allowance paid under section 64 of or Schedule 8 paragraphs 4 or 7(2) to the Social Security Contributions and Benefits Act 1992;]

'contribution' means the contribution payable under section 23(1) of the Act in respect of the costs of representation;

<. . .>

'Court of Appeal' means the criminal division of the Court of Appeal or the Courts-Martial Appeal Court as the case may be;

['disability living allowance' means a disability living allowance under [the Social Security Contributions and Benefits Act 1992];

'disability working allowance' means a disability working allowance under [the Social Security Contributions and Benefits Act 1992];]

'disposable capital' and 'disposable income' mean the amounts of capital and income which are available for the making of a contribution after capital and income have been computed in accordance with Schedule 3;

'family credit' means family credit under [the Social Security Contributions and Benefits Act 1992];

'guardian' has the meaning assigned by section 87 of the Child Care Act 1980;

['income-based jobseeker's allowance' means income-based jobseeker's allowance under the Jobseekers Act 1995;]

'income support' means income support under [the Social Security Contributions and Benefits Act 1992];

['interests of justice criteria' means factors which the competent authority is required to take into account by section 22(2) of the Act;]

'judge of the court' means–

(a) in the case of the Court of Appeal, a single judge of that Court or a judge of the High Court;
(b) in the case of the Crown Court, a judge of the High Court, a Circuit judge, a recorder, or an assistant recorder.

'justices' clerk' includes a person duly authorised by the justices' clerk of a magistrates' court to act on his behalf to the extent that he is so authorised;

'legal aid' means representation under Part V of the Act or representation in care proceedings, as the case may be, and

'legal aid order' means an order granting such representation;

['period of computation' means the period of 3 months next ensuing from the date of the application for a legal aid order;]

'person concerned' means the person whose disposable income and disposable capital are to be determined or the person whose resources are to be treated as the resources of any other person under these Regulations;

'proper officer' means–

(a) in respect of proceedings in the House of Lords, the Clerk of the Parliaments;
(b) in respect of proceedings in the Court of Appeal, the registrar;
(c) in respect of proceedings in the Crown Court, the appropriate officer;

(d) in respect of proceedings in a magistrates' court, the justices' clerk.

'registrar' means the registrar of criminal appeals or the registrar of the Courts-Martial Appeal Court, as the case may be, and includes any person duly authorised to act on his behalf to the extent that he is so authorised;

'statement of means' means a statement of means submitted in accordance with regulation 23;

(2) Unless the context otherwise requires, any reference in these Regulations to a regulation, Part or Schedule by number means the regulation, Part or Schedule so numbered in these Regulations and a form referred to by number means the form so numbered in Schedule 2.

Annotations

Para (1): definitions 'attendance allowance', 'period of computation' added, definition omitted revoked, in definitions 'family credit'and 'income support' words in square brackets substituted, by SI 1993 No 789, regs 3, 4(a), (d)–(g); definitions 'disability living allowance' and 'disability working allowance' added by SI 1992 No 720, reg 3, words in square brackets therein substituted by SI 1993 No 789, regs 3, 4(b), (c); definition 'income-based jobseeker's allowance' prospectively added by SI 1996 No 1258, reg 2, as from 7 October 1996; definition 'interests of justice criteria' added by SI 1995 No 542, reg 4.

[4] [Forms]

[[(1) Forms 1 and 5 in Schedule 2 shall be used where applicable and the remaining forms in Schedule 2, or forms to the like effect, may be used with such variations as the circumstances may require.]

[(2) Each magistrates' court shall make copies of Forms 1 and 5 available free of charge to persons (whether solicitors, prospective applicants or appropriate contributors) intending to use them for the purpose of making legal aid applications to that court or of notifying the court or the proper officer of a change in financial circumstances.]]

Annotations

This regulation was substituted by SI 1992 No 720, reg 4.
Para (1): numbered as such by SI 1995 No 542, reg 5.
Para (2): added by SI 1995 No 542, reg 5.

5 Applicants reaching the age of 16

An applicant who attains the age of 16 after the date on which an application for legal aid is made but before the making of a legal aid order shall be treated for the purposes of these Regulations as not having attained that age.

6 Exclusion of solicitors and counsel

(1) The proper officer of each court shall keep a list of solicitors and counsel, notified to him by the Lord Chancellor, who are for the time being excluded from legal aid work under section 47(2) of the Solicitors Act 1974 or section 42 of the Administration of Justice Act 1985.

(2) Any reference in these Regulations to solicitors or counsel shall be construed as not including any solicitor or counsel who is so excluded.

Annotations

Modification: any reference to solicitor(s) etc modified to include references to bodies recognised under the Administration of Justice Act 1985, s 9, by the Solicitors' Incorporated Practices Order 1991, SI 1991 No 2684, arts 4, 5, Sch 1.

7 Determination in private and in absence of legally assisted person etc

Where it is provided by these Regulations that any matter may be determined otherwise than by a court, it may be determined in private and in the absence of the applicant, the appropriate contributor, the person concerned or the legally assisted person as the case may be.

8 Legal aid records

[(1) The proper officer of each court shall keep a record of every application to that court for a legal aid order.

(2) That record shall state whether the application

(a) was granted;
(b) was refused on the ground that it did not appear that it was desirable to make an order in the interests of justice, or
(c) was refused on the ground that it did not appear that the applicant's disposable income and disposable capital were such that, in accordance with regulation 26(1), he was eligible for legal aid,

and, in the circumstances referred to in sub-paragraphs (a) and (b), shall state the factors relied upon by the applicant and the reasons for the decision.

(3) Where a legal aid order was granted or refused by an area committee following an application for review under regulation 15, the proper officer shall keep a record of the decision and reasons of the area committee as notified pursuant to regulation 17(4)(b).

(4) In the case of proceedings to which section 22 of the Act applies, the statement of reasons required by paragraph (2) shall include specific reference to such of the interests of justice criteria as appear to be relevant to the decision.

(5) The proper officer shall send to the Lord Chancellor such information from the records required to be kept by this regulation as the Lord Chancellor shall request.]

Annotations

This regulation was substituted by SI 1995 No 542, reg 6.
The Act: Legal Aid Act 1988.

9 Area committees and powers of Area Directors

(1) Area committees and Area Directors appointed by the Board pursuant to regulation 4 of the Civil Legal Aid (General) Regulations 1989 shall exercise functions respectively delegated to them by the Board or conferred on them by these Regulations and, where an area committee is required or entitled

to perform any function under these Regulations, that function may, subject to paragraph (3), be performed on behalf of the committee by the Area Director.

(2) An Area Director so appointed shall act as the secretary to the area committee for his area.

(3) Paragraph (1) shall not empower an Area Director to refuse–

(a) an application for review under regulation 17(1);
(b) an application under regulation 52; or
(c) an application referred to the committee under regulation 54.

10 General power to grant legal aid

Subject to the provisions of section 21(2), (3) and (5) of the Act and to regulation 23, nothing in Part II or in regulation 36 shall affect the power of a court, a judge of the court or of the registrar to make a legal aid order, whether an application has been made for legal aid or not, or the right of an applicant whose application has been refused or whose legal aid order has been revoked under section 24(2) to apply to the court at the trial or in other proceedings.

Annotations
The Act: Legal Aid Act 1988.

PART II APPLICATIONS FOR LEGAL AID

11 Proceedings in magistrates' courts

(1) An application for a legal aid order in respect of proceedings in a magistrates' court shall be made–

(a) to the justices' clerk in Form 1, or
(b) orally to the court,

and the justices' clerk or the court may grant or refuse the application.

(2) Where an application for a legal aid order is made under paragraph (1)(b), the court may refer it to the justices' clerk for determination.

(3) Except where the applicant is not required to furnish a statement of means under regulation 23(4), a legal aid order shall not be made on an application under paragraph (1) until the court or the justices' clerk has considered the applicant's statement of means.

12 Notification of refusal of legal aid by a magistrates court

(1) Where an application for a legal aid order is refused by a magistrates' court or a justices' clerk, the court or the justices' clerk shall notify the applicant on Form 2 that the application has been refused on one or both of the following grounds, [namely that it does not appear to the court or the justices' clerk–

(a) desirable to make an order in the interests of justice; or
(b) that the applicant's disposable income and disposable capital are such that, in accordance with regulation 26(1), he is eligible for legal aid,]

and shall inform him of the circumstances in which he may renew his application or apply to an area committee for the decision to be reviewed.

[(2) Copies of the following documents shall be sent to the applicant and to his solicitor, if any:–

(a) Form 2;
(b) if the application was refused on the ground specified in paragraph (1)(a), the record required to be kept by regulation 8(1);
(c) where an application for review under regulation 15 may be made, the completed Form 1.]

Annotations
Para (1): words in square brackets substituted by SI 1993 No 1895, reg 3.
Para (2): substituted by SI 1995 No 542, reg 7.
Modification: any reference to solicitor(s) etc modified to include references to bodies recognised under the Administration of Justice Act 1985, s 9, by the Solicitors' Incorporated Practices Order 1991, SI 1991 No 2684, arts 4, 5, Sch 1.

13 Determination of contribution where legal aid is refused by a magistrates' court

Where a magistrates' court or a justices' clerk has refused to make a legal aid order, the court or the justices' clerk shall determine–

(a) the applicant's disposable income and disposable capital, and
(b) the amount of any contribution which would have been payable and the manner in which it would be payable by the applicant or an appropriate contributor had a legal aid order been made,

and shall notify the applicant of the amounts so determined.

14 Renewal of application

(1) Without prejudice to the provisions of regulation 15, an applicant whose application under regulation 11 has been refused may renew his application either orally to the court or to the justices' clerk.

(2) Where an application is renewed under paragraph (1), the applicant shall return the notice of refusal which he received under regulation 12 or any such notice received under regulation 17(4).

(3) Where an application is renewed to the justices' clerk, he may either grant the application or refer it to the court or to a justice of the peace.

(4) Where an application is renewed to the court, the court may grant or refuse the application or refer it to the justices' clerk.

(5) The court or a justice of the peace to whom an application is referred under paragraph (3) or (6), may grant or refuse the application.

(6) A justices' clerk to whom an application is referred under paragraph (4), may grant the application or refer it either back to the court or to a justice of the peace.

(7) Except where the applicant is not required to furnish a statement of

means under regulation 23(4), a legal aid order shall not be made where an application is renewed under paragraph (1) until the court, a justice of the peace or the justices' clerk has considered the applicant's statement of means.

(8) Regulation 12 shall apply where an application is refused under this regulation with the modification that references to a magistrates' court shall be construed as including references to a justice of the peace.

(9) In this regulation, 'a justice of the peace' means a justice of the peace who is entitled to sit as a member of the magistrates' court.

15 Application for review

(1) Where an application for a legal aid order has been refused after having been considered for the first time by a magistrates' court or a justices' clerk, the applicant may, subject to paragraph (2), apply for review to the appropriate area committee.

(2) An application for review shall only lie to an area committee where–

(a) the applicant is charged with an indictable offence or an offence which is triable either way or appears or is brought before a magistrates' court to be dealt with in respect of a sentence imposed or an order made in connection with such an offence; and
(b) the application for a legal aid order has been refused on the ground specified in regulation 12(1)(a); and
(c) the application for a legal aid order was made no later than 21 days before the date fixed for the trial of an information or the inquiry into an offence as examining justices, where such a date had been fixed at the time that the application was made.

16 Procedure on application for review

(1) An application for review shall be made by giving notice in Form 3 to the appropriate area committee within 14 days of the date of notification of the refusal to make a legal aid order and the applicant shall send a copy of Form 3 to the justices' clerk of the magistrates' court to which the first application for legal aid was made.

(2) An application under paragraph (1) shall be accompanied by the following documents–

(a) a copy of the completed Form 1 returned by the court under regulation 12(2); and
(b) a copy of the notice of refusal received under regulation 12.

(3) The time limit within which the application for review is to be made may, for good reason, be waived or extended by the area committee.

(4) The justices' clerk and the applicant shall supply such further particulars, information and documents as the area committee may require in relation to an application under paragraph (1).

17 Determination of review

(1) On a review, the area committee shall consider the application for legal aid and either–

(a) refuse the application; or
(b) make a legal aid order.

(2) Where the area committee makes a legal aid order, it shall make a contribution order in accordance with any determination made under regulation 13.

(3) Where a magistrates' court or a justices' clerk has determined under regulation 13 that any legal aid order which is made shall not take effect until a contribution from disposable capital is paid, the area committee shall send the legal aid order to the appropriate justices' clerk.

(4) The area committee shall give notice of its decision and the reasons for it in Form 4 to–

(a) the applicant and his solicitor, if any, and
(b) the justices' clerk of the magistrates' court to which the application for legal aid was made.

[(5) In the case of proceedings to which section 22 of the Act applies, the statement of reasons required by paragraph (4) shall comply with regulation 8(4).]

Annotations
Para (5): added by SI 1995 No 542, reg 8.
Modification: any reference to solicitor(s) etc modified to include references to bodies recognised under the Administration of Justice Act 1985, s 9, by the Solicitors' Incorporated Practices Order 1991, SI 1991 No 2684, arts 4, 5, Sch 1.
The Act: Legal Aid Act 1988.

18 Proceedings in the Crown Court

(1) An application for a legal aid order in respect of proceedings in the Crown Court shall be made either to the appropriate officer of the Crown Court in Form 1 or

(a) orally to the Crown Court or to a magistrates' court at the conclusion of any proceedings in that magistrates' court; or
(b) where a magistrates' court has been given a notice of transfer under section 4 of the Criminal Justice Act 1987 (serious fraud cases), to the justices' clerk of that magistrates' court in form 1; or
(c) in the case of an appeal to the Crown Court from a magistrates' court, to the justices' clerk of that magistrates' court in Form 1; or
(d) where the applicant was granted legal aid for proceedings in the magistrates' court and was committed for trial in the Crown Court under section 6(2) of the Magistrates' Courts Act 1980, to the justices' clerk of the magistrates' court ordering the committal in such form as may be required; or
(e) in the case of a retrial ordered under section 7 of the Criminal Appeal Act 1968, orally to the court ordering the retrial,

and the appropriate officer, the court or the justices' clerk may grant or refuse the application.

(2) Where an application for a legal aid order is made orally to the court, the court may refer it to the proper officer of the court for determination.

(3) Except where the applicant is not required to furnish a statement of means under regulation 23(4), a legal aid order shall not be made on an application under paragraph (1) until the appropriate officer, the court or the justices' clerk has considered the applicant's statement of means.

19 Notification of refusal of legal aid

(1) Where an application for a legal aid order is refused by the appropriate officer of the Crown Court, the court or justices' clerk, the appropriate officer, the court or the justices' clerk shall notify the applicant on Form 2 that the application has been refused on one or both of the following grounds, [namely that it does not appear to the officer, the court or the justices' clerk–

(a) desirable to make an order in the interests of justice; or
(b) that the applicant's disposable income and disposable capital are such that, in accordance with regulation 26(1), he is eligible for legal aid,]

and shall inform him of the circumstances in which he may renew his application.

[(2) Copies of the following documents shall be sent to the applicant and to his solicitor, if any:–

(a) Form 2;
(b) if the application was refused on the ground specified in paragraph (1)(a), the record required to be kept by regulation 8(1).]

Annotations

Para (1): words in square brackets substituted by SI 1993 No 1895, reg 4.
Para (2): substituted by SI 1995 No 542, reg 9.
Modification: any reference to solicitor(s) etc modified to include references to bodies recognised under the Administration of Justice Act 1985, s 9, by the Solicitors' Incorporated Practices Order 1991, SI 1991 No 2684, arts 4, 5, Sch 1.

20 Determination of contribution where legal aid is refused

Where the appropriate officer of the Crown Court, the court or a justices' clerk has refused to make a legal aid order, the officer, the court or the justices' clerk shall determine–

(a) the applicant's disposable income and disposable capital, and
(b) the amount of any contribution which would have been payable and the manner in which it would be payable by the applicant or an appropriate contributor had a legal aid order been made,

and shall notify the applicant of the amounts so determined.

21 Renewal of application

(1) An applicant whose application under regulation 18 has been refused may renew his application either orally to the court or to the appropriate officer of the Crown Court.

(2) Where an application is renewed under paragraph (1), the applicant shall return the notice of refusal which he received under regulation 19.

(3) Where an application is renewed to the appropriate officer, he may either grant the application or refer it to a judge of the court.

(4) Where an application is renewed to the court, the court may grant or refuse the application or refer it to the appropriate officer.

(5) A judge of the court to whom an application is referred under paragraph (3) or (6), may grant or refuse the application.

(6) An appropriate officer to whom an application is referred under paragraph (4), may grant the application or refer it to a judge of the court.

(7) Except where the applicant is not required to furnish a statement of means under regulation 23(4), a legal aid order shall not be made where an application is renewed under paragraph (1) until the court or the appropriate officer has considered the applicant's statement of means.

(8) Regulation 19 shall apply where an application is refused under this regulation as if references to a justices' clerk were omitted.

22 Proceedings in the Court of Appeal or the House of Lords

(1) An application for a legal aid order in respect of proceedings in the Court of Appeal or the House of Lords may be made–

(a) orally to the Court of Appeal, to a judge of the court or the registrar, or
(b) by giving written notice of the application to the registrar in such form as he may direct.

(2) Where an application for a legal aid order is made orally to the Court of Appeal, the court may refer it to a judge of the court or the registrar for determination; and, where such an application is made orally to a judge of the court, he may refer it to the registrar for determination.

(3) Where a judge of the court refuses to make a legal aid order, the applicant may renew his application to the Court of Appeal.

(4) The registrar considering an application for a legal aid order shall–

(a) make an order; or
(b) refer the application to the Court of Appeal or to a judge of the court.

(5) A legal aid order shall not be made until–

(a) a notice of appeal or application for leave to appeal to the Court of Appeal or the House of Lords, as the case may be, has been given, and
(b) except where the applicant is not required under regulation 23(4) to

furnish a statement of means, the Court of Appeal, a judge of the court or the registrar has considered the applicant's statement of means.

(6) In making a legal aid order in respect of proceedings in the Court of Appeal, the court, a judge of the court or the registrar may specify the stage of the proceedings at which legal aid shall commence.

(7) Subject to the provisions of this regulation, the powers of the Court of Appeal to determine an application for a legal aid order may be exercised by a judge of the court or the registrar.

(8) The powers of the Court of Appeal to revoke a legal aid order may be exercised by a judge of the court or, where the legally assisted person applies for the order to be revoked, by the registrar.

PART III STATEMENT OF MEANS AND PAYMENT OF CONTRIBUTIONS

23 Statement of means

[(1) A statement of means submitted by an applicant or an appropriate contributor shall be in Form 5 and shall be accompanied by supporting documentary evidence in respect of such matters as may be specified in that Form.

[(2) Subject to paragraphs (3) and (4), where an applicant does not submit a statement of means when he applies for legal aid, the proper officer or the court to which the application is being made shall require him to do so.

(2A) Subject to paragraphs (3) and (4), where an applicant submits a statement of means but neither provides supporting documentary evidence nor supplies an explanation in writing of why it was not reasonably practicable to do so, the proper officer or the court to which the application is being made shall require him to provide such evidence or else supply such written explanation.]]

(3) Where an applicant is under 16, the proper officer may require either the applicant or an appropriate contributor, or both, to submit a statement of means [and supporting documentary evidence] in accordance with this regulation.

(4) A statement of means shall be required unless–

(a) it appears to the court or the proper officer that, by reason of his physical or mental condition, the applicant is for the time being incapable of furnishing such a statement; < . . . >

(b) the applicant has already submitted such a statement in connection with a previous application in respect of the same case and his financial circumstances have not changed[, or

(c) it appears to the court or the proper officer that the circumstance specified in regulation 26(3) obtains.]

(5) Nothing in paragraph (4)(a) shall prevent the court or the proper officer from requiring an applicant to furnish a statement of means after a legal

aid order has been made where it appears that he is no longer incapable of furnishing such a statement.

Annotations

Para (1): substituted by SI 1993 No 1895, reg 5(a).
Paras (2), (2A): substituted for existing para (2) by SI 1994 No 807, reg 4.
Para (3): words in square brackets added by SI 1993 No 1895, reg 5(b).
Para (4): word omitted revoked, and words in square brackets added, by SI 1995 No 542, reg 10.

24 Provision of information

(1) [The court or the proper officer may at any time] require the applicant, the legally assisted person or the appropriate contributor to provide [further] evidence of any information given in a statement of means or of any change in his financial circumstances together with such additional information as the court or the proper officer may require.

[(2) Where representation is granted to an applicant who provided a reasonable explanation of why, at the time of submission of the statement of means, [it was not reasonably practicable to provide supporting] documentary evidence, the court or proper officer may subsequently require the assisted person to provide documentary evidence where it appears that [it has become reasonably practicable to do so].

(3) Where, pursuant to paragraph (2), documentary evidence is provided, the determination or redetermination of any contribution payable or the amount of any contribution order, shall be in accordance with regulations 32 and 33.]

Annotations

Para (1): first words in square brackets substituted by SI 1996 No 1258, reg 3; final word in square brackets added by SI 1993 No 1895, reg 6(a).
Para (2): substituted, together with para (3), for para (2) as originally enacted, by SI 1993 No 1895, reg 6(b); words in square brackets substituted by SI 1994 No 807, reg 5.
Para (3): substituted, together with para (2), for para (2) as originally enacted, by SI 1993 No 1895, reg 6(b).

25 Determination of contributions

(1) The court or the proper officer shall, when making a legal aid order, determine the amount of any contribution payable by the applicant, the legally assisted person or the appropriate contributor in accordance with regulation 26.

(2) Where the applicant or the legally assisted person has paid or is liable to pay a contribution under section 9(6) of the Act in respect of advice and assistance given in relation to the same proceedings, any contribution which he or an appropriate contributor is liable to make under section 23(1) of the Act in respect of the costs of representation shall be reduced by the total amount of any contribution paid or liable to be paid under section 9(6).

Annotations

The Act: Legal Aid Act 1988.

26 Assessment of resources and method of determining contributions

(1) Representation shall not be granted to a person for any purpose unless it appears that his financial resources are such that he requires assistance in meeting the costs which he may incur for that purpose.

(2) The court or the proper officer shall–

(a) consider the statement of means [and supporting documentary evidence] submitted by the applicant or the appropriate contributor and any other relevant information; and
(b) subject to [paragraphs (2A) and (3)], determine his disposable income and disposable capital in accordance with Schedule 3.

[(2A) Where the documentary evidence or information which an applicant or legally assisted person or appropriate contributor is required to produce under regulations 23 or 24(1) is deficient and no reasonable explanation is given for the deficiency, the court or proper officer may–

(a) refuse representation if the court or proper officer considers, on the basis of the information available, that the applicant's financial resources are not such that he requires assistance; or
(b) deem his disposable income and disposable capital as exceeding the limits below which no contribution is payable by virtue of Schedule 4, and fix the contribution payable by him at such an amount as the court or the proper officer may determine or (in the case of a legally assisted person) redetermine.]

(3) The court or the proper officer shall not make a determination under paragraph (2)(b) where–

(a) the applicant,
(b) the appropriate contributor, or
(c) the spouse of the applicant or appropriate contributor, is in receipt of [income-based jobseeker's allowance,] income support[, family credit or disability working allowance] and this paragraph shall apply to a man and a woman who are living with each other in the same household as husband and wife as it applies to the parties to a marriage.

(4) Subject to paragraph (3), the applicant or the appropriate contributor shall pay a contribution in accordance with the provisions of Schedule 4.

Annotations

Para (2): first words in square brackets added, and final words in square brackets substituted, by SI 1993 No 1895, reg 7(a), (b).
Para (2A): added by SI 1993 No 1895, reg 7(c).
Para (3): in sub-para (c) first words in square brackets prospectively added by SI 1996 No 1258, reg 4, as from 7 October 1996; second words in square brackets substituted by SI 1992 No 720, reg 5.

27 Contribution orders

(1) The court or the proper officer of the court shall make a contribution order, in Form 6, in respect of any contribution determined under regulation 26 above and shall endorse the legal aid order accordingly.

(2) A copy of the contribution order shall be sent to the person ordered to make the contribution, to the legally assisted person's solicitor or counsel (where counsel only is assigned) and to the collecting court.

Annotations

Modification: any reference to solicitor(s) etc modified to include references to bodies recognised under the Administration of Justice Act 1985, s 9, by the Solicitors' Incorporated Practices Order 1991, SI 1991 No 2684, arts 4, 5, Sch 1.

29 Payment of contributions

(1) Any contribution which is to be paid out of disposable income shall be payable by weekly (or, at the discretion of the court or the proper officer of the court, by fortnightly or monthly instalments) [for the period during which a legal aid order is in force], and the first such instalment shall fall due 7 days from the making of the legal aid order or of the contribution order, whichever is the later.

(2) Any contribution which is to be paid out of disposable capital shall be paid immediately if the sum is readily available or, if it is not, at such time as the court or the proper officer of the court considers to be reasonable in all the circumstances.

(3) Where a contribution out of disposable capital is to be paid immediately, the legal aid order shall not take effect until such payment is made and the court or the proper officer of the court shall give notice of this fact in Form 7 to –

(a) the applicant and the appropriate contributor, and
(b) the solicitor assigned or, where counsel only is assigned, counsel.

[(4) The period referred to in paragraph (1) above means the period from the grant of the legal aid order to–

(a) the conclusion of the proceedings covered by the legal aid order (whether in the court in which the legal aid order was made or in another court following a committal for trial or sentence or remittal); or
(b) where the legal aid order is withdrawn or revoked, the date of such withdrawal or revocation.]

Annotations

Para (1): words in square brackets substituted by SI 1993 No 789, reg 6(a).
Para (4): added by SI 1993 No 789, reg 3, 6(b).
Modification: any reference to solicitor(s) etc modified to include references to bodies recognised under the Administration of Justice Act 1985, s 9, by the Solicitors' Incorporated Practices Order 1991, SI 1991 No 2684, arts 4, 5, Sch 1.

30 Method of payment of contributions

(1) Subject to paragraph (2), payment of contributions shall be made to the proper officer of the collecting court.

(2) Where a legal aid order is not to take effect until a contribution out of disposable capital is paid, such payment shall be made to the proper officer of the court making the legal aid order unless that court otherwise directs.

31 Change in financial circumstances

The legally assisted person or the appropriate contributor shall inform the court or the proper officer of the court of any change in his financial circumstances which has occurred [since he applied for a legal aid order] and which he has reason to believe–

(a) might make him liable to pay a contribution where such a contribution is not already payable; or
(b) might affect the terms of any contribution order made in connection with a legal aid order.

Annotations
Words in square brackets substituted by SI 1996 No 1258, reg 5.

32 Determination where no contribution previously payable

(1) The court or the proper officer of the court shall determine the amount of any contribution payable by a legally assisted person or an appropriate contributor who is not already liable to make such a contribution where–

(a) further information has become available as to the amount of disposable income and disposable capital available at the time when the legal aid order was made; or
(b) the circumstances upon which the disposable income or disposable capital were determined at the time the legal aid order was made have altered [during the period in which the legal aid order was in force];

and it appears likely that, were such a determination to be made, the legally assisted person or the appropriate contributor would be liable to make a contribution.

(2) Regulation 26 shall apply where a contribution is determined under paragraph (1) as it applies where a contribution is determined on the making of a legal aid order.

Annotations
Para (1): in sub-para (b) words in square brackets substituted by SI 1993 No 789, reg 7.

33 Redetermination of contribution

Except where it appears unlikely that any significant change in liability to make a contribution would result, the court or the proper officer of the court shall redetermine the amount of any contribution payable by a legally assisted person or an appropriate contributor under a legal aid order where–

(a) further information has become available as to the amounts of disposable income and disposable capital available at the time when the contribution order was made; or
(b) the circumstances upon which the disposable income or disposable capital were determined at the time when the contribution order was made have altered [during the period in which the legal aid order was in force] so that–

(i) his disposable income may have increased by an amount greater than £750 a year or decreased by an amount greater than £300 a year; or
(ii) his disposable capital may have increased by an amount greater than £750 a year;

and shall vary or revoke the contribution order accordingly.

Annotations
Words in square brackets substituted by SI 1993 No 789, regs 3, 7.

34 Effect of error or mistake

Where it appears to the court or the proper officer that there has been some error or mistake in the determination of the legally assisted person's or the appropriate contributor's disposable income, disposable capital or contribution and that it would be just and equitable to correct the error or mistake, the court or the proper officer may vary the contribution order accordingly, may revoke it or may make a contribution order.

[35] [Variation and revocation of contribution orders]

[(1) At the conclusion of the proceedings the court in which those proceedings are concluded may, if it thinks fit–

(a) remit any sum due under a contribution order which falls to be paid after the conclusion of the proceedings; or
(b) remit or order the repayment of any sum due or paid under a contribution order where the legally assisted person has been acquitted.

(2) Where the legal aid order in connection with which a contribution order was made is revoked, paragraph (1) shall apply as if the proceedings had been concluded.

(3) Where a legally assisted person–

(a) successfully appeals against his conviction; or
(b) is respondent to an appeal which is unsuccessful,

the court hearing the appeal may remit or order the repayment of any sum due or paid under a contribution order.

(4) Where a contribution order has been varied and the sum of the total contributions paid up to the conclusion of the proceedings exceeds the amount which was due taking into account the variation, the court or the proper officer shall order repayment of an amount equal to the difference between the sums paid and the amount due.

(5) Where–

(a) a contribution order is varied to an amount greater than that which was previously payable; or
(b) a contribution order is made after a determination under regulation 32,

the payment of any contributions shall be made in accordance with the provisions of regulation 29, save that in respect of payments to be made out of disposable income, the court or the proper officer may extend the period within which such payment is to be made beyond the conclusion of the proceedings.]

Annotations
This regulation was substituted by SI 1993 No 789, reg 8.

36 Refusal to pay contribution

(1) Where any sums which are due under a contribution order before the conclusion of the proceedings have not been paid by the legally assisted person, the court or the proper officer of that court may–

(a) serve notice on the legally assisted person requiring him to comply with the contribution order and pay any sums due under it within 7 days of receiving such notice; and
(b) if he does not do so, serve notice on him inviting him to make representations as to why he cannot comply with the contribution order.

(2) A notice given under paragraph (1)(a) shall be in Form 9 and a notice given under paragraph (1)(b) in Form 10 and copies of any notices so given shall be sent to the legally assisted person and to his solicitor or, where counsel only is assigned, to counsel.

(3) The court shall consider any representations made under paragraph (1)(b) and, if satisfied that the legally assisted person–

(a) was able to pay the relevant contribution when it was due; and
(b) is able to pay the whole or part of it but has failed or refused to do so,

may revoke the grant of representation.

(4) The revocation of the grant of representation under paragraph (3) shall not affect the right of any legal representative previously assigned to the legally assisted person to remuneration for work done before the date of the revocation.

Annotations
Modification: any reference to solicitor(s) etc modified to include references to bodies recognised under the Administration of Justice Act 1985, s 9, by the Solicitors' Incorporated Practices Order 1991, SI 1991 No 2684, arts 4, 5, Sch 1.

37 Termination of contribution period

(1) [Where a legal aid order is still in force] and–

(a) the legally assisted person, the appropriate contributor or the spouse of the legally assisted person or appropriate contributor begins to receive [income-based jobseeker's allowance,] income support[, family credit or disability working allowance] (in this regulation referred to as 'income-related benefits'); or
(b) the court remits any sum due under a contribution order which falls to be paid after the conclusion of the relevant proceedings; or

(c) the legally assisted person is sentenced in the proceedings to which the legal aid order relates to an immediate term of imprisonment or a sentence of detention in a young offender institution,

[the liability to pay further contributions shall end] on the date receipt of income-related benefits commenced or on the date of that remission or sentence, as the case may be.

(2) The court making any such remission or passing any such sentence shall inform the collecting court [that the liability to pay further contributions ended] on the date of the remission or sentence.

(3) Without prejudice to regulation 31, the legally assisted person or the appropriate contributor shall inform the collecting court of the date on which receipt of income-related benefits commenced.

(4) Paragraph (1)(a) shall apply to a man and a woman who are living with each other in the same household as husband and wife as it applies to the parties to a marriage.

Annotations

Para (1): first and final words in square brackets substituted by SI 1993 No 789, reg 9(a); second words in square brackets prospectively added by SI 1996 No 1258, reg 4, as from 7 October 1996; third words in square brackets substituted by SI 1992 No 720, reg 5.

Para (2): words in square brackets substituted by SI 1993 No 789, reg 9(b).

38 Disposal of sums received from legally assisted persons after conviction

(1) Where a legally assisted person or an appropriate contributor to whom this regulation applies has been ordered to make a contribution, any amounts falling due under the contribution order after the conclusion of the [proceedings and any extension of the period for the purposes of regulation 35(5)] shall, unless remitted or specifically appropriated by the person paying the money to payment of the contribution, be applied (when paid) first, in accordance with the provisions of section 139 of the Magistrates' Court Act 1980 and any sum paid in addition to the sums referred to in paragraph (2) below shall be paid to the Lord Chancellor in accordance with paragraph 4(2) of Schedule 3 to the Act.

(2) This regulation applies to a legally assisted person who is ordered to pay any sum adjudged to be paid on conviction and to an appropriate contributor who is ordered to pay a fine, compensation or costs under the provisions of section 55 of the Children and Young Persons Act 1933 or section 3 of the Children and Young Persons Act 1969.

Annotations

Para (1): words in square brackets substituted by SI 1993 No 789, reg 10.

The Act: Legal Aid Act 1988.

39 Repayment of contributions

On receiving notification of the amount of the costs of representation determined by the appropriate authority under the Legal Aid in Criminal and Care Proceedings (Costs) Regulations 1989, the collecting court or the proper officer of that court shall, in accordance with section 23(7) of the Act, repay to the legally assisted person or the appropriate contributor, as the case may be, the amount, if any, by which any contribution paid exceeds those costs.

Annotations
The Act: Legal Aid Act 1988.

PART IV LEGAL AID ORDERS

40 Legal aid orders

(1) A magistrates' court inquiring into an offence as examining justices may make a legal aid order which applies, or amend an order so that it applies, both to proceedings before the court and, in the event of the defendant being committed for trial, to his trial before the Crown Court and, where such an order is made,–

(a) Form 11 shall be used; and
(b) copies of the order shall be sent in accordance with paragraph (2) below or with regulation 50(3), as the case may be.

(2) A legal aid order for the purposes of proceedings in a magistrates' court, the Crown Court or the Court of Appeal shall be in Form 11[, 11A], 12 or 13 as the case may be and, subject to regulations 17(3) and 29(3), the court or the proper officer shall send–

(a) one copy to the legally assisted person; and
(b) one copy to the solicitor assigned or to counsel (where counsel only is assigned); and,

where the legal aid order is made for the purposes of proceedings before a magistrates' court, a further copy (endorsed 'Board copy') shall be sent under sub-paragraph (b) above.

(3) Where a legal aid order is made by an area committee for the purposes of proceedings in a magistrates' court, one copy shall be sent to the proper officer of the court to which the application for legal aid was made.

(4) Where a legal aid order is amended under regulation 50, copies of the amended order shall be sent in accordance with paragraph (3) of that regulation.

(5) Where the solicitor assigned instructs counsel, the instructions which are delivered to counsel shall include a copy of the legal aid order and the solicitor shall inform counsel of any amendments made to the legal aid order.

Annotations
Para (2): figure in square brackets added by SI 1991 No 637, reg 3(1).
Modification: any reference to solicitor(s) etc modified to include references to bodies recognised under the Administration of Justice Act 1985, s 9, by the Solicitors' Incorporated Practices Order 1991, SI 1991 No 2684, arts 4, 5, Sch 1.

41 Withdrawal and revocation of legal aid orders

(1) A legal aid order may be withdrawn–

(a) where the legally assisted person declines to accept the terms on which a grant of representation may be made;

(c) at the request of the legally assisted person;
(d) in accordance with the provisions of regulation 50;
[(d)where[, as a result of information which has been provided under these Regulations or otherwise,] it appears to the court or proper officer that the legally assisted person's resources are not such that he requires assistance.]

(2) Where two legal aid orders are made in respect of the same proceedings, the second order so made shall be deemed to be of no effect and shall be withdrawn as if the legally assisted person had made a request under paragraph (1)(b) above.

(3) An order withdrawing a legal aid order shall be in Form 14 and a copy of it shall be sent to–

(a) the legally assisted person, or
(b) the solicitor assigned or to counsel (where counsel only is assigned); and
(c) where the legal aid order is withdrawn by the area committee, to the proper officer of the court to which the application for withdrawal was made.

(4) Where a legal aid order is withdrawn–

(a) the counsel assigned shall send all papers and other items in his possession relating to the proceedings to the solicitor assigned or (where no solicitor was assigned) to the legally assisted person; and
(b) the solicitor assigned shall send all papers and other items in his possession relating to the proceedings to the legally assisted person.

(5) Where a legal aid order is revoked under regulation 36(3), the foregoing paragraphs of this regulation shall apply, with any necessary modifications, as if the order had been withdrawn.

Annotations

Para (1): sub-para (d) added by SI 1993 No 1895, reg 8; words in square brackets substituted by SI 1996 No 1258, reg 6.

Modification: any reference to solicitor(s) etc modified to include references to bodies recognised under the Administration of Justice Act 1985, s 9, by the Solicitors' Incorporated Practices Order 1991, SI 1991 No 2684, arts 4, 5, Sch 1.

[41A] [Withdrawal for abuse of legal aid or for failure to provide information]

[(1) Without prejudice to regulation 41, a legal aid order may be withdrawn where, as a result of information which has been provided under these Regulations or otherwise, it appears that the legally assisted person has–

(a) in relation to any application for a legal aid order, made an untrue statement as to his financial resources or has failed to disclose any material fact concerning them; or
(b) intentionally failed to comply with any provision of regulations made under the Act by not furnishing any material information concerning any matter other than his financial resources or in furnishing such information has knowingly made a false statement or false representation,

and, in this regulation, 'legally assisted person' includes an appropriate contributor.

(2) A legal aid order shall not be withdrawn under paragraph (1) where the legally assisted person satisfies the court that he used due care or diligence to avoid such mis-statement or failure.

(3) A legal aid order may be withdrawn where the court is satisfied that the legally assisted person has failed to attend for an interview or to provide information or documents when required to do so under these Regulations.

(4) Regulation 41(3) and (4) shall apply where a legal aid order is withdrawn under this regulation as it applies where an order is withdrawn under that regulation.]

Annotations
This regulation was added by SI 1996 No 1258, reg 7.
The Act: Legal Aid Act 1988.

42 Notes of evidence and depositions

Where a legal aid order is made in respect of an appeal to the Crown Court, the justices' clerk shall supply, on the application of the solicitor assigned to the appellant or respondent on whose application such an order was made, copies of any notes of evidence or depositions taken in the proceedings in the magistrates' court.

Annotations
Modification: any reference to solicitor(s) etc modified to include references to bodies recognised under the Administration of Justice Act 1985, s 9, by the Solicitors' Incorporated Practices Order 1991, SI 1991 No 2684, arts 4, 5, Sch 1.

43 Transfer of documents

Where a person is committed by a lower court to a higher court or appeals or applies for leave to appeal from a lower court to a higher court, the proper officer of the lower court shall send to the proper officer of the higher court the following documents–

(a) a copy of any legal aid order previously made in respect of the same proceedings;
(b) a copy of any contribution order made;
(c) a copy of any legal aid application which has been refused;
(d) any statement of means already submitted.

PART V LEGAL REPRESENTATION

44 Nature of representation

(1) Subject to the following paragraphs of this regulation, a grant of representation shall provide for the services of a solicitor and counsel.

(2) A legal aid order granting representation for the purpose of such part of any proceedings before a magistrates' court as relates to the giving of bail shall not include representation by counsel.

(3) A legal aid order granting representation for the purposes of proceedings before a magistrates' court shall not include representation by counsel except–

(a) in the case of any indictable offence, where the court is of the opinion that, because of circumstances which make the case unusually grave or difficult, representation by both solicitor and counsel would be desirable; < . . . >
(b) < . . . >

{4} Where a court grants representation for the purposes of an appeal to the Court of Appeal, the court may order that representation shall be by counsel only.

(5) Where the Crown Court grants representation for the purposes of–

(a) an appeal to that court;
(b) proceedings in which a person is committed to or appears before that court for trial or sentence or appears or is brought before the Crown Court to be dealt with;

the court may, in cases of urgency where it appears to the court that there is no time to instruct a solicitor, order that representation shall be by counsel only.

(6) Where the Crown Court or a magistrates' court grants representation for the purposes specified in paragraph (5), the court may, if the proceedings are proceedings in which solicitors have a right of audience, order that representation shall be by a solicitor only.

(7) Where in proceedings in a magistrates' court representation or advice is given before a legal aid order is made, that representation or advice shall be deemed to be representation or advice given under the order if–

(a) the interests of justice required that the representation or advice be provided as a matter of urgency;
(b) there was no undue delay in making an application for legal aid; and
(c) the representation or advice was given by the solicitor who was subsequently assigned under the legal aid order.

Annotations
Para (3): sub-para (b) and word immediately preceding it revoked by SI 1991 No 1925, reg 3.
Modification: any reference to solicitor(s) etc modified to include references to bodies recognised under the Administration of Justice Act 1985, s 9, by the Solicitors' Incorporated Practices Order 1991, SI 1991 No 2684, arts 4, 5, Sch 1.

45 Assignment of solicitor and selection of counsel

(1) Subject to regulations 46 and 49, any person who is granted representation entitling him to the services of a solicitor, may select any solicitor who is willing to act and such solicitor shall be assigned to him.

(2) Subject to regulations 46 and 49, where a legal aid order is made providing for the services of solicitor and counsel, the solicitor may instruct any counsel who is willing to act.

Annotations

Modification: any reference to solicitor(s) etc modified to include references to bodies recognised under the Administration of Justice Act 1985, s 9, by the Solicitors' Incorporated Practices Order 1991, SI 1991 No 2684, arts 4, 5, Sch 1.

46 Assignment of solicitor or counsel for the Court of Appeal or the House of Lords

(1) In the case of proceedings in the Court of Appeal or the House of Lords, counsel may be assigned by the court, a judge of the court or the proper officer making or amending the legal aid order.

(2) In assigning counsel or a solicitor to a legally assisted person in respect of an appeal to the Court of Appeal or the House of Lords, the court, a judge of the court or the proper officer shall have regard, as far as is reasonably practicable, to the wishes of the legally assisted person, the identity of the solicitor or counsel, if any, who represented him in any earlier proceedings and the nature of the appeal.

Annotations

Modification: any reference to solicitor(s) etc modified to include references to bodies recognised under the Administration of Justice Act 1985, s 9, by the Solicitors' Incorporated Practices Order 1991, SI 1991 No 2684, arts 4, 5, Sch 1.

47 Assignment of counsel only

(1) Where a legal aid order granting representation for the purposes of proceedings in the Crown Court is made or amended so as to provide for representation by counsel only, counsel shall be assigned by the court or proper officer making or amending the legal aid order.

(2) Where a legal aid order granting representation for the purposes of proceedings in the Court of Appeal or the Courts-Martial Appeal Court is made or amended so as to provide for representation by counsel only, counsel shall be assigned by the court, a judge of the court or the proper officer.

[48] [Assignment of Queen's Counsel or more than one counsel]

[(1) A legal aid order may provide for the services of a Queen's Counsel or of more than one counsel in respect of the whole or any specified part of any proceedings only in the cases specified and in the manner provided for by the following paragraphs of this regulation.

(2) The cases specified for the purposes of this regulation are trials in the Crown Court or proceedings in the Court of Appeal or the House of Lords–

(a) on a charge of murder;
(b) where it appears to the court making the order that the case is one of exceptional difficulty, gravity or complexity and that a legal aid order for the provision of services in the terms provided for by paragraph (3)(a) or (b) of this regulation is required in the interests of justice; or
(c) where the prosecution is being brought by the Serious Fraud Office.

(3) Subject to paragraphs (4) to (9), a legal aid order may provide for

the services of a Queen's Counsel or of more than one counsel in any of the following terms–

(a) a Queen's Counsel alone;

(b) where two counsel are required–

(i) a Queen's Counsel with a junior counsel, or

(ii) a Queen's Counsel with a noting junior counsel, or

(iii) two junior counsel, or

(iv) a junior counsel with a noting junior counsel.

(4) In proceedings to which paragraph (2)(c) applies, a court making a legal order may, if it considers that three counsel are required, provide for the services of three counsel in any of the terms provided for in paragraph (3)(b) plus an extra junior counsel or noting junior counsel.

(5) The fact that a Queen's Counsel has been or is proposed to be assigned under this regulation shall not by itself be a reason for making an order in any of the terms provided for by paragraph (3)(b) or (4).

(6) Where a Queen's Counsel has been or is proposed to be assigned under this regulation, no order in any of the terms provided for by paragraph (3)(b) or (4) shall be made where it appears to the court at the time of making the order that–

(a) there is reasonable certainty that the indictment will be disposed of by a guilty plea and there are no special circumstances requiring the provision of the services of more than one counsel, or

(b) the case relates to an appeal to the Court of Appeal or to the House of Lords and representation can properly be undertaken by a Queen's Counsel alone.

(7) Unless the court to which the application is made otherwise directs, every application for a legal aid order in any of the terms provided for by paragraph (3) or (4) or for an amendment under paragraph (10) or (11) shall be in writing specifying–

(a) the terms of the order sought and the grounds of the application; and

(b) if the order sought is for the provision of services in any terms provided for by paragraph (3)(b) or (4), the reasons why two counsel are required or an extra junior counsel or noting junior counsel is required as the case may be.

(8) A court may, before making a legal aid order in the terms provided for by paragraph (3) or (4) or amending the order under paragraph (10) or (11), require written advice from any counsel already assigned to the applicant on the question of what representation is needed in the proceedings.

(9) A magistrates' court which is competent as respects any proceedings by virtue of section 20(4) or (5) of the Act may make a legal aid order providing for the services of a Queen's Counsel with one junior counsel where:–

(a) the proceedings are a trial for murder and the order is made upon committal or transfer for trial, or

(b) the prosecution is brought by the Serious Fraud Office and the order is made upon receiving a notice of transfer under section 4 of the Criminal Justice Act 1987

but shall have no other power to make an order under this regulation.

(10) In proceedings to which paragraph (2)(a) or (b) applies, a legal aid order which provides–

(a) for one counsel only may be amended to provide for the services of a Queen's Counsel or of more than one counsel in any terms provided for by paragraph (3);
(b) for two counsel in any terms provided for by paragraph (3)(b) may be amended to provide for the services of the same number of counsel but in other terms provided for by that paragraph, or for a Queen's Counsel alone, or for one counsel only in accordance with regulation 47.

(11) In proceedings to which paragraph (2)(c) applies, a legal aid order which provides–

(a) for one counsel only may be amended to provide for the services of a Queen's Counsel or of more than one counsel in any terms provided for by paragraph (3) or (4);
(b) for two counsel in any terms provided for by paragraph (3)(b) may be amended to provide for the services of three counsel in any terms provided for by paragraph (4), for two counsel but in other terms provided for by paragraph (3)(b), or for a Queen's Counsel alone, or for one counsel only in accordance with regulation 47;
(c) for three counsel in any terms provided for by paragraph (4) may be amended to provide for the same number of counsel but in other terms provided for by paragraph (4), or for two counsel in any terms provided for by paragraph (3)(b), or for a Queen's Counsel alone, or for one counsel only in accordance with regulation 47.

(12) In every case in which a legal aid order is made under this regulation for the provision of services in terms provided for by paragraph (3) or (4), it shall be the duty of–

(a) each legal representative–

  (i) to keep under review the need for more than one counsel to be present in court or otherwise providing services, and
  (ii) to consider whether the legal aid order should be amended as provided for in paragraph (10) or (11);

(b) Queen's Counsel, where the services of a Queen's Counsel are provided, to keep under review whether he could act alone.

(13) It shall be the duty of each legal representative, if of the opinion that the legal aid order should be amended as provided for in paragraphs (10) and (11), to notify that opinion in writing

(a) to the other legal representatives for the assisted person, and
(b) to the court;

and the court shall, after considering the opinion and any representations made by any other legal representatives for the assisted person determine whether and in what manner the legal aid order should be amended.

(14) A decision to make or amend a legal aid order so as to provide for the services of a Queen's Counsel or of more than one counsel may only be made:–

(a) in the cases specified in paragraph (2)(a) or (b), by a circuit judge or a High Court judge where the proceedings are in the Crown Court, or by a judge of the Court of Appeal or the Registrar where the proceedings are in the Court of Appeal;
(b) in the case specified in paragraph (2)(c), by the judge expected to try the case or a High Court judge where the proceedings are in the Crown Court, or by a High Court judge or a judge of the Court of Appeal where the proceedings are in the Court of Appeal.]

Annotations

This regulation was substituted by SI 1994 No 3135, reg 3.
The Act: Legal Aid Act 1988.

49 Assignment of one solicitor or counsel to more than one legally assisted person

A solicitor or counsel may be assigned to two or more legally assisted persons whose cases are to be heard together, unless the interests of justice require that such persons be separately represented.

Annotations

Modification: any reference to solicitor(s) etc modified to include references to bodies recognised under the Administration of Justice Act 1985, s 9, by the Solicitors' Incorporated Practices Order 1991, SI 1991 No 2684, arts 4, 5, Sch 1.

50 Amendment of legal aid orders

(1) A court having power to make a legal aid order may, on application, amend any such order by substituting for any legal representative or representatives previously assigned under the order any legal representative or representatives whom the court could have assigned if it had then been making the legal aid order.

(2) A court having power to make a legal aid order may withdraw any such order if the only legal representative or all the legal representatives for the time being assigned under the order withdraws or withdraw from the case and it appears to the court that, because of the legally assisted person's conduct, it is not desirable to amend the order under paragraph (1) above.

(3) An order amending a legal aid order shall be in Form 15 and a copy of it shall be sent to–

(a) the legally assisted person;
(b) the solicitor assigned by the legal aid order or to counsel (where counsel only is assigned) and to any solicitor and counsel assigned by the amended legal aid order; and
(c) where the legal aid order is amended by an area committee, to the proper officer of the court to which the application for amendment was made.

(4) Where a new solicitor or counsel (where counsel only was assigned) is assigned by an order amending a legal aid order, the solicitor or counsel originally assigned shall send all papers and other items in his possession relating to the proceedings to the new solicitor or counsel.

Annotations

Modification: any reference to solicitor(s) etc modified to include references to bodies recognised under the Administration of Justice Act 1985, s 9, by the Solicitors' Incorporated Practices Order 1991, SI 1991 No 2684, arts 4, 5, Sch 1.

51 Applications for amendment of legal aid orders etc

(1) An application for–

(a) representation by counsel in any proceedings of a kind specified in regulation 44(3); or

(b) the amendment or withdrawal of a legal aid order under regulation 50(1) or (2),

shall be made to the proper officer stating the grounds on which the application is made and the proper officer may grant or refuse the application.

(2) Where an application under paragraph (1) is refused, the applicant may renew his application both to the court and (except where paragraph (6) applies) to an area committee, and the proper officer shall notify the applicant of the circumstances in which an application may be renewed.

(3) Where an application is renewed to the court, the court may grant or refuse the application or refer it to the proper officer.

(4) The proper officer to whom an application is referred under paragraph (3), may–

(a) grant the application; or

(b) where the proper officer is a justices' clerk, refer it either back to the court or to a justice of the peace; or

(c) where the proper officer is not a justices' clerk, refer it to a judge of the court.

(5) The court, a judge of the court or a justice of the peace to whom an application is referred under paragraph (4) may grant or refuse the application.

(6) An application may be renewed under paragraph (2) to an area committee except where–

(a) an application under the same sub-paragraph of paragraph (1) in the same proceedings has previously been refused by an area committee or by the court; or

(b) the application was made–

(i) in the case of proceedings in the Crown Court, more than 14 days after the committal for trial or sentence or the date of giving of notice of appeal; or

(ii) in the case of proceedings in a magistrates' court, less than 14 days before the date fixed for the trial of an information or the inquiry into an offence as examining justices, where such a date had been fixed at the time the application was made; or

(c) the application is an application in respect of proceedings in the Court of Appeal, the Courts-Martial Appeal Court or the House of Lords.

52 Renewal to area committee of application for amendment of legal aid order etc

(1) Where an application under regulation 51 is renewed to an area committee, the legally assisted person shall send to the Area Director the following documents–

(a) a copy of the legal aid order and of the notice of refusal;
(b) any papers presented to the proper officer by the legally assisted person or his solicitor in support of the application; and
(c) any other relevant documents or information.

(2) The proper officer and the legally assisted person or his solicitor shall supply such further particulars, information and documents as the area committee may require.

Annotations
Modification: any reference to solicitor(s) etc modified to include references to bodies recognised under the Administration of Justice Act 1985, s 9, by the Solicitors' Incorporated Practices Order 1991, SI 1991 No 2684, arts 4, 5, Sch 1.

53 Consideration by area committee

(1) The area committee shall consider the application and any further particulars, information or documents submitted to it under regulation 52 and any other relevant information and shall grant or refuse the application and, where necessary, amend or revoke the legal aid order accordingly.

(2) The area committee shall notify the proper officer of the court and the legally assisted person and his solicitor of its decision.

Annotations
Modification: any reference to solicitor(s) etc modified to include references to bodies recognised under the Administration of Justice Act 1985, s 9, by the Solicitors Incorporated Practices Order 1991, SI 1991 No 2684, arts 4, 5, Sch 1.

PART VI AUTHORITY TO INCUR COSTS AND RESTRICTIONS ON PAYMENT OF LEGAL REPRESENTATIVES

54 Power of area committee to authorise expenditure

(1) Where it appears to a legally assisted person's solicitor necessary for the proper conduct of proceedings in a magistrates' court or in the Crown Court for costs to be incurred under the legal aid order by taking any of the following steps–

(a) obtaining a written report or opinion of one or more experts;
(b) employing a person to provide a written report or opinion (otherwise than as an expert);
(c) bespeaking transcripts of shorthand notes or of tape recordings of any proceedings, including police questioning of suspects;
(d) where a legal aid order provides for the services of solicitor and counsel, instructing a Queen's Counsel alone without junior counsel; or

(e) performing an act which is either unusual in its nature or involves unusually large expenditure;

he may apply to the appropriate area committee for prior authority so to do.

(2) Where an area committee authorises the taking of any step specified in paragraph (1)(a), (b), (c) or (e), it shall also authorise the maximum fee to be paid for any such report, opinion, transcript or act.

Annotations

Modification: any reference to solicitor(s) etc modified to include references to bodies recognised under the Administration of Justice Act 1985, s 9, by the Solicitors' Incorporated Practices Order 1991, SI 1991 No 2684, arts 4, 5, Sch 1.

55 Restriction on payment

Where a legal aid order has been made, the legally assisted person's solicitor or counsel shall not receive or be a party to the making of any payment for work done in connection with the proceedings in respect of which the legal aid order was made except such payments as may be made–

(a) out of the legal aid fund or by the Lord Chancellor, or
(b) in respect of any expenses or fees incurred in –

(i) preparing, obtaining or considering any report, opinion or further evidence, whether provided by an expert witness or otherwise; or
(ii) bespeaking transcripts of shorthand notes or tape recordings of any proceedings, including police questioning of suspects;

where an application under regulation 54 for authority to incur such expenses or fees has been refused by the area committee.

Annotations

Modification: any reference to solicitor(s) etc modified to include references to bodies recognised under the Administration of Justice Act 1985, s 9, by the Solicitors' Incorporated Practices Order 1991, SI 1991 No 2684, arts 4, 5, Sch 1.

[56] [Duty to report abuse of legal aid]

[Notwithstanding the relationship between or rights of a legal representative and client or any privilege arising out of such relationship, where the legal representative for an applicant or legally assisted person knows [or suspects] that that person has intentionally failed to comply with any provision of regulations made under the Act concerning the information to be furnished by him or in furnishing such information has knowingly made a false statement or false representation, the legal representative shall forthwith report [the circumstances] to the proper officer.]

Annotations

This regulation was added by SI 1993 No 1895, reg 9.

First words in square brackets added, and second words in square brackets substituted, by SI 1996 No 1258, reg 8.

The Act: Legal Aid Act 1988.

SCHEDULE 1 REGULATIONS REVOKED

Regulation 2

Title	*Reference*
The Legal Aid in Criminal Proceedings (General) Regulations 1968	SI 1968/1231
The Courts-Martial Appeal Legal Aid (General) Regulations 1969	SI 1969/177
The Legal Aid in Criminal Proceedings (General) (Amendment) Regulations 1970	SI 1970/1980
The Legal Aid in Criminal Proceedings (General) (Amendment) Regulations 1976	SI 1976/790
The Legal Aid in Criminal Proceedings (General) (Amendment) Regulations 1980	SI 1980/661
The Legal Aid in Criminal Proceedings (General) (Amendment No 2) Regulations 1980	SI 1980/1651
The Legal Aid in Criminal Proceedings (General) (Amendment) Regulations 1983	SI 1983/1863
The Legal Aid in Criminal Proceedings (General) (Amendment) Regulations 1984	SI 1984/1716
The Legal Aid in Criminal Proceedings (General) (Amendment) Regulations 1985	SI 1985/1632
The Legal Aid in Criminal Proceedings (General) (Amendment) Regulations 1986	SI 1986/274
The Legal Aid in Criminal Proceedings (General) (Amendment) Regulations 1987	SI 1987/422
The Legal Aid in Criminal Proceedings (General) (Amendment) Regulations 1988	SI 1988/468
The Legal Aid in Criminal Proceedings (General) (Amendment) (No 2) Regulations 1988	SI 1988/2303

SCHEDULE 2 FORMS

Regulation 4

PART 1 [FORM 1 APPLICATION FOR LEGAL AID IN CRIMINAL PROCEEDINGS MAGISTRATES OR CROWN COURT]

(This form deals with an application for Legal Aid in criminal proceedings in a Magistrates or Crown Court. Due to its complexity, it has proved impossible to obtain a satisfactory reproduction on the database. It has therefore been omitted. Please see the original.)

Annotations
This Form was substituted by SI 1995 No 542, reg 11, Schedule.
This Form was amended by SI 1996 No 1258, regs 9–11.
Modified by the Solicitors' Incorporated Practices Order 1991, SI 1991 No 2684, arts 4, 5, Sch 1.

PART 2 [FORM 2 NOTIFICATION OF REFUSAL TO GRANT LEGAL AID AND DETERMINATION OF CONTRIBUTION]

(This form deals with notification of refusal to grant Legal Aid and determination of contribution. Due to its complexity, it has proved impossible to obtain a satisfactory reproduction on the database. It has therefore been omitted. Please see the original.)

Annotations
This Form was substituted by SI 1995 No 542, reg 11, Schedule.

PART 2 FORM 3 APPLICATION FOR REVIEW OF REFUSAL TO GRANT LEGAL AID

(This form deals with an application for review of a refusal to grant Legal Aid. Due to its complexity, it has proved impossible to obtain a satisfactory reproduction on the database. It has therefore been omitted. Please see the original.)

Annotations
Modified by the Solicitors' Incorporated Practices Order 1991, SI 1991 No 2684, arts 4, 5, Sch 1.

PART 2 [FORM 4 NOTIFICATION OF DECISION OF THE AREA COMMITTEE ON REVIEW OF REFUSAL TO GRANT LEGAL AID]

(This form deals with notification of the decision of the Area Committee on review of the refusal to grant Legal Aid. Due to its complexity, it has proved impossible to obtain a satisfactory reproduction on the database. It has therefore been omitted. Please see the original.)

Annotations
This Form was substituted by SI 1995 No 542, reg 11, Schedule.

PART 2 [FORM 5 STATEMENT OF MEANS BY APPLICANT OR APPROPRIATE CONTRIBUTOR FOR LEGAL AID PURPOSES]

(This form deals with a statement of means by an applicant or appropriate contributor for Legal Aid purposes. Due to its complexity, it has proved impossible to obtain a satisfactory reproduction on the database. It has therefore been omitted. Please see the original.)

Annotations
This Form was substituted by SI 1995 No 542, reg 11, Schedule.
This Form was amended by SI 1996 No 1258, regs 12–14.

PART 2 FORM 6 LEGAL AID CONTRIBUTION ORDER

(This form deals with a Legal Aid Contribution Order. Due to its complexity, it has proved impossible to obtain a satisfactory reproduction on the database. It has therefore been omitted. Please see the original.)

Annotations

This Form was amended by SI 1992 No 720, reg 6 and SI 1993 No 789, regs 3, 12; amended with savings by SI 1996 No 646, reg 2, for savings see reg 1(3) thereof.

PART 2 FORM 7 NOTICE OF WITHHOLDING OF LEGAL AID ORDER

(This form deals with notice of withholding of Legal Aid Order. Due to its complexity, it has proved impossible to obtain a satisfactory reproduction on the database. It has therefore been omitted. Please see the original.)

Annotations

Modified by the Solicitors' Incorporated Practices Order 1991, SI 1991 No 2684, arts 4, 5, Sch 1.

PART 2 [FORM 8 VARIATION OR REVOCATION OF CONTRIBUTION ORDER]

(This form deals with the variation or revocation of a Contribution Order. Due to its complexity, it has proved impossible to obtain a satisfactory reproduction on the database. It has therefore been omitted. Please see the original.)

Annotations

This Form was substituted by SI 1993 No 789, regs 3, 13, Schedule.

PART 2 FORM 9 NOTIFICATION OF ARREARS OF PAYMENT OF CONTRIBUTION ORDER

(This form deals with notification of arrears of payment of a Contribution Order. Due to its complexity, it has proved impossible to obtain a satisfactory reproduction on the database. It has therefore been omitted. Please see the original.)

PART 2 FORM 10 WARNING OF REVOCATION OF LEGAL AID ORDER FOR NON-PAYMENT OF CONTRIBUTION

(This form deals with warning of the revocation of a Legal Aid Order for non-payment of contribution. Due to its complexity, it has proved impossible to obtain a satisfactory reproduction on the database. It has therefore been omitted. Please see the original.)

Annotations

Modified by the Solicitors' Incorporated Practices Order 1991, SI 1991 No 2684, arts 4, 5, Sch 1.

PART 2 [FORM 11 LEGAL AID ORDER (MAGISTRATES' COURT)]

(This form deals with a Legal Aid Order (Magistrates' Court). Due to its complexity, it has proved impossible to obtain a satisfactory reproduction on the database. It has therefore been omitted. Please see the original.)

Annotations
This Form was substituted by SI 1991 No 637, reg 3.
This Form was amended by SI 1993 No 789, regs 3, 14.
Modified by the Solicitors' Incorporated Practices Order 1991, SI 1991 No 2684, arts 4, 5, Sch 1.

PART 2 [FORM 11A LEGAL AID ORDER (CROWN COURT)]

(This form deals with a Legal Aid Order (Crown Court). Due to its complexity, it has proved impossible to obtain a satisfactory reproduction on the database. It has therefore been omitted. Please see the original.)

Annotations
This Form was added by SI 1991 No 637, reg 3.
This Form was amended by SI 1993 No 789, regs 3, 14 and SI 1994 No 3136, reg 4.
Modified by the Solicitors' Incorporated Practices Order 1991, SI 1991 No 2684, arts 4, 5, Sch 1.

PART 2 FORM 12 LEGAL AID ORDER (AREA COMMITTEE)

(This form deals with a Legal Aid Order (Area Committee). Due to its complexity, it has proved impossible to obtain a satisfactory reproduction on the database. It has therefore been omitted. Please see the original.)

Annotations
This Form was amended by SI 1993 No 789, regs 3, 14.
Modified by the Solicitors' Incorporated Practices Order 1991, SI 1991 No 2684, arts 4, 5, Sch 1.

PART 2 FORM 13 LEGAL AID ORDER (COURT OF APPEAL/COURTS-MARTIAL APPEAL COURT)

(This form deals with a Legal Aid Order (Court of Appeal/Courts-Martial Appeal Court). Due to its complexity, it has proved impossible to obtain a satisfactory reproduction on the database. It has therefore been omitted. Please see the original.)

Annotations
This Form was amended by SI 1993 No 789, regs 3, 14.
Modified by the Solicitors' Incorporated Practices Order 1991, SI 1991 No 2684, arts 4, 5, Sch 1.

PART 2 FORM 14 ORDER WITHDRAWING LEGAL AID

(This form deals with an Order withdrawing Legal Aid. Due to its complexity, it has proved impossible to obtain a satisfactory reproduction on the database. It has therefore been omitted. Please see the original.)

Annotations
This Form was amended by SI 1996 No 1258, reg 15.
Modified by the Solicitors' Incorporated Practices Order 1991, SI 1991 No 2684, arts 4, 5, Sch 1.

PART 2 FORM 15 ORDER AMENDING LEGAL AID ORDER

(This form deals with an Order amending a Legal Aid Order. Due to its complexity, it has proved impossible to obtain a satisfactory reproduction on the database. It has therefore been omitted. Please see the original.)

Annotations
Modified by the Solicitors' Incorporated Practices Order 1991, SI 1991 No 2684, arts 4, 5, Sch 1.

PART 2 FORM 16 APPLICATION FOR LEGAL AID IN CARE PROCEEDINGS IN THE [YOUTH COURT] OR CROWN COURT

(This form deals with an application for Legal Aid in care proceedings in the Youth Court or Crown Court. Due to its complexity, it has proved impossible to obtain a satisfactory reproduction on the database. It has therefore been omitted. Please see the original.)

Annotations
Section heading: words in square brackets substituted by virtue of the Criminal Justice Act 1991, s 70.
This Form was amended by virtue of the Criminal Justice Act 1991, s 70.
Modified by the Solicitors' Incorporated Practices Order 1991, SI 1991 No 2684, arts 4, 5, Sch 1.

SCHEDULE 3 DETERMINATION OF DISPOSABLE INCOME AND DISPOSABLE CAPITAL

Regulation 26(2)

General

1 (1) In computing the disposable income and disposable capital of the person concerned, the financial resources of any spouse of his shall be treated as his resources except where–

(a) the person concerned and his spouse are living separate and apart; or
(b) the spouse has a contrary interest in the proceedings in respect of which an application for legal aid has been made; or
(c) in all the circumstances of the case, it would be inequitable so to do.

(2) Where a spouse fails to provide information as to his financial resources in response to the request of the proper officer, the proper officer may make an estimate of the likely resources of the spouse on the basis of any information which is available.

2 Paragraph 1(1) and (2) above and the provisions of this Schedule shall apply to a man and a woman who are living with each other in the same household a husband and wife as they apply to the parties to a marriage.

[2A (1) Where it appears to the proper officer that:

(a) the person concerned has directly or indirectly transferred any resources to another person;
(b) another person is or has been maintaining the person concerned in the proceedings to which the application relates or any other proceedings, or
(c) any of the resources of another person are or have been made available to the person concerned,

the proper officer shall have power to treat all or any part of the resources of that other person as the resources of the person concerned.

(2) Where sub-paragraph (1) applies:

(a) the question of what is or is not a resource of that other person shall be determined, as nearly as the circumstances permit, in accordance with the provisions of this Schedule excluding this paragraph, and
(b) the proper officer shall assess or estimate the value of those resources to the best of his judgment.

(3) In this paragraph, 'person' (except in the phrase 'person concerned') includes a company, partnership, body of trustees and any body of persons whether corporate or not corporate.]

3 Where it appears to the proper officer that the person concerned has with intent to reduce the amount of his disposable income or disposable capital[, whether for the purpose of reducing his liability to pay a contribution towards legal aid or otherwise]–

(a) directly or indirectly deprived himself of any resources; or
(b) converted any part of his resources into resources which under these Regulations are to be wholly or partly disregarded, or in respect of which nothing is to be included in determining the resources of that person;

the resources of which he has so deprived himself or which he has so converted shall be treated as part of his resources or as not so converted as the case may be.

Disposable income

4 (1) The income which the person concerned receives during the [period of computation] shall be taken to be his income for the purposes of this Schedule.

(2) The income received during the contribution period may be estimated on the basis of the income received by the person concerned during the 3 months prior to the commencement of the [period of computation].

5 (1) Where the person concerned receives the profits from any trade, business or gainful occupation other than employment at a wage or salary, the profit which accrues during the [period of computation] shall be taken to be his income for the purposes of this Schedule.

(2) The income received during the [period of computation] may be estimated on the basis of the profits made during the last accounting period for which accounts have been prepared.

[6 In computing disposable income the following payments made under the Social Security Contributions and Benefits Act 1992 shall be disregarded:–

(a) disability living allowance;
(b) attendance allowance;
(c) constant attendance allowance paid under section 104 as an increase to a disablement pension;
(d) housing benefit;
(e) any payment made out of the social fund.]

7 In computing disposable income there shall be deducted–

(a) the total amount of any tax payable on that income;
(b) the total amount of any contributions payable under [the Social Security Contributions and Benefits Act 1992];
(c) reasonable expenses of travelling to and from the place of employment;
(d) the amount of any contribution paid, whether under a legal obligation or not, to an occupational pension scheme within the meaning of the Social Security Pensions Act 1975 or to a personal pension scheme within the meaning of the Social Security Act 1986; and
(e) reasonable expenses in respect of the making of reasonable provision for the care of any dependent child living with the person concerned because of that person's absence from home by reason of employment.

[7A In computing the income of the person concerned, there shall be deducted any sums payable (net of council tax benefit) by the person concerned in respect of the council tax to which he is liable by virtue of section 6 of the Local Government Finance Act 1992.]

8 (1) In computing disposable income there shall be a deduction in respect of the main or only dwelling in the case of a householder of the amount of the net rent payable, or such part thereof as is reasonable in the circumstances.

(2) For the purposes of this paragraph, 'rent' includes–

(a) the annual rent payable; and
(b) a sum in respect of yearly outgoings borne by the householder including, in particular, [any domestic rates and water and sewerage charges], a reasonable allowance towards any necessary expenditure on repairs and insurance and any annual instalment (whether of interest or of capital) payable in respect of a mortgage debt or heritable security charged on the house in which the householder resides or has an interest and,

in calculating the amount of rent payable, any housing benefit paid under the [the Social Security Contributions and Benefits Act 1992] shall be deducted from amount of rent payable.

(3) In this paragraph, the expression 'net rent' means the rent less any proceeds of sub-letting any part of the premises in respect of which the said rent is paid or the outgoings are incurred except that, where any person or persons other than the person concerned, his or her spouse or any dependent of his or hers is accommodated, otherwise than as a sub-tenant, in the premises for which the rent is paid, the rent may be deemed to be reduced by an amount reasonably attributable to such other person or persons.

[(4) In sub-paragraph (2)(b) above, the amount to be included as 'rent' in respect of any annual instalment payable in respect of a mortgage debt or heritable security shall not exceed an amount bearing the same proportion to the amount of the annual instalment as £100,000 bears to the debt secured.]

9 Where the person concerned is not a householder, there shall be a deduction in respect of the costs of his living accommodation of such an amount as is reasonable in the circumstances [< . . . >]

10 (1) Subject to sub-paragraph (2) below, in computing disposable income, there shall be a deduction–

(a) in respect of the maintenance of the spouse of the person concerned, where the spouses are living together;
(b) in respect of the maintenance of any dependent child and of any dependent relative of the person concerned where such persons are members of his household;

at the following rates–

(i) in the case of a spouse at the rate equivalent to [the difference between the income support allowance for a couple where both members are aged not less than 18 (which is specified in column 2 of paragraph 1(3)(c) of Schedule 2 Part I of the Income Support (General) Regulations 1987), and the allowance for a single person aged not less than 25, (which is specified in column 2 of paragraph 1(1)(e) of Schedule 2 Part I of those Regulations)];
(ii) in the case of a dependent child or a dependent relative, at the rate equivalent to < . . . > the amount specified for the time being in paragraph 2 of Part I of Schedule 2 to the Income Support (General) Regulations 1987 appropriate to the age of the child or relative.

(2) The proper officer may reduce any rate provided by virtue of sub-paragraph (1) by taking into account the income and other resources of the dependent child or other dependent to such extent as appears to the officer to be just and equitable.

(3) In ascertaining whether a child is a dependent child or whether a person is a dependent relative for the purposes of this paragraph, regard shall be had to their income and other resources.

11 Where the person concerned is making and, throughout such period as the proper officer may consider to be adequate, has regularly made bona fide payments for the maintenance of

(a) a spouse who is living apart;
(b) a former spouse;
(c) a child; or
(d) a relative;

who is not a member of the household of the person concerned, there shall be a deduction at the rate of such payments or at such rate (not exceeding the rate of such payments) as in all the circumstances is reasonable.

12 In computing disposable income, there shall be a deduction in respect of any sum or sums payable by the person concerned under an order made by, or arising from any conviction before, the High Court, the Crown Court, a county court, or a magistrates' court in any proceedings other than those in respect of which the legal aid order was made.

13 Where the person concerned is required to, or may reasonably, provide for any other matter, the proper officer may make an allowance of such amount as he considers to be reasonable in the circumstances of the case.

14 In computing the income from any source, there shall be disregarded such amount, if any, as the proper officer considers to be reasonable having regard to the nature of the income or to any other circumstances of the case.

Disposable capital

15 (1) In computing the capital of the person concerned, there shall be included the amount or value of every resource of a capital nature belonging to him on the date of the assessment.

(2) In so far as any resource of a capital nature does not consist of money, its amount or value shall be taken to be–

(a) the amount which that resource would realise if sold in the open market, or if there is only a restricted market for the resource, the amount which it would realise in that market, after deduction of any expenses incurred in the sale, or
(b) if such an amount cannot be ascertained, an amount which appears to the proper officer to be reasonable.

16 In computing the capital of the person concerned, there shall be disregarded–

(a) any savings of mobility allowance paid under the Social Security Act 1975 [or disability living allowance] which the person concerned intends to use in connection with mobility [or his disability];
(b) for a period exceeding 12 months from the date of receipt, any arrears of–

(i) attendance or mobility allowance paid under the Social Security Act 1975–1988 [or disability living allowance]
(ii) [income-based jobseeker's allowance,] income support[, family credit or disability working allowance]; and

(c) any payments made out of the social fund under section 32 of the [the Social Security Contributions and Benefits Act 1992].

17 Except where it is reasonable in the circumstances so to do, no sum shall be included in the amount of the capital of the person concerned in respect of the value of the assets of any business owned in whole or in part by him.

18 Save in exceptional circumstances, no sum shall be included in the amount of the capital of the person concerned in respect of –

(a) household furniture and effects of the main or only residence occupied by him;
(b) articles of personal clothing; and
(c) tools and equipment of his trade.

19 In computing the amount of the capital of the person concerned, the value

of any interest in the main or only residence in which he resides shall be *wholly disregarded* [taken to be the amount for which that interest could be sold in the open market, subject to the following rules:–

(a) the amount to be allowed in respect of any mortgage debt or heritable security shall not exceed £100,000;

(b) the first £100,000 of the value of that interest, after the application of the rule in paragraph (a), shall be disregarded.]

[19A Where the person concerned resides in more than one dwelling in which he has an interest, the proper officer shall decide which is the main dwelling and shall take into account the amount for which any interest in a dwelling which is not the main dwelling could be sold in the open market; provided that the total amount to be allowed in respect of any mortgage debts or heritable securities over all such dwellings, together with any amount allowed, under paragraph 19(a) in respect of the main dwelling, shall not exceed £100,000.]

20 In computing the capital of the person concerned, there may also be disregarded such an amount of capital (if any) as the proper officer decides to disregard taking into account the nature of the capital or any other circumstances of the case.

Annotations

Paras 2A, 19A: added with savings by SI 1996 No 436, regs 4, 7; for savings see reg 3 thereof.

Para 3: words in square brackets added by SI 1990 489, reg 3(1)(a).

Paras 4, 5, 7: words in square brackets substituted by SI 1993 No 789, regs 15, 17(a), (c).

Para 6: substituted by SI 1993 No 789, reg 16.

Para 7A: added by SI 1990 No 489, reg 3(1)(b); substituted by SI 1993 No 789, reg 18.

Para 8: in sub-para (2) first words in square brackets substituted by SI 1990 No 489, reg 3(1)(c), second words in square brackets substituted by SI 1993 No 789, reg 17(b); sub-para (4) added with savings by SI 1996 No 436, reg 5, for savings see reg 3 thereof.

Para 9: words omitted added by SI 1990 No 489, reg (1), revoked by SI 1993 No 789, reg 17(c).

Para 10: words in square brackets substituted, and words omitted revoked, by SI 1993 No 789, reg 19.

Para 16: first, second and third words in square brackets added, and fifth words in square brackets substituted by SI 1992 No 720, regs 5, 7; fourth words in square brackets prospectively added by SI 1996 No 1258, reg 4, as from 7 October 1996; final words in square brackets substituted by SI 1993 No 789, reg 17(b).

Para 19: words underlined revoked with savings and subsequent words in square brackets substituted with savings by SI 1996 No 436, reg 6; for savings see reg 3 thereof.

SCHEDULE 4 CONTRIBUTIONS

Regulation 26(3)

Contributions from disposable income

[The weekly instalment of contribution payable by the applicant or the appropriate contributor shall by £1 for each £3 or part of £3 [by which his average weekly disposable income exceeds £47 [£48]; but any applicant or appropriate contributor whose average weekly disposable income does not exceed £48 [£49] shall not be liable to pay a contribution].]

Contributions from disposable capital

The contribution from capital payable by the applicant or the appropriate contributor shall be such an amount as is equal to the amount by which his disposable capital exceeds £3,000.

Annotations

First words in square brackets substituted by SI 1993 No 789, reg 20, words in square brackets therein substituted by SI 1995 No 796, reg 2, sums underlined therein revoked with savings and subsequent sums in square brackets therein substituted with savings by SI 1996 No 646, reg 3, for savings see reg 1(3) thereof.

Appendix E2

Legal Advice and Assistance Regulations 1989

1989 No. 340

Made – – – 3rd March 1989

1 Citation, commencement, and transitional provisions

(1) These Regulations may be cited as the Legal Advice and Assistance Regulations 1989 and shall come into force on 1st April 1989.

(2) Where a review under paragraph (7) of regulation 29 relates to a claim made before 1st June 1989, paragraphs (8) and (9) of that regulation shall not apply and the solicitor may appeal in writing within 21 days of receipt of notification of the decision on the review to a committee appointed by the Board.

Annotations

Modification: any reference to solicitor(s) etc modified to include references to bodies recognised under the Administration of Justice Act 1985, s 9, by the Solicitors Incorporated Practices Order 1991, SI 1991 No 2684, arts 4, 5, Sch 1.

2 Revocations

The Regulations specified in Schedule 1 are hereby revoked.

3 Interpretation

(1) In these Regulations, unless the context otherwise requires–

'ABWOR' means assistance by way of representation;

'the Act' means the Legal Aid Act 1988;

'appropriate area committee' means the area committee in whose area an application for advice and assistance, or a claim for costs has been dealt with by an Area Director;

'area committee' has the meaning assigned to it in the Civil Legal Aid (General) Regulations 1989;

'Area Director' has the meaning assigned to it in the Civil Legal Aid (General) Regulations 1989;

'assessed deficiency' means the amount by which the sum allowed to the solicitor by the Area Director in assessing his claim under regulation 29 exceeds any contribution payable by the client to the solicitor under section 9 of the Act together with the value of any charge arising under section 11 of the Act;

'board of visitors' means a board of visitors appointed by the Secretary of State under section 6(2) of the Prison Act 1952;

'child' means a person under the age that is for the time being the upper limit of compulsory school age by virtue of section 35 of the Education Act 1944 together with any Order in Council made under that section;
'client' means a person seeking or receiving advice and assistance or on whose behalf advice and assistance is sought;
['contract' means a contract entered into by the Board with other persons or bodies pursuant to its powers under section 4 of the Act;]
'costs' means the cost of giving advice or assistance, including disbursements, charges and fees;
'Costs Regulations' means the Legal Aid in Criminal and Care Proceedings (Costs) Regulations 1989;
['disability working allowance' means a disability working allowance under [the Social Security Contributions and Benefits Act 1992];]
'extension' means the grant of prior authority to exceed the limit prescribed under section 10(1) of the Act and, where appropriate, the grant of prior authority to exceed any further limit imposed under regulation 21(3) or 22(8);
'family credit' means family credit under [the Social Security Contributions and Benefits Act 1992];
['franchisee' means a person or body (other than the Board) acting under the terms of a franchising contract;]
'fund' means the legal aid fund;
'income support' means income support under [the Social Security Contributions and Benefits Act 1992];
'patient' means a person who by reason of mental disorder within the meaning of the Mental Health Act 1983 is incapable of managing and administering his property and affairs;
'Scope Regulations' means the Legal Advice and Assistance (Scope) Regulations 1989;
'serious service offence' means an offence under any of the Army Act 1955, the Air Force Act 1955, or the Naval Discipline Act 1957 which cannot be dealt with summarily or which appears to an interviewing service policeman to be serious;
'volunteer' means a person who, for the purpose of assisting with an investigation, attends voluntarily at a police station or at any other place where a constable is present or accompanies a constable to a police station or any such other place without having been arrested.

(2) Any reference in these Regulations to a regulation or Schedule by number means the regulation or Schedule so numbered in these Regulations.

Annotations

Para (1): definitions 'contract' and 'franchisee' added by SI 1994 No 1823, reg 4; definition 'disability working allowance' added by SI 1992 No 719, reg 3, words in square brackets substituted by SI 1993 No 790, reg 4(a); in definitions 'family credit' and 'income support' words in square brackets substituted by SI 1993 No 790, reg 4(b), (c).

Modification: any reference to solicitor(s) etc modified to include references to bodies recognised under the Administration of Justice Act 1985, s 9, by the Solicitors' Incorporated Practices Order 1991, SI 1991 No 2684, arts 4, 5, Sch 1.

[3A] [Exercise of Area Director's functions by franchisee]

[Where and to the extent that a franchising contract so provides, any functions of an Area Director are conferred on a franchisee, the functions may be exercised by the franchisee on the Area Director's behalf.]

Annotations
This regulation was added by SI 1994 No 1823, reg 5.

4 Limit on cost of advice and assistance

(1) Subject to paragraph (2), the limit applicable under section 10(1) of the Act is–

(a) in respect of advice and assistance given in accordance with regulation 6(1), £90;
(b) in respect of advice and assistance provided to a petitioner for divorce or judicial separation which includes advice or assistance in the preparation of the petition, three times the relevant sum specified for preparation in the table in [paragraph 1 (or paragraph 2 in the case of a franchisee) of Schedule 6];
(c) in respect of all other advice and assistance, twice the relevant sum referred to in sub-paragraph (b);

(2) Section 10(1) of the Act shall not apply to–

(a) advice or assistance specified in regulation 5(1)(b) of the Legal Advice and Assistance at Police Stations (Remuneration) Regulations 1989 where the interests of justice require such advice or assistance to be given as a matter of urgency; or
(b) ABWOR provided under arrangements made by the Board under regulation 7; or
(c) advice or assistance given under arrangements made by the Board under regulation 8.

Annotations
Para (1): words in square brackets substituted by SI 1995 No 949, reg 4.
The Act: Legal Aid Act 1988.
Costs Regulations: Legal Advice in Criminal and Care Proceedings (Costs) Regulations 1989, SI 1989 No 343.

5 ABWOR relating to applications for further detention

ABWOR to which Part III of the Act applies by virtue of regulation 7(1)(c) of the Scope Regulations (application for warrant of further detention) shall be available without reference to the client's financial resources.

Annotations
The Act: Legal Aid Act 1988.
Scope Regulations: Legal Advice and Assistance (Scope) Regulations 1989, SI 1989 No 550.

[5A] [ABWOR in proceedings before a Mental Health Review Tribunal]

[ABWOR to which Part III of the Act applies by virtue of regulation 9(a) of the Scope Regulations (proceedings before a Mental Health Review Tribunal) shall be available without reference to the client's financial resources.]

Annotations
This regulation was added by SI 1994 No 805, reg 5.
The Act: Legal Aid Act 1988.
Scope Regulations: Legal Advice and Assistance (Scope) Regulations 1989, SI 1989 No 550.

6 Provision of advice and assistance at police stations etc

(1) A solicitor may give advice and assistance to any person who–

(a) is arrested and held in custody at a police station or other premises; or
(b) is being interviewed in connection with a serious service offence; or
(c) is a volunteer.

(2) Subject to any arrangements made by the Board under paragraph (3), an application for advice and assistance in the circumstances specified in paragraph (1) may be made by telephone to the solicitor from whom the advice and assistance is sought.

(3) The Board may make arrangements for solicitors designated by the Board to attend at police stations or other premises in order to provide advice and assistance under paragraph (1).

(4) Advice and assistance given under this regulation shall be available without reference to the client's financial resources.

Annotations
Modification: any reference to solicitor(s) etc modified to include references to bodies recognised under the Administration of Justice Act 1985, s 9, by the Solicitors' Incorporated Practices Order 1991, SI 1991 No 2684, arts 4, 5, Sch 1.

7 ABWOR in criminal proceedings in magistrates' courts

(1) The Board may make arrangements for the provision of ABWOR to which Part III of the Act applies by virtue of regulation 7(2) and (4) of the Scope Regulations.

(2) Arrangements under paragraph (1) may provide for solicitors designated by the Board to attend at magistrates' courts.

(3) ABWOR under this regulation shall be available without reference to the client's financial resources.

Annotations
Modification: any reference to solicitor(s) etc modified to include references to bodies recognised under the Administration of Justice Act 1985, s 9, by the Solicitors' Incorporated Practices Order 1991, SI 1991 No 2684, arts 4, 5, Sch 1.
The Act: Legal Aid Act 1988.
Scope Regulations: the Legal Advice and Assistance (Scope) Regulations 1989, SI 1989 No 550.

8 Advice and assistance in criminal proceedings in magistrates' courts

(1) Arrangements under regulation 7 may provide for a solicitor who gives ABWOR in accordance with them also to give–

(a) advice to a defendant who is in custody;
(b) advice to a defendant who is before the court as a result of a failure to pay a fine or other sum which he was ordered on conviction to pay, or to obey an order of the court, where such failure may lead to his being at risk of imprisonment;
(c) advice, where in the opinion of the solicitor the defendant requires it, to a defendant who is not in custody;
(d) assistance to a defendant to make an application for representation under the Act in respect of any subsequent appearance of the defendant before the court.

(2) Advice and assistance given under this regulation shall be available without reference to the client's financial resources.

Annotations
Modification: any reference to solicitor(s) etc modified to include references to bodies recognised under the Administration of Justice Act 1985, s 9, by the Solicitors' Incorporated Practices Order 1991, SI 1991 No 2684, arts 4, 5, Sch 1.
The Act: Legal Aid Act 1988.

9 Applications for advice and assistance

(1) An application for advice and assistance to which this regulation applies shall be made in accordance with its provisions to the solicitor from whom the advice and assistance is sought.

(2) This regulation applies to all advice and assistance except–
(a) advice or assistance given under regulation 6 or 8; and
(b) ABWOR given under regulation 7, or to which Part III of the Act applies by virtue of regulation 7(1)(c) of the Scope Regulations (warrants of further detention).

(3) Subject to [paragraph (3A) and] regulations 10 and 15, the application under paragraph (1) shall be made by the client in person.

[(3A) Where a franchising contract so provides and subject to compliance with any provisions specified in the contract, an application for advice and assistance may be made by telephone or by post.]

(4) Where a client makes an application under paragraph (1) he shall provide the solicitor with the information necessary to enable the solicitor to determine–
(a) his disposable capital;
(b) where appropriate, whether he is in receipt of income support[, family credit or disability working allowance] and
(c) where he is not in receipt of income support[, family credit or disability working allowance] his disposable income.

(5) Where an application under paragraph (1) is for advice or assistance relating to the making of a will, the client shall provide the solicitor with the information necessary to enable the solicitor to determine whether the advice or assistance would fall within regulation 4(2) of the Scope Regulations.

(6) The information required by this regulation shall be furnished on a form approved by the Board.

Annotations
Para (3): words in square brackets added by SI 1994 No 1823, reg 6(a).
Para (3A): added by SI 1994 No 1823, reg 6(b).
Para (4): words in square brackets in sub-paras (b), (c) substituted by SI 1992 No 719, reg 3(2).
Modification: any reference to solicitor(s) etc modified to include references to bodies recognised under the Administration of Justice Act 1985, s 9, by the Solicitors' Incorporated Practices Order 1991, SI 1991 No 2684, arts 4, 5, Sch 1.
The Act: Legal Aid Act 1988.
Scope Regulations: the Legal Advice and Assistance (Scope) Regulations 1989, SI 1989 No 550.

10 Attendance on behalf of a client

(1) Where a client cannot for good reason attend on the solicitor in order to apply for advice and assistance in accordance with paragraph (3) of regulation 9, he may authorise another person to attend on his behalf.

(2) Where a person authorised in accordance with paragraph (1) attends on a solicitor, he shall furnish the solicitor with the information necessary to enable the solicitor to determine–

(a) the client's disposable capital,
(b) where appropriate, whether the client is in receipt of income support[, family credit or disability working allowance], and
(c) where the client is not in receipt of income support[, family credit or disability working allowance], the client's disposable income.

(3) Where the application is for advice or assistance relating to the making of a will, the person authorised in accordance with paragraph (1) shall provide the solicitor with the information necessary to enable the solicitor to determine whether the advice or assistance would fall within regulation 4(2) of the Scope Regulations.

(4) The information required by this regulation shall be furnished on a form approved by the Board.

Annotations
Para (2): words in square brackets in sub-paras (b), (c) substituted by SI 1992 No 719, reg 3(2).
Modification: any reference to solicitor(s) etc modified to include references to bodies recognised under the Administration of Justice Act 1985, s 9, by the Solicitors' Incorporated Practices Order 1991, SI 1991 No 2684, arts 4, 5, Sch 1.
Scope Regulations: the Legal Advice and Assistance (Scope) Regulations 1989, SI 1989 No 550.

11 Eligibility for advice and assistance to which regulation 9 applies

(1) A client is eligible for advice and assistance (excluding ABWOR) to which regulation 9 applies if his weekly disposable income does not exceed [£72] [£75], and his disposable capital does not exceed [£1,000].

(2) A client is eligible for ABWOR to which regulation 9 applies if his weekly disposable income does not exceed [£156] [£162], and his disposable capital does not exceed £3,000.

Annotations

Para (1): first sum in square brackets substituted by SI 1995 No 795, reg 3, further substituted with savings by subsequent sum in square brackets by SI 1996 No 641, reg 3(1)(a), for savings see reg 2(1) thereof; final sum in square brackets substituted by SI 1992 No 719, reg 4(1).

Para (2): first sum in square brackets substituted by SI 1995 No 795, reg 3, further substituted with savings by subsequent sum in square brackets by SI 1996 No 641, reg 3(1)(b), for savings see reg 2(1) thereof.

[12] [Contributions]

[(1) A client shall be liable to pay weekly contributions towards the cost of ABWOR if his weekly disposable income exceeds [£64] [£67] but does not exceed [£156] [£162].

(2) The amount of any contribution under paragraph (1) shall be one third of the amount by which his weekly disposable income exceeds [£64] [£67].

(3) The period during which contributions shall be payable shall start on the date of approval of ABWOR and shall continue until the conclusion of the proceedings to which ABWOR related or until ABWOR is withdrawn.

(4) For ABWOR to which Part III of the Act applies by virtue of regulation 7(1)(b) or 8 of the Scope Regulations, a client shall be liable (subject to paragraphs (1), (2) and (5) of this regulation) to pay one week's contribution towards the cost of ABWOR.

(5) A client whose weekly disposable income does not exceed [£64] [£67]is not liable to pay any contribution [towards the cost of ABWOR] under section 9(6) of the Act.

[(6) A client shall in no case be liable to pay any contribution towards the cost of advice and assistance other than ABWOR.]]

Annotations

This regulation was substituted by SI 1993 No 790, reg 6.

Para (1): first and third sums in square brackets substituted by SI 1995 No 795, reg 4, further substituted with savings by subsequent sums in square brackets by SI 1996 No 641, reg 3(2), for savings see reg 2(1) thereof.

Para (2): first sum in square brackets substituted by SI 1995 No 795, reg 4, further substituted with savings by subsequent sum in square brackets by SI 1996 No 641, reg 3(2)(a), for savings see reg 2(1) thereof.

Para (5): first sum in square brackets substituted by SI 1995 No 795, reg 4, further substituted with savings by subsequent sum in square brackets by SI 1996 No 641, reg 3(2)(a), for savings see reg 2(1) thereof; words in square brackets added by SI 1994 No 805, reg 7(c).

Para (6): added by SI 1994 No 805, reg 7(d).

The Act: Legal Aid Act 1988.

Scope Regulations: Legal Advice and Assistance (Scope) Regulations 1989, SI 1989 No 550.

13 Assessment of disposable income, disposable capital and < . . . > contribution

(1) Subject to paragraphs (2) and (3), a solicitor to whom an application under regulation 9 is made shall assess the disposable income and disposable capital of the client and, where appropriate, of any person whose financial resources may be treated as those of the client in accordance with Schedule 2.

(2) Where the solicitor is satisfied that any of the persons whose disposable incomes are to be assessed under paragraph (1) is directly or indirectly in receipt of income support[, family credit or disability working allowance], he shall take that person's disposable income as not exceeding [the sum for the time being specified in regulation 11(1)].

(3) Where, in the case of an application for ABWOR to which regulation 9 applies, the solicitor is satisfied that any of the persons whose disposable capital is to be assessed under paragraph (1) is directly or indirectly in receipt of income support, he shall take that person's disposable capital as not exceeding the capital sum specified in regulation 11(2).

[(4) The solicitor shall also determine in accordance with the provisions of regulation 12 the weekly contribution, if any, payable to him by the client under section 9(6) of the Act.]

(5) The solicitor shall not provide advice and assistance to any person until either the form referred to in regulation 9(6) has been signed by the client or, where appropriate, the form referred to in regulation 10(4) has been signed on behalf of the client, and in any case, until the solicitor has assessed disposable income and disposable capital in accordance with paragraph (1).

Annotations
Section heading: word omitted revoked by SI 1993 No 790, reg 7(a).
Para (2): first words in square brackets substituted by SI 1992 No 719, reg 3(2); final words in square brackets substituted by SI 1993 No 790, reg 7(b).
Para (4): substituted by SI 1993 No 790, reg 7(c).
Modification: any reference to solicitor(s) etc modified to include references to bodies recognised under the Administration of Justice Act 1985, s 9, by the Solicitors' Incorporated Practices Order 1991, SI 1991 No 2684, arts 4, 5, Sch 1.
The Act: Legal Aid Act 1988.

14 Children and patients

(1) A solicitor shall not, except where paragraph (2) [or 2A] applies, accept an application for advice and assistance from a child unless he has been authorised to do so by the Area Director and the Area Director shall withhold such authority unless he is satisfied that it is reasonable in the circumstances that the child should receive advice and assistance.

(2) A solicitor may accept an application for advice and assistance from a child who–

(a) is arrested and held in custody at a police station or other premises;
(b) is being interviewed in connection with a serious service offence; or
(c) is a volunteer;

where the solicitor is satisfied that the application cannot reasonably be made by any of the persons specified in paragraph (3)(a), (c) or (d).

[(2A) A solicitor may accept an application for advice and assistance from a child in relation to proceedings in which that child is entitled to begin, prosecute or defend without a next friend or guardian *ad litem*.]

(3) A solicitor may accept an application for advice and assistance on behalf of a child or patient from–

(a) in the case of a child, his parent or guardian or other person in whose care he is; or

(b) in the case of a patient, a receiver appointed under Part VII of the Mental Health Act 1983 or the patient's nearest relative or guardian within the meaning of Part II of the Mental Health Act 1983; or

(c) in the case of a child or patient, a person acting for the purposes of any proceedings as his next friend or guardian ad litem; or

(d) in the case of a child or a patient, any other person where the Area Director is satisfied that it is reasonable in the circumstances and has given prior authority for the advice and assistance to be given to such other person on behalf of the child or patient.

Annotations

Para (1): words in square brackets added by SI 1992 No 591, reg 3(a).
Para (2A): added by SI 1992 No 591, reg 3(b).
Modification: any reference to solicitor(s) etc modified to include references to bodies recognised under the Administration of Justice Act 1985, s 9, by the Solicitors' Incorporated Practices Order 1991, SI 1991 No 2684, arts 4, 5, Sch 1.

15 Clients resident outside England and Wales

Where the client resides outside England and Wales, the Area Director may give the solicitor prior authority to accept a postal application for advice and assistance if the Area Director is satisfied that it is reasonable in the circumstances to do so.

Annotations

Modification: any reference to solicitor(s) etc modified to include references to bodies recognised under the Administration of Justice Act 1985, s 9, by the Solicitors' Incorporated Practices Order 1991, SI 1991 No 2684, arts 4, 5, Sch 1.

16 Advice and assistance from more than one solicitor

(1) A person shall not, except where regulation 6, 7 or 8 applies, be given advice and assistance for the same matter by more than one solicitor without the prior authority of the Area Director, and such authority may be given on such terms and conditions as the Area Director may in his discretion see fit to impose.

(2) Where regulation 6 applies, a person may be given advice and assistance for the same matter by more than one solicitor without the prior authority of the Area Director, provided that the cost of that advice and assistance shall not exceed the cost that would have been incurred had it been given by one solicitor.

Annotations

Modification: any reference to solicitor(s) etc modified to include references to bodies recognised under the Administration of Justice Act 1985, s 9, by the Solicitors' Incorporated Practices Order 1991, SI 1991 No 2684, arts 4, 5, Sch 1.

17 Separate matters

Where two or more separate matters are involved, each matter shall be the subject of a separate application for advice and assistance provided that matters connected with or arising from proceedings for divorce or judicial separation, whether actual or prospective between the client and his spouse, shall not be treated as separate matters for the purpose of advice and assistance.

18 Refusal of advice and assistance

A solicitor may for good cause either refuse to accept an application for advice and assistance or (having accepted an application) decline to give, or to continue to give advice and assistance and may, if he thinks fit, refuse to disclose his reasons for doing so to the client or person seeking advice and assistance on his behalf; but he shall give the Area Director such information about such a refusal as the Area Director may require.

Annotations
Modification: any reference to solicitor(s) etc modified to include references to bodies recognised under the Administration of Justice Act 1985, s 9, by the Solicitors' Incorporated Practices Order 1991, SI 1991 No 2684, arts 4, 5, Sch 1.

19 Power to require information

The Area Director may require a solicitor who has given advice and assistance to furnish such information as he may from time to time require for the purposes of his functions under these Regulations; and the solicitor shall not be precluded, by reason of any privilege arising out of the relationship between solicitor and client, from disclosing such information to him.

Annotations
Modification: any reference to solicitor(s) etc modified to include references to bodies recognised under the Administration of Justice Act 1985, s 9, by the Solicitors' Incorporated Practices Order 1991, SI 1991 No 2684, arts 4, 5, Sch 1.

20 Entrusting functions to others

Subject to any arrangements made by the Board under regulations 6, 7 or 8, nothing in these Regulations shall prevent a solicitor from entrusting any function under these Regulations to a partner of his or to a competent and responsible representative of his who is employed in his office or is otherwise under his immediate supervision.

Annotations
Modification: any reference to solicitor(s) etc modified to include references to bodies recognised under the Administration of Justice Act 1985, s 9, by the Solicitors' Incorporated Practices Order 1991, SI 1991 No 2684, arts 4, 5, Sch 1.

21 Extensions

(1) Subject to regulation 22(8), and except where regulation 6, 7 or 8 applies, where it appears to the solicitor that the cost of giving advice or assistance is likely to exceed the limit applicable under section 10(1) of the Act, he shall apply to the Area Director for an extension and shall furnish such information as may enable him to consider and determine that application.

(2) Where an Area Director receives an application in accordance with paragraph (1) he shall consider–

(a) whether it is reasonable for the advice and assistance to be given; and
(b) whether the estimate of the costs to be incurred in giving advice and assistance is reasonable.

(3) If the Area Director is satisfied that it is reasonable for the advice or assistance to be given and that the estimate of the costs to be incurred in giving it is reasonable, he shall grant an extension and shall prescribe such higher limit as he thinks fit and may limit the advice and assistance to such subject matter as he thinks fit.

Annotations
Modification: any reference to solicitor(s) etc modified to include references to bodies recognised under the Administration of Justice Act 1985, s 9, by the Solicitors' Incorporated Practices Order 1991, SI 1991 No 2684, arts 4, 5, Sch 1.
The Act: Legal Aid Act 1988.

22 Applications for approval of ABWOR

(1) The approval of the Board shall not be required for ABWOR to be given in accordance with arrangements made by the Board under regulation 7.

(2) The approval of the Board shall not be required for ABWOR to which Part III of the Act applies by virtue of regulation 7(1)(b), 7(1)(c), or 8 of the Scope Regulations.

(3) Subject to paragraph (1), where it appears to the solicitor that the client needs ABWOR to which Part III of the Act applies by virtue of regulation 7(1)(a), 7(2) or 9 of the Scope Regulations, he shall apply to the Area Director for approval.

(4) The application for approval shall be on a form approved by the Board and the solicitor shall supply such information as may enable the Area Director to consider and determine it.

(5) An application for approval[, except in respect of ABWOR to which Part III of the Act applies by virtue of regulation 9 of the Scope Regulations,] shall be refused unless it is shown that the client has reasonable grounds for taking, defending or being a party to the proceedings to which it relates.

(6) An application for approval may be refused if it appears unreasonable that approval should be granted in the particular circumstances of the case.

(7) The Area Director may grant an application for approval in whole or in part and may impose such conditions as to the conduct of the proceedings to which his approval relates as he thinks fit, and in particular it shall be a condition of every approval that the prior permission of the Area Director shall be required–

(a) to obtain a report or opinion of an expert; or
(b) to tender expert evidence; or
(c) to perform an act which is either unusual in its nature or involves unusually large expenditure;

unless such permission has been included in the grant of approval.

(8) An approval of ABWOR shall include an extension in respect of the matter to which it relates and, without prejudice to paragraph (7), the Area Director may prescribe such higher limit as he thinks fit.

Annotations

Para (5): words in square brackets added by SI 1990 No 486, reg 3(2).

Modification: any reference to solicitor(s) etc modified to include references to bodies recognised under the Administration of Justice Act 1985, s 9, by the Solicitors' Incorporated Practices Order 1991, SI 1991 No 2684, arts 4, 5, Sch 1.

The Act: Legal Aid Act 1988.

Scope Regulations: Legal Advice and Assistance (Scope) Regulations 1989, SI 1989 No 550.

23 Counsel

Where it appears to the solicitor that the proper conduct of proceedings in respect of which ABWOR has been granted under regulation 22 requires the instruction of counsel, he may apply to the Area Director for approval and the Area Director shall grant approval if he considers that the proper conduct of the proceedings requires counsel.

Annotations

Modification: any reference to solicitor(s) etc modified to include references to bodies recognised under the Administration of Justice Act 1985, s 9, by the Solicitors' Incorporated Practices Order 1991, SI 1991 No 2684, arts 4, 5, Sch 1.

24 Notification of approval of assistance by way of representation

Where ABWOR has been approved in respect of proceedings specified in regulation 7(1)(a) of the Scope Regulations and the client becomes a party to proceedings or is already a party to proceedings the solicitor shall as soon as practicable give notice of the approval to any other party to the proceedings and the court in which the proceedings are pending.

Annotations

Modification: any reference to solicitor(s) etc modified to include references to bodies recognised under the Administration of Justice Act 1985, s 9, by the Solicitors' Incorporated Practices Order 1991, SI 1991 No 2684, arts 4, 5, Sch 1.

Scope Regulations: Legal Advice and Assistance (Scope) Regulations 1989, SI 1989 No 550.

25 Withdrawal of approval of assistance by way of representation

(1) The Area Director shall withdraw approval of ABWOR granted under regulation 22 from such date as he considers appropriate where, as a result of information which has come to his knowledge, he considers that–

(a) in respect of proceedings specified in regulation 7(1)(a) of the Scope Regulations, the client no longer has reasonable grounds for taking, defending or being a party to the proceedings, or for continuing to do so; or

(b) the client has required the proceedings to be conducted unreasonably so as to incur an unjustifiable expense to the fund; or
(c) it is unreasonable in the particular circumstances that the client should continue to receive ABWOR.

(2) When approval of ABWOR is withdrawn, the Area Director shall notify the solicitor who shall forthwith–

(a) inform his client; and
(b) in respect of proceedings specified in regulation 7(1)(a) of the Scope Regulations, if proceedings have been commenced, send a copy of the notice to the court and to any other party to the proceedings to which the approval related.

(3) Withdrawal of approval shall not affect or prejudice any subsequent application for representation or for approval of ABWOR in respect of the same proceedings.

Annotations

Modification: any reference to solicitor(s) etc modified to include references to bodies recognised under the Administration of Justice Act 1985, s 9, by the Solicitors' Incorporated Practices Order 1991, SI 1991 No 2684, arts 4, 5, Sch 1.

Scope Regulations: Legal Advice and Assistance (Scope) Regulations 1989, SI 1989 No 550.

26 Appeals against refusal of ABWOR etc

(1) Where the Area Director–

(a) refuses an application under regulation 22 for the approval of ABWOR; or
(b) refuses authority in respect of any of the matters set out in paragraph (7)(a) to (c) of regulation 22; or
(c) withdraws approval of ABWOR under regulation 25;

the client may appeal to the appropriate area committee.

(2) An appeal shall be made by giving notice on a form approved by the Board within 14 days of the Area Director's decision to refuse the application or authority or withdraw approval.

27 Determination of appeals

(1) The area committee shall, on an appeal under regulation 26, reconsider the application for approval or authority or the circumstances set out in paragraph (1)(a) to (c) of regulation 25 and shall–

(a) dismiss the appeal; or
(b) in the case of an application for approval or authority, grant the application subject to such terms and conditions as the committee thinks fit; or
(c) in the case of a decision to withdraw approval, quash that decision.

(2) The decision of the area committee on an appeal shall be final and it shall give notice in writing of its decision, and the reasons for it, to the client and to any solicitor acting for him.

(3) Where the Area Director's decision to withdraw approval is quashed on appeal by the area committee, the solicitor shall, in respect of proceedings specified in regulation 7(1)(a) of the Scope regulations, notify any other party to the proceedings and the court, if any, in which the proceedings are pending.

Annotations

Modification: any reference to solicitor(s) etc modified to include references to bodies recognised under the Administration of Justice Act 1985, s 9, by the Solicitors' Incorporated Practices Order 1991, SI 1991 No 2684, arts 4, 5, Sch 1.

Scope Regulations: Legal Advice and Assistance (Scope) Regulations 1989, SI 1989 No 550.

28 Collection and refund of contributions

[(1) Where a client is required to pay contributions, the solicitor may collect them in weekly instalments or by such other periodic instalments as may be agreed between him and the client.

(1A) Where the total contribution is likely to exceed the cost of giving ABWOR, the solicitor shall not require the client to pay a sum higher than would be expected to defray his reasonable costs.]

(2) Where the reasonable costs of the [ABWOR] are less than any contribution made by the client, the solicitor shall refund the balance.

Annotations

Paras (1), (1A): substituted, for para (1) as originally enacted, by SI 1993 No 790, reg 8(a).

Para (2): word in square brackets substituted by SI 1993 No 790, reg 8(b).

Modification: any reference to solicitor(s) etc modified to include references to bodies recognised under the Administration of Justice Act 1985, s 9, by the Solicitors' Incorporated Practices Order 1991, SI 1991 No 2684, arts 4, 5, Sch 1.

29 Costs payable out of the fund

(1) Where the reasonable costs of the advice or assistance, including charges for disbursements, exceed any contribution payable by the client to the solicitor under section 9 of the Act together with the value of any charge arising under section 11 of the Act, the solicitor shall, except where paragraph (2) applies, submit a claim to the Area Director requesting payment of the deficiency.

(2) A claim for charges or fees properly chargeable for advice and assistance given in the circumstances specified in regulation 6 shall be made in accordance with the Legal Advice and Assistance at Police Stations (Remuneration) Regulations 1989.

(3) A claim for the costs of advice and assistance given in accordance with arrangements made by the Board under regulation 7 or 8 shall be made in accordance with the Legal Advice and Assistance (Duty Solicitor) (Remuneration) Regulations 1989.

(4) Where the claim does not relate to ABWOR in respect of which counsel has been instructed, the Area Director shall assess it and pay the assessed deficiency, if any, to the solicitor.

(5) Where the claim relates to ABWOR in respect of which counsel has

been instructed and the Area Director considers that the proper conduct of the proceedings required counsel, or the instruction of counsel has been approved under regulation 23, the Area Director shall–

(a) assess the solicitor's claim excluding counsel's fee, and pay the assessed deficiency, if any, to the solicitor, and
(b) assess counsel's fee and pay him the amount so allowed less the amount, if any, by which the value of any charge arising under section 11 of the Act together with the amount of any contribution payable by the client under section 9(6) of the Act exceeds the amount allowed to the solicitor on the assessment of his claim.

(6) Where the claim relates to ABWOR in respect of which counsel has been instructed without obtaining prior approval under regulation 23, and the Area Director considers that the proper conduct of the proceedings did not require counsel, the Area Director shall–

(a) determine the assessed deficiency on the basis that counsel had not been instructed and the solicitor had conducted the case on his own;
(b) allow the amount which it would have allowed counsel under paragraph (5) above and pay counsel what it would have paid him under that paragraph to the extent of the assessed deficiency; and
(c) pay the balance of the net assessed deficiency if any to the solicitor.

(7) If any solicitor or counsel is dissatisfied with any decision of the Area Director as to the payment of an assessed deficiency in the costs of advice and assistance, he may within 21 days of receipt of notification of that decision make written representations to the appropriate area committee; and that committee shall review the assessment of the Area Director whether by confirming, increasing or decreasing the amount assessed by the Area Director.

(8) A solicitor or counsel who is dissatisfied with the decision of an area committee on a review under paragraph (7) may within 21 days of receipt of notification of the decision apply to that committee to certify a point of principle of general importance.

(9) Where an area committee certifies a point of principle of general importance the solicitor or counsel may, within 21 days of receipt of notification of that certification, appeal in writing to a committee appointed by the Board against the decision of the area committee under paragraph (7).

(10) On an appeal under this regulation the committee appointed by the Board may reverse, affirm or amend the decision of the area committee under paragraph (7).

Annotations

Modification: any reference to solicitor(s) etc modified to include references to bodies recognised under the Administration of Justice Act 1985, s 9, by the Solicitors' Incorporated Practices Order 1991, SI 1991 No 2684, arts 4, 5, Sch 1.

The Act: Legal Aid Act 1988.

30 Basis of assessments

[(1) Subject to paragraphs (2)[, (3) and (4)], in any assessment or review of a claim for costs made under these Regulations the amount to be allowed shall be assessed under the Costs Regulations as if the work done was work done by a solicitor in criminal proceedings in a magistrates' court, save that–

(a) any reference in regulation 7 to regulation 54 of the General Regulations shall be construed as a reference to regulation 22(7) of these Regulations; < . . . >
(b) the words from 'in taking' to 'given or' in regulation 7(6) < . . . > shall not apply] [, and
(c) Schedule 6 to these Regulations shall apply instead of Part I of Schedule 1 to the Costs Regulations.]

[(2) Where the claim is in respect of ABWOR to which regulation 5 applies and which is given in unsocial hours (as defined in regulation 2 of the Legal Advice and Assistance at Police Stations (Remuneration) Regulations 1989), by a solicitor designated in accordance with arrangements made by the Board under regulation 6(3), the amount to be allowed under paragraph (1) shall be increased by one third.]

[(3) < . . . >]

[(4) Where advice and assistance is provided under a franchising contract, regulations 29 and 30 shall apply except to the extent that the contract makes different express provision.]

Annotations
Para (1): substituted by SI 1992 No 591, reg 4; first words in square brackets substituted by SI 1994 No 1823, reg 7(a); words omitted repealed, and sub-para (c) added, by SI 1995 No 949, reg 5(a)–(c).
Para (2): substituted by SI 1989 No 560, reg 2.
Para (3): added by SI 1991 No 2305, reg 3(b); revoked by SI 1995 No 949, reg 5(d).
Para (4): added by SI 1994 No 1823, reg 7(b).
Modification: any reference to solicitor(s) etc modified to include references to bodies recognised under the Administration of Justice Act 1985, s 9, by the Solicitors' Incorporated Practices Order 1991, SI 1991 No 2684, arts 4, 5, Sch 1.
Costs Regulations: Legal Aid in Criminal and Care Proceedings (Costs) Regulations 1989, SI 1989 No 343.
The Act: Legal Aid Act 1988.
Scope Regulations: Legal Advice and Assistance (Scope) Regulations 1989, SI 1989 No 550.

[30A] [Payment on account]

[(1) A solicitor acting for a client who is in receipt of ABWOR may apply to the Area Director for the payment of a sum on account of disbursements incurred or about to be incurred in connection with the proceedings to which the approval of ABWOR relates.

[(1A) Where ABWOR is provided under a franchising contract, the franchisee may apply to the Area Director for the payment of a sum on account of his charges and fees.

(1B) Where advice and assistance (other than ABWOR) is provided under a franchising contract, the franchisee may apply to the Area Director for the payment of a sum on account of his costs.]

(2) Where a payment is made under this regulation, then notwithstanding that there is no deficiency, the solicitor shall, at the conclusion of the case, submit

to the Area Director a statement of his costs, the amount of any contribution payable and the value of any charge arising under section 11 of the Act.

(3) In the event of any payment under this regulation proving to be greater than the assessed deficiency (if any) found to be due, the solicitor shall, on demand, repay the excess to the fund and, where the assessed deficiency exceeds any payment made under this regulation, the balance shall be paid from the fund.

(4) In this regulation 'deficiency' and 'assessed deficiency' shall have the meanings assigned by regulation 29.]

Annotations

This regulation was added by SI 1992 No 591, reg 5.

Paras (1A), (1B): added by SI 1994 No 1823, reg 8.

Modification: any reference to solicitor(s) etc modified to include references to bodies recognised under the Administration of Justice Act 1985, s 9, by the Solicitors' Incorporated Practices Order 1991, SI 1991 No 2684, arts 4, 5, Sch 1.

The Act: Legal Aid Act 1988.

31 Recovery of costs

(1) Where any sum is payable to the client by virtue of an order for costs made in connection with proceedings for which ABWOR has been approved under regulation 22, the sum shall be paid to the clerk to the justices, who shall pay it to the Board; and only the clerk to the justices shall be able to give a good discharge for it.

(2) The Board shall, except where a payment has been made under paragraph (3), pay to the solicitor such portion of the sum paid to the Board under paragraph (1) as corresponds to the charge created in his favour on that sum by section 11(2)(a) of the Act, and pay any balance to the client.

(3) The Board may in addition to any payment under regulation 29, pay the solicitor a sum not greater than the sum payable to the Board under paragraph (1) and where such a payment is made, the Board shall require the solicitor to assign his charge under section 11(2)(a) of the Act to the Board.

Annotations

Modification: any reference to solicitor(s) etc modified to include references to bodies recognised under the Administration of Justice Act 1985, s 9, by the Solicitors' Incorporated Practices Order 1991, SI 1991 No 2684, arts 4, 5, Sch 1.

The Act: Legal Aid Act 1988.

32 Exceptions to charge on property recovered or preserved

The provisions of section 11(2)(b) of the Act shall not apply to the matters specified in Schedule 4.

Annotations

The Act: Legal Aid Act 1988.

33 Authority not to enforce the charge

Where in the opinion of the solicitor–

(a) it would cause grave hardship or distress to the client to enforce the charge on any money or property recovered or preserved for him, or
(b) the charge on any property recovered or preserved could be enforced only with unreasonable difficulty because of the nature of the property,

the solicitor may apply to the appropriate area committee for authority not to enforce, either wholly or in part, the charge and, if the committee gives authority, any deficiency in the solicitor's costs shall be computed as if section 11(2)(b) of the Act did not apply to that money or property or to such part of it as the committee may have authorised.

Annotations
Modification: any reference to solicitor(s) etc modified to include references to bodies recognised under the Administration of Justice Act 1985, s 9, by the Solicitors' Incorporated Practices Order 1991, SI 1991 No 2684, arts 4, 5, Sch 1.
The Act: Legal Aid Act 1988.

34 Costs awarded against a client

Where proceedings have been concluded in which a client is or was in receipt of ABWOR and an order for costs has been made against him in those proceedings, the amount of his liability for costs (if any) shall be determined in accordance with Schedule 5.

35 Costs of successful unassisted parties out of the fund

Before making any order under section 13 of the Act, the Court shall afford the Area director who dealt with the application under regulation 22 an opportunity to make representations.

Annotations
The Act: Legal Aid Act 1988.

36 False statements etc

Where a client has wilfully failed to comply with the provisions of these Regulations as to the information to be furnished by him or, in furnishing such information, has knowingly made a false statement or false representation, and after the failure occurred or the false statement or false representation was made the client received advice or assistance, the appropriate area committee may declare that the advice or assistance so given was not given under the Act and these Regulations and, if it does, shall so inform the client and the solicitor; and thereafter the Board shall be entitled to recover from the client any sums paid out of the fund in respect of the advice and assistance so given.

Annotations
Modification: any reference to solicitor(s) etc modified to include references to bodies recognised under the Administration of Justice Act 1985, s 9, by the Solicitors' Incorporated Practices Order 1991, SI 1991 No 2684, arts 4, 5, Sch 1.
The Act: Legal Aid Act 1988.

[37] [Computation of time]

[(1) Where, under these Regulations, an act is required to be done within a specified period after or from a specified date, the period of time so fixed starts immediately after that date.

(2) The period within which an act is required or authorised to be done under these Regulations may, if the Area Director thinks fit, be extended and any such period may be extended although the application for extension is not made until after the expiration of the period.]

Annotations

This regulation was added by SI 1992 No 591, reg 6.

SCHEDULE 1

Regulation 2

Regulations revoked	*References*
The Legal Advice and Assistance Regulations (No 2) 1980.	SI 1980/1898.
The Legal Advice and Assistance (Amendment) Regulations 1982.	SI 1982/1592.
The Legal Advice and Assistance (Amendment) (No 2) Regulations 1983.	SI 1983/470.
The Legal Advice and Assistance (Financial Conditions) Regulations 1983.	SI 1983/618.
The Legal Advice and Assistance (Amendment) (No 3) Regulations 1983.	SI 1983/1142.
The Legal Advice and Assistance (Financial Conditions) (No 2) Regulations 1983.	SI 1983/1784.
The Legal Advice and Assistance (Prospective Cost) (No 2) Regulations 1983.	SI 1983/1785.
The Legal Advice and Assistance (Amendment) (No 5) Regulations 1983.	SI 1983/1935.
The Legal Advice and Assistance (Amendment) (No 6) Regulations 1983.	SI 1983/1963.
The Legal Advice and Assistance (Amendment) Regulations 1984.	SI 1984/241.
The Legal Advice and Assistance (Amendment) (No 2) Regulations 1984.	SI 1984/637.
The Legal Advice and Assistance (Amendment) Regulations 1985.	SI 1985/1491.
The Legal Advice and Assistance (Prospective Cost) Regulations 1985.	SI 1985/1840.
The Legal Advice and Assistance (Amendment) (No 2) Regulations 1985.	SI 1985/1879.
The Legal Advice and Assistance (Amendment) Regulations 1986.	SI 1986/275.
The Legal Advice and Assistance (Financial Conditions) (No 2) Regulations 1987.	SI 1987/396.
The Legal Advice and Assistance (Financial Conditions) Regulations 1988.	SI 1988/666.

Regulations revoked	*References*
The Legal Advice and Assistance (Financial Conditions) (No 2) Regulations 1988.	SI 1988/459.
The Legal Advice and Assistance (Amendment) Regulations 1988.	SI 1988/461.

SCHEDULE 2 Assessment of Resources

Regulation 13(1)

1 In this Schedule, unless the context otherwise requires–

'capital' means the amount or value of every resource of a capital nature;
'income' means the total income from all sources which the person concerned has received or may reasonably expect to receive in respect of the seven days up to and including the date of his application;
'the person concerned' means the person whose disposable capital and disposable income are to be assessed.

2 The provisions of this Schedule apply to a man and a woman who are living with each other in the same household as husband and wife as they apply to the parties to a marriage.

3 Any question arising under this Schedule shall be decided by the solicitor to whom the client has applied and that solicitor, in deciding any such question, shall have regard to any guidance which may from time to time be given by the Board as to the application of this Schedule.

4 The disposable capital and disposable income of the person concerned shall be the capital and income as assessed by the solicitor after deducting any sums which are to be left out of account or for which allowance is to be made under the provisions of this Schedule.

5 The resources of any person who, under section 26(3) and (4) of the Social Security Act 1986 is liable to maintain a child or who usually contributes substantially to a child's maintenance, or who has care and control of the child, not being a person who has such care and control by reason of any contract or for some temporary purpose, may be treated as the resources of the child, if, having regard to all the circumstances, including the age and resources of the child and to any conflict of interest it appears just and equitable to do so.

[6 If it appears to the solicitor that the person concerned has, with intent to reduce the amount of his disposable capital or disposable income, whether for the purpose of making himself eligible for advice and assistance, reducing his liability to pay a contribution in respect of the costs of advice and assistance or otherwise–

(a) directly or indirectly deprived himself of any resources; or
(b) converted any part of his resources into resources which are to be left out of account wholly or partly;

the resources of which he has so deprived himself or which he has so converted shall be treated as part of his resources or as not so converted as the case may be.]

7 (1) In computing the capital and income of the person concerned, there shall be left out of account the value of the subject matter of any claim in respect of which he is seeking advice or assistance.

(2) In computing the capital and income of the person concerned, the resources of any spouse of his shall be treated as his resources unless–

(i) the spouse has a contrary interest in the matter in respect of which he is seeking advice and assistance, or
(ii) the person concerned and his spouse are living separate and apart, or
(iii) in all the circumstances of the case it would be inequitable or impractical to do so.

8 In computing the capital of the person concerned –

(a) there shall be left out of account the value of the main or only dwelling in which he resides and the value of his household furniture and effects, of his clothes and of tools and implements of his trade;
[(aa) the value of the main or only dwelling in which he resides shall be taken to be the amount for which that interest could be sold in the open market, subject to the following rules:–

(i) the amount to be allowed in respect of any mortgage debt or heritable security shall not exceed £100,000;
(ii) the first £100,000 of the value of that interest, after the application of the rule in paragraph (i), shall be disregarded;]

(b) where the person concerned resides in more than one dwelling in which he has an interest there shall be taken into account in respect of the value to him of any interest in a dwelling which is not the main dwelling any sum which may be obtained by borrowing money on the security thereof; [the amount for which any interest in a dwelling which is not the main dwelling could be sold in the open market; provided that the total amount to be allowed in respect of any mortgage debts or heritable securities over all such dwellings, together with any amount allowed under paragraph (AA)(i) in respect of the main dwelling, shall not exceed £100,000;]
(c) where the person concerned has living with him one or more of the following persons, namely, a spouse whose resources are required to be aggregated with his, a dependent child or a dependent relative wholly or substantially maintained by him, a deduction shall be made of £335 in respect of the first person, £200 in respect of the second and £100 in respect of each further person.

9 In computing the income of the person concerned–

(a) there shall be left out of account–

(i) any income tax paid or payable on income treated under the provisions of this Schedule as his income;
(ii) contributions estimated to have been paid under the Social Security Acts 1975–1988 or any scheme made under those Acts during or in respect of the seven days up to and including the date of the application for advice and assistance;

(b) there shall be a deduction in respect of the spouse of the person concerned, if the spouses are living together, in respect of the maintenance of any dependent child and in respect of the maintenance of any dependent relative of the person concerned, being (in either of such cases) a member of his or her household, at the following rates–

(i) in the case of a spouse at a rate equivalent to [the difference between the income support allowance for a couple where both members are aged not less than 18 (which is specified in column 2 of paragraph 1(3)(c) of Schedule 2 Part I of the Income Support (General) Regulations 1987), and the allowance for a single person aged not less than 25, (which is specified in column 2 of paragraph 1(1)(e) of Schedule 2 Part I of those Regulations)];

(ii) in the case of a dependent child or a dependent relative, at a rate equivalent to < . . . > the amount specified for the time being in paragraph 2 of Part I of Schedule 2 to the Income Support (General) Regulations 1987 appropriate to the age of the child or relative.

[9A In computing disposable income the following payments made under the Social Security Contributions and Benefits Act 1992 shall be disregarded:

(a) disability living allowance;
(b) attendance allowance paid under section 64 or Schedule 8 paragraphs 4 or 7(2);
(c) constant attendance allowance paid under section 104 as an increase to a disablement pension; or
(d) any payment made out of the social fund.]

10 If the person concerned is making bona fide payments for the maintenance of a spouse who is living apart, of a former spouse, of a child or relative who is not (in any such case) a member of the household of the person concerned, there shall be a deduction of such payment as was or will be made in respect of the seven days up to and including the date of the application for advice and assistance.

11 it appears to the solicitor that there has been some error or mistake in the assessment of the disposable income, disposable capital or < . . . > contribution of the person concerned, he may reassess the disposable income or disposable capital or < . . . > contribution or, as the case may be, amend the assessment and in the latter case the amended assessment shall for all purposes be substituted for the original assessment.

Annotations

Para 6: substituted by SI 1990 No 486, reg 3(3).

Para 8: in para (a) words underlined prospectively revoked with savings by SI 1996 No 435, reg 4(a), as from 1 June 1996; sub-para (aa) prospectively added with savings by SI 1996 No 435, reg 4(b), as from 1 June 1996; in sub-para (b) words underlined prospectively repealed with savings and subsequent words in square brackets prospectively substituted with savings by SI 1996 No 435, reg 4(c), as from 1 June 1996; for savings see reg 3 thereof.

Para 9: in sub-para (b) words in square brackets substituted, and words omitted revoked, by SI 1993 No 790, reg 9.

Para 9A: added by SI 1993 No 790, reg 10.

Para 11: words omitted revoked by SI 1993 No 790, reg 11.

Modification: any reference to solicitor(s) etc modified to include references to bodies recognised under the Administration of Justice Act 1985, s 9, by the Solicitors' Incorporated Practices Order 1991, SI 1991 No 2684, arts 4, 5, Sch 1.

SCHEDULE 4 EXCEPTIONS TO CHARGE ON PROPERTY RECOVERED OR PRESERVED

Regulation 32

The provisions of section 11(2)(b) of the Act shall not apply to–

(a) any periodical payment of maintenance, which for this purpose means money or money's worth paid towards the support of a spouse, former spouse, child or any other person for whose support the payer has previously been responsible or has made payments;

(b) any property recovered or preserved for the client as a result of advice and assistance given to him by the solicitor which comprises the client's main or only dwelling, or any household furniture or tools of trade;

(c) (without prejudice to (b) above) the first £2,500 of any money or of the value of any property recovered or preserved by virtue of–

(i) an order made or deemed to be made, under the provisions of section 23(1)(c) or (f), 23(2), 24, 27(6)(c) or (f), or 35 of the Matrimonial Causes Act 1973;

(ii) an order made, or deemed to be made, under the provisions of section 2 or 6 of the Inheritance (Provision for Family and Dependants) Act 1975;

(iii) an order made, or deemed to be made, under section 17 of the Married Women's Property Act 1882; or

(iv) an order made, or deemed to be made, under the provisions of section 4(2)(b) of the Affiliation Proceedings Act 1957; or

(v) an order for the payment of a lump sum made, or deemed to be made, under the provisions of section 60 of the Magistrates' Courts Act 1980; or

(vi) an order made, or deemed to be made, under the provisions of section 2(1)(b) or (d), 6(1) or (5), 11(2)(b) or (3)(b) or 20(2) of the Domestic Proceedings and Magistrates' Courts Act 1978; or

(vii) an order made, or deemed to be made, under section 9(2)(b), 10(1)(b)(ii), 11(b)(ii) of the Guardianship of Minors Act 1971 or under section 11B, 11C or 11D of that Act; or

(viii) an order made, or deemed to be made, under section 34(1)(c) or 35 of the Children Act 1975; or

(ix) an agreement which has the same effect as an order made, or deemed to be made, under any of the provisions specified in this sub-paragraph;

(d) one-half of any redundancy payment within the meaning of Part VI of the Employment Protection (Consolidation) Act 1978 recovered or preserved for the client;

(e) any payment of money in accordance with an order made under section 136 of the Employment Protection (Consolidation) Act 1978 by the Employment Appeal Tribunal;

(f) any sum, payment or benefit which, by virtue of any provision of or made under an Act of Parliament, cannot be assigned or charged.

Annotations

Modification: any reference to solicitor(s) etc modified to include references to bodies recognised under the Administration of Justice Act 1985, s 9, by the Solicitors' Incorporated Practices Order 1991, SI 1991 No 2684, arts 4, 5, Sch 1.

The Act: Legal Aid Act 1988.

SCHEDULE 5 COSTS AWARDED AGAINST A CLIENT

Regulation 34

1 No costs attributable to the period during which a client was in receipt of ABWOR shall be recoverable from him until the court has determined the amount of his liability in accordance with section 12 of the Act:

Provided that where the ABWOR does not relate to or has been withdrawn so that it no longer relates to the whole of the proceedings the court shall nevertheless make a determination in respect of that part of the proceedings to which the approval of ABWOR relates.

2 The court may, if it thinks fit, refer to the clerk to the justices for investigation any question of fact relevant to the determination, requiring him to report his findings on that question to the court.

3 determining the amount of the client's liability his dwelling-house, clothes, household furniture and the tools and implements of his trade shall be left out of account to the like extent as they are left out of account by the solicitor in determining the client's disposable capital.

4 person, not being himself a client, who is a party to proceedings to which the client is a party may, at any time before the judgment, lodge with the clerk to the justices an affidavit exhibiting thereto a statement setting out the rate of his own income and amount of his own capital and any other facts relevant to the determination of his means in accordance with section 12 of the Act and shall serve a copy thereof together with the exhibit upon the client's solicitor and such affidavit and exhibit shall be evidence of the facts stated therein.

5 The court may, if it thinks fit, order the client and any party who has filed an affidavit in accordance with paragraph (4) of this Schedule to attend for oral examination as to his means and as to any other facts relevant to the determination of the amount of the client's liability and may permit any party to give evidence and call witnesses thereon.

6 The court may direct–

(a) that payment under the order for costs shall be limited to such amount payable in instalments or otherwise as the court thinks reasonable having regard to all the circumstances; or
(b) where the court thinks it reasonable for payment under sub-paragraph (a) not to be made immediately, that payment under the order for costs be suspended either until such date as the court may determine or sine die.

7 The party in whose favour an order is made may within 6 years from the date thereof apply to the court for the order to be varied on the grounds that–

(a) material additional information as to the client's means, being information which could not have been obtained by that party with reasonable diligence at the time the order was made, is available; or
(b) there has been a change in the client's circumstances since the date of the order,

and on any such application the order may be varied as the court thinks fit but save as aforesaid the determination of the court shall be final.

8 Where an order for costs is made against a client who is concerned in the proceedings solely in a representative, fiduciary or official capacity, he shall have the benefit of section 12(1) of the Act and his personal resources shall not (unless there is reason to the contrary) be taken into account for that purpose, but regard shall be had to the value of the property or estate, or the amount of the fund out of which he is entitled to be indemnified.

9 Where a client is a child, his means for the purpose of determining his liability for costs under section 12(1) of the Act shall be taken as including the means of any person whose disposable income and disposable capital has, by virtue of Schedule 2 been included in assessing the child's resources.

10 Where an order for costs is made against a next friend or guardian ad litem of a client who is a child or patient, he shall have the benefit of section 12(1) of the Act in like manner as it applies to a client, and the means of the next friend or guardian ad litem shall be taken as being the means of the child as defined in paragraph 9 or, as the case may be, of the patient.

Annotations

Modification: any reference to solicitor(s) etc modified to include references to bodies recognised under the Administration of Justice Act 1985, s 9, by the Solicitors' Incorporated Practices Order 1991, SI 1991 No 2684, arts 4, 5, Sch 1.

The Act: Legal Aid Act 1988.

SCHEDULE 6 [FEES FOR ABWOR IN MENTAL HEALTH REVIEW TRIBUNALS [AND BEFORE THE PAROLE BOARD]]

Regulation 30(3)

[1 Subject to paragraphs 2, 3 and 4, the amount to be allowed shall be assessed at the following prescribed rates:

Class of work	*Rate*
Preparation	£43.25 per hour – (£45.75 per hour for a fee-earner whose offfice is situated within legal aid area 1)
Advocacy	£54.50 per hour
Attendance at court where counsel assigned	£29.50 per hour
Travelling and waiting	£24.25 per hour
Routine letters written and routine telephone calls	£3.35 per item – (£3.50 per item for a fee-earner whose office is situated within legal aid area 1)

[*Class of work*	*Rate*
Preparation	£44.00 per hour – (£46.50 per hour for a fee-earner whose office is situated within legal aid area 1)
Advocacy	£55.25 per hour
Attendance at court where counsel assigned	£30.00 per hour
Travelling and waiting	£24.50 per hour
Routine letters written and routine telephone calls	£3.40 per item – (£3.55 per item for a fee-earner whose office is situated within legal aid area 1)]

2 Subject to paragraph 4, where advice and assistance is provided by a franchisee, the following rates shall apply instead of those contained in paragraph 1:

Class of work	Rate
Preparation	£44.25 per hour – (£46.75 per hour for a fee-earner whose offfice is situated within legal aid area 1)
Advocacy	£55.50 per hour
Attendance at court where counsel assigned	£30.00 per hour
Travelling and waiting	£24.75 per hour
Routine letters written and routine telephone calls	£3.45 per item – (£3.60 per item for a fee-earner whose offfice is situated within legal aid area 1)

[Class of work	Rate
Preparation	£45.50 per hour – (£48.25 per hour for a fee-earner whose office is situated within legal aid area 1)
Advocacy	£57.25 per hour
Attendance at court where counsel assigned	£31.00 per hour
Travelling and waiting	£25.50 per hour
Routine letters written and routine telephone calls	£3.55 per item – (£3.70 per item for a fee-earner whose office is situated within legal aid area 1)]

3 Subject to paragraph 4, where the claim is in respect of ABWOR to which Part III of the Act applies by virtue of regulation 9(a) or (c) of the Scope Regulations, the following rates shall apply instead of those contained in paragraph 1:

Class of work	Rate
Preparation	£52.00 per hour – (£55.50 per hour for a fee-earner whose offfice is situated within legal aid area 1)
Advocacy	£63.00 per hour
Attendance at court where counsel assigned	£29.50 per hour
Travelling and waiting	£24.25 per hour
Routine letters written and routine telephone calls	£3.70 per item

[Class of work	Rate
Preparation	£52.75 per hour – (£56.25 per hour for a fee-earner whose office is situated within legal aid area 1)
Advocacy	£64.00 per hour
Attendance at court where counsel assigned	£30.00 per hour
Travelling and waiting	£24.50 per hour
Routine letters written and routine telephone calls	£3.75 per item]

4 Where the claim is in respect of ABWOR to which Part III of the Act applies by virtue of regulation 9(a) or (c) of the Scope Regulations and the work is done by a franchisee, the following rates shall apply instead of those contained in paragraphs 1, 2 and 3:

Class of work	*Rate*
Preparation	£53.00 per hour – (£56.50 per hour for a fee-earner whose offfice is situated within legal aid area 1)
Advocacy	£64.25 per hour
Attendance at court where counsel assigned	£30.00 per hour
Travelling and waiting	£24.75 per hour
Routine letters written and routine telephone calls	£3.80 per item

[Class of work	*Rate*
Preparation	£54.50 per hour – (£58.25 per hour for a fee-earner whose office is situated within legal aid area 1)
Advocacy	£66.25 per hour
Attendance at court where counsel assigned	£31.00 per hour
Travelling and waiting	£24.75 per hour
Routine letters written and routine telephone calls	£3.90 per item]

5 In paragraphs 1 to 4, 'legal aid area' means an area specified by the Board under regulation 4(1) of the Civil Legal Aid (General) Regulations 1989, and legal aid area 1 means the area so numbered by the Board.]

Annotations

Cross-heading: words 'and Before the Parole Board' added by SI 1992 No 2654, reg 2(2).
This Schedule was added by SI 1991 No 2305, reg 4.
This Schedule was substituted by SI 1995 No 949, reg 6, Schedule.
Paras 1–4: Tables underlined revoked with savings and subsequent Tables in square brackets substituted with savings by SI 1996 No 641, reg 4; for savings see reg 2(2) thereof.

Appendix E3

Legal Advice and Assistance (Scope) Regulations 1989

1989 No. 550
Made - - - 23rd March 1989

PART I GENERAL

1 Citation and Commencement

These Regulations may be cited as the Legal Advice and Assistance (Scope) Regulations 1989 and shall come into force on 1st April 1989.

2 Interpretation

In these Regulations, unless the context otherwise requires:–

'ABWOR' means assistance by way of representation;
'the Act' means the Legal Aid Act 1988;
< . . . >
'client' means a person seeking or receiving advice or assistance or on whose behalf advice or assistance is sought;
'conditional sale agreement' has the meaning assigned to it in section 189 of the Consumer Credit Act 1974;
['Controller' means a person appointed by the Secretary of State pursuant to section 85(1)(b) of the Criminal Justice Act 1991;]
'conveyancing services' has the meaning assigned to it in section 11 of the Administration of Justice Act 1985;
['discretionary life prisoner' has the meaning assigned by section 34(1) of the Criminal Justice Act 1991;
'governor' has the meaning assigned by rule 99 of the Prison Rules 1964;]
'mental disorder' has the meaning assigned to it in section 1 of the Mental Health Act 1983;
['the Parole Board' has the meaning assigned by section 32 of the Criminal Justice Act 1991;]
'rental purchase agreement' has the meaning assigned to it in section 88 of the Housing Act 1980;
'will' has the meaning assigned to it in section 1 of the Wills Act 1837;

Annotations
Definition omitted revoked, and definitions 'discretionary life prisoner', 'governor' and 'the Parole Board' added, by SI 1992 No 2847, reg 2; definition 'Controller' added by SI 1994 No 2768, reg 3.

PART II EXCLUSIONS FROM PART III OF THE ACT

3 Conveyancing Services

(1) Subject to paragraphs (2) and (3, advice and assistance consisting of conveyancing services are excluded from Part III of the Act.

(2) Paragraph (1) does not exclude from Part III of the Act advice or assistance relating to a rental purchase agreement or a conditional sale agreement for the sale of land.

(3) Paragraph (1) does not exclude from Part III of the Act advice or assistance consisting of such conveyancing services as are necessary in order to give effect to an order of the court or, in proceedings under the Matrimonial Causes Act 1973 or the Matrimonial and Family Proceedings Act 1984, the terms of an agreement.

Annotations
The Act: Legal Aid Act 1988.

4 Wills

(1) Except as provided by paragraph (2), advice and assistance in the making of wills are excluded from Part III of the Act.

(2) Advice and assistance in the making of a will are not excluded by paragraph (1) from Part III of the Act where they are given to a client who is–

(a) aged 70 or over; or
(b) blind (or partially sighted), deaf (or hard of hearing), or dumb, or who suffers from mental disorder of any description, or who is substantially and permanently handicapped by illness, injury or congenital deformity; or
(c) a parent or guardian within the meaning of section 87 of the Child Care Act 1980 of a person to whom any description in (b) applies, where the client wishes to provide in the will for that person; or
(d) the mother or father of a minor who is living with the client, where the client is not living with the minor's other parent, and the client wishes to appoint a guardian for that minor under section 4 of the Guardianship of Minors Act 1971.

Annotations
The Act: Legal Aid Act 1988.

5 Transition

Where advice or assistance has been given before these Regulations come into force, nothing in this Part shall affect further advice or assistance given in relation to the same matter.

PART III ABWOR

6 Application of Part III of the Act to ABWOR

Part III of the Act does not apply to ABWOR except as provided in this Part.

Annotations
The Act: Legal Aid Act 1988.

7 Proceedings in Magistrates' Courts

(1) Part III of the Act applies to ABWOR given –

(a) to a client for the purposes of the proceedings in magistrates' courts specified in the Schedule;
(b) at a hearing in any proceedings in a magistrates' court to a party who is not receiving and has not been refused representation in connection with those proceedings, where the court–

(i) is satisfied that the hearing should proceed on the same day;
(ii) is satisfied that that party would not otherwise be represented; and
(iii) requests a solicitor who is within the precincts of the court for purposes other than the provision of ABWOR in accordance with this sub-paragraph, or approves a proposal from such a solicitor, that he provide that party with ABWOR; or

(c) to a person in connection with an application for a warrant of further detention, or for an extension of such a warrant, made in respect of that person to a magistrates' court under section 43 or 44 of the Police and Criminal Evidence Act 1984.

(2) Subject to paragraph (3), Part III of the Act also applies, in criminal proceedings in magistrates' courts where the client has not previously received and is not otherwise receiving representation or ABWOR in connection with the same proceedings, to ABWOR given to a client–

(a) in making an application for bail;
(b) at an appearance in court where the client is in custody and wishes the case to be concluded at that appearance, unless the solicitor who is advising him considers that the case should be adjourned in the interests of justice or of the client;
(c) who is before the court as a result of a failure to obey an order of the court, where such failure may lead to his being at risk of imprisonment;
(d) who is not in custody and who in the opinion of the solicitor requires ABWOR.

(3) Paragraph (2) does not apply to committal proceedings [the hearing of oral representations supporting or opposing an application for dismissal under section 6 of the Magistrates' Courts Act 1980], to proceedings in which the client pleads not guilty, nor, unless the solicitor considers the circumstances to be exceptional, to proceedings in connection with a non-imprisonable offence.

(4) Part III also applies to ABWOR given to a defendant in proceedings in a magistrates' court where the defendant is before the court as a result of a

failure to pay a fine or other sum which he was ordered on conviction to pay, and such failure may lead to his being at risk of imprisonment.

Annotations

Para (3): words underlined revoked with savings and subsequent words in square brackets substituted with savings by SI 1995 No 1987, reg 3; for savings see reg 2 thereof.

Modification: any reference to solicitor(s) etc modified to include references to bodies recognised under the Administration of Justice Act 1985, s 9, by the Solicitors' Incorporated Practices Order 1991, SI 1991 No 2684, arts 4, 5, Sch 1.

The Act: Legal Aid Act 1988.

8 Proceedings in county courts

Part III of the Act applies to ABWOR given by a solicitor at a hearing in any proceedings in a county court to a party who is not receiving and has not been refused representation in connection with those proceedings, where the court–

(i) is satisfied that the hearing should proceed on the same day;
(ii) is satisfied that that party would not otherwise be represented; and
(iii) requests a solicitor who is within the precincts of the court for purposes other than the provision of ABWOR in accordance with this regulation, or approves a proposal from such a solicitor, that he provide that party with ABWOR.

Annotations

Modification: any reference to solicitor(s) etc modified to include references to bodies recognised under the Administration of Justice Act 1985, s 9, by the Solicitors' Incorporated Practices Order 1991, SI 1991 No 2684, arts 4, 5, Sch 1.

The Act: Legal Aid Act 1988.

9 Other Proceedings

Part III of the Act applies to ABWOR given–

(a) to a person in proceedings before a Mental Health Review Tribunal under the Mental Health Act 1983 whose case or whose application to the Tribunal is or is to be the subject of the proceedings;
(b) [(b) to a prisoner who has been permitted by the governor [or controller] to be legally represented in proceedings before him;
(c) to a discretionary life prisoner whose case is referred to the Parole Board under sections 34(4) or (5) or 39(4) of the Criminal Justice Act 1991.]

Annotations

Para (b): substituted, together with para (c), for para (b) as originally enacted, by SI 1992 No 2874, reg 3; words in square brackets added by SI 1994 No 2768, reg 4.

Para (c): substituted, together with para (b), for para (b) as originally enacted, by SI 1992 No 2874, reg 3.

The Act: Legal Aid Act 1988.

SCHEDULE Proceedings in Magistrates' Courts in which ABWOR is Available

Regulation 7(1)(a)

1 In this Schedule 'proceedings in a magistrates' court' includes giving notice of appeal or applying for a case to be stated within the ordinary time for so doing, and matters preliminary thereto.

2 The proceedings in which Part III of the Act applies to ABWOR under regulation 7(1)(a) are proceedings–

for or in relation to an affiliation order within the meaning of the Affiliation Proceedings Act 1957;

(a) for or in relation to an order under [the Matrimonial Proceedings (Magistrates' Courts) Act 1960 or] Part I of the Domestic Proceedings and Magistrates' Courts Act 1978;

(b) under the Guardianship of Minors Act 1971 and 1973;

(c) under section 43 of the National Assistance Act 1948, section 22 of the Maintenance Orders Act 1950, section 4 of the Maintenance Orders Act 1958, section 18 of the Supplementary Benefits Act 1976, or section 24 of the Social Security Act 1986;

(d) in relation to an application for leave of the court to remove a child from a person's custody under section 27 or 28 of the Adoption Act 1976 or proceedings in which the making of an order under Part II or section 29 or 55 of the Adoption Act 1976 is opposed by any party to the proceedings;

(e) under Part I of the Maintenance Orders (Reciprocal Enforcement) Act 1972 relating to a maintenance order made by a court of a country outside the United Kingdom;

(f) under Part II of the Children Act 1975;

(g) [(h) under section 10A of the Fire Precautions Act 1971].

Annotations

Para 2: words in square brackets in sub-para (b) added, and sub-para (h) added, by SI 1990 No 1477, reg 2.

Appendix E4

Legal Aid in Criminal and Care Proceedings (Costs) Regulations 1989

1989 No. 343
Made – – – 3rd March 1989

1 Citation, commencement, revocations and transitional provisions

(1) These Regulations may be cited as the Legal Aid in Criminal and Care Proceedings (Costs) Regulations 1989 and shall come into force on 1st April 1989.

(2) Subject to paragraph (3) < . . . >

(3) These Regulations shall apply for the determination of costs which are payable in respect of work done on or after 1st April 1989 and costs payable in respect of work done before that date shall be determined as if these Regulations had not been made.

(4) Where a review under regulation 12 relates to a claim made before 1st June 1989, regulation 13(1) and (2) shall not apply and the solicitor may appeal in writing within 21 days of receipt of notification of the decision on the review to a committee appointed by the Board.

Annotations
Para (2): words omitted revoke SI 1988 No 423 and SI 1988 No 2302.
Modification: any reference to solicitor(s) etc modified to include references to bodies recognised under the Administration of Justice Act 1985, s 9, by the Solicitors' Incorporated Practices Order 1991, SI 1991 No 2684, arts 4, 5, Sch 1.

2 Interpretation

(1) In these Regulations, unless the context otherwise requires,–

'the Act' means the Legal Aid Act 1988;
'appropriate authority' has the meaning assigned by regulation 3;
'area committee' has the meaning assigned to it by regulation 4 of the Civil Legal Aid (General) Regulations 1989;
'appropriate area committee' means the area committee in whose area is situated the magistrates' court at which a legal aid order was made;
['contract' means a contract entered into by the Board with other persons or bodies pursuant to its powers under section 4 of the Act;]
'costs' means, in the case of a solicitor, the fees and disbursements payable under section 25 of the Act and, in the case of counsel, the fees payable under that section;

'counsel' means counsel assigned under the legal aid order;
'Court of Appeal' means the criminal division of the Court of Appeal or the Courts-Martial Appeal Court as the case may be;
'determining officer' means an officer appointed under regulation 3(2);
'disbursements' means travelling and witness expenses and other out of pocket expenses incurred by a fee-earner in giving legal aid;
'fee-earner' means a solicitor, a legal executive or any clerk who regularly does work for which it is appropriate to make a direct charge to a client;
['franchisee' means a person or body (other than the Board) acting under the terms of a franchising contract;]
'legal aid' and 'legal aid order' have the meanings respectively assigned by the General Regulations;
'legal aid area' has the meaning assigned by paragraph 1(2) of Schedule 1 Part I;
'legal executive' means a fellow of the Institute of Legal Executives;
'registrar' means the registrar of criminal appeals or the registrar of the Courts-Martial Appeal Court, as the case may be;
'the General Regulations' means the Legal Aid in Criminal and Care Proceedings (General) Regulations 1989;
'solicitor' means a solicitor assigned under the legal aid order;
'trial judge' means the judge who presided at the hearing at which the defendant was substantively dealt with and in respect of which the costs are payable;
'taxing master' means a taxing master of the Supreme Court;
['wasted costs order' has the meaning assigned to it by regulation 3A of the Costs in Criminal Cases (General) Regulations 1986].

(2) Unless the context otherwise requires, any reference in these Regulations to a Regulation or Schedule by number means the Regulation or Schedule so numbered to these Regulations and any reference to a Part of a Schedule by number means the Part so numbered in that Schedule.

Annotations
Para (1): definitions 'contract' and 'franchisee' added by SI 1994 No 1825, reg 4; definition 'wasted costs order' added by SI 1991 No 838, reg 3(1).
Modification: any reference to solicitor(s) etc modified to include references to bodies recognised under the Administration of Justice Act 1985, s 9, by the Solicitors' Incorporated Practices Order 1991, SI 1991 No 2684, arts 4, 5, Sch 1.

3 The appropriate authority

(1) Subject to paragraphs (2), (3) and (4) the appropriate authority shall be–

(a) the registrar in the case of proceedings in the Court of Appeal;
(b) an officer appointed by the Lord Chancellor in the case of criminal proceedings in the Crown Court;
(c) the Board in the case of criminal proceedings in a magistrates' court;
(d) <. . .>

(2) The appropriate authority may appoint or authorise the appointment of determining officers to act on its behalf under these Regulations in accordance with directions given by it or on its behalf.

(3) For costs claimed in respect of advice or assistance as to an appeal from the Crown Court to the Court of Appeal, the appropriate authority shall be:–

(a) (except in the case of an appeal under section 9(11) of the Criminal Justice Act 1987) the registrar where, on the advice of counsel or the solicitor assigned, notice of appeal is given, or application for leave to appeal is made, whether or not such appeal is later abandoned;

(b) an officer appointed by the Lord Chancellor under paragraph (1)(*b*) in all other cases.

(4) For costs claimed in respect of advice or assistance as to an appeal from a magistrates' court to the Crown Court, the appropriate authority shall be the Board.

Annotations
Para (1): sub-para (d) revoked by SI 1991 No 2037, reg 2(a).
Modification: any reference to solicitor(s) etc modified to include references to bodies recognised under the Administration of Justice Act 1985, s 9, by the Solicitors' Incorporated Practices Order 1991, SI 1991 No 2684, arts 4, 5, Sch 1.

4 General

(1) Costs in respect of work done under a legal aid order shall be determined by the appropriate authority in accordance with these Regulations.

(2) In determining costs, the appropriate authority shall, subject to and in accordance with these Regulations,–

(a) take into account all the relevant circumstances of the case including the nature, importance, complexity or difficulty of the work and the time involved, and

(b) allow a reasonable amount in respect of all work [actually and] reasonably done.

Annotations
Para (2): words in square brackets added by SI 1992 No 592, reg 3.

[4A] [Interim payment of disbursements]

[(1) A solicitor may submit a claim to the appropriate authority for payment of a disbursement for which he has incurred liability in criminal proceedings in the Crown Court in accordance with the provisions of this regulation.

(2) A claim for payment may be made where–

(a) a solicitor has obtained prior authority to incur expenditure of £100 or more under regulation 54(1)(a), (b), (c) or (e) of the General Regulations; and

(b) he has incurred liability for a disbursement under that authority of £100 or more.

(3) Without prejudice to regulation 7(6), a claim under paragraph (1) above shall not exceed the maximum fee authorised under the prior authority.

(4) A claim for payment under paragraph (1) may be made at any time before the solicitor submits a claim for costs under regulation 5(2).

(5) A claim under paragraph (1) shall be submitted to the appropriate authority in such form and manner as it may direct and shall be accompanied

by the authority to incur expenditure and any invoices or other documents in support of the claim.

(6) The appropriate authority shall allow the disbursement subject to the limit in paragraph (3) above if it appears to have been reasonably incurred in accordance with the prior authority.

(7) Where the appropriate authority allows the disbursement, it shall notify the solicitor and, where the disbursement includes the fees or charges of any person, that person, of the amount payable and shall authorise payment to the solicitor accordingly.

(8) Regulations 14 to 16 (redetermination etc) shall not apply to a claim for payment under this regulation.]

Annotations

This regulation was added by SI 1993 No 934, reg 5.

Modification: any reference to solicitor(s) etc modified to include references to bodies recognised under the Administration of Justice Act 1985, s 9, by the Solicitors' Incorporated Practices Order 1991, SI 1991 No 2684, arts 4, 5, Sch 1.

[4B] [Interim disbursements and final determination of costs]

[(1) On a final determination of costs, paragraphs (2) and (3)(e) of regulation 5 and regulation 7 shall apply notwithstanding that a payment has been made under regulation 4A.

(2) Where the amount found to be due under regulation 7 in respect of a disbursement is less than the amount paid under regulation 4A ('the interim disbursement'), the appropriate authority shall deduct the difference from the sum otherwise payable to the solicitor on the determination of costs, and where the amount due under regulation 7 exceeds the interim disbursement, the appropriate authority shall add the difference to the amount otherwise payable to the solicitor.]

Annotations

This regulation was added by SI 1993 No 943, reg 5.

Modification: any reference to solicitor(s) etc modified to include references to bodies recognised under the Administration of Justice Act 1985, s 9, by the Solicitors' Incorporated Practices Order 1991, SI 1991 No 2684, arts 4, 5, Sch 1.

[4C] [Interim payments in cases awaiting determination]

[(1) The appropriate authority shall make an interim payment in respect of a claim for costs in criminal proceedings in the Crown Court in accordance with the following provisions of this regulation.

(2) Entitlement to a payment arises in respect of a claim for costs–

(a) in the case of a solicitor, where the total claim for costs is £4000 or more (exclusive of Value Added Tax);
(b) in the case of a barrister, where the basic fee claimed is £4000 or more (exclusive of Value Added Tax);
(c) where the claim for costs is for less than the amounts mentioned in (a) or (b) but is related to any claim falling under (a) or (b).

(3) Entitlement to a payment under paragraph (1) of this regulation shall not arise until three months have elapsed from–

(a) the date on which the bill is ready to tax or, if earlier,
(b) the date three months after the conclusion of the last of any related proceedings.

(4) A bill shall be regarded as being ready to tax on the date on which it is received by the appropriate authority for determination except that where there are related claims for costs all the bills relating thereto shall be regarded as ready to tax on the date the last bill is received.

(5) A solicitor or barrister may submit a claim for an interim payment under this regulation if no payment has been made under paragraph (1) and six months have elapsed from the conclusion of the proceedings against the defendant whom he represented under the legal aid order.

(6) For the purposes of this regulation, proceedings are related to each other in the circumstances set out in paragraph (7) and claims for costs are related to each other in the circumstances set out in paragraph (8).

(7) Proceedings are related to each other:–

(a) where different proceedings involving the same defendant are prepared or heard or dealt with together;
(b) where proceedings involving more than one defendant arose out of the same incident, so that the defendants are charged or tried or disposed of together.

(8) The following claims for costs are related to each other:–

(a) the claims of a solicitor and counsel acting in the same proceedings for a defendant;
(b) the claims of any solicitor or counsel acting in any proceedings mentioned in paragraph (7)(a);
(c) the claims of all the solicitors or counsel acting for the defendants in the circumstances mentioned in paragraph (7)(b).

(9) No payment shall be made under this regulation unless (subject to regulation 17) the solicitor or barrister has submitted his claim in accordance with the provisions of regulations 5(1) and 8(1).]

Annotations
This regulation was added by SI 1993 No 934, reg 5.
Modification: any reference to solicitor(s) etc modified to include references to bodies recognised under the Administration of Justice Act 1985, s 9, by the Solicitors' Incorporated Practices Order 1991, SI 1991 No 2684, arts 4, 5, Sch 1.

[4D] [Amount of interim payment in cases awaiting determination]

[(1) Where entitlement to a payment arises under regulation 4C, the amount payable shall be–

(a) 40% of the total claim for costs
less
(b) any sum already paid.

(2) Regulations 14 to 16 (redetermination etc) shall not apply to a payment under this regulation.]

Annotations
This regulation was added by SI 1993 No 934, reg 5.

[4E] [Interim payments under franchising contracts]

[Where representation under Part V of the Act is provided under a franchising contract for criminal proceedings in a magistrates' court, the franchisee may apply to the Board when the legal aid order is granted for an interim payment in respect of a claim for costs in accordance with the contract.]

Annotations
This regulation was added by SI 1994 No 1825, reg 5.
The Act: Legal Aid Act 1988.

5 Claims for costs by solicitors

(1) Subject to regulation 17 [and paragraph (1A)], no claim by a solicitor for costs in respect of work done under a legal aid order shall be entertained unless the solicitor submits it within three months of the conclusion of the proceedings to which the legal aid order relates.

[(1A) Where proceedings in a magistrates' court have not been concluded but a warrant of arrest has been issued, a claim by a solicitor for costs in respect of work done under a legal aid order shall be made not earlier than 6 weeks and not later than 19 weeks from the date of issue of the warrant and the provisions of Schedule 1 Part III shall apply.]

(2) Subject to paragraph (3), a claim for costs shall be submitted to the appropriate authority in such form and manner as it may direct and shall be accompanied by the legal aid order and any receipts or other documents in support of any disbursements claimed.

(3) A claim shall–

(a) summarise the items of work done by a fee-earner in respect of which fees are claimed according to the classes specified in [regulation 6(1), paragraph 4(2) of Schedule 1 Part II or paragraph 4(2) of Schedule 1 Part III];
(b) state, where appropriate, the dates on which the items of work were done, the time taken, the sums claimed and whether the work was done for more than one assisted person;
(c) in the case of proceedings in the Crown Court or Court of Appeal, specify, where appropriate, the fee-earner who undertook each of the items of work claimed;
(d) give particulars of any work done in relation to more than one indictment or a retrial;
(e) specify any disbursements claimed, the circumstances in which they were incurred and the amounts claimed in respect of them;
(f) [where counsel has been instructed by the solicitor although not assigned under the legal aid order, state

(i) the amount agreed in respect of counsel's fee;
(ii) the time spent by counsel in preparation, advocacy, travelling and waiting;
(iii) the amounts agreed for counsel's travelling and waiting time and travelling costs in proceedings specified in paragraph 2(2) of Schedule 1 Part III.]

(4) Where the solicitor claims that–

(a) regulation 44(7) of the General Regulations, or
(b) paragraph 3 of Schedule 1 Part I, should be applied in relation to an item of work, he shall give full particulars in support of his claim.

(5) Where there are any special circumstances which should be drawn to the attention of the appropriate authority, the solicitor shall specify them.

(6) The solicitor shall supply such further particulars, information and documents as the appropriate authority may require.

Annotations
Para (1): words in square brackets added by SI 1993 No 934, reg 7(a).
Para (1A): added by SI 1993 No 934, reg 7(b).
Para (3): in sub-para (a) words in square brackets substituted by SI 1993 No 934, reg 7(c); sub-para (f) added by SI 1993 No 934, reg 7(d), substituted by SI 1994 No 2218, reg 3.
Modification: any reference to solicitor(s) etc modified to include references to bodies recognised under the Administration of Justice Act 1985, s 9, by the Solicitors' Incorporated Practices Order 1991, SI 1991 No 2684, arts 4, 5, Sch 1.
General Regulations: Legal Aid in Criminal and Care Proceedings (General) Regulations 1989, SI 1989 No 344.

6 Determination of solicitors' fees

(1) [The] appropriate authority may allow work done by fee-earners in the following classes–

(a) preparation, including taking instructions, interviewing witnesses, ascertaining the prosecution case, advising on plea and mode of trial, preparing and perusing documents, dealing with letters and telephone calls which are not routine, preparing for advocacy, instructing counsel and expert witnesses, conferences, consultations, views and work done in connection with advice on appeal or case stated;
(b) advocacy, including applications for bail and other applications to the court;
(c) attendance at court where counsel is assigned, including conferences with counsel at court;
(d) travelling and waiting;
(e) dealing with routine letters written and routine telephone calls.

(2) The appropriate authority shall consider the claim, any further particulars, information or documents submitted by the solicitor under regulation 5 and any other relevant information and shall allow–

(a) such work as appears to it to have been reasonably done under the legal aid order (including any representation or advice which is deemed to be work done under that order) by a fee-earner, classifying such work according to the classes specified in paragraph (1) as it considers appropriate; and

(b) such time in respect of each class of work allowed by it (other than dealing with routine letters written and routine telephone calls) as it considers reasonable

< . . . >

[(2A) In any proceedings which are specified in paragraph 1(2) of Schedule 1 Part II, the appropriate authority shall proceed in accordance with the provisions of paragraph 3 of that Part of that Schedule.

(2B) In any proceedings in a magistrates' court which are specified in the Table in paragraph 2(2) of Schedule 1 Part III, the provisions of that Part of that Schedule shall apply.]

(3) Subject to paragraphs (2) [(2A), (2B)] [and (4)] the appropriate authority shall allow fees for work allowed by it under this regulation in accordance with Schedule 1 Part I; provided that, where any work allowed was done after 30th June 1996 [30th June 1997], it may allow such fees as appear to it to be reasonable for such work having regard to the rates specified in that Part of Schedule 1.

(4) In the case of criminal proceedings in the Crown Court and the Court of Appeal, the fees allowed in accordance with Part I of Schedule 1 shall be those appropriate to such of the following grades of fee-earner as the appropriate authority considers reasonable–

(a) senior solicitor,
(b) solicitor, legal executive or fee-earner of equivalent experience,
(c) articled clerk or fee-earner of equivalent experience.

(5) < . . . >

(6) This regulation applies to work in respect of which standard fees are payable under [Part II or Part III of Schedule 1 only to the extent that those Parts specifically so provide].

Annotations
Para (1): word in square brackets substituted by SI 1992 No 592, reg 4(a).
Para (2): words omitted revoked by SI 1993 No 934, reg 8(a).
Paras (2A), (2B): added by SI 1993 No 934, reg 8(b).
Para (3): first words in square brackets added by SI 1993 No 934, reg 8(c); second words in square brackets substituted by SI 1992 No 592, reg 4(b); words underlined substituted by SI 1995 No 952, reg 4, further substituted with savings by subsequent words in square brackets by SI 1996 No 644, reg 2, for savings see reg 1(3) thereof.
Para (5): revoked by SI 1991 No 2037, reg 2(b).
Para (6): words in square brackets substituted by SI 1993 No 934, reg 8(d).
Modification: except in para (4), any reference to solicitor(s) etc modified to include references to bodies recognised under the Administration of Justice Act 1985, s 9, by the Solicitors' Incorporated Practices Order 1991, SI 1991 No 2684, arts 4, 5, Sch 1.

7 Determination of solicitors' disbursements

(1) Subject to the provisions of this regulation, the appropriate authority shall allow such disbursements claimed under regulation 5 as appear to it to have been reasonably incurred; provided that:

(a) if they are abnormally large by reason of the distance of the court or the assisted person's residence or both from the solicitor's place of business, reimbursement of the expenses may be limited to what would otherwise, having regard to all the circumstances, be a reasonable amount; and

(b) in the case of an appeal to the Court of Appeal, the cost of a transcript, or any part thereof, of the proceedings in the court from which the appeal lies obtained otherwise than through the registrar shall not be allowed except where the appropriate authority considers that it is reasonable in all the circumstances for such disbursement to be allowed.

(2), (3) < . . . >

(4) No question as to the propriety of any step or act in relation to which prior authority has been obtained under regulation 54 of the General Regulations shall be raised on any determination of costs, unless the solicitor knew or ought reasonably to have known that the purpose for which the authority was given had failed or become irrelevant or unnecessary before the costs were incurred.

(5) Where costs are reasonably incurred in accordance with and subject to the limit imposed by a prior authority given under regulation 54 of the General Regulations, no question shall be raised on any determination of costs as to the amount of the payment to be allowed for the step or act in relation to which the authority was given.

(6) Where costs are incurred in taking any step or doing any act for which authority may be given under regulation 54 of the General Regulations, without authority to do so having been given or in excess of any fee authorised under regulation 54 of the General Regulations, payment in respect of those costs may nevertheless be allowed on a determination of costs.

Annotations
Paras (2), (3): revoked by SI 1993 No 934, reg 9.
Modification: any reference to solicitor(s) etc modified to include references to bodies recognised under the Administration of Justice Act 1985, s 9, by the Solicitors' Incorporated Practices Order 1991, SI 1991 No 2684, arts 4, 5, Sch 1.
General Regulations: Legal Aid in Criminal and Care Proceedings (General) Regulations 1989, SI 1989 No 343.

[7A] [Costs in proceedings involving counsel not assigned under the legal aid order]

[(1) Where counsel has not been assigned under the legal aid order but has been instructed by the solicitor in proceedings in a magistrates' court, the appropriate authority shall, subject to paragraph (4), pay counsel the fees agreed between him and the solicitor.

[(1A) In proceedings specified in paragraph 2(2) of Schedule 1 Part III, counsel's agreed fees shall also include any fees agreed in respect of counsel's travelling and waiting time and travelling costs.]

(2) The solicitor shall claim his costs (including the time spent by counsel in [preparation and advocacy]) at the rates applicable to solicitors' fees in magistrates' courts proceedings in accordance with the provisions of Schedule 1 Part I.

(3) Where costs are determined in circumstances to which this regulation applies, the appropriate authority shall determine the costs which would have been payable to the solicitor had he undertaken the case without counsel <. . .>

(4) The costs payable in respect of counsel's agreed fee shall be reduced only where, and to the extent that, they would exceed–

(a) the costs determined in accordance with paragraph (3); or
(b) where a standard fee is payable, the total of the relevant standard fee plus the other costs referred to in paragraph 6(a) of Schedule 1 Part III [and the travelling costs allowed in respect of counsel].

(5) The costs payable by the appropriate authority shall be applied as follows:

(a) payment in respect of counsel shall be paid to counsel direct;
(b) the balance of the costs payable shall be paid to the solicitor.]

Annotations
This regulation was added by SI 1993 No 934, reg 10.
Para (1A): added by SI 1994 No 2218, reg 4(a).
Para (2): words in square brackets substituted by SI 1994 No 2218, reg 4(b).
Para (3): words omitted revoked by SI 1994 No 2218, reg 4(c).
Para (4): in sub-para (b) words in square brackets added by SI 1994 No 2218, reg 4(d).
Modification: any reference to solicitor(s) etc modified to include references to bodies recognised under the Administration of Justice Act 1985, s 9, by the Solicitors' Incorporated Practices Order 1991, SI 1991 No 2684, arts 4, 5, Sch 1.

8 Claims for fees by counsel

(1) Subject to regulation 17, no claim by counsel for fees for work done under a legal aid order shall be entertained unless counsel submits it within three months of the conclusion of the proceedings to which the legal aid order relates.

(2) Subject to paragraph (3), a claim for fees shall be submitted to the appropriate authority in such form and manner as it may direct.

(3) A claim shall–

(a) summarise the items of work in respect of which fees are claimed according to the classes specified in regulation 9(4);
(b) state the dates on which the items of work were done, the time taken where appropriate, the sums claimed and whether the work was done for more than one assisted person;
(c) give particulars of any work done in relation to more than one indictment or a retrial.

(4) Where counsel claims that–

(a) it would be inappropriate to allow a standard fee under regulation 9(2); or
(b) regulation 9(5)(b) should be applied in relation to an item of work, he shall give full particulars in support of his claim.

(5) Where there are any special circumstances which should be drawn to the attention of the appropriate authority, counsel shall specify them.

(6) Counsel shall apply such further particulars, information and documents as the appropriate authority may require.

9 Determination of counsel's fees

(1) The appropriate authority shall consider the claim, any further particulars, information or documents submitted by counsel under regulation 8 and any other relevant information and shall allow such work as appears to it to have been reasonably done.

(2) Where the work allowed has been done by junior counsel in the Crown Court, the appropriate authority shall, subject to paragraph (3), allow such of the standard fees specified in Part I of Schedule 2 as may be applicable to that work, unless it appears to the appropriate authority that the standard fee would be inappropriate taking into account all the relevant circumstances of the case, in which case it shall allow fees in accordance with paragraphs (4) and (5).

(3) The appropriate authority may not allow a standard fee in respect of–

(a) committals for trial in which the indictment includes counts in respect of an offence which is classified as a class 1 or 2 offence in accordance with directions given by the Lord Chief Justice under section 75 of the Supreme Court Act 1981;
(b) proceedings in any other case–
  (i) which lasted more than three days or which at the time of listing were reasonably expected to last more than three days;
  (ii) in which the indictment is disposed of by a plea of guilty but which if contested would reasonably have been expected to last more than three days,

unless counsel requests that a standard fee be allowed.

(4) The appropriate authority may, except in relation to work for which a standard fee is allowed under paragraph (2), allow any of the following classes of fee to counsel in respect of work allowed by it under this regulation–

(a) a basic fee for preparation including preparation for a pre-trial review and, where appropriate, the first day's hearing including, where they took place on that day, short conferences, consultations, applications and appearances (including bail applications), views and any other preparation;
(b) a refresher fee for any day or part of a day during which a hearing continued, including, where they took place on that day, short conferences, consultations, applications and appearances (including bail applications), views and any other preparation;
(c) subsidiary fees for–
  (i) attendance at conferences, consultations and views not covered by sub-paragraph (a) or (b);
  (ii) written advice on evidence, plea, appeal, case stated or other written work;
  (iii) attendance at pre-trial reviews, applications and appearances (including bail applications and adjournments for sentence) not covered by sub-paragraph (a) or (b).

(5) In the case of proceedings in the Crown Court or a magistrates' court, the appropriate authority shall, except in relation to work for which a standard fee is allowed under paragraph (2), allow such fees in respect of such work as it considers reasonable in such amounts as it may determine in accordance with Part II of Schedule 2; provided that:

(a) where any work allowed was done after 30th June 1996 [30th June 1997], the appropriate authority may allow such fees in such amounts as appear to it to be reasonable remuneration for such work having regard to the amounts specified in Part II of Schedule 2; or

(b) where it appears to the appropriate authority, taking into account all the relevant circumstances of the case, that owing to the exceptional circumstances of the case the amount payable by way of fees in accordance with Part II of Schedule 2 would not provide reasonable remuneration for some or all of the work it has allowed, it may allow such amount as appears to it to be reasonable remuneration for the relevant work.

(6) In the case of proceedings in the Court of Appeal, the appropriate authority shall allow such fees in respect of such work as it considers reasonable in such amounts as appear to it to be reasonable remuneration for such work.

(7) Where prior authority has been obtained to instruct a Queen's Counsel alone under regulation 54 of the General Regulations, no question as to the propriety of that act shall be raised on any determination of counsel's fees, unless the solicitor knew or ought reasonably to have known that the purpose for which the authority was given had failed or become irrelevant or unnecessary before the fees were incurred.

Annotations

Para (5): in sub-para (a) words underlined substituted by SI 1995 No 952, reg 4, further substituted with savings by subsequent words in square brackets by SI 1996 No 644, reg 2, for savings see reg 1(3) thereof.

Modification: any reference to solicitor(s) etc modified to include references to bodies recognised under the Administration of Justice Act 1985, s 9, by the Solicitors' Incorporated Practices Order 1991, SI 1991 No 2684, arts 4, 5, Sch 1.

General Regulations: Legal Aid in Criminal and Care Proceedings (General) Regulations 1989, SI 1989 No 344.

9A

[(1) Subject to paragraph (2), where the court has disallowed the whole or any part of any wasted costs under section 19A of the Prosecution of Offences Act 1985 the appropriate authority, in determining costs in respect of work done by the legal representative against whom the wasted costs order was made, shall deduct the amount of the order from the amount otherwise payable in accordance with these Regulations.

(2) Where the appropriate authority, in accordance with these Regulations, is minded to disallow any amount of a claim for work done to which the wasted costs order relates it shall disallow that amount or the amount of the wasted costs order, whichever is the greater.]

Annotations

This regulation was added by SI 1991 No 838, reg 3(2).

10 Payment of costs

(1) Having determined the costs payable to a solicitor or counsel in accordance with these Regulations, the appropriate authority shall notify the solicitor or counsel of the costs payable and authorise payment accordingly.

(2) Where the costs payable under paragraph (1) are varied as a result of any review, redetermination or appeal made or brought pursuant to these Regulations, then–

(a) where the costs are increased, the appropriate authority shall authorise payment of the increase;
(b) where the costs are decreased, the solicitor or counsel shall repay the amount of such decrease; and
(c) where the payment of any costs of the solicitor or counsel is ordered under regulation 15(14) or 16(8) or under paragraph 8(4) of Schedule 1 Part II, the appropriate authority shall authorise such payment.

(3) <. . .>

Annotations
Para (3): revoked by SI 1993 No 934, reg 11.
Modification: any reference to solicitor(s) etc modified to include references to bodies recognised under the Administration of Justice Act 1985, s 9, by the Solicitors' Incorporated Practices Order 1991, SI 1991 No 2684, arts 4, 5, Sch 1.

[10A] [Recovery of overpayments]

[(1) This regulation applies where a solicitor or barrister is entitled to be paid a certain sum ('the amount due') by virtue of these Regulations and, for whatever reason, he is paid an amount greater than that sum.

(2) Where the circumstances in paragraph (1) arise, the appropriate authority may–

(a) require immediate repayment of the amount in excess of the amount due ('the excess amount') and a solicitor or barrister shall on demand repay the excess amount to the appropriate authority, or
(b) deduct the excess amount from any other sum which is or becomes payable to the solicitor or barrister by virtue of these Regulations.

(3) The appropriate authority may proceed under paragraph (2)(b) without first proceeding under paragraph 2(a).

(4) Paragraph (2) shall apply notwithstanding that the solicitor or barrister to whom the excess amount was paid is exercising, or may exercise, a right under regulations 12 to 16 (redetermination etc).]

Annotations
This regulation was added by SI 1993 No 934, reg 6.
Modification: any reference to solicitor(s) etc modified to include references to bodies recognised under the Administration of Justice Act 1985, s 9, by the Solicitors' Incorporated Practices Order 1991, SI 1991 No 2684, arts 4, 5, Sch 1.

11 Notification of collecting court

Having determined the costs payable to a solicitor or counsel in accordance with these Regulations, the appropriate authority shall notify the collecting court of the amount determined in each case in which a contribution order under section 23(1) of the Act has been made.

Annotations
Modification: any reference to solicitor(s) etc modified to include references to bodies recognised under the Administration of Justice Act 1985, s 9, by the Solicitors' Incorporated Practices Order 1991, SI 1991 No 2684, arts 4, 5, Sch 1.
The Act: Legal Aid Act 1988.

12 Review of determinations by the Board

(1) If, in a case in which the Board is the appropriate authority, a solicitor or counsel is dissatisfied with a determination made under these Regulations, the solicitor or counsel may within 21 days of receipt of notification of the costs payable under regulation 10(1) apply to the appropriate area committee to review that determination [(including a decision concerning the application of the provisions for standard fees under Schedule 1 Part III)].

(2) On an application under paragraph (1), the appropriate area committee shall review the determination whether by confirming, increasing or decreasing the amount of it [or in the case of a decision of the type referred to in paragraph (1), by confirming or amending the decision].

Annotations
Paras (1), (2): words in square brackets added by SI 1993 No 934, reg 12.
Modification: any reference to solicitor(s) etc modified to include references to bodies recognised under the Administration of Justice Act 1985, s 9, by the Solicitors' Incorporated Practices Order 1991, SI 1991 No 2684, arts 4, 5, Sch 1.

13 Appeals to committee appointed by the Board

(1) A solicitor or counsel who is dissatisfied with the decision of an area committee on a review under regulation 12 may within 21 days of receipt of notification of the decision apply to that committee to certify a point of principle of general importance.

(2) Where an area committee certifies a point of principle of general importance, the solicitor or counsel may within 21 days of receipt of notification of that certification appeal in writing to a committee of the Board against the decision of the area committee under regulation 12.

(3) On an appeal under this regulation the committee appointed by the Board may reverse, affirm or amend the decision of the area committee under regulation 12.

Annotations
Modification: any reference to solicitor(s) etc modified to include references to bodies recognised under the Administration of Justice Act 1985, s 9, by the Solicitors Incorporated Practices Order 1991, SI 1991 No 2684, arts 4, 5, Sch 1.

14 Redetermination of costs by an appropriate authority other than the Board

(1) Where–

(a) a solicitor or counsel is dissatisfied with the costs (other than standard fees allowed under Schedule 1 Part II or under regulation 9(2)) determined under these Regulations by an appropriate authority for proceedings other than criminal proceedings before a magistrates' court < . . . >; or

(b) counsel is dissatisfied with the decision to allow standard fees [under regulation 9(2)],

he may apply to the appropriate authority to redetermine those costs or to review that decision as the case may be.

(2) Subject to regulation 17, the application shall be made, within 21 days of the receipt of notification of the costs payable under regulation 10(1), by giving notice in writing to the appropriate authority specifying the matters in respect of which the application is made and the grounds of objection and shall be made in such form and manner as the appropriate authority may direct.

(3) The notice of application shall be accompanied by–

(a) in the case of a solicitor, the particulars, information and documents supplied under regulation 5; and

(b) in the case of counsel, the particulars, information and documents supplied under regulation 8.

(4) The notice of application shall state whether the applicant wishes to appear or to be represented and, if the applicant so wishes, the appropriate authority shall notify the applicant of the time at which it is prepared to hear him or his representative.

(5) The solicitor or counsel shall supply such further particulars, information and documents as the appropriate authority may require.

(6) The appropriate authority shall–

(a) redetermine the costs, whether by way of increase, decrease or in the amounts previously determined; or

(b) review the decision to allow standard fees under regulation 9(2) and confirm it or allow fees in accordance with regulation 9(4) and (5),

in the light of the objections made by the applicant or on his behalf and shall notify the applicant of its decision.

(7) The applicant may request the appropriate authority to give reasons in writing for its decision and, if so requested, the appropriate authority shall comply with the request.

(8) Subject to regulation 17, any request under paragraph (7) shall be made within 21 days of receiving notification of the decision.

Annotations

Para (1): in sub-para (a) words omitted revoked by SI 1991 No 2037, reg 2(c); in sub-para (b) words in square brackets added by SI 1993 No 934, reg 13.

Modification: any reference to solicitor(s) etc modified to include references to bodies recognised under the Administration of Justice Act 1985, s 9, by the Solicitors' Incorporated Practices Order 1991, SI 1991 No 2684, arts 4, 5, Sch 1.

15 Appeals to a taxing master

(1) Where the appropriate authority has given its reasons for its decision under regulation 14, a solicitor or counsel who is dissatisfied with that decision may appeal to a taxing master.

(2) Subject to regulation 17, an appeal shall be instituted, within 21 days of the receipt of the appropriate authority's reasons, by giving notice in writing to the Chief Taxing Master.

(3) The appellant shall send a copy of any notice given under paragraph (2) to the appropriate authority.

(4) The notice of appeal shall be accompanied by–

(a) a copy of the written representations given under regulation 14(2);
(b) the appropriate authority's reasons for its decision given under regulation 14(7); and
(c) the particulars, information and documents supplied to the appropriate authority under regulation 14.

(5) The notice of appeal shall–

(a) be in such form as the Chief Taxing Master may direct,
(b) specify separately each item appealed against, showing (where appropriate) the amount claimed for the item, the amount determined and the grounds of objection to the determination, and
(c) state whether the appellant wishes to appear or to be represented or whether he will accept a decision given in his absence.

(6) The Chief Taxing Master may, and if so directed by the Lord Chancellor either generally or in a particular case shall, send to the Lord Chancellor a copy of the notice of appeal together with copies of such other documents as the Lord Chancellor may require.

(7) With a view to ensuring that the public interest is taken into account, the Lord Chancellor may arrange for written or oral representations to be made on his behalf and, if he intends to do so, he shall inform the Chief Taxing Master and the appellant.

(8) Any written representations made on behalf of the Lord Chancellor under paragraph (7) shall be sent to the Chief Taxing Master and the appellant and, in the case of oral representations, the Chief Taxing Master and the appellant shall be informed of the grounds on which such representations will be made.

(9) The appellant shall be permitted a reasonable opportunity to make representations in reply.

(10) The taxing master shall inform the appellant (or his representative) and the Lord Chancellor, where representations have been or are to be made on his behalf, of the date of any hearing and, subject to the provisions of this regulation, may give directions as to the conduct of the appeal.

(11) The taxing master may consult the trial judge, the appropriate authority or the determining officer and may require the appellant to provide any further information which he requires for the purpose of the appeal and, unless the taxing master otherwise directs, no further evidence shall be received on the hearing of the appeal and no ground of objection shall be valid which was not raised under regulation 14.

(12) The taxing master shall have the same powers as the appropriate authority under these Regulations and, in the exercise of such powers, may–

(a) alter the redetermination of the appropriate authority in respect of any sum allowed, whether by increase or decrease as he thinks fit;
(b) confirm the decision to allow standard fees under regulation 9(2) or allow fees in accordance with regulation 9(4) and (5).

(13) The taxing master shall communicate his decision and the reasons for it in writing to the appellant, the Lord Chancellor and the appropriate authority.

(14) Except where he confirms or decreases the sums redetermined under regulation 14 or confirms a decision to allow standard fees, the taxing master may allow the appellant a sum in respect of part or all of any reasonable costs (including any fee payable in respect of an appeal) incurred by him in connection with the appeal.

Annotations
Modification: any reference to solicitor(s) etc modified to include references to bodies recognised under the Administration of Justice Act 1985, s 9, by the Solicitors' Incorporated Practices Order 1991, SI 1991 No 2684, arts 4, 5, Sch 1.

16 Appeals to the High Court

(1) A solicitor or counsel who is dissatisfied with the decision of a taxing master on an appeal under regulation 15 may apply to a taxing master to certify a point of principle of general importance.

(2) Subject to regulation 17, an application under paragraph (1) shall be made within 21 days of notification of a taxing master's decision under regulation 15(13).

(3) Where a taxing master certifies a point of principle of general importance, the solicitor or counsel may appeal to the High Court against the decision of a taxing master on an appeal under regulation 15, and the Lord Chancellor shall be a respondent to such an appeal.

(4) Subject to regulation 17, an appeal under paragraph (3) shall be instituted within 21 days of receiving a taxing master's certificate under paragraph (1).

(5) Where the Lord Chancellor is dissatisfied with the decision of a taxing master on an appeal under regulation 15, he may, if no appeal has been made by the solicitor or counsel under paragraph (3), appeal to the High Court against that decision, and the solicitor or counsel shall be a respondent to the appeal.

(6) Subject to regulation 17, an appeal under paragraph (5) shall be instituted within 21 days of receiving notification of the taxing master's decision under regulation 15(13).

(7) An appeal under paragraphs (3) and (5) shall be instituted by originating summons in the Queen's Bench Division and shall be heard and determined by a single judge whose decision shall be final.

(8) The judge shall have the same powers as the appropriate authority and a taxing master under these Regulations and may reverse, affirm or amend the decision appealed against or make such other order as he thinks fit.

Annotations

Modification: any reference to solicitor(s) etc modified to include references to bodies recognised under the Administration of Justice Act 1985, s 9, by the Solicitors. Incorporated Practices Order 1991, SI 1991 No 2684, arts 4, 5, Sch 1.

17 Time limits

[(1) Subject to paragraph (2), the time limit within which any act is required or authorised to be done may, for good reason, be extended;–

(a) in the case of acts required or authorised to be done under regulation 15 or 16 by a taxing master or the High Court as the case may be;

(b) in the case of acts required or authorised to be done by a solicitor or counsel under any other regulation, the appropriate authority.]

(2) Where a solicitor or counsel without good reason has failed (or, if an extension were not granted, would fail) to comply with a time limit, the appropriate authority, [a taxing master] or the High Court, as the case may be, may, in exceptional circumstances, extend the time limit and shall consider whether it is reasonable in the circumstances to reduce the costs; provided that costs shall not be reduced unless the solicitor or counsel has been allowed a reasonable opportunity to show cause orally or in writing why the costs should not be reduced.

(3) A solicitor or counsel may appeal to [a taxing master] against a decision made under this regulation by an appropriate authority in respect of proceedings other than proceedings before a magistrates' court and such an appeal shall be instituted within 21 days of the decision being given by giving notice in writing to the Chief Taxing Master specifying the grounds of appeal.

Annotations

Para (1): substituted by SI 1991 No 529, reg 4(a).

Paras (2), (3): words in square brackets substituted by SI 1991 No 529, reg 4(b).

Modification: any reference to solicitor(s) etc modified to include references to bodies recognised under the Administration of Justice Act 1985, s 9, by the Solicitors' Incorporated Practices Order 1991, SI 1991 No 2684, arts 4, 5, Sch 1.

18 House of Lords

(1) In the case of proceedings in the House of Lords, the costs payable to a solicitor or counsel under section 25 of the Act shall be determined by such officer as may be prescribed by order of the House of Lords.

(2) Subject to paragraph (1), these Regulations shall not apply to proceedings in the House of Lords.

Annotations
Modification: any reference to solicitor(s) etc modified to include references to bodies recognised under the Administration of Justice Act 1985, s 9, by the Solicitors Incorporated Practices Order 1991, SI 1991 No 2684, arts 4, 5, Sch 1.
The Act: Legal Aid Act 1988.

SCHEDULE 1 SOLICITOR'S FEES

Regulation 6

PART I FEES DETERMINED UNDER REGULATION 6

[1 (1) Subject to paragraphs 1A, 2 and 3, the appropriate authority shall allow fees for work allowed by it under regulation 6 at the following prescribed rates:

(a) Magistrates' court proceedings

Class of work	*Rate*
Preparation	£44.00 per hour – (£46.50 per hour for a fee-earner whose office is situated within legal aid area 1)
Advocacy	£55.50 per hour
Attendance at court where counsel assigned	£30.00 per hour
Travelling and waiting	£24.50 per hour
Routine letters written and routine telephone calls	£3.40 per item – (£3.55 per item for a fee-earner whose office is situated within legal aid area 1)

(b) Crown Court and Court of Appeal proceedings

Class of work	*Grade of fee-earner*	*Rate*
Preparation	Senior solicitor	£52.25 per hour – (£54.75 per hour for a fee-earner whose office is situated within legal aid area 1)
	Solicitor, legal executive or fee-earner of equivalent experience	£44.25 per hour – (£46.50 per hour for a fee-earner whose office is situated within legal aid area 1)
	Articled clerk or fee-earner of equivalent experience	£29.25 per hour – (£33.50 per hour for a fee-earner whose office is situated within legal aid area 1)
Advocacy	Senior solicitor	£63.50 per hour
	Solicitor	£55.25 per hour
Attendance at court where counsel assigned	Senior solicitor	£41.75 per hour

	Solicitor, legal executive or fee-earner of equivalent experience	£33.50 per hour
	Articled clerk or fee-earner of equivalent experience	£20.25 per hour
Travelling and waiting	Senior solicitor	£24.50 per hour
	Solicitor, legal executive or fee-earner of equivalent experience	£24.50 per hour
	Articled clerk or fee-earner of equivalent experience	£12.25 per hour
Routine letters written and routine telephone calls		£3.40 per item – (£3.55 per item for a fee-earner whose office is situated within legal aid area 1)

(2) In paragraphs 1(1) and 1A, 'legal aid area' means an area specified by the Board under regulation 4(1) of the Civil Legal Aid (General) Regulations 1989, and legal aid area 1 means the area so numbered by the Board.

1A Subject to paragraphs 2 and 3, the following prescribed rates shall apply to work done by a franchisee instead of the corresponding rates in paragraph 1(1)(a):

Class of work	*Rate*
Preparation	£44.75 per hour – (£47.25 per hour for a fee-earner whose office is situated within legal aid area 1)
Advocacy	£56.00 per hour
Attendance at court where counsel assigned	£30.50 per hour
Travelling and waiting	£24.75 per hour
Routine letters written and routine telephone calls	£3.45 per item – (£3.60 per item for a fee-earner whose office is situated within legal aid area 1)].

[1 (1) Subject to paragraphs 1A, 2 and 3, the appropriate authority shall allow fees for work allowed by it under regulation 6 at the following prescribed rates:

(a) Magistrates' court proceedings

Class of work	*Rate*
Preparation	£44.75 per hour – (£47.25 per hour for a fee-earner whose office is situated within legal aid area 1)
Advocacy	£56.50 per hour
Attendance at court where counsel assigned	£30.50 per hour
Travelling and waiting	£24.75 per hour

Class of work	*Rate*
Routine letters written and routine telephone calls	£3.45 per item – (£3.60 per item for a fee-earner whose office is situated within legal aid area 1)

(b) Crown Court and Court of Appeal proceedings

Class of work	*Grade of fee-earner*	*Rate*
Preparation	Senior solicitor	£53.00 per hour – (£55.75 per hour for a fee-earner whose office is situated within legal aid area 1)
	Solicitor, legal executive or fee-earner of equivalent experience	£45.00 per hour – (£47.25 per hour for a fee-earner whose office is situated within legal aid area 1)
Advocacy	Senior solicitor	£64.50 per hour
	Solicitor	£56.00 per hour
Attendance at court where counsel assigned	Senior solicitor	£42.25 per hour
	Solicitor, legal executive or fee-earner of equivalent experience	£34.00 per hour
	Articled clerk or fee-earner of equivalent experience	£20.50 per hour
Travelling & waiting	Senior solicitor	£24.75 per hour
	Solicitor, legal executive or fee-earner of equivalent experience	£24.75 per hour
	Articled clerk or fee-earner of equivalent experience	£12.50 per hour
Routine letters written and routine telephone calls		£3.45 per item – (£3.60 per item for a fee-earner whose office is situated within legal aid area 1)

(2) In paragraphs 1(1) and 1A, 'legal aid area' means an area specified by the Board under regulation 4(1) of the Civil Legal Aid (General) Regulations 1989, and legal aid area 1 means the area so numbered by the Board.

1A Subject to paragraphs 2 and 3, the following prescribed rates shall apply to work done by a franchisee instead of the corresponding rates in paragraph 1(1)(a):

Class of work	*Rate*
Preparation	£46.00 per hour – (£48.50 per hour for a fee-earner whose office is situated within legal aid area 1)
Advocacy	£57.75 per hour
Attendance at court where counsel assigned	£31.50 per hour
Travelling and waiting	£25.50 per hour
Routine letters written and routine telephone calls	£3.55 per item – (£3.70 per item for a fee-earner whose office is situated within legal aid area 1)]

2 In respect of any item of work, the appropriate authority may allow fees at less than the relevant [prescribed] rate specified in paragraph 1 [or 1A] where it appears to the appropriate authority reasonable to do so having regard to the competence and dispatch with which the work was done.

[3 (1) Upon a determination the appropriate authority may allow fees at more than the relevant prescribed rate specified in paragraph 1 [or 1A] subject to the provisions of this regulation where it appears to the appropriate authority, taking into account all the relevant circumstances of the case, that

(a) the work was done with exceptional competence, skill or expertise;
(b) the work was done with exceptional dispatch; or
(c) the case involved exceptional circumstances or complexity.

(2) Where the appropriate authority considers that any item or class of work should be allowed at more than the prescribed rate, it shall apply to that item or class of work a percentage enhancement in accordance with the following provisions of this regulation.

(3) In determining the percentage by which fees should by enhanced above the prescribed rate the appropriate authority shall have regard to:–

(a) the degree of responsibility accepted by the solicitor and his staff;
(b) the care, speed and economy with which the case was prepared;
(c) the novelty, weight and complexity of the case.

(4) Except in proceedings to which paragraph (5) applies, the percentage above the relevant prescribed rate by which fees for work may be enhanced shall not exceed 100 per cent.

(5) Where the proceedings relate to serious or complex fraud, the percentage above the relevant prescribed rate by which fees for work may be increased shall not exceed 200 per cent.

(6) The appropriate authority may have regard to the generality of proceedings to which these Regulations apply in determining what is exceptional within the meaning of this regulation.]

Annotations

Paras 1, 1A: substituted, for para 1 as originally enacted, by SI 1995 No 952, reg 5, further substituted with savings, by subsequent paras 1, 1A in square brackets, by SI 1996 No 644, reg 3, for savings see reg 1(3) thereof.

Para 2: first word in square brackets substituted by SI 1994 No 2218, reg 7(1); second words in square brackets added by SI 1995 No 952, reg 6.

Para 3: substituted by SI 1994 No 2218, reg 7(2); words in square brackets added by SI 1995 No 952, reg 6.

PART II STANDARD FEES [IN THE CROWN COURT]

1 Application

(1) Subject to sub-paragraphs (3) and (4), this Part of this Schedule applies to the fees for work done by a fee-earner regardless of his grade in relation to the proceedings in the Crown Court specified in sub-paragraph (2).

(2) The following proceedings are specified for the purposes of sub-paragraph (1)–

(a) committals for trial in which the indictment consisted of counts in respect of an offence which is classified as a class 3 or 4 offence in accordance with directions given by the Lord Chief Justice under section 75 of the Supreme Court Act 1981 and

(i) where the trial (including any case prepared for trial in which no jury was sworn) lasted 2 days or less and at the time of listing was reasonably expected to last 2 days or less; or

(ii) where the case was listed and disposed of as a plea of guilty;

(b) appeals against conviction;

(c) appeals against sentence, and

(d) committals for sentence (including proceedings which arose out of a breach of an order of the Crown Court, proceedings in which sentence was deferred and other similar matters).

(3) Where in any proceedings specified in sub-paragraph (2), the trial judge–

(a) is dissatisfied with the solicitor's conduct of the case; or

(b) considers that, for exceptional reasons, the fees should be determined under regulation 6,

he may direct that the fees should be determined under regulation 6 and in that event this Part of this Schedule shall not apply.

(4) If a solicitor so elects, he may claim standard fees under this Part of this Schedule in respect of work done by him notwithstanding that the proceedings in relation to which the work was done are not specified in sub-paragraph (2), and the provisions of this Part of this Schedule shall apply to such a claim with the necessary modifications, save that, where a solicitor elects to claim the principal standard fee for preparation in respect of a trial which lasted more than 2 days, he shall be paid that fee (together with the appropriate standard fees for the other classes of work specified in paragraph 4(2)) and paragraph 2 shall not apply.

(5) For the purposes of this Part of this Schedule, the standard fees which are payable and the classes of work for which such fees may be paid are specified in paragraph 4 and the 'lower fee limit' and the 'upper fee limit' have the meanings given by paragraph 4(3).

2 Allowance of standard fees

(1) The appropriate authority shall allow the standard fee for preparation which has been claimed by a solicitor (together with the appropriate standard

fees for the other classes of work specified in paragraph 4(2)) unless, where the principal standard fee for preparation has been claimed, such a fee is considered to be excessive in which case the lower standard fee shall be allowed.

(2) A solicitor who has been allowed the lower standard fee instead of the principal fee claimed may–

(a) accept that lower fee;
(b) request the appropriate authority in writing to review its decision, or
(c) provide the appropriate authority with a detailed claim in the form directed by the appropriate authority requesting in writing that the fees for preparation be determined under regulation 6.

(3) Where the appropriate authority is requested to review its decision under sub-paragraph (2)(b), the authority shall either–

(a) allow the principal fee; or
(b) request the solicitor to provide a detailed claim in the form directed by the appropriate authority.

(4) Where a solicitor fails to make a request under sub-paragraph (2)(b) or to supply a detailed claim for the purposes of sub-paragraph (2)(c) or (3)(b) within 6 weeks of the decision to allow the lower fee or the request to supply a detailed claim, whichever is the later, the decision to allow the lower standard fee shall be deemed to be confirmed.

3

(1) Where a solicitor–

(a) submits a claim for determination under regulation 6 in a case to which paragraph 1(2) applies; or
(b) disputes the allowance of the lower standard fee and provides a detailed claim under paragraph 2(2)(c) or (3)(b),

the appropriate authority shall first determine the fees for preparation work within the meaning of paragraph 4(2)(a) of this Part of this Schedule.

(2) If the fees so determined are–

(a) less than the lower fee limit, the appropriate authority shall allow and pay the lower standard fee together with the standard fees for all other classes of work specified in paragraph 4(2);
(b) not less than the lower fee limit and not more than the upper fee limit, the appropriate authority shall allow and pay the principal standard fee together with the standard fees for all other classes of work specified in paragraph 4(2);
(c) more than the upper fee limit, no standard fees shall be payable and all fees shall be determined in accordance with regulation 6.

4 **Standard fees**

(1) The classes of work for which standard fees shall be payable are those specified in sub-paragraph (2) and the fees for classes of work which are not so specified shall be determined in accordance with regulation 6.

(2) The classes of work specified for the purposes of sub-paragraph (1) are–

(a) preparation within the meaning of regulation 6(1)(a) but including routine letters written and routine telephone calls, within the meaning of regulation 6(1)(e);
(b) advocacy [(including waiting)] in respect of applications for bail;
(c) attendance at court (including waiting) where counsel is assigned;
(d) travelling except–

(i) to undertake work for which standard fees are not payable, or
(ii) where sub-paragraph (2)(b) applies,

and, for the purpose of this paragraph, 'travelling' shall be deemed to include waiting in connection with preparation work, within the meaning of sub-paragraph (2)(a) above.

(2) The standard fees payable under this Part of this Schedule are the fees specified in the Table below and in this Part of this Schedule the 'lower fee limit' and the 'upper fee limit' mean the lower and upper fee limits specified in the Table.

[TABLE

PREPARATION *Type of proceedings*		*Lower standard fee*	*Lower fee limit*	*Principal standard fee*	*Upper fee limit*
Jury trials		£127.50	£176	£245.75	£307
(including any case prepared for trial in which no jury was sworn)	London rate	£137.00	£183	£257.75	£321
Guilty pleas		£80.25	£108	£172.50	£222
	London rate	£86.25	£112	£182.75	£231
Appeals against		£50.25	£67	£150.75	£229
conviction	London rate	£53.75	£69	£156.75	£240
Appeals against		£35.75	£51	£91.75	£129
sentence	London rate	£38.75	£53	£96.50	£133
Committals for		£41.75	£50	£96.25	£139
sentence	London rate	£44.25	£52	£101.50	£143
ADVOCACY		£25.75			
IN RESPECT OF BAIL APPLICATIONS	London rate	£28.25			
ATTENDANCE AT COURT (INCLUDING WAITING) WHERE COUNSEL ASSIGNED		£21.10 per hour			
TRAVELLING		£18.25 per hour].			

[TABLE

PREPARATION *Type of proceedings*		*Lower standard fee*	*Lower fee limit*	*Principal standard fee*	*Upper fee limit*
Jury trials (including any case prepared for trial in which no jury was sworn)		£129.50	£179	£249.50	£312
	London rate	£139.00	£186	£261.50	£326
Guilty pleas		£81.50	£110	£175.00	£226
	London rate	£87.50	£114	£185.50	£235
Appeals against conviction		£51.00	£68	£153.00	£233
	London rate	£54.50	£70	£159.00	£244
Appeals against sentence		£36.25	£52	£93.00	£131
	London rate	£39.25	£54	£98.00	£135
Committals for sentence		£42.50	£51	£97.75	£141
	London rate	£45.00	£53	£103.00	£145
ADVOCACY IN RESPECT OF BAIL APPLICATIONS		£26.25			
	London rate	£28.75			
ATTENDANCE AT COURT (INCLUDING WAITING) WHERE COUNSEL ASSIGNED		£21.40 per hour			
TRAVELLING		£18.50 per hour].			

(4) A solicitor shall be entitled to the 'London rate' of the standard fees specified in the Table where his office is situated within legal aid area 1 < . . . > within the meaning of paragraph 1(2) of Schedule 1, Part I.

(5) The hourly rate specified in the Table for attendance at court shall, subject to sub-paragraph (6), be paid in respect of the period of time beginning 30 minutes before the case was listed and ending

(a) where the client was present at court, 15 minutes after the hearing ended on that day, or
(b) where the client was not present at court, when the hearing ended on that day,

and, save in exceptional circumstances, shall not be payable during the luncheon adjournment.

(6) Where a fee earner attends a court centre for the purposes of more than one case, the solicitor may claim the attendance fee in respect of the second or subsequent case only for the time actually spent in attendance in addition to the time for which payment is made under sub-paragraph (5).

(7) The hourly rate specified in the Table shall be paid for time spent travelling (within the meaning of sub-paragraph (2)(d)) and, where a fee-earner travels to appear as an advocate in respect of a bail application, the rate payable shall be the rate appropriate to the grade of fee-earner for travelling and waiting under paragraph 1(1)(c) of Schedule 1, Part I.

(8) Where a solicitor acts for more than one defendant, the appropriate authority shall–

(a) allow whichever of the appropriate standard preparation fees is the greater and increase that fee by 20 per cent for each additional defendant;
(b) increase the standard advocacy fee by 20 per cent for each additional defendant who is represented on a bail application,

but no percentage increase shall be made to the standard fees for attendance at court or for travelling.

(9) Where a solicitor acts for a defendant in respect of more than one–
(a) indictment,
(b) appeal against conviction,
(c) appeal against sentence, or
(d) committal for sentence

or in respect of any combination of (a) to (d) above, the appropriate authority shall allow whichever of the appropriate standard preparation fees is the greater and increase that fee by 20 per cent for each additional indictment, appeal or committal for sentence as the case may be.

(10) Where a solicitor prepares a case with a view to counsel appearing at the substantive hearing without the solicitor or his representative attending court, the standard preparation fee payable after application of any increase required by paragraphs (8)(a) or (9) shall be further increased by [£29.50] [£30.00] (or by [£31.50] [£32.00] for a solicitor whose office is situated within legal aid area 1 < . . . >).

[(11) Where a fee-earner listens to a tape recording of an interview conducted under a code issued by the Secretary of State under section 60 of the Police and Criminal Evidence Act 1984, the standard preparation fee payable after application of any increase required by paragraphs 8(a) or 9 shall be further increased by [£10.75] [£10.90] for every 10 minutes of the total running time of all tapes or parts of tapes listened to and by the same amount for any remaining period.]

(12) Where the standard fee payable is increased by virtue of sub-paragraph (8)(a), (9), (10) or (11), then for the purposes of paragraphs 3, 6 and 8–

(a) the upper fee limit shall be increased by the same amount by which the principal standard fee has been increased, and
(b) the lower fee limit shall be increased by the same amount by which the lower standard fee has been increased.

5 Disbursements

Nothing in this Part of this Schedule applies to disbursements which shall be determined in accordance with regulation 7.

6 Re-determinations and appeals

(1) A solicitor who is dissatisfied with a decision on a determination under paragraph 3 may apply for the costs to be re-determined and, subject to

sub-paragraph (2), the provisions of regulation 14(2) to (8) shall apply with the necessary modifications to an application under this paragraph as they apply to an application under regulation 14.

(2) On a re-determination under this paragraph, the appropriate authority shall determine the fees for preparation work within the meaning of paragraph 4(2)(a) and if the fees so determined are–

(a) less than the lower fee limit, the lower standard fee shall be allowed together with the standard fees for all other classes of work specified in paragraph 4(2);
(b) not less than the lower fee limit and not more than the upper fee limit, the principal standard fee shall be allowed together with the standard fees for all other classes of work specified in paragraph 4(2);
(c) more than the upper fee limit, the fees for all classes of work shall be determined in accordance with regulation 6.

7

Irrespective of any dispute under paragraph 2 as to whether the principal standard fee should have been allowed instead of the lower standard fee, where a solicitor is satisfied with a decision to allow a standard fee but contends that–

(a) a standard fee which is not apt for the type of work done has been allowed; or
(b) the provisions of paragraph 4(4) to (12) have been incorrectly applied,

he may, within 6 weeks of receipt of notification of the decision, make a written request setting out his reasons why the decision should be reviewed and, if the appropriate authority confirms its decision, written reasons shall be given.

8

(1) A solicitor may appeal to a taxing master where he is dissatisfied with–

(a) a decision on a re-determination under paragraph 6, or
(b) a decision on a review under paragraph 7.

(2) Where a solicitor appeals to a taxing master in respect of a decision under paragraph 6, the taxing master shall determine the fees for preparation within the meaning of paragraph 4(2)(a) and if the fees so determined are–

(a) less than the lower fee limit, the lower standard fee shall be allowed by the taxing master together with the standard fees for all other classes of work specified in paragraph 4(2);
(b) not less than the lower fee limit and not more than the upper fee limit, the principal standard fee shall be allowed by the taxing master together with the standard fees for all other classes of work specified in paragraph 4(2);
(c) more than the upper fee limit, the fees for all classes of work shall be determined by the taxing master in accordance with regulation 6.

(3) Where a solicitor appeals to a taxing master in respect of a decision made on a review under paragraph 7, the taxing master shall allow whichever standard fee he considers to be apt for the type of work done or, as the case may be, re-apply the provisions of paragraph 4(4) to (12).

(4) Where a taxing master allows an appeal in whole or in part, he may allow the solicitor a sum in respect of part or all of any reasonable costs (including any fee payable in respect of the appeal) incurred by him in connection with the appeal.

(5) This paragraph only applies to appeals in proceedings for which standard fees are payable and the provisions of regulation 15 shall apply to appeals in proceedings for which standard fees are not payable.

(6) Subject to the foregoing provisions of this paragraph, the provisions of regulation 15 to 17 relating to appeals by solicitors shall apply with the necessary modifications to appeals in proceedings for which standard fees are payable under this Part of this Schedule as they apply to appeals in proceedings for which standard fees are not payable.

Annotations

Section heading: words in square brackets added by SI 1993 No 934, reg 14.

Para 4: in sub-para (2) words in square brackets added by SI 1991 No 529, reg 6(a); in sub-para (3) Table underlined substituted by SI 1995 No 952, reg 7(a), further substituted with savings, by subsequent Table in square brackets, by SI 1996 No 644, reg 4(a), for savings see reg 1(3) thereof; in sub-para (4) words omitted revoked by SI 1991 No 529, reg 6(c); in sub-para (10) sums underlined substituted by SI 1995 No 952, reg 7(b), further substituted with savings, by subsequent sums in square brackets, by SI 1996 No 644, reg 4(b), for savings see reg 1(3) thereof, words omitted revoked by SI 1991 No 529, reg 6(d); in sub-para (11) sum underlined substituted by SI 1995 No 952, reg 7(c), further substituted with savings, by subsequent sum in square brackets, by SI 1996 No 644, reg 4(c), for savings see reg 1(3) thereof.

Modification: any reference to solicitor(s) etc modified to include references to bodies recognised under the Administration of Justice Act 1985, s 9, by the Solicitors' Incorporated Practices Order 1991, SI 1991 No 2684, arts 4, 5, Sch 1.

PART III [STANDARD FEES IN MAGISTRATES COURTS]

1 [Interpretation

In this Part of this Schedule–

a 'case' (except where the context otherwise requires) comprises proceedings relating to one or more charges or informations which are preferred or laid at the same time or which are founded on the same facts or which form or are part of a series of offences;

'Category 1 proceedings' means proceedings of the types referred to in column 1 of the Table in paragraph 2(2), and in paragraph 2(6) and (7);

'Category 2 proceedings' means proceedings of the type referred to in column 2 of the Table in paragraph 2(2);

'Category 3 proceedings' means proceedings of the type referred to in column 3 of the Table in paragraph 2(2),

and references to a category or to a category by number shall be construed accordingly;

'core costs' mean the costs relating to the classes of work specified in paragraph 4(2);

'lower limit' and 'higher limit' mean the lower and higher limits specified in the Table in [paragraph 8(1) (or paragraph 8(1A) in the case of a franchisee)];

'relevant standard fee' means the fee shown in the Table in [paragraph 8(1) (or paragraph 8(1A) in the case of a franchisee)] which corresponds to the type of proceedings, the location and the limit within which the core costs have been allowed under this Part;

'unassigned counsel' means counsel who is not assigned under the legal aid order but who is instructed by the solicitor.

2 Proceedings to which standard fees apply

(1) Subject to paragraph 3, standard fees under this Part of this Schedule shall apply to work done in proceedings in a magistrates' court as specified in sub-paragraph (2).

(2) The proceedings (which include any proceedings preliminary or incidental thereto whether before that or another court, including bail applications made either in a magistrates' court or the Crown Court) are the proceedings specified in the following Table:–

TABLE: CATEGORIES AND TYPES OF PROCEEDINGS

Column 1 **Category 1**	Column 2 **Category 2**	Column 3 **Category 3**
1.1 guilty pleas	2.1 contested trials	3.1 committal proceedings under section 6(2) of the Magistrates' Courts Act 1980 including those which are discontinued or withdrawn
1.2 uncontested proceedings arising out of a breach of an order of a magistrates' court (including proceedings in a magistrates' court relating to a breach of a Crown Court probation order, community service order or suspended sentence)	2.2 proceedings which were listed and fully prepared for trial in a magistrates' court but disposed of by a guilty plea on the day of trial before the opening of the prosecution case	3.2 committal proceedings which are discontinued or withdrawn before the court has fixed the date for a section 6(1) committal hearing
1.3 proceedings (other than committal proceedings) which are discontinued or withdrawn	2.3 proceedings which were listed and fully prepared for trial in a magistrates' court but are discontinued or withdrawn or where the prosecution offers no evidence or which result in a bind over on the day of trial before the opening of the prosecution case	3.3 proceedings transferred under section 4 of the Criminal Justice Act 1987 or section 53 of the Criminal Justice Act 1991
1.4 proceedings (other than committal proceedings) relating to summary or either way offences which result in a bind over	2.4 contested proceedings relating to a breach of an order of a magistrates' court (including proceedings relating to a breach of a Crown Court probation order, community service order or suspended sentence)	

Column 1 **Category 1**	Column 2 **Category 2**	Column 3 **Category 3**
1.5 proceedings arising out of a deferment of sentence (including any subsequent sentencing hearing) under section 1 of the Powers of Criminal Courts Act 1973	2.5 proceedings where mixed pleas are entered	

(3) Proceedings shall be treated for the purposes of this Part of this Schedule as forming part of one case where they relate to one or more charges or informations which are preferred or laid at the same time or which are founded on the same facts or which form or are part of a series of offences.

(4) Subject to sub-paragraph (5), where proceedings forming one case fall within more than one category, the proceedings shall be treated as forming part of the higher or highest in value of the categories concerned.

(5) Where a case includes proceedings referred to in the Table in sub-paragraph (2) above at items 3.1 and 3.2, the case shall be treated as if all the proceedings were Category 3 proceedings.

(6) Subject to sub-paragraph (5), where there is a change of solicitor assigned under a legal aid order in proceedings to which sub-paragraph (2) applies, the proceedings shall be treated as Category 1 proceedings for the purposes of a claim for costs in respect of work done under the legal aid order by the solicitor formerly assigned.

(7) Subject to sub-paragraph (5), where proceedings have not been concluded but a warrant of arrest has been issued, the proceedings shall be treated as Category 1 proceedings.

3 Proceedings to which standard fees do not apply

Standard fees shall not apply to proceedings–

(a) in which counsel has been assigned under a legal aid order; or
(b) in which costs are allowed at an enhanced rate in accordance with paragraph 3 of Schedule 1 Part I.

4 Classes of work covered by the standard fee

(1) The classes of work covered by the standard fee are specified in sub-paragraph (2).

(2) The classes of work are:–

(a) any preparation within the meaning of regulation 6(1)(a), including listening to, or viewing, any tape or video recording of interviews or evidence;
(b) routine letters written and routine telephone calls within the meaning of regulation 6(1)(e);

(c) advocacy, including bail and other applications made in either a magistrates' court or the Crown Court;
(d) work done by a fee-earner acting as agent for the solicitor assigned under the legal aid order;
(e) unassigned counsel's [preparation and advocacy].

5 Standard fees: further provisions

(1) Where the solicitor acts for more than one defendant in the proceedings, the claim for payment of a standard fee shall cover all the legally aided defendants whom he represents.

(2) Where a legal aid order is granted to a defendant in respect of more than one charge or information, the claim for payment of a standard fee shall cover all the charges or informations which form part of one case.

6 Costs additional to the standard fee

The following costs shall be payable in addition to the standard fee, and shall be determined in accordance with regulations 6[, 7 and 7A]:–

(a) travelling and waiting time of fee-earners [and unassigned counsel], which shall be payable at the rate provided in paragraph 1(1)(a) [(or paragraph 1A in the case of a franchisee)] of Schedule 1 Part I; and
(b) disbursements.

7 Allowance of standard fees

(1) The appropriate authority shall allow a lower standard fee where the core costs would not, if they had been determined, have exceeded the lower limit.

(2) Where the core costs claimed by the solicitor exceed the lower limit, the appropriate authority shall determine the core costs in accordance with regulation 6(2) and, if the core costs so determined–

(a) do not exceed the lower limit, allow the lower standard fee;
(b) exceed the lower limit but do not exceed the higher limit, allow the higher standard fee;
(c) exceed the higher limit, allow the core costs as determined.

(3) The rates specified in paragraph 1(1)(a) [(or paragraph 1A in the case of a franchisee)] of Schedule 1 Part I shall apply to the costs claimed, subject to the provisions of paragraph 2 of that Part of that Schedule.

[8 Fees payable

(1) Subject to sub-paragraph (1A), standard fees are payable in accordance with the Table below:–

TABLE

Type of proceedings		*Lower standard fee*	*Lower limit*	*Higher standard fee*	*Higher limit*
Category 1		£144.25	£268	£346.00	£463.75
	London rate	£185.50	£344	£440.00	£581.50
Category 2		£254.50	£460	£583.00	£767.25
	London rate	£326.50	£584	£732.50	£934.75
Category 3		£229.75	£406	£520.25	£709.50
	London rate	£290.50	£493	£611.00	£755.25

(1A) Where the work was done by a franchisee, standard fees are payable in accordance with the Table below:–

TABLE

Type of proceedings		*Lower standard fee*	*Lower limit*	*Higher standard fee*	*Higher limit*
Category 1		£148.25	£276	£357.00	£478
	London rate	£191.00	£354	£453.00	£598
Category 2		£262.25	£474	£601.00	£790
	London rate	£336.25	£602	£755.00	£963
Category 3		£236.50	£418	£536.00	£730
	London rate	£299.25	£507	£629.00	£778]

[(1) Subject to sub-paragraph (1A), standard fees are payable in accordance with the Table below:–

TABLE

Type of proceedings		*Lower standard fee*	*Lower limit*	*Higher standard fee*	*Higher limit*
Category 1		£142.00	£264	£341.00	£457
	London rate	£182.75	£339	£433.50	£573
Category 2		£250.75	£453	£574.50	£756
	London rate	£321.75	£575	£721.75	£921
Category 3		£226.25	£400	£512.50	£699
	London rate	£286.25	£486	£602.00	£744

(1A) Where the work was done by a franchisee, standard fees are payable in accordance with the Table below:–

TABLE

Type of proceedings		*Lower standard fee*	*Lower limit*	*Higher standard fee*	*Higher limit*
Category 1		£144.00	£268	£346.00	£464
	London rate	£185.80	£344	£440.00	£581
Category 2		£254.50	£460	£583.00	£767
	London rate	£326.50	£584	£732.50	£935
Category 3		£229.50	£406	£520.00	£709
	London rate	£290.50	£492	£611.00	£755]

(2) A solicitor shall be entitled to the relevant standard fee at the 'London rate' specified in [the appropriate Table] where his office is situated within legal aid area 1, within the meaning of paragraph 1(2) of Schedule 1 Part I.

(3) The costs payable in proceedings to which this Part applies shall (subject to any deductions or reductions made pursuant to regulations 9A or 17(2)) be:–

(a) the relevant standard fee together with the costs determined in accordance with the provisions of paragraph 6; or
(b) where the core costs allowed exceed the higher limit of the relevant standard fee, the costs as determined in accordance with regulations 6 and 7.

(4) Where, in circumstances to which regulation 5(1A) or paragraph 2(7) of this Part applies, a solicitor has been paid prior to the final disposal of the proceedings, any costs which would have been payable to that solicitor upon the final disposal of the proceedings shall be reduced to the extent that they formed part of the costs previously claimed.]

Annotations
This Part was added by SI 1993 No 934, reg 15, Appendix.
Para 1: in definitions 'lower limit' and 'higher limit' and 'relevant standard fee' words in square brackets substituted by SI 1995 No 952, reg 8(a).
Para 4: in sub-para (2) words in square brackets substituted by SI 1994 No 2218, reg 5.
Para 6: first words in square brackets substituted, and second words in square brackets added, by SI 1994 No 2218, reg 6; final words in square brackets added by SI 1995 No 952, reg 8(b).
Para 7: in sub-para (3) words in square brackets added by SI 1995 No 952, reg 8(b).
Para 8: sub-paras (1), (1A) underlined substituted, for sub-para (1) as originally enacted, by SI 1995 No 952, reg 8(d), further substituted with savings, by subsequent sub-paras (1), (1A) in square brackets, by SI 1996 No 644, reg 5, for savings see reg 1(3) thereof; in sub-para (2) words in square brackets substituted by SI 1995 No 952, reg 8(d).
Modification: any reference to solicitor(s) etc modified to include references to bodies recognised under the Administration of Justice Act 1985, s 9, by the Solicitors' Incorporated Practices Order 1991, SI 1991 No 2684, arts 4, 5, Sch 1.

SCHEDULE 2 COUNSEL'S FEES

Regulation 9

PART I STANDARD FEES [IN THE CROWN COURT]

1 The appropriate authority shall allow the fees specified in the Table and

(a) a standard basic fee shall cover preparation and the first day's hearing including, where they took place on that day, short conferences, applications and appearances (including bail applications), views and any other preparation;
(b) a standard refresher fee shall cover any day during which a hearing continued, including, where they took place on that day, short conferences, applications and appearances (including bail applications), views and any other preparation;
(c) a standard written work fee shall cover written advice on evidence, plea, appeal, case stated and other written work;

(d) a standard appearance fee shall cover attendance at applications and appearances (including bail applications and adjournments for sentence) together with, where they took place on that day, short conferences where attendance is not covered by (a) or (b) but shall not cover attendance at a pre-trial review.

2 For the purpose of determining which of the standard refresher fees specified in the Table should be allowed–

(a) a half day refresher fee shall be allowed where

(i) a hearing begins and ends before the luncheon adjournment, or
(ii) a hearing begins after the luncheon adjournment and ends before 5.30 pm; and

(b) a full day refresher fee shall be allowed where

(i) a hearing begins before and ends after the luncheon adjournment but before 5.30 pm, or
(ii) a hearing begins after the luncheon adjournment and ends after 5.30 pm; and

(c) a more than a full day refresher fee shall be allowed where a hearing begins before the luncheon adjournment and ends after 5.30 pm.

3 The standard basic fee specified for 'committals for sentence' shall be allowed to junior counsel in respect of proceedings arising out of a breach of an order of the Crown Court or other similar matters.

4 Where a case listed for jury trial does not proceed on the day for which it is listed the appropriate authority shall allow a sum equal to half of the standard basic fee for a jury trial.
5 Where counsel attends in respect of–

(a) a case listed for plea which is adjourned for trial; or
(b) a case to which neither paragraph 4 nor paragraph 6 applies, which is listed for hearing but not opened due to the failure of the defendant or a witness to attend or the non-availability of a social enquiry report or for some good reason,

the appropriate authority shall allow the standard appearance fee < . . . >.

[6 Where counsel attends in respect of a case which is listed for plea and on which a guilty plea is taken, and which is adjourned part-heard, the appropriate authority shall allow–

(a) the standard basic fee for the first hearing; and
(b) the standard appearance fee for the hearing at which the case is disposed of.]

7 Where counsel represents more than one defendant the appropriate authority shall

(a) increase the standard basic fee by 20 per cent for each additional defendant who is substantively dealt with at the hearing in respect of which that standard basic fee is to be paid; or

(b) where paragraph 4, 5 or 6 applies, increase the sum payable by 20 per cent for each additional defendant.

8 Where counsel appears on behalf of a defendant on the same day in respect of more than one

(a) indictment,
(b) appeal against conviction,
(c) appeal against sentence, or
(d) committal for sentence,

or in respect of any combination of (a) to (d) above, the appropriate authority shall allow whichever of the standard basic fees is the greater and shall increase it by 20 per cent for each additional indictment, appeal or committal for sentence, as the case may be.

9 Where counsel appears at the substantive hearing of a case without his instructing solicitor or representative attending court, the standard basic fee payable after application of any increase required by paragraph 7(a) or 8 shall be further increased by [£19.00] [£19.25].

[10 Where counsel listens to a tape recording of an interview conducted under a code issued by the Secretary of State under section 60 of the Police and Criminal Evidence Act 1984, the standard basic fee payable after application of any increase required by paragraph 7(a) or 8 shall be further increased by [£10.75] [£10.90] for every 10 minutes of the total running time of all tapes or parts of tapes listened to and by the same amount for any remaining period.]

11 Where counsel is instructed to appear in a court which is not within 25 miles of his chambers, the appropriate authority may allow an amount in respect of counsel's attendance at that court to cover any travelling and hotel expenses reasonably incurred and necessarily and exclusively attributable to counsel's attendance at that court; provided that the amount allowed shall not be greater than the amount, if any, which would be payable to counsel practising from the nearest local Bar unless counsel can justify his attendance having regard to all the relevant circumstances of the case.

[TABLE

Type of proceedings	*Standard basic fee*
Jury trials (including any case prepared for trial in which no jury is sworn)	£218.25
Guilty pleas	£115.25
Appeals against conviction	£115.25
Appeals against sentence	£72.50
Committals for sentence	£72.50
Standard appearance fee	£45.75
Standard refresher fee	
(1) Half day	£80.50
(2) Full day	£1 56.00
(3) More than a full day	£234.50
Standard written work fee	£29.50]

[TABLE

Type of proceedings		*Standard basic fee*
Jury trials (including any case prepared for trial in which no jury is sworn)		£221.50
Guilty pleas		£117.00
Appeals against conviction		£117.00
Appeals against sentence		£73.50
Committals for sentence		£73.50
Standard appearance fee	£46.50	
Standard refresher fee		
(1) Half day	£81.75	
(2) Full day	£158.25	
(3) More than a full day	£238.00	
Standard written work fee	£30.00]	

Annotations
Section heading: words in square brackets added by SI 1993 No 934, reg 16.
Para 5: words omitted revoked by SI 1990 No 488, reg 3(7).
Para 6: substituted by SI 1990 No 488, reg 3(8).
Para 9: sum underlined substituted by SI 1995 No 952, reg 9(a), further substituted with savings, by subsequent sum in square brackets, by SI 1996 No 644, reg 6(a); for savings see reg 1(3) thereof.
Para 10: substituted by SI 1990 No 488, reg 3(10); sum underlined substituted by SI 1995 No 952, reg 9(b), further substituted with savings, by subsequent sum in square brackets, by SI 1996 No 644, reg 6(b), for savings see reg 1(3) thereof.
Table: substituted by SI 1995 No 952, reg 9(c), further substituted with savings, by subsequent Table in square brackets by SI 1996 No 644, reg 6(c); for savings see reg 1(3) thereof.
Modification: any reference to solicitor(s) etc modified to include references to bodies recognised under the Administration of Justice Act 1985, s 9, by the Solicitors Incorporated Practices Order 1991, SI 1991 No 2684, arts 4, 5, Sch 1.

PART II DETERMINATION OF OTHER FEES

1 The appropriate authority shall allow such fee in respect of an item of work allowed under regulation 9(5), not exceeding the maximum amount specified in respect of that item of work, as appears to it to provide reasonable remuneration.

2 Where an hourly rate is specified in a Table in this Part of this Schedule in respect of an item of work allowed under regulation 9(5), the appropriate authority shall determine any fee for such work in accordance with that hourly rate; provided that the fee determined shall not be less than the maximum amount specified.

3 Where a refresher fee is claimed in respect of less than a full day, the appropriate authority shall allow such fee as appears to it reasonable having regard to the fee which would be allowable for a full day.

4 The fees allowed to junior counsel for proceedings in the Crown Court arising out of a breach of an order of the Crown Court or other similar matters shall not exceed the maximum amounts specified for 'committals for sentence'.

5 Paragraph 11 of Part I of this Schedule shall apply where counsel's fees are determined in accordance with this Part of the Schedule as it applies where standard fees are allowed in accordance with Part I of the Schedule.

[TABLE 1: JUNIOR COUNSEL

Court	*Type of* proceedings	*Basic fee*	*Full day* refresher fee	*Subsidiary fees Attendance at consultations, conferences and views*	*Written work*	*Attendance at pre-trial reviews, applications and other appearances*
Magistrates' Court	All cases	Maximum amount: £461	Maximum amount: £159.50	£28.75 per hour Minimum amount: £14.35	Maximum amount: £50.50	Maximum amount: £92.50
Crown Court	Jury trials	Maximum amount: £537.50				
	Cases prepared for trial in which no jury is sworn	Maximum amount: £313				
	Guilty pleas	Maximum amount: £189.50		£33 per hour Minimum amount: £16.50	Maximum amount: £57.50	Maximum amount: £98
	Appeals against conviction	Maximum amount: £207	Maximum amount: £176			
	Appeals against sentence	Maximum amount: £106				
	Committals for sentence	Maximum amount: £106]				

[TABLE 1: JUNIOR COUNSEL

Court	*Type of proceedings*	*Basic fee*	*Full day refresher fee*	*Subsidiary fees Attendance at consultations, conferences & views*	*Written work*	*Attendance at pre-trial reviews, applications and other appearances*
Magistrates' court	All cases	Maximum amount: £468	Maximum amount: £162	£29.25 per hour Minimum amount: £14.50	Maximum amount: £51.25	Maximum amount: £94.00
Crown Court	Jury trials	Maximum amount: £545.50				
	Cases prepared for trial in which no jury is sworn	Maximum amount: £317.75				
	Guilty pleas	Maximum amount: £192.25		£33.50 per hour Minimum amount: £16.75	Maximum amount: £58.25	Maximum amount: £99.50
	Appeals against conviction	Maximum amount: £210	Maximum amount: £178.75			
	Appeals against sentence	Maximum amount: £107.50				
	Committals for sentence	Maximum amount: £107.50]				

[TABLE 2: QUEEN'S COUNSEL

Court	*Type of proceedings*	*Basic fee*	*Full day refresher fee*	*Subsidiary fees Attendance at consultations, conferences and views*	*Written work*	*Attendance at pre-trial reviews, applications and other appearances*
Magistrates' Court	All cases	Maximum amount: £4446	Maximum amount: £297	£54.50 per hour Minimum amount: £28	Maximum amount: £105	Maximum amount: £205
Crown Court	All cases	Maximum amount: £5400	Maximum amount: £330.50	£62.50 per hour Minimum amount: £32	Maximum amount: £119.50	Maximum amount: £257.50]

Annotations

Table 1: substituted by SI 1992 No 592, reg 9; further substituted with savings, by subsequent Table in square brackets, by SI 1996 No 644, reg 7, for savings see reg 1(3) thereof.

Table 2: substituted by SI 1992 No 592, reg 9.

Appendix F

Eligibility and Payment Rates from April 1996

1.1 GREEN FORM: Eligibility rates

Income limit		£75.00 per week
Allowances against income:	**Partner**	£27.30 per week
	Children:	
	Under 11	£16.45 per week
	11–15	£24.10 per week
	16–17	£28.85 per week
	18 and over	£37.90 per week
Capital limit	**no dependants**	£1000.00
	one dependant	£1335.00
	two dependant	£1535.00
	three plus	add £100 per dependant

Contribution system None. Applicant is ineligible if his disposable income exceeds £75.00 per week.

Passporting The applicant automatically qualifies on income if he receives income support, disability working allowance, family credit or income based job seekers allowance. NOTE: Even where an applicant qualifies on income grounds due to receipt of a prescribed benefit he may still be ineligible if his capital exceeds the prescribed limit.

1.2 GREEN FORM – payment rates

	Inside London		**Outside London**	
	Franchisees	Non Franchisees	Franchisees	Non Franchisees
	£	£	£	£
Preparation	48.25	46.50	45.50	44.00
Travel & waiting	25.50	24.50	25.50	24.50
Routine letters and telephone calls	3.70	3.55	3.55	3.40
Costs limit	96.50	93.00	91.00	88.00

2.1 ABWOR – Financial eligibility

Income limit		£162.00 per week
Allowances against income:	**Partner**	£ 27.30 per week
	Children:	
	Under 11	£ 16.45 per week
	11–15	£ 24.10 per week
	16–17	£ 28.85 per week
	18 and over	£ 37.90 per week
Capital limit	**no dependants**	£3000.00
	one dependant	£3335.00
	two dependants	£3535.00
	three plus	add £100 per dependant

Contribution system Free if the weekly disposable income does not exceed £67. If the weekly disposable income exceeds £67 but is less than £162 a contribution of 1/3rd of the excess income will fall due each week.

Passporting The applicant automatically qualifies on income if he receives income support, disability working allowance, family credit or income based job seekers allowance. NOTE: Even where an applicant qualifies on income grounds due to receipt of a prescribed benefit he may still be ineligible if his capital exceeds the prescribed limit.

2.2 ABWOR – Payment rates

	Inside London		Outside London	
	Franchisees £	Non Franchisees £	Franchisees £	Non Franchisees £
All criminal matters except warrants of further detention.				
Preparation	48.25	46.50	45.50	44.00
Advocacy	57.25	55.25	57.25	55.25
Attendance at court where counsel assigned	31.00	30.00	31.00	30.00
Travel & waiting	25.50	24.50	25.50	24.50
Routine letters and telephone calls	3.70	3.55	3.55	3.40
Warrants of further detention.*				
Preparation Advocacy	64.33	62.00	60.67	58.67
Attendance at court where counsel assigned	76.33	73.67	76.33	73.67
Travel & waiting	41.33	39.99	41.33	39.99
Routine letters and telephone calls	4.93	4.73	4.73	4.53

* These rates only apply to duty solicitors providing ABWOR in unsocial hours. Where ABWOR is claimed for warrants of further detention at other times, or by own solicitors the normal ABWOR rate applies.

3.0 DUTY SOLICITOR SCHEME – fee earner rates

	Inside London		Outside London	
	Franchisees	Non Franchisees	Franchisees	Non Franchisees
	£	£	£	£
Court Duty Solicitor				
Standard rate	53.50	52.00	52.25	50.75
Enhanced rate	66.88	65.00	65.31	63.44
Travelling	25.50	25.00	25.50	25.00
Police Station Duty Solicitor				
Availability during duty period	3.85	3.75	3.80	3.65
To maximum of	92.00	89.25	90.75	88.00
Advice and assistance other than by telephone:				
-Duty solicitor unsocial hours	61.75	60.00	61.75	60.00
-Duty solicitor other hours	50.25	48.50	46.50	45.50
-Own solicitor	50.25	48.50	46.50	45.50
Travelling and waiting				
-Duty solicitor unsocial hours	61.75	60.00	61.75	60.00
-Duty solicitor other hours	50.25	48.50	46.50	45.50
-Own solicitor	25.75	25.25	25.75	25.25
Telephone advice	22.00	21.50	21.25	20.75
Routine telephone calls	3.75	3.60	3.60	3.50
Cost limit per case	90.00	90.00	90.00	90.00

4.1 CRIMINAL LEGAL AID SCHEME eligibility rates

Income limit		£49.00 per week
Allowances against income:	**Partner**	£27.30 per week
	Children:	
	Under 11	£16.45 per week
	11–15	£24.10 per week
	16–17	£28.85 per week
	18 and over	£37.90 per week
Capital limit		£3,000.00
Equity in home	Free equity disregard	£100,000.00

Contribution system Free if the weekly disposable income does not exceed £48. If the weekly disposable income exceeds £48 a £1 contribution will fall due for every £3 more than £48 exists as disposable income.

Passporting The applicant automatically qualifies on income if he receives income support, disability working allowance, family credit or income based job seekers allowance.

4.2 CRIMINAL LEGAL AID SCHEME – remuneration rates for magistrates' courts

Hourly rates	**Inside London**		**Outside London**	
Travelling	18.50		18.50	
	Franchisees	Non Franchisees	Franchisees	Non Franchisees
	£	£	£	£
Preparation	48.50	47.25	46.00	44.75
Advocacy	57.75	56.50	57.75	56.50
Attendance at court where counsel assigned	31.50	30.50	31.50	30.50
Travelling and Waiting	25.50	24.75	25.50	24.75
Routine letters written and telephone calls	3.70	3.60	3.55	3.45

Standard fees

	Franchisees Inside London				**Non franchisees inside London**			
	Lower Standard Fee £	Lower Limit £	Higher Standard Fee £	Higher Limit £	Lower Standard Fee £	Lower Limit £	Higher Standard Fee £	Higher Limit £
Category one	191.00	354.00	453.00	598.00	185.50	344.00	440.00	581.50
Category two	336.25	602.00	755.00	963.00	326.50	584.00	732.50	934.75
Category three	299.25	507.00	629.00	778.00	290.50	493.00	611.00	755.25

	Franchisees outside London				**Non franchisees outside London**			
	Lower Standard Fee £	Lower Limit £	Higher Standard Fee £	Higher Limit £	Lower Standard Fee £	Lower Limit £	Higher Standrad Fee £	Higher Limit £
Category one	148.25	276.00	357.00	478.00	144.25	268.00	346.00	463.75
Category two	262.25	474.00	601.00	790.00	254.00	460.00	583.00	767.25
Category three	236.50	418.00	536.00	730.00	229.75	406.00	520.25	709.50

4.3 CRIMINAL LEGAL AID SCHEME – Crown Court Standard Fees

	Franchisees Inside London				**Non franchisees inside London**			
	Lower Fee £	Lower Limit £	Principal Fee £	Principal Limit £	Lower Fee £	Lower Limit £	Principal Fee £	Principal Limit £
Jury Trial	139.00	186.00	261.50	326.00	129.50	179.00	249.50	312.00
Guilty Plea	87.50	114.00	185.50	235.00	81.50	110.00	175.00	226.00
Appeal against conviction	64.50	70.00	159.00	244.00	51.00	68.00	153.00	233.00
Appeal against sentence	39.25	54.00	98.00	135.00	36.25	52.00	93.00	131.00
Committal for sentence	45.00	53.00	103.00	145.00	42.50	51.00	97.75	141.00
Advocacy	28.75				26.25			
Attendance	21.40				21.40			
Travelling	18.50				18.50			

4.4 CRIMINAL LEGAL AID SCHEME – Crown courts ex post facto fees

Hourly Rates

		In London £	Outside London £
Preparation	- own solicitor	55.75	53.00
	- fee earner (or equivalent)	47.25	45.00
	- articled clerk (or equivalent)	34.00	29.75
Advocacy	- senior solicitor	64.50	64.50
	- solicitor	56.00	56.00
Attendance at court			
	- senior solicitor	42.25	42.25
	- solicitor	34.00	34.00
	- articled clerk	20.50	20.50
Travelling and waiting			
	- senior solicitor	24.75	24.75
	- solicitor	24.75	24.75
	- articled clerk	12.50	12.50
Letter and telephone calls		3.45	3.60

4.5 LEGAL AID SCHEME Crown courts counsel's standard fees

		Fee £
Jury trial		221.50
Guilty pleas		117.00
Appeals against conviction		117.00
Appeals against sentence		73.50
Committals for sentence		73.50
Standard appearance fee		46.50
Standard refresher fee	– half day	81.75
	– full day	158.25
	– more than a full day	238.00
Standard written work fee		30.00

Notes:

1. Where counsel appears alone the standard basic fee payable is increased by £19.25
2. Where counsel listens to a taped interview the standard basic fee payable is increased by £10.90 for every ten minutes (or part thereof).

4.6 LEGAL AID FOR CONTEMPT PROCEEDINGS

Standard appearance fee		£ 72.25
Division if both solicitor and counsel appear		
	- Advocate	£ 46.50
	- Solicitor	£ 26.25

4.7 CRIMINAL LEGAL AID mileage rate

Mileage rate	£ 0.36 per mile.

NOTES:

1. Eligibility and payment rates are the subject of annual revision.
2. Increase in eligibility rates are now linked to increased in social security rates and attract parity with them.

Appendix G

Digest of Cases

CONTENTS

NOTE: A quick reference guide is provided at the end of this appendix to enable cases to be located by subject if the case name is not known.

1.0 Scope of the criminal legal aid scheme

1.1 *R v Crown Court at Inner London, ex p Bentham* [1989] 1 WLR 408
1.2 *R v Crawley Justices, ex p Ohakwe* (1994) 158 JP 781
1.3 *R v Crown Court at Liverpool, ex p McCann* [1995] RTR 23
1.4 *R v Redbridge Magistrates' Court, ex p Guppy* (1995) 159 JP 622
1.5 *R v Legal Aid Board, ex p Heptonstalls* [1995] 33 LS Gaz R 23
1.6 *R v Clerk to South Cheshire Justices, ex p Bold* (1996) Times, 15 July
1.7 *R v Egan* (1996) Times, 14 October.

2.0 Obtaining information for criminal legal aid applications

2.1 *R v Highgate Justices, ex p Lewis* [1977] Crim LR 611
2.2 *R v Newham Justices, ex p Mumtaz* (1990) 154 JP 597
2.3 *R v South Western Justices, ex p Doyle and Bennett* (1 November 1995, Unreported)

3.0 Power to grant criminal legal aid orders:

3.1 *R v Tullett* [1976] Crim LR 193:
3.2 *R v City of Cambridge Justices, ex p Leader* (1979) 144 JP 148
3.3 *R v Liverpool City Magistrates' Court, ex p Shacklady and Pender* [1993] 2 All ER 929.
3.4 *R v Liverpool City Magistrates' Court, ex p Pender (No 2)* [1994] 2 All ER 897.
3.5 *R v Crown Court at Isleworth, ex p Willington* [1993] 1 WLR 713
3.6 *R v Highbury Corner Magistrates' Court, ex p Sonn & Co* [1995] 4 All ER 57

4.0 Power to grant duplicate legal aid orders

4.1 *R v Liverpool City Justices, ex p R M Broudie & Co* (1994) 159 JP 330

5.0 The merit test

5.1 *R v Edgehill* [1963] 1 All ER 181
5.2 *R v Serghiou* [1966] 3 All ER 637n
5.3 *R v Crown Court at Cambridge, ex p Hagi* (1979) 144 JP 145
5.4 *R v Liverpool City Justices, ex p McGhee* [1993] Crim LR 609

6.0 Assignment of legal aid orders

6.1 *R v Solihull Justices, ex p Johnson* (1976) 140 JP Jo 189
6.2 *Baker v West Sussex Justices* (1983) 148 JP 129
6.3 *R v O'Brien* [1985] 1 All ER 971
6.4 *Practice Note* [1989] 2 All ER 479

7.0 Renewal of applications

7.1 *R v Bury Justices, ex p N (a minor)* [1986] 3 All ER 789

8.0 Delay in consideration of orders and date of order

8.1 *Welch v Rebridge Justices* (1984) 148 JP 474
See also *R v Newham Justices, ex p Mumtaz* (ibid, paragraph 2.2 above).

9.0 Amendments of legal aid orders to allow representation to cover counsel

9.1 *R v Derby Justices, ex p Kooner* [1971] 1 QB 147
9.2 *R v Guildford Justices, ex p Scott* [1975] Crim LR 286

10.0 Legal aid and costs: consequences of not amending a legal aid order

10.1 *R v Crown Court at Liverpool, ex p Lord Chancellor* (1993) 158 JP 821.

11.0 Disclosure of information within legal aid applications

11.1 *R v Winter* [1980] Crim LR 659
11.2 *R v Stubbs* [1982] 1 WLR 509

1.0 SCOPE OF THE CRIMINAL LEGAL AID SCHEME

1.1 *R v Crown Court at Inner London, ex p Bentham* [1989] 1 WLR 408

NOTE: This case was decided under the provisions of section 28(5) of the Legal Aid Act 1974 which stated:

> 'Where a person convicted or sentenced by a magistrates' court desires to appeal to the Crown Court, either of those courts may order that he shall be given legal aid for the purpose of the appeal, and, where any person gives notice of appeal either of those courts may order that the other party to the appeal be given legal aid for the purpose of resisting the appeal.'

The applicant, Bentham, had laid information before Justices under section 99 of the Public Health Act 1936 on the grounds that the state of a council owned flat was prejudicial to the health of the applicant's family. The Justices found in favour of the applicant and ordered the council to carry out certain works to abate the nuisance. The council appealed to the Crown Court.

In order to defend the appeal the applicant applied for criminal legal aid order at the Crown Court. The court refused to grant an order on the grounds that the applicant was not a person resisting an appeal by a person convicted or sentenced by the Justices.

The High Court held that on determination of the information laid under section 99 of the Public Health Act the Justices had made an order under section 94(2) of the Act. In doing so the Justices had determined that the council had committed the criminal offence of allowing the premises to be in such a state of repair that they were prejudicial to health, and therefore the applicant was entitled to a criminal legal aid order to resist the appeal.

Commentary

Although this case was decided on the basis of the 1974 Act, section 21(1) does permit a grant of legal aid to a person not acting in an official capacity to resist an appeal to the Crown Court of a person convicted of an offence who is appealing against that conviction or sentence.

1.2 *R v Crawley Justices, ex p Ohakwe* (1994) 158 JP 781

The applicant had been found to be in possession of small amounts of cannabis and cocaine at Gatwick Airport and he was arrested. Subsequently he was also found to be in possession of £20,000 in various currencies. He was prosecuted and was granted a criminal legal aid order for his defence. A fine and an order for deportation was imposed by way of sentence. Subsequently H M Customs and Excise seized the cash, except that required to discharge the fine under section 25 of the Criminal Justice (International Co-operation) Act 1980. Applications were made from time to time to extend the order of seizure pending the hearing of an application for forfeiture of the cash.

Ohakwe applied for a legal aid order to resist the application for forfeiture. The Justices refused to grant a criminal legal aid order on the grounds that the proceedings were not criminal proceedings for the purposes of Part V of the Legal Aid Act 1988. The applicant sought an order of mandamus to compel the justices to grant a criminal legal aid order.

The High Court held that these proceedings were not criminal proceedings as defined by section 19(5) of the Legal Aid Act 1988 and dismissed the application.

Commentary

This case is interesting if only because it appears that the original grant of criminal legal aid was made without regard to the £20,000 capital held by the applicant. The case is however unlikely to have a great impact on the ability to grant criminal legal aid orders except for courts which regularly deal with smuggling cases.

1.3 *R v Crown Court at Liverpool, ex p McCann* [1995] RTR 23

The scope of the criminal legal aid scheme is wide enough to allow an order to be granted where the legally assisted person sought to obtain the removal of disqualification from holding or obtaining a driving licence.

Section 19(5) of the 1988 Act states that 'Criminal proceedings includes proceedings for dealing with an offender for an offence or in respect of a sentence or as a fugitive or as an offender'. Balcombe J, said 'sentence in relation to any person includes any order made on his conviction for an offence'.

Commentary

This decision seems to extend the scope of the criminal legal aid scheme to any proceedings where the original sentence or order is to be examined. This would seem to include fines enforcement hearings where the criteria within section 22(2)(a) of the 1988 Act are likely to be established given the obvious risk of a custodial sentence (see also *Ex p Guppy* below).

1.4 *R v Redbridge Magistrates' Court, ex p Guppy* (1995) 159 JP 622

Darius Guppy sought a criminal legal aid order in respect of enforcement proceedings before justices to recover a compensation order of £227,000 imposed by the Court of Appeal in substitution for a fine imposed on conviction by the Crown Court at Snaresbrook. The justices refused to grant a criminal legal aid order on the grounds that the enforcement proceedings were not criminal proceedings.

The High Court held that these proceedings were within the section 19(5) of the Legal Aid Act 1988 definition of criminal proceedings and therefore the justices had erred in deciding that they had no jurisdiction to grant a criminal legal aid order. The matter was remitted to the justices for reconsideration.

Commentary

It is now clear that criminal legal aid orders can be granted in enforcement proceedings to recover financial penalties or orders made on conviction or as part of a sentence. This definition seems to exclude the enforcement of legal aid contribution orders from eligibility for a criminal legal aid order and cases involving the enforcement of rates, community charge or council tax as those sums were not imposed as a result of a conviction (see *R v Clerk to South Cheshire Justices, ex p Bold*, below). This seems to create an injustice as in each type of proceeding there is a real risk of a custodial sentence.

If an application for legal aid is to be made in enforcement proceedings the procedure under regulation 11 would apply and the applicant would have to produce documentary evidence of his means.

1.5 *R v Legal Aid Board, ex p Heptonstalls* [1995] 33 LS Gaz R 23.

Popplewell J held that proceedings under section 6 of the Bail Act 1976 were separate proceedings for the purposes of the legal aid fixed fee regulations, thereby reversing the Legal Aid Board's practice of disallowing a separate fee to be paid on the grounds that such matters were part and parcel of the substantive matter.

Commentary

The case does not assist in providing reasons for the grant of a legal aid certificate in Bail Act cases, however the case of *R v Davis* (1986) 8 Cr App Rep (S) 64 provides some assistance, as it held that where proceedings under theBail Act were commenced the opportunity to be represented by counsel should be extended to the defendent..

1.6 *R v Clerk to South Cheshire Justices, ex p Bold* [1996] 27 LS Gaz R 28

An applicant for legal aid sought to argue that proceedings under regulation 41 of the Community Charges (Administration and Enforcement) Regulations 1989 (SI 1989/438) were criminal proceedings for the purpose of obtaining the benefit of a legal aid order. The applicant relied on the ruling *Benham v United Kingdom* (1995) Independent, 3 February in which the European Court of Human Rights had held that it was desirable that a person facing committal to prison for such arrears should be offered legal aid as proceedings under regulation 41 were 'criminal proceedings' within the definition provided by articles 6.1 and 6.3 of the European Convention for the Protection of Human Rights and Fundamental Freedoms.

The High Court held that the construction of the Legal Aid Act 1988, as it presently stands did not allow such proceedings to be regarded as 'criminal proceedings'. the Court relied on the decision of Mr Justice Henry in *R v Highbury Corner Magistrates, ex p Watkins* [1992] RA 300, 306, in which it was said that '. . . proceedings under regulation 41 are plainly legal proceedings other than criminal proceedings. They are proceedings for the recovery of an unpaid tax'.

Commentary

This case confirms the present situation as regards community charge cases and other matters where civil debts are enforced in the magistrates' court. It should always be remembered that ABWOR may be used in such cases (see Chapter Two). The court did observe in this case that there may be a need for further legislation to be enacted by Parliament to give effect to the Benham decision.

1.7 *R v Egan* (1996) Times, 14 October

The Queen's Bench Division of the High Court held that where a person had been found as being unfit to plead in accordance with the Criminal Procedure (Insanity) Acts of 1964 and 1991, he could not be treated as a convicted or an accused person for the purposes of section 21(1) of the Legal Aid Act 1988 and was not, therefore, entitled to a criminal legal aid order for the purpose of challenging that finding of fact. The whole purpose of such a finding of fact was to spare an accused person suffering from such a disability the stigma of a criminal conviction. The High Court consequently quashed the legal aid order granted by the Registrar of Criminal Appeals.

Commentary

As the consequences of finding that a person is unfit to plead, but none the less carried out some unlawful act, may be that a hospital order is made for an indefinite period, the consequences of this finding may be both draconian and discriminatory in practice. It seems that a person under some mental disability will be entitled to a criminal legal aid order up to the moment that the jury determines that he or she is unfit to plead. At that moment the legally aided person can no longer be regarded as an accused person, and their entitlement to a criminal legal aid order ceases, despite the potentially grave orders available to the court. The case sits uneasily with that of *R v Crown Court at Liverpool, ex p McCann* (para 1.3 above) where legal aid was held to be applicable to an application brought by a person who had been sentenced and where there was no prospect of appeal as the time period had expired, to remove a disqualification to drive a motor vehicle. In the latter case a much more generous definition of the scope of the scheme seems to have been applied.

2.0 OBTAINING INFORMATION FOR CRIMINAL LEGAL AID APPLICATIONS

2.1 *R v Highgate Justices, ex p Lewis* [1977] Crim LR 611

Before a decision on legal aid can be reached there must be adequate knowledge of the circumstances of the case. Per Lord Widgery C J it was highly desirable for information to be given in the magistrates' court and it was much to be hoped that all parties would co-operate in the matter.

Commentary

The legal aid application that gave rise to this case concerned an offence under section 47 of the Offences Against the Person Act 1861. The court indicated that such an offence should not always attract a grant of legal aid as the seriousness of the offence can vary greatly. Although section 29(4) of the 1974 Act suggested in the same terms as section 21(7) of the 1988 Act that doubts should be resolved in the applicants favour the High Court held that there must be adequate information to enable a proper view to be formed. The commentary in the CLR makes the point that, although a competent authority should take account of the maximum sentences available for an offence, when considering legal aid, it is a principal of English law that, with the exception of offences of murder, there is no minimum sentence. This case arose before the advanced information scheme took effect; its ratio, however, remains good law if that has not been served or in summary cases.

2.2 *R v Newham Justices, ex p Mumtaz* (1990) 154 JP 597

The applicants had applied for legal aid and had submitted a statement of their means which did not accord with a statement of their circumstances which had been made to the court by the prosecution. The clerk to the justices had therefore written to the applicants' solicitors seeking accounts and clarification of the applicants' true financial position and did not make an order for legal aid at that stage. The information was not supplied and the applicants were committed for trial. After the committal the applicants sought to persuade the clerk to the justices to give further consideration to the legal aid application and make a retrospective grant of legal aid so that the order was dated as at the date that the application was received. The clerk declined to give further consideration to the matter and doubted he had power to make retrospective orders.

The Divisional Court dismissed the application stating that the clerk to the justices was properly entitled to receive a written reply before making a decision to grant legal aid and that an advocate was not entitled to payment under a legal aid order until he was assigned under that order by a court, except in so far as payment was allowed under regulations for urgent work done prior to the grant of the order.

Commentary

This case was decided on the construction of Part II of the Legal Aid Act 1974 (as amended) as the Legal Aid Act 1988 was not in force at the material time. The 1988 Act and its subordinate regulations, as amended, impose a much greater duty on applicants to provide documentation than was the case under the earlier Act. The principle of section 21(5) of the 1988 Act is the same as that under the 1974 Act in that the competent authority shall not make an order until satisfied that the applicant's means are such as shall require representation. The earlier regulations were not so specific as those that exist at present about the powers available to seek further information and it therefore seems that the ratio of this case remains good law. Consequently there is no power that would allow a competent authority to back date an order or a compulsion upon such an authority to grant legal aid in circumstances where that authority has conflicting information concerning an applicant's means.

2.3 *R v South Western Justices, ex p Doyle and Bennett* (1 November 1995, Unreported)

Latham J held that where the documentary evidence provided by an applicant for a criminal legal aid order was deficient and a reasonable explanation was given in writing with the application form it was not open to a court to grant legal aid on the basis that it would be revoked if the documentary evidence was not provided within a set time. The proper procedure that should be adopted was for the court to grant an order unconditionally. If there was some basis to believe that the condition that had prevented the production of documentary evidence had ceased at some later time, the court could then request fresh documentary evidence to be provided in accordance with regulation 21 of the General Regulations.

3.0 POWER TO GRANT CRIMINAL LEGAL AID ORDERS

3.1 *R v Tullett* [1976] Crim LR 193

The defendant applied for a criminal legal aid order in respect of two offences of driving whilst disqualified at the conclusion of a trial. It was contended by the Crown that this could only be done before the proceedings began.

The High Court held that the power to grant an order for legal aid remained until the end of the trial.

3.2 *R v City of Cambridge Justices, ex p Leader* (1979) 144 JP 148

A juvenile court refused to reconsider an application for legal aid when the defendant entered a not guilty plea. The court held that the court of trial had a duty to reconsider a legal aid application.

Commentary

If the renewal procedure has been exhausted at the time of trial the correct procedure to enable the court to determine a further application for legal aid is for an oral application to be made to the court under regulation 10 of the Legal Aid in Criminal and Care Proceedings (General) Regulations 1989. The restrictions that this case sought to impose as to when such applications could be made have now been overturned by *R v Liverpool City Magistrates' Court, ex p Pender (No 2)* (see paragraph 3.4 below).

3.3 *R v Liverpool City Magistrates' Court, ex p Shacklady and Pender* [1993] 2 All ER 929.

Each applicant had been granted a legal aid order subject to the payment of a contribution order and had failed to comply with the terms of that order. The enforcement process specified within regulation 36 of the 1989 General Regulations had been followed and the orders had been revoked by the justices. The validity of that process was not challenged. Subsequently both applicants applied to the clerk to the justices in writing for a further order. The clerk declined to make such an order arguing that he had no jurisdiction to grant a second order, which, if granted, would in any event be of no effect because of the operation of regulation 41(2) of the 1989 General Regulations. In both cases proceedings were still pending before the magistrates' court but neither applicant made an application to the court for an order.

The court held that there was no power within regulation 11 of the 1989 General Regulations that enabled an application to be made to the clerk to the justices for a further order in circumstances where the original order had been withdrawn. Any further application must be made to the court before which proceedings were taking place under regulation 10 of the 1989 General Regulations, which provides for oral applications for legal aid to be made to the court of trial or during other proceedings. Both applications were dismissed.

3.4 *R v Liverpool City Magistrates' Court, ex p Pender (No 2)* [1994] 2 All ER 897.

After the decision in *Shacklady and Pender* (above) Mr Pender made an application to the stipendiary magistrate, before whom his substantive case was listed, under regulation 10 of the 1989 General Regulations, which provides for oral applications for legal aid to be made to the court of trial or during other proceedings. The stipendiary magistrate had read the cases of *R v Macclesfield Justices, ex p Greenhalgh* (1979) 144 JP 142, which defined 'other proceedings' so as to exclude remand or committal proceedings, and *R v City of Cambridge Justices, ex p Leader* (1979) 144 JP 148 which excluded proceedings before justices as being 'other proceedings'. The proceedings against Mr Pender were committal proceedings and the magistrate concluded that the effect of these two cases was such that he did not have the jurisdiction to entertain a further application at that time. A further application was made for an order of mandamus and the divisional court overturned the two earlier cases on the grounds that, because the two former cases were decided on the construction of an old regulation that made no reference to the revocation of legal aid orders whereas the present regulation does, it would be straining language beyond endurance to exclude proceedings before magistrates as being other proceedings.

Commentary

On first reading the effect of these two cases may appear narrow, however the fact that there is little distinction between the words revocation and withdrawal may aid a legally assisted person who seeks amendment of his order but who finds his initial application declined. It would now seem to be open for him to ask for the original order to be withdrawn and then reapply for an order in terms that he seeks. This procedure may be particularly useful where reassignment is sought. A word of caution should be applied however as the validity of the second order under regulation 41(2), although raised by the clerk to the justices, was never determined by the court as a specific issue. It would of course be open to the paying authority to disallow work that does not seem reasonable, for example work that has been repeated by newly nominated solicitors, and it may be that the Divisional Court would be reluctant to allow this decision to be used to circumvent the established procedure for amendment of orders and may reach a contrary decision on the validity of second orders obtained in this way with the intention of avoiding the renewal procedure.

3.5 *R v Crown Court at Isleworth, ex p Willington* [1993] 1 WLR 713

The facts of this case were that a legally assisted person sought the reassignment of his legal aid order on the grounds that he had lost all confidence in the firm assigned under the order. His application was refused and he subsequently instructed a second firm of solicitors to obtain the discharge of his certificate before Judge Miller, which they did. Thereafter the applicant approached a third firm of solicitors and instructed them to apply for an adjournment in order that they could prepare his case properly for trial. This application was refused although the case was adjourned for a short period to enable the defendant to secure legal representation and apply for legal aid. Counsel for the defendant then applied for legal aid to the court nominating the third firm of solicitors as the solicitors to be assigned under the order. The judge responded to this application by reinstating the original legal aid order which remained assigned to the first firm of solicitors. The defendant applied for judicial review of this decision on three grounds, namely:

1. the judge had no jurisdiction to revoke a previous decision to discharge a legal aid order;
2. the judge had no jurisdiction to reinstate a legal aid order once discharged; and
3. the effect of the judge's order was to circumvent the right of a person entitled to representation to select a solicitor under section 32(1)(a) of the Legal Aid Act 1988.

The court held that it did not have jurisdiction to consider the matter on the grounds that the High Court's jurisdiction to review decisions of the Crown Court was restricted to matters other than those which related to trial on indictment.

Commentary

This case illustrates the problem identified in the *Pender* cases above. Whilst the High Court avoided making a substantive decision in this case, had the action arisen as a result of an order made in the magistrates' court there would have been no inherent jurisdiction that would have defeated the application for judicial review, as magistrates' courts are creatures of statute and lack such discretionary powers. It seems unlikely that justices could have lawfully imposed such an order on a legally assisted person, even if they formed the view that the actions of the legally assisted person were designed to abuse or avoid the legal aid regulations.

3.6 *R v Highbury Corner Magistrates' Court, ex p Sonn & Co* [1995] 4 All ER 57.

A long standing client of the applicants sought their attendance at a summary trial before Highbury Corner Magistrates' Court. An application for a legal aid order was made that same day, but the application was deficient in that the required documentary evidence as to means was not provided. Some days later the documentary evidence was provided and a request was made for an order to be issued. the clerk to the justices concluded that as the case had been concluded he no longer had the power to grant a legal aid order. The court held that the clerks view was an incorrect one as a legal aid order may be made after the conclusion of the criminal proceedings. This will allow the legally assisted persons cost incurred prior to the order to be recovered under the provisions of regulation 44(7) of the Legal Aid in Criminal and Care Proceedings (General) Regulations 1989, which allows urgent work undertaken prior to the grant of a legal aid order to be deemed as work done under the order. The argument that the legal aid order should be backdated to the date upon which it was received was rejected by the court as being unnecessary.

4.0 POWER TO GRANT DUPLICATE LEGAL AID ORDERS

4.1 *R v Liverpool City Justices, ex p R M Broudie & Co* (1994) 159 JP 330

The applicants were a firm of solicitors who had sought the issue of a substantial number of duplicate orders from the clerk to the justices. The clerk to the justices had refused to issue duplicate orders unless the applicant's could give a valid reason for the loss of the original. There were two matters to be resolved by the High Court, firstly had the clerk to the justices power to issue duplicate orders and if he had was his refusal to do so in the instant cases unreasonable.

The court held that the power to issue duplicate orders could be regarded as incidental to that specified by regulation 40 of the Legal Aid in Criminal and Care Proceedings (General) Regulations 1989. A fee of £5 is specified by

Magistrates' Court Fee (Amendment) Order 1992 can properly be levied for the supply of this duplicate document. The power to issue such orders is discretionary and the clerk to the justices can properly make enquiries so as to satisfy himself as to the loss or destruction of the original order, as the ratio of *R v Leigh Justices, ex p Kara* (1980) 72 Cr App Rep 327, which relates to enquiries being made to establish the loss or destruction of a warrant, was held to apply equally to legal aid orders.

Although the primary duty to take good care of a legal aid order rests with the solicitor in the three instant cases, the receipt of the order by the solicitor could not be proved. The refusal to grant a duplicate order was therefore unreasonable.

5.0 THE MERIT TEST

5.1 *R v Edgehill* [1963] 1 All ER 181

In cases where a recommendation for deportation is to be made, legal aid should normally be granted even though the court was at pains to state that it was not laying down a hard and fast rule.

5.2 *R v Serghiou* [1966] 3 All ER 637n

The appellant had pleaded guilty to offences of theft from an employer, making a false instrument, obtaining money by deception and false accounting. The justices had committed her to the quarter sessions for sentence where she asked for a further 62 offences to be taken into account. Concurrent sentences of five years were imposed in circumstances where the appellant was not represented, although there were no grounds to suppose she had applied for legal aid.

In reducing the sentence to one of three years' imprisonment Edmund Davies LJ observed that accused persons facing a substantial custodial sentence should be offered legal aid. This should be something that the court takes upon itself to do even if the accused person has not applied for legal aid himself.

Commentary

There are various provisions that require a person to be offered legal aid in circumstances where he has not received a previous custodial sentence before and is about to receive one or where that sentence is one of detention in a young offenders' institution, detention under the Children and Young Persons Act 1933 or the Criminal Justice Act 1982 but in the case of an adult facing a second or subsequent sentence there is no such compulsion. Although section 21(3)(d) of the Legal Aid Act 1988 requires an accused person who is to be sentenced before a magistrates' or Crown Court and who is to kept in custody pending the receipt of reports, or the results of an enquiry, to be granted legal aid (subject to his means being such that require him to receive representation under the Act), there is no specific requirement under the Act that a person on bail facing similar enquiries should be offered legal aid. This case may assist such an applicant.

5.3 *R v Crown Court at Cambridge, ex p Hagi* (1979) 144 JP 145.

Although Roskill LJ stated that the interests of justice are better served if a person facing trial on indictment is granted legal aid as time and money are generally saved the High Court should be reluctant to interfere with the wide jurisdiction and discretion conferred on competent authorities considering applications for legal aid.

Commentary

This case concerned a student of previous good character who was charged with possessing a small amount of cannabis. The case was decided before the introduction of the 1988 Act which conferred statutory criteria for the grant of legal aid. Given the High Court's subsequent intervention in cases where legal aid has been refused the ratio of this case is somewhat weak.

5.4 *R v Liverpool City Justices, ex p McGhee* [1993] Crim LR 609

The likelihood of an applicant for a criminal legal aid order being sentenced to a community service order was not to be regarded as a sentence that would deprive him of his liberty within section 22(2)(a) of the Legal Aid Act 1988.

The criteria within section 22(2) of the Act are not exhaustive and the prospect of a community penalty may be one of the things the competent authority may want to take into account when considering the application overall.

The phrase 'expert cross examination' qualifies the cross-examination and not the witness.

Commentary

Section 22(2)(a) of the Act is the provision most frequently relied on by applicants for criminal legal aid orders even though the frequency of its use may not accord with actual sentencing practices. The restriction of this provision by removing community penalties from the scope of this provision perhaps emphasises the need to consider carefully what grounds can properly be relied on when making an application. Reliance on section 22(2)(a) alone should be spared for the most serious of criminal cases where such a sentence is almost mandatory.

The qualification of section 22(2)(d) should create few problems for the applicant. In cases where an expert is to be cross-examined the need for expert cross-examination may be easier to establish than in other cases. It is unlikely that competent authorities will be persuaded that every case where a police officer or other similar individual is to give evidence for the prosecution will merit representation under this provision, were that the case legal aid would be available for the majority of offences within the criminal calendar. The need for the applicant to establish the need for expert cross-examination remains paramount.

6.0 ASSIGNMENT OF LEGAL AID ORDERS

6.1 *R v Solihull Justices, ex p Johnson* (1976) 140 JP Jo 189

In this unreported case several youths were charged with offences of affray. Counsel sought to challenge the justices' decision that the white youths should be represented by one counsel and the coloured youths by another as his client desired separate representation. The court held that where several persons were charged with offences which were to be tried together the court was entitled to assign one solicitor otherwise the absurd situation could arise of twenty co-defendants being represented by twenty solicitors or counsel. The court went on to state that there was nothing wrong with an application being made for separate representation where there was a conflict of interests that prevented the same solicitor representing all defendants. In such circumstances the appointed solicitor should certify that a conflict of interests has arisen, not the disappointed solicitor. There is a further safeguard in that the court will intervene if a conflict of interests becomes apparent.

Commentary

This case effectively requires that the court appoint the first solicitor to be assigned under a legal aid order for each defendant in a multi-defendant case unless that solicitor certifies a conflict exists. In circumstances where it is known that other solicitors are acting for co-defendants it would be prudent for a solicitor to obtain a letter or fax from them to confirm that a conflict exists between their client and his client to be exhibited with the application as this will hasten the assignment of the order and may avoid the need to apply for an amendment of the order by way of reassignment at a later date.

6.2 *Baker v West Sussex Justices* (1983) 148 JP 129

In this case the appellant was one of six joint defendants who was granted a legal aid order which was assigned to the solicitor representing his co-defendants. Owing to a conflict of interests that solicitor withdrew from representing Baker and another co-defendant, Cook. The Justices amended the legal aid order and assigned a solicitor who had not been nominated by either defendant. Baker subsequently appeared before the court represented by a solicitor of his choice and applied for the order to be amended in order that he was represented by a solicitor of his own choice. The court rejected that application on the grounds that there was no conflict of interests between Baker and Cook.

The court held that because none of the solicitors assigned to represent the co-accused could properly represent Baker or Cook the court should have assigned a solicitor nominated by one of them. They erred in assigning a solicitor who had not been so nominated and this decision was quashed.

Commentary:

This case provides useful guidance as to how solicitors should be assigned after a conflict is discovered. The court does not suggest how the court should distinguish between solicitors, however it is generally accepted that such disputes should be settled by nominating the solicitor who was identified in the earliest application received by the court.

6.3 *R v O'Brien* [1985] 1 All ER 971

Two defendants were jointly charged with an offence of affray, which was committed by the justices for trial at the Crown Court. The legal aid order provided for representation by the same solicitor and included provision for representation by counsel in each case. The 1968 Legal Aid Regulations allowed the solicitor to instruct any counsel who is willing to act. The solicitor instructed different counsel in each case and, in due course, submitted his bill for taxation. The taxing authority allowed only the costs of one counsel and disallowed the costs of the applicant. This decision was upheld on review and Judicial Review was sought.

The High Court held that even if only one solicitor was assigned to represent several defendants he was not restricted to instruct the same counsel to appear for all of them jointly.

6.4 *Practice Note* [1989] 2 All ER 479

1. Regulation 48(3) of the 1989 General Regulations enables a High Court or circuit judge to make a legal aid order which provides for the services of two counsel.
2. If such an application is made to the Crown Court it shall be placed before the resident or designated judge of the Court except where the substantive case is to be heard by a named High Court Judge in which case the application shall be placed before him.
3. The above does not apply if the application is made during a pre-trial review or during the trial. In those cases the judge seized of the matter shall determine the application.
4. In case of doubt the judge concerned or the presiding judge of the circuit should make such direction as he considers appropriate.

7.0 RENEWAL OF APPLICATIONS.

7.1 *R v Bury Justices, ex p N (a minor)* [1986] 3 All ER 789

In calculating the period in which a person, who has an initial application for a criminal legal aid order refused, may renew the application to the Legal Aid Board's Area Committee, the reference point is the date fixed by the court for trial or inquiry as required by regulation 15(2)(c) of the General Regulations 1989 and not the date of the first appearance.

Commentary

The court relied on the case of *R v City of Cambridge Justices, ex p Leader* (1979) 144 JP 148 in reaching its decision. Although this authority has now been overturned by *R v Liverpool Magistrates' Court, ex p Pender (No 2)* [1994] 2 All ER 897 it would be unfortunate if courts reverted to the previous practice relying on the first appearance as barring the right of renewal to the Legal Aid Board. Although this practice was prevalent in 1984 it was not one that found approval with the Justices' Clerks Society or the Law Society.

8.0 DELAY IN CONSIDERATION OF ORDERS AND DATE OF ORDER

8.1 *Welch v Redbridge Justices* (1984) 148 JP 474

The applicant had been brought before the justices in custody and was remanded in custody. At the hearing a legal aid application was made and was referred to the clerk to the justices who was not minded to grant the application and it was referred to a justice who refused it. At the next hearing a further application was made for legal aid together with an application that it be dated as at the date of submission, some seven days before the second application.

The court determined two questions, namely:

(i) An accused person was not remanded in custody on the date that he was first brought before the justices in police custody and therefore the justices were not compelled to grant legal aid, although they had a discretion to do so.
(ii) Justices were not able to back date a legal aid order.

Commentary

This case resolves two common problems that are frequently encounted by solicitors. It makes it quite clear that there is no power to back date a legal aid order, consequently it must be dated at the date upon which it is considered and not the date on which it was received. A solicitor can claim for urgent work done prior to the order under regulation 44(7) of the General Regulations. This case also clarifies that section 21(3)(c) of the Legal Aid Act 1988, which requires a grant of legal aid to a person remanded in custody for so much of the proceedings as relates to bail, is restricted until the hearing after he was remanded in custody by the justices.

See also *R v Newham Justices, ex p Mumtaz* (ibid, at paragraph 2.2 above) and *R v Highbury Corner Magistrates' Court ex p Sonn & Co* (ibid, at paragraph 3.6 above) which confirm that legal aid orders cannot be backdated.

9.0 AMENDMENTS OF LEGAL AID ORDERS TO ALLOW REPRESENTATION TO COVER COUNSEL

9.1 *R v Derby Justices, ex p Kooner* [1971] 1 QB 147

The justices repeatedly refused to extend a legal aid order to allow the applicant who was charged with an offence of murder to be represented by counsel at committal. The applicant sought an order of mandamus.

The court held that the requirement for the case to be unusually grave or difficult was met in cases of alleged murder for although the case may not be difficult it is undoubtedly grave.

Commentary

Although decided under the Criminal Justice Act 1967, which regulated the administration of legal aid, the phrase 'unusually grave or difficult' is still retained as the relevant test under the 1989 regulations.

9.2 *R v Guildford Justices, ex p Scott* [1975] Crim LR 286

In this case the applicant was charged with 35 offences of burglary and other related charges of conspiracy and handling stolen goods. He sought an extension to his legal aid certificate for representation for counsel on the grounds that the case was unusually grave or difficult.

The Lord Widgery held that at an early stage of many grave or difficult cases a competent solicitor could realise that there was no useful purpose in resisting a committal under section 1 of the Criminal Justice Act 1967 [Note: now section 6(2) of the Magistrates Courts Act 1980 committal without consideration of the evidence] and mere multiplicity of simple straight forward charges could not make representation by counsel desirable

If, even in a single case, there were some good grounds for believing that counsel might discover a basis for a sensible submission of no case to answer, or a sound forensic reason as to why certain statements should not be admitted then an extension to counsel should be allowed.

10.0 LEGAL AID AND COSTS: CONSEQUENCES OF NOT AMENDING A LEGAL AID ORDER.

10.1 *R v Crown Court at Liverpool, ex p Lord Chancellor* (1993) 158 JP 821

The facts of this case were that an accused person, Quinn, had been granted a legal aid order by the Liverpool Justices that entitled him to receive representation by a solicitor, junior counsel and Queen's counsel. The Liverpool Magistrates' Court had written to Quinn's solicitors advising them that any change in representation had to achieved by applying for the amendment of the legal aid order.

Quinn absconded for some time and when recaptured chose to dispense with the services of leading counsel and elected instead to be represented by Mr Riordan, junior counsel. Mr Riordan and the existing junior counsel therefore represented the defendant but no application was made to amend the order.

In due course a bill was submitted for taxation whereupon the taxing authority drew attention to the absence of an amendment to the order to enable representation by second counsel, other than Queen's counsel and declined to pay Mr Riordan's fee. Mr Riordan's clerk sought retrospective amendment of the order before His Honour Judge Sir Sanderson Temple who concluded that he had no power to make a retrospective order of that kind. Mr Riordan then applied to His Honour Judge Paterson who concluded that there was power to make a defendant's costs order under section 16 of the Prosecution of Offences Act 1985 and such an order was made. There was a further hearing at which counsel for the Lord Chancellor sought to persuade the learned judge that he had no power to make the costs order but the order remained. The Taxing Master made an ex gratia payment to Mr Riordan and the Lord Chancellor asked the Divisional Court to consider whether there was power for such an order to be made and to report to him.

The High Court concluded that it had jurisdiction to consider the matter as it arose after trial and was not a matter connected with a trial on indictment.

Quinn was without means and was being totally supported by the legal aid fund and had not incurred any expense at or before his trial so as to bring him within section 16(6) of the Prosecution of Offences Act 1985. Therefore the judge was not competent to make a defendant's costs order. Further Regulation 55 of the Legal Aid in Criminal and Care Proceedings (General) Regulations 1989 clearly applied and restricted counsel to fees paid from the legal aid fund. Having made these decisions the court did not consider it necessary to argue the merits or legality of the retrospective decision as this had no moment.

Commentary

This case is of significance not only in those rare circumstances where solicitors fail to ensure they are covered by a legal aid order but the definition of regulation 55 must also apply to applications for pre-certificate costs, in circumstances where the legally assisted person incurred no expense on his own behalf, being totally reliant on the state to provide such assistance, and prohibit the making of such orders.

11.0 DISCLOSURE OF INFORMATION WITHIN LEGAL AID APPLICATIONS

11.1 *R v Winter* [1980] Crim LR 659

The defendant was charged with defrauding the Department of Health and Social Security. During his evidence at trial the judge questioned him on the basis of information contained within his legal aid application.

The Court of Appeal quashed the conviction and held that a legal aid application was not evidence in the case and should not be used to discredit the accused. A legal aid application form should not be on the bench during the trial and should only be seen by the judge after conviction and only for determining a legal aid application.

11.2 *R v Stubbs* [1982] 1 WLR 509

The prosecution obtained a copy of the defendant's legal aid application and, in circumstances where the accused's credit was in issue, used the information within that application to discredit him.

Held by the Court of Appeal, quashing the conviction, the contents of legal aid applications should not be used, even by judges, to discredit witnesses.

Per curiam, if a witness was properly cross-examined on the contents of a legal aid application he is entitled to be warned against incriminating himself.

DIGEST OF CASES – QUICK REFERENCE GUIDE

NOTE: This guide is designed to supplement the main index to this appendices by identifying the main topic discussed within the authorities cited. Reference to the left hand column should assist the reader identify the cases most likely to deal with the particular enquiry they are investigating. The middle column provides the case name and the right hand column provides a cross reference to the main note within the appendices. Full references are given in the heading to the main note.

SUBJECT	*RELEVANT CASES*	*PARAGRAPH BELOW*
SCOPE OF THE CRIMINAL LEGAL AID SCHEME:		
Appeals from magistrates' courts	*R v Crown Court at Inner London, ex p Bentham*	1.1
Proceeds of drug trafficking	*R v Crawley Justices, ex p Ohakwe*	1.2
Variation of sentences and orders made on conviction (removal of disqualification)	*R v Crown Court at Liverpool, ex p McCann*	1.3
Enforcement of monetary orders (except civil debt)	*R v Redbridge Magistrates' Court, ex p Guppy*	1.4
Bail Act Offences	*R v Legal Aid Board, ex p Heptonstalls*	1.5
Community Charge enforcement	*R v Clerk to the South Cheshire Justices, ex p Bold*	1.6
OBTAINING INFORMATION FOR CRIMINAL LEGAL AID APPLICATIONS:		
Provision of information by third parties	*R v Highgate Justices, ex p Lewis*	2.1
Enquiries before determination of the application	*R v Newham Justices, ex p Mumtaz*	2.2
Conditonal grants pending further information	*R v South Western Justices, ex p Doyle and Bennett*	2.3
Information provided after case concluded	*R v Highbury Corner Magistrates' Court, ex p Sonn & Co*	3.6
PROVISION OF DUPLICATE LEGAL AID ORDERS		
Proper enquiry needed before duplicate order may be issued	*R v Liverpool City Justices, ex p R M Broudie & Co*	4.1
Duty to impose charge for supplying duplicate order	*R v Liverpool City Justices, ex p R M Broudie & Co*	4.1
MERIT TEST		
Deportation	*R v Edgehill*	5.1
Risk of custody	*R v Serghiou*	5.2
Trial on indictment	*R v Crown Court at Cambridge, ex p Hagi*	5.3
Community service	*R v Liverpool City Justices ex p McGhee*	5.4
Expert cross examination	*R v Liverpool City Justices, ex p McGhee*	5.4
Remands in custody	*Welch v Redbridge Justices*	8.1

SUBJECT	*RELEVANT CASES*	*PARAGRAPH BELOW*
ASSIGNMENT OF LEGAL AID ORDERS		
One solicitor to be assigned in respect of co-accused, unless conflict of interest	*R v Solihull Justices, ex p Johnson*	6.1
Appointed solicitor to certify conflict of interest	*R v Solihull Justices, ex p Johnson*	6.1
Assignment of solicitor where conflict exists	*Baker v West Sussex Justices*	6.2
Assignment of separate counsel	*R v O'Brien*	6.3
Assignment of more than one counsel	*Practice Note*	6.4
RENEWAL OF APPLICATIONS		
Relevant dates for rights of renewal to the Area Committee	*R v Bury Justices, ex p N (a minor)*	7.1
DELAY IN CONSIDERING APPLICATIONS AND DATE OF ORDER.		
No power to back date orders	*Welch v Redbridge Justices*	8.1
	R v Newham Justices, ex p Mumtaz	2.2
	R v Highbury Corner Magistrates' Court, ex p Sonn & Co	3.6
Conditional orders	*R v South Western Justices, ex p Doyle and Bennett*	2.3
AMENDMENTS TO LEGAL AID ORDERS		
Murder – extension to cover counsel	*R v Derby Justices, ex p Kooner*	9.1
Multiple charges – extension to cover counsel	*R v Guildford Justices, ex p Scott*	9.2
CONSEQUENCES OF NOT AMENDING A LEGAL AID ORDER		
No power to make a defendant's costs order to cover cost of counsel not assigned under an order	*R v Crown Court at Liverpool, ex p Lord Chancellor*	10.1
No power for counsel not covered under an order to claim against legal aid fund	*R v Crown Court at Liverpool, ex p Lord Chancellor*	10.1

SUBJECT	*RELEVANT CASES*	*PARAGRAPH BELOW*
DISCLOSURE OF INFORMATION WITHIN LEGAL AID APPLICATIONS		
Legal aid application forms must not be on the bench until after the trial	*R v Winter*	11.1
Legal aid application forms cannot be used as evidence in trials for other offences	*R v Winter*	11.1
Content of legal aid applications cannot be used to discredit witnesses	*R v Stubbs*	11.2

Appendix H

National Mode of Trial Guidelines (Practice Note) [1990] 1 WLR 1439

The purpose of these guidelines is to help magistrates decide whether or not to commit 'either way' offences for trial in the Crown Court. Their object is to provide guidance not direction. They are not intended to impinge upon a magistrate's duty to consider each case individually and on its own particular facts.

These guidelines apply to all defendants aged 17 and above.

General mode of trial considerations

Section 19 of the Magistrates' Courts Act 1980 requires magistrates to have regard to the following matters in deciding whether an offence is more suitable for summary trail or trail on indictment:

(1) the nature of the case;
(2) whether the circumstances make the offence one of a serious character;
(3) whether the punishment which a magistrates' court would have power to inflict for it would be adequate;
(4) any other circumstances which appear to the court to make it more suitable for the offence to be tried in one way rather than the other;
(5) any representations made by the prosecution or the defence.

Certain general observations can be made:

(a) the court should never make its decision on the grounds of convenience or expedition;
(b) the court should assume for the purpose of deciding mode of trial that the prosecution version of the facts is correct;
(c) the defendant's antecedents and personal mitigating circumstances are irrelevant for the purpose of deciding mode of trial;
(d) the fact that the offences are alleged to be specimens is a relevant consideration; the fact that the defendant will be asking for other offences to be taken into consideration, if convicted, is not;
(e) where cases involve complex questions of fact or difficult questions of law, the court should consider committal for trial;
(f) where two or more defendants are jointly charged with an offence and the court decides that the offence is more suitable for summary trial, if one defendant elects trial on indictment the court must proceed to deal with all the defendants as examining justices in respect of that offence. A juvenile jointly charged with someone aged 17 or over should only be committed for trial if it is necessary in the interests of justice;
(g) in general, except where otherwise stated, either way offences should be tried summarily unless the court considers that the particular case has one

or more of the features set out below and that its sentencing powers are insufficient.

Features relevant to individual offences

Where reference is made in these guidelines to the property of 'high value' it means a figure equal to at least twice the amount of the limit imposed by statute on a magistrates' court when making a Compensation Order (currently £2000)
Editor's Note
This was increased to £5000 from 1 October 1992.

Burglary

1. Dwelling house

(1) Entry in the daytime when the occupier (or another is present).
(2) Entry at night of a house which is normally occupied, whether or not the occupier (or another is present).
(3) The offence is alleged to be one of a series of similar offences.
(4) When soiling, ransacking, damage or vandalism occurs.
(5) The offence has professional hallmarks.
(6) The unrecovered property is of high value.

Notes
Attention is drawn to paragraph 28(c) of Schedule 1 to the Magistrates' Courts Act 1980, by which offences of burglary in a dwelling cannot be tried summarily if any person in the dwelling was subjected to violence or the threat of violence.
In general, cases should be tried summarily unless the court considers that one or more of the above features is present in the case and that its sentencing powers are insufficient.

2. Non-dwellings

(1) Entry of a pharmacy or doctor's surgery.
(2) Fear is caused or violence done to anyone lawfully on the premises (eg night-watchman; security guard).
(3) The offence has professional hallmarks.
(4) Vandalism on a substantial scale.
(5) The unrecovered property is of high value.

In general, cases should be tried summarily unless the court considers that one or more of the above features is present in the case *and* that its sentencing powers are insufficient.

Theft and fraud

(1) Breach of trust by a person in a position of substantial authority, or in whom a high degree of trust is placed.
(2) Theft or fraud which has been committed or disguised in a sophisticated manner.
(3) Theft or fraud committed by an organised gang.
(4) The victim is particularly vulnerable to theft or fraud (eg the elderly or infirm).

(6) The unrecovered property is of high value.

In general, cases should be tried summarily unless the court considers that one or more of the above features is present in the case *and* that its sentencing powers are insufficient.

Handling

(1) Dishonest handling of stolen property by a receiver who has commissioned the theft.
(2) The offence has professional hallmarks.
(3) The property is of high value.

In general, cases should be tried summarily unless the court considers that one or more of the above features is present in the case *and* that its sentencing powers are insufficient.

Social security frauds

(1) Organised fraud on a large scale.
(2) the frauds are substantial and carried out over a long period of time.

Violence (Sections 20 and 47 of the Offences against the Person Act 1861)

(1) The use of a weapon of a kind likely to cause serious injury.
(2) A weapon is used and serious injury is caused.
(3) More than minor injury is caused by kicking, head-butting or similar forms of assault.
(4) Serious violence is caused to those whose work has to be done in contact with the public, eg police officers, bus drivers, taxi drivers, publicans and shopkeepers.
(5) Violence to vulnerable people, eg the elderly and infirm.

In general, cases should be tried summarily unless the court considers that one or more of the above features is present in the case *and* that its sentencing powers are insufficient.
The case considerations apply to cases of domestic violence.

Public Order Act offences

1. Cases of violent disorder should generally be committed for trial.
2. Affray:

    (1) Organised violence or use of weapons;
    (2) Significant injury or substantial damage;
    (3) The offence has a clear racial motivation;
    (4) An attack upon police officers, ambulance men, firemen and the like.

In general, cases of affray should be tried summarily unless the court considers that one or more of the above features is present in the case *and* that its sentencing powers are insufficient.

Violence to and neglect of children

(1) Substantial injury.
(2) Repeated violence or serious neglect, even if the harm is slight.
(3) Sadistic violence, eg deliberate burning or scalding.

In general, cases should be tried summarily unless the court considers that one or more of the above features is present in the case *and* that its sentencing powers are insufficient.

Indecent assault

(1) Substantial disparity in age between victim and defendant, and the assault is more than trivial.
(2) Violence or threats of violence.
(3) Relationship of trust or responsibility between defendant and victim.
(4) Several similar offences, and the assaults are more than trivial.
(5) The victim is particularly vulnerable.
(6) Serious nature of the assault.

In general, cases should be tried summarily unless the court considers that one or more of the above features is present in the case *and* that its sentencing powers are insufficient.

Unlawful sexual intercourse

(1) Wide disparity of age.
(2) Breach of position.
(3) The victim is particularly vulnerable.

In general, cases should be tried summarily unless the court considers that one or more of the above features is present in the case *and* that its sentencing powers are insufficient.

Note

Unlawful sexual intercourse with a girl ***under*** *13* is triable only on indictment.

Drugs

1. Class A

(1) Supply; possession with intent to supply. These cases should be committed for trial.
(2) Possession. Should be committed for trial unless the amount is small and consistent only with personal use.

2. Class B

(a) Supply; possession with intent to supply. Should be committed for trial unless there is only small scale supply for no payment.
(b) Possession. Should be committed for trial when the quantity is substantial.

Reckless driving

(1) Alcohol or drugs contributing to recklessness.
(2) Grossly excessive speed.

(3) Racing.
(4) Prolonged course of reckless driving.
(5) Other related offences.

In general, cases should be tried summarily unless the court considers that one or more of the above features is present in the case *and* that its sentencing powers are insufficient.

Criminal damage

(1) Deliberate fire-raising.
(2) Committed by a group.
(3) Damage of high value.
(4) The offence has clear racial motivation.

Notes

Offences set out in Schedule 2 to the Magistrates' Courts Act 1980 (which includes offences of criminal damage contrary to Section 1 of the Criminal Damage Act 1971 which do not amount to arson) must be tried summarily if the value of the property damaged or destroyed is £2000 or less.

In general, cases should be tried summarily unless the court considers that one or more of the above features is present in the case *and* that its sentencing powers are insufficient.

Index

ABWOR, 10-20
  application form, 16-19
  bail applications, 14
  claim form for attendance at police station, 23
  concluding case that day where defendant in custody, 14-15
  failure to obey orders of court, 15
  failure to pay fines or other monetary orders imposed on conviction, 15
  persons not in custody but who require ABWOR, in opinion of solicitor, 15
  unrepresented defendants requiring assistance of solicitor already at court, 13-14
  warrants of further detention, 14
Advice
  meaning, 1
Advice and assistance schemes, 4
Advice, assistance and representation, 1-7
Advice by way of representation. *See* ABWOR
Applications
  renewals. *See* Renewals of applications
Assistance
  meaning, 1

Citizens' Advice Bureaux, 7
Client funded self help, 2-3
  costs incurred as result of unnecessary or improper acts or omissions, 2
  defendant's costs orders, 2-3
  private payment of solicitors and counsel, 2

Client funded state help–*contd*
  private prosecutor's costs from central funds, 3
  wasted costs order, 3
Commercial or trade schemes, 3-4
Contribution orders, 93-108
  changes in financial status, 101-107
    dealing with, 102
    determining when re-assessment required, 103-106
    determining whether recalculation required, 106
    documentary evidence required to notify, 104
    duty to report, 101-103
    failure to disclose, 107
    financial limits of change to compel or re-asssessment, 105
    form of notification, 103
  'collecting court', 97-99
    transfer, 98-99
  contributions from capital, 100
  contributions from income, 99-100
  correction of mistakes, 127
  court's powers to seek further information during life of case, 107-108
    process for request, 108
  date payments fall due, 99-100
  duration, 99-100
  enforcing, 109-127
  enforcing payment, 109-124
    advisory leaflet, 121-122
    arrears recovery letter, 118
    complaint for recovery of arrears, 119
    first warning, 111
    means enquiry form, 123

Contribution orders–*contd*
enforcing payment–*contd*
overview, 110
overview of stage two, 116
stage one, 110-115
stage two, 115-124
summons for arrears, 121-123
test to determine whether to revoke legal aid and order, 113
timetable, 124, 125
warning of revocation, 112
form, 96
issue of, 93-99
overview of issuing process, 94
powers of court to withhold orders until contributions from capital are paid, 101
remission of contributions, 125-126
repayment of contributions, 126
specified form showing calculations, 97
Costs, 159-175
appeal against taxation, 175
attendance at formal remand hearings, 165
attendance on clients at a distance, 165
attendance on clients remanded in custody, 166
challenging determination, 174
compliance with court order or undertaking given to court, 166
expenses not covered by legal aid order, 169-170
foreign language ability of solicitor, 165
letters to clients, 165
medical/psychiatric reports, 165
methods of claiming costs, 171
photocopying, 164
power to make defendant's costs in relation to legally assisted persons, 167-170
pre-legal aid order
change in circumstances of applicant, 169
no change in legally assisted person's circumstances, 168-169
refund or remittal of contributions as alternative to order, 159-161
Costs–*contd*
refund or remittal or contributions exceeding solicitor's bill, 161-162
refunding contributions after taxation, 162
relevant taxing authorities, 170
scope of legal aid order, and, 164-167
separate representation by counsel, 166
standard fees in magistrates' courts, 171-175
categories, 172
determining, 173
time limits, 170
use of enquiry agents, 166
wasted costs orders, 169
witness expenses, 166-167, 169
work done after/before reassignment of order, 165
work done prior to grant of legal aid order, 162-164
work done under legal aid order, and, 164-167
Counsel
private payment, 2
Court Duty Solicitor scheme, 4-5, 20-23
report, 21-22
Court staff, 6
Criminal legal aid orders
amendment of, 141-157
assignment of different solicitor, 146-152
overview, 146
amendment to through order, 154
amendments to assign counsel, 152-153
Crown Court orders, 153
magistrates court's orders, 152-153
application and renewal procedure, 151
application form, 88
applications to incur expenditure, 154-157
assignment of different solicitor, 146-152
application form, 148-149
breakdown of solicitor/client relationship, 147
client followings, 150

Criminal legal aid orders–*contd*
assignment of different solicitor–*contd*
conflict of interest, 147
geographical constraints, 150
method of application and renewal, 150
professional difficulties, 147
assignment of solicitors and counsel, 143-145
guidance issued by Lord Chancellor's Department, 144-145
rule in *R v Solihull Justices*, 143
authority to incur costs under, 146
certificate of refusal to grant, 95
level of representation, 141-142
nature of, 141-157
nature of representation, 141-146
Crown Court, 142
magistrates' courts, 141
notice of withholding, 101
withdrawal, 153-154
Criminal legal aid scheme
comparison with costs of civil legal aid, 180
competent authorities, 29
content of applications, 33-34
Court of Appeal, 32
Crown Court, 31-32
future developments, 177-181
House of Lords, 32
increase in costs, 178
magistrates' courts, 28-31
means test, 35-59. *See also* Means test
merits test. *See* Merits test
methods of application, 27-34
problems, 177-178
scope, 27-28
solutions, 178-181
timing of applications, 32-33

Free interviews, 6

Green Form Scheme, 5, 9-10, 11, 12

Judicial review, 140
Law centres, 4
Legal advice and assistance. *See* Green Form Scheme

Medical Defence Union, 4
Means test, 35-59
abbreviated statement of means, 41
allowances and deductions from capital, 50-51
articles of personal clothing, 51
business assets, 51
equipment of trade, 51
household furniture, 51
personal effects, 51
residential property, 50
tools, 51
allowances and deductions from income, 46-47
expenses of employment, 46-47
non passporting state benefits, 46
application, 52-53
calculating amount of income received each week, 45-53
calculating contribution from income, 48-49
calculation of capital contribution, 52
capital, 50
capital sums subject to freezing orders, 51-52
co-habitees, 42-44
housing costs, 47-48
council tax, 48
domestic rates, 48
household maintenance, 48
insurances, 48
mortgage payments, 47
rent, 47
rent or board payments made by non-householder, 48
water rates, 48
income, 44-45
accounts, 44
state benefits, 44
wage slips, 44
requirement to provide statement of means, 35-37
applicants passported to free legal aid, 36
mental or physical disability, 36-37
statement already submitted, 36
resources of third parties, 45
savings, 50
spouses, 42-44
contrary interest in proceedings, 43

Means test–*contd*
spouses–*contd*
income excluded where equitable to do so, 43-44
living separate and apart, 43
statement of means by applicant or appropriate contributor for legal aid purposes, 54-59
Merits test, 61-92
appeals, 61-62
application form, 69
assessment of resources (over 16 year olds), 38-39
assessment of resources (under 16 year olds), 39
Bail Act offences, 62-63
bail applications, 62
first hearing, 62
second hearing, 62
case studies, 81-92
committal for sentence, 63-64
committal for trial, 63
murder, 63
cross-examination of child witness, 63
deeming provisions, 61-92
discretionary provisions, 67-92
overview, 67-69
first sentence of imprisonment, 64
full means enquiries, 40-45
identifying cases for passporting to free legal aid, 42
method of application, 66
overview, 61
passporting applicants to free legal aid, 40
poorly completed application forms, 81-92
powers to grant 'conditional orders' pending receipt of documentation, 38
reasons for wanting legal aid, 83, 84, 86, 87, 90
remands for pre-sentence reports, 64
requirement to provide documentary evidence, 37-38
satisfying statutory criteria, 69-81
section 22(2)(a) - applicant will suffer serious damage to reputation, 73-74
Merits test–*contd*
section 22 (2)(a) - risk of custodial sentence, 69-71
aggravating features, 71
local sentencing practices, 71
offence carrying custodial penalty, 70
usual tariff sentence, 70
sentence 22(2)(a) - sentence that would lead to loss of livelihood, 72
section 22(2)(b) - determination of case may involve consideration of substantial question of law, 74-75
section 22(2)(c) - accused unable to understand proceedings or state case, 75-78
inadequate knowledge of English, 75-76
mental illness or disability, 76-78
physical illnesses or disabilities, 78
section 22(2)(d, 79-80
expert cross examination, 80
tracing and interviewing of witnesses, 79-80
section 22(2)(e) - interests of someone other than accused, 80-81
secure training orders, 66
sentence of custody for life where offender under 21, 65
sentence of detention in young offender institution, 65
sentences of detention - section 53, Children and Young Persons Act 1993, 65
sentencing hearings, 64-66
Motoring organisations, 4

Police Station Duty Solicitor scheme, 6, 26
claim form, 25
Pressure groups, 7
Pro bono work, 6-7

Rejection of applications
common reasons for, 129-130
Renewals of applications, 129-140
Court of Appeal, 138
Crown Court, 138, 139
judicial review, 140

Renewals of applications–*contd*
magistrates' court, 130-132
justices clerk/proper officer, 132
oral applications, 130-132
renewals, 131
oral application, 138
review by Legal aid Board Area Committee, 132-138
application form, 135-136
checklist, 133
notification of decision, 137
procedural requirements, 134

Representation
meaning, 1

Solicitors
private payment, 2

Trade unions, 4

Voluntary sector schemes, 7

Wasted costs orders, 3, 169